CW00866344

OXFORD CLASSICAL MONOGRAPHS

Published under the supervision of a Committee of the
Faculty of Classics in the University of Oxford

The aim of the Oxford Classical Monograph series (which replaces the Oxford Classical and Philosophical Monographs) is to publish books based on the best theses on Greek and Latin literature, ancient history, and ancient philosophy examined by the Faculty Board of Classics.

Terence and the Verb 'To Be' in Latin

GIUSEPPE PEZZINI

OXFORD
UNIVERSITY PRESS

OXFORD

UNIVERSITY PRESS

Great Clarendon Street, Oxford, OX2 6DP,
United Kingdom

Oxford University Press is a department of the University of Oxford.
It furthers the University's objective of excellence in research, scholarship,
and education by publishing worldwide. Oxford is a registered trade mark of
Oxford University Press in the UK and in certain other countries

First Edition published in 2015
Impression: 1

Published in the United States of America by Oxford University Press
198 Madison Avenue, New York, NY 10016, United States of America

British Library Cataloguing in Publication Data
Data available

Library of Congress Control Number: 2014953510

ISBN 978-0-19-873624-0

Printed and bound by
CPI Group (UK) Ltd, Croydon, CR0 4YY

To my Mother

Preface

The origin of this book lies in a conversation with Jim Adams in 2008 in his office at All Souls College, Oxford. At that time I was working on a commentary on Terence's *Heauton Timorumenos*, which was my intended project for the D.Phil. in Classical Languages and Literature. During one of my first supervisions with him, Jim did not pay much attention to my first attempts at commentary but pointed me towards what looked like a very small detail in the first line of the passage I was commenting on, the form *inueniundumst* (*Haut.* 513). With his characteristic urgency he invited and challenged me to write a note on this phenomenon ('prodelision'), to be based on my own research and not just repeating or paraphrasing the *vulgata*. I went back to the Bodleian Library and began my work, which in my mind would not have required more than a day or two. My first step, owing to a combination of chance and curiosity, was to type into a database of Latin texts these 'prodelided' forms. It was a bit like Alice encountering the White Rabbit: that quick search was enough to make me realize that 'prodelision' is not just a feature of Plautus, Terence, and Lucretius (as most Latin scholars and readers believe) but is found in texts of many other authors, both poetry and prose. That was just the tip of the iceberg, as very few modern editors print contractions; but it was enough to intrigue me. I thus decided to follow the rabbit into the hole and I have spent the following years working on Latin contractions, soon realising their linguistic significance and their relationship with the peculiar nature of the verb 'to be' in Latin. That short note became this book, which is thus an account of a journey of research within the 'underworld' of contraction (what 'prodelision' really is) and the cliticization of the verb 'to be' in Latin.

Several of my 'lay' friends often ask me what is the point of research in a subject that has been studied for centuries. I hope that this book, as well as many others, may provide an answer, and show how many mysteries of the Latin language still need to be revealed, and how many of our basic tenets are inaccurate or misleading, including the paradigm of the verb 'to be'.

In my journey Jim Adams has been master and companion, always reminding me of the supremacy of facts over fanciful interpretations, of clarity and precision over 'waffling'; Fraenkel's dedication to Leo, that 'not a single line of this book could have been written without his work and teaching' can appropriately be repeated here. To this I would also append 'and without his affection, kindness, and generosity', if I did not know that Jim would probably frown at these 'sentimentalities'.

The writing of this book would not have been possible without the aid of a number of people, and its quality would be considerably inferior without their comments and criticism; I apologize for any remaining mistakes, which might obscure the calibre of the help I have received.

First of all, I wish to thank warmly the examiners of my D.Phil., in its *fieri* and completion: Peter Brown, David Langslow, Wolfgang de Melo, and Tobias Reinhardt. I did not know it at that time but their help would have been much more precious and extensive than their invaluable comments on my thesis. Each of them, with his rigorous work, inspiration, and guidance, has made and makes possible my growth as a person and as a scholar.

A special thanks also goes to my adviser John Penney, for his patience and advice, and to Peter Kruschwitz, for his constant support and wit, together with the colleagues of the Department of Classics at Reading.

Several other people have read and commented on parts or earlier drafts of this book: among them I am especially grateful to Siobhan Butala, David Butterfield, James Clackson, Anna Chahoud, Luca Grillo, Luke O'Duffy, Costas Panayotakis, John Trappes-Lomax, and Rex Wallace.

Oxford is a special place, in which I have been lucky to find many colleagues and friends who have offered me their expertise and encouragement, both during my D.Phil. and while I was converting the thesis into a book: I would like to mention in particular Amin Benaissa, Felix Budelmann, Stephen Harrison, Matthew Leigh, Tom Mackenzie, Oliver Taplin, Barney Taylor, Alessandro Vatri, and the colleagues at the Dictionary of Medieval Latin, especially Richard Ashdowne, Peter Glare, David Howlett, and Carolinne White. I am also grateful to all the students I have had the privilege to teach in these years, and who have helped me to retain my passion for our subject: a special place is held by the undergraduates of Lady

Margaret Hall with whom I shared a beautiful year after the completion of my thesis.

For the preparation of this book I have visited many libraries, where I have found open doors and kind assistance: I would like to express my gratitude in particular to the staff of the *Bodleian Library*, the *British Library*, the *Biblioteca Apostolica Vaticana*, the *Bibliothèque nationale de France*, the *Biblioteca Ambrosiana*, and the *Biblioteca Laurenziana*.

I also would like to mention the importance of the teaching I received in Pisa, above all from Gian Biagio Conte, Rolando Ferri and Glenn Most, as well as the support I received in the crucial months before I came to Oxford, especially that of Alessandro Banfi and Michele Rosboch.

Finally, I gratefully acknowledge the financial support I received from a generous scholarship of the *Banca Gesfid* (now PKB Privatbank), and a joint scholarship of St. Anne's College and the Faculty of Classics at Oxford.

The years in which this book was written have been a roller-coaster of events, some joyful, some less: I would not have been able to go through them without the presence of many friends with whom I share the greatest of adventures; it would be impossible to name all of them here and I am therefore sadly forced to offer a collective, but sincere thanks. I cannot fail however to single out the names of Beniamino Arnone, Noel Murphy, Stefano Rebeggiani and Marco Sinisi. They know why.

My family of origin supported me from the very beginning and I would never be here without them, especially without my father. The book is dedicated to my mother, the one who is at the root and centre of all.

Last, but certainly not the least, I thank my wife, *in qua maxime delector*: she followed me to the UK to study for my D.Phil., she tolerated with great benevolence all my stress over many days and nights, and, most of all, she bore my wonderful children, who bring light to my life. She will probably never pride herself for it, but this book would not exist without her.

Oxford
April 2015

Contents

A note on cross-references

Cross-references in the book generally point to individual sections, numbered as above. Cross-references in simple Arabic numbers (e.g. 4.2) point to sections of the same chapter; cross-references pointing to sections of other chapters have an initial Roman numeral (e.g. IV.4.2) indicating the number of the chapter. For instance, a reference to section 4.2 of the fourth chapter would appear as 'cf. (section) 4.2' within chapter 4, and as 'IV.4.2' in another chapter.

List of Boxes and Tables

Boxes

Tables

xvi *List of Boxes and Tables*

I

Introduction

oculi dolent . . . quia fumu(s) molestust
Pl. *Most*. 891

1. OVERTURE: LINGUISTIC PUZZLES

I will start my journey, on which I invite the reader to join me, with a quick linguistic puzzle. If you read carefully the following short passages, you will probably notice that something does not look/ sound quite right, apart from the inappropriateness of the content (at least for a book of Latin philology). In each passage some changes have been made to the original text, and I challenge the reader to figure out what and where: this little task will help to introduce the area, topic, and applicability of the research presented in this book.

1) 'The delegations from Beauxbatons and Durmstrang will be arriving in October and remaining with us for the greater part of this year. I know that you will all extend every courtesy to our foreign guests while they are with us, and will give your whole-hearted support to the Hogwarts champion when he or she is selected. And now, it is late . . . bedtime! Chop chop!' . . . 'They cannot do that!' said George Weasley. . . . 'We are seventeen in April, why cannot we have a shot?'[1]

2) 'Rita Skeeter never makes anyone look good. Remember, she interviewed all the Gringotts' Charm Breakers once, and called me "a

---

[1] From J. K. Rowling, *Harry Potter and the Goblet of Fire*, London 2000, ch. 12. Copyright © J. K. Rowling 2000.

long-haired pillock"?' 'Well, it is a bit long, dear,' said Mrs. Weasley gently. 'If you would just let me . . . .' 'No Mum.'[2]

3) 'I saw you coming,' said Lupin, smiling. He pointed to the parchment he had been poring over. It was the Marauder's Map. 'I just saw Hagrid,' said Harry. 'And he said you had resigned. It is not true, is it?' 'I am afraid it is' said Lupin.[3]

4) Harry . . . heard a chorus of eerie voices singing to him from the open egg in his hands: 'Come seek us where our voices sound, | We cannot sing above the ground, | And while you are searching, ponder this: | We have taken what you will sorely miss, | An hour long you will have to look, | And to recover what we took, | But past an hour, the prospect is black, | Too late, it is gone, it will not come back.'[4]

It would probably not take long to realize that all contracted forms in the original texts (*'m, -n't, 're, 's, 'd*) have been converted into the uncontracted, grammatically more 'standard' forms (*am not, are, is, has, would, had*): the original text, with the contracted forms in the right place, is found below on p. 4 (texts 5–8). This shift in spelling, from uncontracted to contracted, is not trivial and is responsible for the loss of important meaning and information.

First, contracted spellings reproduce very common forms of English language, both as they are generally realized in speech and as they are normally written in unfiltered writing. For instance, in normal English speech the sequence *it* + *is* is almost always realized as /its/, and the corresponding contracted spelling *it's* is widely used, except in high-style writing. However, because uncontracted spellings are still considered more 'correct', contracted spellings generally have a colloquial ring (at least in standard varieties of English writing), and therefore may be used in written texts as stylistic markers; for instance, in most of the passages above contracted forms are functional to convey the impression of 'real speech' and contribute to the marking of the context as 'fictional, informal dialogue' (e.g. text 3,

---

[2] J. K. Rowling, *Harry Potter and the Goblet of Fire*, ch. 10. Copyright © J. K. Rowling 2000.

[3] From J. K. Rowling, *Harry Potter and the Prisoner of Azkaban*, London 1999, ch. 22. Copyright © J. K. Rowling 1999.

[4] J. K. Rowling, *Harry Potter and the Goblet of Fire*, ch. 25. Copyright © J. K. Rowling 2000.

original text: 'he said **you'd** resigned. **It's** not true, is it?' '**I'm** afraid it is'; see below text 7). Contracted forms, however, are not only 'colloquial' forms: they may also be used in poetry as poetic forms, which do not necessarily have to be current in speech. For instance, the penultimate verse of the short poem in text 4 (in the original text: 'But past an hour, the **prospect's** black'; see below text 8) displays a contraction after a -*ct* (*prospect's*), which is generally avoided in speech.[5] A reader relying only on the above texts (1–4) for his knowledge of the English language would be unable to realize the existence of contracted forms and their various stylistic values in both speech and writing.

Moreover, in text 4 the regular, iambic rhythm of the octosyllables (in the original text: 'But pást an hóur, the próspect's bláck, | Too láte, it's góne, it wón't come báck'; see below text 8) is disfigured if the contracted forms are converted into uncontracted ones ('But pást an hóur, the próspect is bláck); only in line 3 ('and while you are searching, ponder this'), would the reader probably be able to reproduce unconsciously the iambic rhythm, by pronouncing the form **you are** as a single syllable by means of a sandhi reduction (i.e. happening at word boundaries), which, however, could also be analysed as elision (*y'are*) or synizesis (*youare*).

Finally, from a subtler linguistic perspective, contraction is an interesting phenomenon related to and conditioned by many intriguing aspects of language, such as prosody, syntax, and word order. For instance, one of the main factors accounting for contraction is that English auxiliaries and modals do not normally have an accent of their own, but tend to be pronounced as a single prosodic unit together with the preceding word (= enclisis or cliticization): for instance, the phrase 'and will give' (text 1) is normally pronounced 'Ánd will gíve' and not 'Ánd wíll gíve', unless for emphasis. A non-native English speaker would find it hard to figure out the right intonation, if his only available evidence were the texts quoted above, in which all contracted forms have been converted into uncontracted forms.

At the same time, it would be pointless and counterproductive to restore the contracted forms in *all* places, with the illusion of thereby restoring the original texts (reproduced here below, texts 5–8).

---

[5] In the spoken material of the British National Corpus (BNC), a database containing over 100 million words of contemporary English, there are no cases of contracted '*is*' after words ending in -*ct* (vs. 353 instances of uncontracted -*ct is*).

Original texts (contracted forms in bold, original uncontracted forms in bold italics)

5) 'The delegations from Beauxbatons and Durmstrang **will be** arriving in October and remaining with us for the greater part of this year. I know that **you will** all extend every courtesy to our foreign guests while **they are** with us, **and will** give your whole-hearted support to the Hogwarts champion when he or **she is** selected. And now, **it is** late... bedtime! Chop chop!'... 'They **can't** do that!' said George Weasley... 'We're seventeen in April, why **can't** we have a shot?'

6) 'Rita Skeeter never makes anyone look good. Remember, she interviewed all the Gringotts' Charm Breakers once, and called me "a long-haired pillock"?' 'Well, **it is** a bit long, dear,' said Mrs. Weasley gently. 'If **you'd** just let me....' 'No Mum.'

7) 'I saw you coming,' said Lupin, smiling. He pointed to the parchment **he had** been poring over. **It was** the Marauder's Map. 'I just saw Hagrid,' said Harry. 'And he said **you'd** resigned. It's not true, **is it**?' 'I'm afraid **it is**' said Lupin.

8) Harry... heard a chorus of eerie voices singing to him from the open egg in his hands: 'Come seek us where our voices sound, | **We cannot** sing above the ground, | And while **you're** searching, ponder this: | **We've** taken what **you'll** sorely miss, | An hour long **you'll** have to look, | And to recover what we took, | But past an hour, the **prospect's** black, | Too late, **it's** gone, it **won't** come back.' (For bibliographical references see above nn. 1–4).

In some of the above cases the contracted form would be linguistically unacceptable, because of factors relating to syntax and word order (*I'm afraid **it's** [< I'm afraid **it is**]), prosody (*It's not **true's** it? [< It's not **true is it**?]), phonology (*and'll give [< and will give]) or a combination of these.[6] In other cases, matters of style, pragmatics, and metre would suggest that a contracted form, although possible, is not appropriate in the context. For instance, in the first paragraph of text 5 the colloquial ring of contracted forms (**you'll**, **they're**) would contrast with the formal tone of the speech ('I know that **you will** all extend every courtesy to our foreign guests while **they are** with us'). In the second utterance of text 7 ('Well, **it is** a bit long') the form 'it is' is emphatic and corresponds, in speech, to a prominence in intonation ('Well, **it IS** a bit long') which prevents contraction ('Well, **it's** a bit

---

[6] For restrictions on auxiliary reduction in English and the factors conditioning them cf. Zwicky (1970: 331–5), Anderson (2005: 25–30, 64–74), Spencer and Luís (2012: 94–7 and *passim*).

long'); finally, the second octosyllabic verse of the poem in text 8 would be metrically defective with a contracted 'can't' ('We can't síng abóve the gróund') and the uncontracted form 'cannot' is the one used in the original text. Therefore, the loss of meaning caused by the spelling conversion in the above texts does not pertain only to forms that were originally contracted, but also to forms that were not: the only way to recover the information lost would be to restore the contracted forms only in the right places.

English native speakers would be able to do so without much effort; they would probably rely mostly on their 'ear', and, in some cases, they would not be able to give a rational explanation for their 'linguistic feelings' (unless they were professional linguists). Non-native English speakers, unless counting on their past or present interaction with native speakers, would find the task more difficult: among other things, they should search for printed variants of the above texts, in which contracted spellings (or at least some of them) might not have been deleted; they should also collect instances of contracted spellings in other texts, and consider both in what type of texts these forms are attested (e.g. whether in prose or poetry, whether in an academic article or a text message, and so on), as well as the context, in order to identify (if possible) significant aspects such as register and style; they should collect and analyse patterns in which contracted forms are never (or rarely) attested; they should study the mechanisms and practice of English metre; they should consult grammars to see whether they have anything to say about the matter (excluding the possibility of a good and full treatment of the subject, which would obviously make the research pointless); finally, they should combine and elaborate all the various pieces of evidence, in order to gain useful knowledge that may help them to restore the right form in the right places.

If the task is already challenging at this stage, it becomes very laborious if one's aim is not only to reintroduce the contracted forms only in the right places, but also to gain a full understanding of the factors accounting for the places where contracted forms are impossible or avoided: several PhD dissertations have been dedicated to this latter part of the task, while relying on the linguistic percep-tions of native speakers for the former part.[7]

---

[7] Cf. e.g. Halpern (1995).

Despite the difficulties involved, the risk of approximation and imprecision, and the probable impossibility of obtaining a full picture, the task of reconstructing and analysing English contracted forms would still be worth the effort: among the rewards are the awareness of a very common feature of 'real' speech, an understanding of its stylistic features and potential, a greater appreciation of the context in which contractions are used in writing, and, finally, a better comprehension of key aspects of the language conditioning contraction, such as intonation, syntax, word order, pragmatics, and prosody. As every non-native English speaker knows well, no one can claim a proficiency and comprehension of language without a full knowledge of these aspects, which English native speakers naturally possess, although generally unconsciously due to their complexity. The mastery of these 'real' aspects of language is acquired by prolonged osmotic contact with native speakers rather than studying and linguistic research, however ambitious, competent, and painstaking it may be: nevertheless, in the absence of native speakers, this would be the only way to try to reconstruct and regain this knowledge of 'real' language, and contracted forms might be a good area to begin with.

2. AIMS AND FINDINGS

2.1 'Real' Latin

This book is the account of a journey of research similar to the one just described, as far as content, aims, and methodologies are concerned; the object is a language that is (and deserves to be) still studied nowadays, although, unfortunately, none of its native users are alive.

My focus is on two linguistic phenomena of Latin language (contraction and sigmatic ecthlipsis), both related to one of the most common and important words in Latin, the verb 'to be' (*esse*), and, in particular, to its phonetic, prosodic, and syntactic features.

Many scholars have previously, often with expertise and intelligence, dealt with these phenomena and their nature, and my work would not have been possible without theirs. However, most previous studies did not rely on a comprehensive analysis of the evidence and this affected the validity of their results and explanations. Moreover, traditional Latin grammars, with their focus on accidence and pre-scriptive syntax, generally ignore or neglect these phenomena: as a consequence, the majority of Latin readers and scholars are not very aware of their existence, nature, spread, and significance, especially in written sources; one of the aims of this book is to raise this awareness.

Finally, the area of research which I will explore through the analysis of these phenomena, and which includes aspects of 'real' language such as word order, syntax, or intonation, still conceals from the modern scholar most of its secrets: even after centuries of Latin scholarship we are still far from understanding and recreating the natural perceptions of a Latin native speaker, without which our comprehension and appreciation of any Latin text is bound to be deficient. I believe that the results of my analysis can also form a (small) contribution to our knowledge of this hidden level of 'real' Latin.

Two short passages from the poetry of a Latin author will help to introduce the linguistic phenomena under scrutiny and the main questions I will address in my book.

9) Terence, *Hauton Timorumenos* 509–16 (iambic senarii)

CHREMES Syrus est prendendus atque adhortandus mihi.
a me nescioquis exit: concede hinc domum   510
ne nos inter nos congruere sentiant.
SYRUS hac illac circumcursa; inueniundum est tamen
argentum: intendenda in senem est fallacia.
CHREMES num me fefellit hosce id struere? uidelicet
ille Cliniai seruos tardiusculus est;   515
idcirco huic nostro tradita est prouincia.

CHREMES
I must get hold of Syrus and urge him on. Someone's coming out of my house: go home now—I don't want them to realize we're putting our heads together.

SYRUS
Run around this way and that—but I've still got to find the money: I must aim a trick at the old man.

CHREMES
Didn't I see this was what they were plotting? Obviously that slave of Clinia's is a bit on the slow side: that's why the job's been assigned to our man here. (Trans. Brown 2006)

10) Terence, *Hecyra* 485–94 (iambic senarii)

PAMPHILUS quibus iris pulsus nunc in illam iniquos sim   485

quae numquam quicquam erga me commerita est, pater,
quod nollem, et saepe quod uellem meritam scio?
amoque et laudo et uehementer desidero;
nam fuisse erga me miro ingenio expertus sum;
illique exopto ut relicuam uitam exigat   490
cum eo uiro me qui sit fortunatior,
quandoquidem illam a me distrahit necessitas.
PHIDIPPUS tibi id in manu est ne fiat. LACHES si sanus sies.
iube illam redire. PAMPHILUS non est consilium, pater.

PAMPHILUS
How could anger now drive me to be unfair to the woman who's never
done anything to me that I could complain of, dad, and who I know has
done a lot that I'm happy with? I love her, I approve of her, I desperately
want her; I know from experience how wonderful she's been to me. And
I pray that she spends the rest of her life with a man more fortunate
than me, since necessity tears her away from me!

PHIDIPPUS
It's in your hands to stop that happening.

LACHES
If only you'd be sensible: tell her to come back!

PAMPHILUS
That's not my plan, dad. (Trans. Brown 2006)

The passages above were composed in the second century BC by a
Latin speaker of African origin.[8] They were originally meant to be
used as scripts for theatre but were soon circulated in written form
and eventually became very popular; they are preserved for us in
almost seven hundred manuscripts, dating from the fifth to the
fifteenth century AD, on which modern editions are based. As far as
we understand, these texts aimed to imitate real speech, although
concerned with a conventional content and codified in a (loose)
metrical form (iambic senarii).

Although these texts have often been taken to be among the
samples closest to spoken Latin,[9] many features of 'real' speech that
they aimed to imitate are not immediately accessible to a modern,
non-native reader. Many traces reveal that significant information
has been lost in the transmission of the texts through the centuries.

---

[8] *Pace* Bagordo (2001) there are no strong reasons to doubt that Terence received a
Latin education before puberty and thus that his Latin was native.
[9] For instance, at the end of the sixteenth century students at the Görlitz school
were required to imitate Terence when they spoke Latin.

2.2 Contractions in Latin

The first problem concerns the third person form of the verb *esse* ('to be') in the above passages: although in most manuscripts (> 99%) it is spelt in the standard form that one learns in modern Latin grammars (*est*), yet in at least three cases (*Haut.* 512 *inueniundum est*, 516 *tradita est, Hec.* 486 *commerita est*) a few (early) manuscripts have a spelling in which the initial *e* has been dropped and the resulting *st* (< *est*) is attached to the preceding word (*inueniundumst, traditast, commeritast*). What are these 'contracted' spellings? Why are they found in so few manuscripts and, in these, *only* in these three places? Should we ignore them as misspellings or, conversely, reintroduce them even whey they are not attested (e.g. *Haut.* 513 *in senemst, Hec.* 493 *in manust*)?

In at least two cases this latter option would not seem to be correct; Terence's comedies are written in verse and at *Haut.* 509 and *Hec.* 494 the contracted spellings *Syrust* and *nonst*, besides their different phonologic features (*est* following -*s* and -*n* instead of -*m* or -*a*), would be metrically unacceptable. On the other hand, at *Haut.* 515 the form *tardiusculus est* (spelt 'uncontracted' in all manuscripts) is metrically impossible (the anapaest [i.e. light, light, and heavy syllable] -*ŭlŭs est* does not fit the iambic ending of the senarius),[10] whereas a 'contracted' form *tardiuscŭlust* would produce a metrically perfect line (with the iambus -*ŭlust*), and it is thus printed by most editors.

If the alternation between contracted and uncontracted forms is original, what factors are conditioning it? Is it just a matter of metre, or are emphasis, syntax, word order, prosody, or a combination of these to be taken into account? For instance, in the cases when the verb is contracted, it directly follows a (verbal) adjective (*inueniundumst, traditast, commeritast, tardiusculust*); conversely, when the order is altered (*Syrus est prendendus, intendendam in senem est*), the form is not contracted: what (if any) is the relation between the different word order and contraction of *est*? What levels of 'real' language are involved?

Moreover, do contracted forms have a particular stylistic value? For instance, at *Haut.* 515 the (restored) contracted *tardiusculust* appears together with the archaic form of the genitive *Cliniai*, in the speech of an old man: is this relevant? Finally, what (if any) feature of

---

[10] For a description of the features and terminology of Latin comic metre see V.2.

speech do contracted spellings reproduce? Is it analogous to the contraction of auxiliaries and modals in English? What are its linguistic origin, nature, and features?

All these questions become more challenging if one extends the area of research beyond Terence. Are contracted spellings found only in Terence or other republican authors? Are they also found in prose? Most of Latin literature is transmitted by medieval manuscripts written roughly at the same time as those exemplars of Terence in which contracted spellings are hardly ever attested: can we assume that the original use of these forms was much more widespread than it now appears? And, given this set of circumstances, is there any way to trace the presence of contracted forms, in both speech and writing, and analyse their linguistic significance throughout the history of Latin?

The next three chapters of the present book aim to address these questions systematically.

In chapter II I will examine the transmission of contracted spellings of *esse* in the manuscript traditions of literary authors: I will examine both authors in which the presence of contracted spellings is generally acknowledged (e.g. Terence and Plautus) and authors in which this presence is ignored or neglected, despite being extensive (such as Virgil), meaningful (such as Gellius), or sporadic (such as Horace, Lucan, and others). I will also collect evidence from a large variety of non-literary sources (e.g. inscriptions, Sabellian languages, late-antique grammarians, metrical corpora), which show that contracted spellings are not minor quibbles, only relevant to the (few) scholars of archaic Latin comedy.

In chapter III I will analyse the evidence for contracted forms, assessing the circumstances of their use and their frequency in the history of Latin orthography and speech. I will show that contracted spellings are not misspellings, abbreviations, or phonetic spellings of the sandhi type (i.e. involving alteration at word boundaries, as the type discussed above on p. 3 for the form 'you are searching'), supposedly related to elision (as implied by the standard term 'prodelision'), but instead reflect (en)clitic forms of *esse*, showing phonological reduction. Enclitics or clitics are a special class of linguistic elements, common in many languages; they are accentless words or particles which 'lean' accentually on the preceding host: a common (en)clitic in Latin is the particle -*que* (e.g. *uirumque*),[11] whose clitic nature is also

---

[11] On the prosody of Latin clitic particles see Probert (2002).

displayed in spelling, by univerbation with the host. Enclisis (or 'cliticization') will emerge as the main factor accounting for Latin contractions, and as a key feature of the verb *esse*, which will be a central topic of the book.

Contracted spellings were common in early republican poetry, where they probably reflected a phenomenon current in speech, and were also used in late republican and early imperial Latin as archaisms, poeticisms, or colloquialisms. Contracted spellings went gradually out of use in imperial and late Latin, although it is possible that contraction as a phenomenon of speech became obsolete before (or after) then.

In chapter IV I will investigate further linguistic aspects of contracted forms, considering the reasons for the variation between uncontracted forms (e.g. *factus est, facta est, factum est*) and contracted forms (e.g. *factust, factast, factumst*) in Terence. I will examine the possible influence of metre, semantics, style, syntax, and word order on the blocking of contraction (and cliticization), thereby shedding new light on these hidden aspects of Latin language. The findings of this chapter confirm that contraction is related to cliticization of *esse* and, most particularly, to the strong bond which the verb has, in its copula or auxiliary function, with the preceding predicate (noun, adjective, or equivalent) or participle.

2.3 Omission of Final -s

To introduce the second topic analysed in the book, I can refer again to texts 9 and 10, quoted in section 2.1. Just as for contraction, there are traces in these passages revealing that other linguistic information is hidden to the modern reader.

At *Hec.* 485 and 489 the text as found in most manuscripts and printed on pp. 7–8 is not metrically sound: in particular, the forms *ini|quos sim* (*Hec.* 485) and *exper|tus sum* (*Hec.* 489) end with a prosodic sequence (heavy syllable + heavy syllable) which in both cases is unacceptable in the iambic ending of a senarius (light syllable + heavy syllable).[12] The only possible way of achieving the expected light syllable in the penultimate position (*iniquos sim, expertus sum*) would be to imagine that the final -s in the words *iniquos* and *expertus* was not pronounced (*iniquŏ(s) sim, expertŭ(s) sum*). This solution is

---

[12] Cf. V.2.

adopted by most editors, who print *iniquo' sim, expertu' sum,* or similar forms. What is the nature of this phenomenon? Is it just a metrical technicality or does it reflect a real feature of speech?

Moreover, the omission of final *-s* before a consonant (sigmatic ecthlipsis) has parallels both in other Latin sources (e.g. inscriptions) and in modern languages deriving from Latin (e.g. Italian). Should one speculate that in Latin final *-s* was just a spelling convention phonetically realized only before a vowel, thus having a behaviour similar to that of final *-s* in some Romance varieties (cf. e.g. Fr. *les langues* /le lãg/ vs. *les hommes* /lez om/), or perhaps foreshadowing it? Or did final *-s* have a weak phonetic value only in specific historical (e.g. only in early Latin), social (e.g. only in sub-standard texts), stylistic (e.g. only in 'low' registers of Latin), or linguistic circumstances (e.g. only in or before particular words)?

That final *-s* did not always have a weak phonetic value is suggested by evidence found in the same texts above: at *Haut.* 509 (*adhortandus mihi*) and *Hec.* 493 (*sanus sies*) the final syllable of the (verbal) adjectives *adhortandŭs* and *sanŭs* is metrically heavy, which can happen only if the syllable becomes heavy by position, i.e. if final *-s* is fully pronounced before the following consonant (*-us mi-, -us si-*). What factors may account for this different treatment? Is it relevant that the two words displaying omission of final *-s* are both (verbal) adjectives (*iniquos, expertus*) followed by forms of the verb *esse* beginning with *-s* (*sim, sum*)? And finally, what should one expect when the metre does not help to establish whether final *-s* is silent or not (as for the forms *seruo(?s)* at *Haut.* 515 and *pulsu(?s)* at *Hec.* 485)? Should one follow, for instance, the editors of the Oxford edition of Terence, who believe that omission of final *-s* was a standard rule and print it whenever the metre does not prevent it (*seruo', pulsu'*)?

A native Latin speaker would probably be able to give an answer to these questions without much effort, relying on his own natural experience of Latin pronunciation, prosody, and syntax. For the modern reader, aiming to gain a deeper knowledge of Latin language, the task is more challenging and, in order to be accurate, would require systematic analysis of a large quantity of data.

In chapter V I aim to undertake this task, focusing on the evidence of Terence and other republican sources. I will analyse the prosodic omission of final *-s* before a consonant (sigmatic ecthlipsis), relying in particular on a database of all lines of Terence potentially involving it. I will show that metrical evidence for this phenomenon appears to be limited to cases in which a participle or predicate (noun, adjective, or equivalent) precedes a form of *esse* (cf. e.g. *Haut.* 826 *admirātŭ(s) sis*), which confirms the prosodic distinctiveness of such a sequence. The evidence of sigmatic ecthlipsis thus ties in closely with that of contraction, in so far as it supports the claim that *esse* is clitic in nature.

2.4 Implications

The findings of the research on these linguistic phenomena have many implications which I will review in the final chapter (VI).

First, they throw light on orthographic, phonetic, prosodic, and syntactic aspects of the verb 'to be' in Latin: forms of *esse* have a strong bond with the participle and predicate noun or adjective and may either be reduced phonetically in combination with such hosts, or participate in a prosodic simplification of -V*ss*- which they may share with the host (e.g. *nullŭ(s)sum*).

Second, transmitted contracted spellings, or readings betraying a misunderstanding of them, should be given full consideration by editors and not disregarded. Contracted spellings might be restored in other conditions since manuscripts are often not trustworthy when transmitting uncontracted forms. Contracted forms may be stylistically motivated. For instance, in comedy they occur more frequently in spoken metres, and in late Latin become a spelling archaism. Contracted forms should be taught to students and deserve a place in the paradigm of the present indicative of the verb *esse* (*sum, es / -'s, est / -st, sumus, estis, sunt*).

Finally, sigmatic ecthlipsis in Terence occurs for certain only in restricted conditions: the editorial practice of printing it wherever it is possible even if not necessary is misleading. The large amount of data which has been used in my analysis will not be not included in the body of the book due to limited space and is found in the Appendix.

14   *Introduction*

3. METHODOLOGICAL ISSUES

3.1 Variant Forms

I shall now discuss certain methodological issues which arise in any
linguistic research, but are crucial in a linguistic analysis based only
on written sources and focusing on forms (such as -*st* and -*s*) which
are (or appear to be) variants of forms that are (or appear to be)
standard in a language (such as *est* and *es*). Examples of 'variant'
forms in English are *gonna* (a variant of *going to*), *thou* (a variant of
you), *burned* (a variant of *burnt*), and *donut* (a variant of *doughnut*).
The nature of the variation may differ: *donut* is variant simply at the
level of spelling; *gonna* is a phonological variant generated in speech,
which is then reflected in spelling; the form *burned* is not simply a
variant spelling of *burnt*, but is a morphological variant of *burnt* used
both in speech and spelling (cf. OED s.v. *burn* for the distinction in
usage between the two forms). Therefore, by the loose term 'variant
forms' I refer not only to variant spellings but also to phonological
and morphological variants, which are often stylistically marked, as in
the case of archaisms, colloquialisms, and so on (although the various
notions may overlap).

The methodological issues may be explained in practical terms by
considering a phenomenon familiar to English speakers, namely two
variants of the form *it is*: the contracted forms *it's* (displaying contraction of *is* and nowadays the standard contracted form in speech
and spelling) and *'tis* (displaying reduction of *it*, once common in
speech, now restricted to some varieties of English and used in poetry
as an archaism or poeticism).[13] This is also an appropriate way to
introduce contracted forms of *es* and *est* in Latin, which is the topic of
the next three chapters (II–IV), since these seem to be analogous to
English contracted forms in many respects.

If we assume the perspective of a non-native speaker who
happens to find one of these two forms (*it's* and *'tis*) in a literary
text, a series of questions would probably present themselves. Are
these forms supposed to be orthographically correct? Are they
stylistically marked? What are the stylistic differences (if any)
between them and the uncontracted *it is*? Do these forms reflect a
pronunciation of *it is*? If so, which one reflects the standard

---

[13] On this see Peitsara (2004).

pronunciation of *it is*? I shall apply these same questions to Latin contractions of *esse*.

3.2 Speech and Spelling

In addressing the questions raised above, one must first consider the distinction and relation between speech and spelling.[14]

First, while in the written corpus of a language there can be many spellings representing the same form (e.g. *it is*, *it's*, *'tis*, *it iss*, *it'ss*, *its*, *itss*, *itt is*, *itt iss*, *it iz*, etc.), not all of these spellings are equivalent. Some of them may be typographical mistakes and may not necessarily reflect real speech (such as *itt is* for *it is*). Others do reflect pronunciation, and may be created on purpose (such as *it iz* or *it iss*, which may reproduce the English pronunciation of German speakers) or by mistake (e.g. *its* for *it's*); spellings of such a kind, if considered independently and out of context, may look like misspellings, but if they are found repeatedly and in a meaningful context, may reveal themselves as (intentional) phonetic spellings.[15] Some of these phonetic spellings may reproduce the pronunciation of one or more groups of speakers (such as *'tis*, which may reflect the speech of children or comparatively uneducated people,[16] or indeed the Devon dialect[17]) and be recognizable to speakers as acceptable spellings with a strong stylistic value.

Certain other spellings, on the other hand, reflect the commonplace pronunciation of a word or expression. Users easily recognize them but, since they are not standard in writing, they tend to be considered as inappropriate. Therefore these phonetic spellings normally maintain a strong colloquial if not vulgar stylistic value. Spellings reproducing phonological reductions or sandhi outcomes of common linguistic patterns belong to this group (cf. e.g. *gimme love* for *give me love*, *I'm gonna do* for *I'm going to do*).

[14] On this distinction see Adams (2013: 11–12).

[15] Cf. e.g. G. W. Cable, *Strong Hearts* 1899, ch. 3.9: '*Ach! it iss you? Ach, you must coom—coom undt hellup me! Coom! you shall see someding.*'

[16] Cf. e.g. the use of *'tis* in the speech of the elf Dobby in the Harry Potter books: *'tis part of the house-elf's enslavement, sir. We keeps their secrets and our silence, sir* (J. K. Rowling, *Harry Potter and the Goblet of Fire*, ch. 21. Copyright © J. K. Rowling 2000).

[17] For the spread of the form *'tis* in the Devon dialect see Peitsara (2004: in particular 85–8).

Phonetic spellings that reproduce the commonplace pronunciation of very common words can be 'institutionalized' in written texts, thus becoming variant forms which conserve a colloquial value (strong or less strong according to various factors). Contractions are normally considered to be at this stage (e.g. *I'm* for *I am, doesn't* for *does not, it's* for *it is,* etc.).[18]

Finally, phonetic spellings may lose their colloquial value and eventually be accepted as standard spellings, either replacing the old, formerly more correct spelling (this is the case e.g. with the spelling *jail* which has replaced the archaic spelling *gaol*; cf. OED *s.v.*), or coexisting with it as its conditional variant in particular phonological contexts without any marked stylistic value (such as is the case with the forms of the indefinite article *a/an*).

Many factors intervene in the relation between spelling and speech, such as: (1) movement towards analogy and uniformity in the language; (2) prescriptive factors; (3) the influence of spelling on pronunciation; (4) phonotactics[19] or orthographical rules. For instance in the case of (1), one form may be preferred to another in speech for the sake of uniformity within the inflection in general, and consequently come also to be used as an alternative spelling in writing (such as e.g. the forms *burned* and *dreamed,* sometimes preferred to the irregular *burnt* and *dreamt* in both speech and spelling). It may also happen (2) that prescriptive factors, such as the etymological rule, introduce or fossilize a spelling against pronunciation (such as is the case with e.g. the preservation of the consonant cluster /kt/ in the form *Antarctic,* in conformity with the Greek spelling ἀνταρκτικός). Alternatively (3), the spelling system itself may produce a non-standard pronunciation (this is the case for instance with so-called 'spelling pronunciations', that is pronunciations modelled on spelling, such as e.g. /'ɒft(ə)n/ for *often*). Finally (4), a particular form (in speech and/or spelling) may be restrained or influenced by phonotactics (e.g. in the clause *three sixths is the same as one half* the verb *is* cannot

---

[18] Cf. Quirk (1985: 123): 'Contractions are phonologically reduced or simplified forms which are institutionalized in both speech and writing. As such, they are to be distinguished from cases of phonological reduction only.... A contracted form can undergo additional phonological reduction, and this is very commonly the case with the negative contractions, where the final /nt/ is reduced to /n/; eg.: *haven't* /hævn/, *isn't* /izn/'.

[19] I.e. the set of restrictions in a language on the permissible combinations of sounds.

contract, as English phonotactics does not allow more than four consonants in the coda of a syllable) or by orthographical rules (for instance it is unlikely that the form *'s* will be accepted as a full morphological variant of *is* since in English orthography there are few words which are spelt without at least one vowel).

3.3 Sociolects, Registers, Genres

Other factors which one must take into account in the analysis of variant forms in both speech and spelling is the sociolinguistic background of the user (speaker/writer), i.e. his sociolect, and the circumstances and context in which the form is used, i.e. the register or the genre of writing.[20]

First, a form which is commonly found in the speech or writing of one group of people may be extremely rare in the speech or writing of another group; alternatively, the same form may characterize the speech of two groups of people who do not have contact with each other (for example, the form *'tis* appears to be common both in Devon dialect and in the speech of small children from other parts of the country, as already mentioned). Moreover, the same form may have a different meaning or may be used in a different way according to the group of people using it: the adjective *cool* means one thing if it is used by a teenage schoolboy talking about his new schoolmate, but another if used by a journalist discussing the weather (not to mention *hot*). The factors which define the nature of a group of users can vary, and include geography, education, personal history, job, interests, income, and so on.

Second, the same person may prefer to use different forms in different circumstances and contexts: a politician may prefer to use *it's* if addressing a group of supporters during his electoral campaign but *it is* in his formal inauguration speech.[21] Similarly, a university professor may always write *it is* in her books but use *it's* in emails to her students. The student may prefer to use *it is* in emails to the professor but *it's* in emails to his girlfriend. The factors which define

[20] On sociolects, registers, and genres see Labov (2008), Dickey and Chahoud (2010: 3–6), Clackson (2010, 2011c), Adams (2013: especially 3–27).

[21] For instance, in the electoral speeches of President B. Obama (in 2008) and Prime Minister D. Cameron (in 2010) the contraction *it's* is common; conversely, in their inauguration speeches it is carefully avoided.

the context are many, but often depend on the relationship between the interlocutors and the medium of communication. The terms which are normally used to refer to these domains of linguistic variation are *register* and *genre*.[22]

The stylistic attributes of a word or expression (such as whether it should be considered a colloquialism or not) are also influenced by register: the form *it's* found in an academic book will have a stronger colloquial value than the same form found in an email. Conversely, a form *it is*, which is stylistically neutral in an academic book, is likely to be used only as a formalism in children's books such as the Harry Potter series.[23] Similarly, a university professor who prefers systematically to use *it is* in her speech will sound less awkward to her colleagues than a young guy would to his mates.[24]

3.4 Diachronic Factors

A third factor to take into account is the history of the language. Spoken language evolves, and forms that are nowadays very rarely heard in common speech were possibly very common some centuries ago; for instance, if 'proleptic' contraction of *it is* (*'tis*) was presumably common in speech in Shakespeare's time,[25] it is now unfamiliar in contemporary English (except that of particular dialects or sociolects).[26] Spelling systems also evolve; if in eighteenth-century English the spelling *gaol* was more common than *jail*, the situation is now clearly reversed.

Since speech and spelling do not normally evolve at the same speed, the stylistic value of a variant form varies at different moments in history; a form may be a purely phonetic spelling, with a strong

[22] Registers and genres, although sometimes coinciding (e.g. in technical texts), should not be confounded, especially because many genres (such as *in primis* literary genres) are able to include a wide range of registers (cf. Dickey and Chahoud (2010: 5)).

[23] Cf. e.g. the extract from the speech by the director of the school (of magic) quoted in section 1 (passage n. 1), which does not contain any contractions.

[24] On the issue of 'colloquialism' and in particular on the relation between colloquialism and literary genres see Chahoud (2010: esp. 64).

[25] See the figures offered by Peitsara (2004: 82): *'tis*, 97.75%; *it's*, 2.25%. According to her it is 'not possible to see any tendency in the use of either variant as to any particular period of Shakespeare's career . . . any particular type of play (comedy, tragedy, history) or any particular type of character (noblemen, servants, supernatural beings, etc.).' On colloquial contractions in Shakespeare cf. also Crystal (2008: 137–42).

[26] In the British National Corpus the frequency of *'tis* is less than 1% of the total number of forms *it* + *is*.

colloquial value, in one period (as *it's* probably was until the beginning of the eighteenth century[27]), but be a variant spelling at another, with a weaker colloquial value (as *it's* is nowadays),[28] or a poeticism (as *'tis* is often nowadays,[29] in contrast with its colloquial ring in Shakespeare's time). Moreover, variant forms may have a different colloquial value at different periods; in the 1920s the form *it's* had a stronger colloquial value than it has nowadays.[30]

In periods in which there is no single institutionalized spelling of a particular form (as apparently was the case in the first half of the nineteenth century in respect of *it's* and *'tis*),[31] the practice may be different in different texts, under the influence of register and geographic factors[32] or even just personal taste.

3.5 Linguistic 'Intertextuality'

Another element to be considered is linguistic intertextuality, that is the process by which a form is used by a writer in imitation of another writer or written text (normally considered authoritative), or in adherence to the codified language of a genre of writing. If a sociolect and a dialect are the language of a group of people distinguished socially or geographically, linguistic intertextuality refers to the sociolect or dialect of the users of a particular writing genre. If sociolects and dialects normally vary across historical periods and should therefore be diachronically distinguished, linguistic intertextuality is not chronologically constrained since it does not influence speakers but writers.

---

[27] Cf. Peitsara (2004: 81).

[28] Despite the fact that *it's* is hardly ever used in academic writing and is considered colloquial by many grammars and dictionaries, it is nowadays a standard form in many genres of writing: the figures in the British National Corpus are 75% of contracted *it's* in fiction (out of the total number of cases *it* + *is*), 50% in magazines and newspapers.

[29] Cf. n. 38.

[30] In the Corpus of Historical American English (CHAE), the frequency of *it's* is 26% in texts dating to the 1920s, whereas it is 72% in texts dating to the 2000s.

[31] In the CHAE the frequency of *'tis* in the 1840s (7%) was almost equivalent to that of *it's* (6%).

[32] For this reason one finds in the same period a southern British writer such as Thomas Hardy who chooses to use *'tis* (the common pronunciation of *it is* in his variety of English) as the standard colloquial variant spelling of *it's*, and another such as Charles Dickens who on the contrary hardly ever uses *'tis* but systematically prefers the spelling *it's*. On the different choices of writers concerning the spellings *'tis* or *it's* see also Peitsara (2004: 83–4).

The genres that are normally exposed to linguistic intertextuality are literature, academic language, the language of the law, and generally all technical languages.[33] The longer a text remains authoritative in that particular genre, the longer it may operate as a source of linguistic intertextuality; while the style of contemporary academic English is different from nineteenth-century academic English, there are still poets who imitate Shakespeare.

The process by which a term acquires a technical, poetic, or archaic connotation is often related to linguistic intertextuality. It is important to stress that linguistic intertextuality operates above all the other linguistic processes so far examined; a contemporary poet may decide to use a particular form or spelling independently from the current usage of this form in language or its occurrence in a particular sociolect or register. For instance the form *'tis* found in the verses of a contemporary poet[34] is probably less likely to be an imitation of Devon dialect or of the speech of young children than of the poems of Shakespeare. Among the genres exposed to linguistic intertextuality, poetry is one of the most affected, because of its inclusiveness and the influence on it of metrical factors.[35]

3.6 Syntactic and Pragmatic Factors: Contracted Forms

As if the situation was not already complex enough, contracted forms (such as *it's* and *'tis*) are variant forms of a particular type with particular features, which the linguist has to take into account. Contracted forms are not individual words but reflect a phonological blending (*it's* < *it* + *is*) of two words, both of which maintain their morphological identity in the mind of the speaker. For this reason they can also be influenced by syntax and pragmatics. For instance, as we have seen above (section 1), the verbal part of the form (*is*) may be individually emphasized, thus preventing contraction: 'Remember, she ... called me "a long-haired pillock"?' 'Well, **it is** a bit long,

---

[33] On Latin technical languages and their conservatism see de Meo (1986: 85–98). Cf. also Fögen (2011), Powell (2011).

[34] Cf. e.g. the frequency of the form *'tis* (33%) in the poems of Jonathan Robin, a contemporary writer who publishes on the web.

[35] Linguistic intertextuality is not a familiar term among classicists but the phenomenon to which it refers is well known. Cf. in particular Coleman (1999) and Dickey and Chahoud (2010).

dear.'[36] In other cases, contraction is prevented when the verb *is* is the only element of the verbal phrase: 'Oh here it is', 'But that's where it is.' Since the factors affecting the presence of an uncontracted form in such contexts are syntactic or pragmatic, it would be incorrect to consider the form *it is* found, for example, in the transcription of a dialogue in a pub as necessarily having any particular stylistic value.

3.7 The Latin Linguist

As discussed in the sections above, a study of variant forms should simultaneously take into account a series of different elements: the distinction and interaction between spelling and speech, the sociolect, register and genre, diachronic factors, 'intertextuality', and syntax and pragmatics.

It is difficult to be aware of all these factors, especially if one only works (as often Latin scholars do) with a small corpus of literary texts selected on the basis of non-linguistic criteria, such as taste or chance. This method risks producing misleading results. Moreover, the perception of native speakers is not always trustworthy.[37] Only surveys which rely on extensive and classified corpora can offer reliable figures.

Such an analysis is not straightforward for English; it becomes extremely complex for Latin. There are no Latin speakers to interview and there are no transliterations of Latin speech; we do not have extensive Latin grammars, dictionaries, or orthographic treatises written by Latin native speakers; there are no classified and prepared databases of the Latin language of a size comparable to the corpora of contemporary English; most of the available texts written by Latin native speakers are literary works, which are elaborate forms of writing, belonging to a specific register and written in a codified language. Finally, and most importantly, the vast majority of the extant Latin texts have been preserved in medieval manuscripts, i.e. in typographical supports much less accurate than modern editions, written by non-native speakers (medieval scribes) who, more often than not, modified the texts (including the spelling of individual words) according to their linguistic background. Moreover, the (few) manuscripts of classical authors copied by native Latin speakers in late antiquity do not often reproduce the orthographic practice of the authors themselves.[38]

With an awareness of the complexity of the issues that must be taken into account, I will deal in the next three chapters (II–IV) with a linguistic phenomenon which shares many features with *it's* and *'tis*, namely the contraction of the second and third person singular forms of the verb *to be* in Latin (*esse*). I have used an extensive corpus of sources, in order to identify anomalies and confirm tendencies across various texts. Attention will also be given to sources which are likely to be closer to the Latin of a native speaker, such as inscriptions, papyri, or substandard texts, and to sources from which one could try to deduce the perception of native speakers about these forms. Literary works are considered, but always from the perspective of the textual critic: manuscripts have been examined or, when that has not been possible, the apparatus of editions consulted. Ancient grammarians have been considered and their (rare) discussions of the phenomenon have been analysed. All the different elements which affect similar phenomena and which I have described above are taken into account; each occurrence of the form is diachronically contextualized, and the context examined. Finally, the forms are also considered from a linguistic point of view, and the question of the influence of syntax and pragmatics on them is addressed.

Not surprisingly in view of its complexity, the topic of the contraction of *esse* in Latin has not been systematically addressed before. The concept of contraction is unconventional in Latin; the term which is normally used for these forms, prodelision, implies a phonological (and metrical) phenomenon represented in writing, but does not refer to the concept of independent clitic forms. Moreover, so-called prodelision is familiar only to readers of archaic authors and Lucretius; in general, few classicists know about it and even fewer think it anything other than an oddity.

4. 'TO BE' IN LATIN: A (SHORT) HISTORY

Since the main topic of my book is the Latin verb *esse*, and in particular its two neglected forms (-*st*, -*'s*), it will be useful to present a brief historical overview of the verb within the Indo-European family.

[38] Cf. de Melo (2010–2012: I.cxvii–cxx, 2011: 322–4).

Table 1.1. The verb *to be* in PIE and Latin

Person	PIE	Latin
1st Sg.	*$h_1$és-mi	*sum*
2nd Sg.	*$h_1$és-si > *$h_1$ési	*es(s)*[39]
3rd Sg.	*$h_1$és-ti	*est*
1st Pl.	*h_1s-mé	*sumus*
2nd Pl.	*h_1s-té	*estis*
3rd Pl.	*h_1s-énti	*sunt*

Table 1.1 displays the forms of the present indicative of the verb 'to be' in Proto Indo-European (PIE) and Latin.[40] There are some observations to be made on the synopsis above, relevant to the topic of contracted forms of *est* and *es*, which I will deal with in the following chapters.

First, from an Indo-European perspective one would expect the second and third singular forms to be 'uncontracted' (*es(s)* < *$h_1$és-si* and *est* < *$h_1$és-ti*).[41] The contracted forms *-st* and *-'s* would therefore be secondary forms, displaying a phonological reduction that, as we will see, presumably results from de-stressing and cliticization.[42]

Second, the first person form *sum* is not the expected outcome from PIE *$h_1$és-mi*, which would rather be *esum/esom*, an archaic form occasionally found in Latin sources[43] and related to the Faliscan form *esú(m)*[44] and to the Sabellian form *esu(m)/ezu(m)*.[45] *Sum* seems

[39] The older form *ess*, presumably still common in early Latin, is also reconstructed on the basis of metre, since in republican Latin poetry *es* is generally measured heavy (‾ < *ess*). Possible traces of the spelling *ess* are occasionally found in the manuscripts of republican authors (cf. e.g. Pl. *Merc.* 489, *Rud.* 240). Cf. Meiser (1998: 221), Questa (2007: 20–1, 40), and see below II.3.8.2.

[40] Cf. Clackson (2007: 124). For other etyma of PIE *$h_1$és-mi*, with slight variations, see Sihler (1995: 548; 1st pl. *h_1s-mós*, 3rd pl. *$h_1$sonti/*$h_1$senti*), Meiser (1998: 221; 2nd pl. *h_1s-tés*), Weiss (2009: 425–7).

[41] Cf. Meiser (1998: 221), Clackson and Horrocks (2007: 66).

[42] Cf. Joseph and Wallace (1987: 686–8), Meiser (1998: 221) and see III.1.3. For a different view see Nyman (1974, 1977) and Sihler (1995: 549), who consider *est* and *es* as derived from older *-st* and *-'s* by insertion of a prothetic vowel (see nn. 46 and 47 and III.1.3).

[43] Such as the inscription on the Garigliano bowl (*esom kom meois sociois*; cf. Mancini (1997), Vine (1998), the inscription from the *Ager Signinus* (*morai eṣo[m]*; cf. Colonna (1994)), and a passage of Varro (*L.* 9.100 *de infectis sum quod nunc dicitur olim dicebatur esum et in omnibus personis constabat, quod dicebatur esum es est*). Cf. also Baldi (1999: 172), Clackson and Horrocks (2007: 30), and see III.1.3.

[44] Cf. Bakkum (2009: 162–3, 197).

[45] Cf. Untermann (2000: 245), Bakkum (2009: 162).

to have derived from *esum/esom*, presumably under the influence of the same phenomena which would explain contracted *-st* and *-'s*, namely de-stressing and cliticization, thus providing a parallel for them.[46]

Third, the second plural form (*estis*) is rather odd from an historical point of view (? < *h_1s-té*); the initial *e-* seems to be a later insertion, possibly explained by analogy with the second and third person singular form (*est* and *es*) and/or by the influence of some phonotactic rule of Latin (presumably the same one responsible for the addition of a prothetic vowel, *e-* or *i-*, to words beginning with *s-* + consonant; cf. e.g. *iscola* < *sch(o)la* and see III.1.2 and III.1.3). The preference for the form *estis* instead of the expected **stis* would provide a parallel for the eventual winning out of the uncontracted forms *est* and *es* over *-st* and *-'s* in late Latin (cf. III.2.2).[47]

In conclusion, there seems to be evidence which supports the idea that forms of *esse* were exposed to phonological reduction (*est* > *-st*, *es(s)* > *-'s*) but that, at the same time, an initial consonantal cluster *st-* in a monosyllabic word attracted the addition (or retention) of *e-*. Far from meriting the neglect that they have suffered among modern scholars and readers, the contracted forms *-st* and *-'s*, widely attested in Latin (cf. II.3), find supporting evidence within the stem of *esse* itself and deserve attention.

5. STATISTICS

A final note on statistics. In this book I will often provide statistics, in order to assess the frequency of a form or pattern of distribution. I am

---

[46] Cf. Joseph and Wallace (1987: 687), Dunkel (1998: 89), Meiser (1998: 221), Baldi (1999), Bammesberger (2004), Clackson and Horrocks (2007: 66), Weiss (2009: 425). For a different view see Bonfante (1932, 2000), Bader (1976), Schmalstieg (1998), according to whom *esum* is an analogical form (*//es, est, estis*), and Sihler (1995: 549), who believes that '**esom* is based on **som*, created at the same time that (enclitic) *-ss* and *-st* were evolving into restressed *ess* and *est*.'

[47] Cf. Sihler (1995: 549–50), according to whom *estis* is a restressed enclitic: 'the *e-* is not inherited from PIE but is a sort of prop-vowel . . . the most likely explanation for its source [i.e. that of *estis*] is of the type *-ss* : *ess* = **stes* : X, where X = *estis*.' Sihler also considers *es* and *est* as having undergone the same process (cf. n. 45).

fully aware, however, that statistical figures are not necessarily significant when one is working with a small set of data, which is often the case with a selected corpus of an ancient language. For instance, in Terence young girls apparently use contracted forms of the type *-ust* much more often (five out of six instances, i.e. 83%) than old women (two out of five instances, 40%): is this significant? The answer is negative, as shown by a statistical test, known as the t-test,[48] which establishes that the likelihood that this pattern is significant is between 80–90% (a very low figure by statistical criteria), i.e. that there is a very high probability that these results arise by chance (p > 0.13). Conversely, the same t-test shows that the rarity of contracted forms in non-metrical inscriptions (1%) compared to their higher frequency in metrical inscriptions (11%) is statistically significant, with a likelihood higher than 99.95%.

I have checked the significance of all the sets of data for which I provide statistical figures, by employing the t-test. The results are normally given in footnotes. As a rule, I have preferred not to provide statistical figures and not to draw conclusions based on them whenever the results of the t-test do not point to a very high statistical significance (> 99%, i.e. p < 0.01); I have highlighted and discussed the few exceptions to this rule.

Everything should now be ready for our journey into the foggy land of 'real' Latin: I cannot promise that I will clear away all the fog, but I hope that at the end of the journey our eyes will be able to see a bit more clearly, especially as far as it concerns the verb 'to be'.

---

[48] For an explanation of the t-test and its applicability in linguistic studies see Woods, Fletcher, and Hughes (1986), Évrard and Mellet (1998), Rietveld and van Hout (2005). Cf. also de Melo (2007a: 15).

II

Contraction of *esse*

Collection of Evidence

illa quidem scriptura confusa
Marius Victorinus p. 75 M.

The aim of this chapter is to collect the evidence for the contraction of *esse* in Latin (*-st* < *est*, *-'s* < *es*). After a general introduction to the phenomenon (section 1) and an overview of the different phonological patterns (section 2), I will present a compilation of the evidence for contracted forms of *esse* in Latin (section 3), collected from a large variety of sources (manuscripts, metre, inscriptions, Sabellian languages, grammarians, etc.).[1]

1. INTRODUCTION

By the 'contraction of *esse*' I refer first of all to a reduced spelling of the second and third person singular present of *sum*, in which the verbal forms *est* and *es* lose their initial *e* (*est* > *-st*, *es* > *-'s*) and attach themselves to the preceding word (which is typically polysyllabic).[2] This spelling is found in modern editions of Latin authors (mainly, but not only, Plautus, Terence, and Lucretius) in particular phonological contexts, especially after words ending in vowels, long and short (e.g. Ter. *Eun.* 471 *ex Aethopiast* [*Aethiopiā* + *est*],[3] Lucr. 1.10

---

[1] The main body of this chapter is a revised and extended version of Pezzini (2011).
[2] Cf. section 2 and IV.3.1.
[3] Quotations from Terence, when not specified, are from Kauer and Lindsay's OCT edition (1958).

patefactast [*patefactă* + *est*],[4] Ter. *Eun.* 426 *tute's* [*tutĕ* + *es*]), and after words ending in -V*m* (e.g. Cic. *Brut.* 225 *cauendumst* [*cauendum* + *est*], Frontin. *Aq.* 109 *palamst* [*palam* + *est*]). This 'contracted spelling' is also found after words ending in vowel + -*s* (-V*s*), generally when the vowel before the -*s* is short (cf. e.g. Enn. *Ann.* 238 S. *paratust* [< *paratŭs* + *est*], Ter. *An.* 702 *forti's* [*fortĭs* + *es*]);[5] in cases of this type, the expected cluster -*ss*- (e.g. **paratusst* < *paratŭs* + *(e)st*) normally appears as -*s*- in both editions and manuscripts (e.g. *penest*), owing either to sigmatic ecthlipsis (for this term cf. V.1) or to the simplification of the phonotactically difficult cluster -*sst*.[6] Finally, there are also a few cases of 'contraction' after words ending in long vowel + -*s* (cf. Ter. *Eun.* 361 *rest* [< *rēs* + *est*]) or ending in another consonant (cf. e.g. Pl. *Trin.* 541 *haecst* [< *haec* + *est*][7]), which however are problematic (cf. section 2).

This phenomenon is known among modern grammarians and linguists as 'prodelision'[8] or 'aphaeresis'.[9] As the term 'prodelision' itself suggests, this phenomenon is normally considered to be related to elision (i.e. the omission of a final vowel before a word beginning with a vowel),[10] a sandhi phenomenon common in metrical texts,

---

[4] Quotations from Lucretius, when not specified, are from Martin's Teubner edition (1959).

[5] Cf. section 2.

[6] There are however some counter-examples, e.g. Pl. *Ps.* 713 *opusst* A, 717 *allatusst* A, which are probably to be considered mere misspellings. On sigmatic ecthlipsis and simplification of -*ss(t)*- see III.1.3, V.1.1, and V.5.

[7] In Lindsay's edition (1940a). Quotations from Plautus, when not specified (as in this case), are from Leo's edition (1895–1896).

[8] A modern term, literally an 'inverse elision', originally coined by scholars of Greek metrics to refer to the phenomenon occurring mainly in Greek tragedy and comedy in which the short initial vowel of a word is lost after a long final vowel or diphthong (cf. e.g. Soph. *Trach.* 381 Ἰόλη 'καλεῖτο = Ἰόλη ἐκαλεῖτο). Cf. Platnauer (1960), West (1982: 13 n. 19), Allen (1987: 102–3).

[9] Ancient grammarians already use this term, but by it they refer to the loss of the prefix in simple-for-compound verbs. Cf. e.g. Serv. *Aen.* 1.59 FERANT *auferant; et est aphaeresis*, 203, 430 etc., Diom. *Ars* GL 1.441.23ff. *aphaeresis est ablatio de principio dictionis contraria prosthesi, cum aut littera amputatur aut syllaba aufertur: littera, ut 'ruit omnia late', pro eruit; syllaba, ut 'temnere diuos' pro contemnere, et 'linquere castra' pro relinquere*, GL 4.396.9f., GL 5.297.4ff., GL 6.452.5f. Scholars of Greek metrics have used the term *aphaeresis* in its modern sense as a synonym for prodelision (cf. preceding note). Cf. also Weiss (2009: 426).

[10] According to the standard definition, cf. Allen (1978: 78–82). Some scholars (cf. in particular Soubiran (1966: especially 55–91) and Traina and Bernardi Perini (1998: 258–60)) have denied that the final vowel was completely omitted in pronunciation but believe rather that it was merged with the following syllable; this is a complex

which most likely reflected a practice common in spoken language.[11]
Despite the considerable amount of evidence, the contraction of *esse*
(= prodelision/aphaeresis) has not yet been systematically investigated and comprehensively explained,[12] and this deficiency has led
editors to deal with it in different ways. The case of the text of
Catullus is an example; in Goold's edition (1989) contraction is
always printed when possible (that is, every time *est* and *es* follow a
word ending in a vowel or in an elidible *-m*), whereas in Bardon's
edition (1973) it is printed seven times, in Mynors' OCT edition
(1958) only four times, and in Eisenhut's Teubner edition (1983),
never.

Many issues are still to be fully addressed concerning the nature of
the contraction. Are contracted spellings to be considered simply as
misspellings (such as in English *its nice* for *it's nice*) or as abbreviations (such as Mr for Mister)? Or are they phonetic spellings reflecting a phonological variant current in some varieties of speech (such as
in English *gonna* for *going to*)? Or are they to be considered common
and accepted variant spellings, reflecting the standard pronunciation
of such forms (such as the form *it's* for *it is* in English)? If so, what, if
any, is their stylistic value (colloquial, archaic, poetic, etc.)? Or are
contracted spellings exceptional graphical realizations of a sandhi
phenomenon common in metrical texts (such as the 'elided' spelling
of final *-e* in Shakespeare's verse 'Th' expense of spirit in a waste of

---

problem and this is not the place to discuss the various arguments in detail. However,
statistics (cf. Allen (1978: 79–81)) suggest that complete elision was standard at least
with words ending in a short vowel and with certain classes of common words ending
in a long vowel. Final *-ī* and *-ū* probably underwent synizesis with the following
syllable, thus becoming semivowels. As far as 'prodelision' is concerned, it is beyond
doubt that the vowel *e-* in *est/es* was completely lost, including in cases after *-ī* and *-ū*
(cf. Soubiran (1966: 183–4) and see section 2). This fact itself suggests that 'prodelision' and elision should not be considered equivalent phenomena.

[11] Cf. III.1.2 with n. 7.
[12] Previous discussions (cf. in particular Brinkmann (1906), Questa (2007: 39–49);
also some useful observations in Müller (1894: 364–6), Leo (1912: 279–88), Lindsay
(1922: 74–6, 129–35, 209, 1961: 24–5)) are mainly based on Plautine evidence, which
thus does not require any fresh investigation. An exception is Havet (1884, 1911:
232–3), but the number of cases he quotes is small. The matter is treated briefly by
grammars (cf. Leumann (1977: 123–4), Sommer and Pfister (1977: 215)). Marouzeau
(1908; cf. III.1.1) offers a fairly unconvincing interpretation of contracted spellings,
mainly construed as mere abbreviations. The recent work of Fortson (2008: 134–75)
explicitly aims to investigate the phenomenon from a linguistic point of view only,
and will be taken into account especially in chapter IV.

shame'[13])? And, finally, should diachronic factors be considered in the analysis of the form, as they must be, e.g., in the case of the form *'tis*, whose stylistic value in Shakespeare is different from its value in contemporary texts?[14] In this chapter I will collect evidence for contracted forms of *est* and *es* in Latin in order to provide a comprehensive overview on which one can rely in dealing with the questions posed above, which will be the subject of chapters III and IV.

Before presenting the evidence for contracted forms, it is important to stress that in using the term 'contraction' one may adopt two different approaches: a purely phonetic approach, which considers contracted forms as utterances of speech (e.g. /'faktast/), or an orthographic approach, which considers them as spellings attested in writing (e.g. *factast*). A distinction should be maintained between these two levels, speech and spelling, even if they are related; if a contracted pronunciation (e.g. /'faktast/) may be construed as a mere phonological variant for an uncontracted form (*facta est*), without implications for the spelling of *est* in Latin, a contracted spelling (*factast*) cannot but be pronounced as contracted /faktast/, unless it is an abbreviation.[15]

These issues will be addressed more specifically in chapter III, where the two levels will be analysed separately. In the present chapter, however, I will partially overlook this distinction and simply collect the evidence, often without specifying whether it is relevant to speech or spelling. This decision is due to the fact that individual pieces of evidence can often be considered in either way; it is hazardous to attempt an interpretation of these without first having undertaken an evaluation of contraction as it occurs in a wide range of sources.

2. PHONOLOGICAL PATTERNS

I have briefly mentioned in the previous section the range of phonological contexts in which it is possible to find contracted forms of *est/es*. In this section I will present them in detail.

---

[13] *Sonnet* 129.1 (ed. Burrow 2002).
[14] For all these notions ('phonetic spellings', 'variant spellings', 'diachronic factors', etc.) and the related methodological issues see I.3.
[15] On the distinction between spelling and speech cf. I.3.2.

The largest group[16] (Table 2.1) includes instances of *est/es* following a word ending in a vowel (-V + *est/es*), either long or short. Another large[17] group (Table 2.2) includes instances of *est/es* following a word ending in elidible -*m* (-V*m* + *est*). A third, smaller[18] group (Table 2.3) includes instances of *est/es* following a word ending in -*s* preceded by a short vowel (-*ŭ*, -*ĭ*, and, more rarely, -*ĕ*[19]). This pattern is mainly attested in archaic authors and in inscriptions dated to the republican period.

Table 2.1. Contracted forms after words ending in a vowel

Pattern	Explanation	Examples
-ast/-a's	-ā/ă + est/es	ex Aethopiast (Aethiopiā + est) Ter. *Eun.* 471 patefactast (patefactă + est) Lucr. 1.10 temulenta's (temulentă + es) Ter. *Eun.* 655
-est/-e's	-ē/ĕ + est/es	aegrest aegrĕ + est) Ter. *Ph.* 162 malest (malĕ + est) Catul. 38.1 (Mynors 1958) tute's (tutĕ + es) Ter. *Eun.* 426
-ist/-i's	-ī/ĭ + est/es	relicuist (relicuī + est) Ter. *Haut.* 193 mihist (mihĭ + est) Ter. *Haut.* 742[20] si's (sī + es) Prop. 2.22b.4 (Goold 1999)
-ost/-o's	-ō/ŏ + est/es	modost (modŏ + est) Ter. *Ad.* 386[21] nemost (nemō + est) Lucr. 4.174 ganeo's (ganeō + es) Ter. *Haut.* 1034
-ust/-u's	-ū/ŭ + est/es	scitust (scitū + est) Ter. *Hec.* 296 diust (diŭ+ est) Pl. *Merc.* 541[22] tu's (tū + es) Pl. *Trin.* 454

[16] There are some 650 instances in Leo's edition of Plautus (1895–1896), about 450 instances in Kauer and Lindsay's edition of Terence (1958), about 200 in Martin's edition of Lucretius (1959), and at least another 250 to be found in editions of other authors (excluding cases in editions which *always* print the contracted spelling, cf. section 1); in this last group we find at least forty-seven instances in modern editions of Cicero and about fifty in some modern editions of Virgil (cf. section 3.1.1).

[17] Some 450 instances in Plautus, about 265 in Terence, about eighty in Lucretius, and at least sixty in other authors.

[18] Almost 600 instances in Plautus, about ninety in Terence, six in Lucretius, and at least thirty-four in other authors, mainly republican.

[19] On the pattern -*est* = -*ĕs* + *est* cf. also III.1.4.4, with n. 65.

[20] The pronoun *mihi* appears to be normally scanned pyrrich (˘ ˘) in Terence. Cf. Questa (2007: 63). The only certain exception out of more than 300 instances is at *And.* 112.

[21] The adverbial form *modo* is normally scanned pyrrich (˘ ˘) in Terence (cf. Lindsay 1922: 207) except in particular metrical contexts (cf. Questa (2007: 97, 440)).

[22] In Plautus *diu* is normally scanned pyrrich (˘ ˘) in iambo-trochaic lines (cf. Questa (2007: 97)).

Table 2.2. Contracted forms after words ending in elidible -*m*

Pattern	Explanation	Examples
-amst	-am + est	quoniamst (quoniam + est) Lucr. 1.604
		palamst (palam + est) Frontin. *Aq.* 109
-emst	-em + est	quidemst (quidem + est) Cels. 2.15.4 (Marx 1915)
		autemst (autem + est) Lucr. 4.1058
-imst	-im + est	olimst (olim + est) Pl. *Poen.* 356
		generatimst (generatim + est) Lucr. 2.1089
-umst (-uomst)	-um (-uom) + est	cauendumst (cauendum + est) Cic. *Brut.* 225
		fatendumst (fatendum + est) Lucr. 1.205
		aequomst (aequom + est) Pl. *Asin.* 186

Table 2.3. Contracted forms after words ending in short vowel + -*s*

Pattern	Explanation	Examples
-ust (-uost)/-u's	-ŭs (-uŏs) + est/es	paratust (paratŭs + est) Enn. *Ann.* 238 S.
		mortuost (mortuŏs + est) Pl. *Aul.* 568
		miseritust (miseritŭs + est) Afran. 417 R.[23]
		exercituru's (exerciturŭs + es) Pl. *Amph.* 324
-ist/-i's	-ĭs + est/es	laborist (laborĭs + est) Ter. *Haut.* 82
		forti's (fortĭs + es) Ter. *An.* 702
-est/[24]	-ĕs + est	penest (penĕs + est) Pl. *Amph.* 653

A very small group (Table 2.4) includes contracted forms in problematic phonological contexts: contracted *es* following -*m*, *est* following words ending in long vowel + -*s* or ending in a consonant other than -*s* or -*m*. In this group I also include a particular pattern of forms ending in -*est*, which some scholars have considered as deriving from -*ĭs* + *est*. Each pattern listed in Table 2.4 requires separate consideration.

The first pattern listed in Table 2.4 (-*m's* < '*m* + *es*) is problematic because it is hardly ever attested in manuscripts, a fact which is apparently striking given the frequency of the pattern -*mst*, especially in the manuscripts of Plautus, Terence, and Lucretius (cf. section

---

[23] Quotations from republican playwrights, if not specified, are from Ribbeck (1871–1873).

[24] No instances of the second person form have been found. On -*est* = -*es* + *est* cf. also III.1.4.4 with n. 65.

Table 2.4. Problematic patterns of contracted forms

Pattern	Explanation	Examples
-m's	< -m + es	omnium's (omnium + es) Catul. 49.7
		(*sic* **Trappes-Lomax 2007: 123** : omniums R^{ac} : omnium R^{pc} *cett. codd. edd.*)
-est	< ēs + est	rest (rēs + est) Ter. *Eun.* 361
-lst/-cst/*etc.*	< -C + est	nilst (nihil + est) Ter. *Haut.* 676
		illicst (illic + est) Ter. *An.* 607
-est	< -ĭs + est	similest (? similĭs + est) Ter. *Haut.* 1020

3.1.1 and III.2.1). For this reason, scholars generally do not adopt this spelling in their editions (cf. e.g. Ter. *Hec.* 681 *alteram es*), with the exception of editors who systematically print contraction after -V and -*m*, such as Goold in his edition of Propertius (cf. Prop. 2.28.59, 3.23.12 *quoniam's*). However, the contracted form -'*s* seems to be attested in the Romanus manuscript of Catullus (fourteenth century), which had for the word *omnium* (49.7) the reading *omniums* (cf. Trappes-Lomax (2007: 123) who prints *omnium's*), before someone deleted the -*s*. Although this would apparently be the only direct evidence for the spelling -*m(')s*, it is not inconceivable that this reading is indeed to be construed as a contracted spelling and not as a misspelling (as most editors seem to think). First, the number of instances of the sequence -*m* + *es* in Plautus, Terence, and Lucretius is very low (about twenty-eight) compared to the frequency of the sequence -*m* + *est* in the same authors (> *c.*1300, of which > *c.*600 are spelt uncontracted in manuscripts): the exceptionality of the spelling -*m(')s* might thus be less significant than it seems. Second, the spelling -*m(')s* was presumably very obscure-looking to scribes (as also shown by the textual situation of Catullus' Romanus at 49.7): its non-existence in the manuscript tradition of Plautus, Terence, and Lucretius might be simply due to late antique and medieval interventions. Consequently, it is not impossible that this pattern of contraction (-*m's* < = -*m* + *es*), although scarcely attested in manuscripts, was as standard as the pattern -*mst*: spellings such as *postquam's* (Catul. 67.6, Goold (1989)), or *quoniam's* (Prop. 3.23.12, Goold (1999)), although lacking direct supporting evidence in manuscripts, are not completely implausible (cf. also Lindsay (1922: 74) who proposes the reading *nequam's* at Pl. *Asin.* 710).

The only attested case of the second type of Table 2.4 (*est* following long vowel + -*s*) is the controversial form *rest*, accepted by some scholars[25] but rejected by others.[26] Manuscripts apparently give it only at Pl. *Merc.* 857 (*rest* B;[27] but apparatuses are contradictory) in the fixed expression *certa res (est)*. Lindsay (1904a) accepts it in his text but Leo (1895–1896) prefers to print *res*, presumably having in mind Pl. *St.* 473 where A gives *certa res* with omission of the verb (which is admitted by the metre), while P has *certa res est* (not admitted by the metre). In Kauer and Lindsay's (1958) edition of Terence *rest* is printed three times (*Eun.* 268, 312 *res est* A, 361 *res* A); however, only in the third case is the uncontracted form *contra metrum* (Marouzeau prints the reading of A with omission of the verb: *at nil ad nostram hanc? :: alia res*). Therefore, although it is occasionally found in editions, there is no clear evidence for contracted forms of *est* after a long vowel + *s*, despite the number of potential instances.[28] Other untransmitted cases of this pattern, such as *uerbist* (< *uerbīs est*), are even more implausible (cf. Questa (2007: 44)).

As far as the third type is concerned (-*st* after a consonant other than -*m* or -*s*), there are few cases attested in manuscripts. Apart from the instances listed in Table 2.4, one finds: *Merc.* 285 *quidst* | A, 884 *miserst* | **codd.** (*miser* B[pc]), *Mil.* 469 *quidst* | A, 964 *nuptanst* B, 1139 *quidst* | A, *Pers.* 6 *nonst* A[ac], *Poen.* 407 *quidst* | A, 865 *idst* A, 1333 *hicst* A, *St.* 330 *isst* | A, *Trin.* 541 *haecst* A (*ut videtur*, cf. Studemund (1889: *ad loc.*)), *Curc.* 85 *sat st* | B, *Epid.* 461 *nonst* BE, *Men.* 498 *nomenst* | B[ac] : *nomen sit* CDB[pc].[29] Almost all these forms are *contra metrum* and they are not normally accepted by editors. Moreover,

---

[25] Cf. Havet (1911: 232), Lindsay (1922: 75), Lindsay (1961: 24–5), Nyman (1975).

[26] Cf. Leo (1895–1896: 255), Questa (2007: 43–4).

[27] Capital letters in bold refer to the sigla of the manuscripts used in the appropriate editions.

[28] E.g. in Terence there are about thirty instances of the sequence long vowel + -*s* + *est*, all to be scanned (and printed) uncontracted: *rēs est* (*An.* 368, 459, 588, 693, 845, *Haut.* 158, 318, 490, 564, 689, *Eun.* 748, 979, *Ph.* 479, *Ad.* 206, 418, 643), *spēs est*, (*An.* 304, *Eun.* 295, 1054, *Ph.* 319), *senēs est* (*Haut.* 419), *diēs est* (*Hec.* 185), *crās est* (*Eun.* 338), *paupertās est* (*Ph.* 903), *fās est* (*Hec.* 387), *nōs est* (*Haut.* 182), *mōs est* (*Haut.* 562), *liberōs est* (*Haut.* 949), *uōs est* (*Haut.* 977), *honōs est* (*Eun.* 1023), *uōs estne* (*Ph.* 740), *drachumīs est* (*An.* 451), *aedīs est* (*Haut.* 275), *uīs est* (*Ad.* 943).

[29] Cf. also Lindsay (1904b: 65), who suggests *haecst* and *hicst* at Pl. *St.* 237, and *Poen.* 1333, and his notes in the apparatus of his edition (1904a) at Pl. *Trin.* 563 (uel etiam *hicst locutus*), *Truc.* 693 (an *hicst*?).

the majority of these (except those at *Pers.* 6, *Poen.* 865, 1333, *Trin.* 541, *Mil.* 964, and *Epid.* 461, the last at the end of the half-line) are found at the end of the line (indicated by | in the list above), and therefore are probably to be construed as abbreviations.[30] The only transmitted forms printed in editions are Pl. *Mil.* 964 *nuptanst* and *Trin.* 541 *haecst*, accepted by Lindsay, who resorts to scanning this latter line with a hiatus between *glabrae* and *em* in order to accommodate the form.[31] Kauer and Lindsay (1958) also print in their edition of Terence the two forms reported in Table 2.4 (Ter. *An.* 607 *illicst*, *Haut.* 676 *nilst*); these contracted forms are not transmitted by manuscripts but are supposedly required by metre. Other editors, however, scan the two lines without a contracted form (cf. Marouzeau (1963: *ad loc.*)). Contraction after a consonant other than *-m* or *-s* is in fact a pattern that not only, as pointed out, lacks strong supporting evidence, but would also infringe upon some phonotactic rules of Latin, according to which an *-s* cannot be preceded by a consonant in the coda of a syllable (*-cst*, *-lst*).[32]

The last problematic pattern comprises adjectival forms ending in *-est* in a context that seems to require the morphological sequence *-ĭs* (masculine or feminine) + *est* (cf. e.g. Ter. *Haut.* 1019 [*natus*] *consimilest moribus* [? = *consimilis est*]). These forms are sporadically transmitted in manuscripts and have long been the object of controversy among scholars of Plautus and Terence. I will postpone the analysis of this pattern (*-est* <? *-is est*) to the next chapter (III.1.4), since its interpretation depends on the general phonological assessment of contracted forms.

A last note before I proceed with the collection of evidence: if we consider the forms with strong supporting evidence, the word to which the contracted form of the verb is attached is almost always

---

[30] Cf. also Questa (2007: 315) commenting on *Mil.* 469 and 1139 (*quidst*).

[31] Pl. *Trin.* 541 (ia⁶) *ŏues* | *scăbrae* | *sunt, tam* | *glăbrae* |—*em, qu(am) haecst* | *mănus* |.

[32] According to this rule the pattern *-umst* would be problematic as well: however, in such a combination the consonant *-m(-)* was probably realized as a (long) nasalized vowel (cf. section 3.1.2). On Latin phonotaxis see Weiss (2009: 189–91). On contracted forms after consonants other than *-m* and *-s* see also Leo (1912: 281), Lindsay (1922: 76), Questa (2007: 42, 66).

polysyllabic. Contracted forms after monosyllabic words are rarely attested in manuscripts and rarely required by metre.[33] I will come back to this point in chapter IV, where I will investigate the syntactic limitations of contracted forms (IV.3.1).

3. THE EVIDENCE

Sources of six main types constitute the evidence for contracted forms of *esse*: direct transmission in manuscripts, presented in section 3.1; metre, discussed in section 3.2; readings in manuscripts potentially resulting from a misunderstanding of a contracted spelling, in section 3.3; inscriptions, section 3.4; grammarians, section 3.5; parallels in Sabellian languages, presented in section 3.6. There are also sources of some other types which, to a certain extent, may provide evidence for contraction, and will be analysed in section 3.7.

At this point it will be useful to distinguish between third and second person forms. While contracted forms of *est* are readily found in manuscripts and are also attested in inscriptions, contracted forms of *es* are hardly ever transmitted in manuscripts or inscriptions and are generally reconstructed on the basis of metre. Moreover, the number of restorations of contracted second person forms is much smaller than that of contracted third person forms; in Leo's edition of Plautus there are only about 150 instances of contracted *-(e)s*, against around 1550 of contracted *-(e)st*, and in the OCT edition of Terence only thirty-five against about 800. No contracted *(e)s* is found in Martin's edition of Lucretius, and no more than ten instances are found in editions of other authors (excluding editions where contraction is always printed).

The following discussion will therefore take into account only the third person singular form. I will present the evidence for contraction of the second person form in a separate section (section 3.8).

---

[33] See below IV.3.1 and Fortson (2008: 172). Cf. however Ter. *Hec.* 535 *est* A : *test* A²KL : *te est cett. codd. Mar.*

3.1 Direct Transmission in Manuscripts

3.1.1 Collection of Data

The most extensive evidence for contracted forms is provided by manuscripts, which, in some cases, give the spelling *st* instead of *est*, usually directly attached to the preceding word (*-st*). These spellings are extremely widespread in the manuscript tradition of three authors: Plautus, Terence, and Lucretius; given this concentration it would be unjustifiable to speak of mere misreadings (cf. III.1.1). In Plautus there are around 1300 instances in which the contracted spelling has direct support in manuscripts, out of a total of approximately 2750 relevant instances, i.e. *est* placed after a vowel, after elidible *-m*, or after a sequence of short vowel + final *s*, all occupying the metrical position of a single syllable (rate of transmission = 47%). In Terence there are about 420 instances in which the contracted spelling is found in at least one manuscript (mostly the late-antique A), out of some 970 relevant instances (rate of transmission = 43%).[34] In Lucretius the number of contractions found in manuscripts is about 265, out of around 420 relevant instances of *est* placed after a vowel or *-m* (rate of transmission = 63%).[35] The only form that belongs to the pattern -V*s* + *est* and is contracted in spelling in Lucretius' manuscripts is the archaism *necessust* (cf. pp. 135–6). After Lucretius, contraction after -V*s* is hardly ever found in manuscripts.

Contracted forms of *est* are also found in manuscripts of other authors, although they are generally ignored by editors. Forty-three examples are found in manuscripts of Virgil, listed in Box 2.1 (when the reference is underlined, the form is found at the end of the line). The total number of instances of the pattern -V/-V*m* followed by *est* (i.e. those in which *est* could potentially be contracted in spelling) in Virgil is 197. The percentage of instances found contracted in at least one manuscript is therefore appreciable (22%), and not dramatically lower than in Plautus (47%) and Terence (43%). Most of these instances (thirty-five) are transmitted only by ancient manuscripts of Virgil, i.e. dating to late antiquity.[36] Traces of contracted spellings

---

[34] Cf. Appendix 1.1.   [35] Cf. p. 128.

[36] Seven by **M** (Italy V c.), eleven by **P** (Italy V/VI c.), one by **MP**, eight by **R** (Italy V/VI c.), six by **V** (Italy V c.), one by **F** (Italy, end of IV c.), one by **AV** (both V c.).

Box 2.1 **Contracted forms in manuscripts of Virgil**

(underlined: at the end of the line)

Aen. 1.306 datast P^{ac} : data est P^{pc} *cett.*

2.701 morast V : maior est M^{ac} : mora est M^{pc} *cett.*

2.703 troiast V : troia est *cett.*

3.341 puerost F^{ac} : puero est F^{pc} *cett.*

4.370 amantemst P^{ac} : amanteë p^{ac} : amantem a *Pomp.* : amantem est P^{pc} *cett.*

4.639 perficerest P : perficere est *cett.*

4.691 torost P^{ac}c : toro est P^{pc} *cett.*

5.571 sidoniost P : sidonio es R : sidonio est *cett.*

6.325 turbast M^{ac} : turba est M^{pc} *cett.*

6.455 amorest M^{ac} : amore est M^{pc} *cett.*

6.719 putandust P^{ac} : putandumst P^{pc} : putandum F : putandum est *cett.*

7.263 cupidost V : cupido *Tib. et schol ver. Aen. 9.361* : cupido est *cett.*

7.552 abundest R : abunde est *cett.*

8.71 undest MP : unde sit F^{ac} : unde est F^{pc} *cett.*

9.187 quietest M^{ac} : quiescit P^{ac} : quiete est $M^{pc}P^{pc}$ *cett.*

10.240 certast V : certa est *cett.*

10.710 uentumst P^{ac} : uentum M^{ac} : uentum est $M^{pc}P^{pc}$ *cett.*

10.792 tantost P^{ac} : tanto est P^{pc} *cett.*

11.23 imost M^{ac} : imo **Pra** : imo est M^{pc} *cett.*

11.151 dolorest $M^{ac}P\gamma$: dolori est *Serv. Aen. 12.47* : dolore est M^{pc}R *Don.*

11.178 tuast P^{ac} : tua est P^{pc} *cett.*

11.683 suprast M^{ac} : supra est M^{pc} *cett.*

12.23 latinost P : latino γ^{pc} : latino est γ^{ac} *cett.*

12.678 acerbist P : acerbe est **a** : acerbum est *Serv.* : acerbi est *cett.*

12.739 uentumst P^{ac} : uentum M^{ac} : uentum est $M^{pc}P^{pc}$ *cett.*

12.879 ademptast M : adempta est *cett.*

Ecl. 4.63 cubilest R : cubili est P^{ac} : cubile est P^{pc} *cett.*

6.11 ullast V : ulla est *cett.*

6.74 secutast R^{ac} : secuta M : secuta est R^{pc} *cett.*

7.43 annost $M^{ac}a^{ac}$: anno est $M^{pc}a^{pc}$ *cett.*

8.107 certest $P^{ac}a^{ac}$: certe est $P^{pc}a^{pc}$ *cett.*

10.23 secutast $M^{ac}R^{ac}$a : secuta est $M^{pc}R^{pc}$ *cett.*

Georg. 2.82 miratastque M^{1} : mirataeque M : miraturque M^{7}en : mirata estque γ^{2}ad : miratasque *cett. Porph., Phil. Georg. 1.54, Serv. Georg. 2.82, Serv. Georg. 1.103* (A) (cf. Sabbadini *ad. loc.*) : mirataque *Serv. 1.103* (PHVML)

2.222 oleost γ : oleo c : oleo est **PRadhrs** *Arus.* : oleae est *cett.*

2.257 difficilest Pγ : difficile est *cett.*

2.272 multumst R^{ac} *Velius Longus* : multum est R^{pc} *cett.*

2.420 ullast P : (n)ulla est *cett.*

3.8 uiast V : uia est *cett.*

3.98 uentumst R^{ac} : uentum est R^{pc} *cett.*

3.112 tantaest MPcetv : tantae est Rrγ : tantae *cett.*

3.148 romanumst R^{ac} : (roman)ust F : romanum est R^{pc} *cett.*

3.452 laborumst R^{ac} : laborum est R^{pc} *cett.*

3.478 coortast R^{ac} : co(ho)rta est R^{pc} *cett.*

survive in medieval manuscripts in only eight instances.[37] In twenty-six of the forty-three instances the contracted form is found at the end of the line (60% of instances); this figure is noteworthy especially if compared with the rate of 'uncontracted' instances (i.e. instances never contracted in spelling in the manuscripts) of -V/-V*m est* found at the end of the line, namely fifty-three out of 154 (34%).[38] To put it another way, if we consider only the instances of -V/-V*m est* found at the end of the line in Virgil (fifty-four cases) the percentage of instances found contracted in the manuscripts is higher (twenty-six out of fifty-four = 33%) than the overall percentage of contracted forms in the manuscripts, regardless of their position in the verse (forty-three out of 197 = 22%).[39]

Not all editors of Virgil have considered the evidence for contraction seriously; Mynors (1972) and Conte (2009) never print contracted forms (with the exception of Mynors *ad Georg.* 2.82 *miratastque*) and rarely report them in their apparatus.[40] On the other hand, Ribbeck (1894–1895) and Geymonat (1973) print such forms systematically,[41] normally reporting the different readings of manuscripts in their apparatus. An intermediate (but inconsistent) position is that of Perret (1981), who never prints the contracted form in the first six books of the *Aeneid* but always prints it in the last six, in both cases without commenting on it in his apparatus.[42] Moreover, commentaries on Virgil's works very rarely take the evidence

---

[37] *Aen.* 4.691 *torost* c (IX c.), 11.151 *dolorest* γ (IX c.), *Ecl.* 7.43 *annost* a (IX c.), 8.107 *certest* a, 10.23 *secutast* a, *Georg.* 2.222, *oleost* γ, 2.257 *difficilest* γ, 3.112 *tantaest* cetv (IX c.). On the manuscript tradition of Virgil and on the possibility that the number of forms originally contracted in manuscripts was higher see pp. 128–30.

[38] The likelihood that the difference between the two patterns is statistically significant is between 99.5% and 99.95%, as shown by the t-test.

[39] This fact has led some scholars (cf. in particular Marouzeau (1908)) to consider the contracted forms found in the manuscripts of Virgil as simple abbreviations, chosen in order to save space at the end of the line. The general evidence for contracted forms prevents us from reducing this phenomenon to a simple scribal practice without any phonological or orthographic implications (cf. III.1.1). Nevertheless, the frequency of contracted spellings at the end of the line is undeniable, and may suggest that in some cases they were retained by scribes because they were graphically convenient at the end of the line, while others were eliminated.

[40] Mynors mentions such forms in the apparatus only at *Georg.* 2.82 and 3.112; Conte *ad Aen.* 6.719, 7.263, 10.710, 11.23, 11.151, 12.739.

[41] With the exception of *Georg.* 2.82 (printed uncontracted by Ribbeck) and *Georg.* 2.222 (printed uncontracted by Geymonat).

[42] With the exception of *Aen.* 7.263, 11.23, 11.151, 12.678.

concerning contraction into account;[43] the only direct mention of textual evidence is made by Ribbeck in the *prolegomena* to his edition (1866: 419), but a serious discussion of these forms in manuscripts of Virgil and an attempt at explaining them is still lacking.[44]

Twenty-seven contracted forms are found in the manuscripts of Gellius' *Noctes Atticae*, listed in Box 2.2. In the list some references are in italics, meaning that the form is found in direct speech, whereas others are underlined, meaning that the form is in a quotation from an archaic author. As far as the manuscripts are concerned, contracted forms are transmitted both by ancient manuscripts (**A**, **V** c.), and by medieval (**O**, **X** c.) and even humanistic manuscripts (**N**, **XV** c.).

Many of Gellius' contracted spellings are found in direct speeches (seven); the first four (12.5.7 *ratast, ratiost,* 12.5.13 *east, fortitudost*) appear in the elaborate speech of the anti-Stoic philosopher Taurus (Gellius' own contemporary and teacher) and the other three (20.1.50 *denuntiatast,* 20.1.52 *quitast,* 20.1.53 *disciplinast*) in the speech of the jurist Sextus Caecilius Africanus, a strenuous supporter of the ancient laws of Rome, during a discussion with Gellius' friend Favorinus. The forms uttered by Sextus Caecilius are found just after a quotation from the Twelve Tables.[45] Many other contracted forms in Gellius (ten) occur in quotations of republican authors, both in verse (Volcacius Sedigitus, Ennius, Porcius Licinius, Aedituus) and in prose (Nigidius Figulus, Varro). From this evidence one might draw the conclusion that, in the view of Gellius, the contracted spelling had a connection with archaic, old-fashioned, or high-style Latin, whether

---

[43] Oxford commentaries (Austin (1955, 1964, 1971, 1977), Williams (1960, 1962), Fordyce (1977), Mynors (1990), Harrison (1991), Clausen (1994)) never comment on the contracted forms, with the exception of Mynors (1990) *ad Georg.* 2.82. Mynors, however, simply states that the contracted reading (*miratastque*) is preferable. Norden (1957: cf. in particular 334 *ad Aen.* 6.845, and 449 n. 2) and Horsfall (2000, 2003, 2006, 2008: cf. in particular *ad Aen.* 2.703, 7.263, 7.311, 11.369) neither print nor comment on contracted forms; the only relevant notes are those of Horsfall (2000) *ad* 7.311 *usquam est,* defined by him as a 'common aphaeresis of *est,* with *es* only at 6.845', and Norden (1957: 449 n. 2): 'Nicht mitgezählt ist *Aen.* 9.260 *fidesque est* = Aphaeresis'. These notes and the editorial choice of not printing contracted forms in the text seem to imply the notion that contracted forms were common in pronunciation but not in orthography. On these problems cf. III.2.2.

[44] An exception is Marouzeau (1908), cf. above n. 37 and below III.1.1.

[45] Cf. Gell. 20.1.49 *tertiis—inquit—nundinis partis secanto. si plus minusue secuerunt, se fraude esto* (= Crawford 1996: 580 number 3.6).

Box 2.2 **Contracted forms in manuscripts of Gellius**

(*italics*: in direct speech; <u>underlined</u>: quotations of archaic authors)

1.3.28 difficilest A : difficile est *cett.* (quoting, in a Latin translation, a sentence by Theophrastus)

2.6.5 uastiorest A : uastiore est *cett.*

2.8.6 homost A : homo est *cett.*

<u>12.2.3 dictust ollis *codd.* : dictus ollis *Cic. Brut. 58* (quoting Ennius *Ann.* 306 S.)</u>

<u>12.5.7</u> fundamentum ratast NO^{pc} : fundamentum rata Z : fundatast O^{ac}ΠX : fundamentum rata est *cett.*

12.5.7 ratio st Z : ratio est cett.

12.5.13 east N : ea est cett.

12.5.13 fortitudost N : fortitudo st O : fortitudo Z : fortitudo est cett.

12.7.8 historia st O : historia est *cett.*

13.17.1 datast N : data est *cett.*

13.23.19 priuatiuast O^{pc} : priuatiua O^{ac}N : priuatiua est *cett.*

<u>13.26.1</u> sonost N^{ac} : [.]onost TY : t(h)ono est *cett.* (quoting Nigidius Figulus fr. 9 Funaioli)

<u>13.26.1</u> tonost Q^{ac} : tono st OT : tono est *cett.* (quoting Nigidius Figulus fr. 9 Funaioli)

15.17.3 desitast N : desita est *cett.*

<u>15.24.1</u> tertio st O : tertio TY : tertio est *cett.* (quoting Volcacius Sedigitus fr. 1 Morel)

15.31.4 ratio st O^{pc} : ratio [..] O^{ac} : ratio est cett.

<u>16.16.4</u> nominatast ON : (cog)nominata est *cett.* (quoting Varro fr. 103 Cardauns)

<u>16.17.2</u> syllabast X^{ac}N : syllaba est *cett.* (quoting Varro *ARD* fr. 107 Cardauns)

<u>18.2.7</u> frustra st O : frustra est *cett.* (quoting Ennius *Sat.* 62 V.)

18.2.16 datast Z : data est *cett.*

<u>19.9.12</u> nu(l)last Z : nulla est *cett.* (quoting Aeditus, *uetus poeta*, fr. 2 Baerhens)

<u>19.9.13</u> homost N : homo est *cett.* (quoting Porc. Licin. fr. 6.2 Morel)

<u>19.9.13</u> flaminast Z : flamma est *cett.* (quoting Porc. Licin. fr. 6.2 Morel)

20.1.3 mentiost Z : mentio est *cett.*

20.1.50 denuntiatast N : denuntiata est cett.

20.1.52 quitast O : quita est cett.

20.1.53 disciplina historia st Z : disciplina est historia cett. : disciplinast Hertz

---

in spelling and/or pronunciation.[46] Furthermore, the very fact that in Gellius these contracted forms gather in significant speeches or in quotations from archaic authors suggests that the manuscripts may well preserve the state of the original text; if scribes had introduced

---

[46] For Gellius' use of archaisms and for his grammatical theory grounded on the *auctoritas* of the *ueteres* cf. Holford-Strevens (2003: chs. 2 and 10, in particular pp. 49–54, 172–4).

Box 2.3 Contracted forms in quotations from archaic authors (not in Gellius)

Acc. *Trag.* 200 R. miscendumst H^{pc} *Cic. ND 3.68* : miscendum H^{ac} *Cic. Tusc. 4.77* (Cic. *de Orat.* 3.219)

      215 R. (= 62 D.) in(s)citiast **P** : inscitia est *cett.* (Cic. *Sest.* 102)

Afran. 60 R. (= 70 D.) uiast C^{a} : uias A^{a}B^{a} : uius L^{1} : uisast *Ribbeck* (Non. p. 829 L.)

Enn. *Ann.* 238 S. paratust *codd.* (Fest. p. 166 L.)

      455 S. aquast **N** : aquas istas **C** (Charis. p. 313 B.)

      560 S. gestast H (Cic. *de Orat.* 3.168)

    Trag. 290 J. quidnamst H (Cic. *de Orat.* 3.164)

Lucil. 483 M. ullast *mosaique d'Althiburos (CIL 08.27790), edd.* : ulla *codd.* (Non. p. 855 L.)

      633 M. quost L^{ac} *Non. p. 514* : quo est G L^{pc} *Non. 514, Non. 357* : quos tu *Non. p. 365* (Non. pp. 357, 365, 514 L.)

      895 M. apo(l)lost *codd.* (Non. p. 35 L.)

Nov. 115 R. adductust M : addictus U : addictust *Friedrich* (Cic. *de Orat.* 2.255)

Pac. 330 R. tutela(m)st AH^{ac} (Cic. *de Orat.* 2.193)

---

contracted forms haphazardly (i.e. if they were to be considered misspellings or abbreviations) one would expect a more random distribution.[47]

Other instances of contracted spellings occur in quotations from ancient authors offered by different sources (listed in Box 2.3).

Apart from Virgil, Gellius, and quotations from ancient authors, there is a group of instances in manuscripts of Horace (Box 2.4), mainly **B**, Bernensis 363 (IX c.), and **R**, Vaticanus Reginae 1703 (IX c.). Six of these forms (underlined in the list) are found at the end of the line.

Contracted spellings are not only attested in poetry. In prose, one finds a high number of contracted forms in manuscripts of Cicero (*c.*140 instances), especially those of the *Epistulae ad familiares* and of the treatise *De oratore* (Box 2.5).

Most of these instances are found in early medieval manuscripts (*Fam.* **M**, *de Orat.* **H** and **A**, IX c., *Top.* **Bb**, X c., *Brut.* **C**, IX c.). Two interesting exceptions are instances of *necessest* from *Pro Caecina* (*Caec.* 49), which are found in the leaves of a late antique manuscript in rustic capitals preserved by the Turin palimpsest (**P**, now lost). The

---

[47] On this cf. also III.1.1.

Box 2.4 Contracted forms in manuscripts of Horace

(underlined: at the end of the line)

Serm. 1.1.59 quantostopus B : quanto est opus *cett.*
　　　1.2.37 audirest B : audire est *cett.*
　　　1.2.72 puellast R : puella est *cett.*
　　　1.2.88 pedes tēptorē B : pede est emptorem *cett.*
　　　1.2.132 fugiendum stet B : fugiendum est et *cett.*
　　　1.5.104 uiaequest *Porph.* : uiaeque est *codd.*
　　　1.10.24 falernist R^{ac} : falerni est *cett.*
　　　2.6.33 uentumst F^{ac} : uentum est *cett.*
Ep. 2.1.120 temer est R^{ac} : temere est *cett.*
Ars 304 tantis tergo B : tantis ergo *cett.*
　　　327 remotast C^{ac} : remota est *cett.*
　　　353 ergost B : ergo est *cett.*
　　　386 iudicium stea B : iudicium est ea *cett.*
　　　409 quaesitum stego B : quaesitum est ego *cett.*
Carm. 2.16.25 ultrast R^{ac} : ultra est *cett.*
　　　2.18.10 uenast R^{ac} : uena est *cett.*

Box 2.5 Contracted forms in manuscripts of Cicero[i]

Brut. 89 cognita st UO^{pc} : cognita [. . .] O^{ac} : cognita sit BG : cognita est *cett.*
　　　225 cauendum st CB (pro est B^{mg}) : cauendum est *cett.*
　　　249 ita st B : ita est *cett.*
Caec. 49 necessest P : necesse est *cett.*
　　　necessest P : necesse est k : nec est *cett.*
Top. 78 opiniost β : opinio est *cett.* (Reinhardt)
　　　82 una st B : una sit A : una est *cett.*
　　　95 dandast β : danda est *cett.* *N.D. 2.159* repentest A^{ac}V^{ac} : repente est
　　　A^{pc}V^{pc}B^{ac} : repente sunt B^{pc}
de Orat. 1.6 uisumst H^{ac} : uisum est H^{pc} *cett.*
　　　1.18 neglegendast H^{ac} : neglegenda est H^{pc} *cett.*
　　　1.18 moderandast H^{ac} : moderanda est H^{pc} *cett.*
　　　1.19 carast H^{ac} : cara est H^{pc} *cett.*
　　　1.23 concessast H^{ac} : concessa est H^{pc} *cett.*
　　　1.40 ignarast H^{ac} : ignara est H^{pc} *cett.*
　　　1.157 dictiost H : dictio est *cett.*
　　　1.158 proferendast H : proferenda est *cett.*
　　　1.159 cognoscendast H : cognoscenda est *cett.*
　　　1.178 defensiost H : defensio est *cett.*
　　　1.182 quaesitum st H^{ac} : quaesitum est H^{pc} *cett.*
　　　1.183 adductast H : adducta est *cett.*
　　　1.188 habitast H^{ac} : adhibitast H^{pc} : adhibita est *cett.*
　　　1.193 plurimast H^{ac} : plurima est H^{pc} *cett.*
　　　2.33 oblectatio st AH : oblectatio est *cett.*

(continued)

Box 2.5 **Continued**

2.38 putandast AH : putanda est EO : putanda sit VPUR
2.48 necessest AH[ac] : necesse est H[pc] *cett.*
2.64 persequendumst AH[ac] : persequendum est H[pc] *cett.*
2.86 modost AH[ac] : modo est H[pc]VOPUR : modo stat E
2.140 pertimescendast AH[ac] : pertimescenda est H[pc] *cett.*
2.148 colendast AH[ac] : colenda est H[pc] VOPUR : colenda sunt E
2.151 (pro)positast AH[ac] : (pro)posita est H[pc]VOPURE[pc] : propositae sunt E[ac]
2.170 perspicuumst AH[ac] : perspicuum est H[pc] *cett.*
2.186 cognoscendast AH[ac] : cognoscenda est H[pc] *cett.*
2.207 enitendu(m) st AH : enitendum est *cett.*
2.209 dicendumst H : dicendum est *cett.*
2.212 inflammandumst H : inflammandum est AER : influendum est VOPU
2.215 p(er)spicuu(m)st AH : perspicuum est *cett.*
2.220 dictost AH : dicto est *cett.*
2.230 dictu(m)st A : dictum est HEVOPR : dicendum est U
2.243 positumst H[ac] : positum est H[pc] *cett.*
2.315 primast A : prima est *cett.*
2.327 inpositast A : (in)posita est *cett.* (in a quot. of Ter. *An.* 128–9)
2.328 inpositast AHVOP : posita UR
2.337 admouend(a)st H : admouenda est *cett.*
2.339 uitandast H : uitanda est *cett.*
2.341 adco(m)modatast AH : adcommodata est *cett.*
2.341 quoniam st AHE : quoniam est *cett.*
2.343 aliast AH : alia est *cett.*
2.343 iucunda st H : iudicandast A : iu(di)ca(/u)nda est *cett.*
2.349 perspicuomst AH : perspicu(/o)um est *cett.*
2.360 euocandast H[ac] : euocanda est H[pc] *cett.*
3.11 uitast H : uita est *cett.*
3.118 uitiorumst AH : uitiorum est *cett.*
3.119 longust A[ac] : longumst A[pc] : longum est *cett.*
3.119 perspicuumst H : perspicuum (est) *cett.*
3.122 nostrast A : nostra O[1]P : nostra (est) *cett.*
3.139 uocitata st AH : uoc(it)ata est *cett.*
3.143 dandast AH[ac] : danda est H[pc] *cett.*
3.147 magnast AH : magna est *cett.*
3.160 maximast H : maxima est *cett.*
3.163 uidendu(m)st H : uidendum est *cett.*
3.167 fugiendast H : fugienda est *cett.*
3.167 factumst H : factum (est) *cett.*
3.168 dictumst H : dictum est *cett.*
3.168 sensu(m)st H : sensu(m) (est) *cett.*
3.178 naturast H : natura (est) *cett.*
3.180 consecutast H : consecuta est *cett.*
3.182 longissimast AH : longissima es(se)t *cett.*
3.185 putandast H : putanda est *cett.*
3.186 etia(m) st AH : etiam est *cett.*
3.190 oratiost A : oratio est *cett.*
3.190 effig(/c)ienda(m)st AH : effigienda est E : efficiendum est VOPUR

3.190 utendu(m)st **H** : utendast **A** : utendu(m) est *cett.*

3.190 oratiost **H** : oratio est *cett.*

3.195 qu(a)eda(m)st **AH** : qu(a)edam est *cett.*

3.196 offensu(m)st **AH** : offensum est *cett.*

3.202 percursio stet **H** : percursio est et *edd.*

3.209 demonstratio stet **AHE** : demonstratio est et *edd.*

3.210 perspicuu(m) st **A** : perspicuumst **H**^{ac} : perspicuum est **H**^{pc} *cett.*

3.217 nullumst **H**^{ac} : nullum est **H**^{pc} *cett.*

3.221 animi st **AH** : animi est *cett.*

3.227 suauest **AH**^{ac} : suaue est **H**^{pc} *cett.*

Att. 1.1.1 opiniost **λ** : opinio est **s** : opinio se **M** : opinio si **R**

1.7.1 cura est **Mm** : curae est *cett.* : curaest *Müller*

13.2a.2 necessitudost **M**^{ac} : necessitudo est **M**^{pc} *cett.*

13.32.3 roma est **M** : romaest *cett. edd.*

Fam. 1.9.15 impunitatem stillorum **M** : impunitatem est illorum *cett.*

2.12.2 sordidast **m** : sordida **M** : sordida est *cett.*

2.15.4 necessaest **M** : necesse est *cett.*

5.1.1 benest **M** : bene est *cett.*

5.2.1 benest **M** : bene est *cett.*

5.2.5 imminutast **M** : imminuta **G** : imminuta est *cett.*

5.2.9 appellandast **M** : appellanda sit *cett.*

5.10c.1 expectandumst **M** : expectandam est **R** : exspectandum sit **I** : exspectandum est *cett.*

6.4.1 difficilest **M**^{ac} : difficile est **M**^{pc} *cett.*

6.14.1 uitiumst **M** : uitium est *cett.*

7.1.3 consecutast **M** : consecuta est *cett.*

7.1.4 nullast **M**^{ac} : nulla est **M**^{pc} *cett.*

7.3.3 adiunctast **M** : adiuncta est *cett.*

7.3.4 uisast **M** : uisa est *cett.*

7.7.1 itast **M** : ita est *cett.*

7.17.2 ratiost **M** : ratione **R** : est ratio **G** : ratio est *cett.*

7.29.1 quantist **M** : quanti est *cett.*

7.30.1 sublatast **M** : sublata est *cett.*

7.30.1 incredibilest **M** : incredibile est *cett.*

7.30.3 beneficiost **M** : beneficio est *cett.*

8.1.4 rauennaest *codd.*

8.3.1 neglegentiast **M** : neglegentia est *cett.*

8.10.2 inertiast **M** : inertia est *cett.*

8.11.4 commentariost **M** : commentario est *cett.*

10.3.3 iudiciumst **M**^{ac} : iudicium est **M**^{pc}**HD**

10.3.3 ratiost **M**^{ac} : ratio est **M**^{pc}**HD**

10.5.3 incredibilest **M** : incredibile est *cett.*

10.6.1 patiendast **M** : patienda est *cett.*

10.12.5 uitast **M**^{ac}**D** : uita est **M**^{pc}**D** : est uita **H**

10.13.1 sententiast **M** : sententia est *cett.*

10.20.2 sublatast **M** : sublata est *cett.*

10.22.2 uisumst **M** : uisum est *cett.*

10.23.1 maximest **M** : maxime est *cett.*

10.27.1 restituturast **M**^{ac} : restitutura est **M**^{pc} : restitura est **D** : restituta est **H**

(*continued*)

Box 2.5 Continued

10.30.3 pugnatumst M^{ac} : pugnatum est M^{pc}HD
10.31.2 adeost M^{ac} : adeo est M^{pc}
10.33.1 necessesst M^{ac} : necesse est M^{pc}HD
12.13.2 passast M : passa est *cett.*
12.14.2 dissipatast M : dissipata est *cett.*
12.14.3 mirast M : mira est *cett.*
12.14.3 utilest M : utile est *cett.*
12.16.3 iustast M : iusta est *cett.*
12.22.2 unast M : una est HD : est una L
12.25.1 consecuta est M : consecuta est H : secuta est D
12.29.1 spectatast M : spectata est *cett.*
12.29.1 lamiast M : lamia est *cett.*
14.2.3 faciendast MH^{ac} : facienda est FH^{pc}D
14.3.4 defensast M : defensa est *cett.*
14.5.1 fortunast M : fortuna est *cett.*
14.15.1 benest M : bene est *cett.*
15.1.5 nullast M : nulla si FHD
15.10.1 factust M : factus FH : factu DV : factu est *cett.*
15.14.1 meost M : meo stet FHD : meo est *cett.*
15.14.4 popularest M : populare est FH^{pc}D : populare H^{ac}
15.18.1 molestast M : molesta est FHD
15.19.2 difficilest M : difficile est *cett.*
16.12.1 deductast M : difficile est *cett.*
16.27.2 incredibilest M : incredible est *cett.*

[i] Contracted spellings of manuscript H of *De oratore* have been checked in the facsimile of Beeson (1930). The list of cases from Avranches 238 (A) I owe to the kindness of Sytse Renting. Textual information on the manuscripts of *Fam.* and *Att.* has been gathered from the editions of Mueller (1896–1898; cf. in particular I.viii-ix, II.iv) and Mendelssohn (1893).

---

same manuscript, according to the testimony of the nineteenth-century philologist Amedeo Peyron (in Pesce (1997: 133)) had a contracted spelling at *Scaur.* 19 (*natiost*). It is a surprise to find such an abundance of examples in medieval manuscripts, because after late antiquity scribes tended to steer clear of such spellings. This fact gives the Ciceronian cases a certain authority. Moreover, one of the above instances (*de Orat.* 2.327) is a quotation from a passage of Terence, an author in whom contraction is well attested (cf. p. 37 and Appendix 1),[48] whereas a few others (reported in Box 2.3) are quotations from other archaic authors; this confirms that the manuscripts of Cicero preserve the original text.

---

[48] The form *inpositast* (Ter. *An.* 129) cannot be checked in Terence's A, in which this portion of text is missing. The form is spelt uncontracted in medieval manuscripts of Terence, but this is not significant since contracted spellings were frequently altered by medieval scribes. On this see sections 3.3, III.2.1, Appendix 1.

Contracted spellings are particularly common in the famous manuscript Harleianus 2736 of Cicero's *De oratore*, written by Lupus of Ferrières in the middle of the ninth century: the rate of transmission of contracted forms in this manuscript is 16% (= seventy out of 441 potentially contracted forms in the portions of text preserved in the manuscript), which goes up to 30% for the pattern *-a est*. It is likely that these readings were originally found in the archetype of the manuscript (cf. Beeson (1930: 1)). Contracted spellings in *De oratore* are evenly scattered throughout the text and do not seem to occur in meaningful contexts.

Editions and commentaries do not normally take into account the Ciceronian cases of contracted forms,[49] although these figures are proportionally high. Moreover, most of these forms are found in his *Epistulae*, a natural receptacle of speech-like features, and in the fictional dialogue *De oratore*, which is supposed to reproduce a conversation between *eloquentissimi homines* (cf. *de Orat.* 1.23). The gathering of contracted spellings in texts imitating (up to a point) speech might be significant: although one cannot exclude the possibility that the concentration of contracted forms in these two works is only due to accidents of textual transmission, this evidence may be taken to imply that Cicero used contracted spellings as markers of speech.

Some other examples (twenty-eight), listed in Box 2.6, are found in a manuscript of Quintilian's *Institutio*, **B** (Bernensis 351, IX c.), and in manuscripts of Seneca's letters, mainly **B** (Bambergensis V.14, IX c.). However, most of the above examples (twenty-one) are of the type *-e + est* and therefore are not necessarily relevant, given that they could be considered the result of haplography.

More interesting are the instances (eleven) in a manuscript (**A** Vindobonensis 277, VIII/IX c.) which contains Augustan poet Grattius' minor text, the *Cynegetica*, a poem of 541 hexameters on hunting (listed in Box 2.7). Unlike Virgil's forms, only three of these are found at the end of a line (underlined in the list). Given that the number of relevant instances (i.e. those in which *est* follows a vowel or an elidible *-m*) in Grattius is twenty-five, the rate of transmission of contracted forms is high (44%). Grattius is a close imitator of the poetic language

---

Box 2.6 Contracted forms in manuscripts of Quintilian and Seneca

---

Quint.[i] *Inst.* 1.5.5 difficilest B : difficile est *cett.*
           3.2.4 necessest B : necesse est *cett.*
           3.3.7 sententiast B : sententia est *cett.*
           3.8.2 sententiast B : sententia est *cett.*
           4.1.73 qualest B : quale est *cett.*
           4.2.49 qualest B : quale est *cett.*
           4.4.2 audaciast B : audacia est *cett.* (quoting Cic. *Mil.* 30)
           4.5.3 lucidast B : lucida est *cett.*
           5.11.33 qualest B : quale sit A : quale est *cett.*
           5.13.30 similest B : simile est *cett.*
           5.13.47 culpast B : culpa est *cett.*
           8.4.15 positast B : posita est *cett.*
           9.2.82 credibilest B : credibile est *cett.*
           10.7.14 compositast B : composite si b : composita est *cett.*
           11.3.85 propest B : prope est *cett.*
           11.3.124 deformest B : deforme est *cett.*
           11.3.134 necessest B : necesse est *cett.*
           11.3.138 necessest B : necesse est *cett.*
           11.3.181 necessest B : necesse est *cett.*
           12.9.6 necessest B : necesse est *cett.*
Sen. *Ep.* 90.16 intolerabilest B : intollerabilis est Q[ac] : intolerabile est Q[pc] *cett.*
           90.20 incredibilest B : incredibile est *cett.*
           95.27 grauest B[ac] : graue est B[pc] *cett.*
           95.33 turpest B[ac] : thus pus W : ius potest X : turpe est B[pc] *cett.*
           95.71 fiduciaest BQ : fiducia est CDREWX : fiduciae est *cett.*
           101.11 benest B[ac] : bene est B[pc] *cett.* (quoting Maecenas *poet.* 4 Bl.)
           118.11 talest B[ac] : tale est B[pc] *cett.*
           124.16 uiaest B : uia est QCDREX : uiae est W

[i] Textual information on Quintilian's *Institutio* has been gathered from Winterbottom (1970: 40).

---

of Virgil and Ovid[50] and it would be possible to argue that his imitation worked also at an orthographic level (cf. p. 130). Moreover, the expression *si qua est* (found in Grattius at 224 and 478, both contracted in spelling) seems to be typical of the poetic language of

---

[50] Cf. Verdière (1964: 33–44) who lists eighty-two parallels between the *Cynegetica* and the *Aeneid* and eighty-three parallels between the *Cynegetica* and Ovid's works. See also Kenney (1965) for a discussion of the most relevant parallels, and the apparatus of Formicola's (1988) edition, which lists parallels for almost every line of the poem; Virgil is the most frequently recurring name, followed by Ovid and Lucretius.

Box 2.7 Contracted forms in the manuscript A of Grattius

---

202 petroniost
224 si quast
266 <u>primast</u>
312 illast
336 <u>damnost</u>
346 <u>tuerist</u>
372 ueniast
382 tutelast
394 medicinast
412 malost
478 si quast (sequast *cod.*)

Box 2.8 Contracted forms in manuscripts of other authors

Apul. *Apol.* 50 sanctissimast F[ac] : sanctissima est *cett.*
Cels. 2.15.4 quidemst at F : quidem stat V : quidem at JT
Carmen de figuris uel schematibus 137 meritostultos CP : meritost ultus *edd.*
                              165 dictus talax CP : ut dictust aiax *edd.*
Frontin. *Aq.* 109.6 palamst C : palam s.c. *cett.*
Lucan. 7.532 secutast π^1 : secuta est *cett.*
Mart. 14.100.1 ignotast E : ignota est *cett.*
Stat. *Theb.* 12.561 illest P : ille *cett.*

Virgil; it is found eight times in the *Aeneid,* whereas there are only four instances of it in Ovid (in one case apparently imitating Virgil)[51] and only a further seven in the whole corpus of imperial poets. In both Virgil and Ovid the expression is found uncontracted in the manuscripts, but this is not significant (cf. III.2.1.2).

Finally, there are sporadic instances of contracted forms in other authors (Box 2.8). Among these instances we may note Lucan's *secutast* (from a late-antique fragment) and two instances from the late *Carmen de figuris* (an anonymous handbook of rhetorical figures dated to the fourth or fifth century AD),[52] most probably to be taken as

---

[51] Ov. *Met.* 5.309 *nobiscum,* **si qua est fiducia** *uobis* | (cf. Virg. *Aen.* 11.502 *sui merito* **si qua est fiducia** *forti* |), 5.378, 6.39, *Trist.* 1.1.115.

[52] Found in the *Anthologia Latina* (Buecheler and Riese (1894–1906: I.2 n. 485 pp. 9–19)) and recently edited by D'Angelo (2001). See in particular pp. 43–4 for an

conscious orthographic archaisms (so D'Angelo (2001 *ad* 165)). The *Carmen de figuris* is a text that exhibits many 'archaic' features, both orthographic and morphological (such as sigmatic ecthlipsis, cf. Butterfield (2008b: 188 n. 2)): it is likely that contracted forms also had an archaic ring in this text.

This list does not claim to include all instances of contracted forms in the manuscripts of Latin authors. It relies on the critical apparatuses of major editions and lexica; I have carried out a systematic examination of the manuscripts of Terence, Lucretius, and Cicero's *De Oratore* only. It probably offers a good range of the diffusion of the phenomenon, even though a fair number of instances are presumably not recorded by editors and thus could be located only by examining the manuscripts.

3.1.2 A Particular Type of Reading

Before continuing with the other types of evidence, I will now focus on a class of readings found especially in manuscripts of Plautus, Terence, and Lucretius, which should be considered within the group of direct transmission of contracted forms, but deserves special attention: the spelling *-ust* in place of a form *-umst* (with omission of *-m-*). This type of reading (*-ust*=*-umst*) is found eighty-one times in manuscripts of Plautus,[53] three times in Terence (*Eun.* 612, 959, and *Hec.* 457), and twice in Lucretius (2.516 *remensumst* **Q** *edd.* : *remunsust* **O**, 3.668 *putandust* **QO**[ac] : *putandumst* **O**[pc] *edd.*). One may also include instances of *-us est* for *-umst* (twenty-one instances in Plautus), *-us* for *-umst* (twenty-four in Plautus), and *-unst* for *-umst* (thirty-five in Plautus).[54]

---

analysis of the metrical features of the *Carmen*, and cf. also Schenkeveld (2001). For a general introduction to the *Carmen* and its problems see Schindel (1999). For a metrical analysis see Viparelli (1990), who comments on the two instances *dictust* and *meritost* (43–4); I fail to understand her distinction between 'prodelisione o [di] elisione inversa' (*dictust* and *meritost*) and 'aferesi' (allegedly twenty-one cases in the *Carmen*, presumably all other instances of *est/es* following an elidible syllable).

[53] E.g. Pl. *Most.* 948 *dicendust* A : *dicendum est* BCD : *dicendumst edd.* For the detailed list see Brinkmann (1906: 88–91, category c); cf. also Questa (2007: 41).

[54] See Brinkmann (1906: 91–6, categories d, e, f) and Questa (2007: 41), who points out that 'misspellings' of the same type appear to be gathered in single manuscripts and/or single plays (e.g. *-unst*, 7 in *Merc.* A, 3 in *Bac.* B, 7 in *Trin.* P). This fact may suggest that a uniform system for this spelling never existed in Plautus' text.

How can one explain the confusion over the spelling *-umst*? One explanation might be palaeographical: the form *-ust* might derive from the loss of the macron above the vowel ($\bar{u}$), a common abbreviation in manuscripts for a nasal letter, also word-internal. On this view, the spelling *-umst* would be the oldest, and *-ust* would derive from it, while the other spellings (*-unst, -us, -us est*) would be the result of a combination of palaeographical and phonological factors, under the influence of the pronunciation /factūst/ for *factum+st*, with omission of *-m* and compensatory nasalization and lengthening of the preceding vowel:[55]

-umst > (-ūst) > -ust > -unst,[56] -us, -us est

Another possibility would be that the older reading is *-ust* (=*-um est*)[57] and that this is to be construed as an archaic phonetic spelling reflecting the aforementioned nasalized pronunciation /factūst/. The various types of reading found in Plautine manuscripts corresponding to a sequence *-um+est* (such as *-umst, -unst, -us, -us est*) would be the innovations of later scribes who were trying to introduce a more familiar and/or more phonetic spelling. The few instances of *-ust* = *-um est* would therefore be relics of the original spelling and not later mistakes.

Both hypotheses are possible; in any case, under both scenarios this type of spellings (*-ust, -unst,* etc.) appears to have been influenced by the pronunciation of *-m* at a certain stage: omission or obscuration of final *-m* was apparently a common phenomenon in speech[58] and readings displaying omission of *-m* or assimilation (*-n*) seem to be reflections of this pronunciation. Interestingly, this type of spelling (*-(u)st/-(u)nst=-(u)mst*) is also attested in inscriptions.[59]

[55] For obscuration of final *-m* resulting in the nasalization and lengthening of the preceding vowel cf. Allen (1978: 30–1).

[56] The variant spelling *-unst* would represent the nasal pronunciation of the preceding vowel. Cf. n. 55 and Questa (2007: 41).

[57] Cf. Fortson (2008: 135 n. 6).

[58] Cf. Quint. 9.4.40, Leumann (1977: 223–6), Allen (1978: 30–1), Väänänen (1981: 66–7), and Herman (2000: 39–40).

[59] See below section 3.4.1.

Contraction of esse: Evidence

3.2 Metre

Metre provides further evidence for contracted forms. In a particular case of contraction, i.e. *est* following -V*s*, the form with contraction is not prosodically equivalent to the form without contraction, and therefore sometimes only one of the two can be accepted in metrical texts. For instance, since elision is not permitted over final -*s*,[60] a sequence such as *factus est* (¯ ˘ ¯) is not equivalent to *factust* (¯ ˘ ¯). If the uncontracted form does not fit the metre, it is appropriate to restore the contracted form. We can use as an example Ter. *An.* 102 and *Ad.* 21:

An. 102 iambic senarius (ia⁶)

plăcŭit: | despon|d(i). hic nup|tĭīs | **dictŭs est** | dĭes

(¹ ˘ ˘ ¯ | ² ¯ ¯ | ³ ¯ ¯ | ⁴ ˘ ¯ | ⁵ ˘ ˘ ¯ | ⁶ ˘ ¯)

Ad. 21 iambic senarius (ia⁶)

sū͡ō quis|quĕ tem|pŏr(e) **ūs|ŭs est** sĭnĕ| sŭper|bĭā

(¹ ¯ ¯ | ² ˘ ¯ | ³ ¯ ¯ | ⁴ ˘ ˘ ˘ ˘ | ⁵ ˘ ¯ | ⁶ ˘ ¯)

These are the lines as given by manuscripts. In neither of these lines does the metre work. At *An.* 102 the fifth foot is a cretic (¯ ˘ ¯) and at *Ad.* 21 the fourth foot is a second paeon (˘ ¯ ˘ ˘), two types of metrical feet which are not permitted in such a position in the metre: in an iambic senarius (ia⁶), in place of the standard iambic foot (˘ ¯, compulsory at the end of the line), we could only have a tribrach (˘ ˘ ˘), an anapaest (˘ ˘ ¯), a spondee (¯ ¯), a dactyl (¯ ˘), or, exceptionally, a proceleusmaticus (˘ ˘ ˘ ˘).[61]

In both cases a contracted form seems to be required by the metre:

An. 102 iambic senarius (ia⁶)

plăcŭit: | despon|d(i). hic nup|tĭīs | **dictŭst** | dĭes

(¹ ˘ ˘ ¯ | ² ¯ ¯ | ³ ¯ ¯ | ⁴ ˘ ¯ | ⁵ ¯ ¯ | ⁶ ˘ ¯)

Ad. 21 iambic senarius (ia⁶)

sū͡ō quis|quĕ tem|pŏr(e) **ūs|ust** sĭnĕ| sŭper|bĭā

(¹ ¯ ¯ | ² ˘ ¯ | ³ ˘ ¯ | ⁴ ¯ ˘ ˘ | ⁵ ˘ ¯ | ⁶ ˘ ¯)

---

[60] Cf. III.1.2 with n. 28.
[61] For an analysis of iambic senarius see below V.2 and Questa (2007: 332–41).

Box 2.9 Metrically restored -*st* in Plautus and Terence

Plautus: 156 instances -ŭs + est (-us est *codd.* : -ust *edd.*)[i]
Terence:
thirty-two instances -ŭs + est (-us est *codd.* : -ust *edd.*)
  An. 102 dictust, 165 opust, 255 uisust, 265 peropust, 307 satiust, 527 pollicitust, 530 pollicitust, 576 intumust, 682 opust, 928 mortuost, 937 commotust, 955 uinctust, *Haut.* 515 tardiusculust, *Eun.* 188 gerundust, 474 honestust (honestus CF), 546 ornatust, 645 ludificatust, 708 deductust (deductus A), 758 opust, 772 satiust, *Ph.* 661 oppositust (oppositus A), 715 opust (opus A), 833 facturust (facturus A), 896 conueniundust, *Hec.* 169 elapsust (elapsus A), 517 uisust, *Ad.* 21 usust, 98 iniustiust (iniustius A), 404 adortust (adortus A), 412 plenust, 728 natust (natus A¹), 920 rectiust
three instances -ĭs + est (-is est *codd.* : -ist *edd.*)
  Haut. 82 laborist, *Eun.* 546 hominist (hominis A), *Hec.* 352 tristist

[i] Cf. Brinkmann (1906: 98–101) for the complete list of cases.

Although metrical phenomena are not necessarily displayed in spelling and may appear only in the pronunciation of the line (such as e.g. elision; cf. III.1.2), in this case it seems correct to assume that contracted forms were also graphically displayed and so restore the contracted spellings (*dictust* and *usust*), for three reasons: first, the uncontracted spellings (*dictus est* and *usus est*) would not automatically prompt contracted pronunciation, since final -*s* would normally only be omitted before a consonant (cf. III.1.2 with n. 2); second, contracted spellings in -*ust* are attested in manuscripts and inscriptions (cf. sections 3.1 and 3.4); third, as I will discuss in the next chapters,[62] contracted forms do not appear to be the product of a sandhi phenomenon but independent clitic forms. It is thus not surprising that in both cases above all editors agree in printing a contracted spelling.

There are a good number of instances in which metrical evidence has led editors of Plautus and Terence to restore a contracted form in place of an uncontracted form found in manuscripts. In Box 2.9 I have reported the instances accepted by most editors.

As appears from the list in Box 2.9, in some cases the verb is found uncontracted in one branch of the manuscript tradition, but it is omitted in another branch (cf. e.g. *Ad.* 98 *iniustius* A : *iniustius est* Σ : *iniustiust KL*). As we will see in section 3.3, the omission of the verb seems to be a common misunderstanding of an original contracted spelling (*-ust > us<t>*);[63] in such cases the restoration of a contracted spelling is therefore justified both by metre and by palaeographical factors.

Notably, not all instances of the sequence *-ŭs + (e)st* in the manuscripts of Plautus and Terence can be contracted (*-ust* = ¯): in many cases the form without contraction (*-us est* = ˘ ¯) is the only one that is metrically permissible and the uncontracted spelling is the one printed by editors.[64] Cf. e.g.:

Ter. *An.* 82 ia[6]

egomet continuo mecum certe cap|tŭs est
¯ | ˘ ¯

Ter. *Eun.* 759 tr[7]

immo hoc cogitato: quicum res tibist pereg|rīnŭs est
| ¯ ˘ ¯

In both cases we need an iambic sequence (˘ ¯) at the end of the line, and therefore the contracted form (*-ust*) is not acceptable (*captust* = ¯ ¯, *-grīnust* = ¯ ¯). These examples show that contraction was not obligatory and that the two prosodies (˘ ¯/¯), together with the two corresponding pronunciations (/-us est/, /-ust/) and spellings (*-us est*/*-ust*) coexisted.

Moreover, the number of cases in which a contracted form has been restored on the basis of metre is proportionally high. In the portion of text preserved in the codex Bembinus (**A**), which is the oldest manuscript of Terence and the most conservative as far as contracted forms are concerned,[65] we count some thirty-five instances of contracted forms guaranteed by the metre (*-ust < -ŭs + est*, *-ist < -ĭs + est*), but only eight of these forms are contracted in spelling in **A**, whereas the others have been restored by editors on a metrical (and sometimes also palaeographical) basis.[66]

---

[63] Omission of the verb is particularly common when a second person form (*es*) is expected (cf. 3.8.1). Moreover, there are some cases in which the reading with omission of the verb is transmitted in all manuscripts and is metrically unacceptable; in such cases the contracted spelling is therefore restored on the basis of metrical factors (cf. 3.8.2).

[64] In Plautus *c*.250 instances of the transmitted *-ŭs est* must be spelt uncontracted according to Leo (1895–1896); in Terence *c*.100 according to Kauer and Lindsay (1958) and Marouzeau (1963) (figures vary slightly).

[65] Cf. Appendix 1.1.

[66] For the differences in the rate of alteration of contracted forms in Plautus and Terence, and in different metres in Terence see III.2.1.1.

Box 2.10 **Metrically restored forms in other authors**
[-us est *codd.* : -ust *edd.*]

Acc. *trag.* 268 R. (= 25 D.) illiust
         418 R. (= 491 D.) nullust
Pac. 375 R. factust
Naev. *com.* R. 26a adulescentulust
         45 R. formidolusust
Titin. 153 R. (= 152 D.) condemnatust
Afran. 211 R. (= 217 D.) uisust (uisum est *codd.*)
Pompon. 3 R. miseriust
Porc. 3.8 M. mortuust
pall. inc. fab. 10 R. mortuust
Comm. *instr.* 1.17.17 locutust

Contracted forms have been restored for metrical reasons in some
lines of other authors (listed in Box 2.10).

Almost all the instances in the list above are found in republican
authors. The only interesting exception is a line by Commodianus
(probably third century AD), for which manuscripts give a hexameter
(1.17.17 *maiestas autem illorum nulla locutus est*) which cannot be
accepted even in his loose metrical system.[67] Commodianus' use of
metre is quite different from the classical one; in his poetry heavy
unstressed syllables often become light and light stressed syllables
become heavy (cf. e.g. line endings such as 1.6.21 *in terrā fuisse* and
1.6.23 *illī fēcissent*).[68] In the case above, however, the line does scan
according to the rules of classical metre.[69] The only real flaw would be
the ending *locutus est*; from a metrical point of view *locutust* would
be a good emendation, which would suggest that in the age of

[67] On this see Castorina (1950), Perret (1957).

[68] This system led the way towards the metrical system of Romance languages,
based on a succession of accented and unaccented syllables (taking the place of 'arsis'
and 'thesis', respectively). Another good example of a borderline system is offered by
the lyrics of Church Fathers such as St. Ambrose. The loss of vowel quantities and the
influence of accentual factors is considered by the grammarian Consentius (approximately fifth century AD) as an African vice (GL 5.392.3, 5.392.11), but it is also found
in substandard versification in other parts of the Empire. See Adams (1999: 113–18 in
particular n. 39; 2007: 263–4, in particular n. 244). Cf. also Castorina (1950), Perret
(1957), Holmes (2002).

[69] *Maies|tās au|tem* || *il|lōrum* | *nullā lŏ|cūtŭs est*. Hiatus at the caesura (*autem* ||
illorum) is not very common but is found in hexametric poetry (cf. e.g. Virg. *Ecl.* 3.6 *et
sucus pecori* || *et lac subducitur agnis*).

Commodianus the contracted form was still known, at least as a poetic licence.

3.3 Indirect Transmission in Manuscripts

Manuscripts can also offer indirect evidence for the status of contracted forms. To understand this evidence, we must recall that medieval scribes rarely comprehended the contracted spelling *-st*, which they found in the manuscripts from which they were copying. Consequently they tried to convert the contracted spelling into something with a more standard appearance, such as the uncontracted spelling *est* or another palaeographically similar word, or they simply left it out, thus deleting every trace of the original contracted spelling. Different typologies of this scribal practice are displayed in Table 2.5.

The manuscript traditions of Plautus, Terence, and Lucretius offer good evidence for these scribal practices, derived from both misunderstanding and a desire for uniformity. First (typology a), there are many examples of contracted forms found in one or more manuscripts that are uncontracted in spelling in different branches of the tradition.[70] In particular, the number of contracted spellings of *est* in older and/or better manuscripts is much higher than in more recent and/or inferior ones, in which the normal uncontracted spelling tends to be introduced, until it becomes the only one accepted.[71] Second (typologies b–f),

Table 2.5. Typologies of readings resulting from misunderstanding of contracted spellings

---

a) the uncontracted spelling *est* (the most common solution)

b) another form of *sum* (mainly *sit*, sometimes *sunt*, rarely *sim* or *sis*)

c) paleographically similar forms such as the conjunction *si* or, more rarely, the pronoun *se*

d) an ending in *-s*, derived from the loss of *-t* (e.g. *sagittas* < *sagittast*)

e) omission of *est* (e.g. *adductus* < *adductust*)

f) other misspellings or misreadings, paleographically similar to a contracted spelling (e.g. *certet* < *certest*)

---

[70] I give just a few Plautine examples from hundreds of cases: Pl. *Amph.* 653 *penest* BDE : *penes est* J, *Curc.* 284 *quisquamst* BE : *quisquam est* J, *Mil.* 997 *corporist* P : *corporis est* CD, *Poen.* 356 *olimst* A : *olim est* P, *Rud.* 761 *uenerist* A : *ueneris est* P.

[71] E.g. in Terence out of the *c.*390 contracted forms found in A (IV/V c.), only thirty-three are still present in D (IX c.), three in C, and one in F (IX–X c.). Cf. III.2.1.1 and Appendix 1.1.

Table 2.6. Contracted spelling vs. misunderstanding

b) *-st ~ sit/sunt/sim/sis*	Pl. *Truc.* 789 factumst C : factum sit B Lucr. 1.959 finitumst O : finitum sit Q[72]
c) *-st ~ si/se*	Pl. *Mil.* 1390 formast FZ : forma si P Lucr. 5.1365 libitumst O : libitum si Q
d) *-st ~ -s* ending	Lucr. 4.66 hiscendist O (= hiscendi est) : hiscendis Q Grat. *Cyn.* 202 petroniost A : petronios E
e) *-st ~ -Ø*	Lucr. 4.118 putandumst O : putandum Q[73] Pl. *Cas.* 620 nostrast domo A : nostra domo est P[74]
f) *-st* + another reading (†)	Enn. *Ann.* 455 S. aquast N : aquas istas C, Ter. *Haut.* 819 licitumst A : liceat Σ

Letters b–f refer to the classification of misunderstandings as given in Table 2.5.

Table 2.7. Contracted spelling vs. different misunderstandings

a ~ b	Ter. *Ph.* 538 opust A : opus est D^{pc}CF : opus sit D^{ac} Virg. *Aen.* 8.71 undest MP : unde est F^{ac}R : unde sit F^{pc}
a ~ c	Pl. *Trin.* 338 malitiast B : malitia es(t) A : malitia si CD
a ~ d	Pl. *Cas.* 384 abiegnast B^{pc} : abiegna est JE^{pc} : abiegnas B^{ac}VE^{ac} Ter. *Ad.* 388 psaltriast D : psaltria est A^{pc} : psaltrias A^{ac}
a ~ e	Ter. *Eun.* 826 adductust A : adductus est CF : adductus D Pl. *Poen.* 766 nemost A : nemo est B : nemo CD
c ~ d	Pl. *Men.* 366 tibist B^{pc} : tibi si B^{ac} : tibis CD
e ~ f	Pl. *Mil.* 383 geminast A : gemina B : gemina et CD

Letters a–f refer to the classification of misunderstandings as given in Table 2.5.

there are many instances in which in one branch of the tradition we have the direct transmission of the contracted spelling, while in the other(s) we have a clear misunderstanding. Some patterns are shown in Table 2.6.

In some instances there is more than one type of misunderstanding at the same time. Some good examples are given in Table 2.7.

Relying on this evidence, editors have sometimes opted to restore a contracted spelling in places where manuscripts have a similar range

---

[72] Cf. also Lucr. 1.954 *repertumst* O : *repertum sit* Q, 3.1061 *pertaesumst* O : *pertaesum sit* Q, Ter. *Haut.* 881 *dictumst* A : *dictum sit cett.*

[73] Cf. also Lucr. 3.816 *summast* O : *summa* Q.

[74] This type of reading is very frequent; the omission of the verb (due to the loss of final *-st*) is integrated by reinserting it in a different place.

Table 2.8. Single readings corrected to a contracted spelling by editors

b)	Nov. 105 R. (trochaic septenarius (tr[7]): fixed ending ‾ ˘ x)
	per deam sanctam Lauernam, quae mei cultrix | quaestui sit *codd.* (ametric)

$$\overset{\text{‾ ˘ ˘}}{x}$$

$$\text{\| quaestuist } \textit{Ribbeck}$$
$$\overset{\text{‾ ˘}}{x}$$

d)	*Aegritudo Perdicae*[75] 47 iam fessa sagittas | H
	iam fessa sagittast | *Baerhens*
e)	Afran. 417 R. nescio qui nostri miseritus tandem deus *codd.*
	nescio qui nostri miseritust tandem deus *Ribbeck*
f)	Acc. *Trag.* 96 R. hoc in re est quod *codd.*
	hocinest quod *edd.*

Letters b–f refer to the classification of misunderstandings as given in Table 2.5.

Table 2.9. Multiple readings corrected to a contracted spelling by editors

a + b	Cic. *N.D.* 1.55 aestimanda est B : aestimanda sit ACPNz : aestimandast *Ax*
e + b	*Rhet. Her.* 3.38 ridiculum H : ridiculum sit ПΠBC : ridiculumst *Marx*
a + e	Quint. 8.4.15 posita est AbNP *edd.* : posita E : positast *Radermacher*
d + a	Virg. *Aen.* 10.777 clipeos P : clipeo est *cett.* : clipeost *Ribbeck*
a + d + e	Virg. *Aen.* 3.629 sui est MP^{pc}ωγ : suis P^{ac} : sui abefrv : suist *Ribbeck*
a + b + e	Gell. 7.16.7 uitam est *Cic. Sul. 72* : uitam sit V : uitam *cett.* : uitamst *Hertz*

Letters a–e refer to the classification of misunderstandings as given in Table 2.5.

of readings, even though the direct transmission of the contracted spelling is missing.

In some cases the whole manuscript tradition gives a single reading which is unacceptable (textually and/or metrically) and belongs to one of the categories of misunderstanding listed in Table 2.8.

In other cases the reading of one branch of the manuscript tradition is linguistically acceptable, while the other branch has a different reading (less convincing or clearly wrong), which, if considered together with the acceptable reading, seems to cover up an original contracted spelling. Table 2.9 lists some of the most common patterns.

---

[75] The *Aegritudo Perdicae* is a late Latin poem (around the sixth century) in hexameters, which tells the story of the incestuous love of Perdica for his mother Castalia. It is conserved only by a Renaissance manuscript and was first edited by Baehrens in 1877. The most recent edition is the Teubner of Zurli (1987). It is a very corrupt text, to which many philologists have devoted their attention (cf. e.g. Hunt (1971a, 1971b, 1982, 2004), Watt (1992), La Penna (1997), Vitale (1999)).

I have found about 250 instances of contracted spellings neither attested in manuscripts nor required by metre, but restored by editors on the basis of this type of indirect textual evidence.[76] In many of these cases, however, the decision of the editors is debatable. Within this group we must distinguish at least three types of cases.

First, in many cases the different reading in the other branch of the tradition can be explained by syntactic factors without postulating a misunderstanding of an original contracted spelling. An example of this type is Cic. *N.D.* 1.15:

> quod cum saepe alias tum maxime animaduerti cum apud C. Cottam familiarem meum accurate sane et diligenter de dis inmortalibus **disputatumst**.[77]
>
> disputatumst *Plasberg, Ax* : disputatum est B[ac] : disputatum sit ACNB[pc]

In this case the subjunctive (*disputatum sit*), probably to be considered erroneous, may be explained by the influence of the construction *cum* (narrative/causal) + subjunctive (*cum disputatum sit*) on the construction *cum* (temporal) + indicative (*cum disputatum est*), and not necessarily by the misunderstanding of a contracted form *disputatumst*.[78] A similar case occurs at Cic. *Verr.* 2.4.151:

---

[76] Excluding cases found in Plautus, Terence, and Lucretius (see below n. 84) and in editions in which *est* is always spelt contracted after vowel or -*m*. (cf. p. 133 with n. 113).

[77] 'This has often struck me, but it did so with especial force on one occasion, when the topic of the immortal gods was made the subject of a very searching and thorough discussion at the house of my friend Gaius Cotta.' Trans. Rackham.

[78] *Tum . . . cum* + subjunctive is common in Cicero, but normally the subordinate clause with *cum* takes on a causal-concessive sense (cf. e.g. Hofmann and Szantyr (1965: 625)). This construction occurs in the passage quoted above, in which *tum* may be correlative both with the first *cum* (*cum alias*) and with the second (*cum . . . disputatumst*). The construction *cum* + *alius* (or similar) followed by *tum* + *maxime* (or similar), is common in Cicero (cf. e.g. Cic. *Prov.* 2 **cum propter** alias causas **tum maxime propter** *illud insigne scelus, Marc.* 21, *de Orat.* 332; and see also OLD s.v. *tum* 11). Moreover, the structure *cum saepe alias tum . . .* is frequent in Cicero (cf. *Brut.* 144, *idque* **cum saepe alias tum** *apud centumuiros in M. Curi causa* **cognitum est**, *Tusc.* 4.7 **quod cum saepe alias, tum** *nuper in Tusculano studiose egimus*). Therefore the sentence should be read: *quod cum* ('although') *saepe alias* (i.e. *animaduerterim*) *tum* ('yet') *maxime animaduerti, tum* ('then') *cum* ('when') *. . . disputatumst*. Even if *tum* could be connected only to the first *cum*, the fact that *tum* can be correlative with the second *cum* as well makes the indicative *disputatum est* preferable to the subjunctive *disputatum sit*.

Syracusanam quidem ciuitatem ut abs te **adfectast** ita in te esse anima-
tam uidemus[79]

adfectast *Klotz* : adfecta est α : adfecta sit β

Here the subjunctive was probably introduced either because the *ut*
clause is dependent on an infinitive clause or under the influence of
the final/resultative *ut* + subjunctive construction. Another example
is *Top.* 76:

in hoc genere etiam **illast** in Palamedem coniecta suspicionum prodi-
tionis multitudo[80]

illast *Friedrich* : illa est α *Reinhardt* : illa sunt β

In this case the plural form would have been introduced under the
influence of the collective meaning of the term *multitudo*[81] ('also
the vast variety of suspicions of treason heaped on Palamedes *are* of
the same kind'). And again cf. Sen. *Ep.* 79.9:

illud de quo agitur, quod beatum facit, **aequalest** in omnibus[82]

aequalest *Hense, Reynolds* : aequale ω : aequale est ς

In this case the verb might simply be an interpolation, as the maxim
also works without it.[83] In other cases, the context is heavily corrupted
and the reintegration of the contracted spelling is not cogent. Cf. e.g.:

Pompon. 130 R.

decedo cacatum: <num qu>ae **praestu**<st hic> ueprecula *Ribbeck*

Afran. 58 R.

gingiuestigia aut *codd.* : **gingiuast** gannit hau *Ribbeck*

Suet. *Poet.* 11 p. 29 Reif.

simitur Hecura sexta ex his fabula *codd.* : **exclusast** fabula *Reifferscheid*

---

[79] 'That the feelings of the people of Syracuse towards you correspond to their
treatment by you, we are fully aware.' Trans. Greenwood.

[80] 'Of that kind is also the vast variety of suspicions heaped on Palamedes.' Trans.
Reinhardt.

[81] Cf. e.g. Cic. *Fin.* 1.25 *multitudinem haec maxime allicit, quod ita putant dici ab illo,
recta et honesta quae sint, ea facere ipsa per se laetitiam* ('the thing that most attracts the
crowd is the belief that Epicurus declares right conduct and moral worth to be intrin-
sically and of themselves delightful.' Trans. Rackham). Cf. also ThLL VIII.1601.67ff.

[82] 'But as regards the quality under discussion—the element that produces
happiness—it is equal in them all.' Trans. Gummere.

[83] For the omission of *est* in emphatic sentences, common in particular after the
pronoun *ille/illa/illud*, see Kühner and Stegmann (1955: I.11), Hofmann and Szantyr
(1965: 419–23). Cf. e.g. Cic. *Off.* 1.63 *praeclarum igitur illud Platonis* (quotation follows),
Sen. *Dial.* 3.12.5 *illud pulchrum dignumque, pro parentibus liberis amicis ciuibus prodire
defensorem,* 4.32.3 *ille magnus et nobilis, qui more magnae ferae latratus minutorum
canum securus exaudit,* Ben. 2.1.3 *illud melius, occupare ante quam rogemur.*

Lucil. 245 M.
omni in una homini bul *codd.* : omnis in **unast** res homini bulga
Lachmann

Finally, there are instances of contracted spellings being restored by editors based only on their own 'editorial feelings', without textual or metrical support (unless such forms are to be considered modern typographical errors):

Pac. 179 R.
pigrast *Ribbeck* : pigra est *codd.*
Quint. 11.3.124
deformest *Radermacher* : deforme est *codd.*
    (the uncontracted form is acceptable)
Titin. 166 R.
luculentust *Ribbeck* : luculentaster *codd. Daviault*
    (*luculentaster* is both metrically and linguistically acceptable)

Excluding debatable instances (i.e. readings possibly generated by syntactic factors, *loci desperati*, contracted forms without textual or metrical support) I have collected about 120 instances of contracted forms which seem to have good indirect support in the manuscripts and have been restored by editors.[84]

The complete list of instances is found below in Box 2.11 classified according to the typologies listed in Table 2.5 above. In Box 2.11 these typologies are ordered according to the grade of textual support: first, categories **d.** (-*s* < -*st*) and **c.** (*si/se* < -*st*), in which the reading of the manuscripts is linguistically improbable and the contracted form seems to be a convincing solution; then category **b.** (*sit/sis/sunt/sim* < -*st*) and **e.** (-Ø < -*st*) in which the reading of manuscripts is often linguistically acceptable and thus the contracted form is less necessary; between these two groups (**d.**, **c.** and **b.**, **e.**) I have listed the instances of multiple readings (cf. Table 2.9 above); finally, category **f.** (other readings (†) < -*st*) in which editorial intervention is heavy and the contracted spelling is less plausible. In some cases manuscripts preserve the uncontracted spelling (category **a.**) together with the misunderstanding (e.g. Ter. *Ph.* 538 *opust* A : *opus est* D[pc]CF : *opus*

---

[84] This figure does not include instances found in Plautus, Terence, and Lucretius since they are too many to be mentioned individually (cf. e.g. Pl. *Mil.* 1390 *forma si codd.* : *formast edd.*), and contracted spellings are directly transmitted to a great extent (cf. above, 3.1), thus providing enough evidence for the use of contracted spellings by these authors. See also Lodge (1924–1933) *s.v. sum* for a list of cases.

Box 2.11 **Contracted forms restored by editors**

---

c. *si/se/sic* < *-st* (+ a. *est*)

Catul. 38.2 malest me *edd.* : male sime GOR[ac] : male est si me R[pc]m

Cic. *ad Att.* 4.15.1 gratumst *Buecheler* : gratum si NM : gratum se OR

Germ. *Arat.* 375 B. notast *Orellius* : nota si O : nota est Z : nota similem A

Mart. 8.70.1 tantast *Lindsay* : tanta est B[a] : tanta si C[a] (Lindsay)

Quint. 7.4.19 ponendumst *Gertz, Radermacher* : ponendum si A : ponendum est GH *cett. edd.*

d. *-s* < *-st* (+ a. *est*)

Pompon. 105 R. datast *Ribbeck* : datas *codd.*

Titin. 12 R. necessest *edd.* : necesses NC

Lucil. 491 M. terrast *Lachmann* : terras *codd.*, 493 M. multost *Lachmann* : multos *codd.*, 708 M. usurast *Corpetus* : usuras et *codd.*

Var. *Men.* 267 B. disruptast *Buecheler* : di(s)ruptas *codd.*

Rhet. Her. 4.8 inutilest *Marx* : inutiles M : inutile est CE

Cic. *N.D.* 1.37 sententiast *Ax* : sententias A[ac]B : sententia est A[pc]

Virg. *Aen.* 6.398 fatast *Ribbeck* : fatas F[ac], 9.508 rarast *Ribbeck* : raras P[ac], 10.777 clipeost *Ribbeck* : clipeos P : clipeo est *cett.*, *Georg.* 4.402 umbrast *Ribbeck* : umbras γ : umbras est *cett.*, 4.493 stagnist *Ribbeck* : stagnis FMγ *edd.*: stagni est R

Germ. *Arat.* 31 B. ueterist *Baehrens* : ueteris OZ

Hor. *Serm.* 1.3.50 paulost *Keller and Holder* : paulos x[ac] : paulo est *cett.*, *Ars* 264 ueniast *Keller and Holder* : uenias B

Epigrammata Bobiensia (ed. Munari 1955) 35.1 decimast Cytherea *Munari* : decima Schytera *cod.*

Aegritudo Perdicae 47 sagittast *Baehrens* : sagittas H

multiple readings (e.g. *-s* < *-st* + *sit* + *est*)

Acc. *Trag.* 154 R. (= 180 D.) fortunaest *Buecheler* : fortunae sic H[pc]G[ac]P : fortunae sit LFE *Bamb.*

Rhet. Her. 3.38 ridiculumst *Marx* : ridiculum H : ridiculum sit PBCΠ : est ridiculum b : ridiculum est ld, 4.50 spontest *Marx* : sponte sit Md : sponte se l : se sponte b

Catul. 62.8 certest *Haupt* : certe si V : certe rmg : certes i T

Rhet. Her. 3.23 contentiost *Marx* : contentiosa M : contentio est EC : contentio BP

Cic. *N.D.* 2.123 elephantost *Ax* : elephanto est H : elephantos AV[ac]B[ac] : elephanto B[pc] : elephantis PV[pc], *Caec.* 104 offendendumst *Scholl* : offendendum B : offendendum si T, *ad Att.* 7.11.4 factast *Müller* : factas EORM : facta si H : facta bdms, 11.6.2 cogitatumst *Müller* : cogitatum si MW : cogitatum sensi ORbdms : cogitatum est *edd.*, *ad Fam.* 1.6.2 adflictast *nonn. edd.* : adflicta si M[ac] : adflicta sit M[pc]GR : adflicta est *Victorius cett. edd.* (cf. Shakleton-Bailey *ad loc., sc. ex -tast, quod in textu ponunt plerique*), 1.8.3 totast *Müller:* tota si *codd.* : tota sunt *Madvig* : tota est *Boot*, 8.13.2 stomachust *Mendelsshon* : stomachus M : stomacho est *cett.*, 11.9.2 persuasissimumst *Mendelsshon* : persuasissimum et M : persuasissimum est D : persuasissimum sit H

Virg. *Aen.* 3.629 suist *Ribbeck* : suis P[ac] : sui est MP[pc]γω : sui abefrv

Germ. *Arat.* 385 causast *Orellius* : causa si BP : causa A : causa est Z

Apul. *Apol.* 50 praecipuast *Helm* : praecipua si F : praecipua sit φ

Gell. 7.16.7 uitamst *Hertz* : uitam est *Cic. Sul. 26* : uitam sit V : uitam *cett.*

Disticha Catonis 4.32 B. tibist *Baehrens* : tibi **V** : tua **E** : est tibi **T** : tibi sit **A**

b. *sit/sis/sunt/sim* < *-st* (+ a. *est*)

Nov. 105 R. quaestuist *Ribbeck* : quaestui sit *codd.*

Rhet. Her. 2.16 quaerendumst *Marx* : quaerendum sit **H** : quaerendum est *cett.*

Cic. *Planc.* 50 repudiatast *Olech.* : repudiata est **E** : repudiata sunt **T** : repudiata fuit **AFOPRS**, *Verr.* 1.153 restinguendumst *Klotz* : restinguendum sit **V** : restinguenda est β, 3.187 factast *Klotz* : facta est **b** : facta sis **O**, *ad Fam.* 11.12.2 prouidendumst *Mendelsshon* : prouidendum sit **M** : prouidendum est **HD**, 13.53.2 illast *Mueller* : illa sit *codd.*

Stat. *Theb.* 1.706 ultrast *Mueller* : ultrasim **P**^{ac} : ultra est **P**^{pc}ω

Gell. 4.9.13 inuidiosast *Madvig, Hertz* : inuidiosa sit *codd.*

Aegritudo Perdicae 259 nullast *Baehrens* : nulla sit **H**, 271 nullast *Baehrens* : nulla sit **H**

e. *-Ø* < *-st* (+ a. *est*)

pall. inc. fab. 9 R. facturust *Ribbeck* : facturus *codd.*

trag. inc. fab. 109 R. nanctust *Bentley* : na(n)ctus *codd.*

Lucil. 399 M. spurcust *Mercier:* spurcus *codd.*

Pompon. 77 R. sextust *Fleckeisen* : sextus *codd.*

Var. *Men.* 293 B. secutust *Astbury:* secutus *codd. p. 553* : secutus est *codd. p. 555*

Catul. 62.3 tempust *Trappes-Lomax* : tempus *codd.*, 64.186 nulla spest *Trappes-Lomax* : nulla spes *codd.*, 67.27 quaerendust unde *Terzaghi* : quaerendus unde **V**, 73.3 benignest *Friedrich* : benigne *codd.*, 97.4, culust *Trappes-Lomax* : culus *codd.* [i]

Lutat. *Poet.* fr. 2.4 M. uisust *Ursinus nonn. edd.* : uisus est *ed. Ascensiana 1521* : uisus *codd.*

Cic. *ad Fam.* 4.13.5 necessest *Mendelssohn* : necesset **M** : necesse est *cett.*

Hor. *Serm.* 1.1.20 causaest *Keller and Holder* : causae *nonn. codd.* : causae est *cett.*, 1.7.35 tuorumst *Keller and Holder* : tuorum **gy** : tuorum est *cett.*, 1.9.71, 2.3.257, 2.4.76, 2.5.8, *Ep.*1.1.108, 1.7.72,1.16.79, 2.1.179, *Ars* 72, 76 (-st *Keller and Holder* : *-Ø nonn. codd.* : est *cett. codd.*)[ii]

Disticha Catonis B. 1.38 enimst *Baehrens* : enim **DCE** : enim est *recc.*

Grat. *Cyn.* 249 meritumst *Enk* : meritum **AE** : meritum est **D**

f. † < *-st* (+ a. *est*)

Acc. *Trag.* 96 R. (= 647 D.) hocinest *edd.* : hoc in re est *codd.*, 112 (= 383 D.) terraest *edd.* : terra est *Bamb* : terrae est *cett.*

    Annales 3 D. itidemst *Gronovius edd.* : itidem et *codd.*

Aquil. 8 R. oppidumst *Bothius* : est oppidum *codd.*

Caec. 169 R. infortunatust *Spengelius* : est infortunatus *codd. edd.*

Naev. *trag.* 61 R. opust *Mueller* : est opus *codd.*

    praet. 6 R. menalust *codd.* : min salust *edd.*

Var. *Men.* 32 B. diffusast anima *Vahlen* : diffusus *codd.*

Catul. 22.13 scitiust *Trappes-Lomax* : tristius *codd.*, 78.3 homo bellust *Trappes-Lomax* : homo est bellus *codd.*, 78.5 homo stultust *Trappes-Lomax* : homo est stultus *codd.* (cf. Trappes-Lomax (2007: 253))

Lucr. 2.181 quamquam *codd.* : tanta stat *Lachmann* : quom tantast *Butterfield 2009*

Cic. *N.D.* 2.122 east *Ax* : ea est **B** : ea set **AV**, 2.30 necessest *Ax* : neces sit **A**^{ac} : necesse est **A**^{pc}**VB**, 1.82 auditumst *Ax* : auditum est **HN** : auditu est **ADB**^{2} : auditus est **B**^{ac}, 2.73 dictumst *Ax* : dictum est **A**^{pc}**HVB**^{pc} : dictu est **A**^{ac} : dictus

(continued)

Box 2.11 **Continued**

est B^{ac}, 3.46 fanumst *Ax* : fanum est PVB^{pc} : fanus est A^{ac}H : fanu est A^{pc}B^{ac}, *Verr.* 3.192 eiusmodist *Klotz* : eiusmodi est Vβ : eiusmodi sti O, *Arat.* 448 coronaest *Baehrens* : corona est H^{ac}DVAMS : coronae est H^{pc}BCKT, *ad Att.* 5.18.1 Antiochiast *Müller* : Antiochi(a)e *codd.*, 7.7.1 tuast *Müller* : tu si *codd.* : tua est *edd.*, *ad Fam.* 7.12.2 commodumst *Mendelsshon* : commodum et *codd.* : commodum est *edd.*, 7.17.1 alienissimust *Mendelsshon* : alienissimus et MG : alieni sumus et R : alienissimus est *cett.*, *de Orat.* 3.227 quiddamst et *Friedrich* : quiddam siet HA : quiddam est L

Virg. *Aen.* 11.369 cordist *Ribbeck*, cordis est P^{ac} : cordi est P^{pc} *cett.* : cordi *recc.*, 12.889 morast *Ribbeck* : moraset M^{ac} : mora est M^{pc}PR

Culex 37 certest *Baehrens* : certet O : cernet C, 295 grauest nos *Baehrens* : graues tuos B : graues uos V : tuos graue CH, 300 meritast *Baehrens* : ferit ast GSCL : feritas V

Quint. 9.4.140 necessest *Radermacher* : recesset GH : necesse est PVω

Hor. *Serm.* 1.1.51 suauest *Keller and Holder* : sua ūt (= suauert?) B

Sen. *Ep.* 99.31 nihilost *Hense* : nihilest B : nihilo est *cett.*, 121.5 mobilest *Hense* : mobilem B$\eta\theta$: mobile Qψ, 106.10 corporalest *Windhaus* : corporalis Bϕ : corporale est ψ

Lucan. 8.749 relictumst *Housman*: relictus M^{1}Z^1 : relictum est GUZ^2 : relictu λ : relictum PV

Carmen de figuris uel schematibus 168 mediost *Riese* : medius CP

---

[i] For instances from Catullus cf. Trappes-Lomax (2007: 8–9) and his notes *ad loc.*

[ii] Omission of the verb is common in the textual tradition of Horace; all the cases of contracted spelling listed above are from Keller and Holder (1925), who print a contracted form whenever omission of *est* is found in a branch of the manuscript tradition.

sit D^{ac}GLp^{ac}). Most of the instances listed in Box 2.11 are found in metrical texts (about seventy), several of which are the work of republican authors (about twenty).

The evidence provided by readings resulting from the misunderstanding of contracted spellings is weaker than that provided by their direct transmission in manuscripts. Consequently, there is often disagreement among editors as to whether to restore the contracted spelling or not. Some editors are keen to do so whenever they find a minimum of indirect support in manuscripts,[85] while others tend to print the uncontracted form without even reporting variants in the apparatus. For this reason, it is much more difficult to find instances

---

[85] Ribbeck and Madvig print contracted spellings in many places. Madvig in particular identifies several mistakes (especially of the b. type) in Ciceronian and Livian manuscripts allegedly covering up an original contracted spelling (cf. Madvig (1834: I.184) *infinitis locis vetus scribendi modus errorem* [i.e. the confusion *est/sit* in manuscripts] *peperit*. Cf. also Madvig (1834: I.184, 1860: 585, 1871–1884: I.58, 1876: 44). I have recorded most of these passages in the previous list.

of this type without consulting a large number of editions or, better, checking the complete corpus of Latin manuscripts. Therefore, I expect this list to be less complete that those of the other types of evidence. Nevertheless, I think that it offers a good overview of the spread of readings resulting from the misunderstanding of contracted spellings in a large variety of authors, and I hope that it may be a starting point for a better appreciation by editors of the spread and corruption of contracted spellings in manuscripts.

3.4 Inscriptions

3.4.1 *Collection of Data*

Inscriptions are another source of evidence for the contracted form of *est*.[86] A search in the online Epigraphik-Datenbank Clauss-Slaby, a corpus of more than 450,000 inscriptions, has shown 106 clear instances of the contracted spelling, eighty-six belonging to the pattern -V *est*, ten to the pattern -V*m est*, and ten to the pattern -V*s est*.

The list in Table 2.10 does not claim to record all instances of contracted spellings in inscriptions, especially because editors of CIL are not always accurate.[87] However, it is possible to use it to make some observations.

   1) Even if the number of instances is sufficient to rule out the possibility of mere slips, such examples look relatively few and limited,

---

[86] Diehl (1899: 117–23) offers a good account of contracted spelling in inscriptions. However, he considers only inscriptions recorded by CIL and does not provide references for the pattern -V + *est* (though he offers some figures for this pattern). Moreover, Diehl records only fifty-six instances (with or without references: forty-eight -V*st*, five -*ust* [-*um est*], three -*ust* [-*us est*]. All cases of contracted spellings in CIL 6 are listed in CIL 6.7 p. 7664, together with some forms that have nothing to do with contracted forms of *est* (e.g. *in graecost* = *in graecostasi*, cf. Plin. *Nat.* 33.19). Kruschwitz (2004: 71–6) lists all instances of contracted spellings in republican inscriptions. I have excluded from my list only 1^2.2951a *iud*[*ic*]*ata*[*st* and 1^2.3146 *mole*<*s*>*tus*[*t*] which are heavily corrupted. Even if relying on a smaller corpus, Kruschwitz's conclusions (2004: 74–6) are similar to mine except in one important point: he does not distinguish between inscriptions in verse and those in prose and therefore does not appreciate the proportionally high frequency of contracted forms in republican 'verse inscriptions' (cf. in particular his statements at points I and IV). Some examples of contracted forms in inscriptions are also quoted by Soubiran (1966: 164), Sommer and Pfister (1977: 215), Fortson (2008: 135).

[87] Cf. e.g. an inscription recorded twice in CIL (CIL 8.1495 = 8.26590) which is printed in one place with the uncontracted spelling *pollicita est*, while in the other with the contracted *pollicitast*.

Contraction of esse: *Evidence*

Table 2.10. Contracted forms in inscriptions

Pattern	Spelling	N.	Form	Inscription(s)
-V est (86)	-ast (-a est)	66	sitast (26)	AE 1984.946, AE 1989.476, <u>CIL 1^2.2272</u>, **CIL 1^2.2273**, <u>CIL 1^2.3449k, CIL 1^2.3461</u>, CIL 2.3507, CIL 2.3513, CIL 2.5296 (sita st), **CIL 6.5254**, CIL 6.5789, CIL 6.14013, CIL 6.16401, CIL 6.19176, **CIL 6.25489**, CIL 6.30556, CIL 6.34398, CIL 8.5172, CIL 8.14281, **CIL 8.21275**, CIL 8.25774, CIL 11.5770, CILA 03-02.359, ICUR 6.2961, InscrAqu 2.1864, IRC 4.226
			factast	AE 1940.16
			ueritast	AE 1967.54
			uitast	AE 2005.1673
			priuatast	<u>CIL 1^2.1831</u>
			uocitatast	<u>CIL 1^2.2273</u>
			traductast	<u>CIL 1^2.2662</u>
			deast	<u>CIL 1^2.2954</u>
			fugatast	<u>CIL 1^2.3441</u>
			passast	<u>CIL 1^2.3449d</u>
			sequtast	<u>CIL 1^2.3449h</u>
			finitimast	**CIL 2.3256**
			salitast	CIL 4.8821
			carast	**CIL 6.5302**
			amplesast	**CIL 6.13528**
			consumpsast	**CIL 6.20466**
			inlatast	CIL 6.17144
			probatast	**CIL 6.21200**
			rosast	**CIL 6.22377**
			datast	**CIL 6.25531**
			sui<t>ast	**CIL 6.26011**
			relatast	**CIL 6.26192**
			beatast	**CIL 6.28239**
			cunctast	**CIL 6.30113**
			terrast	**CIL 6.35887**
			iussast	**CIL 6.37412**
			raptast	CIL 6.38598
			sepultast	CIL 8.8092
			paratast	**CIL 8.11824**
			conditast	CIL 8.24406
			pollicitast	**CIL 8.26590**
			ullast	**CIL 8.27790.4**
			iunctast	**CIL 9.3375**
			dedicatast (2)	CIL 10.3682, InscrIt 13.2.17
			positast	**CIL 10.4427**
			sepultast	CIL 11.524
			insitast	**CIL 11.1118**
			uiast	**CIL 2-14.814**
			receptast	ICUR 4.1053b
			co]nsecutast	ICUR 5.13617a

Pattern	Spelling	N.	Form	Inscription(s)
	-as (-a est)	5	sitas(t)	<u>CIL 1².3449i</u>, CIL 8.6916, CIL 8.21087, CIL 8.21308
			factas(t)	ILAlg 2.6384
	-est (-e est)	6	benest	AE 1995.332
			test	**CIL 6.21200**
			qualest	**CIL 9.1164**
			necessest	**CIL 12.5271**
			malest	ILS 8625.23
			credibilest	AE 1912.146
	-ost (-o + est)	9	indiciost	<u>CIL 1².1216</u>
			istost	**CIL 4.4968**
			nostrost	**CIL 4.1791**
			seniost	**CIL 4.1791**
			animost	**CIL 6.25703**
			antrost	**CIL 6.28239**
			ingeniost	**CIL 8.14632**
			tumulost	**CIL 12.882**
			indiciost	**CLE 1076**
-m + est (10)	-anst (-am + est)	1	quisquanst	<u>CIL 1².2662</u>
	-est (em + est)	1	itidest	**CIL 6.13528**
	-umst (-um + est)	2	]tumst seu	CIL 5.8515
			uetitumst	**CIL 6.34185**
	-ust (-um + est)	6	moriendust (2)	AE 2001.1789, CIL 9.3821
			accensust	CIL 3.12013.3
			scriptust	<u>CIL 1².1209</u>
			molestust	**CIL 10.5371**
			moriundust	**CIL 10.5371**
-s + est (10)	-ust (-us + est)	9	situst (5)	AE 2001.312, <u>CIL 1².1861</u>, CIL 6.38824, CIL 6.15089a, Hep 6.119
			uocitatust	<u>CIL 1².584</u>
			satiust	<u>CIL 1².2179</u>
			natust	**CIL 11.1118**
			(a)rsust	CIL 4.10014
	-ost (-os + est)	1	Theorost	CIL 6.10115

(**in bold**: inscriptions in verse; <u>underlined</u>: republican inscriptions)

compared to the number of relevant instances in inscriptions (more than 4600, which means that the contracted forms are about 2% of the total; or, if we exclude the pattern -*us est*, which is contracted only in early Latin, *c.*3000, which means that the contracted forms are about 3% of the total).[88] These figures are shown in Table 2.11 below.

[88] 106 contracted forms out of *c.*4600 = 2.3%; ninety-six contracted forms *not* belonging to the pattern -*ŭs* + *est* (cf. Table 2.11) out of *c.*3000 = 3.2%. These figures are based on a search in the online Clauss-Slaby database and are only approximate.

Table 2.11. Distribution and frequency of contracted spellings in inscriptions

	Total (%)		Metrical (%)	Non-Metrical (%)
CONTRACTED	106 (2%) [96 (3%)]		52 (11%) [48 (17%)]	54 (1%)
		End of line	23	41
		Formula *situs/-a est*	7	28
		Not at the end of line and not formulaic	26	11
TOTAL RELEVANT CASES (-V(*m/s*) + *est*)	*c.*4600 [3000]		*c.*460 [290]	*c.*4140 [2710]

Numbers in square brackets show figures excluding the pattern -us est.

2) As shown in Table 2.11, fifty-two instances are found in inscriptions written in verse (in bold in the list in Table 2.10), almost all included in CLE and/or in the collection of Courtney (1995), henceforth referred to as ML.[89] This figure, by contrast (cf. point 1 above), represents a high proportion: since the number of relevant instances spelt uncontracted in metrical inscriptions recorded in CLE and/or in ML is only about 460, this means that some 11% of the relevant patterns (-V *est*, -V*m est*, -*us est*) are spelt contracted in CLE and ML.[90] If we exclude the controversial pattern -*us est*, the figure rises (about forty-eight out of 290 = 17%). Of these fifty-two instances twenty-three are found at the end of the line (where they might be considered as mere abbreviations) and seven belong to the pattern *sita/situs est*, which looks like a fixed formula in the language of funerary inscriptions and is thus a less convincing piece of evidence for contracted spellings (see below, point 5). However, twenty-six instances are not found at the end of the line and do not belong to a formulaic pattern.

[89] Inscriptions in verse not recorded by these two corpora are CIL 2–14.814, written in elegiac couplets (on this inscription see Cugusi (2007: 51)), 1².3441 (cf. Massaro (2007: 137) 'testo celebrativo, quasi certamente metrico, verosimilmente elegiaco'), and 1².3449i (cf. Kruschwitz (2004: 74); against him Massaro (2007: 159)).
[90] The likelihood that this figure is statistically significant is higher than 99.95%, as shown by the t-test.

Table 2.12. Omission of elidible -V(*m*) in inscriptions ('elided spelling')

Pattern	Form	Inscription
-a est	Cinyr(a) est	**CIL 6.14831**
(9 instances)	sepult(a) est	CIL 6 .21372
	sit(a) est (4)	CIL 8.17350, CIL 10.7848, RIU 3.731, ERPLeon 204
	fix(a) est (2)	CIL 16.118, RHP 509
	depos(i)t(a) est	ICUR 5.13196
-e est (4)[91]	grau(e) est	AE 1985.956
	ment(e) est	**CIL 6.30125**
	funtaqu(e) est	**CIL 8.16674**
	domusqu(e) est	ICUR 3.6628
-um est (5)	script(um) est	AE 1927.87
	centuriari(um) est	AE 1949.215
	cenat(um) est	CIL 6.2104
	fact(um) est	CIL 6.9190
	monument(um) est	**CIL 6.26464**

(**in bold**: inscriptions in verse)

3) Contracted spellings seem to be more frequent in spelling in inscriptions than 'elided spellings', i.e. spellings that reflect elision (cf. e.g. *sepult est < sepulta est*), as shown by comparing the figures of Table 2.11 with the figures for elision involving the patterns -V + *est* and -V*m* + *est* shown in Table 2.12 (-V*s* + *est* is not affected by elision[92]). I have found no more than eighteen instances in inscriptions which present a graphical omission that does not look like a mere abbreviation[93] but rather seems to be a phonetic spelling reflecting elision (listed in Table 2.12). In Table 2.12, I have indicated in parentheses the syllable missing in the inscription (e.g. *sit(a) est = sitest*). Contracted spellings in inscriptions are thus more common than elided spellings for the pattern -V *est* (-*a est*: sixty-six contracted against nine elided; -*o est*: nine against zero; -*e est* is not really relevant since the two spellings cannot be

[91] I have listed in this category the instances in which the verb is NOT univerbated to the preceding word and the vowel *e* is part of the verb (-X *est*).

[92] Cf. III.1.2 with n. 28.

[93] Among the instances excluded from the list as being clear abbreviations, cf. e.g. AE 1987.1045 *D(is) M(anibus) s(acrum)* | ... *Felic(i)o p(ius) u(ixit) an(nos) XXX* | *c(uius) corp(us) hic co(n)dit(um) est*; CIL 6.2104 *ung(uenta) et sportul(as) acc(eperunt) sing(uli)* | *(denarios) C hoc anno **cenat(um) est** [in]* | *dies sing(ulos)*; CIL 4.171 *aed (ilem) o(ro) u(os) f(aciatis) **dign(um) est**/una et uicini o(ro) u(os) f(aciatis)*.

distinguished).[94] This is less true for the pattern -*m est* (-*um est*: eight contracted against five elided; -*am est*: one against zero; -*em est*: one against zero).[95] Only four of the instances of elided spellings (in bold in the list) belong to inscriptions written in verse.

4) Despite the strong evidence for the spelling -*mst* in manuscripts of Plautus, Terence, and Lucretius (cf. 3.1.1 p. 37), this type is not well attested in inscriptions. Moreover, in most instances the -*m* is missing (one instance -*est* = -*em est*, plus six instances -*ust* = -*um est*) or is spelt as -*n* (*quisquanst*). This seems to be a reflection of the omission or obscuration of final -*m* in speech, which would suggest that this type of spelling is influenced by pronunciation.[96] As pointed out, this uncertainty concerning the spelling of the reduced form -*umst* is attested in the manuscripts of Plautus, Terence, and Lucretius as well.[97]

5) As shown in Table 2.11, fifty-four instances are found in inscriptions that are not in verse or are too mutilated to be analysed. This means that in non-verse inscriptions (i.e. inscriptions not recorded in CLE and/or in ML) the contracted spellings are only about 1% of the total (fifty-four out of *c*.4200). Of these fifty-four instances, forty-one are found at the end of the line, where they were probably preferred to the uncontracted spellings for reasons of space.[98] Moreover, in twenty-eight of these fifty-four instances the contracted form is found in a fixed expression of the type *situs/sita est*, which looks like a traditional formula in the context of funerary inscriptions; in this case the contracted spelling is less telling, since its presence might simply be due to imitation and adherence to a convention.[99] In non-metrical inscriptions there are thus only eleven instances that are not at the end of the line and do not belong to the pattern *situs/sita est*, which is a low figure compared with the number of equivalent instances in metrical inscriptions (twenty-six; see above point 2).[100] Consequently, the evidence of contracted spellings in non-metrical inscriptions is

---

[94] The likelihood that this difference in frequency is statistically significant is higher than 99.95%, as shown by the t-test.

[95] For an account of elision in inscriptions see Soubiran (1966: 56–9), although he quotes only from CLE. However, my figures confirm his general claim that elision in inscriptions is exceptional.

[96] Cf. 3.1.2 and below pp. 74–5.   [97] Cf. 3.1.2.

[98] Cf. e.g. CIL 2.4402 *sitas^t*| and CIL 1^2.3461 *sitas^t*| (*t* written over the *s*), CIL 1^2.5271 *leg$_e$ n$_e$cssest* (small *e* written inside the consonants *g* and *c*). On contractions as abbreviations cf. III.1.1.

[99] Perhaps the contracted spelling entered funerary language as a high-style archaism, thus confirming the presence of contracted spellings in the orthographic system of early Latin (cf. III.2.1.1).

[100] The likelihood that this pattern is statistically significant is between 99.5% and 99.95%, as shown by the t-test.

relatively weak. Nevertheless, such instances may still be considered as evidence for the existence of contracted forms of *est* (at least at one stage in the evolution of Latin) and should not simply be dismissed en masse as abbreviations.

6) Lachmann (1871: *ad* 1.993) pointed out that there seem not to be many instances of contracted spellings in republican inscriptions (nineteen cases, underlined in Table 2.10 above).[101] This would be unexpected, given that direct transmission of contracted spellings is well attested in the manuscripts of republican authors. However, the overall number of occurrences of the relevant patterns (-V + *est*, -V*m* + *est*, -V*s* + *est*) is about 140 in republican inscriptions recorded in CIL 1², as shown in Table 2.13.[102] Therefore, the frequency of contracted forms in CIL 1² is higher than the general frequency of contracted forms in the whole corpus of inscriptions: nineteen out of *c.*140 (14%)[103] or, excluding the pattern -*us est*, fifteen out of about eighty (19%), against 106 out of *c.*4600 in the whole corpus of inscriptions (2%).[104] Moreover, the number of republican inscriptions written in verse is small. Only some ninety inscriptions from CIL 1² are recorded in CLE or ML. In these, I have found only ten relevant instances spelt uncontracted (1².11 *uictus est*, CIL 1².1202 *gratum est*, 1².1210 *tantum est*, 1².1211 *paullum est*, 1².1212 *conditus est*, 1².1219 *proprium est*, 1².2138 *ueniundum est*, 1².1924 *prosecutus est*, 1².2173 *curuom est*, 1².2274 *situs est*) against twelve contracted spellings, recorded in the list above (CIL 1².1209 *scriptust*, 1².1216 *indiciost*, 1².1861 *situst*, 1².2179 *satiust*, 1².2273 *sitast*, *uocitatast*, 1².2662 *quisquanst*, *traductast*, 1².3441 *fugatast*, 1².3349d *passast*, 1².3449h *sequtast*, 1².3449i *sitas*). Consequently, it would seem that Lachmann's claim about the rarity of contracted forms in archaic inscriptions is not correct.

[101] CIL 1².1861 (Samnium, *c.*169 BC.) *situst*, CIL 1².584 (Genoa, 116–17 BC) *uocitatust*, CIL 1².1209 (Rome, second half 2nd century BC) *scriptust*, CIL 1².1216 (Rome, second half 2nd century BC) *indiciost*, CIL 1².2662 (Corinth, 102 BC) *traductast, quisquanst*, CIL 1².1831 (Samnium, first half 1st century BC?) *priuatast* CIL 1².2179 (late republic) *satiust*, CIL 1².2272 (Cartagena, 1st century BC) *sitast*, CIL1².2273 (Cartagena, early 1st century BC) *sitast, uocitatast*, CIL 1².2954 (Isauria, 1st century BC) *deast*, CIL 1².3441 (Samothrace) *fugatast*, CIL 1².3449d (Cartagena, 1st century BC) *passast*, CIL 1².3449h (Cartagena, 1st century BC) *sequtast*, CIL 1².3449k *sitast*, 1².3449i *sitas(t)*, CIL 1².3461 *sitast*, AE 2001.312 (1st century BC) *situst*. Only six are found in inscriptions dated before the first century BC; no instances are found in the *inscriptiones uetustissimae* (CIL 1². 1–580).

[102] Cf. also the index of CIL 1² p. 787, which however does not record about thirty cases.

[103] I exclude from these figures one contracted spelling found in a republican inscription not recorded by CIL 1² (AE 2001.312 *situst*).

[104] The likelihood that the patterns of table 2.13 are statistically significant is higher than 99.95%, as shown by the t-test.

Table 2.13. Contracted and uncontracted spellings in republican and imperial inscriptions

Republican inscriptions	Contracted (e.g. *deast, satiust*)	Uncontracted (e.g. *sita est, factus est*)
Metrical (CLE and ML)	12	10
Non-metrical	7	*c.*110
TOTAL	19 (14%) [15 (19%)]	*c.*120 (86%) [65 (81%)]
Imperial inscriptions	**Contracted** (e.g. *ulast, situst*)	**Uncontracted** (e.g. *bona est, dictus est*)
Metrical (CLE and ML)	40	*c.*400
Non-metrical	47	*c.*4000
TOTAL	87 (2%)	*c.*4400 (98%)

Numbers in square brackets show figures excluding the pattern -us est. *ML = Courtney 1995*

7) Diachronic observations are difficult to make since few inscriptions have been dated precisely. The phenomenon seems to be attested from the second century BC (CIL 1^2. 1861 = CLE 361: *c.*169 BC) until at least the third century AD (CIL 8.11824 = CLE 1238: written in uncials dating at the earliest to the third century AD). The majority of instances are found in imperial inscriptions, even if, as shown in Table 2.13, they are proportionally more frequent in republican inscriptions, especially of the first century BC (cf. n. 101). As far as the pattern *-s est* is concerned, four instances are found in republican inscriptions, while the others (six) are found in inscriptions dated to the imperial age (cf. e.g. the form *(a)rsust*, attested in an inscription from Pompei).

3.4.2 Some General Remarks

With the caution required in dealing with the artificial medium of inscriptions on stone, we can try to draw some conclusions from the above observations.

First, the results of the survey show that contracted forms are mainly a feature of metrical inscriptions (cf. Tables 2.11 and 2.13). This fact excludes the possibility that we are always dealing with mere graphic abbreviations (if they were just abbreviations, it would be difficult to explain the different proportion of contracted forms in metrical and non-metrical texts).[105] Second, the figures suggest that the contracted spellings are proportionately much more common in republican inscriptions than in later inscriptions (see Table 2.13).

While evidence from inscriptions supports the idea that contracted spellings were a feature of poetry and/or republican Latin, it is difficult to use this evidence to draw conclusions about speech and pronunciation.[106] A number of methodological problems arise when dealing with inscriptions since many different factors may influence a particular spelling. First, writers may simply be imitating the spelling of an older and/or model inscription, as presumably was the case with the funerary formula *sitast/situst*. This 'horizontal transmission' may be either conscious (such as in the case of an archaism) or mechanical. Second, there may be the influence of the spoken language either of the writer himself (and thus filtered by his degree of literacy and sociolect) or of other people whom the writer wanted to imitate. Third, 'material' factors may account for an apparent orthographic quirk, such as the need to save space by using abbreviations, or even just imprecision or oversight on the part of the writer.[107] Therefore, the same form found in two different inscriptions might have two different origins. To give an example, the non-standard spelling *oi = ū*, found in some republican inscriptions (e.g. CIL 1^2.9 *ploirume*), may reflect local Oscan orthography/pronunciation in an inscription from Capua, whereas it may be taken as an orthographical archaism in an inscription from Rome, its relationship to Oscan being merely coincidental.[108]

In the case of contracted spellings, given that we cannot regard a contracted form as a 'standard' spelling (except perhaps in the case of republican metrical inscriptions) or as a simple abbreviation, should we attribute this deviation to pronunciation or to orthography? Or, to put the same question in other words: in a particular inscription, was the engraver writing a contracted form under the influence of speech, or was he copying from another inscription/text, perhaps deliberately

---

[105] Cf. III.1.1.   [106] Cf. III.2.2.

[107] For a discussion of the methodological problems of an analysis relying on inscriptions see Adams (2007: chs. II and X, in particular pp. 39–40, 629–35) and Clackson (2011b). Cf. also Soubiran (1966: 58).

[108] For this example cf. Adams (2007: 45).

inserting an old-fashioned form, and/or adhering to a particular orthographic code?

It is impossible to give a firm answer to these questions since it is hazardous to argue from inscriptions to pronunciation. The higher frequency of contracted spellings in republican inscriptions (both in prose and in poetry) compared to their frequency in later inscriptions, together with their almost complete absence from republican high-style documents,[109] might be taken to suggest that at least in the republican age contracted forms were common in spoken language.[110] On the other hand, no firm inference can be drawn from these data about the pronunciation of contracted forms in later ages.

I will come back to this issue in chapter III (especially section III.2.2). Nevertheless, before moving on, I mean to focus on three pieces of epigraphic evidence which, although not very strong, might be advanced to support the hypothesis that the contracted pronunciation did not completely disappear from spoken Latin until at least the first or second century AD.

1) The number of occurrences of contracted forms (-V*st*, -V*s*) in post-republican inscriptions, belonging neither to poetic nor to formulaic contexts (twenty-three), is higher than the number of occurrences of elided spellings (twelve). On the one hand we have to note that the grapheme with contraction (*factast*, etc.) apparently had orthographic status at a certain stage of Latin, whereas the grapheme with elision (e.g. *fact'est*) did not, and was not likely to have, since it would have obscured inflectional information. On the other hand, if in post-republican spoken Latin the only way to pronounce a sequence -V/-V*m* + *est* was with elision (a phenomenon common in speech, cf. III.1.2), we would perhaps expect different proportions.

2) The confusion over the pattern -V*m* + *(e)st* (five times spelt -V*st*, and one time -V*nst* in imperial and late inscriptions) is better explained as being the result of the influence of pronunciation than of horizontal transmission (see sections 3.1.2 and 3.4.1 p. 70). Therefore, it might also be possible to explain the contracted spelling of -*st* in the form *moriendust* (= *moriendum est*), found in an inscription dated to the first

---

[109] No contracted spellings are found in the *inscriptiones uetustissimae* (cf. n. 101) or in the more official poetic inscriptions in Saturnian verse; on these cf. Kruschwitz (2002). Moreover, contracted spellings are very rare in legal texts; on this cf. Kruschwitz (2004: 75 n. III).

[110] Kruschwitz (2004: 74) draws a similar conclusion ('Prodelision ist gleichwohl ein so konventionelles Merkmal der gesprochenen Sprache').

century AD (AE 2001.1789), as having been influenced by contemporary pronunciation.

3) In post-republican inscriptions, most instances are admittedly found in metrical texts or formulaic phrases where they might reflect artificial writing conventions, or are found at the end of the line, where they could have been preferred for reasons of space. However, there are a number of cases al found in post-republican inscriptions which would be more difficult to consider as poeticisms, formulae, or abbreviations. Cf. e.g.:

AE 1940.16 Chubur cellam promam aedificandam /]um mponendum opere tectorio perficiendam / **factast** penes Mastliuam Sucan exactorem

CIL 8.1495 [V]ibiae Asicianes fil(iae) suae HS C / mil(ia) n(ummum) **pollicitast** ex quorum re/[d]itu ludi scaenici et sportulae / decurionibus darentur.

3.5 Grammarians

Grammarians offer further evidence for the status of the contraction of *est*, in spelling and/or pronunciation.

3.5.1 *Marius Victorinus*

A first passage is in the grammarian and philosopher Marius Victorinus (fourth century AD), who explicitly refers to forms of this type in his treatise *Ars grammatica* (Mariotti 1967: pp. 85–6[111] (= GL 6.22.14ff.)):

cum fuerit autem scriptum 'audiendus est' et 'scribendus est' et 'mutandus est' et similia generis masculini, primam uocem integram relinquetis, ex nouissima autem E et S detrahetis. idem facietis in femininis ut prima uox cuius generis sit appareat idemque in neutris.

Furthermore, when there is written 'audiendus est,' 'scribendus est,' and 'mutandus est' and similar expressions with the masculine gender, you will preserve the first word intact and cut out the E and the S from the second one [= audiendus t]. You will do the same with feminine words so that the gender of the first word remains clear and (you will do) the same with neuter words as well.

---

[111] Quotations from Marius Victorinus are from Mariotti's (1967) edition, which provides a useful linguistic commentary. Henceforth I will refer to his edition with the abbreviation 'M.' following the page number.

Even if Victorinus does not bother to consider the implications for the feminine and neuter of the rule 'e *et* s *detrahetis*' (which would produce *audiendat* and *audiendumt*, not *audiendast* and *audiendumst*), nevertheless it would seem clear that he is referring to forms such as *audiendust*, *audiendast*, and *audiendumst* (assuming that for the feminine and neuter Victorinus means only 'e *detrahetis*').[112] However, to make further observations based on this passage, we need to place it in the context of Victorinus' 'spelling philosophy'.

Victorinus is a radical grammarian who tends to advocate spellings that reflect pronunciation (phonetic spellings),[113] polemicizing both against the ancients, who were not consistent in spelling and pronunciation (pp. 75–6 M.):

> 'cum' aduerbium temporis antiqui quattuor litteris scribebant [in] his, 'quum'; apud Catonem 'quum' rursus per O, 'quom'. sed antiqui cum ita scriberent, pronuntiabant tamen perinde ac si per 'cum' scriptum esset, illa quidem **scriptura confusa** ... in quibus **peccabant** et aliis litteris scribebant, quam quibus enuntiabant, et aliter legebant, quam scribebant.[114]

and against those moderns who follow the rules of ancient writers (p. 85 M.):

> inducti fortasse eo quod legistis praeceptum antiquorum qui aiunt scribi quidem omnibus litteris oportere, in enuntiando autem quasdam litteras elidi. in quo, ut idem saepius dicam, bis peccatis.[115]

His principle is that the ear (=the phonetic realization) is the criterion of spelling (cf. p. 72 M. *nam ut color oculorum iudicio, sapor palati, odor narium dinoscitur, ita sonus aurium arbitrio*

---

[112] Mariotti (1967: 219) states that after *idemque in neutris* we should understand 'm *detrahetis*' only (thus producing *multu est*); this does not seem to be correct, since in this passage Marius Victorinus is referring to something other than the loss of final -*m*.

[113] On phonetic spellings cf. I.3.2.

[114] 'The ancients used to spell *cum* the temporal adverb with these four letters: *quum*; Cato instead spelt *quum* with an *o*: *quom*. However, even if the ancients spelt it this way, they pronounced it as if it was written *cum* and this is definitely a confused way of writing. They were wrong to do so, [since] they wrote different letters from those they actually pronounced, and they read it otherwise than how they wrote it.'

[115] 'Perhaps you [are] under the influence of the written rules of the ancients, who say that you must write all the letters, even if some of them are lost in pronunciation. To repeat it again: you are twice wrong to do so.'

subiectus est);[116] one must write the letters which are required by the
sound of a word in pronunciation (cf. p. 73 M. *quae uoces Z litterae
sonum exigunt, eas per Z sine ulla haesitatione debemus scribere*;[117]
p. 78 M. *attamen has etiam uoces, quae V potius quam O* **sonant**, *per
duo V scribite, ut 'uulua, uultus' et similia, sicuti sine ulla dubitatione
per V et O, quae [ita]* **sonant** *ita, uti 'uoluit, uoluo, uolutus, conuolutus'*).[118] This 'grammatical theory' is different from that advocated by
other grammarians such as Aulus Gellius[119] but has some illustrious
antecedents.[120]

The spellings recommended by Victorinus in his treatise, apparently on the basis of this 'phonetic principle', are (pp. 84–5 M.):
posquam (instead of *postquam*),[121] *hiems, sumsit, consumtum,
emtum, redemtum,* and *temtat* (instead of *hiemps, sumpsit, consump-
tum, emptum, redemptum, temptat*), *sepulcrum* (instead of *sepul-
chrum*), *improles* (instead of *inproles*).[122] Moreover, Victorinus

---

[116] 'For as a colour is identified by the eyes, a taste by the palate, and a smell by the
nose, so a sound falls under the judgement of the ear.'

[117] 'Words which require the sound of the letter Z must be spelt without any doubt
with the Z.'

[118] 'However, you spell with two Us also the words which sound with a U rather
than with an O, such as *uulua, uultus* and similar. In the same way [you must] without
any doubt [spell] with U and O those words which sound so, such as *uoluit, uoluo,
uolutus, conuolutus*'

[119] Cf. above n. 46.

[120] Another notorious advocate of phonetic spelling was the emperor Augustus (cf.
Suet. *Aug.* 88). For similar *quaestiones* cf. e.g. the polemics of Velius Longus against
Scaurus on the analogical reduplication of *l* in *paulum* and *paullum* (GL 7.80.10ff.
*quia pullum per duo scribimus, obseruauerunt quidam ut 'paullum' repetito eodem
elemento scriberent. quod mihi non uidetur, quoniam enuntiari nullo modo potest et
non est necesse scribere quod in uerbo non sonet*).

[121] The spelling *posquam* is found in inscriptions (cf. CIL 1².2540a) and in
manuscripts of literary texts, cf. Titin. 40 R., Accius *trag.* 118 R. and *inc. trag.* 165
R., Virg. *Aen.* 1.723 *posquam* R^ac *Ribbeck* (interestingly the passage quoted by
Victorinus), Ter. *Eun.* 645 *posquam* G^il ε, Catul. 3 *posquam* RvenD. It is also possible
that this spelling was accepted by some authors. For another popular simplification of
this type entering the literary language, cf. the adjective *posmeridianus*, used three
times by Cicero (*de Orat.* 3.17, 3.121, *Orat.* 157), 'with the permission of custom and
for the sake of agreeable effect', as he himself states (*Orat.* 157). Cicero's concession to
the spoken language for the sake of *lenitas* (= euphony) was noted and praised by the
grammarian Velius Longus (GL 7.79.2ff. *sequenda est uero non numquam elegantia
eruditorum uirorum, qui quasdam litteras lenitatis causa omiserunt, sicut Cicero, qui
foresia et Megalesia et hortesia sine n littera libenter dicebat et, ut uerbis ipsius utamur,
'posmeridianas quoque quadrigas' inquit 'libentius dixerim quam postmeridianas'*).

[122] It is debatable whether all these spellings reflected the standard pronunciation of
the forms at the time of Victorinus, especially because Victorinus himself, infringing his
own rule, sometimes prescribes a spelling explicitly different from pronunciation (cf.

seems to recommend, at least in poetry,[123] the omission in orthography of that which (according to Victorinus) is elided in pronunciation (85 M.):

> eliduntur autem uocales singulae, cum duae concurrerunt, ut 'men incepto desistere uictam' (Virg. *Aen.* 1.37), non 'mene'; et 'ten inquit miserande puer' (Virg. *Aen.* 11.42), non 'tene'. T quoque ex consonantibus eliditur, ut 'posquam res Asiae' (Virg. *Aen.* 3.1) non 'postquam'. M autem: 'mult ille et terris' (Virg. *Aen.* 1.3), uocalis et consonans pariter, 'non equid[em] inuideo' (Virg. *Ecl.* 1.11), 'et breuiter Troiae suprem[um] audire laborem' (Virg. *Aen.* 2.11).[124]

Spellings such as *equid inuideo* were certainly not familiar and it is not a surprise that later scribes of the manuscripts of Victorinus introduced the full spelling (*equid[em] inuideo, suprem[um] audire*).[125]

The passage quoted at the beginning of this section, in which Victorinus seems to recommend the contracted spelling of *est*, directly follows and precedes arguments of this type. At a superficial

---

p. 84 M. *quae* ψ *sonant et non declinantur . . . per B S scribite, ut 'abscedit'*). It is safer to say that most of these forms (*posquam, hiems*, etc.), in the perception of Victorinus, were close enough to current pronunciation to influence the spelling of the others by analogy. We may however observe that assimilation (*improles*), loss of aspiration (*sepulcrum*), and simplification of consonantal clusters (*posquam, temtat*, etc.), were common phenomena in Latin speech (cf. Väänänen (1981: 55, 60–6)). On the other hand the epenthesis of a labial was also a common phonetic phenomenon in Latin speech (cf. e.g. *sumptum*, and see Weiss (2009: 187)), and therefore, at least in early Latin, spellings such as *sumpsit* were probably closer to speech than *sumsit* (the morphologically expected form). Nevertheless, Romance reflexes (cf. e.g. It. *tentare* < *temptare*; *assunse* < *adsumsit*) suggest that in late Latin earlier epenthetic consonants were also exposed to the process of consonantal simplification.

[123] This limitation of the elided spelling to poetic texts is suggested by the fact that Victorinus' quotations are all taken from poetic texts (Virgil in particular; on this cf. Mariotti (1967: 218)). However, it must be observed that the instances of contracted spellings (of *audiendus est, scribendus est*, and *mutandus est*, cf. above p. 75), which are quoted in the following section, are apparently not taken from poetic texts.

[124] 'Moreover, single vowels must be elided [= *in spelling*?] when they are followed by another vowel, such as *"men incepto desistere uictam"*, not *"mene"*; and *"ten inquit miserande puer"*, non *"tene"*. Also, in a consonantal cluster the T must be elided, such as *"posquam res Asiae"* not *"postquam"*. As far as the M is concerned: *"mult ille et terris"*, the consonant [must be elided] together with the vowel: *"non equid inuideo"*, *"et breuiter Troiae suprem audire laborem."*'

[125] Other unfamiliar spellings apparently proposed by Marius Victorinus are *hicc* and *hocc*, discussed at p. 86 M. (= GL 6.22.17ff.): *at hicce et hocce pronominibus, si uox sequens a uocali incipiat, e nouissimam detrahetis, ut 'hicc alienus ouis custos bis mulget in hora'* (Virg. *Ecl.* 3.5) *et 'manibusque meis Mezentius hicc est'* (Virg. *Aen.* 11.16) *et 'hocc erat alma parens'* (Virg. *Aen.* 2.664) *et 'hocc Ithacus uelit'* (Virg. *Aen.* 2.104).

level, Victorinus would seem therefore to consider the contracted spelling of *est* to be just another one of the phonetic spellings recommended by his orthographical theory and could therefore possibly reflect phonetic phenomena current in Latin speech at his time.

The problem with this view is that it is difficult to evaluate to what extent Victorinus' work is to be trusted. Two issues especially should be taken into account.[126] First, late-antique grammarians were often elaborating previous material, which possibly they did not understand and/or which reflected a different linguistic situation; consequently, Victorinus' remarks on contraction might not have any connection with the Latin spoken and written at his time. Second, the unity of the text itself is problematic; it is not implausible that the *Ars grammatica* of Victorinus, in the form transmitted by manuscripts and printed by editors, is, to some extent, a compilation by some later scribes or scholars.[127] Individual passages might therefore have been extracted from other works and assembled or interpolated into a new text. Thus, the sense that a passage seems to have in the context of the *Ars* might be different from the sense that the same passage had in the original text. In this respect, it is relevant to point out that in the passage on elided spelling (p. 85 *eliduntur autem uocales singulae cum duae concurrerunt*), which directly precedes the remarks on contractions (quoted at the beginning of this section), there exist some traditional elements of metrical treatises. For instance, the quotation *multum ille et terris* (Virg. *Aen.* 1.3) is used as an example of metrical reductions of -V*m* before V- by many late-antique metricists.[128] Consequently, both the passage on elided spelling and the remarks on contracted spelling which follow it might originally have had not an orthographic reference but a metrical one (prescribing or describing the scansion of a line) and thus might not be related to Victorinus' general defence of phonetic spellings (as discussed above) at all.

In conclusion, the passage of Victorinus provides evidence for the existence of contracted spellings but it does not necessarily support

---

[126] Cf. Mariotti (1967: 3–62).

[127] Cf. Mariotti (1967: 45–55) for an overview of the discrepancies between the editions of Victorinus' *Ars* by Keil and Mariotti, and the textual difficulties of this text.

[128] Cf. Consentius p. 29 N. [*De arte metrica*]: *paene omnes in ecthlipseos exemplis non aliud dent quam 'multum ille et terris'*. 'As an example of *ecthlipsis* [i.e. omission of -*m* and/or vowels at word boundaries] almost all quote nothing other than *multum ille et terris*.' Cf. also Aphthonius GL 6.66.15, Audax GL 7.339.28.

the view that at his time contracted forms were standard in speech.
I will come back to this issue in chapter III.

3.5.2 *Consentius*

Another piece of evidence for contracted forms is offered by some
passages by the grammarian Consentius (fifth century AD), referring
to the phenomenon of *synaliphe*:

> Niedermann 1937: p. 7 (= GL 5.389.30ff.)
> post hos sunt duo metaplasmi, quos partim iam poetae factos in scrip-
> tura ipsi relinquunt, partim faciendos nobis tradunt, synaliphe et ecth-
> lipsis. synaliphe uel syncrisis est, cum per conlisionem concurrentium
> uocalium subtrahendi ex his aliquam praebetur occasio. hoc, sicut dixi,
> aut ipse poeta ita iam scriptum reliquit aut nobis subtrahendum tradit.
> scriptum reliquit, ut est illud 'nec non aurumque animusque **Latinost**'
> (Virg. *Aen.* 12.23); nobis subtrahendum permittit, ut est illud 'atque ea
> diuersa penitus dum parte geruntur' (Virg. *Aen.* 9.1).

After these, there are two types of 'metaplasm',[129] 'synaliphe', and
'ecthlipsis', which phenomena (as I said) in part the poets already
themselves hand down, represented in writing, and in part leave us to
put into practice. 'Synaliphe' or 'syncrisis' is when there is the oppor-
tunity, in a clash of two vowels running together, of deleting one of the
two. This either the poet himself has left in written form, or he leaves it
to us to effect the removal. An instance he has left written is: 'nec non
aurumque animusque Latinost'. An instance which the poet leaves us to
remove is: 'atque ea diuersa penitus dum parte geruntur'.

> Niedermann pp. 29–30 (= GL 5.402.24ff.)
> scire debemus . . . esse aliquam potestatem poetis ut ipsi interdum cor-
> rumpant metaplasmo dictionem quale est 'nec non aurum<que> ani-
> musque **latinost**'. quod cum euenit, metaplasmum in dictione inuenimus,
> non in scandendo adferimus. quod utique faceremus, si reliquisset 'latino
> est', sicut 'excussaque pectore Iuno est' (Virg. *Aen.* 5.679).

We must know that occasionally there is the possibility for the poets
themselves to corrupt their diction with a metaplasm such as 'nec non
aurumque animusque latinost'. When this happens, we find the metaplasm
in the diction, we do not add it in the scansion, a thing which necessarily
we would do, if he had left latino est, such as 'excussa pectore Iuno est'.

---

[129] I.e. phonetic phenomena unfamiliar in non-literary orthography, yet already
found in classical literature. On this term see Abbott (1909: 236).

Niedermann p. 31 (= GL 5.403.19ff.)

'Thybris ea fluuium, quam longa est, nocte tumentem' (Virg. *Aen.* 8.86). 'gast' enim dicendo e excludimus. tale est 'regina e speculis' (Virg. *Aen.* 4.586), inter uocalem a et consonantem s perit e.

'Thybris ea fluuium, quam longa est, nocte tumentem'. In saying 'gast' we leave out the e. The same is the case with 'regina e speculis', between the vowel a and the consonant s the e is lost.

First, these passages confirm the authenticity of the reading *latinost* (Virg. *Aen.* 12.23), which is contracted in spelling in one manuscript of Virgil (cf. 3.1.1 p. 38), thus confirming that this contracted form is not an abbreviation but a real form. In this regard, the first passage is particularly interesting, as Consentius distinguishes between phenomena which are displayed in the orthography (contraction) and phenomena which are not (elision).

Second, these passages show that Consentius scanned a sequence -V + *est* as '-V*st*', regardless of the spelling of the manuscripts, as he explicitly says in the second passage ('*latinost*' ... *quod utique faceremus, si reliquisset* '*latino est*'). However, this cannot necessarily be taken as a proof that contracted forms were still common in normal speech at the time of Consentius; in the section of the work to which the above passages belong, he is analysing phonetic phenomena produced in poetry ('metaplasms', cf. n. 129), which might well not have any direct contact with the language of his contemporaries. Furthermore, as already observed for Victorinus (cf. p. 79), much of the material of late antique grammarians is 'traditional'. It is not implausible that Consentius was extracting his material from earlier grammarians; consequently he might be reporting things which he did not even understand himself.

Before moving on, a few remarks must also be made about the phenomenon of ecthlipsis (a Greek term corresponding to the Latin *elisio*), mentioned by Consentius in the first extract cited above (p. 7 N.). What exactly Consentius refers to by this word is not clear; the definition that he provides is not straightforward[130] and the examples that he quotes as illustrations apparently do not stand out as being

---

[130] Cf. p. 27 N. *ecthlipsis est, cum concursus uocum non solum praeterit syllabas, sed excludit et uelut expressas strangulatasque diplodit. ideo denique hic metaplasmus ecthlipsis dicitur quasi exprimens et eiciens quae uelut superfluo duabus obstant uocibus altrinsecus positis. ille quoque superior metaplasmus uelut lenior secundum suam uim etiam nomine censetur, quasi transiliat, quae possunt transiliri. nam ideo denique synaliphe dicta est quasi saltu quodam praetermittens.*

essentially different from the cases of *synaliphe* (cf. e.g. pp. 27–8
N. *item eius* [i.e. *ecthlipseos*] *potestas est, ut interdum dipthongon
excludat, ut 'femineae ardentem'. item eius potestas est, ut interdum
uocalem cum m expellat, ut 'interea medium Aeneas', 'fuit Ilium et
ingens'*). However, the difference between *synaliphe* and ecthlipsis
seems to become clearer in a series of examples quoted by Consentius
in the following passage, in which he discusses possible ambiguities
between the two phenomena (pp. 28–9 N.):

> sic dubium erit, utrum hoc an illo modo scandas, utrum synalipham an
> ecthlipsin facias, 'coniugio Anchise'. nam si sic scandas: 'coniugi Anchi',
> synalipham fecisti, transiluisti enim o syllabam; quae transilitur, non
> exclusa est. si sic scandas: 'coniugi Onchise', ecthlipsis erit; exclusa est
> enim <a> et quasi expressa. simile est et illud 'accipio agnoscoque
> libens'. nam si sic scandas: 'accipi agnoscoque li', synaliphe est, si sic
> 'accipi. ogno.scoque li', ecthlipsis est. tale est 'femineae ardentem'. nam
> potes scandere 'femine. arden.tem' et erit synaliphe. item potes scandere
> 'femine. aerden.tem' et erit ecthlipsis. item similiter incertum, sit syna-
> liphe an ecthlipsis 'fuit Ilium et ingens'. nam si sic scandas 'Iliet',
> synalipha est, si sic 'Iliut', ecthlipsis est. simile est 'egregium Antorem'.
> nam utroque modo scandi potest 'egregi. Anto' et 'egregi unto'.

> It will be thus uncertain whether you should scan 'coniugio Anchise' in
> this or that way, whether you should have synaliphe or ecthlipsis.
> Indeed, if you scan 'coniugi Anchi', you have synaliphe. In fact, you
> have skipped the o syllable, and this syllable is skipped not cut off. If you
> scan 'coniugi Onchise' it will be ecthlipsis, in fact the a is cut off and as it
> were squeezed out. It is the same with 'accipio agnoscoque libens'.
> Indeed, if you scan 'accipi agnoscoque li', it is synaliphe, [but] if [you
> scan] 'accipi. ogno.scoque li', it is ecthlipsis. Similar is 'femineae arden-
> tem'. Indeed, you can scan 'femine. arden.tem' and it will be synaliphe.
> Conversely you can scan 'femine. aerden.tem' and it will be ecthlipsis.
> Similarly it is uncertain whether there is synaliphe or ecthlipsis in 'fuit
> Ilium et ingens'. Indeed, if you scan 'Iliet', it is synaliphe, if you scan
> 'Iliut', it is ecthlipsis. Similar is 'egregium Antorem'. Indeed it can be
> scanned in either way, 'egregi. Anto' and 'egregi unto'.

In all cases quoted in the passage above, Consentius uses the term
synaliphe when it is the last syllable of the first word that is to be
omitted in the scansion (e.g. *coniugi Anchise*), and the term *ecthlipsis*
when it is the first syllable of the second word to be omitted (e.g.
coniugi Onchise). However, in the first passage quoted at the beginning of this section Consentius considers *latinost* as a case of *synaliphe* and not of *ecthlipsis* (p. 7 N. *synaliphe . . . aut ipse poeta ita iam*

scriptum reliquit . . . ut est illud 'nec non aurumque animusque Lati-nost') and in another passage he himself states that the two phenomena are often confused.[131] Nevertheless, there seems to be evidence that some late-antique grammarians contemplated the loss of the second, word-initial, vowel in a sequence -V(*m*) + V-. It is possible however, that this phenomenon is merely a fabrication of grammarians and metricists, perhaps modelled on Greek prodelision,[132] with the exception of the contracted spelling of *est* (for which there is other supporting evidence).

3.5.3 *Velius Longus*

Another grammarian who provides evidence on contracted spellings is Velius Longus (second century AD). After quoting an orthographic proposal made by Verrius Flaccus, namely that the phonetic weakness of final -*m* (cf. above p. 51) should be indicated by writing only the first bit of the letter,[133] he adds a note on the possibility of 'removing vowels' (*uocales subducebantur*) from a word (GL 7.80.20ff.):

> est etiam ubi uocales subducebantur, si id aut decor compositionis aut metri necessitas exigebat, ut 'adeo in teneris consuescere multum est' (Virg. *Georg.* 2.272).
>
> Sometimes vowels were dropped if required by the elegance of the composition or by metrical needs, such as 'adeo in teneris consuescere multum est'.

Velius Longus' concern is with orthography and thus the expression *uocales subducebantur* presumably refers not only to a phonological but also to a graphic phenomenon, just as the quotation from Verrius

---

[131] P. 29 N. *cum . . . ita hi duo metaplasmi* [i.e. *synaliphe* and *ecthlipsis*] *distare uideantur, tamen iam communi quasi consensu in scandendo non solum nostra aetate, sed etiam a scriptoribus synaliphae nomen praeualuisse uideo.*

[132] Cf. above n. 8.

[133] GL 7.80.17ff. *non nulli circa synaliphas quoque obseruandam talem scriptionem existimauerunt, sicut Verrius Flaccus, ut, ubicumque prima uox m littera finiretur, sequens a uocali inciperet, m non tota, sed pars illius prior tantum scriberetur, ut appareret exprimi non debere.* 'Some thought that we should adhere to this way of writing [i.e. phonetic spelling: cf. GL 7.80.13 *non est necesse id scribere, quod in uerbo non sonet*] also when dealing with *synaliphe* (= elision), such as Verrius Flaccus, so that whenever the first word finishes with the letter *m* and the following word begins with a vowel, we should not write the complete *m* but only its first part, so that it would be clear that it must not be pronounced.'

Flaccus involved a graphic change. But to what does this refer in our case? In the quotation from Virgil there appears to be no 'removal of vowels' but presumably this occurred before the simplifying intervention of some later scribe: the vowels which are prosodically dropped (and thus could be graphically omitted) might be *ade(o) in teneris, mult(um) est*[134] (elision) or *multum (e)st* (contraction). However, while the spelling *ade'in* (= *adeo in*) or *mult'est* would be quite unusual, the spelling *multumst* is precisely what we find in the Romanus manuscript of Virgil (fifth century AD) in this line (cf. p. 102). This coincidence seems to make the words of Velius Longus trustworthy, thus confirming the observations we made on Consentius' passages (above p. 81). Therefore, it is possible that at a certain point in the development of Latin, earlier than Velius' time[135] (perhaps at the time of Verrius Flaccus, i.e. the beginning of the first century AD), there were some authors (such as Virgil) who knew and used the contracted spelling *multumst* for the sake of, allegedly, '*decor compositionis aut metri necessitas*'. This contracted spelling had probably already become unusual at the time of Velius Longus.

It is uncertain how Velius explained this spelling and whether it was for him the graphical display of a normal pronunciation or not, especially because one does not even know for sure that he was referring to a contracted form of *est*. One may simply observe that the above-mentioned passage follows the discussion of the spelling proposed by Verrius for the loss of final *-m* before a vowel,[136] which is considered by Velius as a phonetic spelling, reflecting a phenomenon of speech but unusual in the current orthography.[137]

---

[134] This possibility is less plausible, since Velius is referring to the dropping of vowels (*uocales subducebatur*) and not of vowel + *m*.

[135] Velius uses the imperfect *subducebantur*, thus implying that he is referring to an earlier period, just as a few lines before he used the perfect *existimauerunt*, referring to Verrius Flaccus.

[136] Cf. above n. 133.

[137] Cf. in particular his programmatic statement at the beginning of the section, in which the loss of final *-m* in pronunciation is quoted as an example of a letter written but not pronounced: GL 7.54.1ff. *ingredienti mihi rationem scribendi occurrit statim ita quosdam censuisse esse scribendum, ut loquimur et audimus. nam ita sane se habet non numquam forma enuntiandi, ut litterae in ipsa scriptione positae non audiantur enuntiatae. sic enim cum dicitur, 'illum ego' et 'omnium optimum', illum et omnium aeque m terminat nec tamen in enuntiatione apparet*; 'at the very beginning of a discussion on orthography, I notice that some [earlier grammarians] have recommended that we have to write in the way we speak and hear it. Indeed, it is quite evident that sometimes the system of pronunciation is such that letters which are

3.6 Sabellian Languages

Another piece of evidence is offered by phenomena apparently parallel to the contraction of *est*, occurring in Sabellian languages. First, we have in Oscan inscriptions at least two instances of contracted spelling of the third person of the verb *to be*, attached to the preceding word:

Po 1 (p. 103)[138]	**teremnatust**	*Lat.* terminatast
Cp 8.4 (p. 97)	**destrst**[139]	*Lat.* dextrast

We may add two other more problematic instances from another Oscan inscription, found recently at Aufidena, Castel di Sangro.[140]

Aufidena 3.3	**úpstúst**	*Lat.* obsitast?
Aufidena 3.6	**angítúst**	*Lat.* statutumst?[141]

A few remarks may also be offered on the univerbation of *est* in Sabellian languages. In Oscan the standard form of the copula

---

found in the spelling itself are not heard in pronunciation. So it is indeed when "*illum ego*" and "*omnium optimum*" are said, both *illum* and *omnium* end with *m* and yet this letter does not appear in pronunciation.'

[138] The sigla, lines, and page numbering of the Sabellian material come from the edition of Rix (2002).

[139] Lejeune (1993: 264–5) takes **destrst** to be just an abbreviation (= *destru stait*, 'is located on the right') but, as Fortson (2008: 135 n. 8) demonstrates, his argument is not convincing.

[140] First published by La Regina (2010). I would like to thank John Penney for pointing out to me the two instances of contraction from the Aufidena inscription.

[141] These forms are however problematic. While the form **úpstúst** is not attested elsewhere, the form **angítúst** is apparently found in the inscription of the Tabula Bantina (cf. Crawford (1996: 271–92)) and is normally construed as a third person singular of the future perfect (cf. Crawford (1996: 285) and Untermann (2000: 100)), equivalent to Latin *dixerit/statuerit*. The suffix *-ust* is found in other Sabellian forms (e.g. *fefacust, dicust, andersafust*) normally construed as third person singular forms of the future perfect (cf. Buck (1904: 173), Bottiglioni (1954: 142)). The parallel with **teremnatust** however shows that the suffix *-ust* might also be construed, theoretically, as the ending of the third person singular of the perfect passive (deriving from the feminine ending *-u*+clitic *est*; cf. Untermann (2000: 747)): in the context of the Aufidena inscription this interpretation seems to be possible. For another interpretation of the two forms from the Aufidena inscription see La Regina (2010), who considers them as forms of the pluperfect, equivalent to Latin *statuerat* (**angitust**) and *fecerat* (**úpstúst**; cf. **úpsannúm**).

corresponding to Latin *est* is **íst**, even though **est** is attested as well.[142]
In some possible instances of **íst**, the form, though fully spelt, is found
written together with the preceding word:

Pg 9.4 (p. 73)	*clisuist*	*Lat.* clusa est
Cp 8.4 (p. 97)	**sakruvist**	*Lat.* sacra est?
Cp 9 (p. 98)	**sakruvi(s)t**	*Lat.* sacra est?[143]

All counter-instances belong to the Cippus Abellanus (Cm 1,
pp. 114–15), where **íst** is never written together with the preceding
word (with the exception of **pússtíst**, which is not a clear word; cf.
Untermann (2000: 619)). However, this text is not particularly relevant since it is a very high-style text, modelled on the style of
Latin official formulae (cf. Adams (2003: 138)). If one excludes the
instances from the Cippus Abellanus, in Oscan the third person **íst**
seems to be always written together with the preceding word, a
probable sign of its clitic nature. Moreover, the form **íst** itself may
already suggest a clitic reduction, with its phonetic raising of *ĕ* to *ĭ*.[144]
This evidence therefore seems to indicate the existence of a phonetic
reduction of the forms *est/es* in Sabellian languages, probably origin-
ating in their (en)clitic nature.

[142] Cp 29 (p. 99) **nik(ú). est**, Cp 30 (p. 100) **múiník(ú). est**. (Lat. *communis est*).
Interestingly, in both cases the vowel which ends the preceding word is elided, thus
suggesting a strong syntactic and phonological bond between the copula and the
predicate.
[143] The interpretation of the form **sacruvi(s)t** as **sakru* (lat. *sacra*) + **ist** (lat. *est*) is
however not certain, cf. Untermann (2000: 651–2 with bibliography).
[144] Cf. Bader (1976: 50), Joseph and Wallace (1987: 686). The phonetic change of
long *ē* towards an open *ĭ*, that is the merger of *ē* and *ī* into a vowel whose quality was in
between (written í in the native alphabet or sometimes i or e), seems to be a common
phenomenon in Oscan: cf. e.g. **lígatúís** (= Lat. *legatis*), **líkítud** (= Lat. *liceto*). Cf. Buck
(1904: 33–4), Bottiglioni (1954: 28–9), Clackson and Horrocks (2007: 57) and see pp.
120–2 for the analogous merger of *ē* and *ī* in late Latin. However, in our case the shift
would be of *short ĕ* (*ĕst*) into *ĭ* (written í), which is a 'greater' phonetic change in
quality than long *ē* > *ĭ*, thus suggesting the interference of some other phonetic
phenomenon. On this issue cf. also Cipriano and Mancini (1984: 49–50) who derive
the vowel í in **íst** from a form **ēst*, supposedly a back-formation from a contracted
*ne esti.

3.7 Other Types of Evidence

Finally, there are some independent pieces of evidence that may be
quoted to support an analysis of the phenomenon of contraction in
Latin. First, some passages of Latin literature have been quoted by
scholars to argue for the use of contracted forms in Latin spelling and/
or pronunciation.[145]

Ov. *Rem.* 187–8
poma dat autumnus; **formosa est** messibus aestas;
uer praebet flores; igne leuatur hiems.

Ov. *Met.* 15.429–31
Oedipodioniae quid sunt, nisi nomina, Thebae?
quid Pandioniae restant, nisi nomen, Athenae?
nunc quoque Dardaniam **fama est** consurgere Romam

Ov. *Met.* 15.426–8
clara fuit Sparte, magnae uiguere Mycenae,
nec non et Cecropis, nec non Amphionis arces.
uile solum **Sparte est**, altae cecidere Mycenae

In all three Ovidian passages there seems to be a fixed structure: in the
first two passages every line is composed of two parts of three words
each (cf. e.g. *quid Pandioniae restant | nisi nomen, Athenae?*); in the
third passage in each line the half-line before the caesura has the same
number of words as the half-line after the caesura (cf. *nec non et
Cecropis, | nec non Amphionis arces*). In all instances the sequence
with *est* (*formosa est, sparte est, fama est*) must be counted as a
single word in order for the symmetry to be maintained. Kenney
(1986) and Kershaw (1987) used this evidence to argue for the
restoration of the contracted spellings *formosast, spartest, famast*.

A similar example is offered by a passage of Apuleius (*Apol.* 103):

'dentes splendidas': ignosce munditiis. 'specula inspicis': debet philosophus. 'uorsus facis': licet fieri. 'pisces exploras': Aristoteles docet. 'lig-
num consecras': Plato suadet. 'uxorem ducis': leges iubent. 'prior **natu**
is<ta> est': solet fieri, 'hierum **sectatus es**': dotalis accipe, donationem
recordare, testamentum lege. (ed. Helm).

The whole passage seems to be constructed with a series of sentences
composed of two words (*dentes splendidas | ignosce munditiis | etc.*).

[145] Cf. Kenney (1986), Kershaw (1987), Hunink (1996).

The only sequences that do not respect the symmetry are *prior natu is<ta> est* and *hierum sectatus es*. Hunink (1996) resolves the problem by printing *natust* in place of the reading *natu is est* given by the manuscripts and by postulating contraction in the expression *sectatus es* (i.e. *sectatu's*), at least in pronunciation.[146]

However, the fact that in the passages quoted above the verb *esse* seems to form a single prosodic word with the preceding element does not necessarily point to contraction of the verb, in spelling and/or pronunciation. There are instances of monosyllabic words that, in similar contexts, form a single prosodic word with the preceding element, without displaying any graphic and/or phonetic reduction. In the monostichs of the so-called *Carmina duodecim sapientum* (fourth or fifth century AD, in Buecheler and Riese 1894–1906: II.59–61[no. 495–506]), every line is made up of six words (cf. ll. 1–2 *sperne lucrum: uersat mentes insana cupido* | *fraude carete graues, ignari cedite doctis*). However, in three lines containing forms of *sum* this rule seems to not be respected:

> 499 ludite securi, quibus **aes est** semper in arca
> 502 sancta probis **pax est**: irasci desine uictus
> 504 inicio furias: **ego sum** tribus addita quarta

The use of the verb *esse* in the passages above, causing the lines to exceed six words, does suggest that the verb forms a prosodic word with the preceding element (*aés est, páx est, égo sum*), but there is no sign of phonetic reduction in spelling and/or in pronunciation.[147] Therefore, the use of the verb *esse* in the passages from Ovid and Apuleius quoted above points to a 'univerbating' capability of the verb *esse* in Latin which is most likely related to its clitic nature, a theme which will be extensively discussed later in the book.[148] However, this evidence does not prove that the verb was contracted in such contexts, and indeed it could still have been in elision with the preceding word (*formós est, spárt est, fám est*).

Another piece of evidence may be the epistolary formula S.V.B.E.V., found in Cicero's letters, which is apparently an acronym for *si uales benest*

---

[146] Cf. Hunink (1996: 166–7), who also quotes 46.10 *pollicitus* F (= *pollicitu's?*) as a possible parallel.

[147] For this argument on the *Carmina duodecim sapientium* cf. Baehrens (1879–1886: I.XII–XIII).

[148] Cf. in particular III.1.3, V.5.2, VI.4. For the clitic nature of *esse* cf. also Adams (1994a: in particular 86–9).

ego ualeo (cf. Shackleton Bailey (1977: I.274 at *Fam.* 5.1.1)).[149] In Cic.
Fam. 5.14, where elision is apparently avoided (cf. Ehrhardt (1985)),
the abbreviated *ben(e) est* would be the only exception (cf. Shackleton
Bailey (1987)). The presence of such a form in a text otherwise lacking
reduction of vowels at word boundaries may thus be taken to imply
that the verb *esse* was contracted (*benest*).

Similar (and more convincing) evidence on the contraction of *est* is
offered by the metrical treatment of this form in poetry. For instance,
in Horace's fourth book of *Odes* the only case of elision of a long
vowel would be *tuī est* at *Od.* 4.3.21, which scholars have taken as a
case of contraction.[150] Similarly, in Lucretius and most imperial
poetry elision is avoided after iambic words (e.g. *ĕquī atque*), except
with *est/es* (e.g. *tuō est*).[151] Also possibly relevant, especially in view of
his lateness, is the case of Vegetius' *De re militari* (fourth or fifth
century AD), in which elision is almost completely avoided in clausu-
lae, except when the second, vowel-initial, word is *est*.[152] Finally, in
classical poetry (especially in Virgil[153]) elision before a monosyllable
is almost completely avoided at the end of the line.[154] The only
exception would be the pattern with *est* (or *es*) preceded by a final
vowel or elidible *-m*. Similar figures are found for the end of the first
hemistich (before the caesura) in both hexameter and pentameter,
and for the second hemistich of the pentameter; in classical poetry

---

[149] Cf. Sen. *Ep.* 15.1 *mos antiquis fuit, usque ad meam seruatus aetatem, primis
epistulae uerbis adicere 'si uales bene est, ego ualeo'*; Plin. *Ep.* 1.11.1 *at hoc ipsum scribe,
nihil esse quod scribas, uel solum illud unde incipere priores solebant: 'si uales, bene est;
ego ualeo.'* In Shackleton Bailey's edition of Cicero's *Epistulae ad familiares* one finds
it unabbreviated only once, at the beginning of letter 14.8 (cf. also 5.1 and 14.15 *si
uales, bene est,* 14.14 *si uos ualetis, nos ualemus*). The abbreviation SVBEV is the most
common abbreviation in Cicero's *Epistulae ad familiares* and one finds it at the
beginning of a letter ten times (5.14, 12.13, 13.6, 14.11, 14.16, 14.17, 14.21, 14.22,
14.23, 14.24). One finds also the abbreviation SVBEEV (*si uales bene est ego ualeo*)
twice (5.9, 10.34), SVBEEQV (*si uales bene est ego quoque ualeo*) four times (5.10a,
10.33, 12.11, 12.12), SVB (? *si uales benest*) six times (7.29, 11.3, 12.16, 15.19, 8.11c,
9.7b).
[150] Cf. Lachmann (1871: *ad* 1.993).
[151] Cf. Butterfield (2006–2007: 89, 2008a: 117 n. 31).
[152] Cf. Holmes (2002: 361–3).
[153] After Virgil elision tends to be less used by poets (cf. Soubiran (1966: especially
587–612), and the figures of Lyne (2004: 16–17)). For an account of a non-imperial
poet cf. also Ferguson (1970: 173–5), who analyses all the cases of elision in the
Catullus' hendecasyllables, pointing out that elision in the last foot is permitted only
with *est*.
[154] Cf. Soubiran (1966: 160–2, 543–4).

elision in these positions is generally avoided, except with *est* (or *es*).[155] These metrical figures may be taken to imply that phonetic reduction with *est* was something different from general elision and that contracted forms (at least in pronunciation) were still common in classical Latin.[156]

If the first conclusion is most likely correct, the second seems to be less cogent, since other explanations can be found for this particular metrical treatment of *est*: for instance, it has been argued (cf. Fortson (2008: 135 n. 7)) that the rarity of elision in the last foot might be due to the avoidance of tonic monosyllables in this position. Since other vowel-initial atonic monosyllables are very rare, the anomaly of *est* might be explained by its being a clitic monosyllable and not by its being contracted in such a position.

In conclusion, although none of these pieces of evidence is conclusive if taken individually, on the whole there seems to be at least partial evidence supporting the idea of a continuity in the treatment of the verb *est* from (late) republican (Cicero) to late Latin (Vegetius); the form *est* (in spelling and/or speech) seems to form a prosodic word with the preceding element (cliticization) and in this it may undergo phonological reduction, with features different from those of elision. However, metrical figures are not available for all classical authors[157] and it is not clear whether they tell us something about the spelling of *est*, its phonological realization in speech, or both (cf. III.2.2). Whether this phonological reduction involved contraction and whether this was also reflected in spelling can be discussed only with reference to other evidence. I will discuss these issues in chapter III.

3.8 The Second Person Form

I will conclude this chapter by presenting the evidence on contraction of the second person form *'s* (= *es*),[158] which, as pointed out (cf. p. 36), is weaker than that concerning the third person.

---

[155] Cf. Siefert (1956: 29 n. 15), Soubiran (1966: 90, 155, 162).

[156] Cf. Soubiran (1966: 159–62).

[157] For Virgil's *Eclogues* see Nougaret (1966), for Virgil's *Aeneid* (third book), Valerius Flaccus (seventh book) and the *Aratea* of Germanicus see Lienard (1980). General figures for hexametric poetry are found in Siedow (1911: 133), and Soubiran (1966: *passim*). Cf. also Tordeur (1994).

[158] On the forms *ess* and *'ss* cf. p. 23 with n. 43 and Questa (2007: 20–1, 40).

3.8.1 *Direct and Indirect Transmission in Manuscripts*

After a vowel, there are a few cases of forms ending in *-s* < *es* (e.g. *factas* = *facta's* < *facta (e)s*) in the manuscripts of Plautus and Terence, which are listed in Box 2.12. In most of the instances listed below, the other manuscripts have either an uncontracted form or a reading with omission of *es* (cf. e.g. Pl. *Cas.* 1007 *iratas* **A** : *irata es* **cett. Lindsay** : *irata's* **Leo**; *Rud.* 467 *accepturas* **CD** : *acceptura* **B** : *acceptura es* **cett. Leo** : *acceptura's* **Lindsay**; Ter. *Haut.* 1034 *ganeos* **A** : *ganeo* **cett.** : *ganeo's* **edd.**). Apart from these instances, in Plautus and Terence the standard spelling of *es* in this phonological context (i.e. after -V) is uncontracted.

After *-m*, the contracted spelling is apparently attested only once, in the Romanus manuscript of Catullus (49.7 *omniums* **R^ac** : *omnium's* **Trappes-Lomax 2007** : *omnium es* **Oksala** : *omnium* **R^pc cett. codd. edd.**): as discussed above (pp. 32–3), contraction of *es* (*-'s*) was probably admitted also after *-m*, despite the fact that there is no trace of it in the manuscript tradition of Plautus, Terence, and Lucretius.

The situation is different when *es* follows a word ending in *-s*. In speech, a form ending in *-s* used absolutely (e.g. *bonus*) was probably quite distinct from a form followed by a contracted *-'s* (e.g. *bonu's*), the latter actually being pronounced *bonuss* < *bonus* + *'s*, at least in Plautus and Terence.[159] However, in spelling the two forms would be difficult to distinguish, unless we postulate that geminated *-ss* was

---

Box 2.12   **Contracted forms -V's (-Vs in *codd.*) = -Vs + *es* in Plautus and Terence**

Pl. (eleven instances): *Cas.* 1007 iratas **A**, *Epid.*553 fabulatas **A**, *Men.* 1079 patres **P**, *Merc.* 529 redemptas **A**, 682 sanas **B**, *Mil.* 1155 tutes **P**, *Pers.* 207 dignas **P**, *Ps.* 978 tunes[i] **A**, *Rud.* 467 accepturas **CD**, *Trin.* 454 tus **P**, 988 ipsusnes **B**, *Truc.* 262 solitas **AP**[ii]
Ter. (one instance): *Haut.* 1034 ganeos **A**

    [i] *Ps.* 978 and *Trin.* 988 are not completely relevant since they involve the merging of the verb with a weak enclitic particle ending in *-e*. Even so, I have added them to the list since they show the kind of univerbated spelling that may point to contraction rather than to elision.
    [ii] The fact that this case is transmitted by both branches of the manuscript tradition, suggests that the spelling is ancient.

---

[159] Cf. p. 23 with n. 39.

Box 2.13 Restored -'s in Plautus and Terence

Plautus:
132 instances -*us* (*codd.*) : -*u's* (*edd.*) = -ŭs + es[i]
one case -*is* (*codd.*) : -*i's* (*edd.*) = -ĭs + *es Men.* 1007 quisqui's (Ritschl)

Terence:
twenty-two instances -*us* (*codd.*) : -*u's* (*edd.*) = -ŭs + *es*
   An. 621 meritu's, 724 incepturu's, 202 locutu's, 749 sanu's, *Eun.* 286 relictu's, 559
   sanu's, 651 dignu's, 696 dicturu's, *Haut.* 580 functu's, 815 meritu's, 823 pollicitu's,
   Hec. 392 consciu's, 825 nactu's, exanimatu's, *Ph.* 295 servu's, 550 facturu's, 798
   locutu's, *Ad.* 234 passu's, 394 quantu's, 852 fortunatu's, 957 germanu's, 961 bonu's.
four instances -*is* (*codd.*) : -*i's* (*edd.*) = -ĭs + *es*
   An. 702 forti's, *Haut.* 848 homini's, *Ph.* 324 forti's *Ad.* 321 quisqui's

[i] For a detailed list of cases in Plautus see Brinkmann (1906: 101–5, cat. *b*, instances marked by ˙˙)
who construes all these instances as transmitted contracted spellings and not as cases featuring
omission of *es* (cat. *c*). Cf. also below 3.8.2.

---

consistently written (which is not obvious, since simplification of -*ss*-
seems to be standard in the case of the contraction of the third person
form, e.g. *factus*+*(e)st* > *factust*[160]). Contracted forms of *es* after -*s* are
thus unidentifiable in writing and even in modern editions they are
normally differentiated only by a diacritic mark ('). Consequently, it
is conceivable that in some cases a spelling such as *bonus* could be
construed as standing for *bonu*+'s, thus providing evidence for direct
transmission of contracted *(e)s*. In fact, in most of the instances where
editors of Plautus and Terence print a contracted spelling -V's (= -V*s*
+ *es*), one finds in the manuscripts a reading (e.g. *factus*) which looks
like a word ending in -V*s* used absolutely without being followed by
the verb *es* (cf. Box 2.13). In some of these instances another branch
of the tradition has restored the verb in the (unmetrical) uncontracted
form. Cf. e.g. Pl. *Merc.* 767 *molestus* **AB** : *molestus es* **CD** : *molestu's*
edd.; *Pers.* 484 *auctus* **A** : *auctus es* **P** : *auctu's edd.*; Ter. *Eun.* 651
dignus **A**ᵃᶜ : *dignus es* **A**ᵖᶜΣ (unmetrical) : *dignu's edd.*

   It is difficult to say whether the spelling -*us* without verb can always
be considered as direct evidence of a contracted form,[161] since the
metre rarely helps to establish whether the contracted form -*u's* is the

---

[160] Cf. p. 28 with n. 6 and below III.1.3.
[161] Perhaps the original contracted spelling might have been written with a double
sigmatic ending -*ss* (< *ess*), e.g. *factuss* (< *factu ss < *factus ess), if one can trust Pl. *Mil.*
825 *sppm' seho* **B** (< *suppromuss* [= *suppromus* + *es(s)*] *eho*) : *suppromus eho* **CD** :
suppromu's eho edd.). This, however, is an isolated example, and moreover not
palaeographically clear.

only one admissible in the context (cf. 3.8.2). Moreover, the omission of the verb may be emended in other ways,[162] or even accepted in some cases.[163] Nevertheless, the high number of omissions of this type in Plautus and Terence, the need in most of cases of a second person verb form, and the metrical impossibility of a different form (either uncontracted *-ŭs es* or *-ŭs* with omission of the verb) in some instances,[164] make the contracted spelling (*-u's* i.e. *-ŭs + es*) a plausible editorial amendment in such contexts. Some examples of this pattern are found in other archaic authors:

Pac. 327 R.	ausu's *Ribbeck* : ausus *codd.*
Var. *Men.* 211 B.	insciu's *Astbury* : inscius *codd.*
Afran. 364 R.	gnatu's *edd.* : gnatus *codd.*

Two examples are found in Virgil (*Aen.* 1.237, 5.687, cf. n. 163) but many editors prefer not to amend the text and maintain the omission of the verb in their editions. It is likely that there are several analogous cases in the manuscript tradition of other imperial authors; however, since editors do not always indicate such omissions in their apparatus, it is difficult to collect all relevant examples.[165]

Instances of readings which possibly result from the misunderstanding of a contracted second person form are scarce (I have found no more than twenty cases) and few are persuasive. Among them, the most relevant are: third person contracted forms, directly[166] or

---

[162] The uncontracted spelling is sometimes acceptable: cf. Ter. *Ad.* 321 *quisquis* A : *quisqui's* **KL** : *quisquis es* **cett. edd.**; *Haut.* 848 *hominis* A : *homini's* **KL** : *hominis es* **cett. edd.** In other cases editors insert the verb in another place in the line: cf. Ter. *Haut.* 823 *argentum ad eam deferes quod* <*ei*> *pollicitu's* **KL** : *quod pollicitus* A : *quod es pollicitus* Σ *Bentley*; *Ad.* 957 *nunc tu germanu's pariter animo et corpore* **KL.** : *tu es germanus* Σ *Bentley Prete.*

[163] Cf. e.g. Ter. *Hec.* 392 *parturire eam nec grauidam esse ex te solus consciu's* **KL** : *conscius* **codd. Umpfenbach, Marouzeau;** Virg. *Aen.* 1.237 *qui mare, qui terras omnis dicione tenerent,* | *pollicitus* **codd., Mynors** : *pollicitu's Ribbeck*; 5.687 *Iuppiter omnipotens, si nondum exosus ad unum* | *Troianos . . . da flammam euadere classi* **codd.** *Mynors* : *exosu's Ribbeck.*

[164] Cf. 3.8.2.

[165] For a similar case in the text of an imperial poet cf. Propertius 3.11.41, 2.14.1, 3.7.1 with Heyworth's apparatus (2007a).

[166] Cf. e.g. Pl. *Mil.* 409 *absumptust* B[1] : *absumptus es* B[2]CD : *absumptu's edd.*; *Trin.* 264 *adhibendumst* B : *adhibendust* ACD : *adhibendu's edd.*

indirectly[167] transmitted; omission of the verb (with the patterns -V + *es* and -V*m* + *es*);[168] other readings.[169] An example showing a probable misunderstanding of a contracted form, which manifests itself differently in two different manuscripts, is Pl. *Mil.* 49:

> memoriast **BD** : memoria **C** : memoria's *edd.*

Apart from Plautus and Terence, a few contracted forms have been restored in other authors:

Acc. *Trag.* 417 R. (= 495 D.)	Diomedes et *codd.* : dia Mede's **Ribbeck**
Naev. *Com.* 55 R.	pausillus sis *codd.* : pausillu's **Ribbeck**
Nov. 62 R.	nactus est *codd.* : nanctu's **Ribbeck**
Catul. 66.27	adeptus **GR** : adeptos **O** : adepta's *Scaliger*

3.8.2 Metre

For the pattern -V + *es* and -V*m* + *es* the metre does not help much, at least in archaic authors where *es* is generally measured heavy (= *ess*);[170] in this case both elision and contraction would give the same prosodic result, a heavy syllable: *bŏn(a) ēs = bŏnā's* (˘ ˉ).

In late republican and classical Latin, where *es* is measured light, the two forms are not prosodically equivalent if the elided syllable is heavy and if *es* does not become heavy by position (i.e. if it is followed by a vowel). Cf. e.g. Lucil. 1238 M. *hex.*

> 'ō Pub|l(i), ō gur|ges Gal|lōnī, ĕs hŏ|mō mĭsĕr' | inquit.

The second half of the fourth foot must be a pyrrhic (˘ ˘) in order for the metre to scan. This can happen only if the final -*i* of *Galloni* is elided (*Gal|lōn(i), ĕs hŏ|mō*), but not if *es* is 'prodelided' or contracted (*Gal|lōnī's hŏ|mō*). However, this pattern (word ending in heavy or closed elidible syllable + *es* + V-) is not common. Apart from this passage from Lucilius, I have found only two other cases in Latin:

Phaed. 4.26.16 *ia⁶*	hŏdi(e) in|uītā|rĕ **quō|rum ĕs** in | nŭmĕrō | mĭhi
Anth. Lat. 462.28 *pent.*	impĭŭs | hoc **tē|lō ĕs** ;|| hoc pĭŭs | essĕ pŏ| tes.

---

[167] Cf. e.g. Pl. *Truc.* 167 *habitus est* CD (unmetrical): *habitus si* B : *habitu's edd.*
[168] Cf. e.g. Ter. *Eun.* 750 *merita* A : *merita es Σ* : *merita's edd.*
[169] Cf. e.g. Pl. *Pers.* 220 *maleas* B : *mala es* CD : *mala's edd.*
[170] Cf. p. 23 with n. 43.

The first instance is not particularly compelling since both quantities
are permitted in the foot (*quō|rum's in* | = ‾ ‾, *quō|r(um) ĕs in* | = ˘ ‾:
that is to say, both a spondeus and an iambus are permitted as the
third foot of an iambic senarius). It is not a surprise that no editor of
Phaedrus (e.g. Postgate (1920), Brenot (1961)) prints the form
quorum's.

The second instance, which is from an elegiac poem on the
Augustan poet Mevius, probably dating to the first century AD, is
more interesting:[171] in a naturally heavy element of the pentameter
one would normally expect a heavy syllable,[172] which is not given by
eliding the final *-ō* of the word preceding the verb (*tēl|(ō) ĕs* = ‾ | ˘)[173]
but is given by scanning the verb *es* contracted (*tēl|ō (ĕ)s* = ‾ | ‾).[174]
Although isolated, this example may be taken to imply that
in imperial literature contracted forms of *es* were still used by
poets.

As far as the pattern *-Vs* + *es* is concerned, the contracted spelling
(*-V's* = one syllable) is not metrically equivalent to the uncontracted
one (*-Vs es* = two syllables) and it is sometimes possible to restore a
contracted form in such instances. However, I have found few cases in
which the uncontracted form *-V es* is the only one transmitted and
the two forms (contracted and uncontracted) are not both metrically
acceptable:

[171] This poem has been attributed to Seneca. Cf. Roller (1996: 333 n. 32).

[172] *Breuis in longo* (or 'lengthening in arsis') before the median *caesura* in a
pentameter is extremely rare in classical Latin poetry; a search in the digital archive
Pede Certo (developed by a research team led by Emanula Colombi based at the
Università di Udine and the Università Ca'Foscari Venezia) has shown only eighteen
cases, fourteen with the noun *uultus* (Ov. *Am.* 3.2.16, *Ep.* 13.150, 14.104, 17.222,
18.64, 21.180, *Fast.* 3.690, *Tr.* 1.2.34, 4.3.50, *Pont.* 2.8.60, *Ibis* 142, *Epic. Drusi* 260,
Mart. 3.66.2, Sen. *Epigr.* 52.19), three with *omnis* (Prop. 2.28.56, Ov. *Am.* 2.4.48, *Priap.*
33.4), and one with *rediit* (Ov. *Rem.* 6).

[173] Although in the history of Latin *o* + *vowel* contracted to *ō* (e.g. *cōmo* < **coemo*;
cf. Leumann (1977: 119), in classical Latin poetry it is standard to elide a final *-ō*
placed before an open syllable beginning with *ĕ-*. Although there are not many cases
and often the length of the final *-o* is ambiguous (cf. Soubiran (1966: 207–18)), in
classical Latin poetry all cases of the sequence *-ō ĕ-* not in hiatus must be scanned as a
short syllable, thus implying elision of final *-ō* (cf. e.g. Virg. *Aen.* 4.12 |*crēd(ō) ĕqui̯|
dem nec uana fides genus esse deorum*, Hor. *S.* 2.7.53 *tu cum proiectis insignibus |ānŭl
(ō) ĕ|questri*, Ov. *Am.*1.4.3 |*erg(ō) ĕgŏ| dilectam tantum conuiua puellam*, Mart. 3.41.4
tu magnus quod das? |imm(ō) ĕgŏ | quod recipis).

[174] Housman makes the same point in a letter to H. E. Butler (in Leach (2009:
230)). Cf. also Soubiran (1966: 177), Cipriano and Mancini (1984: 16).

Pl. *Bac.* 602   improbus es *codd.* : improbus's *edd.*
Cas. 734   seruus es *codd.* : seruo's *edd.*
Ter. *Eun.* 273   tristis es *codd.* : tristi's *edd.*
Laber. *com.* 29 R (= 20 Pan.)   lentus es Fγδ : lentu's *Fleckeisen edd.*[175]

As has been pointed out the normal reading of the manuscripts where a contracted form occurs in editions displays an apparent omission of the verb (*factus* for *factu's*).[176] A form without the verb and a contracted form are not prosodically equivalent (*factu's* = ‾ ‾, *factus* = ‾ ˘), at least in early Latin; however, in iambic and trochaic metres, only rarely are the two forms metrically distinguishable. Before a consonant the forms -*ŭs* and -*ū's* are prosodically equivalent (cf. e.g. Ter. *Eun.* 286 *relictu's custos*). Before a vowel the two forms are prosodically different (˘ vs. ‾) but are metrically distinguishable only when the -V*s* syllable occupies a monosyllabic heavy or light element.[177] This particular condition is not common in Plautus and Terence,[178] but there are some cases in which the form without the verb (apparently transmitted by the manuscripts) is not metrically admissible. I have found at least four instances in Plautus:[179]

Ep. 284 (tr⁷)   et plă|cet. tum| t(u) ĭgĭtur| călĭdē| quidquĭd| actū|rū's ăge
acturus *codd.* : acturū's *edd.*
Mil. 824 (ia⁶)   ĕhŏ tū | scĕlē|stĕ, qu(i) il|lī sup|prōmū's| eho
suppromus *codd.* : suppromū's *edd.*[180]
Merc. 726 (ia⁶)   sc(io) inno|xiū's| audac|ter quam|uis dī|cĭto
innoxius *codd.* : innoxiu's *edd.*
Rud. 871 (ia⁶)   ădŭles|cens Plē|sidip|pŭs. ut | nanctū's,| hăbe.
nanctus *codd.* : nanctū's *edd.*

In all cases the -V*s* syllables (-*rus*, -*mus*, -*ius*, -*tus*) occupy a mono-syllabic heavy element and must be naturally heavy, since they cannot

---

[175] On this passage of Laberius, cf. Panayotakis (2010: 211–13). He adopts Fleck-eisen's emendation *lentu's*, but does not explicitly mention the phenomenon of aphaeresis/prodelision and simply speaks of 'a weak final *s*' (p. 212).
[176] Cf. section 3.8.1 with Box 2.13.   [177] For this terminology cf. V.2.
[178] In most cases the syllable -V*s* occupies an anceps element, the two forms thus being metrically indistinguishable: cf. e.g. Pl. *Amph.* 1138 (both *prŏfectŭs* and *profec-tū's* are metrically admissible). Other analogous cases are *Amph.* 411, 780, *Asin.* 25, 411, 662, *Bac.* 160, *Cas.* 245, 812, *Men.* 293, *Merc.* 622, *Ps.* 272, 1177 (*es* BD), *Rud.* 847, 982, *St.* 263, 759, *Truc.* 949, 955, Ter. *An.* 234, *Haut.* 580, *Hec.* 825, *Ad.* 724.
[179] Cf. also Postgate (1904: 451–2).
[180] On the form *suppromus* see above n. 161.

become heavy by position, being followed by a vowel. Therefore the forms *actūrŭs, suppromŭs, innoxiŭs*, and *nanctŭs* would be *contra metrum*. Such cases may also provide evidence for the view that the spelling *-us* transmitted in the manuscripts might actually represent *-ū's* (cf. above 3.8.1).

3.8.3 *Inscriptions and Other Types of Evidence*

There are no cases of the contracted form *'s* in inscriptions, at least so far as I have been able to find out.[181] Only one case is potentially relevant:

CIL 1². 3449i: Septumia | (mulieris) l(iberta) Scuti[a] | heic **sitas** ui[ua] / plaquit salu[e] / et uale.

CIL editors consider *sitas* as being equivalent to *sitast* (= *sita est*, with contracted form) and thus I have recorded it (cf. Table 2.10). *Sitas* might also be considered as an instance of a contracted second person form (= *sita es*), but since there are no instances of the formula *sita/situs* with *es* (e.g. *sita es*), this interpretation is not convincing.

As far as other types of evidence are concerned, Marius Victorinus does not mention the second person form in his passage about contracted forms (cf. 5.3.1), and no mention of it is found in other grammarians either. As already pointed out (pp. 87–8), some evidence from a passage of Apuleius (*Apol.* 103 *sectatus es*) does seem to support a contracted spelling and/or pronunciation of *es*. Finally, the metrical behaviour of *es* in classical poetry is analogous to that of *est*, thus suggesting similar phonological features (cf. pp. 89–90).

In conclusion, evidence about the status of the contracted form of *es* is weaker than that concerning the third person form; nevertheless, its existence seems to be confirmed at least in republican authors. It is possible to envisage that it was also used in classical Latin (in spelling and/or pronunciation), presumably only after a vowel or *-m*.

---

[181] Exceptions might be CIL 4.4504 *ua(le) Modesta ua(le) ualeas* **ubicumq(ue)** *es*, AE 2004.963 **hered(es)** *es testam(ento) f(aciendum) c(urauerunt)*, which however look like abbreviations rather than contracted spellings. Cf. also CIL 4.8617 *P(ublius) Pro/pesi/cunius/uerp(a) es*, CIL 4.8931 *Mentul(a) es*, where it is elision that is marked in spelling.

III

Contraction of *esse*

Phonological Analysis and Historical Appraisal

non recte uinctust

Ter. *An.* 955

The aim of this chapter is to discuss the nature of the contraction of *esse* and evaluate its use in Latin. I begin the chapter (section 1) with a phonological analysis: contracted spellings are not abbreviations (section 1.1) or phonetic spellings of a sandhi phenomenon somehow related to elision (section 1.2), as implied by the standard term 'prodelision', but rather reflect clitic forms of *est* and *es* displaying phonological reduction (section 1.3). I will then (section 1.4) consider the problematic pattern *-est* < *-ĭs* + *est* (cf. II.2 p. 35), which probably has a morphosyntactic rather than phonological explanation. In the second part of the chapter (section 2), I will analyse the evidence on contracted forms collected in chapter II, in order to assess their spread, use, and stylistic value in the history of Latin speech and spelling.

1. PHONOLOGICAL DISCUSSION

To begin with, it is necessary to present an overview of the various ways in which scholars and editors have considered contracted forms.

1.1 Contracted Spellings as Abbreviations

A first view assumes that the vast majority of contracted spellings in manuscripts do not reflect a phenomenon of speech, but are abbreviations used by scribes.[1] This would have been the practice of late-antique scribes since, as we have seen, contracted spellings are frequent in late-antique manuscripts whereas they are rare in medieval manuscripts, with the uncontracted spellings found in their place (cf.II.3.1.1, II.3.3, Appendix 1). In support of the view that contracted spellings were used as abbreviations, there is the fact that several instances, in both manuscripts and inscriptions, are found at the end of the line (e.g. 60% of the cases in Virgil),[2] where the scribes might have resorted to abbreviations owing to a lack of space.

However, this view is not convincing. First, the metrical evidence for the pattern *ŭs + (e)st* shows that contracted forms are not always prosodically equivalent to uncontracted forms, thus suggesting that contracted spellings were phonologically relevant (cf. II.3.2). Second, a large number of contracted spellings, in both inscriptions and manuscripts, are found in places other than at the end of the line; in Plautus and Terence only a small number of instances of contracted spellings are found in such a position,[3] and in Lucretius there are more than 120 instances which are not found at the end of the line (about 46%). In inscriptions as well, there are a good number of contracted spellings in positions other than at the end of the line (cf. II.3.4.1). Finally, the distribution of contracted spellings within and across manuscripts does not seem to be random (which is what one would expect if contracted spellings were just abbreviations). In Gellius they are often found in quotations of or references to archaic texts (cf. II.3.1.1 pp. 40–2), and in both inscriptions and manuscripts they are frequent in verse texts but are very rare in prose texts (cf. II.3.1.1, II.3.3, II.3.4). For instance, in the oldest manuscripts of Livy contracted spellings are hardly ever found, whereas in the oldest manuscripts of Virgil, which date to the same age as those of Livy (fifth or sixth century), contracted spellings are common.[4] Finally, late-antique grammarians refer to cases of contracted spelling attested in manuscripts and discuss them as real metrical phenomena (cf. II.3.5).

---

[1] This is, in part, the view held by Marouzeau (1908).
[2] Cf. II.3.1.1 p. 39, and II.3.4.1 with Tables 2.10 and 2.11.
[3] Taking Terence's *Adelphoe* as an example, only twenty out of the seventy-nine forms spelt contracted in A are found at the end of the line.
[4] Cf. 2.1.2, pp. 127–8.

In conclusion, there are cases in which contracted spellings were presumably introduced or retained by scribes for their graphic convenience,[5] but they seem to be exceptional and do not undermine the view that contracted spellings reflect a phonological phenomenon, current in speech either at the time of the author or at an earlier stage (cf. section 2.2).

1.2 Contractions as Sandhi Spellings

Contracted spellings are therefore to be seen as reflecting (at least in origin) a phenomenon of speech and not as misspellings or abbreviations. There are, however, different interpretations about the nature of this phenomenon.

First, there is the interpretation implied by the standard term 'prodelision', accepted by most scholars and editors,[6] according to which contracted spellings reflect a sandhi phenomenon related to elision (i.e. vowel-deletion in a pre-vocalic context). Elision is standard in metrical Latin texts, where it clearly reflects a common phenomenon of speech.[7] Its existence is further confirmed by some Latin compound words featuring internal elision (cf. e.g. in Latin *magnŏpere* < *magnŏ ŏpere*, *animaduerto* < *animum aduerto*), by the testimony of ancient grammarians (cf. Riggsby (1991)), and by the occasional 'elided' spellings attested in badly-spelt prose texts.[8]

---

[5] On contracted spellings after a consonant other than -*s* or -*m* see II.2 pp. 34–5; on contracted spellings as abbreviations in inscriptions see II.3.4.1 p. 70.

[6] Cf. e.g. Allen (1978: 122, note on the Chapter 'Vowel junction'): 'Mention should also be made of "prodelision"... which occurs when a final vowel is followed by the copula *est* (or *es*)... in such cases it was the initial *e* that was eliminated in the juncture.' Goold (2002: 88) 'When two vowels (or diphthongs) come together and en elision takes place, one of three things must occur: (1) the first vowel is completely eliminated; (2) the second vowel is completely eliminated (prodelision or aphaeresis); (3) *synaliphe*, which I believe to happen most of the time—the first vocalic component is sounded, but so lightly as not to consume any metrical time.' Gaisser (2009: 76) 'If *es* or *est*... is the second word in hiatus after either a vowel or *m*, its *e* is suppressed; in this case the process is called *prodelision*. Examples of all three types of elision (between vowels, of final *m* before an initial vowel, and prodelision) are found ....'

[7] On elision and its occurrence in Latin speech cf. Allen (1987: 79–82), Sihler (1995: 233), Coleman (1999: 33), Weiss (2009: 132–6).

[8] The number of instances is not very high: Soubiran (1966: 57) lists fewer than twenty cases of 'elided' spellings in inscriptions (e.g. CIL 4.4385 *audomnia* [= *aude omnia*?], 8931 *mentules* [= *mentula es*]) and I have not found many other examples in other substandard, badly-spelt texts: e.g. Bu Njem 99.4 *un asinu* < *unum asinum* (on

Elision is a sandhi phenomenon,[9] in the sense that it is a consequence of, and limited to, a particular phonological context at word boundaries, and does not affect the realization of the same words when they appear in other phonological contexts. An example from modern Italian would be the sequence *che ora è?* (= *what time is it?*) which, if uttered rapidly, may be pronounced /kor'e/ as if it were written *ch'or'è*, although *ch* (= *che*) and *or* (= *ora*) do not exist as morphologically independent forms. A sandhi phenomenon in spoken English is, for example, the assimilation of final consonants;[10] e.g. *that case* is pronounced /ðæk keɪs/ in normal speech, even if the speaker's perception is generally /ðæt/, which is the pronunciation of the word in isolation and careful speech.[11] On the other hand, the contraction of *it is* into *it's* does not seem to be a sandhi phenomenon;[12] though phonetically strictly connected both forms exist in the mind of the speaker/writer, and their alternation does not depend on phonological but on stylistic factors (e.g. contractions are normally avoided in very formal speech), syntactic factors (e.g. if placed at the end of a complex clause the combination does not normally contract[13]) and pragmatic factors (e.g. the uncontracted form might be preferred by the speaker for emphasis or clarity). Sandhi phenomena do not necessarily appear in spelling, but there are some languages in which phonetic spellings of sandhi phenomena are common, such as Sanskrit (cf. e.g. the assimilation of final consonant

this example see Adams (1994c: 97)). See II.3.4.1 with Table 2.12 for a list of 'elided' spellings before *est* and II.3.8.3 with n. 181 for 'elided' spellings before *es*.

[9] An alternative definition might be a 'transitional phenomenon of connected speech'.

[10] For a definition and an exhaustive treatment of sandhi phenomena see Andersen (1986). For an introduction to sandhi in spoken English see Carr (1999: 116–27), Roach (2000: 134–49). For elision in English cf. Carr (1999: 116–18). Two notable cases of sandhi in spoken English are the intrusive and the linking *r*. For these cf. in particular Vogel (1986: 55–64) and recently Heselwood (2009), McCully (2009: 206–8).

[11] Cf. also *meat pie* pronounced /miːp piɛ/ in rapid, casual speech, as opposed to the simple /miːt/. Cf. Roach (2000: 138–42).

[12] Roach (2000: 143) considers it a phenomenon of connected speech, yet specifying that 'it is difficult to know whether contractions of grammatical words should be regarded as examples of elision or not. The fact that they are regularly represented with special spelling forms makes them seem rather different from the above examples.'

[13] Cf. e.g. the sequence *I don't know where it is* in which there cannot be contraction of *is* (**where it's*). On this see I.3.6; cf. also Fortson (2008: 137) and the bibliography quoted.

in Sk. *tanmanaḥ* < *tád* ('that') + *manas* ('mind') i.e. 'that mind'),[14] and there are some genres in which they occasionally appear (such as poetry, cf. e.g. Dante *Inferno* 1.37 **temp'** *era dal principio del mattino* [*temp'* = *tempo*: elided spelling]).

In the development of a language, phonetic spellings of sandhi phenomena may be institutionalized in the orthographic system, such as e.g. the article *l'* in Italian.[15] A phenomenon of English that seems to be on the way to being institutionalized is, for example, the reduction of 'going to' to 'gonna'.[16]

Contraction of *esse* has normally been explained in the same terms as elision: there was a single form, *est* (or *es*), which 'lost' its vowel in a post-vocalic phonological context. The term 'prodelision', which is the standard term used to refer to the contraction of *esse* and is borrowed from Greek metre,[17] implies this view. Contracted spellings of *est/es* in Latin (e.g. *factumst*) would therefore be equivalent to the 'prodelided' spellings, found e.g. in Dante *Inferno* 1.38 *e 'l sol montava 'n su con quelle stelle* (*'l = il , 'n = un*).

There are several flaws in this explanation. First, unlike in Greek, this type of 'inverted elision' (i.e. aphaeresis/prodelision) does not have strong parallels elsewhere in Latin. Forms such as *sclusa* (= *exclusa*) or *strumentum* (= *instrumentum*), which show a similar development superficially, constitute an independent category; they are late,[18] non-standard forms, with particular phonological

[14] Cf. *Mahabharata* 12.46.
[15] Cf. also I.3.2.
[16] Cf. Bybee (2001: 11, 60–1) who remarks that in speech this kind of institutionalization happens only with some high frequency words. See also I.3.2.
[17] In Greek 'prodelision' is clearly phonologically motivated, as it always involves a short vowel following a long vowel or diphthong, thus suggesting that in Greek it is actually to be considered a subtype of elision. On prodelision in Greek cf. II.1 with n. 8.
[18] They are mainly found in late-antique sources, such as the *Epistula* of Anthimus (early sixth century AD; cf. *stiuus* < *aestituus* p. 12.4, *scaldetur* < *excaldetur* p. 28.7; cf. Liechtenhan (1963: 48–9)), the translations of Oribasius (fifth or sixth century AD; cf. Svennung (1932: 78) and Adams (2007: 472–501)), or the *Codex Diplomaticus Langobardorum* (late eighth century AD; *aut sclusa* 150.1, *sub stimatione* 146.1; cf. Löfstedt (1961: 112–14)). Already the grammarian Diomedes (late fourth century) mentions this phenomenon (cf. GL 1.441.20ff.). Perhaps one of the first instances of this type of aphaeresis is *spectemus* (= *exspectemus*), found in the letters of Claudius Terentianus (early second century AD) at 471.24 (cf. Adams (1977: 21–2)). However, this instance is problematic because the form *spectemus* might be construed as a case of *simplex pro composito* (against this view Pighi (1964: 71)) or even in its genuine

features,[19] they are found mainly in prose,[20] in all types of phonological contexts,[21] and do not seem to result from a sandhi phenomenon.[22] Other, more relevant forms that have been quoted as parallels for contracted forms of *est/es*, such as contracted forms of *iste*,[23] *ille*,[24] *et*,[25]

---

sense of 'to watch', 'consider', possible in the context (*spectemus illum dum uenit*). On the aphaeresis *exs-* > *s-* see also Väänänen (1981: 47–8).

[19] All these forms feature the loss of an initial atonic syllable in polysyllabic words beginning with *i(n)s-*, *(h)is-*, *aes-*, *ex-* + consonant. Cf. also *Spania* (< *Hispania*), *storia* (< *historia*), *strumentum* (< *instrumentum*). This type of aphaeresis is closely connected to another phonological phenomenon common in late and medieval Latin and in the Romance developments which is known as prothesis and consists in the adjoining of a euphonic prothetic vowel (*i-* or *e-*) before a word beginning with *s-* + consonant: cf. e.g. *iscola* < *sch(o)la*, *estercus* < *stercus*. Prothesis is apparently already attested in an inscription from Pompei (CIL 4.7721 *Ismurna*, but note however that *Smyrna* is not a Latin word; cf. Sampson (2010: 56)). On prothesis see Löfstedt (1961: 107–12), Väänänen (1981: 47–8), Sampson (2010: in particular 53–60), Wright (2011: 68). Cf. also below p. 108 and section I.4 p. 24.

[20] All the examples quoted in n. 18 are found in prose texts.

[21] See e.g. after a vowel: Anthimus 27.8 *bene scaldetur*; after a consonant: Anthimus 12.4 *et stiuo . . . nam stiui*. Cf. also Löfstedt (1961: 113–14).

[22] Presumably they are hypercorrective forms arising against prothesis. On this view cf. Löfstedt (1961: 114), Adams (1977: 22). On hypercorrection against prothesis see also Sampson (2010: 56–9, 113).

[23] Found in some inscriptions (cf. AE 1967.549 |*sta dies*, 1981.872 *locus ste*, AE 1981.873 *locus ste*, ILCV 365 *r.p. stius ciuitatis stituit*, 1096 *lapis ste*, 3330 *in lucesta*, 3463 *cineres sti*; cf. Carnoy (1906: 112)) and in the manuscripts of literary authors, such as Plautus (cf. *Trin.* 333 *nihil storum* B, *Bac.* 679 *iam stoc* **Nonius**; cf. Skutsch (1892: 124 with n. 2)) and Virgil (cf. *Aen.* 6.389 *iam stinc* M^ac). See also ThLL VII.2.494.60ff. These aphaeretic forms have been construed as resulting from hypercorrection against prothesis (cf. n. 22). Cf. Sommer and Pfister (1977: I.215), Sampson (2010: 101).

[24] Cf. Corrsen (1870: 626). An aphaeretic pronunciation of the pronoun *ille* in late Latin, presumably caused by a proclitic use precursory to Romance definite articles (cf. Bloch and Von Wartburg (1968: 363)), can be reconstructed from its outcome in Romance languages: cf. Fr. *le/la* (< *ille/illa*), It. *la/lo* (< *illa/illud*). Müller (1894) thought that this pronunciation was already common in early Latin, citing in support a passage from Afranius (67 R. *immo li mitem faxo faciant* **codd.** : *immo illi* **edd.** : *immo olli* **Ribbeck**). However, the form *li* is probably a mere misspelling.

[25] Cf. Shipley (1924: 151–5) and Soubiran (1966: 181–2) who notice in Virgil the frequency of 'elided' *et* before the caesura (cf. e.g. *Aen.* 1.90 *intonuere poli et* || *crebris micat ignibus aether*) and argue that in such cases *et* was probably pronounced with 'aphaeresis' [poli't]. Cf. also the unmetrical reading of Servius *ad Aen.* 12.709 (*inter se coiisse uiros et cernere ferro* **codd. edd.** : *decernere ferro* **Seru.**) which becomes acceptable if one reads *et* with aphaeresis (*uiros't*), and the scansion *iliut* (< *ilium et*) proposed by Consentius (p. 29 Neidermann '*fuit Ilium et ingens.*' *nam si sic scandas Iliet, synaliphe est, si sic Iliut, ecthlipsis est*; on this cf. II.3.5.2 pp. 81–3).

and *in*,[26] are not clearly attested and/or are found only in late sources.[27]

Moreover, if elision and prodelision are related, why is the prodelided spelling common in manuscripts and inscriptions and the elided spelling is not (see II.3.4.2 p. 74 and cf. e.g. CIL 10.4427, in which contraction is displayed and elision is not, [pent.] *quis ara haec positast poena hominis miseri*)?

Finally, the contracted pattern *-s* + *(e)st* is not well described by this idea of 'prodelision', which implies a phonological condition analogous to that which produces elision—that is, the adjacency of two vowels (e.g. *bona est*, analogous to *bona eram*)—in order to make one of the two vowels fall. In forms such as *-ust*, the vowel originally dropped follows a consonant rather than a vowel (*factust* < *factus est*). In order to justify the standard explanation one would have to assume the loss of final *-s* before a vowel (*factus est* > *factu est* > *factust*), but this cannot be easily accepted.[28] Prosodic omission of final *-s* (sigmatic ecthlipsis) is common in republican poetry (cf. V.1.3) and is paralleled by the omission of final *-s* in republican inscriptions (cf. V.1.2), but in these cases it occurs (always in poetry and regularly in inscriptions) after a short vowel and before a consonant.[29]

In conclusion, the notion of 'prodelision', which implies that contracted spellings are phonetic spellings of a sandhi phenomenon, seems to be inadequate.

---

[26] Cf. CIL 3.2 *quadamensitate* (?< *quadam immensitate*), and CIL 13.1855 *sancta necclesia* (< *sancta in ecclesia*) which however is the reading of Lebeuf alone: CIL editors print *sancta [in] ecclesia*.

[27] All cases quoted in the preceding notes (23–6) are from late sources; cf. Soubiran (1966: 179–83) with his bibliography.

[28] Leo (1912: 253–333), in a notorious discussion, argued that final *-s* could also fall before a vowel, but his argument has been refuted by many scholars (cf. in particular Lindsay (1922)). Brinkmann (1906), followed by Allen (1978: 123) held that the proximity of two sibilants (*factus est -> factus st*) was responsible for the alleged fall of *-s* before *est/es*, but his argument lacks convincing parallels. Gratwick (1993: *ad* Pl. *Men.* 36) states that 'such forms [as *subruptust*] probably arose by analogy with *subrupta est, subruptum est* pronounced *subruptast, subruptu(m)st*.' This explanation is not convincing because it does not explain a phonological peculiarity of the pattern *-Vst*, i.e. the fact that there is no clear evidence for contraction of *-st* after a long vowel + *s* and for contraction of *-st* after a consonant other than *-s* or *-m* (cf. II.2).

[29] Cf. e.g. CIL 1².8 *Corneliŏ(s) L(uci) f(ilius)*, Enn. *Ann.* 71 S. *Rōmŭlŭ(s) praedam* (at the end of a hexameter). On omission of final *-s* see chapter V.

1.3 Contractions Reflecting the Cliticization of *esse*

The starting point for a phonological discussion of contraction is the pattern *-s* + *est*. As mentioned in the previous section, the main difficulty of this pattern is the apparent loss of initial *e-* after a consonant (*-s*). A more convincing interpretation of this pattern postulates that the dropping of the vowel *e-* from *est* is independent of the phonological context (i.e. the fact of its being placed after *-s*):

1) *factus* + *st* -> 2) *factusst*[30] -> 3) *factust*

On this view *st* would be an independent form, displaying phonological reduction, and *factus_(s)t* would not be derived phonologically from *factus est* (just as in English the form *a book* is not derived phonologically from **an book*). The passage from stage 2 to stage 3 could be due to the degemination of *-ss-* or to the simplification of the disallowed consonant cluster *-sst* to *-st*:

2) *factus(s)t* -> 3) *factust*[31]

or to sigmatic ecthlipsis:

2) *factu(s)st* -> 3) *factust*[32]

This last explanation may be more likely, especially because this type of contraction after *-s* shares a phonetic property with sigmatic ecthlipsis: the vowel preceding the final *-s* is always short. As already pointed out (II.2 p. 34), there is no clear evidence for contracted forms of *est* occurring after a long vowel + *s* (cf. e.g. the genitive form *domūst*) despite the number of potential instances. Likewise, there is no evidence for sigmatic ecthlipsis to occur after a long vowel;[33] moreover, omission of final *-s* in republican inscriptions is mainly attested after a short vowel (cf. V.1.2 and Appendix 2). This fact might suggest that the two phenomena (contraction after *-s*

---

[30] Spellings with *-sst* are occasionally attested in manuscripts, cf. Pl. *Ps.* 713 *opusst* A, 717 *allatusst* A, 1068 *meliusst* A. However, these instances are few and might simply be misspellings. Cf. also 3.8.1 with n. 161, II.1 with n. 6.

[31] Cf. Fortson (2008: 134). The degemination of *-ss-* might be paralleled (to a certain extent) by the treatment of final *-s* before clitic forms of *esse* beginning with *s-*; on this see V.5.2.

[32] For this view cf. Nyman (1974, 1977) and Bettini (1978).

[33] On sigmatic ecthlipsis occurring only after a short vowel in early Latin poetry see V.1.3. Cf. also Questa (2007: 32–5).

and sigmatic ecthlipsis) are connected. The final reconstruction would be: *factŭs* + *st* > *factusst* > [sigmatic ecthlipsis or simplification of -*ss*(*t*)] *factust*.[34]

The existence of independent contracted forms has been recognized by some scholars,[35] as has its clitic origin.[36] The clitic nature of these forms is phonetically self-evident (consonantal cluster without vowel) and it is confirmed by the fact that they are normally univerbated to the preceding word in spelling (*bonast*, not *bona st*), in both manuscripts and inscriptions (cf. II.1 and II.3.4.1 with Table 2.10).[37] These forms would derive from *es/est* (the historically expected outcomes of PIE *$*h_1és$-si*/*$*h_1$ési* and *$*h_1$és-ti*)[38] by a process of clitic reduction, which is paralleled in other languages (cf. VI.4), including Sabellian dialects (cf. II.3.6).

Moreover, the first person form *sum* might be considered a contracted clitic form, derived from an older *esum/esom*, a form occasionally attested in Latin which is paralleled in Faliscan and in Sabellian languages (cf. Bakkum (2009: 162–3), Untermann (2000: 245)) and would be the expected outcome from an Indo-European point of view (< PIE *$*h_1$ésmi*; cf. I.4). The development *esum* > *sum* would provide a parallel, within the stem of the verb *esse* itself, for the type of clitic reduction that would be visible in -*st* < *est* and -*s*(*s*) < *es* (cf. I.4).

The notion that contracted forms are clitic forms of *est/es* implies that they do not result from a sandhi phenomenon but are instead

---

[34] This view is defended by Nyman (1974, 1977) and Bettini (1978), and is implicitly postulated in Havet (1884).

[35] Cf. in particular Soubiran (1966: 160–2), Nyman (1977), Gratwick (1981: 349), Joseph and Wallace (1987), Sihler (1995: 549), Meiser (1998: 221), Fortson (2008: 136–7), de Melo (2010–2012: I. lxxxvii).

[36] Wackernagel (1892: 428–9) already recognized that 'aphaeresis' (i.e. contraction) was due to the cliticization of *est*.

[37] Only rarely is the non-univerbated spelling found in manuscripts: cf. e.g. Lucr. 4.281 *cumque st* Q, Cic. *Brut.* 249 *ita st* B.

[38] Cf. I.4, and see Joseph and Wallace (1987: 686–8), Meiser (1998: 221), Weiss (2009: 425–7). Cf. also Untermann (2000: 250) on the analogous forms in Oscan. Other scholars have suggested that -*st*/-*'s* are older than *est/es*, whose development would be explained by a process of restressing (Sihler (1995: 549)) and/or by the insertion of a prothetic vowel in post-consonantal contexts (i.e. *$*idst$ > *id est*) eventually extended to non-clitic postvocalic contexts (Nyman (1974: 22, 1977)). This process would essentially be the same as that which generated *estis* (cf. I.4). However, this reconstruction is probably less convincing because it implies more phonological steps (*$*h_1$és-ti* > *est*(*i*) > *st* > *est* against *$*h_1$és-ti* > *est* > *st*).

variant forms of the second and third person singular forms of the verb *esse*. This does not mean that phonological factors are not involved in the formation of contracted forms, but that the phonological reduction of contracted forms is consequent on the clitic nature of the verb *esse* in Latin, rather than triggered by the phonological context (i.e. by the ending of the preceding word).

From an historical point of view, clitic forms (*-'s, -st,* and also *sum*) look like posterior forms,[39] which were presumably common in speech at the time of Plautus and Terence (cf. section 2.2). The older *est* and *es(s)* were probably preferred after certain consonants (e.g. *-t, -d*), because of phonotactic factors (cf. II.2 p. 35). Uncontracted spellings eventually became standard orthography (cf. 2.1.3), under the pressure of a desire for uniformity (there are few monosyllabic words in Latin not containing a vowel) and the tendency to insert a prothetic *e-* before the consonantal cluster *sC*, a phenomenon apparently also attested within the stem of *esse* itself in the second person plural form *estis* (< PIE *h_1s-té*; cf. I.4).

In conclusion, at a certain stage of Latin, *-st* and *-'s* were variant forms of *est* and *es*, and, in texts in which both contracted and uncontracted forms were accepted (such as those of Plautus and Terence), they were presumably chosen by the speaker/writer according to factors analogous to those affecting contracted forms of the verb 'to be' (e.g. *is/'s*) in English.[40] I will investigate these factors in chapter IV.

1.4 The Pattern *-est* < ? *-ĭs + est*

After having established the clitic nature of contracted forms, I now turn to discuss in detail a controversial pattern that I had temporarily left out of my analysis (cf. II.2 p. 35): the pattern *-est* < ? *-ĭs + est*.

1.4.1 The Evidence

The pattern *-est* < *-ĭs est* (cf. e.g. Ter. *Haut.* 1019 *consimilest* [= *consimilis est*] *moribus* [*sc. natus*]) has attracted the attention of several scholars,[41] since it differs from the outcome expected for a

---

[39] Cf. n. 38.   [40] Cf. I.1 and I.3.
[41] See in particular Brinkmann (1906: 61–74), Leo (1912: 285–8), Lindsay (1922: 76), Leumann (1977: 360), Questa (2007: 43–9), Fortson (2008: 161–74). Cf. also Timpanaro (1978: 175–85).

sequence -*ĭs* + *(e)st*, according to the phonological reconstruction presented in section 1.3 (-*ŭs st* -> -*ust*, -*ĭs st* -> -*ist*).

Allegedly transmitted instances of the type -*est* < -*ĭs est* are found only in Plautus, in four places[42]:

Amph. 538	condignum donum, qualest [*sc.* Alcumena] cui dono datumst[43]
	qualest **BDE** : qualis est **J**
Merc. 451	communest illa mihi cum alio[44]
	communest **B** : communis est **CD**
Truc. 170	amator similest oppidi hostilis[45]
	similest **B** : similis est **CD**
Truc. 507	nimium tui similest [*sc.* puer][46]
	similest **P** (= similis est)

In all instances the subject (explicit or implicit) is masculine or feminine, whereas the predicate adjective seems to display the ending -*e*, not the expected -*ĭs* (cf. in contrast Pl. *Amph.* 856 *ecquis alius Sosia intust, qui mei **similis** siet?*, *Mil.* 448, 519, *Pers.* 14, etc.).

There is also another instance where -*est* is not directly transmitted, but the transmitted reading looks like a misunderstanding of an original spelling -*est* (metrically acceptable).[47] This reading is found

---

[42] Two other instances quoted by some scholars (Pl. *Mil.* 1062 *talentum Philippi huic opus auri est; minus ab nemine accipiet* :: *eu ecastor nimis uilest tandem* [= *uilis est*? Leo (1912: 286), cf. also Questa (2007: 43)], *Asin.* 8 *ut sciretis nomen huius fabulae;* | *nam quod ad argumentum attinet, sane breuest* [= *breuis est*? Leo (1912: 286)]) are unconvincing, since in both cases a neuter adjective fits well in the context: in *Mil.* 1062 the subject of *uile* is *talentum* or the general concept of 'money, sum' ('he needs a Philippian Talent, he will take less from no one :: good Lord, that's too cheap!'), in *Asin.* 8 the subject of *breue* may well be an implied antecedent *id* or the implied noun *argumentum* ('as for what concerns the plot, that is quite simple').

[43] 'A worthy gift, matching the one it has been given to.' Trans. de Melo.

[44] 'She's the joint property of myself and a third party.' Trans. de Melo.

[45] 'A lover's like a hostile city.' Trans. Nixon.

[46] 'He (i.e. the boy) is the very image of you.' Trans. Nixon.

[47] Leo also quotes Pl. *St.* 765 (*prostibiles tandem* **P** : *prostibilest tandem* **edd.**) and *Trin.* 828 (*nobilis* **B** : *nobiles* **CD** : *nobilest* **edd.**) but in both instances the form ending in -*est* (*prostibilest* and *nobilest*) is most likely a neuter adjective, referring to the following infinitive clause: *prostibilest tandem* | *stantem stanti sauium dare amicum amicae*? 'Why, it's the way of a common strumpet, for a damsel to give a kiss standing to her sweetheart as he stands'; *Trin.* 828 *et nobilest apud homines,* | *pauperibus te parcere solitum* 'and it's well known among men, that you usually spare the poor and punish and tame the rich.' Trans. de Melo. See n. 49 and cf. section 1.4.2.

in an analogous grammatical context, in which a masculine/feminine
ending in *-ĭs* + *est* seems to be required (Pl. *Merc.* 1005):

> non **utibilest** hic locus
> utibile si **CD** : ut si **B** : utibilest *edd.*

One of the directly transmitted readings (Pl. *Amph.* 538 *qualest*) is
confirmed by the testimony of Nonius, who quotes it (p. 292 L.) and
explains it as a case of *neutrum positum pro masculino* (the manuscripts have *culest* instead of *qualest*), a fact which suggests that
Nonius presumably did not read *qualis est* (otherwise his comment
would be pointless) but either *quale est* or *qualest*.[48]

Moreover, there is a group of other instances (all from Plautus) in
which the context seems to require a masculine/feminine ending *-ĭs* +
est but (some) manuscripts read *-e est*.[49]

Amph. 442–3	nimis **similest** mei │ ... tam **consimilest** atque ego [*sc.* ille] 442 simile est **BDE** : similis est **J** 443 consimile est **P**
Amph. 537	ecastor condignum donum, **qualest** qui donum dedit [*cf. above Amph.* 538] quale est **BD** : qualis est **JE**
Amph. 601	neque lac lactis magis est simile quam ille ego **similest** mei simile est **P**
Aul. 324	cocus ille **nundinalest** nundinale est *Festus 176 L.* : nundinalis est **BVJ** (mund- **J**) : nundinatlis est **D**
Truc. 505	ehem, ecquid mei **similest**? [*sc.* puer; *cf. above Truc.* 507] si mille est **BD** : simille est **CD**³
St. 74	**exorabilest** (*sc.* pater) exorabile est **P** : exorabilist **A**

---

[48] It should be pointed out that **F**³, a correcting hand who apparently had access to
another good manuscript, read either *quale* or *quale est* (cf. Fortson (2008: 170–1)).

[49] Leo (1912: 286) also quotes Pl. *Bac.* 6 (*simile est* **Prob.** 7, **Pomp.** 5.199) and *Trin.*
679 (*facile est* **P**), but in both instances the form may be taken as a neuter: in the
former (*Bac.* 6 *sicut lacte lactis similest*) the adjective is referring to a neuter noun (*lac*)
and therefore the ending *-e* does not appear to be derived from *-ĭs*, while in the second
(*Trin.* 679 *ne scintillam quidem relinques, genus qui congliscat tuom.* │ :: *facilest
inuentu.*) the subject is impersonal ('it is easy to find it': cf. Cic. *Lael.* 64.6 *ad quas
non est facile inuentu qui descendant*). See above, n. 47 and cf. section 1.4.2.

Finally, there are some other instances from other archaic poets, quoted by Nonius, in which a form *-e est/es* is commented on as being an example of *neutrum pro masculino*, in a context which would seem to require a masculine form of the adjective *(-ĭs)*:

Non. pp. 332–3 L.
simile est, pro similis est; pro masculino positum neutrum.
Titinius Fullonibus (34 R.): 'formicae pol **persimile est** rusticus homo'
Naeuius Gymnastico (60 R.): 'pol haut parasitorum aliorum **simile est**'
Nouius in Militibus Pometinensibus (62 R.): 'tu pueri pausilli **simile es**'
   [simile est *codd.* : simil es *Ribbeck* : simili's *Ritschl*; cf. *Lindsay app. ad loc.* : 'simile's (i.e. -lis es) *Nouius*']

Non. p. 337 L.
tale positum pro talis.
Titinius Setina (106 R.): 'accede ad sponsum audacter. uirgo nulla **tale est** Setiae'

In all these instances one finds a morphosyntactic context analogous to the ones presented above, with a predicate adjective ending in *-e* referring to a masculine/feminine subject.

There have been different attempts at explaining this evidence. The first question to be raised is whether the spelling *-est*, directly transmitted in only four cases, is to be considered as reflecting the phonological outcome of the sequence *-ĭs + est* or not.

1.4.2 Incongruence in Gender

First, it is possible that Nonius was correct; the *-est* spelling is to be construed as a contracted form of a nominalized neuter adjective ending *-e + (e)st*. According to this view, there would be no phonological relation between *-ĭs est* and *-est* (*-e est*); the apparent difficulty would be morphosyntactic in nature, involving a lack of agreement in gender between the subject and the adjective in the predicate.

Would this incongruence of gender be 'original'? I.e. would forms such as *(con)similest, qualest* (cf. *Truc.* 170, 507, *Amph.* 538) be the original Plautine readings and the equivalent uncontracted forms such as *(con)simile est, quale est* (cf. *Amph.* 442, 443, 537, 601, *Truc.* 505) be later emendations, eventually 'corrected' in medieval manuscripts into the (uncontracted) *similis est, qualis est* (cf. *Amph.* 442, 537) in order to emend an apparent grammatical mistake?

The use of a nominalized neuter adjective in the predicate referring to a masculine or feminine subject is occasionally attested in Latin,[50] though not as commonly as in Greek;[51] among the instances quoted by scholars[52] cf. e.g. Var. *L.* 10.4.2 *nam simile est homo homini* ('for a human being is like a human being'),[53] which seems to provide a parallel for the Plautine instances listed in section 1.4.1 (cf. e.g. *Amph.* 538 *condignum donum, qualest cui dono datumst, Truc.* 170 *amator similest oppidi hostilis*). In Plautus himself there are at least two examples of this morphosyntactic pattern: Pl. *Mil.* 685 *bona uxor suaue ductust* ('a good wife is a pleasure to marry') and *Poen.* 238 *modus omnibus rebus . . . optumum est* [**Lindsay** : *optimus est Leo*] *habitu* ('moderation is the best thing to have in all circumstances').[54]

Therefore, one might argue that many instances of the pattern *similest* in Plautus are to be considered as cases of this type of syntactic anomaly, especially because in some instances the neuter adjective (grammatically referring to a masculine/feminine subject) is found in a context in which a disagreement of gender is plausible

---

[50] Cf. Kühner and Stegmann (1955: I.32–3) and Hofmann and Szantyr (1965: 444–5), who state that the phenomenon is uncommon in Latin, is restricted to poetic language, and is influenced by Greek syntax (see n. 52 on Virg. *Ecl.* 3.80).

[51] Cf. Kühner and Gerth (1890: II.1.58–60).

[52] Cf. e.g. Virg. *Ecl.* 3.80 *triste lupus stabulis* [which is an imitation of a passage of Theocritus, cf. Clausen (1994: 111)], *Aen.* 4.569 *uarium et mutabile semper femina,* Ov. *Am.* 1.9.4 *turpe senex miles, turpe senilis amor,* Cic. *N.D.* 3.15 *quid simile medicina . . . et diuinatio?, Off.* 1.11 *commune animantium omnium est coniunctionis appetitus, Rhet. Her.* 3.22 *utile est ad firmitudinem sedata uox in principio.* For other cases of lack of agreement between subjects and predicate adjectives or nouns see Kühner and Stegmann (1955: I.20–53), Hofmann and Szantyr (1965: 435–45, esp. p. 442, discussing the use of a neuter predicate noun with a masculine/feminine subject: cf. e.g. Ter. *Phorm.* 94 *paupertas mihi onus uisum est*).

[53] This nominalized use of the neuter adjective seems to be common in particular with *simile.* Cf. e.g. Hor. *S.* 2.3.99–100 *quid simile isti Graecus Aristippus,* Mart. 3.11.4 *quid simile est Thaïs et Hermione?,* Tert. *Apol.* 1.12 *Christianus uero quid simile?,* 46.18 *quid simile philosophus et Christianus,* Jer. *Ep.* 60.3.2 *quid simile infernus et regna caelorum?* However, it is also possible to argue that in some cases the verb implied is not *est* but *habet/habent* (cf. Cic. *Div.* 2.65 *quid simile habet passer annis;* Sen. *Nat.* 1.5.8 *quid enim simile speculis habent nubes*). A different case is that of a predicate *simile* referring to a masculine noun as a lemma (cf. Var. *L.* 8.68 *sic item quoniam simile est recto casu 'surus' 'lupus' 'lepus',* Serv. *A.* 1.306 *simile est et 'iocus'*).

[54] However, in both cases the text is problematic: *Mil.* 685 *suaueduc[tu]st* A : *sua deductust* CD : *sua deducta est* B[1] (*sit* B[2]) : *si ea deducta est* F *nonn. edd.* : *suaue ductust* **Ritschl**, **Leo** (*apparatus: i.e. suauis*), **Lindsay**, **Goetz-Schoell** (*apparatus: uel deducta est*); *Poen.* 238 *modus . . . optimum est* B **Lindsay** (*optum-, apparatus: ?-must*) : *modis . . . optimum est* CD : *modust . . . optumum* **Spengel** : *modus . . . optumumst* **Goetz-Schoell** (*appartus: uel modis*) : *optimus est* **Leo**.

for other reasons. For instance, in *Amph.* 537 and 538 (*ecastor con-dignum donum,* **qualest** *qui donum dedit.* :: *immo sic: condignum donum,* **qualest** *cui dono datumst*)[55] the neuter form *quale est* might be explained by an attraction of gender; in both instances the adjective is placed after a neuter noun (*donum*), to which it refers in a comparison. Even if according to the norms of grammar *qualis* might have been preferred in both cases, a confusion of gender might have occurred in such a context. Similarly, in *Amph.* 601 the form *simile(st)* is in parallel with the neuter adjective *simile* referring to the neuter *lac* (*neque lac lactis magis est simile quam ille ego* **similest** *mei*).

Another possibility would be to ascribe this syntactic anomaly not to Plautus but to late-antique scribes; according to this view the original reading of Plautus would have been *similist* (with the expected contracted spelling *-ist* < *-īs est*), which was not grammatically understood by later scribes[56] who altered it into the neuter form *similest* (and eventually *simile est* and *similis est*), possibly under the influence of the Grecizing construction with the nominalized neuter adjective in the predicate.[57]

It is difficult to date this confusion of gender, i.e. to determine whether it is Plautine in origin or not. Nevertheless, the possibility that we are dealing with a syntactic and not with a phonological phenomenon seems plausible, since the pattern *-est* (= *-ist*?) is attested in manuscripts only with forms of the nominative of a masculine/feminine adjective (e.g. *similest* = *similist*) and never with other cases (e.g. **Venerest = Veneris + est*); if this contraction was dictated by phonological considerations alone then other case contractions would be just as likely.[58]

---

[55] 'Honestly, a worthy gift, matching the one who gave it. :: No, a worthy gift, matching the one it has been given to.' Trans. de Melo.

[56] An analysis of the manuscript tradition of Terence suggests that already in late antiquity contracted spellings after *-Vs* were no longer familiar; they are hardly ever found in late-antique manuscripts, which do nonetheless extensively preserve contracted spellings after *-V* and *-Vm.* Cf. 2.1.1 and Appendix 1.

[57] One might also observe that examples of gender incongruence are not uncommon in late Latin, although this is not necessarily relevant to the question of contraction. On this cf. Löfstedt (1956: I.1–10), Svennung (1941: 133), Norberg (1944), Väänänen (1981: 149–50). See also Adams (1976: 88–9) commenting on some instances from the Anonymus Valesianus II, such as *omnia ... quod, synagogas ... quae, factum est ... modius.*

[58] See section 1.4.4.

Nevertheless, in the following sections I will take into consideration a phonological approach to the problem, because, although one might explain all the above instances as cases of incongruence of gender (except perhaps *Merc.* 1005 *non utibilest hic locus*), yet the fact remains that many scholars and editors have readily accepted such instances (? -*est* < *ĭs est*) as contracted forms deriving from -*ĭs* + *est* and have in consequence debated the question of how to explain the phonological transition -*ĭs est* > *est*.

Table 3.1. Reconstructions of the pattern *similest* (= *similĭs est*?)

Number	Plautus	Phenomena	> Later Scribes	Character of the Later Scribal Treatment
1 (Questa) [1.4.3]	*similĭs (e)st > *similĭ(s) st > *similĕ st > **similest**	sigmatic ecthlipsis opening of final -ĭ	simile est	removal of contraction
2 (Leo) [1.4.3]	similĭs est > *similĭ(s) est > *similĕ est > **similest**	'elision' of final -*s* (?) opening of final -ĭ	similist	restoration of the masculine/ feminine ending -*i(s)* (for the sake of the agreement or sim.)
3 (Fortson) [1.4.3 and 1.4.5]	*similĭs (e)st > similist > **similest**	analogy with *similest* (n.), *potest*, etc.	similis est	*idem* +removal of contraction
4 (Brinkmann) [1.4.5]	*simil est > **similest**	different adj. root (*simil*)		
5 (Leumann) [1.4.6]	*similĭs (e)st > **similist**		similest	confusion of *i/e* (< blending of [ĭ]/[ē]) AND/OR influence of the neuter
			simile est	*idem* + 'uncontraction'
			similis est	restoration of the masculine/feminine ending -*i(s)* (for the sake of the agreement)

* Forms not transmitted by manuscripts.

An analysis of these forms is complicated by the fact that they are textually problematic (cf. section 1.4.1) and there is therefore disagreement as to whether to consider them original or not. Moreover, there are different phonological explanations adduced, often by the same scholar. For this reason, I have placed here a table (Table 3.1) summarising the different reconstructions, to which I invite the reader to refer in the following sections. In the first column I have indicated the section in which that particular reconstruction is discussed.

1.4.3 -est *as the Original Phonological Outcome of* -ĭs + est

I shall begin by considering the phonological reconstruction cautiously formulated by Questa (2007: 48), which is probably the most convincing (no. 1 in Table 3.1).

1. *similĭs st*	adjective + contracted form of *est*
2. *similĭ(s) st*	dropping of final *-s*
3. *similĕ st*	opening of final *-ĭ*
4. *similest*	univerbation
5. *simile est*	alteration of the contracted spelling by later scribes, occurring before the time of Nonius (third/fourth centuries AD), with consequent confusion with the neuter form
6. *similis est*	correction into the masculine form (attested in later manuscripts)[59]

This phonological reconstruction is supported by the parallel with some indeclinable disyllables ending in *-ĭs* (especially *potis* and *magis*), which in early Latin have a secondary form in *-ĕ* (*potĕ* and *magĕ*), deriving from sigmatic ecthlipsis + opening of final *-ĭ* (i.e. from the same phonetic phenomena that would allegedly explain the passage *similis (e)st > similest*).[60] These forms are however

---

[59] Cf. e.g. *Truc.* 170 *similest* B : *similis est* CD.

[60] There is a frequent confusion in spelling in early Latin between *i* and *e*, which reflects at least two phonological phenomena. First, opening (> *ĕ*) of weak short *i* in a final position in order to avoid loss (the phenomenon which would be at work in our case), which appears to be regular during this period (cf. *facile* < **facili*, *mare* < **mori*:

problematic and a full discussion would require far more space than is available here.[61] There is also the expression *corpore custos* (i.e. 'bodyguard' < *corporis* (gen.) + *custos*; cf. Leumann (1977: 384))[62] found in some imperial inscriptions (e.g. CIL 6.4340, 4342, 4343, 4437, 8810, all dating to the first century AD), which seems to be an

see Sihler (1995: 65), Meiser (1998: 73–4), Clackson and Horrocks (2007: 52–3); cf. also n. 61). Second, the orthographic instability of *ĭ* and *ĕ* in early Latin texts, attested e.g. in the Scipionic *elogia* (cf. e.g. CIL 1².9 **aidiles** *cosol cesor . . . consol censor* **aidilis**; cf. Adams (2007: 70–1, 137)), which might suggest that the two vowels were articulated in a very similar way in early Latin (cf. Wachter (1987: 305–6)). See also Bakkum (2009: 97–8) for a similar phenomenon in Faliscan.

[61] The forms *potĕ* < *potis* and *magĕ* < *magis* seem to have good supporting evidence: both *pote* and *mage* are well attested spellings in Latin (cf. ThLL *ad loc.*), found not only in archaic authors but also in classical poets (cf. e.g. Prop. 2.1.46, Mart. 9.15.2 *pote*, Virg. *Aen.* 10.481, Prop. 4.8.16 *mage*). They are possibly used as archaisms (cf. Don. Ter. *And.* 264 *pote pro potis ut mage pro magis* τῷ ἀρχαισμῷ, Tränkle (1960: 35), Fedeli (1980: *ad* 1.11.9)) or perhaps colloquialisms (cf. Fedeli (2005: 84)), and they are also found in late-antique texts (cf. e.g. Cassiod. *Var.* 12.3.1 *pote sit*, *Carmen de figuris* 168, 178 *pote* [on this text see pp. 49–50 with n. 52], Optat. *Carm.*14.13, 28, Maur. 1483, 2893 *mage*). However, the relation between *potis* and *pote* may be morphological (masculine/feminine vs. neuter) and not phonological, since *pote* might also be construed as an archaic neuter form of the adjective *potis* (cf. Leumann (1977: 525), Meiser (1998: 222), Questa (2007: 36)), with a history (< *potĭ* with the Ø ending of the neuter adjectives, cf. *facile* < **facili*) different from that of *potis*. Similarly *mage* might be construed as a neuter form, coined by analogy with *pote*; cf. Leumann (1977: 228). Therefore, the alternation *potis/pote* and *magis/mage* might be due to an interchange of gender (cf. also Priscian GL 2.251.17f. *hic et haec potĭs et hoc pote nomina esse, ostendit comparatio potior et potissimus*). On the other hand, in early Latin *potis* and *magis* (at least before a consonant) were presumably close in pronunciation to [*pote*] and [*mage*], under the influence of sigmatic ecthlipsis and opening of final *-ĭ*. Apart from *potĕ* and *magĕ* scholars mention also the forms *plurĕ*, used as equivalent to a genitive by Plautus, Lucilius, and Cicero, according to Charisius, p. 274 B. (cf. Hofmann and Szantyr (1965: 130)); *nimĕ*, which is transmitted at Pl. *Ps.* 1274a but is apparently *contra metrum* and precedes a word beginning with a vowel; and **sate*. There is a large bibliography on this issue: cf. in particular Neue and Wagener (1892–1905: II.594–5), Leo (1912: 292–301), Lindsay (1922: 204), Niedermann (1953: 133), Leumann (1977: 228), Sommer and Pfister (1977: I.215), Timpanaro (1978: 182–5), Sihler (1995: 538–9), Questa (2007: 35–8).

[62] The form *corpore* might also be construed as a dative equivalent to *corpori* (cf. Nettleship (1889: 423)). The ending *-e* would derive from the old dative ending *-ei*. The spelling *-e* (representing long close *e*) for *-ei* is well attested in Latin inscriptions and reflects an intermediate stage between *-ei* and *-ī* and (on this see Adams 2007: 52–64). For an overview of early Latin case endings see also Clackson and Horrocks (2007: 16).

archaism conserved in a formulaic expression and possibly provides further evidence for the transition -*ĭs* > -*e*.[63]

Another similar reconstruction (no. 2 in Table 3.1) is given by Leo (1912); however, Leo did not understand the notion of clitic forms and explained the first two passages by assuming the drop of final -*s* before a vowel, which, as pointed out (section 1.2 with n. 28), is difficult to accept.

1. *similĭs est*
2a. *similĭ est*   'elision' of final -*s* before a vowel
2b. *similĕ est*   opening of final -*ĭ*
3. *similĕ st*

A parallel but slightly different hypothesis is offered by Fortson (2008), who explains the passages from stage 2 *similĭ(s) st* to stage 4 (*similest*) of Questa's reconstruction on an analogical and not a phonological basis (no. 3 in Table 3.1).

3. *similist*   standard contraction -*is est* > -*ist*
4. *similest*   under the pressure of the neuter form *simil(e) est* and the 'constant presence lurking in the background (Fortson (2008: 171))' of *est* and compounds

1.4.4 Two Problematic Pieces of Evidence

The main problem with these phonological reconstructions is that they do not fit well with two aspects of the evidence. First, as pointed out (p. 113), both the spelling -*est* (< -*ĭs est*) and the spelling -*e est* (which looks like a misunderstanding of -*est*) are attested only for a circumscribed class of words; that is, adjectives in the nominative case (*qualis, communis, similis, utibilis, nundinalis, exorabilis*; cf. above 1.4.1); if -*e (e)st* was the phonological realization of -*ĭs* + *est*, we would expect also to find it in spelling with other morphological endings (e.g. **Venerest*). Second, the form -*est* is not the only

---

[63] Leo (1912: 288–91) also mentions the alternation of the verbal endings -*ris*/-*re* of the second person passive form as evidence of the phonological transition -*ĭs* > -*ĕ*. However, as pointed out by Lindsay (1922: 131 'Leo defies Comparative Philology by insisting that *sequeris* is older than *sequere*'), the ending -*re* probably derives from the Indo-European ending **-so*; -*ris* is a later form, deriving from -*re* + -*s*, cf. Meiser (1998: 218).

spelling attested for contracted -*ĭs* + *est*, but the spelling -*ist* (i.e. the expected contraction according to the phonological reconstruction of contracted forms[64]) is found as well, especially in the manuscripts of Plautus.[65]

Mil. 997	corporist **B** : corporis est **CD**
Merc. 672	oneri st **B** : oneris est **CD**
Rud. 761	Venerist **A** : Veneris est **P**
St. 74	exorabilist **A** : exorabile est **P**
Ps. 954	mala mercist **P** *Leo Lindsay* : malast mers **Brinkmann**
Pers. 580	potist **A** : potes **P** : potis *edd.*

The last two cases (*Ps.* 954, *Pers.* 580) are not accepted by all editors, but the first four are printed contracted in most editions of Plautus, especially because they are confirmed by the metre. There is also one instance from Terence (*Eun.* 546 *hominis* **A** *Mar.* : *hominis est* **cett. codd.** : *hominist* **KL**), in which the linguistic context seems to require a verb but the metrical context does not allow an uncontracted form -*ĭs est*: the form *hominis* transmitted by **A** might derive from a contracted form *hominist*, with an easy loss of final -*t* (cf. II.3.3 pp. 56–8, Appendix 1.1). Moreover, one finds in manuscripts a series of readings in -*is* in a context which seems to require a second person verbal form *es*. Just as the contracted spelling -*u's* (< -*ŭs* + *es*) is not graphically distinguishable from an absolute form -*us* without verb (cf. II.3.8.1), so the result of a sequence -*ĭs* + (*e*)*s* > (-*i's*) would not be distinguishable from an absolute form -*ĭs* without verb. Consequently, a reading -*ĭs* in the manuscripts, especially in a context

---

[64] Cf. section 1.3 and II.2.

[65] There is also one instance of the pattern -*ĕs* + *est* printed contracted in modern editions of Plautus: *Amph.* 653 *omnia adsunt bona quem penest uirtus* [*penest* **BDE edd.** : *penes est* **J**]. The contracted form *penest* is generally preferred to the uncontracted form *penes est*, transmitted by **J**, even though the line belongs to a *canticum* and thus its scansion is not straightforward (cf. Palmer (1890: 69), Lindsay (1922: 76), Questa (1995: 69), Christenson (2000: *ad loc.*)). Although a single instance would appear to be insufficient evidence for the existence of contraction after -*ĕs*, the number of instances of a sequence -*ĕs* + *est*/*es* is very low (there is only one other case, Pl. *Truc.* 858a). Therefore, it seems correct to accept the form *penest* and to assume that contraction of *est*/*es* was also possible after a word ending in -*ĕs* (on this pattern cf. also Lindsay (1922: 209), Questa (2007: 43)).

in which the verb *es* seems necessary, might be construed as *-ĭ's* (= *-ĭs es*), thus providing evidence for the contraction *-ĭs* + *es* > *-ĭ's*:

Pl. *Curc.* 407   cuiatis *codd.* : cuiati's **Leo, Lindsay, de Melo** (quoi-)
                    Questa (2007: 43)
Ter. *An.* 702   fortis *codd.* : forti's *edd.*
     Haut. 848 hominis v^{ac} : hominis *es cett.* : homini's **KL**
     Ad. 321   quisquis **A** : quisquis es *cett.* : quisqui's **KL**

In conclusion, the absence of spellings *-est* <*-ist* with non-adjectival morphological endings, and even more the presence in the manuscripts of the spelling *-ist* reflecting *-ĭs est* pose some problems for the idea that *-est* was the normal phonological development of a sequence *-ĭs* + *est*.

1.4.5 Different Ways of Dealing with the Evidence

One way to deal with the morphological and orthographic inconsistency in manuscripts (i.e. *similest* vs. *corporist*) is to retain it in modern editions. That is the choice of Leo who, in his edition of Plautus, prints *-est* when the word ending in *-is* is an adjective (e.g. at *St.* 74 he prints *exorabilest* against the reading *exorabilist* transmitted by **A**) and *-ist* when it is a noun (cf. e.g. *Aul.* 421 *testis est codd.* : *testist* **Leo** : *testest* **Lindsay**). However, Leo does not explain the reasons for this different treatment of nouns and adjectives, which would remain problematic, although it is already attested in manuscripts to a certain extent. Kauer and Lindsay (1958), on the other hand, are inconsistent in their edition of Terence, in which we find *tristist* printed at *Hec.* 352 (but *triste'st* is given as an alternative in the apparatus), for the unmetrical *tristis est* of the manuscripts, whereas at *Haut.* 1019 and 1020 they print *consimilest* and *similest* for the *consimilis est* and *similis est* of the manuscripts.

Another approach is that of Brinkmann (1906: 61–74) who supposes that the form *similest* results from a reduced form **simil* (< *similis*) to which the verb is attached (no. 4 in Table 3.1). This view is not persuasive (cf. Fortson (2008: 169–70)); apart from the fact that the form *simil* does not have supporting evidence anywhere else (cf. Leumann (1977: 449)), Brinkmann's theory would not be able to explain spellings with *-est* (< *-ĭs est*) which do not involve *similis* as the host word of *(e)st* (e.g. *qualest* or *communest*).

More plausible, on the other hand, is the view of Fortson (2008: 171) who rejects the spelling *-ist*, claiming that 'the ms. spelling *-ist* is a clear *lectio facilior*, explicable by simple restoration of the *i*' (no. 3 in Table 3.1). Fortson does not state it explicitly, but following his view, the spelling *-est* should be restored even when *-ist* is transmitted by manuscripts. This editorial possibility is contemplated by Lindsay (cf. e.g. his apparatus *ad Mil.* 997 *uel corporest*, and *ad Merc.* 672 *uel onerest*). The problem with this view is that it seems arbitrary to consider the spelling *-ist* (< *-ĭs est*) less accurate than spelling *-est* (< *-e est*). Even if there are more instances of *-est* indirectly transmitted (twelve instances of *-e est* < *-est*? + one instance of *-es* < *-est*? vs. four instances of *-is* < *ist*? and four of *-is* < *-i's*?), the number of directly transmitted instances of *-ist* is higher than that of directly transmitted instances of *-est* (six: four).[66]

1.4.6 -est *as a Misspelling of* -ist

Another way of explaining the evidence would be to argue that the spelling *-ist* is not a misreading (as claimed by Fortson) but the original reading, with *-est/-e est* being a later change (no. 5 in Table 3.1). Leumann (1977: 123) holds this view, explaining the transition *-is est/-ist* > *-e est/-est* as the fabrication of grammarians or later scribes.[67] The idea that *-ist* is the original spelling is also contemplated by Lindsay (1922: 76) and Questa (2007: 48). In addition to their main reconstructions (cf. section 1.4.3), they leave open the possibility that the change of *-ist* into *-est* (later converted into *-e est*) might merely be a graphic confusion on the part of the scribes. This graphic confusion would be caused by two factors already mentioned, namely the obscurity of a contracted form after *-ĭs* and the influence of the neuter form *-est* (cf. section 1.4.2).

There are some further points supporting the view that *-est* is a later innovation by scribes; the confusion of *is* ~ *e* in orthography may actually have been influenced by a late-antique pronunciation of the ending *-ĭ*, being close to [ẹ]. As we have seen (pp. 115–16 with n. 60), in early Latin an ending *-ĭs* might have been pronounced *-ĕ* before

---

[66] However, these figures are too small to be statistically significant, as shown by the t-test.

[67] On the possibility of the influence of some grammatical theory on these spellings see Timpanaro (1978: 180 n. 46).

a consonant, under the influence of two phonetic phenomena that are both independently attested in pre-historic and/or early Latin: sigmatic ecthlipsis (-*ĭs* > -*ĭ*) and the opening of final -*ĭ* (-*ĭ* > -*ĕ*). Therefore, a spelling -*e* for -*ĭs* found in an archaic text or inscription (cf. e.g. CIL 1².1334a *rege Mitredatis*) might rightly be construed as a phonetic spelling influenced by pronunciation (cf. above n. 60). Instances of orthographic confusion of -*ĭs* > -*e* are also noticeable in inscriptions and manuscripts of late antiquity and the early Middle Ages (cf. e.g. Greg. Tur. *Franc.* 2.5 *auxilium bonitate eius* B).[68] These instances have been construed by some scholars as cases of phonetic spellings, implying that -*ĭs* was pronounced -*e* (i.e. *ę*[69]) in late antiquity.[70] Following this approach, it has been argued that many instances of the spelling -*e est*/-*est* for -*is est*/-*ist* in Plautus might also be considered cases of phonetic spelling to be ascribed to late-antique scribes (cf. Lindsay (1922: 132), Fortson (2008: 168)).

This reconstruction is far from unproblematic, especially because a pronunciation of -*ĭs* as *ę* is not expected in late antiquity. The spelling *e* for *ĭ* is indeed a well-attested phenomenon in late Latin inscriptions and substandard texts[71] reflecting the pronunciation [*ę*] of *ĭ* in late Latin.[72] On the other hand, final -*s* was reintroduced in the late republic[73] and it was retained during late antiquity both in spelling and in speech.[74] While there are a few cases of sigmatic ecthlipsis in late-antique poetic texts, on the basis of the style of these writings they ought to be considered

[68] Cf. also CIL 6.23818 (= CLE 977) *aetate hic parua iaceo lacrimabile* [= *lacrimabilis?*] *semper*. Scholars also mention some cases of spelling in -*e* found in the manuscripts of Lucretius corrected into -*ĭ(s)* by modern editors: Lucr. 5.949 *umore* OQU : *umori(s) Bentley*, 1410 *dulcedine* OQ : *dulcedini(s) Lambinus*, 2.263 *tempore* : *tempori(s) Butterfield 2008a* (= 2.456, 2.1006, 6.320). There are also some instances from Plautus (cf. e.g. *Merc.* 880 *caelum ut est splendore plenum*) but these can be explained by syntactic factors (i.e. interchange of genitive/ablative). On this cf. in particular Leo (1912: 301–9), Timpanaro (1978: 175–7).

[69] Cf. n. 72.

[70] Cf. Lindsay (1922: 134), discussing forms such as *similest*: '[I]n late Latin -*ĭs* definitely passed into -*e*.' See also Timpanaro (1978: 179).

[71] Cf. Adams (2007: 138, 151–2, 228, 247–8, 441–2, and in general chapter X, pp. 624–83).

[72] On the merger of *ĭ* and *ē* in late Latin and the outcome [*ę*] in Romance languages see Allen (1978: 47–9), Väänänen (1981: 36–7), Meiser (1998: 60–2). This phenomenon appears to be different from the opening of final -*ĭ* which we have seen at work in early Latin (cf. n. 59), but it does seem to be paralleled in Sabellian dialects (cf. II.3.6).

[73] Cf. V.1.1 and Adams (2007: 140–1).

[74] Cf. V.1.1 and Väänänen (1981: 67–8), Herman (2000: 40–1), Adams (2007: 636).

archaisms.[75] Moreover, despite the claim of Timpanaro (1978: 179: 'la grafia *-e*... per *-is* è molto diffusa in iscrizioni e codici della tarda antichità')[76] instances in which *-e* stands for *-ĭs* are not in fact frequent, and they can often be explained by non-phonetic factors.[77] Furthermore, they are generally found in texts later than the time of Nonius,[78] which is the *terminus ante quem* for the spelling *similest* in Plautus.

I would not completely reject the possibility that phonological factors influenced late-antique scribes in 'correcting' an original *-ist* spelling to *-est*: in a form like *similist* the ending *-s* of the adjective is not distinguishable from the *s-* of the verbal form (*st*) and thus scribes might have construed the form as *simili* + *st* and considered *simili* as a misreading for *simile*, influenced by the contemporary pronunciation of final *-ī* in late Latin.[79]

1.4.7 Final Remarks

As is evident from the range of different reconstructions, it is difficult to establish the origin and morphological nature of the spelling *-est* < ? *-ĭs* + *est*. Different factors might potentially have been influencing each other; phonetic factors, such as the development of *-ĭs* into *-ĕ* in early Latin and of *-ī* into *-ę* in late Latin, might have 'authenticated' a neuter form *simile* in a context in which one would expect a masculine (or feminine) form, just as morphosyntactic factors (such as incongruence in gender) might have authenticated a phonetic spelling *simile* (= *similis*).

---

[75] Cf. V.1.1, Butterfield (2008b: 188).

[76] Timpanaro does not quote many instances but refers to the evidence collected by other scholars (e.g. Schuchardt (1866: II.45)), which is generally scarce and unconvincing, apart from that collected by Bonnet (1890: 340–2). Bonnet lists a series of instances (*c*.30) in the manuscripts of Gregory of Tours of nouns ending in *-e* in a context where one would expect a genitive: cf. e.g. *Franc.* 3.15 *quid opere sciret,* 6.28 *latere dolore detentus; Glor. mart.* 1.88 *alta nocte silentia.* However, Bonnet himself does not consider these forms as genitives displaying phonological change (*-is* > *e*), since in the Gallic area final *-s* was retained during the Middle Ages, and instead suggests that this is a morphosyntactic phenomenon, derived from the confusion between genitive and ablative.

[77] See the preceding note.

[78] Most instances are found in Gregory of Tours (sixth century AD) and are problematic (cf. n. 76). The inscriptions quoted by Schuchardt (1866–1868: II.45) date all to the sixth or seventh century. The manuscripts of Lucretius are medieval (cf. n. 68).

[79] See n. 72.

For these reasons, perhaps an agnostic position is advisable (cf. Lindsay (1922: 133)). Nevertheless, an editor must choose whether to print -*est* or -*ist*, when metrical or textual factors point to the presence of contracted -*ĭs est*. It would probably be too arbitrary to 'correct' the -*est* spelling to -*ist* in all cases, especially because it might be a case of a nominalized use of the neuter adjective (cf. 1.4.2). At the same time, it seems equally arbitrary to restore -*est* whenever a contracted -*ĭs* + *est* is required (cf. e.g. Pl. *Aul.* 421 *testis est codd.* : *testest* **Lindsay**); the spelling -*ist* is attested in manuscripts and cannot easily be considered a *lectio facilior* (which would rather be -*is est*) and the form -*est* is attested only for a particular class of words, thus suggesting the inter-ference of some non-phonological factors. All things considered, the wisest choice for an editor would probably be to print the spelling -*est* (< -*ĭs est* ?) only when transmitted by manuscripts, and to print -*ist* for a transmitted -*is est* whenever the metre requires a contracted spelling.

2. HISTORICAL APPRAISAL OF CONTRACTED FORMS

The aim of this section is to trace the history of contracted forms in Latin, both in speech and in writing. Until when, if ever, was a form such as *bona est* pronounced /bonast/? When did a contracted spell-ing such as *bonast* become uncommon, unfamiliar, and eventually obscure? Were contracted forms, in speech and/or writing, stylistic-ally marked? In which authors, genres, periods? Should a reader assume that *est/es* were always pronounced contracted, regardless of the way they were spelt? Should an editor restore contracted spellings whenever possible? In order to deal with these questions, one has first to draw a clear distinction between the fields of spelling and speech.[80]

2.1 Orthography

2.1.1 *Early Latin (Third and Second Centuries* BC*)*

Evidence collected in chapter II suggests that in early Latin contracted spellings were common in poetic texts. Contracted spellings are

---

[80] For this distinction cf. I.3.2.

extensively transmitted in the manuscripts of early republican playwrights, Plautus and Terence especially, but also in fragmentary republican poets (Ennius, Naevius, Accius, etc.) quoted by later authors such as Cicero, Gellius, or Nonius (cf. II.3.1.1).

Moreover, there is evidence indicating that many cases of contracted spellings have been altered in the process of transmission of the texts. First, in texts and fragments of early poets there are many cases of readings presumably resulting from the misunderstanding of a contracted spelling (cf. II.3.3).

Second, in early Latin poetry one finds contraction of *est/es* after -V*s*: in this case the contracted form is not equivalent to the uncontracted one and is often required by the metre, and thus the contracted spelling is generally restored by editors in the place of a transmitted uncontracted spelling (cf. II.3.2). As a general rule, metre can only be used to determine the number of syllables pronounced and their individual quantity in a line, but in this case it seems safe to assume that contraction of *est/es* (guaranteed by the metre) was also reflected in spelling, given the frequency of contracted spellings in manuscripts (cf. II.3.1), the clitic nature of contracted forms (cf. section 1.3), and the fact that a contracted pronunciation of an uncontracted spelling -*us est* would have implied multiple phonological steps for the reader to make (-*us est* > -*us st* > -*ust*).[81]

Third, an analysis of the manuscript tradition of comic playwrights shows that the contracted spellings were probably standard in the original texts. For instance, in the portion of Terence's text transmitted by the codex Bembinus (**A**), the oldest and most conservative exemplar, there are about thirty-five instances where contracted forms -*ust* (< -*ŭs* + *st*) and -*ist* (< -*ĭs* + *st*) are required by the metre but only eight of these forms are spelt contracted in **A**. This means that in about 77% of the cases the contracted form has been altered.[82] In the same portion of text, we find in the manuscript *c.*380 cases of contracted -*st* after -V or -V*m*. If one applies to the figure of 380 the same rate of alteration as exists for the alteration of the pattern -*ŭst* (77%), one would expect to find more than 1600 instances of the pattern -V + *est* and -V*m* + *est*. However, the number of instances of such a pattern in **A** is only *c.*750. Even if one assumes that contracted spellings after -V and -V*m* were less exposed to the process of alteration than -*ust* (< -*ŭs* + *est*), it is difficult to imagine that many cases of this pattern have not been altered in A as well. In confirmation of this, one may observe that there are several cases of contracted spellings transmitted in the medieval manuscript D that are found uncontracted in A (cf. Appendix 1.1).

This evidence supports the idea that a high number of uncontracted forms -V *est* and -V*m est* were originally spelt contracted in Terence; contracted forms were probably the standard spellings used by Terence and one may safely assume that they were also standard in Plautus and in other comic authors, on the basis of metrical evidence and of the frequency of contracted forms in manuscripts of these authors (cf. II.3.1.1, II.3.2, and II.3.3).

Contracted spellings are also attested in early inscriptions in verse (cf. II.3.4 and Table 2.13 with no. 101), thus confirming that the contracted spellings found in manuscripts were not introduced by (late) imperial scribes (who produced the oldest extant manuscripts of early authors) but were already common in early republican times. I would only question the spelling -V*mst* < -V*m est*, given its rarity in inscriptions (cf. II.3.4) and the high number of instances in Plautus' manuscripts of the spelling -*ust* (= -*umst*):[83] was -*ust* (= -*umst*) another acceptable spelling in Plautus, and was the nasal (*m* but sometimes *n*) introduced by imperial scribes?[84]

While contracted spellings were common in early poetry, they were probably avoided in early prose. No instance of contracted spelling is transmitted, either directly or indirectly, in manuscripts or fragments of early texts in prose (cf. II.3.1.1 and II.3.3 with Box 2.11), and metre obviously cannot be used as a criterion in prose texts. Moreover, contracted spellings are less common in early inscriptions in prose than in early inscriptions in verse.[85] This fact confirms that contracted spellings found in early inscriptions in verse are not abbreviations or misspellings (otherwise one would expect a more random distribution) and suggests that in early Latin they were associated with the poetic style.

---

[83] Cf. II.3.1.2.

[84] Fortson (2008: 135 n. 6) takes this view for granted, following Marouzeau (1908), but I do not think the evidence is conclusive; in Terence A (fourth or fifth century AD) the spelling -*umst* is standard, whereas -*ust* (= *um est*) is transmitted only three times (cf. II.3.1.2).

[85] Cf. II.3.4.1 with Table 2.13 and n. 101.

However, despite (or together with) their poetic character, some factors suggest that in early Latin contracted spellings were not purely artificial or high-style poetic forms but had also a 'colloquial' ring and an association with normal speech. First, although they are also found in epic and tragedy, contracted spellings are frequently attested in literary genres featuring low-register elements and imitation of low-class characters, such as the *palliatae* of Plautus and Terence, the *togatae* of Titinius, the satires of Lucilius, and also (in first-century BC literature) the *atellanae* of Novius and Pomponius.[86] Second, if one considers the pattern *-us + est/es*, there is a change in the use of contracted and uncontracted forms from Plautus to Terence: in the language of Plautus, apparently more open to lexical and mor- phological colloquialisms, contracted forms account for about 65% of the total,[87] while in Terence they account for only 34%.[88] Third, while in Plautus the proportion of contracted *-ust* versus uncontracted *-us est* is essentially the same in every type of metre,[89] in Terence contracted forms are slightly more common in ia[6] (the metre spoken in performance and the one that most closely resembles the rhythms of normal speech) than in tr[7] (a more poetic, high-style metre, performed in recitative).[90]

2.1.2 *Classical Latin (First Century BC to Second Century AD)*

It is more difficult to state whether contracted spellings were still used in classical Latin poetry, of the late Republic (first century BC) and the early Empire (first to second century AD).[91] Some direct

---

[86] Excluding Plautus and Terence (> 2000 instances), there are twenty-two instances of contracted forms with supporting evidence in republican comedy and satire vs. thirteen in tragedy and epic. See Box 2.2, 2.3, 2.10, and 2.11 for a detailed list of instances.

[87] According to Brinkmann (1906: 51–2) in Plautus there are *c.*570 contracted forms (*-u's/-ust*) against *c.*310 uncontracted (*-ŭs es/-ŭs est*). Among the contracted forms, there are *c.*200 cases already found contracted in spelling in manuscripts. Cf. II.3.1, IV.1.5.1 with Table 4.5 (only pattern *-ust*).

[88] Cf. IV.1.5.1 with Table 4.6. The likelihood that this difference in frequency is statistically significant is higher than 99.95%, as shown by the t-test.

[89] Cf. IV.1.5.1 with Table 4.5.

[90] Cf. IV.1.5.1 with Table 4.7. However, the likelihood that this difference in frequency is statistically significant is not extremely high (between 98% and 99%), as shown by the t-test.

[91] I use the term 'classical Latin' in a chronological rather than stylistic sense, to refer to the Latin spoken and written in the period between the first century BC and

contemporary evidence for this period apparently indicates a (gradual) decrease in their use; in late republican verse inscriptions contracted spellings are still frequent but they appear to be relatively rare
in imperial verse inscriptions.[92] There is also a fragment of papyrus
dating to the first century AD (PapHercul 817), preserving some
passages from a *Carmen de bello Actiaco*,[93] in which the only relevant case is spelt uncontracted (*incertum est*). Finally, contracted
spellings are hardly ever attested in the manuscripts of many late
republican and imperial poets (e.g. Catullus, Ovid, Tibullus, Propertius, Persius, Juvenal, Statius).

On the other hand, there is evidence suggesting that contracted
spellings had not disappeared from classical Latin poetry, of both the
late republican and early imperial period. It should first be pointed
out that almost all classical authors are entirely transmitted by medieval or even renaissance manuscripts,[94] which do not provide reliable
evidence for the spelling of *est/es*. As explained (see section 2.1.1 and
cf. II.3.3, Appendix 1.1), medieval scribes were not familiar with
contracted spellings and tended to alter them, to the point of deleting
any traces of them from the manuscripts.

Second, contracted spellings remain more common in imperial
inscriptions in verse (9%) than in prose (1%),[95] thus pointing to
a stylistic differentiation in their use also in the imperial period,
possibly influenced by imitation of contemporary poetry (especially

---

the second century AD, and not to the standardized form of Latin codified in
dictionaries and grammars (for this distinction cf. Clackson (2011a)).

[92] Cf. II.3.4.1 with n. 101 and Table 2.13.

[93] Found in Courtney's edition (1993: 334–40).

[94] Some notable exceptions are: twenty-five lines from Ovid *Ep.* 4 (from the fifth-
century AD codex Guelferbytanus 13.11.Aug. 4⁰) where the only relevant case (4.9.105
mea est) is spelt uncontracted; some fragments from Lucan (from books 5, 6, and 7, in
Pal. Vat. 24, IV/V c. AD, and Vind. 16, Neap. 4.A.8, V c. AD) in which most instances
(twelve out of thirteen) are spelt uncontracted (7.475 *inuecta est*, 490 *exact]a est*, 500
peruentum est, 501 *extremum est* in Pal. Vat. 24, 5.644 *unda est*, 6.407 *datum est*, 6.416
palam est, 6.561 *usu est* in Neap.4.A.8, 5.62 *donata est*, 5.64 *ereptum est*, 5.274 *parum
est*, 5.298 *relictum est* in Vind. 16) but, notably, one case is spelt contracted (5.644
secutast in Neap. 4.A.8); three fragments of late-antique manuscripts of Juvenal (Bob.,
Ambr., and Ant.) which contain respectively 14.324–15.43, 14.250–6, 268–91, 303–19,
and 7.149–98 in which there are only four relevant cases (14.254 *habendum est*, 14.276
hominum est, 14.281 *praetium est*, 14.304 *misera est*) all spelt uncontracted; a fragment
from Persius (Bobiense, VI c. AD) where the only relevant case is spelt uncontracted
(1.63 *populi sermo est*; note however that the precise reading of the manuscript is the
erroneous *populis sermo est*: could it cover up an original *populist sermo*?). For a survey
of the manuscript traditions of classical poets see Reynolds (1986).

[95] Cf. II.3.4.1.

128   *Contraction of* esse: *Phonology and History*

in the case of inscriptions in elegiac verse). Moreover, there are some cases in which an inscription displaying contracted spelling seems to imitate the poetry of a classical author, such as Ovid or Tibullus: e.g. CIL 6.20466 *Felicula hic misera* **consumptast** *morte puella* (cf. Tib. 1.3.55 *hic iacet inmiti consumptus morte Tibullus*)[96] or CIL 2–14.814 *indignor misera[m] non licuisse frui | dulces anplexus morientis et oscula data | nec tenuit moriens deficiente manu | in supero(s) it si qua* **uiast** *aditusque sepulcro* (cf. Tib. 1.1.60 *te teneam moriens deficiente manu*, and Ov. *Am.* 3.9.58 *me tenuit moriens deficiente manu*).[97] In imitating classical poetry, were the drafters of inscriptions perhaps recalling contractions that they had seen in the manuscripts of poetic texts?

Finally, contracted spellings are occasionally attested in some late republican and imperial poets, whose text is transmitted by late-antique or early medieval manuscripts. For instance, in Lucretius contracted spellings are well attested in the early medieval manuscripts Q and O (cf. II.3.1 p. 37). Moreover, an analysis of the manuscript tradition of Lucretius shows that the original number of contracted forms was probably higher. In the tradition of Lucretius, the two oldest manuscripts, O and Q, preserve a high number of contracted spellings. In *De rerum natura* the total number of cases of sequence -V + *est* and -V*m* + *est* (contracted or uncontracted) is *c.*420: 186 of these are spelt contracted both in Q and O, sixty-seven are spelt contracted only in Q, and twelve only in O. These figures show that contracted spellings were altered in both manuscripts independently and suggest that in the archetype of Q and O the number of contracted spellings was higher than the number of cases transmitted either in O or Q (*c.*265). Moreover, since the process of alteration had already started in late-antique manuscripts (cf. above pp. 124–5 and Appendix 1) it is probable that in the archetype of Q and O many cases of contracted forms had already been altered. Therefore contracted spellings were possibly the standard spellings for *est* after -V or -V*m* in Lucretius as well.

In manuscripts of Virgil the number of contracted forms transmitted is smaller than that in Lucretius but it is still significant in proportional terms. Forty-three contracted forms are found directly transmitted in manuscripts[98] and another six have been restored by

---

[96] On this example cf. Cugusi (2007: 44).
[97] On this example cf. Cugusi (2002: 2, 2007: 51 n. 269).   [98] Cf. Box 2.1 p. 38.

some editors relying on a good degree of textual evidence.[99] Since the
number of potentially contracted cases is 197, the proportion of
contracted spellings with supporting evidence in Virgil is about
25%. Cases of direct transmission of contracted spellings are mainly
found in late-antique manuscripts: twelve in **M**, eighteen in **P**, nine in
R, six in **V**, and one in **F** (forty-six cases, including instances found in
more than one manuscript).[100] Most instances are transmitted only
by one of these manuscripts; only in four cases is a contracted form
found in more than one late-antique manuscript (three cases in **MP**
and one case in **MR**). The total number of independent contracted
forms found in late-antique manuscripts is therefore forty-two,[101] to
which we must add a contracted spelling transmitted only by a
medieval manuscript (*Georg.* 2.222 *oleost γ*). Such a distribution is
improbable if all the original instances of contracted forms had been
transmitted as indicated by a statistical analysis of these data; this is
described below.

Considering only **MPR** and the portion of text transmitted in all
three manuscripts,[102] we have the following figures: twenty-one forms
found only in one of the three manuscripts (five in **M**, ten in **P**, and
six in **R**), four forms found in two of these manuscripts (three in **MP**
and one in **MR**) and another four spelt uncontracted in **MPR** but
transmitted contracted by other manuscripts (three by **V**, one by *γ*), for
an overall total of twenty-nine different contracted forms transmitted
in this portion of text. The scattered distribution of contracted forms
(only four cases transmitted by more than one manuscript) is such that
the number is unlikely to coincide with the original number of contracted forms in the archetype. A probabilistic calculation on these data
suggests that the original number of contracted spellings in the archetype would have been at least sixty-three (out of 143 potentially

---

[99] Virg. *Aen.* 3.629, 6.398, 9.508, 10.777, *Georg.* 4.402, 4.493. Cf. Box 2.11 pp. 62–4.

[100] Cf. Box 2.1 p. 38.

[101] I.e. forty-six cases in total, from which I subtract cases of the same instance
spelt contracted in more than one manuscript (four).

[102] I exclude therefore *Ecl.* 1–6.47, 3.72–4.51, 7.1–10.9, *Georg.* 1.323–2.215,
4.37–566, *Aen.* 1.1–276, 2.73–3.684, 4.116–5.36, 7.277–644, 10.460–508, 11.645–90,
11.737–92, 12.47–92, 12.651–86, 12.759–830, 12.939–52. For an overview of missing
portions of text in these manuscripts cf. Mynors (1972: p. V). Excluding these
portions of text, there are 143 instances of patterns -V + *est* and -V*m* + *est*, twenty-
nine of them spelt contracted in at least one manuscript. The manuscripts F and V
have been excluded as they are in a fragmentary state and most spellings cannot be
confirmed.

contracted instances in this portion of text).[103] However, it is possible that the number might have been higher, since the calculation takes into account only three manuscripts and only a reduced portion of text.

Contracted spellings are also found in the manuscript tradition of Grattius, who is a close imitator of Virgil;[104] apart from providing further evidence for the use of contracted spellings in classical Latin poetry, the case of Grattius suggests that the cases of contracted spellings found in Virgil's manuscripts are original, as also confirmed by the testimony of late-antique grammarians (cf. II.3.5.2 p. 81). Moreover, there are some isolated cases of contracted spellings, directly or indirectly transmitted, in the manuscripts of other late republican and early imperial authors, such as Horace and Lucan (cf. II.3.1.1 with Boxes 2.4 and 2.8), which may be construed as relics of an ancient orthographic stage.

In conclusion, evidence supports the view that contracted spellings were still used in classical poetry,[105] although it is probably impossible to determine to what extent and to give precise chronological indications. As far as the phonological context is concerned, contracted spellings were admitted only after -V and -Vm in classical poetry: already in Lucretius the pattern -Vs + *(e)st/(e)s* is hardly ever attested (cf. 2.2). This is possibly related to the reintroduction of final -s after short vowels in classical Latin (cf. V.1), the loss of which, as we have seen (cf. above 1.3), had probably been involved in the pattern -*ust* found in early Latin poetry. Consequently, contracted spellings after -V and -Vm transmitted in the manuscripts of classical authors (Virgil, Grattius, Lucan, Martial, etc.) or readings possibly resulting from misunderstanding of such contracted spellings (cf. especially the cases of omission of the verb in Horace, listed in Box 2.11) should be given full attention by editors.

Contracted spellings seem to be less frequent in classical prose texts: they are rare in late republican prose inscriptions and almost

---

[103] This number is the result of a calculation which assumes that all the instances of contracted spelling in Virgil are original and that the three manuscripts taken into account (**MPR**) are direct copies of the archetype. Both these assumptions are arbitrary, and therefore the number is simply meant to be indicative of the probability that some contracted forms have been lost in the process of transmission.

[104] Cf. II.3.1 pp. 47–9.

[105] On this view cf. Lachmann (1871: *ad* I.193), who, however, does not postulate contracted spelling in all syntactic contexts (on this cf. IV.1.6). Lachmann lists a series of instances from Ovid, Tibullus, Propertius, Martial, and Catullus which, according to him, should be printed contracted. His view was accepted by Müller (1894), but criticized by Baehrens (1879–1886: I.XII) and eventually dismissed by most editors.

completely absent from imperial prose inscriptions and from the oldest manuscripts of Latin prose writers,[106] with the notable (and somewhat puzzling) exception of Cicero's *Epistulae ad familiares* and *De oratore.* It seems safe to assume that contracted spellings were generally avoided in classical prose, but it is likely that they might have occasionally or exceptionally appeared in some registers; in these contexts they were presumably used as stylistic markers, even more so than they might have been in early Latin. Cicero might have used contracted spellings as markers of speech (cf. p. 37); in Gellius they seem to be used as archaisms (cf. pp. 40–2), and elsewhere (i.e. in imperial Latin poetry) they may be construed as poeticisms. However, it is difficult to discriminate between the three values ('colloquial', archaic, poetic) and it is not excluded that they overlapped to a certain extent (on this type of overlapping cf. I.3). At a certain point in classical Latin contracted spellings lost their connection with real speech and became purely artificial forms, but it is difficult to establish a *terminus ante quem*, as we will see in section 2.2 below.

2.1.3 *Late Latin (Third to Sixth Centuries* AD)

Contracted spellings fell out of use in late Latin,[107] and were presumably used only in exceptional cases as archaisms (as in the *Carmen de figuris*, cf. II.3.1 pp. 49–50). In late Latin poetry and even more patently in prose the standard spelling for *est* and *es* was uncontracted, including in cases after -V and -V*m*. This is suggested by several elements. First, contracted spellings are hardly ever found in late-antique inscriptions. Second, late-antique grammarians seem to refer to the phenomenon either as a practice of the past as or an innovation (cf. II.3.5.3 p. 84). Third, contracted spellings are absent

---

[106] For example, no instances are apparently found in the late-antique manuscripts of Livy: Verona 38 (early V c. AD), Paris Lat. 5731 (first-half V c. AD), Vat. Lat. 10696 (IV/V c. AD), Bamb. Class. 35ᵃ (V c. AD). This rarity contrasts with the number of contracted spellings found in the oldest manuscripts of Virgil, dating to about the same time (cf. p. 37 n. 36). Other late-antique manuscripts of Livy have either been lost (**Ta**, V c., destroyed in a fire), or are in a fragmentary state (Bodl. Lat. class. f.5, P. Oxy. 11.1379).

[107] For the term 'late Latin' (here used in a purely chronological sense) and its problems cf. Adams (2011).

from sources dating to late antiquity, such as the Latin literary papyri collected by Cavenaile (1958), all dated to the fourth or fifth centuries AD, and various other corpora of non-literary late Latin documents.[108] In these corpora *est* and *es* placed after -V or -V*m* are always spelt uncontracted.[109] Finally, the tradition of Latin authors shows that in late-antique manuscripts contracted spellings were exposed to alteration, both in prose and in poetry, thus suggesting that scribes were not acquainted with them. In manuscripts of Virgil contracted spellings are rarely found in more than one manuscript; in manuscripts of Plautus and Terence many contracted spellings transmitted in one branch of the tradition are spelt uncontracted in another.[110]

2.2 Speech

If it is difficult to assess the use of contracted forms in the evolution of Latin orthography, it seems even more complicated to trace a history of their use in speech. Some scholars, explicitly[111] or implicitly,[112]

---

[108] ChLA, TAlb, CEpLat, PItal, TVindol, OBuNjem (for the abbreviations see Reference List). All these corpora collect documents later than the third century AD.

[109] E.g. in the corpus of Cavenaile (1958) in all thirty-two instances of *est/es* the spelling is uncontracted: Cavenaile 5.38 *reuoluta est* (Virg. *Aen.* 4.691), 7.601 *ubique est* (Virg. *Aen.* 1.601), 7.604 *iustitiae est* (Virg. *Aen.*1.604), 8.141 [*iust*]*itiae est* (Virg. *Aen.* 5.605), 8.314–15 *fabricata est* (Virg. *Aen.* 2.46), 8.945 *effata es* (Virg. *Aen.* 4.456 : *effata codd. edd.*), 16.9.459 *ima es*[*t*] (Virg. *Aen.* 6.459), 16.13.737 *neces*[*s*]*e est* (Virg. *Aen.* 7.737), 17.8 *facta est* (Virg. *Aen.* 2.534), 17.37 *uia est* (Virg. *Aen.* 3.8), 23.34 [*o*]*diosa est* (Cic. *Div. Caec.* 36), 23.40 *parum es*[*t*] (Cic. *Div. Caec.* 36), 25.1 *ante* [*es*]*t*, 25.5 *audita ē* (Cic. *Cael.* 27), 25.33 *conuicium est* (Cic. *Cael.* 30), 25.75 *necesse es*[*t* (Cic. *Cael.* 35), 25.80 *qui est* (Cic. *Cael.* 36), 25.95 *reliqu*]*um est* (Cic. *Cael.* 37), 25.99 *ille est* (Cic. *Cael.* 38), 25.154 *pruden*[*tia e*]*s*[*t* (Cic. *Cael.* 45), 27.1 *coepisse est* (Cic. *Verr.* 2.1.60 : *confecisse est edd.*), 32.6 *facta est* (Sall. *Catil.* 6.2), 32.10 *orta est* (Sall. *Catil.* 6.4), 33.3 *data est* (fr. Liv. 37), 33.17 *datum e*[*s*]*t* (fr. Liv. 37), 33.125 *dimicatum* [*es*]*t* (fr. Liv. 37), 33.188 *uota est* (fr. Liv. 37), 39.12 *picta est* (fr. *Aesopica*), 41.15 *con*]*dita est* (fr. on *Seruius Tullius*), 45.a.9 *namque est* (literary fragment?), 45.b.10 *quae est* (literary fragment?), 54.6 *quae est* (fragment from the Bible). Moreover, all these instances are spelt uncontracted in manuscripts of Virgil, Cicero, and Livy. Not taking into account the prose authors (in whose manuscripts contraction is hardly ever attested), there are no cases of forms spelt contracted in manuscripts of Virgil which can be checked in the corpus of papyri.

[110] Cf. 2.1.1.

[111] Cf. Lachmann (1871: *ad* 1.993), Baehrens (1879–1886: I.xii–xiii), Müller (1894: 301–4), Trappes-Lomax (2007: 107).

[112] Cf. e.g. Heyworth (2007b) who uses the word 'prodelision' every time he refers to an 'elision' involving *est/es* (cf. pp. 258, 340).

have claimed that *est/es* were always pronounced contracted when placed after a word ending in -V or -V*m*, regardless of the spelling. Following this idea, some editors have systematically printed contracted spellings in such conditions, even when there are no transmitted cases in the manuscripts of the author.[113] Apart from the doubtful legitimacy of introducing systematically a phonetic spelling, the alleged persistence of the contraction of *est/es* in speech, from early to late Latin, has not been supported by any kind of demonstration.

An orthographic survey of contracted spellings (section 2.1) has shown that they are almost exclusively attested in poetic texts, as represented either in manuscripts or in inscriptions, and therefore it seems justifiable to consider them as 'poetic spellings', which do not necessarily reflect a phonological phenomenon common in normal speech at the time of the author using them.

On the other hand, it is likely that these poetic spellings did derive from a phonological phenomenon which was common in speech at least at a certain stage in the history of Latin. Poets did not normally invent new phonetic phenomena but adopted the phenomena of normal speech to fit their poetic needs.[114] Moreover, a phonological analysis (cf. section 1.3) has shown that contraction of clitic *est/es* is indeed a phonological phenomenon of the Latin language more broadly, with parallels in other Italic languages (cf. II.3.6).

It is certain, however, that at some stage of Latin contracted forms were no longer used in spoken language, and therefore they presumably sounded very artificial if found in a literary text.[115] This is evident from a number of facts. First, as observed,[116] medieval scribes were not familiar with contracted spellings. Second, some medieval and later Latin writers were not aware of contraction. The earliest evidence that I have found is Bede, who at the beginning of the eighth century AD prescribes elision even before *est*: GL 6.247.1ff. *'arta uia est uerae quae ducit ad atria uitae' scanditur enim ita, 'artaui'*

---

[113] Cf. Wunder in his edition of Cicero's *Pro Plancio* (1830), Ehwald in his edition of Ovid's works (1888), and, recently, Goold in his editions of Catullus (1989) and Propertius (1999).

[114] On this issue cf. Coleman (1999: in particular pp. 40–1).

[115] For the preservation in Latin poetry of pronunciations obsolete in current speech see Coleman (1999: in particular pp. 33–5).

[116] Cf. 2.1.1. II.3.3, and Appendix 1.

dactylus, 'estue' spondeus intercepta 'a' syllaba per synalipham.[117]
Three centuries later Marbod of Rennes wrote a Leonine verse
(*Anal. Hymn.* 50, 300.39 *si sterilis grauis est, si uirgo puerpera uisa
est*) in which the rhyme requires an elided (*grauis est // uisest*) and
not a contracted (*uisast*) scansion. These are only a few of several
instances which show that in medieval poetry contracted forms were
no longer known and had presumably disappeared from spoken
language,[118] as also indicated by the fact that *est/es* eventually came,
in Romance languages, to be pronounced /e/ (cf. e.g. Fr. *tu es, il est*).

Is it possible to establish more exactly the chronological boundaries
of the period in which contracted forms were, if not standard, at least
common in normal speech? It seems easier to fix a *terminus post
quem* for the disappearance of the phenomenon in speech, namely
the second century BC. As pointed out (2.1.1), it is likely that in
Plautus and Terence contracted spellings had a 'colloquial' ring and
thus that contracted forms were current in the spoken language.[119]
The evidence of inscriptions seems to confirm this view, since, as
we have seen, contracted forms are proportionally more common
in republican inscriptions (the earliest instance dating to *c.*169 BC)
than in later inscriptions, thus possibly suggesting that they had a
different status in speech in republican Latin. Moreover, contracted
spellings are less frequent in republican high-style texts (in both literary
texts and inscriptions), where colloquialisms were probably avoided.[120]

We can try to take a further chronological step and consider the
case of Cicero and Lucretius (cf. above 2.1.2, II.3.1.1). Although
contracted spellings are rare in most of Cicero's manuscripts (including
some dating to late antiquity), they are surprisingly common in a
few early medieval manuscripts of *Epistulae ad familiares* and *De
oratore* (cf. II.3.1.1 pp. 42–7). Since both texts imitate speech to a
certain degree, one may infer that contracted spellings were used as
markers of speech, thus implying that they were still current in (some
varieties of) speech in late republican times.

---

[117] (= 119 K.) "*arta uia est uerae quae ducit ad atria uitae.*" The scansion is the
following: *artaui* dactyl, *estue* spondee, with the last syllable *-a* [of *uia*] cut by
synaloepha [= *elision*].'

[118] For a complete list see Leonhardt (1988), who exhaustively presents evidence in
support of the idea that in the Middle Ages contracted forms were no longer used in
spoken Latin. For an (artificial) use of contracted forms in neo-Latin poetry see
Harsting (2000: 316).

[119] Cf. section 2.1.1.

[120] On this issue cf. also Kruschwitz (2004: 75–6) and see II.3.4.1.

The use of contracted spellings in Lucretius is extensive. However, it is difficult to determine the stylistic value of contracted forms in Lucretius and therefore whether they still reflected a phenomenon of speech or not. On the one hand, one has the impression that Lucretius uses contracted forms artificially: 50% of such forms are found at the end of the line,[121] which is a place where poets normally put archaic forms.[122] Excluding the possibility that we are dealing with mere abbreviations (cf. above 1.1), the frequency of contractions at the end of the line may be taken to imply that they were used by Lucretius as archaic poeticisms, without any relation to speech. This seems to be the case for the type -V*st* (= -V*s* + *est*), which in Lucretius' manuscripts is attested only in the form *necessust* (2.710, 2.725, 4.1006, 5.351 in Q, 6.206 in O *ut uidetur*), which is found at the end of the line in all cases. The form *necessus* (= CL *necessum*) is archaic and appears elsewhere in the *Senatus Consultum de Bacchanalibus* (CIL 1².581) and in Gellius (5.19.16, 16.8.1, the former being a quotation from an oration of Scipio the younger), suggesting that Lucretius used it as an intentional archaism. Its connection with -*st* might indicate that contraction of *est* had also an archaic flavour in Lucretius (at least when attached to a word ending in -*s*).[123] In fact, contraction after -V*s* (e.g. -*ust*) is mainly attested in writing in republican sources[124] and it is likely that, as a phonological phenomenon, it was going to disappear (or had already disappeared) from speech in the first century BC. Consequently, one may assume that such a contracted spelling (-*ust*) was artificial at the time of Lucretius. On the other hand, if all contracted spellings (e.g. -*umst*, -*ast*, etc.) were regarded as representing the same degree of poetic artificiality, one would expect them to be used with equivalent frequency, which is

---

[121] Cf. II.3.1.1 p. 37.

[122] On the use by Lucretius of archaisms at the end of the line see Bailey (1947: 75-6). On the frequency of archaic or unusual forms at the end of the line in Latin comedy cf. also de Melo (2007a: 226), Questa (2007: 31 [on *face*], 50 [on *antidhac*], 51 [on *nihil* dysillabic], 53 [on *dextera* and *sinistera*], 80 [on the perfect ending -*ĕrunt*)], 183-4 [on *fieri*], 287 [on *sies, siet, sient, fuas*]).

[123] On the form *necessus* cf. p. 37 and see also Trappes-Lomax (2007: 8). On the use of phonological and morphological archaisms by Lucretius, see Bailey (1947: I.72-87, especially 75-6). Cf. also Coleman (1999: especially 44), de Melo (2007a: 226).

[124] Cf. II.2. However, the form -*ust* is still found in Pomponius 3 R. *miseriust*, Novius 115 R. *adductust*, and in a few imperial inscriptions (cf. in particular the form (*a*)*rsust* found in the Pompeian inscription CIL 4.10014; cf. Table 2.10 and II.3.4.1).

not the case (cf. II.3.1.1 p. 37): contractions after -V and -V*m* appear to have been more acceptable in Lucretius' time, possibly because the time of their use in speech was more recent. In conclusion, contracted spellings presumably had a poetic flavour in Lucretius, but it seems impossible to determine whether one should construe all of them as 'archaic' poeticisms (i.e. merely inherited from previous poets) or 'colloquial' poeticisms (i.e. influenced by the pronunciation of such forms in speech).[125]

In authors later than Cicero and Lucretius contracted spellings are more rarely found, and it becomes even more difficult to determine whether they retained a colloquial flavour, i.e. whether they were still reflecting a phenomenon of speech; a good number of contracted forms are found in Virgil, but these might be construed as mere poeticisms inherited from previous poets, possibly Lucretius himself. The poetic flavour of contracted spellings seems clear in Grattius, whose poetic language is strictly modelled on that of Virgil.[126] In later authors contracted spellings are hardly ever transmitted in manuscripts; even if one accepts the implication that they were not used by these authors, this still makes it difficult to argue about the reasons why they were not used and their possible stylistic value.

On the other hand, there are some pieces of evidence which support the view that contracted forms had not completely disappeared from real speech in imperial Latin. First, in imperial poetry the metrical treatment of *est* and *es* after -V and -V*m* is different from that of other monosyllables, thus pointing to a special phonological treatment of these forms in such conditions (cf. II.3.7); for instance, in Virgil (in whose manuscripts contracted spellings are attested) *est* and *es* are the only monosyllabic forms admitted at the end of the hexameter even when they are preceded by an elidible syllable. *Est* and *es* display similar metrical features in the corpus of other imperial poets, such as Ovid and Propertius, although they are hardly ever spelt contracted in the manuscripts of these authors. This distinct metrical treatment of *est/es* in imperial Latin poetry (whether displayed in the spelling or not) may be taken to imply that contraction had some sort of existence in imperial Latin. Moreover, there is at least one instance in imperial Latin poetry in which the contracted form *'s* is mandatory since the uncontracted *es* does not fit the metre

---

[125] For this distinction cf. Coleman (1999: 33–5).
[126] Cf. 2.1.2 and II.3.1.

(*Anth. Lat.* 462.28 *telo's*; cf. II.3.8.2).[127] However, the scansion *telō's* does not necessarily reflect the standard pronunciation of an uncontracted spelling *(telo) es* in classical Latin, but may simply be the prosody of a contracted spelling *telo's*, which might be a mere poetic mannerism (like the contraction *'tis* in English poetry). Therefore, while metrical evidence from imperial poetry might be added to the evidence for contracted spellings (listed in section 2.1.2), it would not necessarily justify a suggestion that contraction was standard in imperial Latin speech.

Second, there is the testimony of some grammarians. In the second century AD Velius Longus seems to quote a contracted spelling as an example of phonetic spelling (II.3.5.3). Moreover, in the fourth century AD, Marius Victorinus mentions spellings such as *audiendust*, *scribendust*, and *mutandust* and seems to consider them as phonetic spellings, although this evidence is not conclusive, as we have seen (cf. II.3.5.1). Finally, the grammarian Consentius (fifth century AD) still recommends a scansion with the contracted form (cf. II.3.5.2).

Third, there are some pieces of evidence from inscriptions which might back up the idea that contracted forms had not completely disappeared from speech: the number of cases of contracted spelling in imperial inscriptions is higher than the number of cases of elided spelling (cf. II.3.4.1 pp. 69–70); there are cases of contracted spelling in imperial inscriptions in prose which may be construed as phonetic spellings (cf. II.3.4.2). The confusion over the pattern -V*m est*, occasionally spelt -V*st* or -*nst* in manuscripts and inscriptions, seems to suggest the influence of pronunciation (cf. II.3.1.2, II.3.4.1 p. 70). Finally, there are cases of contracted spellings in non-poetic imperial sources, which might possibly be considered as misspellings influenced by pronunciation.[128]

If one takes as true the hypothesis that contracted forms persisted in imperial Latin speech, we are led to wonder whether the contracted pronunciation /factast/ was the only one used for the sequence *facta est*, or whether the elided version /factest/ was also used.[129]

---

[127] On this see 2.1.2 and II.3.7. Cf. also Soubiran (1966: 160).

[128] Eight instances of direct transmission in Seneca, one in Apuleius (*Apol.* 50), one in Celsus (2.15.4), one in Frontinus (*Aq.* 109), twenty in Quintilian (*Inst.* 9.4.140), plus other cases of indirect transmission (cf. II.3.1.1 and II.3.3).

[129] As seen, (II.3.4.1 with Table 2.12) there are some instances of elided spelling in inscriptions; cf. in particular the forms *fixest*, *depostest*, *sepultest*.

Certainly, if a poet wrote *factast*, both he and his readers would read it and pronounce it *factast*, but, as seen, a spelling *factast* might simply be an archaic and/or poetic mannerism. There is no solution to this problem. However, it is worthwhile to remark that the two phenomena (elision and contraction) have different origins and different phonological features. Contraction of *est/es* is not a sandhi phenomenon and involves the total loss of the vowel from the verb *est*, which is univerbated with the preceding word in spelling.[130] On the other hand, elision is a sandhi phenomenon that rarely shows up in spelling and most likely does not involve the loss of any vowel, but rather a blurring of the vowels in contact.[131] If one assumes that in imperial Latin the two phenomena were confused, this would imply that contraction, as a specific phenomenon connected to the cliticization of *esse*, had already started to disappear from speech and that the initial *e-* of *est* was regaining the strong phonological status that it eventually came to have in Romance languages (cf. Fr. *est*, It. *é*). This view is not implausible, especially because none of the pieces of evidence listed above is sufficient in itself to prove beyond doubt that *est* and *es* were always pronounced contracted in speech in imperial Latin. On the other hand, neither is there strong evidence for the view that contracted forms had completely disappeared from (early) imperial Latin speech.

3. FINAL REMARKS

The evidence collected in chapter II suggests that contracted spellings were the graphic reflection of a phonological phenomenon of Latin speech, namely the cliticization and contraction of *est* and *es*, and not a phonetic spelling reflecting a sandhi phenomenon somehow related to elision. Contracted spellings were common in early Latin but they were probably stylistically marked as 'poetic colloquialisms'; they were common in poetic texts (both literature and inscriptions) but they were generally avoided in prose. Contracted spellings were also used by (some) classical authors, of both the late republican period (e.g. Lucretius, Cicero, Virgil) and (less extensively) the (early) Empire (e.g. Grattius and Gellius); it is also plausible that other authors

---

[130] Cf. 1.2 and 1.3.   [131] Cf. 1.2.

(e.g. Catullus, Ovid, Horace and perhaps also Lucan, Martial, Statius, etc.) made (extensive) use of them and that the traces were deleted by late-antique and medieval scribes. In late republican Latin (first century BC) contracted spellings were stylistically marked, although the frequency in inscriptions and the case of Cicero, who seems to use them as markers of speech, may suggest that they still reflected a phenomenon of speech; in imperial Latin, and especially by the time of Gellius, contracted spellings were probably artificial forms, construable as poeticisms and/or archaisms, but there is the possibility that contraction as a phonological phenomenon had not completely disappeared from spoken language, at least until the first century AD (cf. 2.1.2, 2.2 and II.3.1.1). In late antiquity (third to sixth centuries AD) contracted spellings went out of use and started to be altered in manuscripts; similarly, contraction as a phonological phenomenon of speech disappeared from the language, and at the beginning of the Middle Ages it was no longer understood. Although it is probably impossible to establish a precise chronology, one may note that by the second century AD the grammarian Velius Longus seems implicitly to consider contraction and contracted spellings as somehow unfamiliar phenomena (cf. II.3.5.3).

There is a final question to be addressed: given that, as pointed out (cf. especially sections 1.3, II.3.2), contracted forms may alternate with uncontracted forms in the same text, what are the factors (e.g. semantic, syntactic, pragmatic, stylistic, etc.) that influence or regulate the alternation between contracted and uncontracted forms? I will address this question in the next chapter by analysing the evidence for contraction of *est/es* in Terence, and in so doing I will determine some linguistic patterns that might be relevant to the variation between contracted and uncontracted forms. Since it seems clear that contracted forms are the result of a process of clitic reduction, linguistic observations on the behaviour of contracted forms in early Latin poetry might also contribute to a better understanding of the behaviour and the syntactic status of clitics in Latin and of the nature of the verb *esse*.

IV

Analysis of Contracted Forms
in Terence

non opus est dicto . . . at scito huic opust

Ter. *Ph.* 1003

The aim of this chapter is to investigate the reasons for the variation between uncontracted (e.g. *factus est, facta est, factum est*) and contracted forms (e.g. *factust, factast, factumst*) in Terence. In the first section (1) I will limit my analysis to the pattern -*ŭs* + *(e)st/(e)s*, for which one can rely on the metrical evidence to determine the type of form (cf. II.3.2). In the following section (2) I will take into account the other two patterns (-V + *(e)st/(e)s* and -V*m* + *(e)st/(e)s*), undertaking a statistical analysis of the rate of transmission of contracted spellings in the manuscript tradition of Terence. I will conclude the chapter with an overview of the limits on the situations in which contraction is a possibility (3), followed by some final remarks (4).

1. THE PATTERN -*ŬS* + *(E)ST/(E)S*

As I have mentioned in previous chapters (cf. in particular II.3.1.1, II.3.2, III.1.3), textual and metrical evidence shows that contracted forms may alternate with uncontracted forms within the same text, and especially in the comedies of Plautus and Terence. Are there reasons for this alternation? Is it regulated by semantic factors (related to the meaning of the verb), syntax (involving the relation of the verb to other elements of the sentence, and in particular to the host word), word order (concerning the position of the verb in the clause), pragmatic factors (depending on the emphasis given to the verb and/or the host word in the context), stylistic factors, or simply metrical factors?[1]

In the following section I will analyse the alternation between contracted and uncontracted forms for the pattern *-ŭs + (e)st/(e)s*. A contracted form of the type *-ust* is not metrically equivalent to the uncontracted form *-us est*,[2] and therefore in certain cases only one of them is admitted by the metre (regardless of its spelling in the manuscripts). I will exclude forms of the type *-ĭs + (e)st/(e)s* and *-ĕs + (e)st*, because of their particular phonological features and limited occurrence.[3]

1.1 'Minimal Pairs'

A starting point might be to analyse the passages in which one finds the same expression repeated twice in a short sequence, one case with the contracted form and the other with the uncontracted form. I have found in Terence at least two good examples, both confirmed by the metre:

An. 953–5
PAMPHILUS. recte admones. Dauo ego istuc dedam iam negoti.
                                                SIMO. non potest
PAM. qui? SI. quia habet aliud magis ex sese et maius. PAM. quidnam?
                                                SI. **uinctus est.**
PAM. pater, non recte **uinctust.**

PAM. That's good advice. Now I'll put Davus in charge of these things. SIM. He can't.
PAM. Why? SIM. He's got something greater and more important on his hands. PAM. What is it? SI. **He has been tied up.** PA. Father, it's not right that **he's been tied up.**

Ph. 1002–3
NAUSISTRATA. mi uir, non mihi narras? CHREMES at . . . NAU.
                                                quid 'at'?
CH. non **opus est** dicto. PHORMIO tibi quidem; at scito huic **opust.**

NAU. Aren't you going to tell me, my dear? CH. But . . . NAU. How do you mean, 'But'?

---

[1] On these factors and the related methodological problems cf. I.3.
[2] Cf. II.3.2.   [3] Cf. III.1.4

CH. **There is no need** for me to tell you. PH. Not for *you*, indeed; but **there's need** for *her* to know it.

The explanation of the forms *est/-st* in these passages is not self-evident; there is more than one way to explain the alternation of contracted and uncontracted forms.

First, in both passages the uncontracted form (*uinctus est, opus est*) is used by a *senex* (Simo in the *Andria* and Chremes in the *Phormio*), a character type allegedly using many old-fashioned and long-winded expressions (cf. 1.5.2), whereas the contracted form is used by a different character (the young Pamphilus in the former case, the parasite Phormio in the latter). Following a popular (although not always convincing) approach,[4] one might argue for linguistic characterization; in Terence uncontracted forms would have an old-fashioned flavour and would characterize the speech of old people (in the ageist perspective allegedly at work in comedy),[5] whereas contracted forms would be the forms of normal speech and would be used by more dashing, younger characters.

Second, in both cases the contracted form is placed at the end of the clause (*'pater, non recte uinctust'*, *'at scito huic opust'*), whereas the uncontracted form is either not at the end of the clause (*non opus est dicto*) or constitutes the only element of the sentence together with the preceding participle (*uinctus est*): this may be taken to imply that contraction was avoided when the form was not placed at the end of a complex clause, possibly under the influence of some syntactic or pragmatic factor, to be investigated.

Third, in both cases the uncontracted form seems to be used when the emphasis of the clause is on the expression with *est*, whereas the contracted form is used when the emphasis is on another part of the clause. In the passage from the *Andria*, the verb *uinctus est* (with the uncontracted form) conveys a new piece of information. It sounds like a revelation and it is emphatic in its context: 'PAM. What is it? SIM. He has been TIED UP.' In the second utterance, the emphasis is

---

[4] See in particular Adams (1984) on the characterization of the speech of women; Fantham (1972: 75–6) and Maltby (1985: 118–23) on the use of Greek words in the speech of lower character types; Maltby (1979) and Karakasis (2005: 62–82) on the linguistic characterization of old men; Arnott (1970: 53–6), Katsouris (1975: 132–4), Martin (1995), Barsby (1999: 26), and Karakasis (2005: 101–20) on the characterization of individual characters. Cf. also Petersmann (2002–2003: 99–100), Clackson (2011c).

[5] For the alleged *makrologia* of *senes* in Terence cf. Karakasis (2005: 62–82) and Clackson (2011c).

instead on the adverbial phrase (*non recte*): 'it's NOT RIGHT that he's been tied up.' The verb with the contracted form (*uinctust*) is redundant and might be left out without any loss of information. In Barsby's translation (2001) it is omitted: 'PAM. What is it? SIM. He's tied up. PAM. Father, that's not proper.' Similarly, in the passage from the *Phormio*, the first, uncontracted, *opus est* is in an emphatic position since it represents a riposte to the inquisitiveness of Nausistrata ('NAU. How do you mean, "But"?' 'CH. There is NO NEED for me to tell you'). On the other hand, in the second utterance, the contracted *opust* is redundant and might also be omitted, since the focus on the sentence is on the personal pronouns ('Not for YOU, indeed; but there's need for HER to know it').

Finally, the choice between a contracted or an uncontracted form might simply depend on their different prosody (*-st*/-'*s* being asyllabic, *est*/*es* being a heavy syllable) and thus on metrical factors. At *An.* 954 the expression with the contracted form (*uinctust* ¯ ¯) is not metrically acceptable at the end of an ia^8 (which requires the scansion ˘ ¯) and therefore the uncontracted form (*uinctus est* ¯ ˘ ¯) is mandatory. Likewise, in *Ph.* 1003 (an ia^6) the second *opus* + *est* expression cannot be uncontracted (*huic opus est* ¯ ˘ ˘ ¯) since it would break the metre (which in such a position requires an iambic sequence, *huic opust* ¯ ˘ ¯). If these observations do not prove that the metre is the only factor responsible for the alternation between contracted and uncontracted forms in the two passages, they certainly show that it might be, thus reducing the persuasiveness of the other explanations.

The variety of the arguments outlined above shows that an analysis of minimal pairs does not allow us to draw firm conclusions about the factors responsible for the alternation of contracted and uncontracted forms. Nevertheless, it has suggested some hypotheses which I will try to verify over the course of the chapter, with the support of a statistical examination of all instances of contracted and uncontracted *-ŭs* + *(e)st/(e)s* in Terence.

1.2 The Evidence

Table 4.1 shows the figures for the occurrence of contracted and uncontracted forms in Terence for the patterns *-ŭs* + *(e)s* and + *-ŭs* + *(e)st*.

Only ten instances of the contracted form are spelt contracted in manuscripts, eight in **A** and two in **D**. Interestingly, six of

Table 4.1. Frequency of contracted and uncontracted -*ŭs* + *(e)st/(e)s* in Terence

	Contracted		Uncontracted	Uncertain
	64		122	16
TOTAL		186		

these instances belong to the fixed expression *opus est*. For all the other instances, the manuscripts have a different reading, mainly with the uncontracted spelling or with omission of the verb (cf. e.g. *Ph.* 833 *facturus* AP^ac : *est facturus* D : *facturus est* **cett.** : *facturust* **edd.**). Most contracted forms have been restored by editors, generally on the basis of the fact either that the reading transmitted by manuscripts seem to result from a misunderstanding of an original contracted spelling, that the sentence is defective without the verb *est/es*, or that the manuscripts transmit an uncontracted spelling that is metrically unacceptable (cf. II.3.2, II.3.3, II.3.8.1, and II.3.8.2). However, since the scansion of comic metre is not always unambiguous, the proportion of contracted and uncontracted forms varies among different editions. In my analysis I have considered all cases in which the scansion of the line is sufficiently plain that the form of the verb is printed in the same way (contracted or uncontracted) by most editors of Terence; instances found in lines with major corruptions or with metrical ambiguities have been excluded (sixteen, in the top right column of Table 4.1). Nevertheless, these instances will be mentioned in case they might provide evidence against the results which will emerge in the course of the analysis.

The following analysis is therefore based on a corpus of 186 instances of the pattern -*ŭs* + *(e)st/(e)s*, sixty-four contracted and 122 uncontracted.

1.3 Metre

As has been speculated in section 1.1, the alternation between contracted and uncontracted forms may be influenced by metrical factors. The very fact that most contracted forms have been restored by editors relying on metre shows that prosodic convenience is an important factor to be taken into account. However, this does not necessarily mean that the preference for a contracted or uncontracted form in a particular passage depends *only* or *primarily* on metrical convenience. Some other factors might determine or influence which form (contracted or uncontracted) was considered more suitable in a particular context, independent of the poet's arrangement of the line into its metrical form.

However, there is one place in the line where metrical considerations are most likely to be a key factor; the second last element in the line, which has a fixed quantity in all comic metres (light in ia⁶, tr⁷, ia⁸, heavy or pyrrhic in ia⁷). When the verb *est* is found in this position, the choice between the contracted and uncontracted form may depend on the prosodic quantity of the word ending *-ŭs* that precedes *est/es*. In particular, at the end of an ia⁶, tr⁷, or ia⁸ (in which the penultimate element must be light):⁶

A- if the word ending in *-ŭs* is a trochee (¯ ˘) or has a trochaic ending (as almost all participles), the verb form must be uncontracted (*est/es*);⁷

B- if the word ending in *-ŭs* is a dactyl (¯ ˘ ˘) or has a dactylic ending, the verb form must be contracted (*-st/- 's*);⁸

C- if the word ending in *-ŭs* is a pyrrhic (˘ ˘), the verb form must be contracted (*-st/-'s*) except if it is preceded by a light monosyllable (in this case either form is acceptable);⁹

D- if the word ending in *-ŭs* is a tribrach (˘ ˘ ˘) or has a tribrach ending, the verb form must be uncontracted (*est/es*) except in

---

⁶ For these abbreviations and the metrical terminology used in this section see V.2.
⁷ The contracted form would result in a spondaic ending (¯ V*st*/V's = ¯ ¯), which is not admissible at the end of the line. Cf. e.g. *laudātŭs* + *est*: *laudātŭs est* (¯ ˘ ˘) fits the iambic ending of an ia⁶ (or tr⁷, ia⁸), while *laudātust* (¯ ¯) does not.
⁸ The choriambic ending with the uncontracted form (¯ ˘˘ *est/es*) is not admissible at the end of the line. Cf. e.g. *rēctĭŭs* + *est*: *rēctĭŭst* (¯ ˘ ¯) fits the line ending whereas *rēctĭŭs est* (¯ ˘ ˘ ¯) does not.
⁹ An anapaestic ending (˘ ˘ *est/es*) might be admissible at the end of the line, but only if the first light syllable of the anapaest is the second syllable of the preceding heavy resolved element (for this terminology cf. V.2). In this case the second light syllable of the anapaest would come to occupy the penultimate element of the line (i.e. ˘˘ | ˘ | ¯, cf. e.g. in an ia⁶: ˘˘10 ˘ 11 ¯ 12). However, the law of Ritschl (cf. V.4.2.1 and Questa (2007: 207–13)) does not allow a disyllabic element (in our case the tenth in ia⁶) to be formed from a word beginning before the element and ending inside it. This would be the case if the line ended with a pyrrhic word + uncontracted *est/es* (˘ || ˘ | ˘ *est/es*), except if the pyrrhic word was preceded by a light monosyllable (or a disyllable become monosyllable after elision). Compare e.g. Ter. *Ph.* 75 (ia⁶) *quid uerbis ŏpust?* with *Hec.* 865 (ia⁸) *nĕqu(e) ŏpŭs est*. On the linguistic implications of this apparent exception cf. Fortson (2008: 7).

Table 4.2. Instances of *-ŭs* + *(e)st/(e)s* determined by metrical factors

	Contracted (*-ust*)	Uncontracted (*-us est*)
	Category B, C, E	Category A, D
Auxiliary	2	17
Copula	5	20
Other	3	2
TOTAL	10	39

the case that the tribrach is preceded by a light monosyllable or by a light syllable belonging to the same word (in this case either form is acceptable).[10]

At the end of an ia[7]:

E- if the word ending in *-ŭs* is a trochee ($^-$ $^\smile$) or has a trochaic ending, the form of the verb must be contracted (*-st,-'s*);[11]

F- if the word ending in *-ŭs* is a pyrrhic ($^\smile$ $^\smile$) or has a pyrrhic ending, both forms are generally acceptable.[12]

Forty-nine instances of *-ŭs* + *(e)st/(e)s* conform to one of these patterns, in which the form of the verb may be strictly determined by the metre. Table 4.2 shows the figures.

In theory, one should also take into account the instances placed in the second last element of the half-verse, in an ia[7] or an ia[8] with medial caesura,[13] a place that shares the metrical features of the second last position of the verse (i.e. it must be light). However, there are no such cases in Terence.

1.4 Semantics

A second level of enquiry involves semantics: is the meaning of the verb responsible for the alternation between contracted and uncontracted forms? Are contracted forms equally attested according to the

---

[10] The metrical conditions are analogous to those discussed in n. 9 ($^{\smile\smile}$*est/es* = $^{\smile\smile}$ -V*st*).

[11] The cretic ending with the uncontracted form ($^-$ $^\smile$ *est/es*) is not admissible at the end of an ia[7]; cf. e.g. *laudātŭs* + *est: laudātust* ($^-$ $^-$) fits the spondaic ending of an ia[7], while *laudātŭs est* (= $^-$ $^\smile$ $^-$) does not.

[12] Both the anapaestic ($^{\smile\smile}$ *est/es*) and the iambic ($^\smile$ -V*st/-'s*) ending (this latter necessarily preceded by a light syllable) are acceptable at the end of an ia[7].

[13] Cf.V.2 p. 207 and Questa (2007: 341–2 and 348–9).

different functions of the verb, namely auxiliary, copula, locational, existential, or forming an idiomatic expression with *opus*?

Before continuing with this investigation, however, it is necessary to clarify the meaning of these terms, as used in the following analysis. By 'auxiliary function' I refer to senses 20 and 21 in the Oxford Latin Dictionary (OLD) *s.v. sum*, that is to cases of the verb *esse* used with a participle, past (e.g. *An.* 527 *pollicitust*, 954 *uinctus est*) or future (e.g. *Ph.* 833 *facturust*, 835 *acturus est*), or with a gerundive (e.g. *Eun.* 188 *gerundust*, *An.* 167 *expurgandus est*). By 'copula use' I refer to senses 12–19 in the OLD, i.e. to cases in which the verb links the subject (expressed or implied) with a predicate noun (e.g. *Ph.* 295 *tu seruo's*), pronoun (e.g. *Eun.* 974 *ille . . . ipsus est*) or adjective (e.g. *Haut.* 515 *seruos tardiusculust*), or with an adverb (e.g. *Ad.* 639 *melius est*), or another element filling the role of a predicate noun or adjective, such as a complement (e.g. *Hec.* 343 <u>odio ipsus est</u>) or a clause (e.g. *Eun.* 940 <u>nosse omnia haec salus est adulescentulis</u>). By 'locational use' I refer to sense 11 in the OLD, i.e. to instances of the verb used with a locative complement (e.g. *Eun.* 816 *animus est in patinis*), except when the verb may be translated as 'there is' (e.g. *Ph.* 332 *quia enim in illis fructus est*, to be construed as 'because **there is** profit in them,' not as 'the profit is in them'). By 'existential use' I refer to senses 1–10 in the OLD, i.e. to cases in which the verb does not link the subject with another element of the clause, but itself forms a complete predicate, expressing existence or an analogous notion, and thus may generally be translated in English as *there is* (e.g. *Haut.* 187 *atque etiam nunc tempus est* ['And there's still time' (Barsby), 'Actually, there's still time now!' (Brown); for other cases see below Box 4.1]).[14] Finally, I will consider separately the fixed expression *opus est*, which seems to be a special case (see section 1.7).

This is not the first attempt at explaining the alternation of contracted and uncontracted forms on a semantic basis. Soubiran (1966: 165) analysed the use of *est* and *es* in Virgil and claimed that the

[14] McGlynn (1963–1967 s.v. *sum* I.5) and Fortson (2008: 143 n. 25) consider the locational as a sub-sense of the existential use, whereas the OLD (*sum* 11) considers it as a sub-sense of the copula use (B). Soubiran (1966: 166–72) makes further over-subtle distinctions (between strong and weak existential, strong and weak locational). In the following analysis I have considered the locational sense as a category distinct from both the existential and the copula use, in order to give more precise figures. For the idea that there was no distinction between the existential and the copula function, cf. VI.5.

phonological reduction of these forms is connected to their seman-tics; if the verb is auxiliary or copula (i.e. if it is 'grammatically weak', in Soubiran's terminology) it is exposed to phonetic reduction, whereas if it is existential (i.e. if it is 'grammatically strong') it is not.[15]

However valid these conclusions may be, the method by which Soubiran comes to them is not completely satisfactory. First, since the alternation *-us est/-ust* is not attested in Virgil, Soubiran resorts to analysing only the instances in which *est* is placed after an elidible syllable (*-V est*, *-Vm est*), all of which he construes as undergoing 'aphaeresis'[16] (thus as being 'phonetically weak').[17] He then compares these instances (*-V/-Vm + est*) with the instances of *est* placed after a consonant or at the beginning of the line (where it cannot undergo a prosodic reduction and should allegedly be considered 'phonetically strong').[18] His figures show, despite some discrepancies,[19] that exist-ential *est* (including the use with a pronominal dative of possession, except *sibi*) is normally placed after a non-elidible syllable (thus being, according to him, 'phonetically strong'); on the contrary, *est* used in a copula function (i.e. having, according to him, a 'weak grammatical role'), is usually placed after an elidible syllable (thus being, according to him, 'phonetically weak'). Soubiran thus argues for a relation between phonetics ('weak' *-st* and 'strong' *est*) and semantics ('strong' and 'weak' grammatical value), which is based on two assumptions: (1) that in Virgil the verb *always* loses its initial *e-* if placed after an elidible syllable (i.e. *-V* or *-Vm*), and (2) that *est* is phonetically weak (i.e. clitic) *only* if placed after an elidible syllable. Both these assumptions are arbitrary,[20] and thus Soubiran's argument is not fully persuasive.

[15] Cf. Soubiran (1966: 166): '[E]n règle générale, Virgile place *est* après consonne ou au début du vers lorsqu'il possède un sens fort; il place *est* après finale élidable lorsqu'il n'est qu'une copule ou un outil grammatical.'

[16] I.e. contraction.

[17] Cf. Soubiran (1966: 166): 'après voyelle [le monosyllabe] est exposé à perdre [son intégrité phonétique].'

[18] Cf. Soubiran (1966: 165): 'après consonne... le monosyllabe conserve son intégrité phonétique.'

[19] In order to support his argument with incontrovertible figures he creates complicated subcategories, distinguishing e.g. between 'existence fortement affirmée' and 'existence virtuelle' (cf. above n. 14).

[20] On the impossibility of contraction under certain circumstances and the elision of the preceding *-V* or *-Vm* syllable in such contexts see section 3; on the fact that the verb *esse* may be prosodically weak and form a single unit with the preceding word even when this does not end in *-V* or *-Vm* see II.3.7.

Second, many of his statistical observations take no account of metre and word order, a fact that significantly diminishes the value of his results. For example, Soubiran (1966: 173) observes that in Virgil auxiliary *est* with a masculine *-us* participle is never placed directly after the participle and is generally (fifteen times out of seventeen) placed after an elidible syllable (-V or -V*m*). His conclusion is that Virgil, aware of the grammatical weakness of the auxiliary, tended to place it in a position where it could undergo 'aphaeresis' (i.e. contraction).[21] However, the displacement of the verb from the participle might depend only on metrical factors; most participles have a trochaic ending ($\bar{\ }\ \smile$)[22] and therefore they cannot be placed before *est* in a hexameter (which does not allow a cretic sequence $\bar{\ }\ \smile\ \bar{\ }$).[23] Soubiran's figures should not be completely dismissed, but his results are not conclusive, since they only consider the patterns -V *est* and -V*m est*, which do not provide good evidence for the alternation between contracted and uncontracted forms.

Apart from Virgil, a semantic analysis of contracted forms has also been attempted for Plautus. Recently, Fortson (2008: 143) wondered if semantics played a role in the variation of contracted and uncontracted forms in Plautus, but his conclusions were negative: 'If we turn now to aphaeresis in Plautus, the first fact to be noted is that semantics do not appear to play any role in whether *est* contracts or not, contrary to Soubiran's claims about elision before *est* in Virgil.' However, Fortson does not provide figures for the occurrences of contracted forms for each meaning of the verb, but simply lists a small number of cases of contracted *est* (four auxiliary, three copula, four existential/locational).

The aim of this section is to verify Soubiran and Fortson's results by providing detailed figures for the occurrence of contracted forms in Terence, considered according to their semantic use. Table 4.3 displays the results of this survey in the corpus of Terence, the result of my own collation of the manuscripts and metrical analysis of all cases.

---

[21] Cf. Soubiran (1966: 173): '[C]ela montre assez l'intention du poète de réduire dans le vers la place occupée par un auxiliaire totalement inexpressif.'

[22] E.g. all the participles in *-ātŭs* and *-ītus*, the sigmatic (cf. e.g. *lapsŭs*) and apophonical participles (cf. e.g *uīsŭs*), etc. With a pyrrhic ending there are *stătus*, *dătus*, *sĭtus*, *lĭtus*, *rŭtus* (and compounds), plus few other participles in *-nĭtus* and *-dĭtus*. Cf. Fortson (2008: 142 n. 22).

[23] Cf. also section 2 p. 177.

Table 4.3. Distribution of -*ŭs*+ *(e)st/(e)s* by semantic function in Terence

Function	Contracted		Uncontracted	
	Tokens	%	*Tokens*	%
AUXILIARY	33	49%	34	51%
COPULA	20	26%	56	74%
EXISTENTIAL	0	0%	9	100%
LOCATIONAL	0	0%	2	100%
opus est	11	34%	21	66%
TOTAL	64	34%	122	66%

First, no instances of contracted forms are found when the verb has an existential or a locational meaning. All instances of existential or locational *(e)st/(e)s* following a word ending in -*us* are found uncontracted in Terence (listed in Box 4.1).[24]

Second, contracted forms are proportionally more common when the verb is used as an auxiliary than when it is used with a different function: 49% auxiliary as opposed to 26% copula and 34% *opus + (e)st* (cf. Table 4.3).[25]

However, these figures are not completely accurate, since they also consider the instances (forty-nine, see Table 4.2 above) in which the form is found at the end of the line. These instances are less relevant since the form of the verb strictly depends on prosodic and metrical factors (cf. section 1.3). Table 4.4 offers figures that exclude instances strictly determined by metre. The table shows the great gap between the frequency of contracted auxiliary *est* and that of contracted *est* used in any another sense: 65% versus 29% (copula), 0% (existential/locational), and 29% (*opus est*).[26] Only in seventeen cases (excluding cases at the end of the line) is auxiliary *est* found uncontracted in Terence. Moreover, this figure can be further lowered: in five of these cases uncontracted *est* does not follow the participle directly but is

---

[24] The likelihood that the absence of this pattern (contracted existential/locational *est/es*) is statistically significant is higher than 99.95%, as shown by the t-test.

[25] The likelihood that this difference in frequency is statistically significant is between 99% and 99.5%, as shown by the t-test.

[26] The likelihood that this difference in frequency is statistically significant is higher than 99.95%, as shown by the t-test.

Box 4.1 Existential and locational *(e)st/(e)s* after *-us* in Terence

EXISTENTIAL:

An. 183 **erus est** neque prouideram.
[*catching sight of Simo*] 'There's the master. I didn't see him.'

An. 846 **erus est**. quid agam?
[*catching sight of Simo*] 'There's the master. What shall I do?'

Haut. 187 atque etiam nunc **tempus est**.
'and there is still time.'

Haut. 240 dum moliuntur, dum conantur, **annus est**.
'While they're making preparations and getting themselves going, a year goes by.'

Haut. 717 **unus est** dies dum argentum eripio.
'It'll take me one day to get my hands on the money.'

Ph. 332 quia enim in illis **fructus est**
'because there is profit in them'

Ph. 482 quantum **metus est** mihi uidere huc saluom nunc patruom
'How I'm dreading [= how much fear there is for me about seeing] my uncle's safe return'

Ph. 1026 exsequias Chremeti quibus est commodum ire, em, **tempus est**.
'Anyone who is intending to go to Chremes' funeral, now is the time.'

Hec. 204 et ei ludo, si **ullus est**, magistram hanc esse satis certo scio.
'I'm quite sure that, if there is such a school, she's the headmistress.'

LOCATIONAL:

Eun. 816 iamdudum **animus est** in patinis.
'My mind has been on my pans for some time.'

An. 789 est Simo **intus**? :: **est**.
'Is Simo at home?' :: 'yes [he is].'[i]

[i] The last instance is probably not relevant since contraction is phonologically impossible at the beginning of a clause (cf. below section 3.2). All translations are from Barsby (2001), with slight variations. No instance of locational or existential *est/es* is found in the group of uncertain instances that have been excluded from the analysis (cf. above section 1.2, with Table 4.1).

Table 4.4. = Table 4.3 not considering instances strictly determined by metre

Function	Contracted		Uncontracted	
	Tokens	%	*Tokens*	%
AUXILIARY	31	65%	17	35%
COPULA	15	29%	36	71%
EXISTENTIAL	0	0%	8	100%
LOCATIONAL	0	0%	2	100%
opus est	8	29%	20	71%
TOTAL	54	39%	83	61%

attached to another element (ending in *-us*).[27] As we will see below (section 1.6), this pattern (not found with the contracted form[28]) is to be considered separately. Consequently, the proportion of instances of the pattern *participle + est/es* (e.g. *factus + est*) found contracted (e.g. *factust*) versus uncontracted (e.g. *factus est*) rises further, to 75%. This figure is high, if compared with the proportion of examples of *est* used in its copula or existential/locational senses or in the fixed expression *opus est*.[29] These figures suggest that when the verb is used as an auxiliary, it has a marked tendency to undergo phonological reduction, that is to cliticize (cf. III.1.3). This may be taken to imply that it is the strength of the syntactic bond between the auxiliary and the participle or gerundive that triggers cliticization (cf. below 1.6 and VI.6).

Conversely, when the verb is used as a copula or in the fixed expression *opus est*,[30] the uncontracted spelling seems to be preferred to the contracted;[31] for this pattern there are probably other factors affecting contraction and its blocking, which we will investigate in the following sections.

Finally, when the verb is used in its locational or existential sense, the full, 'strong' uncontracted form seems to be mandatory; this would confirm Soubiran's claim about the 'stronger' phonological form of *est* being used as existential, i.e. having a 'strong grammatical sense' (cf. pp. 148–9).

[27] *Haut.* 509 *Syrus est prendendus, Hec.* 286 *quibus est ... obiectus, Ph.* 422 *tuos est damnatus,* 872 *tuos est pater inuentus, Ad.* 115 *meus est factus.*

[28] I.e. no instances of *-ust/-u's factus, -ust/-u's ... factus, factus ... -ust/-u's* are attested (cf. section 1.6.1).

[29] Seven instances (four uncontracted and three contracted in KL) belong to the group of instances that have been excluded from the analysis as uncertain cases (cf. section 1.2 and Table 4.1). Even if we considered all these cases (contracted or uncontracted as in Kauer and Lindsay's edition), the relative frequency of contracted forms according to semantic function would be the same.

[30] McGlynn (1963–1967 s.v. *sum* II.13) considers the verb in the expression *opus est* as having a copula sense. However, in my analysis I have preferred to consider this phrase separately, both because of its formularity and because the verb may also be construed as having a stronger, quasi-existential sense ('there is a/the need').

[31] If we also include in the figures the sixteen uncertain cases (cf. Table 4.1) the proportions do not vary greatly: 35% show contracted *opus est* (31% excluding cases at the end of the line), 31% show contracted copula *est* (35% excluding cases at the end of the line).

1.5 Style

Another factor affecting the choice between a contracted and an uncontracted spelling might be their different stylistic values. Early on, Lindsay (1904b: 142) stated that '...-*ust* was the form of rapid, -*us est* of more deliberate utterance.' Even though this may be no more than saying that -*ust* is clitic whereas -*us est* is not, we might also infer from it the assumption that the contracted spelling was associated with a casual attitude, haste, or carelessness: is this statement in accordance with evidence? How could we verify it?

It is not straightforward to give an answer to these questions since it is difficult to determine the stylistic value of every single microsequence in which we find a form -*us* + *est*. As Lindsay (1922: 45) also asserted, commenting on an analogous phenomenon: 'We could not frame a hard-and-fast rule for the use of "I'll" and "I will", "he's" and "he is" (or "he has") in English: and a foreign dissertation which should attempt it would make amusing reading.'

Nevertheless, a possible way of investigating the stylistic value of contracted versus uncontracted forms might be to relate the two forms to elements which seem to be connected with a particular style, such as type of verse (i.e. metre) and type of character.

1.5.1 Verse Type

The main distinction in the metres of Latin comedy is between *deuerbia* (spoken verses) and *cantica* (verses accompanied in performance by the music of the *tibicen*),[32] i.e. between iambic senarii and all other metres.[33] A further division made by modern scholars lies between the iambic-trochaic stichic metres (the 'recitative' verses, i.e. tr[7], ia[7], ia[8], tr[8]) and the *mutatis modis cantica* (the lyric songs, especially the Plautine ones, that exhibit a complex variation of

---

[32] For this distinction, already found in ancient grammarians and commentators, cf. e.g. Diomedes *GL* 1.491, Don. *De Com.* 8.9, *ad An.* Praef. I.7, *ad Eun.* Praef. 1.7, *ad Ph.* Praef. 1.7, *ad Hec.* Praef. 1.7, *ad Ad.* Praef. 1.7, Marius Victorinus *GL* 6.79, Liv. 7.2.8–11. Cf. Moore (1998, 2008: 19–31, 2012), Fortson (2011), de Melo (2010–2012: I.xciv–xcvi).

[33] According to the standard theory of Ritschl and Bergk, widely accepted among scholars of Latin comedy (cf. e.g. Marshall (2006: 203–44). For a different view cf. Questa (2007: 359), who thinks that trochaic septenarii might also be declaimed without melody and without accompaniment (as the ia[6]). For a full description of the problem and a defence of the standard theory see Moore (1998, 2008).

metres).[34] As far as the stylistic value of these verses is concerned, there seems to be a clear differentiation between spoken verses (ia⁶) and 'recitative' and sung verses (all the others), supported by accompanying differences in language and theme.[35] It is more difficult to argue about the differences in style between the recitative metres.[36] In my analysis I will be content with a basic distinction: the iambic senarius is presumably the metre most similar to speech,[37] while musical verses (recitatives and/or songs) are on the contrary more sophisticated, 'artificial' metres.

A precedent for this type of survey may be found in some brief remarks by Fortson (2008: 137), who states that in Plautus the variation between contracted and uncontracted forms does not depend on the type of metre: according to him 91% of the occurrences of the contracted form -*ust* and an identical 91% of uncontracted -*us est* are in 'iambo-trochaic verses'. Even if Fortson does not offer detailed figures to ground this claim and considers ia⁶ and the recitative metres together, his conclusions appear to be consistent with the evidence. In Table 4.5 I offer more detailed figures, based on Leo's edition of Plautus. These figures consider the evidence from another

<hr>

[34] On this see in particular Beare (1964: 219–32), Sandbach (1977: 119–21), Hunter (1985: 42–4), Duckworth (1994: 361–75), Barsby (1999: 27–9), Gratwick (1999: 209–11), Marshall (2006: 204). Cf. however Moore (1998, 2012) for the view that all comic metres were sung (apart from iambic senarii) and thus that the distinction between 'recitative' metres and *cantica* is much less significant than that between unaccompanied (i.e. iambic senarii) and accompanied verses (all the others).

[35] Cf. Moore (2012: especially 174–7, 237–66). See also Haffter (1934: ch. 6) on the low stylistic features of ia⁶ as opposed to the high and poetic stylistic features of tr⁷, and Happ (1967) who analyses some linguistic features of Plautine songs not found in ia⁶. Cf. also Bagordo (2007) who argues against a stylistic differentiation between ia⁶ and the other metres in Terence.

[36] See however Moore (2012) for a (generally) persuasive investigation of the stylistic features and dramatic function of each comic metre, as well as the purpose of the variations within each metre and across metres. Cf. also Haffter (1934), Hunter (1985: 44–6), Moore (1998, 1999).

[37] Cf. Cic. *Orat.* 184 *at comicorum senarii propter similitudinem sermonis sic saepe sunt abiecti, ut non numquam uix in eis numerus et uersus intellegi possit.* 'And the senarii of the comic poets, **because of their likeness to speech**, are often so loose that sometimes one can hardly discern metre and verse in them' (trans. Moore). Cf. also Cic. *Orat.* 189 (*senarios uero...effugere uix possumus; magnam enim partem ex iambis nostra constat oratio.* 'We can hardly avoid iambic senarii since **our speech consists largely of iambs**') and the description by Aristotle of the Greek iambic trimetre (the equivalent and the progenitor of Latin iambic senarius) as the metre closest to ordinary speech (*Poet.* 1449a24–6, *Rhet.* 1404a32).

Table 4.5. Distribution of *-us* + *(e)st* in Plautus
by type of verse

	Contracted	Uncontracted
ia^6	60%	40%
tr^7	68%	32%
ia^7	62%	38%
ia^8	71%	29%
tr^8	86%	14%
Others	67%	33%
TOTAL	65%	35%

perspective; that is, they show the distribution of contracted and uncontracted forms (*-us* + *(e)st*) within each metre.

Table 4.5 shows that the percentage figures for contracted forms do not significantly vary in different verses (they range from a minimum of 60% in ia^6 to a maximum of 71% in ia^8; the rate in tr^8 should not be taken into account since there are only seven instances in total).

An analysis of evidence from Terence gives slightly different figures. In Terence the variety of verses is much more limited than in Plautus: there are only five main metres, the iambic senarius (ia^6), the iambic septenarius (ia^7), the iambic octonarius (ia^8), the trochaic septenarius (tr^7), and the trochaic octonarius. (tr^8).[38]

The figures for the alternation between contracted and uncontracted forms by type of verse are displayed in Table 4.6.

Apart from the generally lower frequency of contracted forms in Terence than in Plautus (34% in Terence, 65% in Plautus), these figures show a slight preference for uncontracted forms in tr^7 (78%) and ia^8 (68%) than in ia^6 (61%; given the small number of instances in tr^8, ia^7, and other metres, the figures for contracted forms in these metres are less meaningful), although the likelihood that this difference in frequency is statistically significant is not very high.[39] This impression becomes stronger if we exclude the cases in which the spelling is strictly determined by the metre. Table 4.7

---

[38] In all, about 3200 ia^6, 1300 tr^7, 900 ia^8, 400 ia^7, 90 tr^8 to which we have to add less than thirty lines of lyric verses.

[39] Between 95% and 96% (as shown by the t-test) which is not a very high figure by conventional criteria.

Table 4.6. Distribution of *-ŭs + (e)st/(e)s* by type of line in Terence

	Contracted		Uncontracted	
	Tokens	*%*	*Tokens*	*%*
ia⁶	32	39%	50	61%
tr⁷	12	22%	43	78%
ia⁸	12	32%	25	68%
ia⁷	5	63%	3	37%
others	3	75%	1	25%
TOTAL	64	34%	122	66%

Table 4.7. = Table 4.6 not considering instances strictly determined by metre

	Contracted		Uncontracted	
	Frequency	*%*	*Frequency*	*%*
ia⁶	27	47%	30	53%
tr⁷	10	23%	33	77%

summarizes the figures for the frequency of contracted *-ust* in ia⁶ and tr⁷, which are the most common metres in Terence.[40]

Although the figures are still not extremely statistically significant,[41] I would point out that contracted forms seem to be less frequent in tr⁷ (a metre which, as noted, seems to be more 'poetic' than ia⁶), whereas they are as common as uncontracted forms in ia⁶. Moreover, among the ten cases of contracted forms in tr⁷, only in one case is the verb used as a copula (in six cases it is auxiliary, in the other three it occurs in the expression *opust*), whereas in ia⁶ there are eleven cases of contracted *-ust* with copula *-st* (out of twenty-seven).

1.5.2 Character Type

Another factor that might be considered is character type. Are contracted forms used more by a particular type of character, thus

---

[40] Cf. n. 38.
[41] The likelihood that the difference in frequency is statistically significant is between 98% and 99%, as shown by the t-test.

Table 4.8. Distribution of -*ŭs* + *(e)st/(e)s* by character type in Terence

	Contracted		Uncontracted	
	Frequency	*%*	*Frequency*	*%*
Senex	17	27%	47	73%
Seruus	12	25%	36	75%
Adulescens	18	47%	20	53%

possibly being construed as a mark of linguistic characterization? The assumption that Terence tends (allegedly much more than Plautus) to characterize the language of a type or even of a single character is quite common in recent studies on Terence's language (cf. p. 143 with n. 4), although it has not yet been convincingly demonstrated. According to the most recent monograph on this topic (Karakasis (2005)), Terence concentrates allegedly 'collo-quial' features and Graecizing constructions in the speech of low-class characters (slaves, parasites, pimps and soldiers), whereas archaisms, pleonastic, and high-style expressions are more often used in the speech of old people. Although many of these claims do not seem firmly grounded in evidence, and linguistic character-ization in Terence seems to be a topic over-exploited in recent interpretations of his writing, yet, for the sake of completeness, I will take into account this possibility, not least because there are undoubtedly some (limited) linguistic features restricted to certain types of character (cf. e.g. the 'feminine' oaths *ecastor* and *mecastor*).[42]

In the following discussion I have considered only the three char-acter-types *senex*, *seruus*, and *adulescens*, since the number of relevant occurrences in the speech of other character types (such as the *mer-etrix* or the *ancilla*) is too small for a statistical analysis. Table 4.8 shows the figures for contracted forms according to character type in Terence. The figures are low and not very statistically significant.[43] However, contracted forms seem to be more common in the language of *adulescentes* than in the language of *senes* and *serui*. If one excludes the

---

[42] Cf. Adams (1984).
[43] The likelihood that these figures are statistically significant is between 97% and 99%, as shown by the t-test.

cases in which the spelling is strictly determined by the metre, we find similar proportions: 36% contracted forms for the *senes*, 25% for the *serui*, and 52% for the *adulescentes*.

1.5.3 Some General Remarks

Is it significant that contracted forms seem to be less frequent in tr[7] than in ia[6], and that they seem more common in the speech of *adulescentes* than in those of *serui* and *senes*? A possible explanation is that contracted forms were associated with ordinary speech; as observed, tr[7] seems to be a more poetic type of metre (cf. 1.5.1); the ia[6] metre, on the other hand, was associated by the ancients with normal speech (cf. n. 37). The speech of *adulescentes* might perhaps be expected to be more natural than the speech of old men, full of long-winded expressions according to some scholars (cf. p. 143 with n. 4). This last conclusion is however not very convincing, since uncontracted forms are as frequent in the speech of *senes* as they are in the speech of *serui* (cf. Table 4.8), and the alleged fondness of old men for unnatural long-winded forms of expression is still to be convincingly demonstrated.

On the other hand, the evidence of the higher frequency of contracted forms in ia[6], although not enough to prove their strong colloquial value, would seem to contradict the idea that contracted spellings were used as 'poetic', artificial spellings, and to suggest rather that they reflected a phenomenon current in speech (cf. III.2.1.1).

1.6 Syntax and Word Order

Other possible factors that might regulate or limit the use of contracted forms relate to syntax and word order. Are contracted forms more frequent, or conversely avoided, if the verb is found in a particular syntactic sequence? If we consider for instance different possible sequences of the same expression (e.g. *tuus filius amicus meus est / tuus filius est amicus meus / tuus filius amicus est meus*), are contracted forms used in all these patterns? Are there any syntactic constraints on contraction? Are contracted forms more common in a particular position within the clause?

1.6.1 *Type of Host Word and Clausal Position of the Verb*

There seems to be evidence to support the view that contraction is affected by factors related to syntax and word order. First, contraction seems to depend on the type of host word taking the contracted form and on its syntactic bond with the verb. In particular, excluding the expression *opus* + *est* (which will be analysed separately in section 1.7) in all cases of contraction in Terence the host word is a participle (e.g. *Ad.* 728 *natust*) or a predicate noun (e.g. *Ph.* 295 *seruo's*),[44] adjective (*Ad.* 412 *plenust*), or adverb (*An.* 307 *satiust*), with which the verb has a strong syntactic bond. The figures are displayed in Table 4.9. Conversely, as displayed in the table above, all cases of *(e)st/(e)s not* following a participle or predicate (noun, adjective, or adverb) are found uncontracted in Terence.[45] Apart from the cases of existential and locational *est/es* (eleven cases, listed in Box 4.1) in which by default the verb is not preceded by a participle or predicate, there are fifteen cases of auxiliary or copula *est/es* which are displaced from the participle or predicate (noun, adjective, or adverb) and they are all found uncontracted (Box 4.2).[46] In the list in Box 4.2 I have underlined the participle or the predicate noun, adjective, or adverb from which the verb has been displaced. The only exceptional case would be *Ad.* 480 *ut captust seruolorum*, which however is textually problematic, and belongs to the group of excluded cases.[47]

Second, contraction of *est/es* seem to be related to the position that the verb occupies in the clauses, as shown by the figures displayed in Table 4.10. Apart from the expected absence of cases of contracted *-st/'s* in first position (cf. section 3.2), one may first note that there are only three instance of contracted *-st/-'s* in second position in a clause, i.e. following a host word placed at the beginning of the clause. In one

---

[44] The ending *-uos* (i.e. *-uus*) has been considered within the pattern *-us* + *est*. Cf. II.2 with Table 2.3.

[45] The only exception might be *An.* 102 *hic nuptiis **dictust** dies*, in which the verb *-st* could be construed as a copula and the host word *dictus* as attributive to the subject *dies* (cf. Barsby's (2001) translation: 'today is the day fixed for the wedding'). However, it is probably preferable to construe *-st* as an auxiliary following the participle (cf. Brown's (2006) translation: 'today was fixed for the wedding').

[46] The likelihood that this pattern is statistically significant is higher than 99.95%, as shown by the t-test.

[47] Cf. p. 145 with Table 4.1 and below n. 66.

Table 4.9. Distribution of *-ŭs* + *(e)st/(e)s* in Terence according to host word (excluding *opus (e)st*)

Host word	Contracted		Uncontracted	
	Tokens	%	*Tokens*	%
Participle	33	53%	29	47%
Predicate (noun, adj., adv., pron.)	20	30%	46	70%
Other (e.g. subject, complement)	0	0%	26	100%

Box 4.2 Uncontracted auxiliary or copula *est/es* displaced from the participle or predicate

An. 232 <u>compotrix</u> eius est.
She is her drinking partner. [verb attached to the adjunct *eius*]

Haut. 168 <u>ut</u> diei tempus **est**
Haut. 212 <u>ut</u> tempus **est** diei
[seeing] what time of day it is

Haut. 509 <u>Syrus</u> **est** prendendus . . . mihi.
I must get hold of Syrus.

Haut. 645 tuos **est** <u>animus</u> . . . ignoscentior.
Your disposition is more forgiving.

Haut. 667 nunc <u>ita</u> tempus est mi ut cupiam filiam.
Now my situation is such that I'm eager for a daughter.

Ph. 422 tuos **est** <u>damnatus</u> gnatus.
Your son was condemned.

Ph. 732 <u>quae</u> haec **anus est** exanimata
who is this prostrated old woman

Ph. 872 patruos tuos **est** pater <u>inuentus</u>.
Your uncle has been recognized as the father.

Ph. 1026 quibus **est** <u>commodum</u> ire, em, tempus est.
Anyone who is intending to go, now is the time.

Hec. 198 <u>quod</u> hoc genus **est**.
What a breed is this!

Hec. 286 nos omnes quibus **est** . . . <u>obiectus</u> labos
all of us for whom some trouble has been lined up

Hec. 343 amat cui <u>odio</u> ipsus **est**.
He loves someone who can't stand him.

Hec. 759 uobis quibus est minime <u>aequom</u>
to you, for whom it is least appropriate

Ad. 115 is meus **est** <u>factus</u>.
He has been made mine.

Table 4.10. Position of *(e)st/(e)s* after *-ŭs* in the clause (excluding *opus (e)st*)

Position in the Clause		Contracted		Uncontracted	
		Tokens	%	*Tokens*	%
First		0	0%	1	1%
Second	Complex clause	1	2%	16	16%
	Simple clause (*host + est/es*)	2	4%	21	21%
Other clause-internal		16	30%	22	22%
End of a complex clause		34	64%	41	41%

of these instances the clause is complex and some other material
follows the verb (*Ad.* 404 *adortust iurgio fratrem apud forum*); in
the other two cases the clause is simple and the clause ends with the
verb (*Eun.* 474 *ita me di ament, honestust*, 852 *fortunatu's qui isto
animo sies*). In contrast, there are thirty-seven counter-examples with
the uncontracted form in second position, sixteen in a complex
clause[48] and twenty-one in a simple clause.[49] Therefore, in second
position (in either a simple or complex clause) contracted forms are
much less frequent (7%) than uncontracted forms (93%).[50] In particular, contraction is avoided altogether when the sequence *host
word + (e)st/(e)s* constitutes the only material of the sentence.[51]

---

[48] *An.* 340 *laetus est nescioquid*, 915 *bonus est hic uir*, 940 *dignus es | cum tua
religione*, 976 *tuos est nunc Chremes*, *Haut.* 509 *Syrus est prendendus atque adhortandus mihi*, 717 *unus est dies dum argentum eripio*, *Eun.* 759 *quicum res tibist,
peregrinus est | minus potens quam tu*, 1079 *fatuos est, insulsus, tardus*, *Hec.* 286
omnes quibus est alicunde aliquis obiectus labos, 639 *natus est nobis nepos*, 759 *quibus
est minime aequom*, *Ph.* 422 *tuos est damnatus gnatus*, 562 *solus est homo amico
amicus*, 1026 *quibus est commodum ire, em tempus est*, *Ad.* 252 *laetus est | de amica*,
326 *alienus est ab nostra familia.*

[49] *An.* 183 *erus est neque prouideram*, 973 *solus est quem diligant di*, *Haut.* 240
dum conantur annus est, 969 *satius est quam te . . . possidere Bacchidem*, 1011 *iniquos
es qui me tacere de re tanta postules*, *Hec.* 455 *ipsus est de quo hoc agebam tecum*, *Ph.*
179 *nullus es, Geta nisi iam aliquod tibi consilium celere reperis*, 555 *saluos est, ut
opinor*, 1026 *quibus est commodum ire, em, tempus est*, *Ad.* 639 *melius est, quandoquidem . . . uoluit credere*, 897 *bonus es quom haec existumas*. There are ten further
cases of sentences formed only by the sequence *host word + est/es*, listed in n. 51.
Instances with an infinitive clause preceding a main clause have been excluded (cf. e.g.
Ph. 961 *nosmet indicare placabilius est*).

[50] The likelihood that this difference in frequency is statistically significant is
higher than 99.95%.

[51] *An.* 846 *erus est*, 954 *uinctus est*, *Haut.* 545 *stolidus est*, 776 *tardus es*, *Eun.* 546
ipsus est, 1088 *dignus est*, *Ph.* 215 *ipsus est*, 350 *iratus est*, 426 *iratus est*, *Ad.* 951
bonus est. The only analogous case with the contracted form would be *Ad.* 538 *ipsust,*

In addition, and related to this, there seems to be a tendency for *est/ es* to contract especially when placed at the end of a (complex) clause (64%).[52] Moreover, if one excludes auxiliary *est* (which, as seen in section 1.4, seems to be more exposed to contraction), there are twenty cases of contracted *-ŭs -st/-s* in Terence, sixteen of which are found at the end of a complex clause (80%).[53] Conversely, there are fewer cases of non-auxiliary uncontracted *est/es* at the end of a (complex) clause (twenty-five out of sixty-six, 38%),[54] and most of these instances (fifteen) are found at the end of the line, thus presumably depending on metrical factors and so being less significant (cf. section 1.3).

To sum up the main points emerging from the analysis above: contraction of *est/es* (auxiliary, copula, locational, and existential) is altogether avoided when the host word is not a participle or predicate (noun, adjective, or adverb) and it tends to be avoided when the verb is not at the end of a (complex) clause, especially when the host word is in an initial position in the clause (i.e. when the verb is in second position). One may infer from this evidence that the standard pattern of contraction in Terence is clause-final *est/es* following a non-initial host word. Alterations to this standard pattern appear to result in the blocking of contraction. Such alterations are presumably caused by syntactic and/or pragmatic factors. One might speculate that a verb displaced from the default position (end of the clause after participle or predicate) is given a stronger pragmatic role and/or does not have a strong bond with the host word. Therefore the full, uncontracted form is preferred in such a context, whereas the weak, contracted form is preferred when the verb is in a neutral position at the end of the clause. I will discuss this view at greater length in chapter VI.

which, however, is a modern conjecture for *ipsest* of A and has been excluded from the analysis (cf. 1.2 with Table 4.1).

[52] The likelihood that this frequency is statistically significant is between 99% and 99.5%.

[53] One of the cases in which non-auxiliary *-st/-'s* is not found at the end of a complex clause is textually problematic and metrically questionable (*Ad.* 957 *germanu's* **KL**, **Mar.** : *es germanus* **Bentley, Prete**).

[54] The likelihood that this difference in frequency is statistically significant is higher than 99.90%.

1.6.2 Syntactic Constraints on Contraction

Another way to investigate the influence of syntax and word order on
contraction is to follow the approach adopted by Fortson (2008:
144–61) in his analysis of contracted forms in Plautus. Having dismissed semantic, metrical, and stylistic factors (the first allegedly
insubstantial, cf. 1.4, and the last two too complex to investigate),
Fortson focuses on the host word preceding *(e)st* (to which the verb
'cliticizes') and its syntactic relation with the rest of the phrase. In his
analysis (which takes into account only the third person form *est*),
Fortson does not aim to investigate the factors responsible for the
alternation of contracted and uncontracted forms, but rather to
determine the syntactic constraints on the contraction of *est*.

First (category 1; see Table 4.11), Fortson lists thirty-five cases of
contracted forms occurring after nouns[55] and compares them with
the parallel cases of uncontracted forms. He observes that contraction
is normally avoided (cat. 1a in Table 4.11) if the verb is phrase-
internal in a noun phrase (NP)[56] occurring between a noun and its
modifier (noun/adjective), element in apposition, or genitive or dative
of possession, i.e. when the verb breaks a strong syntactic bond (cf.
e.g. Pl. *Men.* 1070 *erus est meus* vs. **erust meus*). Consequently,
Fortson (2008: 150) concludes, 'cliticization of *est* to a nominal was
free when that nominal was at the right edge of its phrase [i.e. cat. 1b],
and strongly constrained otherwise.'

Second (2), Fortson considers the cases of contracted forms after
adjectives and participles. He states (p. 151) that there seem to be 'no
constraints on the ability of *est* to cliticize (i.e. to contract) to adjectives that are at the right edge of their phrases'[57] (cat. 2c), whereas '*est*

---

[55] Eleven after a bare noun (e.g. *Aul.* 389 *et strepitust intus*, *Bac.* 946 *miles
Menelaust*), fifteen after a noun modified by a nominative adjective or pronoun
(e.g. *Trin.* 712 meus *ut animust eloquar*, 901 *hic* noster *architectust*), five after a
noun modified by a genitive or dative (e.g. *Amph.* 381 *quis* tibi *erust?*, *Trin.* 368
sapiens aetati *cibust*), four after a noun modified by another complement (e.g. *Trin.*
432 **tempust** adeundi).

[56] By noun phrase (NP) Fortson refers to the syntactic segment in a clause formed
by a noun (or a pronoun), i.e. the so called 'head' of the phrase, and the elements
logically depending on it (adjectives, pronouns, complements). Conversely, a verb
phrase (VP) is the syntactic segment in a clause formed by the verb and the elements
depending on it. Cf. e.g [*Caius Marci pater*]^{NP} [*meus amicus est*]^{VP}. 'Caius, father of
Marcus, is my friend.'

[57] I.e. the VP (verb phrase).

Table 4.11. Fortson's analysis of contraction in Plautus

Grammatical category of the host word	Cat.	Position of the sequence host word + *(e)st, (e)s* in the phrase (NP or VP)	Contracted	Uncontracted
1) NOUN	1a	breaking a syntactic bond	1	12
	1b	FINAL/WITH ADJUNCTS	34	22
2) ADJECTIVE	2a	breaking a strong syntactic bond[58]	0	3
	2b	breaking a weak syntactic bond[59]	11	?
	2c	FINAL	*dozens*	?
PARTICIPLE	2d	breaking a syntactic bond	*unconstrained*	
	2e	FINAL	(no figures offered)	
3) PRONOUN	3a	breaking a syntactic bond	2	12
	3b	FINAL	22	34
ADVERB	3c	breaking a syntactic bond	0	1
	3d	FINAL	5	4

cliticizes much less commonly to a phrase-internal adjective' (cat. 2a and 2b): in the few cases where it does (eleven),[60] the verb never comes between the adjective and its 'head' (i.e. it never breaks a strong syntactic bond, cat. 2a). Moreover, there appears to be no constraints when the verb is auxiliary and follows the participle directly (cat. 2d and 2e). However correct Fortson's statements might be, he does not give complete figures to support these claims (e.g. he does not say how many cases there are of contracted forms 'at the right edge of their phrases'; see Table 4.11).

Finally (3), Fortson analyses the cases of contracted forms following a pronoun or an adverb (Table 4.11), and his conclusions are analogous to those presented in the previous paragraph: contracted forms are freely used if the pronoun/adverb is placed at the end of its (noun) phrase (cat. 3b and 3d),[61] whereas they are normally avoided when the verb is phrase-internal (cat. 3a and 3c).

---

[58] I.e. (according to Fortson's analysis) separating an adjective from its head.

[59] I.e. (according to Fortson's analysis) separating an adjective from an adjunct or complement.

[60] Cf. e.g. *Aul.* 196 *nemini credo qui large* **blandust** diues pauperi.

[61] After a pronominal genitive in *-ius*: three contracted, one uncontracted when the verb is phrase-final in a NP; one contracted, six uncontracted when the verb is phrase-internal. After a possessive adjective (*meus, tuos*): eight contracted, fourteen

Though Fortson's concept of 'phrase-internal' is sometimes indefinite and the number of corroborating counter-examples for a particular category is often small (cf. in particular cat. 2a), his analysis is generally convincing, and shows that in Plautus contracted forms are normally avoided when the verb breaks a syntactic bond (clearly if the syntactic bond is strong, less patently if the syntactic bond is weak). The few exceptions are discussed in detail[62] and are rejected on the basis of either philological or linguistic factors.

Before we move on, we might note the high proportion of contracted forms in Plautus attached to a phrase-final noun (i.e. a noun in final position in an NP, not followed by adjectives, other modifiers, or adjuncts): twenty-nine contracted cases, as opposed to only eleven uncontracted, excluding instances of clauses formed only by the noun + *est* (four instances, always spelt uncontracted).[63] Moreover, in most of the contracted cases (twenty-two out of twenty-nine), the noun is not only at the end of the NP but also at the end of the clause (cf. e.g. *Bac.* 774 *hic quidem, opinor, Chrysalust*). Conversely, a phrase-final noun followed by an uncontracted verb is clause-final only in three instances.[64] This seems to confirm, from a different perspective, the tendency of contracted -*st*/-'*s* to be found at the end of a complex clause in Terence, which was observed in the previous section (1.6.1).

I will now verify Fortson's results by considering the evidence from Terence, taking into account both the third and the second person forms. Following Fortson's approach, I first consider instances of contracted forms following a noun (Table 4.12). Interestingly, the

---

uncontracted when the verb is phrase-final; none contracted, five uncontracted when the verb is phrase-internal. After an adverb in -*us*: four contracted, four uncontracted when the verb is phrase-final; none contracted, one uncontracted when the verb is phrase-internal. Only two cases of *est* after the dative/ablative of nouns, both contracted and phrase-final. No cases of contracted forms after the dative/ablative of pronouns. No clear figures are offered for the verb following a pronominal nominative singular (*nullus*, *totus*, *ipsus*): however, of the eight contracted cases listed by Fortson, only one is phrase-internal. No cases of contracted forms are found in Plautus after *is*, *quis*, *quisquis* (cf. section 3.1).

[62] Cf. p. 153 on *St.* 50 and p. 159 on *Capt.* 990.

[63] Cf. e.g. *Amph.* 533 *tempus est*, *Capt.* 888 *Boius est*.

[64] *Rud.* 1052 *tuosne hic seruos est* | (remarkably at the end of an iambic-ending verse), *Capt.* 574 *quis seruos est*, *Men.* 72 *haec urbs Epidamnus est* (this latter before the medial caesura).

Table 4.12. *(e)st/(e)s* after nouns (*-ŭs*) in Terence

Cat.	Pattern	Contracted	Uncontracted
1a	breaking a syntactic bond[65]	0	5
1b	phrase final	2	10
	TOTAL	2	15

overall number of occurrences of contracted forms coming after a noun is much more limited in Terence than in Plautus (only two instances). Therefore, the (expected) lack of contracted forms breaking a syntactic bond (i.e. occurring between the noun and its modifier, cat. 1a)[66] is not statistically significant. As expected (cf. 1.6.1), both cases of contracted forms found at the right edge of an NP (cat. 1b) are also clause-final (*Ph.* 295 *tu seruo's*, *Eun.* 546 *qui hic ornatust?*).

The second group includes the instances of *est/es* following an adjective or a participle. Comparative adverbs in *-iŭs* (e.g. *melius, satius*) have been treated as equivalent to adjectives. The figures for this pattern are offered in Table 4.13. These figures show that contracted forms are not found between an adjective and its head (i.e. breaking a strong syntactic bond, cat. 2a). However, the number of counter-examples with the uncontracted form is low (only two instances[67]) and therefore the absence of contracted forms for this category is probably not significant. Contracted forms seem less common when they are attached to a phrase-internal adjective with

---

[65] I.e. separating the noun from a modifier, dative of possession, or element in apposition.

[66] The only exception would be *Ad.* 480 (ia[6]) *praetĕrĕ(a)* |, *ut cap|tust ser|uōlō|rum, non |mălus* ('besides, as far as slaves go, [he is] not bad'), which however is textually problematic; this is the text as printed in the OCT and Marouzeau editions, following the medieval tradition. However A and the indirect tradition (followed by some editors) have a different text which metrically requires the uncontracted form: *praetĕrĕ(a)* |, *ut cap|tŭs est* | *seruō|rum, non* | *mălus*.

[67] *Haut.* 717 *unus est dies dum argentum eripio* ('It will take me one day to get my hands on the money'), *Ph.* 562 *solus est homo amico amicus* ('He's the only and one friend to his friend').

Table 4.13. *(e)st/(e)s* after adjectives/participles (*-ŭs*) in Terence

Cat.	Pattern	Contracted	Uncontracted
2a	Adj. + V + N	0	2
2b	Adj. + V + adjunct	3	8
2c	Adj. + V (phrase final)	15	31
2d	Part. + V + subj./compl./adv.	12	9
2e	Part. + V (phrase-final)	21	20
	TOTAL	51	70

a predicate function (i.e. breaking a weak syntactic bond, cat. 2b),[68] in accordance with Fortson's observations on Plautus,[69] but again the number of instances is low and not statistically significant. As expected (cf. 1.6.1), all instances of phrase-final contracted forms after an adjective (cat. 2c) are also clause-final; conversely, we find at least one instance of a phrase-final uncontracted form not at the end of the clause (*An.* 915 *bonus est hic uir*).

As already pointed out (cf. 1.6.1) contracted forms are more common in Terence when the verb follows a participle, as they are in Plautus according to Fortson, but they do not appear to be much more common when the participle is phrase-final (twenty-one cases vs. twenty uncontracted, cat. 2e)[70] than when it is phrase-internal

---

[68] Contracted: *An.* 576 *qui intumust eorum consiliis, Ad.* 412 *praeceptorum plenust istorum ille*, 957 *nunc tu germanu's pariter animo et corpore*. Uncontracted: *An.* 340 *laetus est nescioquid*, 940 *dignus es | cum tua religione, Haut.* 475 *talentum hoc pacto satius est quam illo minam*, 707 *satis sanus es aut sobrius?, Eun.* 759 *quicum res tibist peregrinus est, | minus potens quam tu* (in this case the adjective phrase *minus potens* is appositive), *Eun.* 1079 *fatuos est, insulsus, tardus, Ad.* 252 *laetus est | de amica, Ad.* 326 *alienus est ab nostra familia.* I do not consider in this list *Ph.* 179 (*nullus es, Geta nisi iam aliquod tibi consilium celere reperis*) because the vocative (*Geta*) can hardly be considered an adjunct of the verb phrase.

[69] Cf. Fortson (2008: 151): '*est* cliticizes much less commonly to a phrase-internal adjective.'

[70] Cf. *An.* 202 *ita aperte ipsam rem modo locutu's*, 255 *id mihi uisust dicere*, 527 *quod mi pollicitust ipsus gnatus*, 530 *nam gnatus quod pollicitust haud dubiumst mihi . . .*, 621 *quid meritu's?*, 724 *quidnam incepturu's?*, 928 *is ibi mortuost*, 955 *pater non recte uinctust, Haut.* 815 *ita meritu's*, 823 *quod ei pollicitu's, Eun.* 696 *monstrum hominis, non dicturu's?*, 708 *et pro te huc deductust?*, 826 *quam ob rem adductust?, Ph.* 550 *aut quidnam facturu's?*, 833 *quidnam nunc facturust Phaedria?*, 896 *nunc conueniundust Phormio, Hec.* 433 *qui mecum una uectust*, 825 *quid exanimatu's obsecro? aut unde anulum istum nactu's? |, Ad.* 234 *quor passu's?*, 728 *puer natust.*

(twelve cases vs. nine uncontracted, cat. 2d).[71] Forston's claim that auxiliary *est* freely contracts in Plautus (Forston 2008: 152 'Aphaeresis of *est* in its role as an auxiliary verb in periphrastic tenses after participles was unconstrained.') finds support in evidence from Terence, in line with what has been pointed out in previous sections (cf. sections 1.4 and 1.6.1). Moreover, these figures confirm the relation between contraction and the position of *est/es* in the clause: first, the only instance of a sentence formed only by a sequence *participle + verb* is found with the uncontracted form (*An.* 954 *uinctus est*); second, in most cases (seventeen out of twenty-one)[72] a phrase-final contracted form is also clause-final.

The last group includes the instances in which contracted forms are found after a pronoun. These figures are shown in Table 4.14.

Contracted forms are apparently not used by Terence after pronouns; that is, they are only found after nouns, adjectives (or comparative adverbs), and participles. Moreover, contracted forms are not found after an adverb ending in *-ŭs*, but this may not be significant since there are no cases of uncontracted *est* after an adverb ending in *-us* either.[73]

Table 4.14. *(e)st/(e)s* after pronouns *(-ŭs)* in Terence

Cat.	Pattern	Contracted	Uncontracted
3a	Pron. poss. adj. (*meus/tuos*) + V + adj./compl./adv.	0	1
	Pron. poss. adj. (*meus/tuos*) + V + head N	0	4
	quibus + V	0	3
3b	Pron. nom. sing. + V (phrase-final)	0	5
	Pronominal genitive + V (phrase-final)	0	1
	TOTAL	0	14

[71] *An.* 102 *hic nuptiis* **dictust** *dies,* 937 *ita animus* **commotust** *metu,* Haut. 580 *hominis frugi et temperantis* **functu's** *officium,* Eun. 188 *ita facere certumst, mos* **gerundust** *Thaidi,* 286 *numnan hic* **relictu's** *custos,* 645 *postquam* **ludificatust** *uirginem,* Ph. 661 *ager* **oppositust** *pignori* | *ob decem minas,* 798 *ecquid* **locutu's** *cum istac,* Hec. 169 *paullatim* **elapsust** *Bacchidi atque huc transulit,* 517 *nam audiuisse uocem pueri* **uisust** *uagientis, Ad.* 21 *suo quisque tempore* **usust** *sine superbia,* 404 **adortust** *iurgio fratrem apud forum.*

[72] Exceptions are *An.* 255, 527, *Ph.* 833, 896 (cf. n. 70). In all these instances the participle is preceded by the adjuncts of the VP and it is followed by the NP or an equivalent element.

[73] Apart from *An.* 789 (*est Simo intus? :: est*), where however there is a strong syntactic break between the verb and the preceding adverb (cf. section 3.2).

In conclusion, the evidence for contracted forms in Terence does not contradict Fortson's conclusions on the constraints on contraction in Plautus (and especially that contracted forms are prohibited if the verb divides a modifier from its head), but at the same time they do not confirm them, since the number of instances considered is often too low and not statistically significant. In general, the figures presented in the tables above reflect, from a different perspective, the frequency of contracted *est/es* at the end of the clause, which has been discussed in the previous section (cf. 1.6.1).

In the following section I will assess the tendency of clause-final *est/es* to contract, by considering the distribution of contractions in the fixed expression *opus est*, which so far has been excluded from the analysis and discussion.

1.7 *opus (e)st*

1.7.1 *Terence*

In the OCT edition of Terence there are thirty-five instances of the expression *opus est*, excluding the cases in which the verb is split from the noun and the sequence appears in different orders (*est opus*, *opus . . . est*, *est . . . opus*). In thirteen of the thirty-five cases OCT editors print *est* contracted to *-st* (cf. e.g. *Ph.* 75 *quid uerbis opust?*), six of which are already spelt contracted in A, which is a high incidence (50%).[74] Of the remaining seven instances not preserved by A (the most important source of evidence for contracted spelling), four belong to passages missing in A,[75] two are spelt uncontracted in A,[76] and one shows the omission of the verb in A.[77] Of these seven cases, five are assured by the metre,[78] whereas the two others are not[79] and will therefore be excluded from the following analysis.

---

[74] Cf. in contrast the figures given at II.3.1.1 p. 37 and VII.1.

[75] *An.* 165 *quid* **opust** *uerbis*, 265 *nunc* **peropust** *aut hunc cum ipsa aut de illa aliquid me aduorsum hunc loqui*, 638 *illi ubi nil* **opust**, 682 *at iam hoc* **opust**.

[76] *Eun.* 758 *atqui ita opus est* A, *Ph.* 559 *iam opus est* A.

[77] *Ph.* 715 *ut cautust ubi nil opus* A; for a parallel omission of *est* in this construction cf. perhaps *An.* 638 *si roges, nil pudet hic, ubi opus* [*est*].

[78] *An.* 165, 265, 682, *Eun.* 758, *Ph.* 715.   [79] *An.* 638, *Ph.* 559.

Table 4.15. *opus* + *(e)st* construction in Terence

Sequence	Contracted	Uncontracted	Total
opus (e)st	11	21	32

As far as the uncontracted forms are concerned (twenty-two cases), six are found in sections of text not transmitted by A,[80] five of which are metrically assured,[81] whereas the last one (*An.* 704) might be replaced by the contracted form without excessively disturbing the metre.[82] The first five instances will be included in the survey, and the last one excluded. The final figures for the instances analysed are shown in Table 4.15.

A survey of the position in the clause of the thirty-two instances of the expression *opus est* gives interesting results. A first group consists of the instances (fifteen) in which the expression *opus (e)st* is *not* the last element of the clause, but is followed either by the complementary ablative (e.g. *An.* 722–3 *opus est tua | . . . memoria atque astutia*) or by another element (e.g. *Ph.* 557 *quantum opus est tibi argenti*). In most of these instances (thirteen vs. two) the verb is found uncontracted (Box 4.3).[83] The only two cases with the contracted form (*An.* 165 and *Eun.* 632) are found in the question *quid opust uerbis*, which looks like a fixed expression with a fixed word order;[84] these cases are probably less significant.

---

[80] *An.* 32, 99, 446, 523, 704, 722.   [81] *An.* 32, 99, 446, 523, 722.

[82] *An.* 704 (ia[7]) *iăm — hŏc ŏpŭs | est. quin| i(am) hăbeō. |quĭd est?| huic, non| tĭbĭ — hăbe|ō, n(e) er|rēs* vs. *iăm — hŏc ŏ|pust. quin|* etc.

[83] Other cases might be *Eun.* 770 *perii, huic ipsist* **opus** *patrono quem defensorem paro* ('Damn it! It's this very man, whom I'm setting up as my defender, who needs a protector.') and *Ph.* 227 *em nunc ipsast* **opus** *ea aut, siquid potest, meliore at callidiore* ('yes! This is just what we need now, or something better and cleverer, if we can find it'). These two instances have not been included in the analysis since the verb *(e)st* does not follow the noun *opus*. Moreover, in both instances the host word is an emphatic term (*ipsi/ipsa*): this might be connected to an apparent rule of Latin word order, which leads *esse* to attach to a focused word in the clause (on this cf. Adams (1994a: in particular 15–33)).

[84] Found at Pl. *Amph.* 615, *Aul.* 468, 472, *Bac.* 486, 1164, *Capt.* 937, *Cist.* 94, *Curc.* 79, *Mil.* 1213, *Most.* 993, *Poen.* 436, 579, *Rud.* 590, Ter. *An.* 165, *Eun.* 632. The expression is found also with the uncontracted form (*quid uerbis opus est*) which perfectly fits the first half of an ia[6] (cf. Pl. *Merc.* 106, *An.* 99). For other occurrences of the expression in later authors cf. [Cic.] *Sall.* 12, Sen. *Ep.* 98.18 (*quid opus est uerbis*).

Box 4.3 Clause-internal *opus (e)st* in Terence

UNCONTRACTED (thirteen)
An. 32 nil istac **opus est** arte
An. 722–3 nunc **opus est** tua | . . . memoria atque astutia.
Eun. 765 nil **opus est** istis, Chreme.
Haut. 187 caue faxis: non **opus est** pater.
Hec. 865–6 neque **opus est** | adeo muttito.
Ph. 204 atqui **opus est** nunc quom maxume ut sis, Antipho.
Ph. 557 quantum **opus est** tibi argenti, loquere.
Ph. 560 sed **opus est** mihi Phormionem ad hanc rem adiutorem dari.
Ph. 584 sin spreuerit me, plus quam **opus est** scito, sciet.
Ph. 666 **opus est** sumptu ad nuptias.
Ph. 1003 non **opus est** dicto.
Ad. 601 ita **opus est** facto
Ad. 740 maxume **opus est** iactu

CONTRACTED (two)
An. 165 quid **opust** uerbis?
Eun. 632 quid **opust** uerbis?

We might also note that in many of these instances (*Eun.* 765, *Haut.* 187, *Hec.* 865–6, *Ph.* 1003) the clause is negative and the expression *opus* + *est* is placed after the negative adverb. The very fact that this sequence (*non/neque/nihil opus est*) is admitted suggests that the expression *opus est* should be considered a grammatical unit, as in Latin the normal placement of the verb *esse* in a negative clause is immediately after the negative adverb,[85] as e.g. at *Haut.* 376 *iam nunc haec **non est** tua*, 549 ***non est** mentiri meum*.[86] Apparent exceptions to this rule depend normally on a strong

---

[85] On this see in particular Adams (1994a: 9–13). Cf. also Devine and Stephens (2006: 183, 202, 211).

[86] Cf. also *An.* 354 *item alia multa quae nunc **non est** narrandi locus*, *Haut.* 204 *quod illum insimulat durum id **non est**,* 741 ***non est** temere,* 995 *si **non est** uerum*, *Eun.* 83 *quod heri intro missus **non est**,* 381 ***non est** profecto*, *Ph.* 495 ***non est** longum*, 912 *tum **non est** data*, 927 *nam **non est** aequom me propter uos decipi*, *Hec.* 104 ***non est** opus prolato hoc*, 494 ***non est** consilium*, 509 *si huic **non est**,* 666 *uxor quid faciat in manu **non est** mea*, 669 ***non est** nunc tempus*, 700 *nam is quidem | in culpa **non est**, Ad.* 40 *ex me hic natus **non est** sed ex fratre*, 101 ***non est** flagitium*, 112 ***non est** flagitium facere haec adulescentulum?*, 341 ***non est** utile hanc illi dari*, 578 *id quidem angiportum **non est** peruium*, 596 *id quia **non est** a me factum agis gratias?*

connection between the adverb *non* and another element of the clause; cf. e.g. *An.* 698 *non <u>Apollinis</u> mage uerum atque hoc respon-sumst* ('not even Apollo's oracle speaks more truly'), *Ph.* 303 *non, non sic futurumst* ('no, no, it's not going to happen *like that*'), *Hec.* 277 *sed non <u>facile</u> est expurgatu* ('but it is *not easy* to clear myself').[87] The fact that the negative adverb is normally followed by *opus* suggests that this sequence was almost considered as a single word.[88] Moreover, the rarity of contraction in non-clause-final *opus est* may be taken to imply that in such a position the whole expression was somehow emphasized and that this resulted in the blocking of contraction (as in English, where contraction of *it's* is blocked if the sequence is emphasized: e.g. 'It's nice that you are here' vs. 'You're right, it is nice').

A second group consists of the instances (seventeen) in which *opus (e)st* is placed at the end of a complex clause (listed in Box 4.4).[89]

For this pattern the contracted form seems to be about as common (seven) as the uncontracted one (eight). Although metrical factors might possibly be influencing the form,[90] the evidence seems to support the view that contraction was less constrained at the end of a complex clause than inside it.

In this respect, it may be useful to consider in brief the group of instances in which the standard sequence *opus est* is split and the verb is placed after another element of the clause. In three cases the verb is placed at the end of the clause, after the ablative: *Haut.* 80 *tibi ut opus factost, face*, *Ph.* 716 *atque ita opus factost*, *Ad.* 996 *plus scis quid opus factost*. In all three instances the verb is found contracted and is attached to the complement *facto*; the sequence *opus factost* looks

---

[87] However, Terence's syntax appears not to be so strict and there are some instances (probably influenced by metrical needs) in which the rule is not respected. Cf. in particular *Ad.* 709 *hicine non gestandus in sinust?*, *Eun.* 980 *culpa non factumst mea.*

[88] The sequence *opus est* appears to be standard also in classical Latin. Cf. e.g. Cicero, where there are 132 instances of *opus est* (cf. in particular *Verr.* 2.3.196 *mihi frumentum non opus est*, *Pis.* 73 *non opus est uerbis sed fustibus*) against only four of *est opus* (*Verr.* 2.3.192 *tametsi ne uectura quidem est opus*, *Parad.* 44, *Div.* 2.59, *Att.* 5.18.3).

[89] By 'complex clause' I mean any clause which does not consist only of the sequence *opus* + *(e)st* (cf. also 1.6.1 p. 162). All the cases of *opus* + *est* in Terence are found in 'complex' clauses.

[90] At *An.* 99, *Hec.* 431, *Ph.* 666 and perhaps also *An.* 446 the uncontracted form fits well at the end of the half line before the caesura; at *Eun.* 1083, *Ph.* 75, 715, 1003 the contracted form *opust* fits well at the end of the line.

Box 4.4 Clause-final *opus (e)st* in Terence

UNCONTRACTED (eight)

An. 99 quid uerbis **opus est**?

An. 446 nunc uxore **opus est**.

An. 523 ibi me opperire et, quod parato **opus est**, para.

Haut. 612 non **opus est**?

Haut. 941 sed ita dictu **opus est**, si me uis saluom esse et rem et filium

Ph. 665–6 tum pluscula | supellectile **opus est**.

Hec. 431 in arcem transcurso **opus est**.

Ad. 335 lacrumas mitte ac potius quod ad hanc rem **opus est** porro prospice.

CONTRACTED (nine)

An. 682 at iam hoc **opust**.

An. 265 sed nunc **peropust** aut hunc cum ipsa aut de illa aliquid me aduorsum
 hunc loqui.[i]

Eun. 758 atqui ita **opust**.

Eun. 1083 mirum ni illoc homine quoquo pacto **opust**. |

Ph. 75 quid uerbis **opust**? |

Ph. 100 quid uerbis **opust**? |

Ph. 538 quin, cum **opust**, beneficium rursum ei experiemur reddere?

Ph. 715 ut cautust ubi nil **opust**! |

Ph. 1003 at scito huic **opust**. |

[i] I take *peropust* as being at the end of the (main) clause, since the following infinitive clause is complex and contains a disjunctive construction (*aut . . . aut*), which suggests the presence of a syntactic pause between the main clause and the infinitive clause (*nunc peropust* || *aut hunc cum ipsa aut de illa aliquid me aduorsum hunc loqui*).

---

like a fixed expression[91] and this fact might be responsible for the splitting of *est* from *opus*.

In the other seven cases the verb is displaced from the noun *opus* but is not found at the end of a complex clause: *An.* 715 *ita factost opus*, *Haut.* 611 *non est opus*, *Hec.* 104 *non est opus prolato hoc*, 409 *hunc minimest opus* | *in hac re adesse*, *Ph.* 985 *enimuero uocest opus*, *Ad.* 342 *quapropter quoquo pacto tacitost opus*, 625 *quod minimest opus* | *usquam efferri*. In most of these cases the verb is found contracted, thus contrasting with what has been observed before (contraction is normally found at the end of the clause). However, in all these cases (including the uncontracted *non est opus* at *Haut.* 611 and *Hec.* 104) the verb attaches itself to a 'focal' word; that is, a word which for various reasons takes on a particular emphasis in the clause.[92] This focal word may be either an adverb of quantity (*Ad.* 625

[91] Cf. also *An.* 715 *ita factost opus* (quoted in the previous list), Pl. *Bac.* 604, *Cas.* 587, *Epid.* 288, *Poen.* 319, *Trin.* 887.

[92] For the concept of 'focal words' I refer in particular to the work of Adams (1994a: especially 15–33).

Table 4.16. Position of *opus* + *(e)st* in Terence

Cat.	Position	Contr.	Uncontr.
1	NOT AT END OF CLAUSE	2	13
2	AT END OF CLAUSE	9	8

quod **minimest** *opus, Hec.* 409 *hunc* **minimest** *opus),*[93] a demonstrative,[94] an emphasized word (cf. *Ph.* 985 *enimuero* **uocest** *opus*), or a negative adverb (*Hec.* 104 *non est opus*). The only exception would seem to be *An.* 715 *ita factost opus*, which however appears to be a particular case (see pp. 173–4 with n. 91).

In conclusion, contracted forms seem to be avoided when the expression *opus est* is *not* placed at the end of a complex clause; with the exception of *An.* 165 and *Eun.* 632 (which seem to be particular cases), all instances of this type (thirteen) are found uncontracted. On the other hand contracted forms seem to be common when the expression *opus (e)st* is at the end of a complex clause (nine out of seventeen).[95] Other cases of contracted forms not placed at the end of a complex clause do not necessarily contradict this view since they involve a displacement of the verb from *opus* and are apparently affected by a general syntactic and pragmatic rule of Latin, according to which the verb *esse* is attracted to focal words (cf. Adams (1994a: in particular 15–33)). These results are displayed in Table 4.16.

The analysis of *opus est* in Terence seems therefore to support the view which emerged in the previous sections (1.6.1 and 1.6.2): in Terence contracted forms seem to be more common when the verb stands at the end of a (complex) clause.

1.7.2 Plautus

It will be useful to present briefly the evidence on *opus est* in Plautus, in order to compare it with that from Terence. I am not going to discuss the evidence from Plautus as systematically as I have that from Terence, mainly because for Plautus I have to rely on

---

[93] For the focal character of these words see Adams (1994a: 19–25) and n. 83.
[94] Cf. n. 83.
[95] The likelihood that this frequency is statistically significant is higher than 99.5%, as shown by the t-test.

Table 4.17. Position of *opus* + *(e)st* in Plautus

Cat.	Position	Contr.	Uncontr.
1	NOT AT END OF CLAUSE	22	22
2	AT END OF CLAUSE	34	16

editions (which, as we have seen, are not always accurate) and not on my own collation of the manuscripts and metrical analysis.

Table 4.17, modelled on Table 4.16, displays the results of a survey based on Leo's text.[96] These data are not very different from those from Terence, although there are proportionally more cases of contracted *est* found when *opus est* is not clause-final and the statistical significance of the different is frequency is not extremely high.[97] Although these figures should be verified by a careful metrical analysis (often seriously hindered by the textual difficulty of the Plautine manuscripts), they nevertheless seem to support the results offered by the survey of evidence from Terence: contracted forms are more common when the expression *opus est* is placed at the end of the clause.

2. CONTRACTIONS AFTER -V AND -V*m*

Having considered the pattern *-ŭs* + *est/es* in Terence, I will now analyse the instances in which the verb follows an elidible syllable (-V or -V*m*). The aim of this section is to verify the factors which have emerged as being responsible for the variation between the contracted and the uncontracted forms. However, while for the former pattern, as we have seen, metre constitutes a crucial tool in determining whether the form of the verb is contracted or uncontracted, for the latter pattern the contracted and the uncontracted forms (i.e. the contracted and the elided scansion) are prosodically equivalent;[98] a

---

[96] I have excluded from this analysis the instances of the fixed expression *quid opust uerbis* (twenty-four instances in Plautus, with the verb always contracted except at *Merc.* 106). Cf. n. 84.

[97] Between 90% and 95%, as shown by the t-test.

[98] Apart from in exceptional circumstances (cf. II.3.8.2), which, however, never occur in Plautus or Terence.

sequence *factum est* is spondaic both if scanned *factumst* (with contraction) and if scanned *fact(um) est* (with elision). It would seem, therefore, that the only way to determine the form (contracted or uncontracted) of any single instance is to rely on the reading of the manuscripts, and these are not trustworthy. This fact, however, does not necessarily imply that nothing can be said about this pattern at all; on the contrary, there are at least two possible methods for analysing the data.

The first method is that employed by Soubiran in his analysis of Virgil (cf. pp. 148–50): to compare all instances of *est*/*es* placed after an elidible syllable (e.g. *non **facta est** = non **factast**) with the instances of *est*/*es* placed after a non-elidible syllable (e.g. *non **est facta***). This method does not take philological or orthographical data into account but simply assumes that every time *est*/*es* is placed after an elidible syllable it should be considered (and scanned as) contracted (i.e. phonologically weak), whereas when it is placed after a non-elidible syllable it should be considered as uncontracted (i.e. phonetically strong). As observed (cf. p. 150), the main problem with this method is that it fails to take into account certain general patterns of the Latin language that impact the positioning of *est*/*es* after an elidible syllable. For example, in Terence auxiliary *est*/*es* is placed after an elidible syllable more frequently (87%) than copula (63%) or locative/existential (67%) *est*/*es*,[99] but this may simply be due to the fact that auxiliary *est*/*es* is most frequently preceded by the participle (e.g. *laudata*/*laudatum*), which by its very nature often ends with an elidible syllable (*-a* or *-um*).[100] This method might still be employed to verify whether the alternation between the contracted and the uncontracted spellings depends on the type of metre; such an analysis, however, does not produce particularly interesting results: *est*/*es* is placed after an elidible syllable in 70% of the instances in ia[6], 66% in tr[7], 74% in ia[8] and 72% in ia[7].

The second method is a purely textual one. It only considers the instances of *est* placed after an elidible syllable (-V, -V*m*) and compares the figures for the forms which are spelt contracted in the manuscripts with those for the forms spelt uncontracted. In this type

---

[99] These figures do not include the instances of *(e)st*/*(e)s* following a word ending in *-ŭs*.

[100] Cf. p. 150 and Fortson (2008: 142).

of analysis I exclude the second person form, since its contracted spelling (*'s*) is hardly ever transmitted (cf. II.3.8.1) and therefore cannot be compared with the rate of transmission of the contracted spelling of the third person form.

In carrying out this type of analysis, I do not take the readings of the manuscripts as being 'correct'; my aim is rather to verify whether the process of alteration of contracted spellings in the manuscripts (due to the misunderstanding of the contracted form, cf. II.3.3) is uniform at all the possible levels of statistical analysis. For instance, if we assumed that in origin all instances of *est/es* were spelt contracted, we would expect the rate of alteration to be the same within the various categories one could consider (e.g. type of metre, semantics, syntactic position, etc.). If this were not the case, the evidence might be taken to imply that at a certain stage of the development of Latin (presumably, but not necessarily, that of the author himself) the contracted form was not permitted in certain circumstances and the uncontracted form was preferred.

In the following analysis I will take into account only the evidence from the manuscript **A** (Bembinus), in which contracted spellings are well attested (cf. pp. 124–5 and Appendix 1). Table 4.18 shows the results of this analysis, summarizing the distribution of contracted forms that occur in **A** (excluding the pattern -*ŭs/ĭs/ĕs* + *est*), as classified by semantic function and type of host word, the two main factors that have emerged in the preceding analysis (cf. 1.4 and 1.6.1).

From Table 4.18 we may observe that in **A** the rate of alteration[101] for the contracted auxiliary and copula *est* (61%) is higher than that of locational (43%)[102] and existential (36%) *est*.[103] We may explain this fact in two possible ways: either some instances of uncontracted locational *est* and even more cases of uncontracted existential *est* were already found uncontracted in the original text (and were supposed to be scanned uncontracted, with elision of the preceding syllable), or else the later scribes responsible for the process of

---

[101] I.e. assuming that all examples were contracted in the first place.

[102] For the reasons why I insist on considering the locational sense as a separate group, cf. p. 148 with n. 14.

[103] The likelihood that the difference in frequency between auxiliary/copula and locational/existential -V*st*/-*mst* is statistically significant is higher than 99.95%, as shown by the t-test.

Table 4.18. *(e)st* after -V and -V*m* in the Bembinus of Terence

	Total	% Contracted spellings
GRAMMATICAL FUNCTION		
Auxiliary	221	61%
Copula	327	61%
Locational	60	43%
Existential	89	36%
TYPE OF HOST WORD		
Participle	153	75%
Predicate (noun, adj., adv., etc.)	217	68%
Other element (subject, non-predicate adv. or complement, etc.)	327	39%

alteration felt that the contracted spelling was less suitable when the verb was used in its locational or existential sense than when it had a copular or auxiliary function, and thus altered the former types more often than the latter. I believe the first reconstruction to be more plausible, since contracted forms had probably a degree of artificiality in imperial and late Latin;[104] at any rate, in both cases these data suggest that at a certain stage of Latin contracted forms tended to be avoided when the verb was used in its locational and existential senses, i.e. when it had a stronger grammatical function (cf. 1.4).

Second, the rate of transmission of contracted spellings seems to depend on the type of host word; contraction is much more frequently attested in spelling when the verb is attached to a participle (75%) or to a predicate noun, adjective, adverb, or equivalent element (68%),[105] than when it follows another element of the clause, such as the subject or a non-predicate complement (39%).[106] These figures tie in with the observations made in the preceding sections (cf. in

[104] Cf. III.2.1.2 and III.2.1.3.

[105] Cf. e.g. *Eun.* 121 *hoc* **falsumst**, *Hec.* 843 *hoc* **itast**, *Ph.* 840 *quis egreditur.* :: **Getast**. I consider as being syntactically equivalent to a predicate (adjective, noun, or adverb) other elements of the clause with a predicative function, such as nouns in oblique cases (cf. e.g. *An.* 440 **biduist** ... *haec sollicitudo*, *Hec.* 193 *sane* **curaest**, *Ad.* 904 *hoc mihi* **moraest**; see OLD *s.v.* sum 15) or prepositional complements (cf. e.g. *An.* 424 *haud* **clam me est**).

[106] Cf. e.g. *Eun.* 131 *frater* ... *ad* **remst** *auidior*, 1005 *quid hoc* **autemst**, *Haut.* 804 *ea* **quaest** *nunc apud uxorem*, 989 **postquamst** *inuenta*. The likelihood that this difference in frequency is statistically significant is higher than 99.95%, as shown by the t-test.

particular 1.6.1) and supports the view that contraction was triggered by the syntactic bond of the verb with the host participle or predicate (noun, adjective, etc.).[107]

In conclusion, the analysis of the pattern -V/-V*m (e)st* seems to confirm some of the results that emerged from the analysis of the pattern -*ŭs (e)st/(e)s*; in particular, the evidence for the rate of transmission of contracted spellings in A supports the view that contraction tended to be avoided when the verb had a strong semantic function (i.e. locational or existential) and/or when it did not have a strong bond with the host word (i.e. when this was not a participle, or a predicate noun, adjective, pronoun, adverb, or equivalent element).[108]

This said, however, it is still difficult for an editor to establish a rule in order to determine decisively when a transmitted uncontracted *est* should be printed uncontracted. Contracted spellings *are* attested in manuscripts when the verb is locational and/or existential, although less frequently, and when it does not have a strong syntactic bond with the host word. It would thus probably be incorrect to consider all these cases as misreadings for an uncontracted form and claim that contraction was altogether forbidden in such conditions.

In the following section I will analyse some of the circumstances in which contracted forms do seem to be avoided altogether and thus should be printed uncontracted in editions.

---

[107] One might also observe that the rate of transmission of contracted spellings after -V and -V*m* is slightly higher in ia⁶ (61%) than in other types of verse (tr⁷ 48%, ia⁸ 49%, ia⁷ 56%); thus, one might infer that, at a certain stage in the transmission of the text (presumably the redaction itself), contracted forms were considered as being more appropriate in ia⁶—the verse which more closely resembled normal speech— than in other types of metre (cf. 1.5.1). However, the figures are not significant enough to establish this. Perhaps, as already observed (cf. section 1.5.3 above), one might only point out that if contracted spellings had a strong poetic and artificial value in Terence we would expect different figures.

[108] On this cf. Ferri (2003: 265, commenting on [Sen.] *Oct.* 478 *complexus astra est*) who argues that *scriptio plena* of 'aphaeresis' (= contracted spelling *astrast*) is less acceptable when *est* and the preceding word belong to different syntactic constituents (*complexus* astra *est*). In such circumstances Ferri seems to envisage a discrepancy between spelling (*astra est*) and pronunciation ([*astrast*]); however, it is also possible that in such cases contraction was avoided in both spelling and pronunciation, and that the phonetic reduction occurring between the two words was elision (*astr(a) est*).

3. LIMITS OF CONTRACTION

3.1 Contraction after Monosyllables

As some scholars have pointed out[109] contraction was probably avoided after monosyllables.

First, contracted forms after monosyllables ending in -V or -V*m* (e.g. *cum/quom, dum, tum, nam, quam, iam, si, tu, me, te, se, re, rem, qui, quae, quis, qua, quo*), are not firmly attested in manuscripts of Plautus or Terence. Table 4.19 presents the number of instances of *est/es* following a monosyllable ending in a vowel or (in the case of *est* only) in elidible -*m* (= -V*m*) in Plautus and Terence, together with the evidence of contraction in the manuscripts. As Table 4.19 displays, the number of instances of a contracted spelling after a monosyllable is small;[110] the figure is more striking if we compare the percentages of the contraction of *est/es* after monosyllables (7% for Plautus, 2% for Terence) with the general percentages of transmitted contracted forms of *est/es* after elidible syllables (-V, -V*m*) in manuscripts of Plautus and Terence (about 47% in Plautus, about 43% in Terence).[111] After monosyllables ending in *short vowel* + -*s* (*ĭs* and *quĭs*), the contracted spelling (*quist, ist*) is hardly ever attested (Table 4.20). The only exception would be *isst* found in A at Pl. *St.* 330.[112] Apart from the fact that it would be the only case of contraction after the pronoun *is*, the metre seems to require the uncontracted spelling *is est*.[113] Moreover, the metre always confirms the uncontracted spelling -*is est* for the all other instances. The reading *isst* is therefore to be considered erroneous and perhaps to be explained as an abbreviation or a misreading.[114]

---

[109] Cf. in particular Questa (2007: 40), Fortson (2008: 172).

[110] Six cases in Plautus, one in Terence: Pl. *Pers.* 491 *mest, Bac.* 713 *test, Ps.* 71 *test, Merc.* 684 *quaest, Merc.* 257 *quast, Mil.* 193 *quast,* Ter. *Hec. test* (A²). One might also mention the conjecture *quist* (< *qui est*) proposed by Fleckeisen for Pl. *Pers.* 120 *quist Argentumdonides* (*qui argentum domidest* P : *qui Argentumdonidest* **Lindsay**), which is palaeographically convincing, given the frequency of transposition of -*st* in P (cf. Lindsay (1904a: *ad Merc.* 330)).

[111] Cf. p. 37.

[112] Cf. Questa (2007: 40–2).

[113] All major editors print the uncontracted spelling. Cf. also Brinkmann (1906), Fortson (2008: 161, n. 70).

[114] Cf. Fortson (2008: 161, n. 70).

Table 4.19. *(e)st/(e)s* after monosyllables ending in -V or -V*m* in Plautus and Terence

	Plautus	Terence
POTENTIALLY CONTRACTED	86	49
CONTRACTED IN MSS.	6	1
%	7%	2%

Table 4.20. *(e)st/(e)s* after monosyllables ending in *short vowel + -s* (*is, quis*) in Plautus and Terence

	Plautus	Terence
TOTAL NUMBER	58	14
CONTRACTED IN MSS.	1	0

Also the evidence for contraction found in the manuscripts of other authors or testified to by other sources suggests that contraction was normally avoided after monosyllables. Out of the *c.*300 instances of contracted spellings directly transmitted in the manuscripts of literary authors (cf. II.3.1) plus *c.*120 restored by editors (cf. II.3.3), there are only three instances of a contracted form after a monosyllable (Lucil. 633 M. *si quost* L^ac *Non. 514. 327,* Gratt. 224, 478 *si quast*), which are not completely relevant (see below p. 184). Moreover, out of the 106 instances of contracted forms found in inscriptions (cf. II.3.4.1), there is only one instance of a contracted spelling after a monosyllable (CIL 6.21200 *test*) which, however, is not very significant since the two adjacent vowels are the same (*te, est-*) and therefore the elided scansion *t(e) est* is not clearly distinguishable from the contracted one *te (e)st*. One might also add that all instances of *est/es* following *is* or *quis* in archaic poets (where a contraction *-ist* might theoretically be possible) are confirmed by the metre to be uncontracted, although the number of relevant instances is not very high.[115]

Finally, we should consider the metrical evidence from other poets, in which the contracted spelling is not attested but might originally have appeared (cf. in particular III.2.1.2). In the manuscripts of Catullus there are no instances of contracted spellings but this fact is not significant since this author is transmitted only by late medieval

---

[115] Cf. *is est* Pac. 119 R., *quis est* Pompon. 145a, Enn. 2 R., Pac. 25 R.

manuscripts (cf. III.2.1.2). It is nonetheless of interest to note that in Catullus *est/es* is *never* placed after an elidible monosyllable (i.e. ending in -V or -V*m*). This fact is noteworthy since Catullus often places *est/es* after a non-elidible monosyllable[116] and frequently places an elidible monosyllable before another monosyllable beginning with a vowel, thus freely allowing elision between two monosyllables;[117] consequently, it appears that in Catullus the pattern *elidible monosyllable* + *est/es* must have had some particular phonetic features of its own, which the patterns *monosyllable* + *est/es* and *elidible monosyllable* + *vowel-initial monosyllable* do not share.

The evidence from Lucretius is also relevant, since his textual tradition preserves the contracted spelling frequently (cf. pp. 37 and 128). In Lucretius there are only four transmitted instances of *est/es* placed after an elidible monosyllable (2.190 *se est*, 2.974 *iam est*, 5.900 *quae est*, 5.1150 *rem es*),[118] against about ninety instances of *est/es* placed after a non-elidible monosyllable,[119] and thirty-three instances of elision between two monosyllables,[120] thus suggesting a situation similar to

---

[116] 33 instances: *nox est* (5.6), *mos est* (9.8), *non est* (14A.10, 24.5, 41.5, 42.15, 44.2, 68A.17, 68A.30, 68B.135, 89.5), *non es* (44.17), *quid est* (29.15, 52.1, 52.4), *hoc est* (31.7, 76.15, 83.6, 94.2, 100.3, 107.2, 107.3), *et est* (38.2), *dens est* (39.20), *fas est* (50.21), *res est* (56.4), *par est* (62.9, 111.3), *pars est* (62.58), *mons est* (66.43), *huc est* (75.1), *haec est* (76.15), *sat est* (23.27).

[117] Thirty instances: *te in* (31.6, 55.3, 55.4, 55.4, 55.5, 55.14), *qui in* (15.7, 62.39, 115.4), *quam in* (59.2), *qui ut* 89.5, *si ad* (39.2, 39.4), *si in* (98.1), *si ut* (14A.8), *dum in* (44.14), *me ex* (16.3), *me a* (66.76), *me ut* (76.23), *te a* (6.134), *te ut* (30.12), *te his* (14a.20), *qui ut* (89.5), *si ut* (14a.8), *quem in* (2.2, 64.216), *te ac* (6.16, 30.9), *me ac* (15.1, 28.9).

[118] Three other instances have been excluded, being only the conjectures of modern editors: 5.44 *tumst* (sunt **codd.**), 2.205 *se est* (*inest* **codd.**), and 2.247 *se est* (*inest* **codd.**).

[119] *hic est* (1.722, 2.1066, 3.914, 3.992, 4.317), *haec est* (2.286, 4.1089, 6.238), *hoc est* (3.1000, 5.446, 6.379), *nunc est* (3.678, 3.848, 5.1135, 5.1165), *quod est* (1.523, 1.958, 1.969, 3.518, 3.804, 5.865), *id est* (2.886, 3.135, 3.1008, 4.795, 5.577, 5.1252, 6.139), *nil est* (1.993), *non est* (1.459, 1.508, 1.901, 1.944, 1.979, 2.308, 2.496, 3.103, 3.867, 4.19, 4.595, 4.768, 4.858, 4.920, 4.950, 4.1081, 5.126, 5.146, 5.539, 5.546, 5.590), *par est* (1.189, 1.361, 1.458, 2.125, 2.849, 4.1184, 6.1082), *mors est* (1.671, 1.793, 2.754, 3.520, 3.830), *quis est* (2.250), *uis est* (2.540, 3.277, 3.296, 4.888, 5.1286, 6.354), *pars est* (2.1017, 4.292, 4.438, 6.368), *plus est* (2.1183, 3.294), *os est* (3.122), *mens est* (3.299, 3.548, 3.647, 4.748), *res est* (3.424), *spes est* (4.1086), *ut est* (1.419, 4.181, 4.910, 5.583, 6.1167, 6.1199), *post est* (6.1033).

[120] *cum in* (1.882, 2.54, 3.101, 4.474), *cum et* (2.812), *quam in* (3.394, 3.916), *quae in* (3.916, 2.126, 2.436, 3.390, 4.887), *dum in* (4.1130), *te in* (5.91, 6.245), *se in* (3.77), *si in* (1.234, 2.35, 2.36, 3.888, 5.192), *qui in* (2.617, 5.74, 6.844, 6.1037), *re et* (1.826), *rem e* (1.150), *se ac* (4.961, 6.689), *si ac* (4.1026), *si e* (1.185), *si ex* (4.515), *iam ad* (6.8).

that in Catullus (see above). Moreover, all of these four instances are spelt uncontracted in manuscripts.

In other classical poets (in whom, with the exception of Virgil and Grattius, direct transmission of contracted spellings is rarer) *est* and *es* are hardly ever placed after an elidible monosyllable ending in a vowel or -V*m*. In a corpus including the works of the most important imperial poets (Virgil, Horace, Ovid, Propertius, Tibullus, Statius, Valerius Flaccus, Lucan, Manilius, Persius, Martial, Juvenal, Phaedrus, Silius Italicus) I have found only twenty-five instances of *est*/*es* placed after a monosyllable,[121] seventeen of which involve the sequence *si qua* preceding *est*/*es* (which possibly has some particular phonetic features[122]). In order to appreciate these figures, we might compare them with some evidence from prose; e.g. in Cicero *est*/*es* is placed after an elidible monosyllable in more than 700 instances.

Looking at these facts from Soubiran's perspective (cf. pp. 148–50, 177), one might interpret this evidence as a further sign of the phonetic peculiarity of *est*/*es* in classical Latin (on this cf. also pp. 89–90) and associate it with the avoidance attested in Plautus and Terence (see above) of contracted forms after monosyllables (ending in -V, -V*m*, or -*ŭs*). However, elision between two monosyllables is not very frequent in these imperial authors. I have found only 118 instances of elision between two monosyllables, twenty-eight in Virgil, fifteen in Horace, thirteen in Propertius, one in Tibullus, twelve in Statius, three in Valerius Flaccus, one in Manilius, seven in Persius, one in Juvenal, seven in Phaedrus, and thirteen in Silius Italicus. To appreciate the smallness of these figures, we might consider more detailed data for the preposition *in*, the most common monosyllable placed after another, elidible monosyllable: the total number of occurrences of the preposition *in* in these authors is more than 8000, but only in thirty-eight instances (less than 0.5%) is *in* placed after an elidible monosyllable. On the contrary, in Lucretius and even more in Catullus (authors who, as has been said,

---

[121] *si qua est* (Virg. *Aen.* 2.142, 2.536, 2.433, 7.4, 9.493, 10.828, 10.903, 11.502, Stat. *Theb.* 5.629, *Sil.* 13.151, Ovid. *Met.* 5.309, 5.378, 6.39, *Trist.* 1.1.115, Iuv. 12.118, Mart. 11.45.5, Tib. 3.6.25), *cum est* (Hor. *Serm.* 1.2.122, 2.1.62), *me est* (Virg. *Ecl.* 5.4, Hor. *Carm.* 3.29.5, Tib. 1.7.9), *te es* (Hor. *Serm.* 2.3.273), *tum est* (Ovid. *Met.* 11.71), *quo est* (Hor. *Serm.* 2.3.137), *qui est* (Phaed. 4.21.15).

[122] The sequence *si* + indefinite pronoun is probably to be construed as a single prosodic phrase, with cliticization of the indefinite pronoun, which therefore would not count as a monosyllable; cf. also pp. 48–9, 182.

apparently allow elision between monosyllables) the figures are significantly different: in Lucretius *in* occurs 898 times and is placed after an elidible monosyllable twenty-four times (3%), in Catullus it occurs 160 times and is placed after an elidible monosyllable sixteen times (10%).

Consequently, while metrical data from classical poets are not completely relevant, since the rarity of *est/es* after elidible monosyllables does not necessarily point to contraction (given that other monosyllables behave in a similar way), on the other hand the evidence from Lucretius and particularly from Catullus is more interesting: both Lucretius and, to an even greater extent, Catullus freely allow elision between monosyllables except when the second monosyllable is *est/es*. We might thus imagine that both these authors used contracted forms, a fact already known with regard to Lucretius but which is not evident for Catullus (cf. II.3.3 and III.2.1.2).

Furthermore, the evidence from Catullus and Lucretius may be compared with the evidence from Plautus and Terence, leading us to conclude that the absence of contracted forms after elidible monosyllables, attested in the manuscripts of these two playwrights, is original. Therefore, one may assume that after an elidible monosyllable contracted forms were not possible and the uncontracted forms were mandatory. In the case of *est/es* following an elidible monosyllable not in hiatus, the phonetic reduction occurring between the two syllables was elision; in Plautus and Terence (and apparently also in Lucretius and Catullus) a sequence *iam* + *est* not in hiatus should always be printed *iam est* (with the uncontracted spelling) and scanned *i(am) est*.[123]

3.2 Contraction after Syntactic Breaks

Another condition in which contraction was presumably avoided was when *est/es* was placed at the beginning of the clause, i.e. after a syntactic break. Let us consider for example the lines listed in Box 4.5.

---

[123] The rarity of contraction after monosyllabic words in general might be related to another feature of monosyllabic words in early Latin metre, namely the fact that, if ending in -V or -V*m* and placed before a vowel, they are often found not elided and stand in hiatus. On this see Skutsch (1914: 137–40), Questa (2007: 185–96).

Box 4.5 *est/es* after change of speaker in Plautus and Terence

---

Pl. *Cist.* 735 crepundia una. :: **est** quidam homo, qui illam ait se scire ubi sit.
Pl. *Epid.* 153 noui ego te. :: **est** Euboicus miles locuples, multo auro potens
Pl. *Merc.* 563 quid ais, Demipho? :: **est** mulier domi?
Pl. *Mil.* 794 at scietis. sed ecquae ancillast illi? :: **est** prime cata.
Pl. *Trin.* 934 eho an etiam Arabiast in Ponto? :: **est**.
Ter. *Eun.* 395 deducam. sed eccum militem. :: **est** istuc datum
Ter. *Ad.* 375 rationem :: **est** hercle inepta, ne dicam dolo

---

In all these instances the verb *est* is the first word pronounced by a new speaker. Contraction is presumably impossible in these instances (as a contracted form would have to attach to the preceding word), and the phonetic reduction occurring between *est* and the preceding syllable, as required by the metre,[124] is therefore elision: *un(a) est, t(e) est, Dempih(o) est, ill(i) est, Pont(o) est, milit(em) est, ration(em) est.* It is probably not a coincidence that in all these instances the manuscripts have the uncontracted spelling, which is most likely to be the original one.[125]

A similar group includes instances in which *est/es* is placed at the beginning of a sentence or of a clause, without a change of speaker (listed in Box 4.6). In these instances too, the contracted form is presumably not admissible. It is therefore not a coincidence that here again the manuscripts have the uncontracted spelling in all cases.[126]

A final group worth considering includes the instances in which the verb *est/es* is placed after a parenthetic element, either a single word or a clause; in these cases, listed in Box 4.7, the verb is not at the beginning of a new clause, but it is preceded by a syntactic break, either strong (as when the preceding word is a vocative or a reporting

---

[124] Cf. e.g. Pl. *Epid.* 153 (tr⁷) *nōu(i) ĕgŏ | t(e)*. :: **est** *Eu|bŏïcus| mīles| lŏcŭples |, mult(o) au|rō pŏ|tens* (₁ ˘˘˘ |₂ ⁻ ⁻ |₃ ˘˘˘ |₄ ⁻ ⁻ |₅ ˘˘˘ |₆ ⁻ ⁻ |₇ ⁻ ⁻).
[125] For Plautus I rely on the apparatuses of the most important modern editions, in particular those in Ritschl's (1848–1858) edition and Loewe, Goetz, and Schoell's (1878–1894) large Teubner (which has a very accurate apparatus but whose reliability is diminished by the editors' lack of awareness of Studemund (1889)), and those in Leo's (1895–1896) and Ernout's editions (1952–1962). For Terence I rely on my own collation of A and of other medieval manuscripts (cf. Appendix 1).
[126] See n. 125.

> **Box 4.6** *est/es* at the beginning of a sentence or clause in Plautus and Terence
>
> ---
>
> Pl. *Asin.* 233 non omnino iam perii, **est** relicuom quo peream magis.
> Pl. *Curc.* 94 num muttit cardo? **est** lepidus.
> Pl. *Epid.* 302 face modo, **est** lucrum hic tibi amplum.
> Pl. *Poen.* 1049 agedum huc ostende. **est** par probe, quam habeo domi.
> Pl. *Poen.* 1119 foras Giddeneni. **est** qui illam conuentam esse uolt.
> Pl. *Ps.* 171 uel opperire, **est** quod domi dicere paene fui oblitus.
> Pl. *Rud.* 947 eho mane dum, **est** operae pretium quod tibi ego narrare uolo.
> Pl. *St.* 186 promitte uero, ne grauare. **est** commodum?
> Pl. *St.* 449 potius quam inuidiam inueniam, **est** etiam hic ostium
> Ter. *An.* 980a te expectabam: **est** de tua re quod agere ego tecum uolo.
> Ter. *An.* 917 antehac numquam? **est** uero huic credundum
> Ter. *An.* 789 noui omnem rem. **est** Simo intus?
> Ter. *Haut.* 981 modo liceat uiuere, **est** spes...
> Ter. *Ph.* 989 uel oculum exclude: **est** ubi uos ulciscar probe.
> Ter. *Ad.* 411 saluos sit! spero, **est** similis maiorum suom.

verb)[127] or weak (as when the preceding word is an interjection, an imprecation, or term of endearment).

Even if one might be led to scan the instances of this type with the elided and not with the contracted scansion (cf. e.g. Ter. *Ad.* 622 *hem quid istuc obsecro—inqu(am)—est* as opposed to *hem quid istuc obsecro inquamst*), it must be pointed out that, for this group, manuscripts often have a contracted spelling: Pl. *Asin.* 261 *herclest*, *Bac.* 840 *obsecrost*, *Cist.* 316 *herclest* (**A**), *Epid.* 480 *inquamst . . . inquamst* (**A**), *Trin.* 433 *herclest*, *Truc.* 296 *obsecrost*, 535 *herclest*, Ter. *Eun.* 1006 *obsecrost* (**A**), *Eun.* 1020 *Parmenost* (**A**), *Haut.* 321 *herclest* (**DG**), *Ph.* 421 *Demiphost* (**A**), *Ad.* 622 *inquamst* (**A**). Therefore, as far as this category is concerned, the proportion of transmitted contracted forms out of the total number of potentially contracted forms is thirteen out of forty (33%), which does not differ greatly from the general percentage of transmitted contracted forms in Plautus and Terence. Consequently, there are apparently no strong reasons for excluding this group from the cases of limitations of contraction.

---

[127] For the view that vocatives normally mark transitions between two cola, cf. Fraenkel (1965).

Box 4.7 *est/es* after a parenthetic element in Plautus and Terence

---

Pl. *Asin.* 261 certum hercle **est** uostram consequi sententiam.

Pl. *Aul.* 199 paucis, Euclio, **est** quod te uolo

Pl. *Bac.* 121 o Lyde, **es** barbarus.

Pl. *Bac.* 416 paulisper, Lyde, **est** libido homini suo animo obsequi.

Pl. *Bac.* 840 quis igitur obsecro **est**?

Pl. *Cist.* 316–17 haec hercle **est**... quae corrumpit filium

Pl. *Epid.* 480 haec, inquam, **est**. non haec, inquam, **est**

Pl. *Epid.* 715 quid illuc, Epidice, **est** negoti?

Pl. *Mil.* 62 immo eius frater, inquam, **est**.

Pl. *Mil.* 1084 iam iam sat, amabo, **est**.

Pl. *Pers.* 488 libera, inquam, **est**.

Pl. *Poen.* 1265 ubi ea, amabo, **est**?

Pl. *Rud.* 253 sed quid hoc, obsecro, **est**?

Pl. *Rud.* 339 sed Plesidippus tuos erus ubi, amabo, **est**?

Pl. *Rud.* 527 edepol, Neptune, **es** balineator frigidus.

Pl. *Rud.* 1304 quid tu? num medicus, quaeso, **es**?

Pl. *Trin.* 433 is hercle **est** ipsus.

Pl. *Trin.* 508 Philto, **est** ager sub urbe hic nobis.

Pl. *Truc.* 296 quid id obsecro **est**? |

Pl. *Truc.* 513 ubi illa, obsecro, **est** quae me hic reliquit

Pl. *Truc.* 535 hoc quidem hercle **est** ingratum donum.

Pl. *Truc.* 586 impudens mecastor, Cyame, **es**.

Pl. *Truc.* 941 quid id, amabo, **est** quod dem?

Ter. *An.* 721 quid istuc obsecro **est**?

Ter. *An.* 919 sic, Crito, **est** hic.

Ter. *An.* 950–1 dos, Pamphile, **est** | decem talenta.

Ter. *Eun.* 756 num formidulosus obsecro **es**, mi homo?

Ter. *Eun.* 896 quam tu rem actura obsecro **es**? |

Ter. *Eun.* 1006 sed ubi obsecro **est**?

Ter. *Eun.* 1020 sed in diem istuc, Parmeno, **est** fortasse quod minare

Ter. *Haut.* 320–1 multimodis iniurius, | Clitipho, **es**

Ter. *Haut.* 321 audiundum hercle **est**, tace.

Ter. *Haut.* 440 uehemens in utramque partem, Menedeme, **es** nimis

Ter. *Ph.* 421 tecum nil rei nobis, Demipho, **est**.

Ter. *Ph.* 742–3 non obsecro **es** | quem semper te esse dictitasti?

Ter. *Hec.* 803 adulescens, dicdum quaeso mi, **es** tu Myconius?

Ter. *Ad.* 138–9 et est dis gratia | quom, ita ut uolo, **est**.

Ter. *Ad.* 622 'hem quid istuc obsecro' inquam 'est?'

Ter. *Ad.* 989 si ob eam rem uobis mea uita inuisa, Aeschine, **est**[i]

---

[i] I have not edited the text myself but have preferred to keep the editors' punctuation, though sometimes inconsistent (cf. e.g. Pl. *Bac.* 840 *quis igitur **obsecro** est?*, *Rud.* 253 *sed quid hoc, **obsecro**, est?*).

Before concluding, we might consider one last instance in which the verb is placed after a syntactic break of a type which cannot be included in any of the categories listed above (Ter. *Haut.* 228):

tum quod dem ei 'recte' **est**   (*KL*)

In this instance too one might prefer the uncontracted spelling (*recte est*), in order to maintain the independence of the word in quotation marks; **A**, however, has the contracted form (*rectest*), and this should probably be accepted (with Umpfenbach).

In conclusion, it seems plausible to state that in Plautus and Terence contraction was altogether avoided only when the verb was placed after a major syntactic break, such as a change of speaker or the beginning of a new clause or sentence. In such a context the uncontracted form was preferred and the preceding syllable, if elidible (i.e. ending in -V or -V*m*) and not in hiatus, was elided in the scansion.

4. FINAL REMARKS

I will now conclude my analysis of contracted forms and collect the results that have emerged in this chapter. The analysis has been based primarily on evidence from Terence, for which I have carried out my own collation of the manuscripts and scansion of the lines, although I have also taken into account evidence from other authors, Plautus in particular (cf. sections 1.5.1, 1.7.1, and 3). Therefore, the following observations claim to be valid only for the corpus of Terence, although they probably reflect a wider picture.

Contracted forms were common in Terence after -V, -V*m*, and -*ŭs*, but they were not the only forms possible in these phonological contexts. Contraction was sometimes avoided and the uncontracted form, with or without elided scansion (e.g. *fact(a) est* / *fact(um) est* or *factŭs est*), preferred.

The presence of an uncontracted form may be explained by the influence of a number of factors, which can be summed up by considering the group of uncontracted cases of -*ŭs est/es*, confirmed by the metre (122 examples, cf. Table 4.1): in eleven of these cases (-*ŭs est/es*) the verb has a locational or existential sense, a pattern for which there are no counter-examples with the contracted form (cf. section 1.4); in one case (*An.* 789 *est Simo intus?* :: *est*) the verb is placed in the first position of the sentence, where contraction is phonologically impossible (cf. 3.2); in twenty-six cases the verb is not attached to a participle or predicate noun, adjective, or adverb, a pattern for which there are no counter-examples with the contracted form (cf. 1.6.1). Moreover, in thirty-eight cases[128] the verb is placed in second position after the host word, a pattern for which there are only three counter-examples with the contracted form (cf. 1.6.1); in fifty-five cases[129] non-auxiliary *est* is not at the end of a (complex) clause, a pattern for which there are only six counter-examples with the contracted form, one of which is textually uncertain (cf. 1.6.1 p. 160 with n. 45) and two of which are of the particular type *opus est* (cf. Box 4.3); finally, in thirty-nine cases the form is found at the end of the line, where the uncontracted form is likely to have been preferred for metrical reasons (cf. 1.3).

If one excludes cases that belong to one of the above groups, there remain only twenty-three cases of uncontracted *est* in Terence. In eight of these the verb follows *opus* (i.e. a particular case, cf. section 1.7), and in seven cases it is not found at the end of a (complex) clause, which in general seems to be the standard position of contracted forms (cf. sections 1.6.1 and 1.6.2). Therefore, there remains a group of eight cases (that is, twenty-three minus eight minus seven). The blocking of contraction in this group (eight out of 122) possibly depends on metrical, pragmatic, or stylistic factors, which however are difficult to evaluate; although we have remarked that uncontracted forms appear to be slightly less frequent in ia[6] (cf. sections 1.5.1 and 2), the evidence does not allow us to draw definite conclusions on the stylistic value of contracted forms in Terence (although it is probably valid to exclude the possibility that they were used as mere poeticisms).[130]

Conversely, contracted forms in *-ust/-u's* appear to be found in a specific pattern: the verb is always auxiliary or copula and is attached to a participle or predicate noun, adjective, or adverb. Moreover, in the majority of cases (forty-three out of sixty-four, 67%) contracted *-st/-'s* is at the end of a (complex) clause. In fifteen out of the twenty-one cases of contracted *-st/-'s* that are not at the end of a (complex) clause, the verb is an auxiliary attached to a participle: this suggests that in this pattern the verb was more exposed to contraction (cf. 1.6.1).

---

[128] This figure includes one case of *opus est*.

[129] This figure includes thirteen cases of *opus est*.　　　[130] Cf. III.2.1.1.

A statistical analysis of the pattern -V / -V*m* + *est* (section 2) has shown that contracted forms probably behaved in the same way in other phonological contexts as well; they are not attested in manuscripts at the beginning of the clause and they are less frequently attested when the verb has a strong semantic sense and/or is not attached to a participle or predicate noun, adjective, or equivalent. Finally, contracted forms were avoided after monosyllabic words and at the beginning of the clause, in all phonological contexts (cf. section 3).

The evidence discussed in this chapter ties in with the phonological analysis presented in chapter III (cf. in particular III.1.3), confirming the clitic nature of contracted forms, a position I will further expand in chapter VI. First, however, I will analyse another complex phenomenon of early Latin that provides further evidence for the clitic nature of *esse*: sigmatic ecthlipsis.

V

Sigmatic Ecthlipsis and Cliticization of *esse*

s nostrum et semigraecei quod dicimu(s) sigma | nil erroris habet
(Lucil. 379–80 M.)

In this chapter I will consider another complex phenomenon of early
Latin, the prosodic omission of final -*s* (sigmatic ecthlipsis). The aim
of this chapter is to analyse the evidence for sigmatic ecthlipsis in
Terence (sections 3–4) and make some linguistic observations on it
(section 5), which will be confirmed by a comparison with the
evidence from Plautus (section 6). These observations will provide
further evidence for the clitic nature of *esse* in Latin, discussed in the
previous chapters. Two necessary premises precede the central discussion: the first premise introduces the problematic status of final
-*s* in Latin and (re)assesses some relevant evidence (section 1); the
second describes the metre of Roman comedy and the metrical
terminology used in the following analysis (section 2).

1. FIRST PREMISE: FINAL -*s* IN LATIN

1.1 Weak Articulation of -*s*

By the term 'sigmatic ecthlipsis' I refer to the prosodic omission of
final -*s*, which, after a short vowel and before a word beginning with a
consonant, does not make position, thus preventing the expected
heaviness of the syllable. Cf. e.g. Enn. *Ann.* 71 S. (hexameter):

occī|duntŭr. ŭ|bī pŏtĭ|tur rătŭ(s) | Rōmŭlŭ(s) | praedam |

The final syllables of *rătus* and *Rōmŭlus* should be scanned heavy according to the prosodic rules valid for classical hexameter, as in both cases final -*s* is followed by another consonant (*R*-, *p*-); as a result of sigmatic echtlipsis this does not happen in the line above.

Sigmatic ecthlipsis is attested especially (but not exclusively) in early poetry (see section 1.3) and is often considered a manifestation of the weak pronunciation of final -*s* in speech. Therefore, before I discuss its occurrence and nature, it is necessary to consider the problematic status of final -*s* in Latin, to which sigmatic ecthlipsis is normally considered to be related.[1]

Not all final consonants in (written) Latin had a full phonological status in speech: for instance, it seems beyond doubt that in classical Latin final -*m* was 'obscured' in pronunciation (cf. Quint. 9.4.40) before a following vowel (thus allowing elision of the preceding vowel, e.g. *fact(um) ĕrăt*); in normal speech it was probably replaced by nasalization of the preceding vowel (e.g. *factū*); in writing, final -*m* was only a retained graphic mark, which was often omitted in vulgar texts.[2] The loss of final -*m* in Romance (cf. e.g. It. *dono* < Lat. *donum*) is thus in continuity with the weak phonologic status of -*m* in Latin, which can be traced back to early republican times, since there are several omissions of final -*m* already in republican inscriptions and elision of -V*m* is standard in early poetry.

There is some evidence to suggest that -*s* was also weakly articulated, at least at certain stages in the history of Latin.[3] Apart from sigmatic ecthlipsis, scholars refer in particular to the (allegedly) common omission of final -*s* in Latin inscriptions[4] and to some remarks of Cicero and Quintilian, which it is useful to quote in full.

---

[1] For an overview with extensive bibliography see Butterfield (2008b: 188 nn. 2, 4), Adams (2013: 132–47). Cf. also Havet (1891), Leo (1912: 248–333), Lindsay (1922: 126–35), Dressler (1973), Wallace (1982, 1984), Skutsch (1985: 56), Coleman (1999: 33–4), Questa (2007: 325).

[2] On this see Allen (1978: 30–1), Adams (2013: 128–32).

[3] For some attempts at explaining the phonological reasons of the drop of final -*s* see Havet (1891), Proskauer (1910), Sullivan (1970: 12–15), Bernardi Perini (1974), Hamp (1974), Mańcsak (1975), Giannini (1986). Cf. also Vine (1993: 222), Fortson (2008: 252).

[4] On this see section 1.2 and Appendix 2. Cf. also Proskauer (1910), Harsh (1952), Hamp (1959), Wachter (1987: Index p. 547), Coleman (1999: 33–4), Adams (2007: 51–2, 74–5, 104 with n. 319, 140–1 with n. 74; 2013: 132–47). See Bakkum (2009: 93–4) for omission of final -*s* in Faliscan.

Cic. *Orat.* 161
quin etiam, quod iam subrusticum uidetur, olim autem politius, eorum
uerborum, quorum eaedem erant postremae duae litterae, quae sunt in
optimus, postremam litteram detrahebant, nisi uocalis insequebatur. ita
non erat ea offensio in uersibus quam nunc fugiunt poetae noui. sic
enim loquebamur: 'qui est omnibu' princeps', non 'omnibus princeps',
et 'uita illa dignu' locoque', non 'dignus'.[5]

Quint. 9.4.37–8
ceterum consonantes quoque, earumque praecipue quae sunt asper-
iores, in commissura uerborum rixantur, ut s ultima cum x proxima,
quarum tristior etiam si binae collidantur stridor est, ut 'ars studiorum'.
quae fuit causa et Seruio Sulpicio, ut dixi, subtrahendae s litterae
quotiens ultima esset aliaque consonante susciperetur, quod reprehen-
dit Luranius, Messala defendit. nam neque Lucilium putat uti eadem
ultima, cum dicit 'Aeserninus fuit' et 'dignus locoque', et Cicero in
Oratore plures antiquorum tradit sic locutos.[6]

In the first passage Cicero seems to consider the omission of final -*s*
before consonant as a rustic habit (*subrusticum*), once admitted in
poetry; in the second passage Quintilian mentions the idiosyncratic
practice of some authors, who omitted final -*s* before consonant, and
reports Cicero's opinion that archaic authors 'spoke like this' (*sic
locutos*).

In classical sources final -*s* is generally attested in spelling, a fact
which is normally taken to imply that by that time the sound was
restored in speech; however, there are some occasional cases of
omission of -*s* also in classical inscriptions.[7] Omissions become

---

[5] 'Furthermore—something that now seems somewhat rustic but was once considered refined—they dropped the last letter of words ending in the same two letters as
optimus, unless a vowel followed. Thus in verse that feature was not objectionable
which today the "new poets" shun. We used to say. . . .' (Trans. Adams).

[6] 'Consonants also, and especially the harsher ones, clash violently where words
meet, for example a final *s* with a following initial *x*; the hiss produced by the collision
of *s* with *s* (as in *ars studiorum*, "art of studies") is even more disagreeable. This is why
Servius Sulpicius dropped the final *s* whenever it was followed by another consonant.
Luranius criticized him for this, but Messala stood up for him. He thinks that Lucilius
does not pronounce the final *s* in *Aeserninus fuit* and *dignus locoque*, and certainly
Cicero in the *Orator* [161] reports that many of the ancients spoke like this.' (Trans.
Russell).

[7] Cf. e.g. CIL 4.2260 *uictor | ualea(s) qui bene | futues*, CIL 4.4287 *si qui(s) muria(m)
| bona(m) uolet*, CIL 6.377 *Siluani cum fratribus | et sororibu(s) dedica|uerunt*. For an
overview of omission of final -*s* in imperial inscriptions see Proskauer (1910).

(again) more frequent in some early medieval manuscripts, in which hypercorrect additions of -*s* are also attested (cf. Löfstedt (1961: 130–2), Adams (2013: 146)). Finally, in certain areas of Romance (Italy and the Eastern Provinces) final -*s* is lost (cf. It. *dici*, Rum. *zici* < Lat. *dicis*).

Relying on this and other evidence, some scholars have reconstructed the development of final -*s* in terms analogous to that of final -*m* (cf. e.g. Löfstedt (1961: 131), Wallace (1984: 570)): accordingly, final -*s* was weakly pronounced in speech since early times, and, despite its classical restoration in the educated language of the elite, it continued to be omitted in the practice of non-educated or non-urban speakers, to which one should trace back the Romance situation. However, some recent studies (cf. especially Adams (2013: 132–47)) have challenged this view, presenting strong evidence against the loss of final -*s* in imperial and late Latin[8] and against the continuity between early Latin and Romance, highlighting the phonological peculiarity of sigmatic ecthlipsis in early Latin (normally attested after a short vowel and before a consonant; see 1.3), in contrast with the generalized loss of -*s* in Romance. The significance of Cicero's and Quintilian's remarks has also been questioned (cf. Adams 2007: 140–1, 146), and one cannot exclude the possibility that they were both referring to an archaizing mannerism (cf. Cic. *Orat.* 161 **olim** *autem politius*, Quint, 9.4.38 *plures* **antiquorum**…*sic locutos*).

Loss of final -*s* in Romance and medieval Latin is thus an independent phenomenon, while in classical and late Latin final -*s* was both common in spelling and strongly articulated in speech; the only evidence for the weak status of final -*s* in Latin would thus be found in early sources and consists of the omission of final -*s* in republican inscriptions and of sigmatic ecthlipsis in early poetry. However, both these pieces of evidence are not without problems, as will be shown in the following sections (1.2 and 1.3).

---

[8] In particular, Adams points out that most of the cases of omission of final -*s* in imperial inscriptions can be explained by the operation of non-phonological factors, such as morphological conflation and the need for abbreviation (cf. also Proskauer (1910: 187)); the few remaining cases are not significant. Moreover, in non-literary documents other than epigraphic, in which omission of final -*m* is common, final -*s* is hardly ever omitted (cf. Adams (2013: 135–4)). See also Pezzini (2015) on the repetition of final -*s* in classical poetry as evidence for a full phonological status in speech.

1.2 Omission of Final -*s* in Early Latin Inscriptions

Table 5.1 displays the figures from a survey of the evidence for sigmatic ecthlipsis in CIL 1². In total, I have found at least 319 cases of the omission of final -*s* in inscriptions recorded in CIL 1².[9]

I will comment on these figures at greater length in Appendix 3, which contains a complete list of all occurrences of the omission of final -*s* in CIL 1². Here, I will only point out that the evidence for the omission of final -*s* in republican inscriptions does not appear as strong as is normally stated by scholars. In many cases the omission is found at the end of the line (116) and may therefore be irrelevant, owing to a need for abbreviation. Of the remaining cases (203), the vast majority (164) involve a particular pattern: a nominative of the second declension with the ending -*o(s)*. It is difficult to believe that particular factors are not involved in the omission of -*s* in such cases, especially because the form -*os* is rarely found written complete without omission,[10] and, conversely, omission of -*s* is extremely rare in equivalent nominatives ending in -*us*,[11] which are generally written complete (-*us*);[12] moreover, there are some cases of word spelt

Table 5.1. Omission of final -*s* in CIL 1²

		Nominative Second Declension		Other	Total
		-*us* (-*ius*)	-*os* (-*ios*)		
AT END OF LINE		22 (7)	73 (66)	21	116
NOT AT END OF LINE		12 (6)	164 (154)	27	203
BEFORE VOWEL		3	9	6	18
BEFORE CONSONANT	Any	6	147	19	172
	s-	3	8	2	13
TOTAL		34	237	48	319

[9] An excellent survey of omission of final -*s* in republican inscriptions is given by Proskauer (1910), although her figures are not complete. For further bibliography on omission of final -*s* in inscriptions see n. 4.

[10] Less than forty tokens in CIL 1² (cf. p. 256, Table 7.4). One of the few cases is found in the controversial *Praeneste fibula* (CIL 1².3 *Manios med fhe fhaked Numasioi*).

[11] Only twelve cases not at the end of line. Cf. Appendix 2 and Proskauer (1910).

[12] More than 2000 cases in CIL 1². Cf. Appendix 2, Table 7.4.

differently in different inscriptions belonging to the same series, in one case with the ending -*us* without the omission of -*s*, in the other with the ending -*o(s)* with omission; cf. e.g. CIL 1².406n *L(ucius) Canoleio(s) T(iti) f(ilius) fecit* and CIL 1².406o *L(ucius) Canoleius L(uci) f(ilius) fecit*.

Therefore, omission of -*s* in nouns ending in -*o(s)* might possibly be interpreted as a formulaic and/or archaizing feature of epigraphic style: interestingly, omission of final -*s* in second declension nominative singular ending -*os* is also standard in Middle Faliscan inscriptions (164 instances in all, out of 175 cases of omission of -*s* and 172 cases of -*o(s)*; cf. Bakkum (2009: I.93–4)).[13]

The small group of cases of the omission of -*s* remaining in early inscriptions (twenty-seven) is again not particularly significant. In five cases the word is a Greek personal name in -*as* and the form -*a* could be construed as a nominative of the Latin first declension (see Appendix 2).[14] In fourteen cases the vowel before the -*s* is long: such instances cannot be easily related to sigmatic ecthlipsis, which is only attested (and attestable) after a short vowel, as discussed in the following section.

1.3 Sigmatic Ecthlipsis in Latin Poetry: A Short History

As already mentioned, sigmatic ecthlipsis is the prosodic omission of final -*s*, attested under particular phonological circumstances. Final -*s* is never lost before a vowel since elision is not allowed after -*s* (e.g. *factŭs ĕrăt* never becomes **fact(us) erat*),[15] a fact which, in itself, shows that the phonological status of -*s* is different from that of -*m*; sigmatic ecthlipsis does not affect -*s* in such an environment. Final -*s* after a long vowel is prosodically uninfluential, as the weight of the syllable is already determined by the vowel (e.g. both *rēs* and *rē(s)* give a heavy syllable); omission of final -*s* in such an environment cannot be metrically verified, nor it can be excluded. Consequently, sigmatic ecthlipsis is attested only in a specific phonological environment: before a consonant and after a short vowel.

---

[13] In Middle Faliscan inscriptions there is no instance of -*us*/-*u'* as Faliscan does not have vowel weakening.

[14] On such Latinized Greek forms see Adams (2003: 371–2) with bibliography.

[15] On the old (unfounded) theory of Leo on the omission of final -*s* before vowel cf. III.1.2 with n. 28.

Sigmatic ecthlipsis is a metrical archaism of Latin: it is metrical in so far as it is (and can be) attested only in metrical texts, and in non-metrical texts is referred to as a metrical phenomenon (cf. Cic. *Orat.* 161 *non erat ea offensio in uersibus*), yet somehow related to speech;[16] it is archaic both because it is mainly found in poets of the third and second centuries BC (e.g. Ennius, Plautus, Terence, Lucilius) and because, when used by later authors (e.g. Lucretius, Cicero, Catullus), it is often found in passages with an archaizing ring. Sigmatic ecthlipsis is almost completely absent from imperial poetry, but reappears in a very late text, the *Carmen de figuris*, which imitates the language and metre of archaic authors (cf. II.3.1.1 pp. 49–50).

Two instances of sigmatic ecthlipsis are attested in two problematic verses attributed to the first known Latin author, Livius Andronicus (fr. 25 M. *inferus an superus tibi | fert deŭ(s) | funera, Ulixes?*, fr. 32 M. *cum socios nostros mandisset | impĭu(s) | Cyclops*). Although these verses scan as hexameters, it is likely that they originally were Saturnians, which were rewritten by a later author who was unfamiliar with the old metre.[17]

Ennius is a poet who is fond of sigmatic ecthlipsis: in the fragments of his *Annales* there are *c.*110 instances of sigmatic ecthlipsis (i.e. one every five lines) as against only forty-six cases of retained -*s* (i.e. 71% rate of omission).[18] Moreover, instances of sigmatic ecthlipsis (seven tokens) are found in fragments of his other poetry.[19]

---

[16] In both Cicero's and Quintilian's passages (see p. 195) sigmatic ecthlipsis is explicitly associated with speech, either archaic (*sic enim loquebamur; plures antiquorum tradit sic locutos*), non-standard (*subrusticum*), or distinctive of some peculiar people (Servius Sulpicius and Messalla). However, it will be preferable to maintain the two levels (speech and metre) distinct, and to use the term sigmatic ecthlipsis to refer only to the metrical phenomenon, since, as discussed below, the relation between the two levels is problematic. Moreover, it cannot be excluded that ancient authors misunderstood the linguistic nature of sigmatic ecthlipsis. In this respect, it is interesting that in Quintilian's passage the idea that sigmatic ecthlipsis is a manifestation of the omission of final -*s* in (archaic) speech (*neque Lucilium . . . uti eadem ultima, cum dicit 'Aeserninus fuit'*) is presented as a mere opinion (*Messala . . . putat*).
[17] Cf. Mariotti (1952: 76–7). On Saturnian verse see recently Parsons (1999) and Mercado (2012). For classical accounts cf. Lindsay (1893), Leo (1905), Pasquali (1981).
[18] Cf. Skutsch (1985: 56).
[19] *Sat.* 66 V. *piscĭbŭ(s) pascit, Var.* 15 V. *imāgĭnĭ(s) formam |*, 18 V. *uĭuŭ(s) pēr ōra,* 19 V. *cĭuĭ(s) nĕqu(e) hostis |*, 21 V. *Maeōtĭ(s) pălūdes |*, 40 V. *cĕrĕbrum Iŏuĭ(s) paenĕ sŭprēmi |*, 43 V. *Pōlўpŭ(s) Corcÿrae ||, Praetex.* 4 R. *ingentĭbŭ(s) uentis |*.

Sigmatic ecthlipsis is normally taken for granted in the plays of Plautus and Terence,[20] and, in the OCT edition of the latter, is printed (e.g. *factu'* = *factus*) whenever the metre allows it; however, this editorial choice—as well as the general assumption about sigmatic ecthlipsis in Plautus and Terence—is questionable, as will be shown in the course of this chapter.

Another author who makes extensive use of sigmatic ecthlipsis is Lucilius: in the corpus of his complete lines I have counted *c.*225 instances, whereas the total number of instances, including incomplete and problematic verses, might well be around 240 (cf. Skutsch 1985: 56). Moreover, according to Harsh (1952: 268), in the first hundred complete, non-obelized lines, there are 35 cases of sigmatic ecthlipsis (i.e. one every three lines) as against 15 cases of retained *-s* (i.e. 70% rate of omission). In one interesting case (580 M. *situ(s) Metrophanes*) the line displaying sigmatic ecthlipsis is quoted by Martial (11.90.4) in a passage displaying several archaic forms (such as the archaic genitive *terrāī frugiferāī* [= Enn. *Ann.* 510 S.]) and openly disparaging archaizing taste.

Sigmatic ecthlipsis is found in the fragments of other republican authors, in both theatrical texts[21] and hexametrical/elegiac poetry (fourteen instances),[22] and also in some metrical inscriptions,[23] although complete figures are not available.

In the course of the first century BC sigmatic ecthlipsis becomes less common: despite Cicero's (later) remarks, it is occasionally found in his juvenile poem *Aratea* (seven instances) and in an epigram

---

[20] Cf. Shipp (1960: 30–1), Barsby (1999: 297), Questa (2007: 32–5). Wallace (1982, 1984) analyses the evidence for sigmatic ecthlipsis in Plautus, without however providing detailed figures.

[21] Cf. e.g. Acc. *Trag.* 308 R. *sătĭs armātŭ(s) sum.*

[22] Hostius (second century BC) fr. 2 M. *pastĭbŭ(s) pulsae* |, Accius (170–85 BC) *Annales* fr. 4 D. | *fraxĭnŭ(s) fixa ferox*, Valerius Aedituus (second/first century BC) fr. 2 M. (eleg.) *ĭbĭmŭ(s) sic, lūcet* || . . . *candĭdŭ(s) praecĭpĭtans*|, Lutatius Catulus (second/first century BC) fr. 1 M. (eleg.) *ĭbĭmŭ(s) quaesītum* || . . . *dā Vĕnŭ(s) consĭlium*|, Sevius Nicanor (second/first century BC) fr. 1 M. *libertŭ(s) nĕgābit* | . . . *Marcŭ(s) dŏcēbit* |, Valerius Aedituus (second/first century BC) fr. 2 M. (eleg.) *nil ŏpŭ(s) nōbis* | *ĭbĭmŭ(s) sic lūcet* || . . . *candĭdŭ(s) praecĭpĭtans*, Sueius (first century BC) fr. 1 M. *finĭbŭ(s) Grāis* | . . . *mortālĭbŭ(s) dantes* |, Egnatius (first century BC) *labentĭbŭ(s) Phoebe* | . . . *lūcĭbŭ(s) fratris.*

[23] Cf. CIL I².1603 (*dēdĭtŭ(s) fāto*|; *trādĭtŭ(s) morti* |; *in maerōrĭbŭ(s) matrem* |), and the inscription of the temple of Ardea (*dignis dignŭ(s) lŏcŏ pictūris condĕcŏrāuit* | *rēginae Iunōnĭ(s) sŭprēmĭ cōniŭgĭ(s) templum* | *Plautiŭ(s) Marcŭ(s) cluēt Āsiā lāt(a) ess(e) ŏriundus*), which is quoted by Plinius (*NH* 35.17) and was reportedly written 'antiquis litteris Latinis'.

attributed to him by Quintilian (8.6.73 = fr. 4 B.); Lucretius uses it at most forty-four times (one every 169 lines), as a metrical licence (especially in the fifth foot of the hexameter) and in passages 'of a deliberately more archaic and lofty tone' (cf. Butterfield (2008b: 204)); in Varro's Menippean satires there are eight cases of sigmatic ecthlipsis,[24] in addition to one instance in a quotation of the poet Pompilius and one in the epigram of Plautus (quoted by Gellius at 1.24.3 *Lūdŭ(s) Iŏcusque* |); the last certain classical example of sigmatic ecthlipsis is found in Catullus (116.8 *at fixus nostris* | *tū dăbĭ(s)* | *supplĭcium*) an author who, as witnessed by Cicero (*Orat.* 161 *offensio... quam nunc fugiunt poetae noui*), notoriously avoided this practice, together with his fellow poets.

Ennian poetic language is most likely the model for these late republican uses, and in some cases sigmatic ecthlipsis is found in allusions to or direct citations of Ennius (e.g. Lucr. 5.1442 *tum mare* **ueliuolis** *florebat nāuĭbŭ(s) ponti,* cf. Enn. *Ann.* 380 S. *nauibus ue-liuolis*; Lucr. 3.1025 = Enn. *Ann.* 137 S.). In one interesting case (Pompilius *Ep.* 2 M. *Ennĭŭ(s) Mūsārum* || *Pompĭlĭŭs clŭĕor,* quoted by Varro) sigmatic ecthlipsis appropriately affects the final *-s* of the name *Ennius,* at the beginning of the first half of a pentameter, whereas the name of the 'modern' poet (Pompilius), opening the second half-line, is not affected by sigmatic ecthlipsis. Finally, the Catullan example (116.8 *tu dabi(s) supplicium*) could itself be a parody of a verse of Ennius (*Ann.* 95 S. *tu nam mi calido dabi(s) sanguine poenas;* cf. Timpanaro (1978: 179 n. 45), Lightfoot (1999: 55 n. 164)) or of an imitation of it by the poet Gellius, disparaged by Catullus in the poem.

After Catullus sigmatic ecthlipsis disappears from classical poetry, except in quotations of archaic authors.[25] It re-emerges in late antiquity, especially in the already mentioned *Carmen de figuris* (seven instances),[26] where it is clearly used as a metrical archaism.

[24] 9.1 *cedĭt cĭtŭ(s) celsŭ(s) tŏlūtim* |, 36.1 *pectŭ(s) sŏlūtum*|, 36.3 *dĭuĭtĭ(s) Crassi* |, 71.1 *mortālĭbŭ(s) fēcit,* 252.2 | *lēgĭbŭ(s) nec luxu,* 289.3 | *magnŭ(s) cŏmest,* 417.2 *purissĭmŭ(s) multost*|.

[25] This is probably also the case for the phrase *omnĭbŭ(s)* | *maior* | *et mĕli*|*or,* found in a passage of the grammarian Caper (GL 7.102.11), which is taken as an hexameter by Keil ('*omnĭbŭ(s)* | *māior* | *et mĕli*|*or', cum* |*syncrĭsĭs* | *omnis*).

[26] Always in the fifth foot, before the last heavy element (31 *fingĭmŭ(s) dici* |, 46 *dĭcĭmŭ(s) multa* |, 100 *claudĭmŭ(s) quaedam* |, 106 *uariantĭbŭ(s) quod fit* |, 165 *infortissĭmŭ(s) Graium* |, 166 *nectĭmŭ(s) uerbo,* 177 *subtraxĭmŭ(s) grate* |). On the *Carmen de figuris* cf. II.3.1.

Finally, there are a couple of instances in two late *centones*, both dated to the fifth century, *De alea* (52 *est lŏcŭ(s) quem*, ed. Carbone 2002 = *Anth. Lat.* 8 R.) and *Alcesta* (145 *oblĭtŭ(s) nātōrum*, ed. Salanitro 2007 = *Anth. Lat.* 15 R.), and one instance in the panegyric *In laudem Justini Minoris* by the sixth-century poet Corippus (2.254 *omnĭbŭ(s) sufficiunt*); these instances are most likely mere metrical 'errors', possibly influenced by the accentual system arising in late Latin.

Given this diversified evidence, it is not straightforward to relate sigmatic ecthlipsis to the status of final *-s* in current speech at the different stages of Latin. It would be clearly incorrect to take the exceptional occurrence of sigmatic ecthlipsis in an archaizing poem such as the *Carmen de figuris* as a manifestation of the phonological weakness of *-s* in late Latin speech; similarly, the total absence of sigmatic ecthlipsis from classical texts (first to fourth centuries AD) argues against the idea that final *-s* was dropped in classical Latin.[27]

Given its archaic/Ennian ring, sigmatic ecthlipsis might well be a mere metrical licence already in late republican authors (first century BC), without any strong link to current speech, in which final *-s* might well have been fully pronounced; this possibility seems to also be suggested by the remark of Cicero, who refers to sigmatic ecthlipsis as a practice of earlier speech (*Orat.* 161 *sic enim* **loquebamur** 'this is the way we used to speak'; cf. also Quint. 9.4.38 *plures antiquorum tradit sic locutos*, '[Cicero] reports that many of the ancients spoke like this').

Sigmatic ecthlipsis seems to be standard in authors of the third and second century BC, and especially in Ennius and Lucilius, and may well reflect a current practice in speech: however, the use of sigmatic ecthlipsis in these two authors also presents some problematic elements. In both Ennius and Lucilius, the treatment of final *-s* after a short vowel and before a consonant seems to follow a strict rule, with few exceptions; it is *always* prosodically silent when the syllable ending in *-s* is in one of the even elements[28] of the line (the 'thesis'

---

[27] On this cf. Pezzini (2015).

[28] By the term 'element' I refer to a metrical unit that, in the hexameter, may consist of either a heavy syllable (a 'heavy' element, e.g. trŏ-iae), two light syllables (a 'pyrrhic' or 'resolved' element, e.g. pătŭ-lans), or by either a light or a heavy syllable indifferently (an 'indifferent' element). The hexameter consists of twelve elements, grouped in pairs (known as 'feet') in which the first is a heavy element, and the second is either a heavy (making the foot a spondee) or a resolved element (making the foot a dactyl): cf. e.g. [ītălĭ][ām fă]to, i.e. dactyl (heavy + resolved) and spondee (heavy + heavy).

or 'fall' in old metrics), i.e. the elements that are supposedly not affected by the metrical 'ictus'.[29] Cf. e.g.:

Lucil. 22 M.
Iānŭ(s) Quī|rīnŭ(s) pă|ter siet ac dicatur ad unum
first light place of the second element (trochaic ending) *and*
first light place of the fourth element (trochaic ending)

Enn. *Ann.* 8 S.
oua parire so|let gĕnŭ(s) | pennis condecoratum
second place of the sixth element (dactylic ending)

Enn. *Ann.* 75 S.
solus auem seruat at | Rōmŭlŭ(s) | pulcer in alto
second light place of the eigth element (dactylic ending)

Lucil. 195 M.
lippus edenda acri assiduo cep|āriŭ(s) | cepa
second light place of the tenth element (dactylic ending).

Conversely, final -*s* before a consonant is *always* prosodically influential and renders the preceding syllable heavy by making position when it is found in one of the odd elements of the line (the 'arsis' or 'rise' in old metricology), i.e. the elements that are supposedly affected by the metrical 'ictus'. Cf. e.g.:

Enn. *Ann.* 1 S.
Musae quae pedi|būs mag|num pulsatis olympum
first heavy place of the fifth element

Odd elements in the hexameter are thus always heavy, whereas even elements (apart from the last) are either heavy or resolved. The tenth element (i.e. the second element of the fifth foot) is normally resolved, whereas the last element (i.e. the second element of the sixth foot) is always indifferent, making the last foot either a spondee (heavy + heavy element) or a trochee (heavy + light element). Cf. e.g the line *arma uirumque cano, troiae qui primus ab oris*, whose division into elements (in round brackets, with number subscript) and feet (in square brackets, with number superscript) would be: $^1[(ar)_1|(mă~uĭ)_2]$ $^2[(rum)_3|(quĕ~că)_4]$ $^3[(nō)_5|(trō)_6]$ $^4[(iae)_7|(quī)_8]$ $^5[(prī)_9|(mŭ|s~ă|b)_{10}]$ $^6[(ō)_{11}|(ris)_{12}]$. In this line all odd elements (1, 3, 5, 7, 9, 11) are heavy, elements 2, 4, and 10 are resolved, elements 6 and 8 are heavy, and element 12 is indifferent, consisting of a heavy syllable. See also section 2.

[29] By metrical 'ictus' I refer to that sort of verse 'beat' or 'accent', which is traditionally believed to affect the odd elements in the hexameter (i.e. the elements in 'arsis'), and the equivalent heavy elements in other metres. The existence and nature of the 'ictus' are very controversial (cf. n. 32); in the present discussion I will not take a stance on this issue, and I will use the term 'ictus' in inverted commas, by which I mean that I am not arguing for its existence but at the same time I am not excluding it.

Lucil. 262 M.
concursans ueluti Ancari|ūs clā|reque quiritans
first heavy place of the seventh element.

The interesting (and puzzling) aspect of the behaviour of final -*s* in Ennius and Lucilius is not that it is always prosodically influential in odd elements (which *always* and *necessarily* are heavy), but that it never is in even elements (which can be and often are heavy). For instance, out of 112 cases in Ennius there is only one case of -*s* making position in an even element (*Ann.* 305 S.):

ōrĕ Cĕth|ēgū̱s |Marcŭ(s) Tŭdītānō collēga
fourth element, made heavy by position (*Cĕth|ēgū̱s Marcus*).

This line is problematic and perhaps we should accept the emend-ation of Havet (1891), and invert the order of *Tuditano* and *Marcus*, thus giving a more 'regular' line:

ōrĕ Cĕth|ēgŭ(s̱) Tŭ|dītā|nō Mar|cū̱s col|lēga.

Similarly, there are only eight cases of this type in Lucilius (3%), probably all corrupt (cf. Havet (1891: 318–21)).

Why do Ennius and Lucilius retain -*s* only in odd, heavy elements? Is there any relationship between sigmatic ecthlipsis and the metrical 'ictus'?[30] Also, is it relevant that in most cases (93% in Ennius, 89% in Lucilius) the word ending in -*s* affected by sigmatic ecthlipsis has a dactylic or trochaic ending (often filling the fifth foot, in 50% of the cases in Ennius, 55% in Lucilius), and thus features the syllable bearing the word accent occupying one of the odd, heavy elements (e.g. Enn. *Ann.* 34 S. | ártŭbŭ(s) | lumen |, 280 S. con|téntŭ(s) be|atus, Lucil. 173 M. | dígnŭ(s) pu|ellus, 493 M. Trĕ|bélliŭ(s) | multost |)? Is there any relation between the retention of final -*s* in Ennius and Lucilius and iambic shortening (see section 5), a phenomenon that is not allowed when the syllable is accented and (at least according to the 'traditional' definition)[31] concerns syllables unaffected by the metrical 'ictus'? I will not try to address these questions here, as they bring in one of the most controversial issues of Latin philology, i.e. that concerning the existence and nature of the metrical 'ictus' and

---

[30] For this controversial term and notion see n. 29.
[31] Against this 'traditional' definition see now the severe words of Questa (2007: 134–51).

its relation to the word accent, which deserves a much fuller treatment.[32]

As far as the present discussion is concerned, I will only highlight that sigmatic ecthlipsis in Ennius and Lucilius displays a certain degree of artificiality and complexity, which we would not expect if it were merely the manifestation of the drop of final *-s* in speech.

The only remaining important evidence for sigmatic ecthlipsis consists of the comedies of Plautus and Terence, in which sigmatic ecthlipsis is generally considered to be as standard as it is in Ennius and Lucilius—but is it really so? In the central section of the chapter I will address this question: I will assess in particular the corpus of Terence, and provide systematic and detailed figures, which I will compare in the final section with the figures for Plautus taken from previous studies.

2. SECOND PREMISE: THE METRE OF ROMAN COMEDY

Before I present the evidence for sigmatic ecthlipsis in Terence, it is necessary to provide a summary of the terminology I use in this chapter, which is derived from recent treatises on Latin comic metre (especially Questa (2007) and de Melo (2010–2012: I.lxxxv–xcviii).[33] The following examination relies on an analysis of iambic and trochaic lines, which form about 99% of the metres used by Terence. Iambic lines consist of a series of iambic feet, trochaic lines of a series of trochaic feet. An iambic foot (˘ ¯) is a sequence of a light element + a heavy element, a trochaic foot (¯ ˘) is a sequence of a heavy element + a light element.

A light element (˘) is always monosyllabic and is formed by a light syllable (e.g. *fă-cis*), a heavy element (¯) is naturally monosyllabic and formed by a heavy syllable (e.g. *făc-tus*) but may occasionally be disyllabic (a 'resolved' element) and formed by two light syllables (e.g. *făcĭ-o*). Although this may seem simple at first glance, it is complicated by

---

[32] For an overview of the history of the *quaestio* see Fortson (2008: 30–4), with bibliography. For a recent study see Stroh (1990). Cf. also Allen (1973: 335–59), Questa (2007: *passim*).

[33] For other treatments of comic metre see Lindsay (1922), Raven (1965), Gratwick (1993: 40–63), Fortson (2011).

the fact that in the iambic and trochaic lines of Terence a light element is normally treated as an *anceps element* (x), i.e. an element that may be either light or heavy and thus may be formed either by a light syllable or by a heavy syllable, or even by two light syllables. We should note here that heavy and anceps elements may be either monosyllabic or disyllabic, whereas light elements are always monosyllabic.

Since each heavy element may be resolved into two light syllables, and each light element (i.e. each anceps element) can be replaced by a heavy element, an iambic or trochaic foot may actually result in a dactyl (⁻ ˘ ˘), anapaest (˘ ˘ ⁻), spondee (⁻ ⁻), tribrach (˘ ˘ ˘), or proceleusmatic (˘ ˘ ˘ ˘).

Some restrictions and exceptions are found, but mainly at the end of the line: the last element of each line is *indifferent* (∩), i.e. it can be either heavy or light but is necessarily monosyllabic; the penultimate syllable, if originally light, is always treated as light and is therefore always formed by a light syllable.

Terence mainly uses five metrical patterns: they are, in order of frequency, iambic senarii (ia^6: six iambic feet, i.e. twelve elements), trochaic septenarii (tr^7: seven trochaic feet + one element, i.e. fifteen elements), iambic octonarii (ia^8: eight iambic feet, i.e. sixteen elements), iambic septenarii (ia^7: seven iambic feet + one element, i.e. fifteen elements), and trochaic octonarii (tr^8: eight trochaic feet, i.e. sixteen elements).[34] Box 5.1 shows the structure of each of these metrical patterns.

Box 5.1 Iambo-trochaic metres used by Terence

Iambic senarius (ia^6)	x ⁻ | x ⁻ | x ⁻ | x ⁻ | x ⁻ | ˘ ∩ |
Trochaic septenarius (tr^7)	⁻ x | ⁻ x | ⁻ x | ⁻ x | ⁻ x | ⁻ x | ⁻ ˘ ∩
Iambic octonarius (ia^8)	x ⁻ | x ⁻ | x ⁻ | x ⁻ | x ⁻ | x ⁻ | x ⁻ | ˘ ∩ |
Iambic septenarius (ia^7)	x ⁻ | x ⁻ | x ⁻ | x ⁻ | x ⁻ | x ⁻ | x ⁻ | ∩
Trochaic octonarius (tr^7)	⁻ x | ⁻ x | ⁻ x | ⁻ x | ⁻ x | ⁻ x | ⁻ x | ⁻ ∩ |
⁻ *heavy element*	(= one heavy syllable or two light syllables)
- *light element*	(= one light syllable)
× *anceps element*	(= heavy element or light element)
∩ *indifferent element*	(= one heavy or light syllable)
| *end of foot*	

In Box 5.1 I have not taken into consideration the various metrical
laws that affect iambo-trochaic lines (for these cf. Questa (2007:
199–413)), since its aim is simply to give a general overview of the
metrical concepts to which I will refer in the following discussion.

The final technical term I will use in this chapter is *caesura*
(indicated in this chapter by the symbol ||), i.e. a metrical break inside
the line that coincides with the end of a word. In my analysis I will
refer only to a particular type of *caesura*, i.e. the *median caesura* in ia[7]
and ia[8], which occurs when there is the end of a word after the eighth
element. Cf. e.g.:

Haut. 724 (ia[7])
dĕcem | mĭnās | quās mī | dărĕ || pollĭcĭ|tust. quod| sī nunc| me
Eun. 541 (ia[7])
praefē|cĭmus| dăt(ī) ā|nŭlī || lŏcŭs tem|pus con|stĭtū|tŭmst|.

This type of caesura is relevant to my discussion because the iambic
foot that precedes the caesura (i.e. that formed by the seventh and
eighth elements) is treated as though it were the last foot of the line;
consequently the eighth heavy element is indifferent (i.e. it must be
monosyllabic but can be either light or heavy) and the seventh
element is necessarily light. The schema of ia[7] and ia[8] with median
caesura would therefore be the following:

Iambic octonarius (ia[8])
x – | x – | x – | ˘ ⌒ || x – | x – | x – | ˘ ⌒ |
Iambic septenarius (ia[7])
x – | x – | x – | ˘ ⌒ || x – | x – | x – | ⌒

3. SIGMATIC ECTHLIPSIS: EDITORS' CHOICES

In the OCT edition of Terence we find printed about 990 cases of
sigmatic ecthlipsis, out of a total of about 1450 instances of final -*s*
following a short vowel and preceding a consonant, which are the two
conditions necessary for the realization of the phenomenon.
Instances of final -*s* preceding a vowel will therefore not be considered
in the following analysis and are excluded from the figures given.

With regard to the *c.*460 instances in which sigmatic ecthlipsis is
not printed by the OCT editors, about seventy involve monosyllabic

words (*bis*, *is*, *quis*). Sigmatic ecthlipsis is never found printed in monosyllabic words in the OCT of Terence, even when the two conditions are met and they are metrically to be scanned light.[35] The remaining group consists mainly of cases of syllables occupying a heavy element and which therefore are necessarily to be scanned heavy; cf. e.g. *Ph.* 890 ia[6]:

nunc ges|tus mĭhĭ | uoltus|qu(e) est căpi|**undus** | nŏuōs|

The syllable -*dus* of the gerundive *capiundus* occupies the tenth, heavy element of the line and therefore cannot be scanned light.

The rationale behind this choice is clear: OCT editors *always* print sigmatic ecthlipsis except in the case of monosyllabic words ending in -*s* and except when the syllable ending in -*s* is metrically heavy (i.e. if it occupies a monosyllabic heavy element). The question that remains uncertain is whether all *c.*990 instances of sigmatic ecthlipsis printed by OCT are justified by the evidence.

In fact, the impression that a reader may have when consulting the OCT edition of Terence is that sigmatic ecthlipsis is such a wide-spread phonetic phenomenon as to be considered standard; accordingly, one might argue that in the Latin of Terence's contemporaries final -*s* was so phonetically weak that, though not weak enough to allow elision, it was always silent before a consonant. But is this really true? What is the evidence for sigmatic ecthlipsis in Terence?

To try to answer these questions a complete scansion of Terence's text is needed. Since the evidence for sigmatic ecthlipsis is metrical, we need clear figures concerning the metrical position of the syllable ending in -*s* in each of the lines concerned in order to evaluate whether that syllable is to be scanned heavy or light.

The following analysis is based on the scansion of all the lines in Terence that contain the sequence *short vowel + -s + consonant*: *c.* 1230 lines have been analysed, consisting of 591 iambic senarii, 288 trochaic septenarii, 244 iambic octonarii, eighty-six iambic septenarii, and twenty-one trochaic octonarii. The complete list of these lines with their scansion is found in Appendix 3. Given their complexity, lines belonging to lyric sections have been excluded, together with a

---

[35] In these cases the OCT edition of Terence displays the light weight of the syllable but not the dropping of final -*s*, thus implying the operation of iambic shortening (cf. section 4.2.3). Cf. e.g. *Ph.* 124 *quid ĭs fecit?* (cf. also *An.* 577, *Ph.* 124, 477, 1046).

few other lines (about twelve) which, if not *desperata*, are excessively obscure as far as prosody and metre are concerned. This does not mean that the scansion of all lines examined has been straightforward or that no other scansions could be allowed. However, I have tried to be as inclusive as possible; since the purpose of this analysis is to evaluate the evidence for sigmatic ecthlipsis, not that for the retention of final -*s*, even the simple fact that a scansion without sigmatic ecthlipsis is potentially admissible is relevant. For the lines of which the scansion is debatable or ambiguous, I have preferred to follow the prosody suggested by OCT editors, for the sake of consistency.[36]

4. TERENCE: THE METRICAL EVIDENCE

4.1 Overview

Excluding *cantica* and problematic lines, I have found in Terence c.1422 instances of the pattern *short vowel + final -s + consonant* (including instances in which the word following -*s* is a univerbated clitic -*que*, -*ne*, or -*ue*)[37] for a total of c.1230 lines. As mentioned above, this prosodic sequence can count either as a light syllable (with sigmatic ecthlipsis) or as a heavy syllable (without sigmatic ecthlipsis and with final -*s* making position, as expected). The only way to determine its prosody is to scan the line without considering the weight of the syllable ending in -*s* and to establish in each case which metrical position it occupies.

---

[36] A good treatment of sigmatic ecthlipsis in Plautus and Terence is by Sullivan (1970) in his (neglected) PhD dissertation on final -*s* in early Latin. However, Sullivan does not provide detailed and complete figures and lists for iambo-trochaic lines, and only focuses on cases occupying a light element (cf. section 6).

[37] Fourteen instances in total: in nine instances the syllable ending in -*s* must be scanned heavy, and thus final -*s* makes position (*An.* 748 *quisue*, *Haut.* 594 *minúsque*, 616 *ísne*, *Eun.* 507 *magísque*, *Ph.* 102 *uoltisne*, 480 *mansurúsque*, 554 *minúsue*, 890 *uoltúsque*, *Ad.* 853 *pergísne*); in three instances the syllable occupies an anceps element and thus the weight of the syllable cannot be determined (*An.* 161 *pedibus-que*, *Eun.* 136 *ignarusque*, *Hec.* 848 *uenustatisque*); in two instances the syllable ending in -*s* must be scanned light (*Haut.* 46 *nimisque*, *Ph.* 852 *isne*), but both cases could be explained as an effect of iambic shortening (see section 4.2.3). For a certain case of sigmatic ecthlipsis before a univerbated clitic cf. Pl. *Bac.* 192 *minus ualet moribundŭ(s)que est* | (cf. also Fortson (2008: 248)).

In an iambo-trochaic line a syllable that may be either heavy or light can occupy many different metrical positions: it can form a light element (thus being necessarily light), a monosyllabic heavy element (thus being necessarily heavy), a monosyllabic anceps or indifferent element (thus often making it impossible to determine its weight), or it can be one of the two syllables of a resolved anceps or heavy element (thus being necessarily light).[38] To clarify, I offer here some examples. In the examples below the symbol | indicates the borders of the iambic foot, the symbol || indicates the end of the line.

fac|tus sit || (˘ ˉ)
-*us* occupies a light element

| mĕlĭus | dicas (˘ ˘ ˉ)
-*us* occupies a monosyllabic heavy element

gră|uis mā|ter (x ˉ)
-*is* occupies a monosyllabic anceps element

| bŏnus tū | (˘ ˘ ˉ)
-*us* occupies the second place of a resolved anceps element

pa|ter tuus | dictus (ˉ ˘ ˘)
-*us* occupies the second place of a resolved heavy element

Table 5.2 presents the results of the analysis, displaying the distribution of the phonetic sequence *short vowel + -s + C-* according to its metrical position in the line.

As displayed in Table 5.2, in some cases (cat. 1, thirty cases) it has been impossible to determine with precision the metrical value of the syllables ending in -*s*, since there are two acceptable scansions of the line, in each of which the syllable occupies a different metrical position. I quote as an example *An.* 21 (ia⁶):

pŏtius| qu(am) istō|r(um) obscū|ram dī|lĭgen|tiam|

In this line the first foot might be scanned either as an anapaest (*potius* = ˘ ˘ ˉ) with the syllable ending in -*s* heavy by position and occupying the second, heavy monosyllabic element of the foot (ˉ), or as a tribrach (*potius* = ˘ ˘ ˘) with the -*s* syllable affected by sigmatic ecthlipsis and occupying the second syllable of the second, resolved

---

[38] For this terminology see above section 3.

Table 5.2. Metrical position and prosody of the sequence -Vs + C- in Terence

Category	1	2		3	4	5	6
ELEMENT	?	*anceps monosyllabic element*	*indifferent element*	*heavy monosyllabic element*	*one of the two syllables of a resolved element (heavy or anceps)*	*light element*
WEIGHT		HEAVY OR LIGHT			HEAVY	LIGHT	
TOTAL (1422)	30	849	34	281	205	23
%		64%		20%	16%	

heavy element (˘ ˘). Consequently, it is impossible to establish the weight of the syllable ending in -*s*, which might be either heavy or light.[39]

This group (cat. 1) is not the only group of instances for which it is impossible to determine the weight of the syllable involved. As displayed in Table 5.2, in the vast majority of cases (cat. 2, 849 instances) the syllable ending in -*s* occupies a monosyllabic anceps element. Cf. e.g.:

Ad. 714 (ia[6])
monstrā|tiō|nĕ **mag|nus** per|dat Iup|pĭter|
mag|nus seventh element, anceps, monosyllabic

Haut. 70 (ia[6])
nullum | **rĕmit|tis tem|pus** nĕquĕ | tē res|pĭcis|
rĕmit|tis fifth element, anceps, monosyllabic
tem|pus seventh element, anceps, monosyllabic

Haut. 905 (tr[7])
sōlus | **sōlus** | tĭmeō | **Bacchis** | consĕ|cūtas|t ĭlĭ|co
sōlus second element, anceps, monosyllabic
sōlus fourth element, anceps, monosyllabic
Bacchis eighth element, anceps, monosyllabic

Ph. 1051 (tr[7])
făciam|qu(e) et dī|cam bĕ|nignĕ | **dīcis** | pol mĕrĭ|tumst tu|om
dīcis tenth element, anceps, monosyllabic

Ph. 236 (ia[8])
inuī|tus fē|cī lex | coē|git au|diō | făteor | plăces|
inuī|tus third element, anceps, monosyllabic

---

[39] Normally, a tribrach word cannot form an iambic foot since this would break Hermann-Lachmann's norm (cf. Questa (2007: 213–21) and see below pp. 218–19). However, the second element of the line is not affected by this norm (cf. Questa 2007: 221–44) and therefore the scansion of *potius* as a tribrach is acceptable in *An.* 21.

Ad. 162 (tr^8)

tū quod | tē **pos|tĕrius** | purgēs | hanc in|iūri|am mī | nollĕ|
pos|*tĕri̱us̱* sixth element, anceps, monosyllabic

Instances considered in this group involve syllables occupying anceps monosyllabic elements, which may be formed by either a heavy or light syllable.[40] It is generally impossible to determine the weight of syllables found in such a metrical position.

Another group (cat. 3) consists of instances in which the syllable potentially affected by sigmatic ecthlipsis occupies an indifferent element (thirty-four cases, see Table 5.2). Since for obvious reasons sigmatic ecthlipsis cannot occur at the end of a line, this group includes only instances that occupy the last element before a median caesura in ia^7 and ia^8. Cf. e.g.:

Ad. 254 (ia^8)

abs quī|uīs hŏmĭ|nĕ qu(om) es|t **ŏpus** || bĕnĕfĭci|(um) accĭpĕ|rĕ gau| deas|
ŏp̱us̱ eighth element, indifferent, monosyllabic, before median caesura

Haut. 744 (ia^7)

ancil|lās om|nis **Bac|chĭdis** || transdū|c(e) hūc ad | uos prŏpĕ|re|
Bac|*chĭdis* eighth element, indifferent, monosyllabic before median caesura

Again, syllables occupying indifferent elements might scan either as heavy or light and therefore the weight of the syllable ending in -*s* cannot be determined. Instances belonging to one of the three groups described above (cat. 1, 2, 3 in Table 5.2, i.e. ambiguous scansions, syllables occupying anceps or indifferent elements) do not provide evidence for sigmatic ecthlipsis, since the weight of the syllables involved cannot be determined and they might potentially all be heavy.

---

[40] Some scholars (cf. especially Gratwick (1993: 40–63)) have argued that some anceps elements in iambic metres (e.g. the third and seventh element in ia^6) and the corresponding elements in trochaic metres (e.g. the second, sixth, and tenth element in tr^7) should be distinguished from the other anceps elements (i.e. the first, fifth, and ninth element in ia^6; the fourth, eighth, and twelfth in tr^7), since the former are less frequently realized as heavy elements than the latter; however, since this would be, in any case, a tendency rather than a rule, and heavy elements would still be possible in every anceps elements (although in a different proportion), I have not taken into account this distinction and have considered together all cases of sigmatic ecthlipsis occupying a (monosyllabic) anceps element.

Another large group (cat. 4, 281 instances, cf. Table 5.2) includes cases in which the syllable ending in -*s* occupies a monosyllabic heavy element. Cf. e.g.:

Haut. 832 (ia⁶)
quīn **ac|cĭpis** | cĕdŏ sā|nē sĕquĕ|r(e) hac m(e) ō|cius|
ac|cĭpis fourth element, heavy, monosyllabic

Eun. 611 (ia⁷)
n(e) **intus** | sit por|r(o) autem | păter | nē rū|rĕ rĕdĭ|ĕrit | iam|
intus second element, heavy, monosyllabic

Eun. 648 (ia⁸)
ŭt ĕg(o) **un|guĭbus** | făcĭl(e) il|l(i) ĭn ŏcŭ|lōs in|uŏlem | uĕnē|fĭco|
un|guĭbus fourth element, heavy, monosyllabic

Hec. 104 (ia⁶)
nōn es|t **ŏpus** | prōlā|t(o) hoc per|contā|rier|
ŏpus fourth element, heavy, monosyllabic

Hec. 144 (ia⁶)
post **Pam|phĭlus** | mē sō|lum sē|dūcit | fŏras|
Pam|phĭlus fourth element, heavy, monosyllabic

Ad. 9 (ia⁶)
mĕrĕtrī|c(em) in prī|mā fā|bŭl(a) eum | **Plautus** | lŏcum|
Plautus tenth element, heavy, monosyllabic

Syllables occupying this type of element are necessarily scanned heavy. Therefore, instances of syllables ending in -*s* which occupy one of these elements provide evidence *against* sigmatic ecthlipsis.

Finally, there is a group of instances (cat. 5 and 6, cf. Table 5.2) in which the syllable ending in -*s* must for metrical reasons be scanned light, since it occupies one of the two places in a resolved element (cat. 5, 205 cases) or a light element (cat. 6, twenty-three cases). As displayed in Table 5.2, the proportion of this group in the total number is about 16%, which is a lower rate than the one found in Plautus (58%), according to the figures given by Wallace (1984: 217). All syllables that are found in these positions are necessarily scanned light. Instances of syllables ending in -*s* occupying one of these positions *seem* to provide evidence for sigmatic ecthlipsis. I say *seem* because, contrary to what we might superficially expect, this evidence presents such homogeneous features as to suggest that we are perhaps dealing with a different phenomenon, as will become clear in the following sections (4.2.1 and 4.2.2).

At this point, it will be useful to consider separately on the one hand the instances in which the syllable ending in -*s* occupies a place in a resolved element, which form the larger group (205 cases), and on the other those in which it occupies a light element (only twenty-three cases). I will consider first the former group of 205 instances (section 4.2.1), and postpone the analysis of the latter group of twenty-three instances to a later section (4.2.2), because, as we will see, the twenty-three instances seem to provide evidence concerning both sigmatic ecthlipsis and other issues such as the cliticization of the verb *esse* in Latin.

4.2 Sigmatic Ecthlipsis in a Resolved Element

Table 5.3 provides further details on the distribution of syllables ending in *short vowel* + -*s* (before a consonant) occupying one of the places in a disyllabic resolved element. It displays in particular whether the syllable ending in -*s* occupies the first or the second place in the resolved element, and the type of word ending in -*s*.

4.2.1 Syllables Occupying the Second Place of a Resolved Element

First, we must note that in most cases (200) the syllable ending in -*s* occupies the second place in a resolved element. Cf. e.g.:

Ad. 810 (ia[6])
quod sătĭs | pŭtā|bas tuă | bŏn(a) am|bōbus | fŏre|
săt ĭs| second place in the second, resolved heavy element

Eun. 645 (tr[7])
quīn ĕti|(am) insŭ|per scĕlŭs | postquam | lūdĭfī|cātust | uirgĭ|nem|
scĕlŭs|second place in the sixth, resolved anceps element

Table 5.3. Metrical position of syllables ending in *short vowel* + -*s* in a resolved element

Metrical Position	First place	Second place			Total
	5	200			205
TYPE OF WORD	Monosyllabic word	Disyllabic word		Polysyllabic word	
		Iambic	Trochaic		
	5	191	5	4	

I have found only five instances in which the syllable ending in -*s* occupies the first place in a resolved element:

An. 377 (tr⁷)

ipsŭs sĭ|b(i) ess(e) in|iŭri|ŭs uĭde|ātŭr | nĕqu(e) ĭd in|iŭri|a
-*ŭs sĭ*- first place in the second, resolved anceps, element

An. 857 (tr⁷)

tristĭs sĕ|uĕrĭ|tās ĭ|nest in | uolt(u) at|qu(e) in uer|bīs fĭ|des
-*ĭs sĕ*- first place in the second, resolved anceps element

Haut. 339 (tr⁷)

sĭnĕ pĕ|rīcl(o) es|s(e) huiŭs mŏ|d(i) obsĕ|cr(o) ălĭquid | rĕpĕrī |
maxŭ|me
-*ŭsmŏ*- first place in the sixth, resolved anceps element

Haut. 812 (ia⁶)

huiŭs mŏ|dī mĭhĭ | rēs sem|per com|mĭnis|cĕre|
-*ŭs mŏ*- first place in the second, resolved heavy element

Ph. 529 (tr⁷)

n(am) hic m(e) hui|ŭs mŏdī | scībat| ess(e) ĕg|(o) hunc es|s(e) ălĭter |
crēdĭ|di
-*ŭs mŏ*- first place in the third, resolved heavy element

All these cases are, however, problematic. First, *An.* 377 and 857 would be the only two cases of breaking of the law of Ritschl (see below) in an anceps element in trochaic septenarii in Terence and are thus suspected by scholars.[41] Moreover, in the last three instances of the list above the word that ends in -*s* is the demonstrative *huius* followed by the genitive *modi*, a sequence that might also be scanned in other ways (apart from the fact that it could be considered a single prosodic word and thus the omission of -*s*- could be something different from sigmatic ecthlipsis[42]). In particular, in the last two lines we could treat *modi* as a pyrrhic (i.e. with iambic shortening, just as OCT editors do twice in the Terence corpus at *Haut.* 205, *Ad.* 441), thus giving:

Ph. 529 (tr⁷)

n(am) hic m(e) hui|us mŏdĭ | scība|t ess(ĕ) ĕgŏ | hunc es|s(ĕ) ălĭter |
crēdĭ|di

Haut. 812 (ia⁶)

huius | mŏdĭ mĭhĭ | rēs sem|per com|mĭnis|cĕre|

---

[41] See Questa (2007: 212–13, 230, with bibliography). Cf. also n. 43.

[42] The omission of -*s* would not in this case be operating at a word boundary (*huiu(s) modi*) but would rather be word-internal (*huiu(s)modi*). On this cf. section 5.

In *Haut.* 339, we might instead scan *huius* as a monosyllable, as is common in Plautus and Terence (cf. e.g. *Hec.* 168, and see Questa (2007: 70)), thus giving:

(tr⁷) sĭnĕ pĕ|rīcl(o) es|s(e) h͡uius mŏ|d(i) obsĕ|cr(o) ălĭquĭd | rĕpĕrī | maxŭ|me

According to the scansions above, the last syllable of *huius* would necessarily be scanned heavy in all three cases.

The rarity of cases in which the syllable ending in -*s* occupies the first place of a disyllabic resolved element is most likely due to the influence of an acknowledged norm in the iambo-trochaic lines of Plautus and Terence, the law of Ritschl (cf. Questa (2007: 207–13)). According to this, a disyllabic element cannot be formed from a polysyllabic word beginning before the element and ending inside it. To put it in another way, a word cannot end after the first place in a disyllabic element (cf. e.g. in a forbidden sequence such as *tam|ĕn ĕ| go*, where the disyllabic element is formed by the last syllable of *tamen* and the first of *ego*), except if the word is a monosyllable. The metrical condition 'forbidden' by the law of Ritschl would be found, for instance, at *An.* 857 (see above) where the second disyllabic resolved element is formed from the last (light) syllable of the word *tristĭs* and the first (light) syllable of *sĕuērĭtās.*[43]

4.2.2 Final -s in Prosodically Iambic Words

We must also note that in most cases (191, cf. Table 5.3) the syllable potentially involving sigmatic ecthlipsis is the last syllable of an original prosodically iambic word (= a pyrrhic word ending in -*s* before a consonant, cf. e.g. *sătĭs sunt*), which becomes pyrrhic because of sigmatic ecthlipsis and which occupies a disyllabic resolved element, e.g.:

---

[43] This metrical sequence could also be accepted in this case since breakings of metrical norms are often admitted in the second position in the line (cf. Questa (2007: 221–4)). However, in trochaic verse in Terence breaking of the norm of Ritschl is hardly ever attested in the second, anceps element (cf. Questa (2007: 230)); moreover, breaking of the norm of Ritschl is occasionally found in Terence, also beyond the second position, but never in anceps elements and always in heavy elements. Cf. e.g. *Eun.* 813 (ia⁸) ĭ|gĭtŭr ŭ|bĭ, *Haut.* 339 (tr⁷) accĭ|pĭt hŏmō (for lists of cases with discussion see Raffaelli (1982: 19–59), Minarini (1987: 106–46)).

An. 736 (ia⁶)

ŏrā|tiō|n(i) ut quom|qu(e) **ŏpŭs** sit | uerbis | uǐde|
ŏpŭs seventh element, disyllabic resolved

Hec. 541 (tr⁷)

multō | **priŭs** scī|uī quam | t(u) ill(um) hă|bēr(e) ă|mīcam | Myrrǐ|na
priŭs third element, disyllabic resolved

Haut. 617 (ia⁸)

e(um) es|s(e) at ut | **sătǐs** con|templā|tă mŏdŏ | sis meă | nūtrix | sătis
sătǐs fifth element, disyllabic resolved

Although they are not displayed in editions,[44] there are also five
instances of what might look like sigmatic ecthlipsis with a monosyllabic word (*is*). These instances are normally considered as undergoing a different metrical phenomenon, i.e. iambic shortening: in all of
these the demonstrative *is* follows another light monosyllable, thus
creating an iambic sequence that is often shortened to a pyrrhic (on
iambic shortening see below 4.2.3 and Questa (2007: ch. 5, especially
108–17)). For this reason editors tend not to print sigmatic ecthlipsis
in these cases.

An. 577 (ia⁷)

ět **ǐs** mǐhǐ | persuā|det nup|tias | quantum | que(am) ut | mātū|rem
ět ǐs second place in the first resolved element

Ph. 124 (ia⁶)

quǐd **ǐs** fē|cit hoc | consǐlǐ|um quod | dīcam | dědit|
quǐd ǐs second place in the first resolved element

Ph. 477 (ia⁸)

quǐd **ǐs** fē|cit con|fūtā|uit uer|bīs ad|mŏd(um) ī|rātum | sěnem|
quǐd ǐs second place in the first resolved element

Ph. 852 (tr⁷)

sěd **ǐsn(e)** est| quem quae|r(o) an nō|n ipsust| congrědě|r(e) actū|tum
quǐ|d est
sěd ǐsne second place in the first resolved element

Ph. 1046 (tr⁷)

quŏd **ǐs** iǔ|bēbit | făciam | mŭlier | săpiens | es Nau|sistră|ta
quŏd ǐs second place in the first resolved element

There are only five instances of sigmatic ecthlipsis in non-iambic,
trochaic dysillabic words (e.g. *ipsŭs, tristǐs*). These are the ones discussed above (4.2.1 p. 215), in which the syllable ending in *-s* occupies

the first place in a dysillabic element (*An.* 377, 857, *Haut.* 339, 812, *Ph.* 529): as shown, all these cases are problematic.

Finally, sigmatic ecthlipsis in trisyllabic or longer words is extremely rare. I have found only four instances of such a type in Terence:

Haut. 205 (ia^8)
ūniŭs | mŏdī | sunt fer|mē paul|lō qu(i) est | hŏmō | tŏlĕrā|bĭlis|
-*iŭs* second place in the second resolved heavy element[45]

Hec. 380 (tr^7)
omnĭbŭs | nōbīs | ut res | dant sē|s(e) ĭtă ma|gn(i) atqu(e) hŭmĭ|lēs
sŭ|mus
-*nĭbŭs* second place in the second resolved anceps element

Hec. 701 (ia^6)
omnĭbŭs | mŏdis | mĭser | sum nec | quĭd ăgam | scio|
-*nĭbŭs* second place in the second resolved heavy element

Ad. 971 (tr^7)
omnĭbŭs | grāti|(am) hăbe(o) et | seorsum | tĭbĭ prae|tĕreā | Dēme|a
-*nĭbŭs* second place in the second resolved anceps element

Moreover, also these instances may be considered as undergoing iambic shortening rather than sigmatic ecthlipsis: in all of these the reduced syllable occupies the second element of an originally iambic sequence occupying a single element, a sequence which is often shortened to a pyrrhic (on iambic shortening see 4.2.3).

Again, one can see by the rarity of this pattern (i.e. sigmatic ecthlipsis at the end of trisyllabic or longer words) the influence of a well-known norm regulating the iambic and trochaic lines in Plautus and Terence, the law of Hermann-Lachmann (cf. Questa (2007: 213–21)). According to it, no disyllabic element can be formed from a word beginning before the element and ending together with it. In other words, no trisyllabic or longer word can end with the second place of a disyllabic element (cf. e.g. in the forbidden sequence *scrup|ŭlŭs | etiam*, the disyllabic element is formed by the last two syllables of the polysyllabic word *scrupulus*). The metrical condition 'forbidden' by the law of Hermann-Lachmann is, for instance, found at *Hec.* 380 (see above) where the second disyllabic resolved element

---

[45] The scansion of this line does not seem straightforward since *modi* might also be scanned as a pyrrhic (cf. 4.2.1 p. 215); consequently the last syllable of *unius* would be scanned with a long *ī*, coming to occupy a monosyllabic anceps element: *Haut.* 205 ūnī|*us mŏdĭ* ($\times$ ˘ ˘) | *sunt fer|mē paul|lō qu(i) est | hŏmō | tŏlĕrā|bĭlis|*.

is formed from the last two syllables of the trisyllabic word (*omnĭbŭs*). The fact that the exceptions above are all found in the second element (which is a place less affected by these metrical norms, cf. n. 39) strongly suggests that the influence of the law of Hermann-Lachmann is at work in other parts of the line.

4.2.3 Sigmatic Ecthlipsis vs. Iambic Shortening

To sum up, in Terence sigmatic ecthlipsis seems to be metrically justified in only 228 out of the *c*.1422 instances of the sequence *short vowel* + *-s* + consonant (cf. Table 5.2), twenty-three occupying a light element, and 205 occupying one of the two places in a disyllabic resolved element. Moreover, if we exclude instances occupying a light element (which I will consider separately in the next section, as they are very few and have specific features) in the majority of the remaining cases (191 out of 205) the syllable involved is the second syllable of a prosodically iambic, disyllabic word that occupies a pyrrhic resolved element (cf. Table 5.3). In this section we will see how even this group of 191 cases does not necessarily provide strong evidence for sigmatic ecthlipsis.

As discussed in the previous sections (cf. 4.2.1 and 4.2.2), the figures reported above may be influenced by two metrical norms (those of Ritschl and Hermann-Lachmann), which reduce the possibility of having a polysyllabic word ending with a light syllable occupying a light metrical place. Is the application of these metrical norms the only factor accounting for the fact that sigmatic ecthlipsis is attested virtually only in iambic words? Is the evidence that such iambic words ending in *-s* can be scanned as pyrrhic sufficient to prove the operation of sigmatic ecthlipsis?

First, one must note that there is little variety among the prosodically iambic words apparently affected by sigmatic ecthlipsis; most of the instances belong to a small number of very common words.[46] In particular, out of the 191 cases (cf. Table 5.3) there are forty-nine instances of the adverb *satis*, twenty-five of *prius*, twenty-three of *minus*, and twenty-one of *opus*, giving a total of 118 instances of just four different words (62%).

---

[46] The low variety of words affected by sigmatic ecthlipsis has been noticed in Plautus as well (cf. Wallace (1982, 1984)), for whom, however, there are no detailed figures.

Table 5.4. Distribution of prosodically iambic words before a consonant in Terence

	Pyrrhic scansion (with sigmatic ecthlipsis)	Both scansions possible	Iambic scansion (no sigmatic ecthlipsis)
satis	49	2	5
prius	25	1	1
minus	23	1	3
opus	21	11	1
OTHER FORMS			
Verbal	9	40	1
Non-verbal	64	6	5
TOTAL	191	61	16

Second, as displayed in Table 5.4, there are few cases in which prosodically iambic words in Terence *must* be scanned as iambs (i.e. with the second syllable not affected by sigmatic ecthlipsis); I have found no more than ten cases of the four most common words (five of *satis*, one of *prius*, three of *minus*, one of *opus*), and six of other words. In total, of the approximately 268 instances of prosodically iambic words in Terence (ending in -*s*), 191 are *necessarily* scanned as pyrrhic, sixty-one *may* be scanned as pyrrhic,[47] and only sixteen *cannot* be scanned as pyrrhic but must be scanned as iambic (cf. Table 5.4).

Third, there are very few certain cases of sigmatic ecthlipsis with iambic verbal forms (nine, with six instances of the form *sumus*). All others involve a nominative noun or adjective ending in -*ŭs*, an adverb ending in -*ĭs* or -*ŭs*, or a pronoun in the genitive singular ending in -*ĭs* or in the dative/ablative plural ending in -*bŭs*. Table 5.4 sums up the figures discussed in the paragraphs above. The distribution displayed in Table 5.4 is interesting; if sigmatic ecthlipsis were simply a phonological phenomenon, perhaps we would not expect a significant variation in the treatment of different morphological endings, as in fact appears to exist. Moreover, these figures suggest that it

---

[47] I.e. with the syllable occupying an anceps or indifferent element shortened by sigmatic ecthlipsis. However, as I will discuss below, in Terence the evidence of sigmatic ecthlipsis is weak and might be explained in most cases as depending on iambic shortening. According to this view, all the cases of *short vowel* + -*s* + C-occupying an anceps or indifferent element should be scanned heavy, since iambic shortening operates only within a disyllabic element (cf. Questa (2007: 85–151)).

is almost standard for prosodically iambic words ending in -*s* (and especially for non-verbal forms) to be scanned pyrrhic in Terence.

As already mentioned (p. 215), the phenomenon by which a prosodically iambic word is scanned as pyrrhic is by no means restricted to words ending in -*s* in Terence; there are many other originally pyrrhic words ending in other consonants that, if placed before a consonant, thus promising to be prosodically iambic, are regularly 'shortened' and scan as pyrrhic. We may consider for instance the words *ăpud* and *ĕnim*; before a consonant the adverb *ĕnim* must always be scanned pyrrhic (twenty-four instances), and this also obtains for the preposition *ăpud* in 63% of occurrences (thirty out of forty-eight). Moreover, originally iambic words ending in long vowels are also often, if not always, scanned as pyrrhic: e.g. this is always true for instances of the imperative *căuē* (twelve out of twelve). This phenomenon is known as *iambic shortening* and consists in the pyrrhic scansion of a prosodically iambic sequence, iambic either by nature (e.g. *uĭdē*) or position (*ăpud| te* = ˘ ˉ |), occupying a disyllabic element in the line. Its importance and spread is now widely acknowledged by scholars.[48] Further to this, it has been suggested that iambic shortening (at least in certain cases) should be considered more a form of metrical licence than a phonetic phenomenon (cf. Questa (2007: 145)).[49]

Some scholars of archaic metre tend to distinguish between the two phenomena (sigmatic ecthlipsis and iambic shortening), and recommend an explanation of the pyrrhic scansions of words such as *sătis* and *mĭnus* as depending on sigmatic ecthlipsis and not iambic shortening (cf. Questa (2007: 94); for an opposite view see Gratwick (1993: 50 and 1999: 226), Fortson (2008: 50)). However, in Terence the evidence for sigmatic ecthlipsis is overwhelmingly based, as we have seen, on prosodically iambic words of this type which are shortened to pyrrhic; it would therefore seem appropriate to question the spread of sigmatic ecthlipsis and leave open the possibility that the pyrrhic scansion of many (if not all) cases of prosodically iambic words

---

[48] On iambic shortening see in particular Bettini (1990), Questa (2007: (85–151), Fortson (2008 chs. 7–9). Cf. also Lindsay (1922), Drexler (1969), Allen (1973: 179–85), Dressler (1973), Devine and Stephens (1980), Gratwick (1999: 228–9).

[49] For a different view, cf. Devine and Stephens (1980), and Fortson (2008), who consider iambic shortening a characteristic of 'fast' or 'colloquial' speech, with possible relations to phrasal-stress patterns.

ending in *-s* depends on iambic shortening, and not on the prosodic omission of final *-s*.

This view would reduce substantially the quantity of evidence for sigmatic ecthlipsis in Terence: out of *c.*990 cases of sigmatic ecthlipsis printed by OCT editors, we would be left with only five problematic cases of verse-internal sigmatic ecthlipsis (*An.* 377, 857, *Haut.* 339, 812, and *Ph.* 529),[50] plus twenty-three cases of sigmatic ecthlipsis in a light element (see Table 5.2), which I will analyse in the next section.

4.3 Sigmatic Ecthlipsis in a Light Monosyllabic Element

As has already been displayed in Table 5.2, there are twenty-three cases in which the syllable ending in *-s* occupies a light element. In twenty of these cases, the element involved is the penultimate element of an ia[6], tr[7], or ia[8]. These instances provide the best evidence for sigmatic ecthlipsis, since the scansion at the end of the line is generally straightforward and sigmatic ecthlipsis would seem therefore to be certain. I list in Box 5.2 all the instances belonging to this group.

Box 5.2 Sigmatic ecthlipsis in the penultimate element of the line

ia[6]
Haut. 15 dicturŭs sum |
Haut. 826 admiratŭs sis |
Ph. 413 abusŭs sis |
Ph. 660 incertŭs sum |
Ph. 683 iussŭs sum |
Ph. 943 sepultŭs sum |
Hec. 334 auctŭs sit |
Hec. 443 defessŭs sum |
Hec. 450 incertŭs sum |
Hec. 485 iniquŏs sim |
Hec. 489 expertŭs sum |
Hec. 653 nullŭs sum |
Ad. 429 usŭs sit |
Ad. 839 tempŭs fert |

---

tr^7
Hec. 878 usŭs sit |
Ad. 873 desertŭs sum |
ia^8
An. 619 fretŭs sim |
An. 599 nullŭs sum |
Eun. 1045 ausŭs sim |
Hec. 730 satiŭs sit |

The remaining three instances, listed in Box 5.3, are cases in which the syllable ending in -*s* occupies the penultimate element before a median *caesura* in an ia^8.

Box 5.3 Sigmatic ecthlipsis in the seventh element before a median caesura in ia^8

An. 203 ŭbĭuis | făcĭli|us pas|sŭs sim || qu(am) ĭn hac | rē mē | dēlū|dier|
An. 582 ĕgŏ dū|dum nōn | nil **uĕrĭ|tŭs sum** || Dāu(e) abs | tē nē | făcĕrēs | ĭdem|
Eun. 555 quid ges|ti(am) aut | quid lae|tŭs sim || quō per|g(am) und(e) ē|merg
                                                                    (am) ŭbĭ | siem|

The second instance is less certain because the median caesura might be substituted with a ninth-element caesura (after *Dāu(e)*), which is a pattern commonly used by Terence in this type of line (cf. Questa (2007: 348–55)).

We can make some observations on the two tables above. First, twenty-two of the twenty-three examples are very similar, i.e. they consist of a participle or a predicate adjective ending in -*s* followed by a form of the verb *sum* beginning with s- (*sum/sim/sis/sit*). The only exception is *Ad.* 839, the scansion of which is somewhat problematic:

expor|ge fron|tem :: scī|lĭcĕt ĭ|tă tem|pŭs fert|

The eighth element is split between two different words (*scilicĕt* and *ĭta*), thus infringing the law of Ritschl (cf. section 4.2.1). We might perhaps scan *scīlĭcēt*, but this would be a prosody without clear parallels in Plautus or Terence.[51] Moreover, the expression *ita tempus fert* ('that's

---

[51] Gratwick (1999) seems to consider this scansion as a case of *breuis in longo* in a *locus Jacobsohnianus*: however, this metrical 'licence', which is well attested in Plautus, is hardly ever found in Terence (cf. Questa (2007: 279–99)).

what the occasion requires') is without parallels in Latin. Perhaps the ending of the line might be emended with the reading *tempus est*, which is an idiomatic expression in both Plautus and Terence.[52]

Does this particular morphological and phonological pattern (-*s* before a participle or adjective followed by a form of the verb *sum* beginning in *s*-) suggest anything about the features of sigmatic ecthlipsis in Terence? One might point out that sigmatic ecthlipsis in the penultimate syllable requires a monosyllable beginning with a consonant at the end of the line (or the half-line). Since monosyllables beginning with a consonant at the end of the line are apparently rare (cf. Questa (2007: 317)) the frequency of sigmatic ecthlipsis with monosyllabic forms of *esse* at the end of the line or the half-line would simply depend on the fact that these are the only forms which may be found in such a position. However, a first riposte to this might be that monosyllabic forms of the verb *esse* are not more common at the end of the line than other monosyllables beginning with a consonant; I have counted eighty-three lines in Terence that end in a monosyllable beginning with a consonant (including those listed in the table above), forty involving forms of the verb *sum* (nineteen of which are preceded by sigmatic ecthlipsis and are listed in the table above), forty-three involving other monosyllabic words (*fert, nunc, quin, fit, uah, rem, phy, uos, uis, uir, nos, mos, nox, iam, fit, qui, me, se, te*). Therefore, it seems remarkable that there are no cases (with the exception of the problematic *Ad.* 389) of sigmatic ecthlipsis before one of these other monosyllables in Terence.

For this reason, the lexical and phonological uniformity of sigmatic ecthlipsis in Terence in a light element (shown in Box 5.2 and Box 5.3) is remarkable and calls for explanation.

5. LINGUISTIC OBSERVATIONS

5.1 Phonological Explanation: The Sequence -*s s*- at Word Boundaries

As we have seen, the prosodic omission of final -*s* in Terence is uniformly confirmed before a monosyllabic form of the verb *esse*

---

[52] Cf. e.g. Ter. *Haut.* 667 *nunc ita tempus est*, 187, *Ph.* 1026, Pl. *Trin.* 432 *tempust adeundi*, *Ps.* 958 *nunc occasio est et tempus*, *Pers.* 724.

starting with *s-*. An explanation for this should take into account both aspects of this uniformity: the lexical (i.e. the fact that all the words following final *-s* are forms of the verb *esse*) and the phonological (the fact that all such words start with *s-*). Which of the two, however, is the determining factor?

A first explanation would emphasize the phonological factor; omission of final *-s* would occur in such contexts in order to avoid a sequence *-s s-* at word boundaries. The lexical uniformity would be due to the rarity of monosyllables starting with *s-* which are not forms of the verb *esse*.[53] Such an explanation would be supported by some evidence that seems to imply that in Latin, both in archaic and classical times, omission of *-s* was influenced by the type of the following consonant. First, Quintilian (9.4.37–8) states that a sequence *-s s-* at word boundaries was problematic for speakers. In the passage quoted in section 1.1 (p. 195) Quintilian seems to connect omission of final *-s* explicitly to cacophonous phenomena at word boundaries (*in commissura uerborum rixantur*). Moreover, Quintilian states that the cacophony given by a final *-s* followed by a consonant is greater when the second letter is another *s* (*quarum tristior etiam si binae collidantur*).[54] Second, there is some other sporadic evidence from Latin authors and inscriptions which supports the idea that the sequence *-s s-* was avoided. For instance, in the letters of Terentianus, the only case of omission of final *-s* after short vowel is before a word starting with *s-* (P.Mich. VIII.471.21 *pater meu sopera*).[55] In Plautus it seems that *qui* is preferred to *quis* before a consonant[56] and that words of three syllables or more are rarely affected by sigmatic ecthlipsis except when they precede an *s-*.[57] Finally, some scholars have claimed that in inscriptions there are many cases of omission of final *-s* before another *s-*.[58]

This evidence is however not sufficient to prove that a sequence *-s s-* at word boundaries was avoided in Latin texts and that omission of

---

[53] Note, however, that there are four instances of *se* found at the end of the line in Terence (*An.* 407, 575, *Eun.* 599, *Hec.* 161).

[54] For a discussion of this passage see Adams (2007: 141).

[55] On this see Adams (1977: 30 n. 112). Cf. also Adams (2003: 734) for a similar omission in a Latin translation from Babrius' fables (P.Amh. II.26 line 5 *frigiti(s) spebus*).

[56] Cf. Löfstedt (1956: II 82–3).

[57] Cf. Butterfield (2008b: 194 with n. 23).

[58] Cf. Carnoy (1906: 183), Väänänen (1966: 70, 77).

final -*s* was influenced by the type of consonant following the -*s*. First, although Quintilian speaks of the greater cacophony of the sequence -*s s*- (*tristior . . . stridor*), he does not necessarily imply that omission of final -*s* was restricted to or more frequent in such cases; in the statement that follows, the reference is to sigmatic ecthlipsis in general (*quotiens ultima esset aliaque consonante susciperetur*) and the examples provided do not involve a sequence -*s s*- (*Aeserninus fuit, dignus locoque*). The second type of evidence is weak too; a single case of the omission of final -*s* in Terentianus might just be a slip, and the other pieces of evidence (such as the omission of final -*s* in inscriptions before another *s*- and the ostensible preference for *qui* before *s*- in Plautus) would require a careful textual and statistical analysis of the corpora before we could consider them conclusive.[59] Finally, most of the evidence above is taken from texts much later than Terence (e.g. Quintilian, Terentianus).

Moreover, there are other elements which suggest that in republican Latin the omission of final -*s* was not determined by the type of consonant that followed. First, if we consider the omission of final -*s* in republican inscriptions, we find that there are only thirteen cases (4%) of omission of final -*s* before another *s*- in CIL 1^2 (cf. section 1.2 with Table 5.1). If sigmatic ecthlipsis was a common way to avoid a sequence -*s s*- we would expect a much higher rate. Moreover, most of these thirteen cases (eleven) involve a nominative of the second declension, which, as noted (section 1.2), is a particular pattern.

Another piece of evidence which suggests that in Terence sigmatic ecthlipsis may not be related to a need to avoid the sequence -*s s*- at word boundaries is provided by the text of Terence itself. First, such a sequence does not seem to be avoided in Terence. Excluding cases in which omission of final -*s* is metrically justified (i.e. cases in which the -*s* follows a short vowel and occupies part of a disyllabic resolved element, cf. section 4.2) or *might* be possible (i.e. cases in which the -*s* follows a short vowel and occupies an anceps element, cf. section 4.1 pp. 211–12), there are at least 380 cases in which a word ending in -*s* (preceded by either a short or long vowel) is followed by a word

---

[59] For instance, in Plautus there are no cases of *quis* introducing an indirect question before a word beginning with *s*-. However, there is only a single case of this type of *quis* before a consonant (*Amph.* 1016 *quis fuerit*), whereas it is quite common before a vowel (cf. e.g. *Merc.* 634 *quis esset*, *Men.* 302 *quis ego sim*, *Aul.* 716 *quis eam abstulerit*). Consequently, the absence of *quis* before an *s*- might be simply due to a general preference for *qui* before a consonant.

starting with *s*-. A statistical calculation shows that this frequency is roughly that which we would expect if the words had been arranged randomly. If Terence had felt the need to avoid the sequence -*s s*- we would expect a lower frequency. Moreover, in at least fifty of these 380 cases, the vowel preceding the -*s* is a short vowel and the syllable becomes heavy by position (i.e. -*s* occupies a heavy monosyllabic element): this clearly shows that final -*s* was not necessarily lost before *s*-. Finally, if one considers the cases in which sigmatic ecthlipsis is metrically justified (205, cf. Table 5.2), one finds that *s*- follows the word ending in -*s* in only forty-one instances (20%), a rate which is not significantly higher than that of other consonants (e.g. 14% *p*, 13% *q*). Again, if sigmatic ecthlipsis were used to avoid the sequence -*s s*- one would expect different figures.

In conclusion, it seems that one can dismiss a purely phonological explanation of the uniformity of sigmatic ecthlipsis in Terence. There is no evidence to demonstrate that in Terence the sequence -*s s*- was avoided, that sigmatic ecthlipsis was influenced by the following consonant, or that -*s* was necessarily lost before -*s*. Consequently, we are led to assume that the frequency of prosodic omission of final -*s* before forms of the verbs *esse* is not due simply to the fact that they all start with another *s*-.

5.2 Cliticization of the Verb *esse*

Another explanation for the uniformity found in cases of the prosodic omission of final -*s* in Terence would emphasize its lexical side, i.e. the fact that in all cases the word following the -*s* is a form of the verb *esse*. Since such prosodic omission appears to be attested in Terence only before a form of *esse* and since the fact that these forms begin with *s*- is not a primary factor, we are led to reflect on the nature of the verb *esse* in Latin.

As has been shown in the previous chapters (cf. in particular III.1.3 and IV.1.6.1), the verb *esse* had clitic status in Latin. Evidence supports the view of the existence, at least for the second and third person singular, of clitic forms of *esse*, undergoing a process of phonetic reduction and contraction and becoming prosodically dependent on the previous word. These reduced forms are found univerbated to the preceding word (cf. e.g. *factast*), thus representing in spelling the bond between the contracted forms and the host word.

Cliticization of the verb *esse* might also be involved in the frequency of the prosodic omission of final -*s* in Terence before forms of
the verb *esse* starting with *s*-. If we assume that in Latin the verb *esse* is
clitic and forms a prosodic word with certain types of host word (in a
way similar to that of other clitic particles such as -*que*), the reconstruction of the development of a cretic ($-\,\smile\,-$) scansion of the
sequence *factus sum* (cf. *An.* 599 *nullŭs sum*, Ad. 873 *desertŭs sum*)
might well adhere to one of these scenarios:

1) *factŭs sum* > *factussum* ($-\,-\,-$) > *factŭsum* ($-\,\smile\,-$)
2) *fáctŭs sum* > *fáctussum* ($-\,-\,-$) > *fáctŭssum* ($-\,\smile\,-$)
3) **factu(s)* + *sum* > *factŭsum* ($-\,\smile\,-$)

In the first scenario, what we have hitherto considered as sigmatic
ecthlipsis (*factus sum* > *factu(s) sum*) might instead be a different
phonological phenomenon, i.e. the simplification of the cluster -*ss*- in
a prosodic word, perhaps analogous, to a certain extent, to the
phenomenon by which the sequence *factusst* (*factus* + *st*) is simplified
to *factust* (cf. pp. 27–8, 106–8).[60] Another parallel for such simplification of -*ss*- simultaneous with cliticization and univerbation of *esse*
might be the omission of final -*s* before univerbated forms of *esse*

---

[60] The simplification of internal -*ss*- is a phonological phenomenon attested in
republican Latin, but generally after a long vowel or diphthong: cf. e.g. *causa* < *caussa*
(thirty instances in CIL 1^2, cf. e.g. 583, 590, 592, 593, etc.), *quaeso* < *quaesso, nasus* <
nassum, diuisio < *diuissio*, etc. See also Quint. 1.7.20 *quid quod Ciceronis temporibus
paulumque infra, fere quotiens s littera media uocalium longarum uel subiecta longis
esset, geminabatur, ut 'caussae' 'cassus' 'diuissiones'?*, Marius Victorinus p. 70 M *iidem
(antiqui) uoces quae pressiore sono eduntur, 'ausus' 'causa' 'fusus' 'odiosus', per duo* s
scribebant, Consentius p. 17 N. *s litteram Graeci exiliter ecferunt adeo ut com dicunt
'iussit', per unum s dicere existimes*. On the simplification of geminated *s* cf. Nettleship
(1889: 580), Leumann (1977: 220–1), Meiser (1998: 125), Weiss (2009: 157). The
graphic simplification of internal -*ss*- (spelt -*s*-) is attested in republican inscriptions
(cf. CIL 1^2 index p. 815) but is simply an orthographic phenomenon related to the
practice, common in republican times, of not writing geminated consonants; for
instance, in the *Senatus Consultus de Bacchanalibus* (CIL 1^2.581) all geminated
consonants are indicated with a single letter (e.g. *deicerent necesus ese Bacanal habere
. . . Bacas uir nequis adiese velet*). On this see Traina (1973), Bernardi Perini (1983),
Fontaine (2006), and cf. Penney (2011), Wallace (2011). There are however some
cases of degemination of -*ss*- in inscriptions which might not be related to this
orthographic practice since they are found in texts in which geminated consonants
are used (cf. e.g. CIL 1^2.614 *leiberei essent agrum oppidumqu(e)* | *quod ea tempestate
posedisent* | *item possidere habereque / iousit dum poplus senatusque / Romanus uellet
act(um)*), but they are few in number.

starting with *s-* in some inscriptions (cf. e.g. Vetter (1953), 7 = CIL 1^2.1614 (in a mixture of Latin and Oscan) *rectasint < rectas sint*).[61]

In the second scenario, the simplification would not be phonological but only prosodic, consisting in the shortening of the unaccented, closed syllable *-tuss-* (expected to be heavy by position), under the effect of the accentuation of the prosodic word *fáctussum*. One might speculate that the prosodic shortening of the internal syllable *-uss-* functioned as a way of avoiding the displacement of the accent to the last syllable of the host word, which, without reduction, would possibly be treated as the penultimate heavy syllable of the prosodic word *host word + verb* (cf. e.g. *fáctŭs + sum = fáctŭ(s)sum* and not *factússum [with *-uss-* heavy by position]). A possible parallel for this prosodic simplification would be iambic shortening, which often affects unaccented closed syllables (cf. e.g. *Eun.* 384 *hăbĕnt des|picatam, Hec.* 848 *uĕnŭs|tatisqu(e)*, and see 4.2.3) and which is probably related to the influence of accentuation on unaccented syllables.[62]

In both these scenarios (1 and 2), evidence for what looks like the prosodic omission of final *-s* in Terence might be explained as being triggered by the cliticization of the verb *esse*. Simplification of *-ss-* (e.g. *factussum > factu(s)sum*) or prosodic shortening of *-(u)ss-* (*fáctussum > fáctŭssum*) would mark the univerbation of the verb and point to a strong prosodic and syntactic bond between forms of *esse* (which in all cases is auxiliary or copula) and the preceding word (which in all cases is a participle or a predicate adjective).

Finally, in the third scenario (3), the cretic scansion of the sequence *factŭsum* would indeed be related to the loss of final *-s* (*factŭ(s)*), which, however, would be an obsolete phenomenon, fossilized in the univerbated formula *participle/adjective + esse*. According to this reconstruction, the prosodic unit *factu(s) sum* had become formulaic at an early stage of Latin, when final *-s* was weakly pronounced, and was in the process of being lexicalized as *factŭsum*. By the time of Terence final *-s* had regained its full phonological status in speech, but fossilized expressions such as *factŭsum*, with ancient omission of final *-s*, persisted to be used. Consequently, sigmatic ecthlipsis might

---

[61] On this example see Mancini (1988: 220–2) and Adams (2003: 129–30). Cf. also Cipriano and Mancini (1984).

[62] Cf. however instances such as *uŏlŭptās mea*, where iambic shortening affects an originally accented syllable (*uolúptas*), which are normally considered as involving re-accentuation on the final syllable (*-tás*), due to cliticization of *mea* (see Bettini 1990: 361–2, Fortson 2008: 256–7).

be an appropriate term to use for Terence, provided that by it one refers to an archaic remnant, only admitted in formulaic, quasi-lexicalized expressions.[63]

It is difficult to establish which of the above scenarios is correct: scenario 1 does not fit well with the fact that sigmatic ecthlipsis in Plautus is also attested before pronouns (*me, te*), which do not begin with -*s* (see section 6); the prosodic shortening envisaged by scenario 2 is not supported by exact parallels; scenario 3 does not explain how sequences *participle/adjective + esse* could become fossilized, given the lexical variety of participles/adjectives, combined with their syntactic bond with the verb *esse*. It is also possible that all three scenarios are valid and that the correct reconstruction should envisage a combination of the various factors, phonological and prosodic.

The common element in all these scenarios, however, is that cliticization of *esse* is a primary factor for the cretic scansion of sequences such as *factus sum*, since it creates the conditions (i.e. prosodic univerbation) necessary for the simplification (phonological and/or prosodic) of the sequence -*(u)s(s)*- (scenarios 1 and 2), or at least for the fossilization of such simplification in a formulaic, quasi-lexicalized expression (scenario 3). The generic concept of sigmatic ecthlipsis would not appropriately describe the prosodic omission of -*s* in such cases, which would be treated not as a final -*s* but almost as a word-internal -*s*- (cf. e.g. *factu(s)sum*).

In conclusion, the evidence for sigmatic ecthlipsis in Terence is weak and cannot easily be used to prove that in the Latin of Terence's time final -*s* was dropped in pronunciation. Editorial choices that encourage this idea do not find sufficient support in the facts. Moreover, the distinctive features of the omission of final -*s* in Terence undermine the idea of a continuity between the omission of -*s* in early Latin and the loss of final -*s* in some Romance languages.[64]

On the other hand, the concentration of the prosodic omission of -*s* in participles or predicate adjectives preceding a form of *esse* supports the view that *esse* was clitic and formed a single word with the preceding participle or predicate noun or adjective. The fact that in every case of such a phenomenon the vowel preceding -*s* is short

---

[63] For this scenario cf. Sullivan (1970: 27–32).

[64] On the treatment of final -*s* in Romance languages see also Löfstedt (1961: 129), Rohlfs (1966: I.431–4), Väänänen (1981: 68), Weiss (2009: 514); cf. also Adams (2013: 132).

might simply be due to the fact that the verb forms a unit with the participle or predicate noun or adjective, which if ending in -*s* at all would normally end in -*ŭs*. Univerbation of *esse* in such cases is not displayed in the spelling (as in the case of contracted forms) but contracted forms and simplified forms of the verb *esse* following an -*s* seem to have very similar features, since both imply the clitic univerbation of the verb to the host word.

6. EPILOGUE: SIGMATIC ECTHLIPSIS IN PLAUTUS

In this final section I will offer a short overview of sigmatic ecthlipsis in Plautus and compare the results with those of Terence, which have been presented in the previous sections. For this analysis I have not conducted a systematic scrutiny of the Plautine corpus but I rely on the data given by Sullivan (1970) in his excellent (and still neglected) PhD dissertation on final -*s* in early Latin.

In his survey Sullivan does not provide detailed and complete figures for sigmatic ecthlipsis in Plautus, and he lists, for iambo-trochaic lines, only cases occupying a light element (i.e. the penultimate before the line end or the median caesura), excluding all the verse-internal cases;[65] moreover, he offers figures for the retention of final -*s* (i.e. of -*s* making a position in a heavy element) only from a small sample of verses (*c*.1000). Nevertheless, although they may be partial, his results are interesting and tie in with the analysis presented above.

According to the survey of Sullivan, there are only fifty-one certain cases of sigmatic ecthlipsis in the whole corpus of Plautus:[66] thirty-six

---

[65] Sullivan excludes all the verse-internal instances on the ground that in these cases the brevity of the syllable ending in -*s* can be explained as the effect of iambic shortening (*breuis breuians*). Although this may be true (as is partly true for Terence, as discussed above, 4.2.3), Sullivan does not provide any figures in support of his claim; this fact undermines the reliability of his results, since, as we have seen above (4.2.1), sigmatic ecthlipsis can affect metrical places in which iambic shortening is not possible, such as the first place of a disyllabic element. Cases of such a type, although problematic, are found in Terence, and it is likely that they may be found in Plautus as well, an author who seems less restricted than Terence in his use of sigmatic ecthlipsis.

[66] These figures are in neat discrepancy with those provided by Wallace (1982, 1984), who claims to have collected 1828 cases of sigmatic ecthlipsis in Plautus. The reason for this discrepancy is that Wallace (1984: 219–20) includes in his analysis cases of a pyrrhic scansion of prosodically iambic words, which, as shown (4.2.3),

instances are found in iambo-trochaic lines of the type analysed in the previous sections (ia⁶, tr⁷, ia⁷, tr⁸), all occupying a light element (the penultimate before the end of the line or the median caesura); fifteen instances are in other types of verses (anapaestic, reiziani, glyconic, iambic, and trochaic dimeters), where the scansion, however, is not always unambiguous.[67]

In the majority of cases (twenty-eight) the form affected by sigmatic ecthlipsis is followed by a form of the verb *esse*;[68] in particular, most of these instances (twenty) display the same pattern which, as shown, appears to be standard in Terence: a participle or adjective ending in *-ŭs* followed by a form of the verb *esse* beginning with *-s*: cf. e.g. *Amph.* 979 *commentŭ(s) sis* |, *Capt.* 14 *rupturŭ(s) sum* |.[69] This frequency is noteworthy and suggests that in Plautus, too, sigmatic ecthlipsis is associated with the linguistic sequence *participle/adjective + esse*, a sequence that Sullivan (1970: 29) defines as 'formulaic'; sigmatic ecthlipsis in this pattern, as discussed above, is presumably related, in some way, to the cliticization of *esse*.

The second large group of instances displaying sigmatic ecthlipsis features another interesting pattern, a verbal form ending in *-s* followed by a personal pronoun (nine tokens): cf. e.g. *Bac.* 313 *occidistĭ(s) me* |, *Poen.* 562 *seruastĭ(s) me*|.[70] This group of instances is

could be well explained as the effect of iambic shortening rather than sigmatic ecthlipsis.

[67] From this number I have excluded two instances recorded by Sullivan (*Asin.* 469 and *Truc.* 187), as in both cases the syllable allegedly affected by sigmatic ecthlipsis could be scanned heavy: in *Asin.* 469 the syllable ending in *-s* occupies the third from last element of an iambic septenarius, which is generally anceps (see above Box 5.1); in *Truc.* 187 it occupies the seventh element of an iambic septenarius, which is anceps unless there is a median caesura, which does not seem to be the case in this line.

[68] (ia⁶) *Asin.* 60 *qualĭ(s) sit* |, *Bac.* 193 *moribundŭ(s)que est* |, 786 *qualĭ(s) sit* |, 856 *qualĭ(s) sit* |, (tr⁷) *Amph.* 411 *Amphitruonĭ(s) sum* |, (ia⁷) *Mil.* 1278 *huiŭ(s) sunt* ||, (an⁸) *Trin.* 832 | *fidŭ(s) fuisti*, (an⁷) *Bac.* 1083 *natŭ(s) foret*. For the pattern *-ŭ(s) s-* see following note.

[69] Other cases: (ia⁶) *Merc.* 232 *uisŭ(s) sum* |, 245 *uisŭ(s) sum* |, *Most.* 555 *confessŭ(s) sit* |, 566 *saluŏ(s) sum* |, *Pers.* 144 *facturŭ(s) sis* |, *Rud.* 103 *saluŏ(s) sis* |, *Stic.* 57 *usŭ(s) sit* |, (tr⁷) *Asin.* 286 *frausŭ(s) sit* |, 376 *facturŭ(s) sum* |, *Aul.* 811 *uisŭ(s) sum* |, *Curc.* 680 *expertŭ(s) sum* |, *Merc.* 217 *nullŭ(s) sum* |, 978 *nullŭ(s) sum* |, *Mil.* 1183 *facturŭ(s) sim* |, *Most.* 1124 *ludificatŭ(s) sit* |, *Trin.* 1050 *commonitŭ(s) sum* |, (ia⁷) *Asin.* 427 *claudŭ (s) sim* ||, (an⁸) *Trin.* 827 *usŭ(s) sum*.

[70] Other instances: (ia⁶) *Merc.* 324 *perdĭ(s) me* |, (tr⁷) *Stic.* 591 *scitĭ(s) uos* |, 622 *eamŭ(s) tu* |, (ia⁸) *Men.* 999 *fertĭ(s) me* ||, (ia⁷) *Truc.* 154 *estĭ(s) uos* ||, (ia²) *Capt.* 206 *scimŭ(s) nos* |, (tr²) *Epid.* 30a *dicĭ(s) tu* |.

interesting: personal pronouns are another important class of clitic words in Latin; they are generally unstressed and form a prosodic unity with the preceding word;[71] moreover, in all our cases the preceding word is a verb with which the personal pronoun has a strong syntactic bond. The frequency of sigmatic ecthlipsis in this pattern thus seems to provide further evidence that sigmatic ecthlipsis and cliticization are somehow related, although in this case it would clearly not be a matter of simplification of -*ss*- (the pronouns involved are *tu, me, nos, uos*), a fact which confirms that the nature of the consonant following the -*s* is secondary (cf. 5.1).

Finally, we are left with a group of fourteen cases of sigmatic ecthlipsis in which the word following is not the verb *esse* or a personal pronoun: most of these instances (ten) are found in metres other than iambic-trochaic, in which the scansion is not always unambiguous: cf. e.g (an⁸) *Poen.* 1180 | *festŭ(s) dies*, (reiz.), *Aul.* 422 *ullŭ(s) cinaedus*.[72] Only four certain cases of this type are found in iambic-trochaic metres: (ia⁶) *Rud.* 512 *estĭ(s) nunc* |, (tr⁷) *Poen.* 565 *tenetĭ(s) rem* |, 575 *tenetĭ(s) rem* |, (ia⁸) *Epid.* 39 *rebŭ(s) iam* |.

In conclusion, there are both differences and similarities between sigmatic ecthlipsis in Plautus and Terence. On the one hand Plautine use is less restricted than that of Terence, as sigmatic ecthlipsis is found, unlike in Terence, also before words other than forms of *esse* and also in metrical positions other than the penultimate element before the line end (or the median caesura). This may be taken to imply, as suggested by Sullivan (1970: 31–2) and already argued by Proskauer (1910), that by the time of Terence sigmatic ecthlipsis had been restricted, possibly because in Plautus' lifetime 'final -*s* was still susceptible of suppression' whereas 'in Terence's day it was no longer regarded as proper'. This idea may also be supported by a comparison of the treatment of final -*s* in a heavy element in Plautus and Terence: if Terence uses final -*s* to make position in a heavy element in about one of every twenty lines, Plautus (according to Sullivan's figures) does so much less frequently, only in about one of every thirty-seven lines.

---

[71] On unstressed, clitic pronouns in Latin see Adams (1994b) with bibliography.

[72] Other instances: (an⁸) *Ps.* 1103 *seruŏ(s) facit* |, 1315 | *onerabĭ(s) scio*, (an⁷) *Bac.* 1077 *inscitŭ(s) capessat* |, (an²) *Rud.* 919 *parcŭ(s) mea* |, *Stic.* 326a *hostĭ(s) uenis* |, (reiz.) *Cas.* 934 *intŭ(s) reliqui* |, *Most.* 891 *fumŭ(s) molestust* |, (glyc.) *Cas.* 938 *rebŭ(s) scio* |.

On the other hand, the use of sigmatic ecthlipsis in Plautus and Terence shares an important feature: in both authors the word following the -*s* belongs to a particular lexical group, either a form of *esse* (including only iambic-trochaic lines: 70% in Plautus, 100% in Terence, excluding the problematic *Ad.* 839) or a personal pronoun (20% in Plautus). A possible explanation for this situation might be found to be a relation between sigmatic ecthlipsis and cliticization, a linguistic feature that both the verb *esse* and the Latin personal pronouns seem to have. Further implications of this possibility will be discussed in the following chapter, which will consider the results of my analysis of sigmatic ecthlipsis together with the evidence concerning contracted forms in Latin, and draw some general conclusions.

VI

Conclusions

iam iam nulla morast

Virg. *Aen.* 2.701

The aim of this final chapter is to review some of the findings of the book and discuss one of its main themes, the cliticization of the verb *esse* in Latin.

1. CONTRACTED SPELLINGS OF *EST*/*ES*

The first finding is philological, and concerns the contracted spellings of *est*/*es* (e.g. *bonast*, *dictumst*), whose prevalence in Latin is significantly underestimated. The analysis conducted in chapter II has shown that the evidence for contracted spellings of *est*/*es* is not restricted to the manuscripts of Plautus, Terence, and Lucretius (as widely believed), but is found in a large variety of sources, ranging from Sabellian languages to late-antique grammarians, from Cicero's *De oratore* to inscriptions.[1] In order to evaluate this evidence correctly it has been necessary to take into account the various factors that might have influenced the occurrence of what looks like a non-standard spelling: pronunciation, style, intertextuality, syntax, register and genre; the discussion of such factors has been complemented by viewing them from a historical perspective, since the occurrence of a particular spelling may be influenced by different factors at different times.[2]

In early Latin contracted spellings had a degree of orthographic 'acceptability', although they had a marked stylistic value, which was

---

[1] Cf. II.3.   [2] Cf. I.3, III.2.1.

probably colloquial and poetic at the same time.[3] One is led to assume a gradual diminution in their use in writing in classical Latin;[4] contracted spellings are still relatively common in the late republican period, but are rare in (early) imperial sources. Also their stylistic value, probably varied with time; Cicero seems to use them as markers of speech; their occurrence in Grattius is probably due to his imitation of earlier poets, such as Lucretius and Virgil; in Gellius they appear to be used as artificial archaisms.[5] These stylistic values ('colloquial', poetic, and archaic) may have overlapped to a certain extent. Moreover, it is highly possible that contracted spellings were used in writing by classical authors more often than their textual transmission seems to indicate. Finally, in late Latin contracted spellings fell out of use.[6]

The implications of these philological findings is that contracted spellings should not be ignored or relegated to notes in the apparatus as misspellings or orthographic idiosyncrasies. From the point of view of the textual critic, instances of the direct transmission of contracted spelling or cases of readings that might have resulted from the misunderstanding of an original contracted spelling should be given full consideration and might lead in many places to a restoration by the editor of the contracted spelling, in both early and classical authors.[7] From the point of view of the exegete, the stylistic value of a contracted spelling should be taken into account in the interpretation of the context; for instance, disregarding contracted forms in the speech of Sextus Caecilius in Gellius (20.1.20–54) would cause one to miss the archaic flavour intended by the author for the passage.[8] Finally, from the point of view of the linguist and grammarian, the occurrence of contracted spellings in a variety of sources suggests that they are not merely a metrical or orthographical quirk but reflect a phenomenon of speech; moreover, contracted *-st* and *-'s* are not just variant phonetic spellings (cf. e.g. *afficere* for *adficere*) but rather 'institutionalized' variants reflecting phonologically reduced forms (cf. III.1.3). Contracted forms should be taught as such to students of Latin and deserve a place in the paradigm of the present indicative of the verb *esse* (*sum, es / -'s, est / -st, sumus, estis, sunt*), especially given their phonological nature, which I will discuss in the next section.

---

[3] Cf. III.2.1.1.   [4] Cf. III.2.1.2.
[5] Cf. II.3.1.1, III.2.1.2 and III.2.2.   [6] Cf. III.2.1.3.
[7] Cf. II.3.3.   [8] Cf. II.3.1.1 pp. 40–2.

2. CONTRACTION OF *ESSE* AS SPEECH
PHENOMENON

There are (at least) two possible phonological interpretations of contracted spellings of *est/es*. The first is implied by the term 'prodelision' (or 'inverse elision') commonly used to refer to this phenomenon: contracted spellings would merely be the orthographic reflection of a phonological phenomenon of connected speech (i.e. a sandhi phenomenon), similar and parallel to elision. From the phonetic point of view, the phenomenon by which the sequence *factum est* is scanned *factum st* would be similar to that by which the sequence *factum habeo* is scanned *fact habeo* with elision; though not identical, both would derive from the same phonological rule operating at word boundaries. This (widespread) interpretation is not convincing for several reasons (see III.1.2).

The second way to consider contracted spellings, which seems better suited to the evidence, emphasizes the nature of the verb *esse* in Latin and its particular prosodic bond with the word preceding it.[9] There is much evidence[10] which supports the idea that the involvement of the verb *esse* in the process of phonological reduction is not incidental but rule-governed, leading to the conclusion that the verb *esse* is *by its nature* exposed to a process of phonological reduction. As we will review more clearly below, the cause of this reduction appears to be the prosodic weakness of the verb *esse* in Latin and its close bond with the preceding word. Therefore, the concept of the 'contraction of *esse*' seems to be more appropriate than that of 'prodelision' or 'aphaeresis'; moreover, the concept of contraction is closely connected to that of cliticization, as we will discuss in section 4.

A final point. The contraction of *esse* was, at least until the early Empire, a real phenomenon of speech and contracted spellings were its reflection in orthography.[11] Moreover, it is reasonable to think that the spoken contraction of *est/es* was not always displayed in spelling and that in early Latin prose texts a sequence spelt *factum est* was pronounced *factumst*, though this is probably unverifiable. This does not mean that *est/es* were *always* pronounced contracted in all circumstances; apart from phonological constraints,[12] there is evidence

---

[9] Cf. III.1.3.
[10] Cf. in particular II.3.6, II.3.7, III.1.3, IV.1.6.1, IV.4, and V.5.2.
[11] Cf. III.2.2.   [12] Cf. II.2.

that suggests that metrical, stylistic, and especially linguistic factors could also affect and block contraction in speech.[13] Lack of contraction is more frequent in recitative than spoken metres in Terence and is more common in Terence than Plautus,[14] but more often it can be explained by the influence of semantics, syntax, and word order as we will see in sections 5–7.

If this account seems valid for early (third–second centuries BC) and probably late republican Latin (i.e. Cicero's time), it is more difficult to verify it in (early) imperial Latin (first and second century AD), in which contracted spellings seem to be used in an artificial manner, as poeticisms or fossilized archaisms. Certainly, in imperial Latin a contracted spelling must reflect a contracted pronunciation; on the other hand, one probably cannot rule out the possibility that this was just a relic of the past and that contraction of *est/es* was no longer current in speech (as is clearly the case in late Latin) and/or was restricted to some substandard or regional variety (cf. the aphaeretic pronunciation of the pronoun *it* in the form *'tis* in English, which is nowadays poetic/archaic, regional, and substandard at the same time).[15] The positive evidence is not sufficiently cogent to prove that in imperial Latin contraction of *est/es* was still a common feature of speech, although there is not enough counter-evidence to prove that this was not the case (cf. III.2.2).

3. PROSODIC REDUCTION IN -*s* + *SUM/SIM/SIS/SIT*

The second important finding of this book is metrical and concerns the prosodic treatment of final -*s* before a consonant. The analysis conducted in chapter V, mainly based on the corpus of Terence, has shown that in the vast majority of cases in which a final -*s* before a consonant is prosodically silent (i.e. in which the lengthening by position of the preceding light syllable does not occur), the syllable involved is the second syllable of a pyrrhic word ($\smile\smile$, e.g. *sătĭs*).[16] This fact might simply be due to the effect of two metrical norms of comic metre, the law of Hermann-Lachmann and the law of Ritschl. Nonetheless, this class of instances (sigmatic ecthlipsis at the end of a

---

[13] Cf. IV.1 and IV.3.   [14] Cf. III.2.1.1 and IV.1.5.1.
[15] Cf. I.3.   [16] Cf. V.4.2.

pyrrhic word) is not necessarily significant; the pyrrhic scansion of a pyrrhic word ending in a closed syllable before a consonant (cf. e.g. *sătĭs crēdĭs* = ˘ ˘ ¯ ˘) is also common in words which do not end with -*s* (such as *ăpŭd* or *ĕnĭm*) and is a subtype of iambic shortening (pyrrhic scansion of an iambic sequence). Iambic shortening might be a mere metrical licence, possibly influenced by accentual factors, and is not related to sigmatic ecthlipsis.[17] Consequently, the aforementioned class of instances (sigmatic ecthlipsis at the end of pyrrhic words) does not provide strong evidence for sigmatic ecthlipsis in Terence and should be excluded, thus severely limiting the evidence for sigmatic ecthlipsis in this author.

The only good evidence for sigmatic ecthlipsis consists of instances in which the prosodic omission of final -*s* is not found at the end of pyrrhic words. An analysis of such instances is interesting, since it shows that in almost all cases the omission of the -*s* precedes a form of the verb *sum* starting with *s*-.[18] This prevalence is most likely not accidental, and its explanation cannot be merely phonological (i.e. related to the mere sequence -*s s*-) since other evidence (in comic texts and republican inscriptions) does not support the idea that sigmatic ecthlipsis was more common before *s*- than other letters, and in Terence sigmatic ecthlipsis is not clearly attested before words beginning in *s*- other than forms of the verb *esse*.[19] Therefore, it is the nature of the verb *esse* which is presumably the main determinant of the omission of final -*s* in such contexts. The most likely explanation is that the verb *esse* in such cases had a close prosodic connection with the preceding word (in all cases a participle or a predicate), which led or contributed to the prosodic simplification of -V*ss*-.[20] This prosodic unity of the copula/auxiliary with the preceding predicate/participle should be considered in relation to the clitic nature of the verb *esse* in Latin, a theme which unifies the various findings of the book and which I will discuss in the next section.

4. CLITICIZATION OF *ESSE*

The two phenomena analysed in this book, the contraction of *est/es* and the phonetic reduction attested in the sequences -*s* + *sum/*

---

[17] Cf. V.4.2.3.   [18] Cf. V.4.3.   [19] Cf. V.5.   [20] Cf. V.5.2.

sim/sis/sit, seem to require a common condition; in both cases the
verb *esse* is treated (whether this is displayed in the orthography or
not) as being attached to the previous word and, in particular in the
case of contraction, as being exposed to phonetic reduction. The
concept that best explains these features is cliticization.[21]

By the term 'clitics' I refer to a special class of linguistic elements,
found in many languages, which display a singular type of phonological and/or syntactic behaviour. This singularity is first of all
phonological; according to traditional grammar, clitics are 'accentless words (or particles) which depend accentually (or "lean": hence
the name, from Greek κλίνω "lean") on an adjacent accented word,
and form a prosodic unit together with it.'[22] This prosodic or accentual unity may be orthographically expressed by univerbation; in
Latin, for instance, the connective *-que* and the interrogative particle
-ne are clitics, and both are written together with the preceding word.
Another feature of clitics, already noticeable in these examples, is that
their behaviour is similar to that of affixes;[23] in some extreme cases
what looks like a clitic is actually an affix, such as is apparently the
case in English with the negative *-n't.*[24] The concept of the clitic is a
broad one; a concise but comprehensive definition is given by
Anderson (2005: 33): '[clitics] are linguistic elements that display
prosodically deficient phonology, anomalous morpho-syntax, or
both.'[25] Various classes of clitics have been identified according to
their syntactic behaviour and the presence or absence of a corresponding independent, non-clitic form.[26] A frequent feature of clitics
that are variant forms of independent words (such as contracted *'s* vs.
uncontracted *is* in English) is phonological reduction; clitics often are
reduced from a corresponding non-clitic form (cf. the clitic forms of
the English auxiliary, *'re* < *are,* *'m* < *am,* etc.).[27] Moreover, such
reduction generally cannot be explained by the effect of sandhi rules

[21] On cliticization of *esse* see III.1.3, IV.1.6.1, V.5.2.
[22] Anderson and Zwicky (2003).   [23] Cf. Anderson (2005: 9–14, 33–6).
[24] Cf. Zwicky and Pullum (1983).
[25] There are other linguistic elements displaying singular morpho-syntactic behaviour that have been normally defined and treated as clitics, regardless of their
phonological behaviour (such as personal pronouns in Romance languages). On
this cf. Anderson (2005: 31–2), Maiden, Smith, and Ledgeway (2011: 325–8). See
also Adams (1994b) for the behaviour of similar pronouns in classical Latin.
[26] Cf. Zwicky (1977), Anderson (2005: especially 9–14, 22–36).
[27] Cf. Zwicky (1977), Anderson (2005: 25–30).

but is idiosyncratic in each clitic form, which is therefore to be considered as a lexical variant.[28]

The clitic nature of the verb *esse* in Latin is not a completely unfamiliar notion,[29] although it has not yet been generally accepted by scholars.[30] Contraction and sigmatic ecthlipsis before forms of *esse* in Terence provide good evidence for this clitic character, at least under some conditions: forms of *esse* behave as if they were forming a single prosodic word with the preceding host, and contracted forms look like clitic forms of *esse*, displaying both univerbation and an idiosyncratic type of phonological reduction (as pointed out in section III.1.3).

However, this is not the only observation we can make from the analysis of contraction and sigmatic ecthlipsis, and especially the former. Since contracted (clitic) forms may alternate with uncontracted forms, it has been possible to assess the determinants for this alternation in the authors who use both sets of forms. Apart from metrical and stylistic considerations (cf. IV.1.3, IV.1.5), the contraction of *esse* appears to be affected by various factors of linguistic significance, which I will analyse in the following sections.

5. THE SEMANTICS OF *ESSE*

The first factor seems to be related to the semantics of the verb *esse*; in Terence the contraction of *esse* is more frequently confirmed metrically when the verb is auxiliary than when it is copula, and is rarely attested in manuscripts and hardly ever confirmed metrically when it is existential (meaning 'there is').[31]

This would support the traditional distinction in lexicography (cf. e.g. OLD *s.v. sum*) between the various uses of the verb (auxiliary, copula, existential) and contrast with the view that the verb *to be* is always used as a copula in every context; even clauses in which the copula function of *esse* is less evident (as in the Latin sentences *est uir*

---

[28] Cf. Kaisse (1985), Anderson (2005: 26–8).   [29] Cf. III.1.3.

[30] Cf. e.g. Devine and Stephens (2006: 191). Moreover, Romance scholars have objected to the clitic interpretation of some Latin elements, such as personal pronouns, whose clitic value allegedly emerged only in Romance languages (cf. Van Kemenade and Vincent (1997: 20–1, 150)).

[31] Cf. IV.1.4 and IV.2.

and the English and Italian equivalents *there is a man, c'è un uomo*)
have been considered to have an implicit predicate[32] or a predicate
expressed by a particle (Eng. *there,* It. *ci*). According to this view, in
clauses of this type (e.g. *uir est*) the verb *to be* would essentially have
the same meaning as in copula clauses (e.g. *uir est bonus*), just as the
verb *teach* has the same meaning in both the sentences *he teaches* and
he teaches Latin.[33] The absence of a semantic distinction within the
verb *to be,* and in particular of the semantic distinction between
copula and existential uses, is the view of many general linguists
(cf. e.g. Moro (1997)) and has also been proposed for the classical
languages, especially by the work of Kahn on the Greek verb *einai.*[34]

As we have seen, the evidence concerning the contraction of *esse*
might suggest that this 'unitary' view of *esse* is not completely
adequate. The frequency of contraction with auxiliary and copula
esse and its rarity with existential *esse* may be taken to imply that the
semantic distinction between auxiliary, copula, and existential *esse* is
not artificial but corresponds to intrinsic features of the language. In
particular, existential *esse* might be considered a 'strong' version of
the verb *esse,* distinct from the 'weak' auxiliary/copula meaning,
exposed to cliticization and univerbation.

The emergence of a full, non-clitic, existential meaning of *esse* has a
possible parallel in the existence of the inceptive verb *escit* functioning
as an existential in the Twelve Tables, alongside *est* (copula).[35] The
form *escit* is found in the Twelve Tables I.3 (Crawford (1996: 586–8)
= Gell. 20.1.25) *si morbus aeuitasue escit,*[36] at Cic. *Leg.* 3.9 *ast quando
duellum grauioresue discordiae ciuium escunt,*[37] and at Lucr. 1.619
ergo rerum inter summam minimamque quid escit |.[38] There are also
three other conjectured cases, two from the Twelve Tables: V.7
(Crawford (1996: 643–6)) *si furiosus ... ess<i> t (esse codd. : esset Nonius :
escit Bouhier)* and X.8 (Crawford (1996: 710)) *cui auro dentes iuncti*

[32] Cf. Kahn (2009: 202–3, quoting Brown (1999)) 'our locution "there is" which
implies or suggests existence, easily admits a complement. "There is an X (which is)
Y." So in Greek, every absolute or quasi-existential use of *einai* can be thought of as
awaiting further specification; that is, as pregnant with the copula construction.'
[33] For this example see Brown (1999).
[34] See in particular Kahn (2003, 2009). Cf. also Brown (1994, 1999).
[35] On verbs in -*sc*- see Keller (1992), Haverling (2000).
[36] 'If there is illness or age'. Trans. Crawford.
[37] 'But when a serious war or civil dissensions arise'. Trans. Keyes.
[38] 'Then what difference will there be between the sum of things and the least of
things?'. Trans. Smith. Cf. also Bailey (1947: *ad* 1.619).

ess\<i\>nt (*essent codd.* : *escunt* **Pithou** : *essint* **Crawford**),[39] and one in Virgil (*Aen.* 8.65 *celsis caput urbibus exit codd.* : *escit* **Faber**). We may also note the form *superescit*, found in Ennius and Accius (Enn. *Ann.* 514 S. *dum quidem unus homo Romanus toga superescit*,[40] Acc. *Trag.* 266 R. *quoi si hinc superescit*;[41] both instances are quoted by Festus (p. 394 L. *superescit significat supererit*)) along with the forms *adescit* and *obescet*, found in glossaries.[42] The above verbal forms seem to derive from a verb **esco*, a sort of 'strong' non-clitic form of *sum* with an existential meaning ('there is'),[43] sometimes (possibly) used in a future sense.[44] This verbal form was probably already archaic at the end of the third century BC.[45]

6. THE SYNTACTIC NATURE OF *ESSE*

Another factor affecting the contraction of *esse* is syntactic; in all cases of contraction metrically confirmed in Terence the word preceding *esse* is a predicate noun or adjective (e.g. *bonust*) or a participle (e.g. *factust*), the only exceptions being a few special cases with the expression *opus est*;[46] moreover, contraction is less frequently attested in manuscripts when the preceding word is not a predicate (noun or adjective) or a participle.[47] Contraction seems to be especially avoided

---

[39] On these two not very convincing cases of **esco* cf. Crawford (1996: 643 and 710 with his bibliography), Dyck (2004: 408). Relevant to the excerpt from the *Tusculanae* (*si furiosus escit*) are also *Inv.* 2.148 and *Rhet. Her.* 1.23, where the authors quote the same passage of the Twelve Tables; in the former case the verb used is *est*, in the latter *existet*.

[40] '[My poetry will survive (?)] as long as there will be a single Roman in toga.' Cf. Skutsch (1985: *ad* 514).

[41] Cf. Dangel (1995: 114 *ad* 266 R.): 'si, lui, vient à y *survivre*.'

[42] Gloss. V 262.8, 625.22 *adescit: aderit*, Paul. Fest. p. 188 *obescet: oberit uel aderit*. On these forms see Haverling (2000: 276, 316, 395).

[43] Cf. Fraenkel (1925: 442–3), Crawford (1996: 588).

[44] So apparently in Lucretius (1.619) and Ennius (514 S.). Cf. Bailey (1947: *ad loc.*), Skutsch (1985: 668), and Festus p. 394 L. (*superescit significat supererit*). See also Keller (1992: 79–84), Haverling (2000: 53, 143–4) for the view that *escit* is also used in a future sense in the passages from the Twelve Tables.

[45] On **esco* see Fraenkel (1925: 442–3), Keller (1992: 79–86), Haverling (2000: in particular 143–4, 395). On analogous formations in other Indo-European languages see Keller (1985), Rix (2001: 241–2).

[46] Cf. IV.1.6 and IV.1.7.   [47] Cf. IV.2.

when the verb is placed between a noun and its modifier, although the causes for this are still to be clearly defined.[48]

The frequency of the contraction of *esse* directly following a predicate (noun or adjective) or participle seems to confirm that there exists a sort of unity between the auxiliary or copula and the preceding predicate or participle, and that this unity might be expressed in the univerbation of the verb and the host.[49] Moreover, the fact that in such cases the verb *esse* undergoes phonological reduction seems to imply the syntactic 'marginality' of this verb in copula clauses,[50] which is reflected in many languages in the omission of the copula in the present tense.[51] Moreover, there are languages (such as e.g. Turkish) in which the verb *to be* in its copula function is replaced by a clitic predicative suffix attached to the predicate (cf. e.g. Turk. *sen* [you] *mutlusun* [are happy], with the clitic suffix -*sun*, which is originally a suffixed form of the second person personal pronoun; *kızın* [girl's] *adı* [name] *Fatma'dır* [is Fatma], with the clitic suffix -*dir* (normally omitted in ordinary speech), which is originally a suffixed form of the third singular person of the verb 'to stand').[52] The contraction of *esse* may be taken to imply that in Latin the

---

[48] Cf. IV.1.6.2 and Fortson (2008: 144–61).

[49] Another concept which one might possibly use to refer to this phenomenon would be that of 'verb incorporation'. On this concept see Baker (1988: 147–228).

[50] This syntactic 'marginality' of the copula has been argued for in the field of formal grammar. According to some works (cf. e.g. Moro (1997)), the verb *esse* should not to be considered as a predicate (i.e. the part of a sentence stating something about the subject) as other verbs, nor as a part of the predicate (as it is according to traditional grammar); in copular clauses (such as *homo animal est*) the predicate role would be filled by the noun that is not the subject (*animal*). The function of the verb *esse* in such clauses would be to link the subject and the predicate and to convey tense indication (T). Tense indication is normally expressed in the sentence by the verbal inflection, to which in copular clauses the verb *to be* would be equivalent from a syntactic point of view. According to this interpretation, the phrase *homo est animal* should not be construed as SUBJECT *homo* + PREDICATE [COPULA *est* + PREDICATE *animal*] (or, in formal terms NP[VP[V NP]]) but as SUBJECT *homo* COPULA *est* PREDICATE *animal* (in formal terms [NP[T SN]]). This interpretation of the copula as a third element of the sentence, linking subject and predicate (which could also be an NP) is already found in Aristotle (cf. *Int.* 10.19b.21 and see Moro (1997: 249–51)).

[51] This is for instance the case with Russian, in which the copula is normally omitted in the present tense, but is used in the past tense and the future. Ellipsis of the copula is well attested also in Latin. Cf. Rubio (2009: 218).

[52] Cf. Lewis (2000: 93–104), Mel'čuk (2009: 46–8).

behaviour of the copula was similar (to a certain extent) to that of a predicative suffix, at least at an early stage of Latin.[53]

In conclusion, the frequency of the contraction of copula and auxiliary *esse* after a predicate noun or adjective and its rarity in other circumstances leads to the conclusion that in Latin contraction is triggered by and conditional on the bond between copula/auxiliary and predicate/participle. Conversely, alterations of this bond seem to block the clitic reduction of the verb. One type of blocking alteration is presumably the existential use of *esse* (as discussed in section 5). Existential *esse* is less likely to form a unity with the host word since by its nature it is not preceded by a participle or predicate noun or adjective. Consequently, existential *esse* is likely not to have a 'connective' function (i.e. 'copula') and is presumably syntactically equivalent to all other verbs, itself fulfilling the syntactic role of the

---

[53] One might also argue for an analogy between the copula and the verbal inflection; both the copula and the verbal inflection would work as tense indicators in the sentence and the sequences *factust* (*participle + esse*), *bonust* (*predicate + esse*), and *fecerit* (*perfect stem + verbal inflection*) might therefore be considered syntactically similar (*predicate + tense*), as they already behave similarly at the orthographic and prosodic levels. Moreover, from a historical point of view, the clitic, syntactically 'marginal' and quasi-affixal value of the verb *to be* may be a feature inherited from Proto-Italic, as suggested by the fact that univerbation of the copula is also attested in Sabellian languages (cf. e.g. VIa 38 *mersi* [Lat. *ius sit*], Cp 8.4 (p.97) *destrst* [Lat. *dextrast*]), especially when the verb is auxiliary: as pointed out (cf. II.3.6) in Sabellian the third person form indicative form **íst** (Lat. *est*) is often written together with the host form (cf. e.g. Pg 9.4 (p.73) *clisuist* Lat. *clusa est*) and cases of univerbation are also found with the subjunctive form *se* (Lat. *sit*), cf. e.g. **anteruakaze** (Ib 8), *anteruacose* (VIb 47) [Lat. ? *intermissum sit*]. Moreover, in Oscan inscriptions there are also some instances of contracted spelling of the third person of the verb *to be*, as auxiliary attached to the participle (cf. II.3.6). Furthermore, there are in Sabellian some active periphrastic forms displaying univerbation of forms of the verb *ezum* (cf. e.g. *andersafust* VIIb 3 Lat. *circumdederit*), thus suggesting that univerbation of the verb *to be* is also related to verb formation. The clitic nature and syntax of contracted forms of *est/ es* seem to provide evidence for a 'univerbated' use of *esse* in Latin, analogous to that attested in Sabellian languages. Although this hypothesis should be verified by further research, cliticization of *est/es* and its syntax might lead one to speculate that univerbation of *esse* (and its syntactic implications) is a general feature of Latin as well. This fact might also explain the origin of new verbal formations of Latin, such as the future perfect *fecerit*, and perhaps even the future *laudabo*, the imperfect *agebat*, the imperfect subjunctive *ageret*, etc. (cf. Clackson and Horrocks 2007: 27); as already proposed by some scholars (cf. Meiser 1998: 204–5, 215), these forms may result from univerbation of forms of *esse* (cf. e.g. *fecerit* < *fec* + *$^*h_1$es-et(i)* instead of + **-is-eti*). This would also corroborate Rix's theory about the origin of the perfect in *u/w-* as derived from univerbation of *esse* to the perfect active participle (e.g. *portauisti* < **portāwis(s)* (< **portā* + **-wos* [perfect active participle] + -s(s) [second person copula]) + **-tay*; cf. Rix (1992), Meiser (1998: 204–5), de Melo (2007b: 51)).

predicate. The behaviour of existential *esse* is also interesting for another reason; not only are there no contracted cases of existential *esse* in Terence metrically confirmed (see section 5), but neither are there any cases of existential *esse* placed at the end of the clause,[54] which seems to be the standard position of copular and auxiliary *esse*, as we will see in the next section.

7. WORD ORDER: THE POSITION OF *ESSE*

There is some evidence that seems to suggest the influence of word order on contraction. First, in Terence metrically confirmed contraction is frequent when the verb is at the end of a clause (e.g. *erus bonust*).[55] Some studies have argued that in Latin the copula tends to occupy the final position in the clause,[56] and explain its appearance in a non-final position as a 'movement' (in generativist terms) of the verb towards the beginning of the sentence ('raising', 'fronting'), which is due to pragmatic factors; accordingly, verbs are generally placed in an initial position in the sentence for reasons of focus or emphasis.[57] The frequency of contraction with clause-final *est/es* might support the view that the standard position of the verb was clause-final and that in this position the verb was pragmatically neutral and exposed to contraction, as also suggested by the analysis

[54] It must be added that existential *esse* is often placed in first position in the clause, a position in which cliticization is phonologically impossible and contraction is never confirmed by metre or attested in the manuscripts (cf. IV.3.2). This however does not significantly undermine the evidence that the absence of contraction is related to the existential use of *esse*; there are cases in which existential *esse* is not found in first position and is not found contracted (cf. e.g. *Hec.* 204 *ei ludo, si ullus est* 'in the same school, if there is such a school', *Ph.* 332 *quia enim in illis fructus est* 'because there is profit in them').

[55] Cf. IV.1.6.1 and IV.2.

[56] Cf. Devine and Stephens (2006: 79 and ch. 2 especially pp. 145, 171); see also Marouzeau (1949) and Bauer (2009).

[57] Cf. Devine and Stephens (2006: 145–72), Bauer (2009: 275–82). Other factors seem to influence the 'displacement' of the verb from its final position and involve the 'movement' of noun phrases towards the end of the sentence, but they are difficult to evaluate; some of the observations which have been made (cf. e.g. Devine and Stephens (2006: 179) on the raising of non-focused material) seem to be too dependent on a theoretical framework rather than on an analysis of the actual linguistic evidence.

of individual cases (cf. IV.1.1). The 'displacement' of the verb from this position would result in the blocking of contraction, possibly under the influence of pragmatic factors, which however are hard to assess.

Second, contraction is hardly ever metrically confirmed when the verb is in second position in the clause, following a first-position predicate (cf. e.g. *Ad.* 326 *quid is ergo?* :: *alienus est ab nostra familia*).[58] The fact that cliticization seems to be avoided in such circumstances casts doubt on the idea that second position (in a clause, colon, or other intonational unit) is the archetypal position for clitics:[59] on the contrary, in Terence contraction (and therefore cliticization) is metrically confirmed especially when the verb is clause-final[60] but is hardly ever attested when it is in second position in a clause. There are cases of contracted copula *esse* 'displaced' from its final, post-predicate position, and attached to a focal word, a fact which seems to confirm that the verb *esse* was subject to attraction from the focus.[61] However, this attraction does not necessarily have to be phonetic/prosodic but might also be syntactic in nature, as the rarity of contraction in second position seems to suggest, and as has already been proposed by Devine and Stephens (2006: 191–8).

8. FINAL REMARKS

This paragraph will attempt to sum up the linguistic findings of this book. The evidence discussed within it supports the idea that in Latin the verb *esse* was essentially clitic in its copula and (especially) auxiliary functions. The standard position of *esse* was presumably clause-final, following the subject and the predicate (noun, adjective, or equivalent) or participle, to which it was attached. The clitic value

[58] This also includes cases in which the second-position verb ends the clause (cf. e.g. *erus est neque prouideram*; see IV.1.6.1).

[59] On this issue see Wackernagel (1892), Collinge (1985: 217–19), Anderson (1993, 2005: 142–51, 178–82), Adams (1994a, 1994b), Janse (1994, 2000), Harris and Campbell (1995: 233–9), Kruschwitz (2004). Cf. also Wackernagel in Langslow (2009: 924 *Index*, s.v. enclitics).

[60] This does not include cases in which the clause is formed only by the sequence *host word + est*, i.e. in which the verb is in second position following a first-position predicate. Cf. n. 58 and IV.1.6.1.

[61] Cf. IV.1.7.1 with n. 83 and Adams (1994a, 1994b). See also Devine and Stephens (2006: 181–3, 199–202).

of *esse* and the bond with such a predicate or participle exposed it to a process of phonetic reduction and prosodic univerbation to the preceding word, making it to a certain extent resemble a (coalescent) inflexional or predicative suffix. This process of the 'clitic incorporation' of *esse* is visible in the prosodic treatment of forms of *esse* after -*s* and even more in contracted spellings of the second and third person singular of the indicative, for which the univerbation is also displayed in spelling. These contracted spellings underwent orthographic standardization in early Latin, although they probably maintained a marked stylistic value.[62] The cliticization of *esse* was closely connected to syntax. Alteration of what appears to be the standard structure of copula clauses (*subject + predicate + esse*) seems to result in the blocking of contraction. Further aspects of this alteration are the existential use of *esse*, which seems to have a syntactic and semantic distinctiveness in Latin, and the rarity of contraction when the verb is not clause-final (and especially when it is in second position), which possibly depends on pragmatic factors. Metrical and stylistic factors might also have contributed to the blocking of contraction but are difficult to evaluate.

The results that have been described are mainly based on an analysis of the corpus of Terence and thus appear to be valid at a particular stage of the development of Latin, at least for the second and the third person of the indicative of *esse*. The situation might be different in classical and late Latin, where sigmatic ecthlipsis is hardly ever attested and contracted spellings gradually become artifical and eventually obscure, thus no longer reflecting phenomena of speech. Another hypothesis is possible, though: the linguistic features of *esse* and its clitic nature (at least in certain contexts) might have been the same even if cliticization of *esse* was no longer reflected in spelling, a fact that might also be explained as due to the influence of orthographic standardization. In any case, since in classical and late Latin the status of contraction and its relation to cliticization are problematic the clitic nature of *esse*, its conditions, and in general the various findings that have been described in this chapter should be verified by an analysis of the behaviour of *esse* in classical and late Latin. This, however, is a subject for another book.

---

[62] Cf. sections 1 and 2.

Appendix

1. Evidence for Contraction in Terence

1.1 Contracted Spellings in the Manuscript Tradition of Terence

The aim of this section is to present the textual evidence for contraction of *est/es* in the manuscript tradition of Terence. Given the high number of manuscripts (more than 700),[1] a selection has been necessary. In the following analysis I will report figures from these documents:

- Vaticanus Latinus 3226, A Bembinus, IV–V c. in rustic capitals, collated in the original and in the reproductions of Prete (1970) and Coury (1982);

- three manuscripts of the medieval MS family γ: Vat. Lat. 3868 C, IX c., collated in the facsimile of Jachmann (1929); Ambros. S.P. 4bis F, IX–X c., collated in the facsimile of Bethe (1903); Ox. Bodl. Auct. F.2.13 O, XII c., collated in the original);

- one manuscript of the medieval MS family δ, Laurent. 38.24 D, X c., collated in the original.

In the OCT edition of Terence we find printed 795 contracted spellings (760 *-st*, thirty-five *-'s*). The range of different patterns is displayed in Table 7.1. There are also other five particular cases, *Eun.* 268, 312, 361 *rēst KL*, *Haut.* 676 *nilst KL*, and *An.* 607 *illic[e]st KL*, in which the contracted form

Table 7.1. Patterns of contraction in the OCT edition of Terence

	//		+ m		+ s	
	est	es	est	es	est	es
-a	198	2	18	0	0	0
-e	79	2	11	0	0[2]	0
-i	76	0	0	0	5	5
-o	79	3	0	0	0	0
-u	6	1	236	0	52	22
TOTAL	438	8	265	0	57	27
		446		265		84

---

[1] Cf. Villa (1984), Reeve in Reynolds (1986: 433–6).
[2] The pattern *rēst* has been excluded. On this problematic form see II.2, p. 34.

follows a word ending in *long vowel* + *-s* or is attached to a consonant other than *-m* and *-s*. These problematic patterns (cf. II.2 p. 34) have been excluded.

The results of the survey are the following:

A   Of the 795 forms printed contracted in the OCT edition, 661 can be checked in the manuscript. The remaining ones belong to lines missing in A (*An.* 1–914 [with the exception of *An.* 896 *peccarest*], *Hec.* 1–37, *Haut.* 851a, *Ad.* 915–97, 139 forms in total). 391 of the 661 forms checkable in the manuscript are already contracted in A, 270 have been altered by A and have been restored by editors. In their place we find in A either the uncontracted spelling (*est/es*, 216 instances), the omission of the copula (twenty-nine instances), or other readings (twenty-five instances). In eight cases the reading of A is likely to be a misunderstanding of an original contracted spelling, as confirmed by two cases in which the contracted spelling is attested in another manuscript (*Hec.* 568, *Ad.* 388); these eight cases are: *An.* 971 (*ullast KL* : *mor*]*ast ulla* A), *Eun.* 386 (*aequomst KL* : *aecumsit* A), 708 (*east* A^pc *KL* : *ast* A), *Hec.* 535 (*test* A^pc *KL* : *est* A), 568 (*leuiust* D *KL* : *leuius et* A), *Ad.* 344 (*sitast KL* : *siest* A), 388 (*psaltriast* D *KL* : *psaltrias* A), *Ad.* 904 (*moraest KL* : *morast* A). Among the cases in which the copula is omitted in A (twenty-nine), nine might derive from the dropping of final *-t* from an original contracted spelling (*Eun.* 546 *hominis<t>*, 708 *deductus<t>*, *Hec.* 169 *elapsus<t>*, *Ph.* 661 *oppositus<t>*, 715 *opus<t>*, 833 *facturus<t>*, *Ad.* 98 *iniustius<t>*, 404 *adortus<t>*, *Ad.* 728 *natus<t>*)[3] and eighteen might be construed as contracted spellings, as they feature omission of *es* after final *-s* (e.g. *Eun.* 651 *dignus* A : *dignus es* A^pc : *dignu's KL*).[4] These thirty-five cases (eight plus nine plus eighteen) seem to provide further evidence for contracted spellings in A, for a total of 426 cases of contracted spelling with supporting evidence in A. Finally, there are eight cases of contracted spelling in A which are not printed uncontracted in the OCT (*Haut.* 228 *rectest*, *Eun.* 761 *admitterest*, 1006 *obsecrost*, *Eun.* 1020 *Parmenost*, *Hec.* 831 *indest*, *Ph.* 421 *Demiphost*, *Ad.* 305 *quidnamst*, *Ad.* 622 *inquamst*) plus one case of contracted spelling which is omitted in the OCT (*Ph.* 247 *incredibilest* A : *incredibile KL*).

Manuscript A is conservative as far as contracted spellings are concerned. However, there is evidence that the process of alteration of contracted spellings had already started in late antiquity; in some cases one of the late antique hands of A adds an *e-* to the contracted spelling of A (cf. e.g. *Haut.* 574 *nemost* A : *nemo est* A^pc, *Ad.* 402 *optumest* A : *optume est* A^pc); moreover, there are several cases in which a form uncontracted in A is found contracted in another manuscript (see below p. 252).

While in the late antique exemplar A contracted spellings are common (*c.*400 out of 800 cases potentially contracted), they are much less frequent in medieval manuscripts of the *γ* and *δ* families.[5]

---

[3] Cf. II.3.3.   [4] Cf. II.3.8.1.

[5] For an overview of the medieval tradition of Terence and its families see Reeve in Reynolds (1986: 433–6), Grant (1986), Posani (1990), Victor (1996, 1999, 2007).

γ family

C In this manuscript there are only three cases of contracted spelling: *Ph.* 346 (*coitiost* C[ac] : *coitio est* C[pc]), *Hec.* 831 (*indest* C[ac] : *inde est* C[pc]), *Ad.* 904 (*moraest* C). However, in one case (*Ad.* 904) the contracted spelling follows an ending -*e* and thus in the context might be construed as belonging to the verb and not to the preceding word (*mora* + *est*). There are also three readings (all *contra metrum*) that presumably result from the misunderstanding of an original contracted spelling: *Haut.* 881 (*dictumst* A *KL* : *dictum sit* C), *Ad.* 39 (*ipsest* A *KL*: *ipse sit* C), *Ad.* 950 (*multum est KL* : *multum sit* C). One might also consider thirteen interesting cases of omission of the copula, out of which two might be explained as resulting from the dropping of final -*t* (*Eun.* 474 *honestus est* A : *honestust KL* : *honestus* C; *Ad.* 538 *ipsest* A : *ipsust KL* : *ipsus* C) and eleven as contracted spellings, as they are of the type -*s* (=?*es*) (*Eun.* 286, 696, *Haut.* 580, 815, 823, *Hec.* 392, 825, *Ph.* 295, 324, *Ad.* 234, 852).[6] With the exception of *Ad.* 950 (missing in A) and *Eun.* 474 (uncontracted in A), in all these cases the form with supporting evidence in C has also supporting evidence in A, being contracted or featuring an interesting reading.

F In this manuscript there is only one possible case of contracted spelling: *Ad.* 904 (*moraest* F), which however is problematic (see above). There are also five readings that probably result from the misunderstanding of an original contracted spelling: *Haut.* 881 (*dictumst* A *KL* : *dictum sit* F), *Ad.* 950 (*multum est KL* : *multum sit* F), *Hec.* 411 (*data est* A : *datast KL* : *data sit* F : *vel data est* F[il]), *Hec.* 568 (*leuius est* A[pc] : *leuius et* A[ac] : *laeuius sit* F), and *Ph.* 546 (*parumn est* F[ac] : *parumne est* F[pc]A). Weaker cases are *Eun.* 474 (*honestus est* A : *honestust KL* : *honestus* F[ac] : *honestus est* F[pc]) and ten instances of the type -*s* (=?*es*) (*Eun.* 696, *Haut.* 580, 815, *Hec.* 392, 825, *Ph.* 295, 324, *Ad.* 234, 394, 852).[7] In all the above cases the form has also supporting evidence in A, with the exception of *Ad.* 950 (missing in A), *Eun.* 474 (uncontracted in A), *Hec.* 411 (uncontracted in A), and *Ph.* 546 (uncontracted in A).

O In this manuscript there are no cases of contracted spellings or readings which may result from the misunderstanding of a contracted spelling.

The first generation of manuscripts of the γ family (C and F) preserves few traces of contracted spellings. The presence of interesting readings in both C and F (*Haut.* 881, *Ad.* 950, *Eun.* 474) together with that of spellings preserved by only one of the two manuscripts (*Ph.* 346, *Hec.* 831, *Ad.* 39, 538 in C, *Hec.* 411, 568 in F) suggests that the process of alteration had already started in the archetype of C and F. The second generation of manuscripts (O) has deleted every trace of contracted spellings, thus standardizing the uncontracted spelling. However isolated, the case of *Hec.* 411 (*data est* A : *datast* D *KL*: *data sit* F : *vel data est* F[il]) may suggest that the archetype γ preserved contracted spellings that had already been altered in A.

---

[6] Cf. II.3.8.1.   [7] Cf. II.3.8.1.

δ family

D   In this manuscript there are sixty-eight instances for which the first hand of
the manuscript gives the contracted spelling. In all except nine cases a second
hand adds a little vowel *e* before *st*. Thirty-three of these sixty-eight cases are
also spelt contracted in A (one also in C): in all except one case (*Hec.* 831,
possibly a typographical error) they are printed contracted also in the
OCT. On the other hand, there are thirty-five cases which are contracted in
D but are uncontracted in A (thirty-one) or belong to portions of text
missing in A (four): in three of these cases, the form is printed uncontracted
in the OCT (*Haut.* 321 *hercle est* A *KL* : *herclest* D, *Hec.* 760 *de me est* A *KL* :
de mest D^1, *Hec.* 308 *quidem est* A *edd.* : *quidemst* D^{ac}). Furthermore, there is
a series of readings (ten) in D that seem to result from the misunderstanding
of a contracted spelling. Three of these are spelt contracted in A: *Haut.* 881
dictumst A *KL* : *dictum sit* D, *Ph.* 538 *opust* A *KL* : *opus sit* D^{ae}, 812 *futurumst*
A *KL*, *futurus est* D^{ac}; another six are instead spelt uncontracted in A: *Eun.*
315 *si quae est* A : *siquaest KL* : *si qua est* D^{ac}, *Hec.* 304 *necesse est* A : *necessest*
KL : *necesse sit* D^{ac}, 583 *certum est* A : *certumst KL* : *certum sunt* D^{ac}, 736 *tibi*
est A : *tibist KL* : *tibi sit* D^{ac}, *Ad.* 301 *erili est* A : *erilist KL* : *erilis est* D^{ac}, 389
domi est A : *domist KL* : *domi sit* D^{ac}; one instance is found in a portion of
text missing in A: *Ad.* 996 *factost KL* : *facto sit* D^{ac}. Finally, there are cases of
omission of *es*/*est* after a word ending in -*s* (twenty-one), which may provide
further evidence for an original contracted form (omission of *est*: *Eun.* 826,
Haut. 903, *Ph.* 661; omission of *es*: *An.* 202, 621, 702, 724, 749, *Eun.* 286, 696,
Haut. 580, 815, *Hec.* 392, 825 (x2), *Ph.* 295, 324, *Ad.* 234, 394, 852, 957). In all
these cases of omission, the form has supporting evidence also in A, apart from
An. 202, 621, 702, 724, 749, *Ad.* 957 (missing in A) and *Hec.* 825 (*exanimatus*
obsecro es A : *exanimatus obsecro* D^{ac} : *es exanimatus obsecro* $D^{pc}CF$:
exanimatu's obsecro KL).

The δ family seems to be more conservative than the γ family. The high
number of cases in which the second hand of D adds an *e*- to the contracted
spelling of D provides evidence for the process of alteration of contracted
spellings in medieval manuscripts. The group of cases of contracted spellings
preserved by D but not by A (thirty-two directly transmitted and six reconstructed) suggests that the archetype δ preserved cases of contraction already
altered in A.

In conclusion, out of the *c.*795 contracted spellings found in the OCT,
476 have supporting evidence in the manuscript tradition: 423 are spelt
contracted in manuscripts (391 in A, thirty-two only in D), and in the
cases of another fifty-three the manuscripts have a reading that may
conceal an original contracted spelling, in most cases featuring omission
of *est*/*es* after a word ending in -*s* (thirty-seven tokens). Finally, there is a
group of twelve cases (eight in A, three in D, and one in ADC) which are
spelt contracted in the manuscripts but are printed uncontracted in the
OCT edition.

1.2 Metrically Reconstructed Forms

Out of the 795 forms printed contracted in the OCT, there are eighty-four instances of the pattern *short vowel* + -*s*, for which the contracted form is not prosodically equivalent to the uncontracted form and which thus may be determined by metrical factors (cf. II.3.2). In only ten of these eighty-four cases is the contracted spelling directly transmitted in manuscripts while in seventy-four cases it is not. In some of these seventy-four cases the manuscripts have a reading with omission of the verb, especially in the second person form (see 1.1), which could be construed as a contracted spelling without affecting the metre (cf. II.3.8.2). In other cases the manuscripts have an uncontracted spelling, which is normally metrically unacceptable. Finally, in the remaining cases the manuscripts have another reading which is sometimes metrically acceptable but generally unsuitable in the context. In almost all of the above cases the uncontracted form would be against the metre whereas the contracted form would fit both the metre and the sense. However, for this category there is sometimes disagreement between editors. For this reason I have considered as having strong metrical support only those cases which are printed contracted by most editors (twenty-seven, i.e. twenty-three -*ŭs* +*est*, three -*ĭs* + *est*, one -*ĭs es*).

In conclusion, there are 501 cases of contracted OCT forms with supporting evidence: 423 are spelt contracted in manuscripts, fifty-one are indirectly transmitted by manuscripts, twenty-seven are reconstructed only on the basis of metre. Conversely, there is a group of *c.*292 forms printed contracted in the OCT without supporting evidence. Table 7.2 presents summarizing figures.

1.3 Editors' Choices

As we have seen in the previous section, in *c.*292 cases the OCT editors restore a contracted spelling without clear supporting evidence. What is the rationale behind this? It cannot be simply phonological or prosodic (i.e. systematically printing contraction after -V and -V*m*); there are at least 174 cases which might potentially have been printed contracted, but which the OCT editors have decided to print uncontracted, generally reproducing the reading of the manuscripts. One might speculate about syntactic factors that could have influenced their choice, but OCT editors do not comment on this issue and the criteria remain somewhat unclear and arbitrary.

The criterion used by Marouzeau for dealing with contracted spellings is only apparently more straightforward: he generally prints a contracted spelling only when it is found contracted in A, otherwise he prints an uncontracted spelling (*c.*345 cases). However, in about fifty cases he does not follow this rule but prints a contracted spelling against A without commenting on it. Moreover, in about another fifty cases he prints an

Table 7.2. Contracted forms in Terence

Patterns -V, -V*m* + *est*/*es*

	Total	Contr. in Oct	Contracted in Manuscripts					Indirect Transmission			
			A	AD	AC	ACF	D	A	D	CF	F
Text transmitted in A	752	592	349 (1 *es*)	32	1	1	26	6	6	0	1
Text missing in A	133	119	/	/	/	/	4	/	1	1	1

	Uncontr. in OCT	A	ADC	D
	174	8	1	3

Pattern *short vowel* + *-s* + *est*/*es*

	Contr. in Oct	Contracted In mss.		With Omission of *EST*/*ES* in mss.		Metrically Reconstructed		Total
		est	*es*	*est*	*es*	*est*	*es*	
-*us* + *est*/*es*	74	10 (8 A, 2 D)	0	9	22	23	0	64
-*is* + *est*/*es*	10	0	0	2	4	3	1	10
TOTAL	84	10	0	11	26	26	1	74

Contracted in OCT	Contracted in A	Contracted in D (not in A)	Indirect transmission	Metrically reconstructed	Total
795	391 (+9 not in OCT)	32 (+3 not in OCT)	53	27	503

uncontracted form whereas A gives a contracted form. The characteristics that make these fifty cases unsuitable for the contracted spelling are not evident. Marouzeau's criterion for dealing with forms belonging to portions of text missing in A (*c*.150) is also unclear: he follows KL in printing contraction in about 105 cases, but prints the uncontracted spelling in about forty cases. In conclusion, editors of Terence do not seem to have a clear rationale for dealing with contracted and uncontracted spellings.

2. Omission of Final -s in CIL 1^2

Table 7.3 displays the figures for the omission of final -s in the republican inscriptions collected in CIL 1^2. The table has already been given in chapter V (Table 5.1) and is repeated here for the sake of convenience.

Observations:

1) Omission of final -s is often determined by the lack of space at the end of the line (116 out of 319 cases, 37%).

2) Omission of final -s does not appear to be influenced by the fact that the following word begins with s- (only thirteen cases in total, 4%). The idea (suggested by Quintilian, see V.1.1 and V.5.1) that a sequence -s s- was avoided by authors as cacophonous is not supported by the evidence of republican inscriptions.

3) Omission of final -s is most common with nominatives of the second declension (thirty-four cases in -us, 237 in -os for a total of 271 cases, 87%). Out of the remaining cases (forty-eight), many are found at the end of a line (twenty-one) and are thus not necessarily significant.

4) Of the twenty-seven cases which are not found at the end of a line and which do not involve a nominative of the second declension, only eight may be associated with sigmatic ecthlipsis; in five of these twenty-seven cases the name is a Greek name in -as and the apparent omission of the -s might simply represent a morphological Latinization (cf. e.g. CIL 1^2.2691 *Apella(s) Careisi P(ubli) s(ervus)*)[8]; in another

Table 7.3 (= Table 5.1). Omission of final -s in CIL 1^2

		Nominative Second Declension		Other	Total
		-us	-os		
At End of Line		22	73	21	116
Not at End of Line		12	164	27	203
Before Vowel		3	9	6	18
Before Consonant	Any	6	147	19	172
	s-	3	8	2	13
TOTAL		34	237	48	319

[8] On this cf. Quint. 1.5.61, Adams (2003: 371–2).

Appendix

Table 7.4. Nominatives in *-us* and *-os* in CIL 1²

Ending	Total	*-s* Omitted	*-s* Not omitted
-us	> 2000	34	> 2000
-os	c.272	237	c.35

fourteen the vowel preceding the *-s* is long, a phonological context in which sigmatic ecthlipsis is not attested.

5) The evidence for sigmatic ecthlipsis in republican inscriptions is weaker than is normally believed and is restricted to nominatives of the second declension, especially when ending in *-os* (237 cases, 220 of which ending in *-ios*). It is difficult to believe that phonological factors are not involved in the omission of *-s* in such cases; as displayed in Table 7.4, omission of final *-s* is almost standard in nominatives of the second declension in which we find an *-o(s)* ending; conversely it is extremely rare in equivalent nominatives ending in *-us*. Moreover, we sometimes find the same word spelt differently in two inscriptions belonging to the same series, in one case with the ending *-us* without the omission of *-s*, in the other with the ending *-o(s)* with omission; cf. e.g. CIL 1².406n *L(ucius)* Canoleio(s) *T(iti) f(ilius) fecit* and CIL 1².406o *L(ucius)* Canoleius *L(uci) f(ilius) fecit.*

Evidence:

1- Omission of Final *-s* at the End of a Line

Nominative of the 2nd Declension (twenty-two in *-us*, seventy-three in *-os*)
CIL 1⁽²⁾.46 **Muluio(s)**/don(um) d(at) [*Ariccia*]
CIL 1.53 Cn(aeus) **Fourio(s)** [*Tusculum*]
CIL 1.57 **Fourio(s)** [*Tusculum*]
CIL 1.59 **Metilio(s)**/[*Palestrina*]
CIL 1.70 L(ucius) **Anicio(s)** [*Palestrina*]
CIL 1.120 Po(m)po **Cestio(s)** [*Palestrina*]
CIL 1.133 M(arcus) **Coriario(s)** [*Palestrina*]
CIL 1.142 Sta(tius) **Cupio(s)** [*Palestrina*]
CIL 1.150 M(arcus) **Epoleio(s)** [*Palestrina*]
CIL 1.156 C(aius) **Fabrecio(s)** [*Palestrina*]
CIL 1.176 P(ublius) **Herenio(s)** [*Palestrina*]
CIL 1.187 M(arcus) **Macolnio(s)** [*Palestrina*]

CIL 1.202 Q(uintus) **Mutilio(s)** [*Palestrina*]

CIL 1.213 C(aius) **Opio(s)** [*Palestrina*]

CIL 1.258 A(ulus) **Roscio(s)** [*Palestrina*]

CIL 1.304 L(ucius) **Tampio(s)** [*Palestrina*]

CIL 1.307 Pac(uius)//**Tampio(s)** [*Palestrina*]

CIL 1.315 C(aius) **Tiliano(s)** [*Palestrina*]

CIL 1.346 C(aius) **Usoro(s)** [*Palestrina*]

CIL 1.354a]**anio(s)** [*Palestrina*]

CIL 1.377 Sta(tios) **Tetio(s)**/dede [*Pesaro*]

CIL 1.389 Pe(tro) **Pagio(s)**/Fougno/aram [*Trasacco*]

CIL 1.394 T(itus) **Vetio(s)**/duno/didet [*Prata*]

CIL 1.402 Q(uintus) **Rauel[i]o(s)** [*Roma*]

CIL 1.405a K(aeso) **Atilio(s)** [*Calvi Vecchia*]

CIL 1.405d K(aeso) **Atilio(s)** [*Paestum*]

CIL 1.405e K(aeso) **Atilio(s)** [*Napoli*]

CIL 1.405f K(aeso) **Atilio(s)** [*Napoli*]

CIL 1.405g K(aeso) **Atilio(s)** [*Napoli*]

CIL 1.405i K(aeso) **Atilio(s)** [*Capua*]

CIL 1.405m K(aeso) **Atilio(s)** [*Mondragone*]

CIL 1.405n K(aeso) **Atilio(s)** [*Calvi Vecchia*]

CIL 1.408 L(ucius) **Canoleio(s)** [*Cerveteri*]

CIL 1.409a L(ucius) **Gabinio(s)** [*?*]

CIL 1.409b L(ucius) **Gabinio(s)** [*Calvi Vecchia*]

CIL 1.409c L(ucius) **Gabinio(s)** [*Capua*]

CIL 1.425a Tr(ebius) **Loisio(s)** [*Trapani*]

CIL 1.425b Tr(ebius) **Loisio(s)** [*Erice*]

CIL 1.425c Tr(ebius) **Loisio(s)** [*Erice*]

CIL 1.425d Tr(ebius) **Loisio(s)** [*Licata*]

CIL 1.425f Tr(ebius) **Loisio(s)** [*?*]

CIL 1.425h Tr(ebius) **Loisio(s)** [*Tarentum*]

CIL 1.425i [Tr(ebius)] **Loisio(s)** [*Tarentum*]

CIL 1.425k [T]r(ebius) **Loisio(s)** [*Roma*]

CIL 1.425l Tr(ebius) **Loisio(s)** [*Ischia*]

CIL 1.425m Tr(ebius) **Loisio(s)** [*Caulonia*]

CIL 1.425n Tr(ebius) **Loisio(s)** [*Illis*]

CIL 1.427 Cn(aeus) **Iunio(s)**/C(ai) l(ibertus) Pobleios [*Narnia*]

CIL 1.476.2 At(tus) **Fertrio(s)** [*Leprignano*]

CIL 1.476.5 K(aeso) **Vomanio(s)** [*Leprignano*]

CIL 1.476.11 **Metorio(s)** [*Capena*]

CIL 1.521 L(ucius) **Manilio(s)** [*Roma*]

CIL 1.534 L(ucius) **Tetio(s)** [*Roma*]

CIL 1.571a Na(uios) **Acrio(s)** [*Palestrina*]

CIL 1.572 L(ucius) **Poulilio(s)** [*Palestrina*]

CIL 1.620 M(arcus) **Aemiliu(s)**/M(arci) f(ilius) [*Grottaminarda*]

CIL 1.918 **Philarguru(s)**/Procili [*Roma*]

CIL 1.1257 Niceporus **patronu(s)**/[*Roma*]

CIL 1.1311 M(arcus) **Granio(s)**/M(arci) [*Roma*]

CIL 1.1315 Hordionius Q(uinti) l(ibertus) **Catamitu(s)**/[*Roma*]

CIL 1.1477 [Felici]tat(i) L(ucio) **Dindio(s)** [*Palestrina*]

CIL 1.1585 **Teophilo(s)**/Terenti [*Capua*]

CIL 1.1750 f(ilius) Fal(erna) **uiuo(s)**/fecit [*Gioia Sannitica*]

CIL 1.1989 M(arcus) **Cl[i]peario(s)**/M[a(ni) [*Civita Castellana*]

CIL 1.2308a **Ant{h}ioc(h)u(s)**/Curti [*Roma*]

CIL 1.2331 **Tyrsu(s)**/Sari L(uci) s(eruus) [*Arezzo*]

CIL 1.2370b Popi(lius)/**Bitu(s)** [*Roma*]

CIL 1.2370d Popi(llius)/**Bitu(s)** [*Roma*]

CIL 1.2373 **Olu(s)** [*Orbetello*]

CIL 1.2383 T(itus) **Volesio(s)** [*Firenze*]

CIL 1.2393c **Lusimacu(s)** [*Roma*]

CIL 1.2477 L(ucius) **Roscio(s)** [*Palestrina*]

CIL 1.2637 Sortes L(uci) l(ibertus) **Dionisiu(s)** [*Perugia*]

CIL 1.2836b M(arcus) Fol]**uio(s)** [[*Roma*]

CIL 1.2873a C(aius) **Cisiedo(s)**/Aplone/ded(et) [*Trasacco*]

CIL 1.2878a [**V**]**alerio(s)** [*Minturnae*]

CIL 1.2878b [**V**]**alerio(s)** [*Minturnae*]

CIL 1.2878c [**V**]**alerio(s)** [*Minturnae*]

CIL 1.2902a L(ucius) **Aimelio(s)** [*Palermo*]

CIL 1.2903c St(atius) **Clanidio(s)** [*Capena*]

CIL 1.2903e M(arcus) **Peio(s)** [*?*]

CIL 1.2914 Q(uintus) **Sabino(s)** [*Rimini*]

CIL 1.3034 D(ecimus) **Numisiu(s)**/D(ecimi) [*Ostia Antica*]

CIL 1.3050 Q(uinti) l(ibertus) **Phi(i)lp(p)u(s)**/ [*Palestrina*]

CIL 1.3105a Ter(etina) **Rufu(s)**/Q(uinto) [*Villetta*]

CIL 1.3176 M(arci) f(ilius) Cla(udia) **Rufu(s)**/ [*Ruvo di Puglia*]

CIL 1.3182 Curtius P(ubli) f(ilius) **Salassu(s)** [*Canosa di Puglia*]

CIL 1.3353 D(ecimus) **Quenniu(s)**/ann(orum?) XX[1] [*Tuscania*]

CIL 1.3362 Senti(us) **Alchu(s)**/Clepatras [*Chiusi*]

CIL 1.3439 Marai(os) [**G**]**erillano(s)**/N(umerius) Varaios et s{e}i qui(s)
alius eri(t) [*Delos*]

CIL 1.3549 L(ucius) **Flauio(s)** [*Alba Fucens*]

CIL 1.3596 P(ublius) **Campatiu(s)** [*Ampurias*]

CIL 1.3619 **Barbaru(s)** [*?*]

CIL 1. p. 68 L(ucius) **Semproniu(s)**/ [*Roma*]

CIL 1. p. 68 Coelius C(ai) l(ibertus) **Pamphilu(s)**/ [*Roma*]

Other (twenty-one)

CIL 1.22 C(aius) Cinci(os)/**aidile(s)**/ [*Roma*]

CIL 1.59 **magistere(s)**/corauero(nt) [*Palestrina*]

CIL 1.379 **Pisaure(n)se(s)**/dono ded(e)ro(n)t [*Pesaro*]

CIL 1.593 praerit in **tabula(s)**/publicas [*Pisticci*]

CIL 1.671 C(aius) Mispius **mute(s)** [*Samothraki*]

CIL 1.1016 C(aius) Aemili(us) K(alendis) **Iuni(s)** [*Roma*]

CIL 1.1017 D(ecimus) Aimil(ius) **Noni(s)**/Octob(ris) [*Roma*]

CIL 1.1049 a(nte) d(iem) III K(alendas) **Nou(em)bri(s)** [*Roma*]

CIL 1.1062 Mai(os) Fabricia/a(nte) d(iem) IIX **Eidu(s)**/Sept(embres)
[*Roma*]

CIL 1.1114 A(ulus) Minuci(us)/a(nte) d(iem) IV **Eidu(s)** [*Roma*]

CIL 1.1259 castu(s) **amabili(s)**/omnibus [*Roma*]

CIL 1.1277 et liber(tis) **libertabu(s)**/in [*Roma*]

CIL 1.1308 in front(e) **pede(s)**/ [*Roma*]

CIL 1.1614 pus olusolu **fancua(s)**/ [*Cumae*]

CIL 1.2332b **So/crate(s)** [*Arezzo*]

CIL 1.2504 magistreis Mirquri **Apollini(s)** [*Delos*]

CIL 1.2567 M(arci) l(ibertus) **Diocle(s)** [*Cerveteri*]

CIL 1.2871 ui[x(it)] **an(n)o(s)**/XXII [*Orte*]

CIL 1.3176 q]uinq(uennales) muru(m) et **turri(s)**/ [*Ruvo di Puglia*]

CIL 1.3339 neque mors **sati(s)**/laudari [*Visentium*]

CIL 1.3380 Bia opset/**marone(s)**/T(ito) Foltonio [*Foligno*]

2. Omission of final -*s* not at the end of a line (underlined before *s*-)

Nominative of the second declension (12 in -*us*, 164 in -*os*)

CIL 1.6 [L(ucius) Corneli]**o(s)** Cn(aei) f(ilius) Scipio [*Roma*]

CIL 1.8 L(ucius) **Cornelio(s)** L(uci) f(ilius) Scipi [*Roma*]

CIL 1.9 L(ucius) **Cornelio(s)** L(uci) f(ilius) Scipi [*Roma*]

CIL 1.20]**ilio(s)** M(arci) f(ilius) C(aius) [*Roma*]

CIL 1.21 C(aius) **Fourio(s)** [C(ai) f(ilius)]/ [*Pontinia*]

CIL 1.21 **Claudio(s)** A[p(pi) f(ilius)]/ [*Pontinia*]

CIL 1.28 M(arcus) **Populicio(s)** M(arci) f(ilius) [*Roma*]

CIL 1.30 C(aius) **Pomplio(s)** No(ni) f(ilii) [*Roma*]

CIL 1.31 M(arcus) **Bicoleio(s)** V(ibi) l(ibertus) Honore [*Roma*]

CIL 1.33 M(arcus) **Terebonio(s)** C(ai) l(ibertus) donum dat liben[s]
[*Roma*]

CIL 1.40 **Manlio(s)** Ac() f(ilius) [*Boccanera*]

CIL 1.41 M(arcus) **Liuio(s)** M(arci) f(ilius) [*Nemi*]

CIL 1.48 **Fourio(s)** C(ai) f(ilius) [*Tusculum*]

CIL 1.49 **Fourio(s)** C(ai) f(ilius) [*Tusculum*]

CIL 1.56 Q(uintus) **Fourio(s)** A(uli) f(ilius) [*Tusculum*]

CIL 1.58 C(aius) **Turpleio(s)** C(ai) f(ilius) [*Tusculum*]

CIL 1.58 Q(uintus) **Turpleio(s)** C(ai) f(ilius) [*Tusculum*]

CIL 1.61 **Cestio(s)** Q(uinti) f(ilius) [*Palestrina*]

CIL 1.62 **Gemenio(s)** L(uci) f(ilius) [*Palestrina*]

CIL 1.64 **Agilio(s)** L(uci) l(ibertus) [*Palestrina*]

CIL 1.67 L(ucius) **Acutilio(s)** L(uci) f(ilius?) [*Palestrina*]

CIL 1.72 V(ibius) **Anicio(s)** V(ibi)/f(ilius) [*Palestrina*]

CIL 1.76 **Maio(s)** Anicia C(ai) f(ilia) [*Palestrina*]

CIL 1.79 C(aius) **Antonio(s)** M(ani) f(ilius) [*Palestrina*]

CIL 1.84 M(arcus) **Aptronio(s)** M(arci) f(ilius) [*Palestrina*]

CIL 1.104 C(aius) **Camelio(s)** L(uci) l(ibertus) [*Palestrina*]

CIL 1.105 **Camelio(s)** N(umeri) l(ibertus) [*Palestrina*]

CIL 1.110 L(ucius) **Caruilio(s)** L(uci) f(ilius) [*Palestrina*]

CIL 1.119 Ce]**stio(s)** C(ai) f(ilius) C(ai) n(epos) [*Palestrina*]

CIL 1.126 **Mino(s)** Colionia Artoro Mai(oris) (uxor) [*Palestrina*]

CIL 1.129 C(aius) **Comio(s)** Pes(i) f(ilius) [*Palestrina*]

CIL 1.132 C(aius) **Coriario(s)** L(uci) l(ibertus) [*Palestrina*]

CIL 1.136 **Coutio(s)** C(ai) l(ibertus) [*Palestrina*]

CIL 1.148 L(ucius) **Dindio(s)** L(uci) f(ilius) [*Palestrina*]

CIL 1.157 C(aius) **Fabric[i]o(s)** f() [*Palestrina*]

CIL 1.161 **Maio(s)** Fabricia [*Palestrina*]

CIL 1.164 C(aius) **Flauio(s)** L(uci) f(ilius) [*Palestrina*]

CIL 1.173]o(s) Ges(s)ia [*Palestrina*]

CIL 1.181 L(ucius) **Lorelano(s)** M(arci) l(ibertus) [*Palestrina*]

CIL 1.182 L(ucius) **Luscio(s)** M(arci) [[*Palestrina*]

CIL 1.189 C(aius?) **Magolnio(s)** Pla(uti) f(ilius) [*Palestrina*]

CIL 1.193 Tr(ebius) **Mamio(s)** Mai(oris) f(ilius) [*Palestrina*]

CIL 1.201 M(arcus) **Mutilio(s)** Q(uinti) f(ilius) [*Palestrina*]

CIL 1.214 Cn(aeus) **Opio(s)** Cn(aei) f(ilius) [*Palestrina*]

CIL 1.218 M(arcus) **Opio(s)** M(arci) f(ilius) [*Palestrina*]

CIL 1.219 M(arcus) **Opio(s)** M(arci) f(ilius) L(uci) n(epos) [*Palestrina*]

CIL 1.221 P(ublius) **Opio(s)** P(ubli) f(ilius) [*Palestrina*]

CIL 1.222 **Sexto(s)** Opio(s) C(ai) f(ilius) [*Palestrina*]

CIL 1.222 Sexto(s) **Opio(s)** C(ai) f(ilius) [*Palestrina*]

CIL 1.228 C(aius) **Orc(e)uio(s)** M(arci) f(ilius) [*Palestrina*]

CIL 1.229 L(ucius) **Orcuio(s)** C(ai) f(ilius) [*Palestrina*]

CIL 1.230 M(arcus) **Orceuio(s)** M(arci) f(ilius) [*Palestrina*]

CIL 1.234 Q(uintus) **Oueio(s)** T(iti) f(ilius) [*Palestrina*]

CIL 1.238 **Pescno(s)** l(ibertus) [*Palestrina*]

CIL 1.239 L(ucius) **P(e)tronio(s)** C(ai) l(ibertus) [*Palestrina*]

CIL 1.240 P(ublius) **P(e)tronio(s)** L(uci) l(ibertus) [*Palestrina*]

CIL 1.242 C(aius) **Plautio(s)** C(ai) f(ilius) [*Palestrina*]

CIL 1.243 L(ucius) **Plautio(s)** M(arci) f(ilius) L(uci) n(epos) [*Palestrina*]

CIL 1.244 M(arcus) **Plautio(s)** M(ani) f(ilius) [*Palestrina*]

CIL 1.252 M(arcus) **Pulio(s)** L(uci) f(ilius) [*Palestrina*]

CIL 1.265 **Samiario(s)** M(arci) f(ilius) [*Palestrina*]

CIL 1.268 **Samiario(s)** C(ai) f(ilius) [*Palestrina*]

CIL 1.280 C(aius) **Saufio(s)** Q(uinti) f(ilius) Sca(tus) [*Palestrina*]

CIL 1.283 Op(p)i(us) **Saufio(s)** L(uci) l(ibertus) [*Palestrina*]

CIL 1.291 M(arcus) **Segnino(s)** M(arci) f(ilius) [*Palestrina*]

CIL 1.296 L(ucius) **Selicio(s)** Nu(meri) f(ilius) [*Palestrina*]

CIL 1.309 C(aius) **Tapio(s)** Sex(ti) l(ibertus) [*Palestrina*]

CIL 1.310 **C(a)io(s)** Tapio(s) M(arci) l(ibertus) [*Palestrina*]

CIL 1.310 C(a)io(s) **Tapio(s)** M(arci) l(ibertus) [*Palestrina*]

CIL 1.316 C(aius) **Tiliano(s)** C(ai) f(ilius) [*Palestrina*]

CIL 1.317 C(aius) **Titilio(s)** C(ai) f(ilius) [*Palestrina*]

CIL 1.319 L(ucius) **Titionio(s)** C(ai) f(ilius) [*Palestrina*]

CIL 1.322 C(aius) **Tilanio(s)** C(ai) f(ilius) [*Palestrina*]

CIL 1.332 C(aius) **Vatronio(s)** L(uci) f(ilius) [*Palestrina*]

CIL 1.349 **Oufilio(s)** C(ai) f(ilius) [*Palestrina*]

CIL 1.351] **Cl[]io(s)** C(ai) l(ibertus) [[*Palestrina*]

CIL 1.363 L(ucius) **Rahio(s)** L(uci) f(ilius) [*Sermoneta*]

CIL 1.375 P(ublius) **Popaio(s)** Pop(li) f(ilius) [*Pesaro*]

CIL 1.382 V(ibius) **Auilio(s)** V(ibi) f(ilius) [*Massaccio*]

CIL 1.382 **Alfieno(s)** Po(bli) f(ilius) [*Massaccio*]

CIL 1.383 **Terentio(s)** L(uci) f(ilius)/ [*Fermo*]

CIL 1.383 **Aprufenio(s)** C(ai) f(ilius [*Fermo*]

CIL 1.383 L(ucius) **Turpilio(s)** C(ai) f(ilius) [*Fermo*]

CIL 1.383 T(itus) **Munatio(s)** T(iti) f(ilius [*Fermo*]

CIL 1.384 L(ucius) **Opio(s)** C(ai) l(ibertus) [*Mosciano Sant' Angelo*]

CIL 1.386 Sa(luios) **Burtio(s)** V(ibi) f(ilius) [*Avezzano*]

CIL 1.388 Sa(luios) **Magio(s)** St(ati) [*Trasacco*]

CIL 1.388 **Anaiedio(s)** St(ati) f(ilius) [*Trasacco*]

CIL 1.395 A(ulus) **Ceruio(s)** A(uli) f(ilius) [*Benevento*]

CIL 1.398 Q(uintus) **Lainio(s)** Q(uinti) f(ilius) praifectos [*San Vittorino*]

CIL 1.399 **Hinoleio(s)** C(ai) l(ibertus) [*Calvi Vecchia*]

CIL 1.400 **Autrodiu(s)** C(ai)/ [*Carinola*]

CIL 1.400 **Racectiu(s)** S(puri) [*Carinola*]

CIL 1.400 **Teditiu(s)** S(puri)/ [*Carinola*]

CIL 1.402 **Cominio(s)** P(ubli) f(ilius)/ [*Roma*]

CIL 1.402 L(ucius) **Malio(s)** C(ai) f(ilius)/ [*Roma*]

CIL 1.406c L(ucius) **Canoleio(s)** T(iti) f(ilius) fecit [*Vasto*]

CIL 1.406n L(ucius) **Canoleio(s)** T(iti) f(ilius) fecit [?]

CIL 1.406q L(ucius) **Canoleio(s)** [L(uci) f(ilius) fecit] Calenos [*Pompei*]

CIL 1.410 **Gabinio(s)** [L(uci) f(ilius)] T(iti) [*Capua*]

CIL 1.410 n(epos) **Caleno(s)** [. . .] [*Capua*]

CIL 1.412a Retus **Gabinio(s)** C(ai) s(eruus) [*Tarquinii*]

CIL 1.412c Retus **Gabinio(s)** C(ai) s(eruus) [*Tarquinii*]

CIL 1.413 **Seruio(s)** Gabinio(s) T(iti) s(eruus) fecit [*Capua*]

CIL 1.413 Seruio(s) **Gabinio(s)** T(iti) s(eruus) fecit [*Capua*]

CIL 1.416 K(aeso) **Serponio(s)** Caleb(us) fece(t) [?]

CIL 1.467b [P(ublius) Sext]**io(s)** V(ibi) f(ilius) [*Roma*]

CIL 1.478 Rustiae **Rustiu(s)** iousit sapere [*Roma*]

CIL 1.498 **Claudio(s)** non sum tua [*Roma*]

CIL 1.518 T(itus) **Iuilio(s)** Ste(llatina) S(purius) Hel(uius) [*Roma*]

CIL 1.541 **Serg[i]o(s)** O[]ani [*Roma*]

CIL 1.545 C(aius) **Ouio(s)** Ouf(entina) fec(i)t [*Roma*]

CIL 1.546 C(aius) **Pomponio(s)** Virio(s) pos(uit) [*Orvieto*]

CIL 1.546 C(aius) Pomponio(s) **Virio(s)** pos(uit) [*Orvieto*]

CIL 1.1259 **castu(s)** amabili(s)/ [*Roma*]

CIL 1.1429 L(ucius) **Octauio(s)** Vi(?)/ [*Lanuvio*]

CIL 1.1731 **Suessiano(s)** C(ai) [f(ilius)] [*Benevento*]

CIL 1.1731 **Amio(s)** N(umeri) f(ilius) [*Benevento*]

CIL 1.1731 **Nonio(s)** M(arci) f(ilius) [*Benevento*]

CIL 1.1731 Cn(aeus) **Suellio(s)** Cn(aei) f(ilius) [*Benevento*]

CIL 1.1731 L(ucius) **Munatio(s)** L(uci) f(ilius) [*Benevento*]

CIL 1.1731 **Vaterrio(s)** C(ai) f(ilius) [*Benevento*]

CIL 1.1731 C(aius) **Freganio(s)** N(umeri) f(ilius) [*Benevento*]

CIL 1.1766 P(ublius) **Haruiu(s)** S(erui) [f(ilius)] [*Trasacco*]

CIL 1.1848 T(itus) **Coruio(s)** A[p(pi?)] f(ilius) [*San Vittorino*]

CIL 1.1990 Polae Abelese / **lectu(s)** I datus/ [*Civita Castellana*]

CIL 1.1990 **lectu(s)** I amplius nihil [*Civita Castellana*]

CIL 1.2308d [**Antioc**]**u(s)** Qurti(us) [*Roma*]

CIL 1.2349 L(ucius) **Iunio(s)** Cn(aei) f(ilius) [*Tarquinia*]

CIL 1.2352 **Comatu(s)** Da[[*Roma*]

CIL 1.2362 **Liciniu(s)** Ruli s(eruus) [?]

CIL 1.2436 **Numesio(s)** M(arci) f(ilius) [*Capena*]

CIL 1.2438 C(aius) **Carulio(s)** C(ai) f(ilius) [*Minturnae*]

CIL 1.2439 C(aius) **Saufeio(s)** C(ai) f(ilius) [*Palestrina*]

CIL 1.2439 C(aius) **Orceuio(s)** M(arci) f(ilius) [*Palestrina*]
CIL 1.2442 **Aidicio(s)** Q(uinti) f(ilii) T(itus) [*Lanuvio*]
CIL 1.2442 T(itus) **Rebinio(s)** Q(uinti) f(ilius) [*Lanuvio*]
CIL 1.2443 C(aius) **Scautio(s)** L(uci) f(ilius) aidile(s) faice[//]mqu [*Roma*]
CIL 1.2448 L(ucius) **Auilio(s)** L(uci) l(ibertus) [*Palestrina*]
CIL 1.2450 L(ucius) **Aulio(s)** L(uci) f(ilius) [*Palestrina*]
CIL 1.2452 C(aius) **Canio(s)** M(arci) f(ilius) [*Palestrina*]
CIL 1.2454 M(arcus) **Canio(s)** M(arci) f(ilius) [*Palestrina*]
CIL 1.2457 M(arcus) **Cestio(s)** M(arci) l(ibertus) [*Palestrina*]
CIL 1.2464 C(aius) **Opio(s)** C(ai) f(ilius) [*Palestrina*]
CIL 1.2472 C(aius) **Plautio(s)** L(uci) l(ibertus) [*Palestrina*]
CIL 1.2480 C(aius) **Terentilio(s)** T(iti) l(ibertus) [*Palestrina*]
CIL 1.2486 Sal(uios) **Seio(s)** L(uci) f(ilius) [*Superaequum*]
CIL 1.2486 L(ucius) **Seio(s)** Sa(lui) f(ilius) [*Superaequum*]
CIL 1.2675a Turp(ilios) **Orcio(s)** P(ubli) f(ilius) [*Cantalupo*]
CIL 1.2678 **Philaro(s)** Tucci M(arci) [s(eruus)] [*Minturnae*]
CIL 1.2730 M(arcus) **Cipio(s)** Larcia u[xor] [*Cerveteri*]
CIL 1.2752 **Marcio(s)** Car() [*Cerveteri*]
CIL 1.2834 L(ucius) **[C]ornelio(s)** Cn(aei) f(ilius) [*Roma*]
CIL 1.2835 P(ublius) **Cornelio(s)** P(ubli) f(ilius) [*Roma*]
CIL 1.2838]**io(s)** M(arci) f(ilius) [*Roma*]
CIL 1.2856 L(ucius) **Camelio(s)** L(uci) f(ilius) [*Palestrina*]
CIL 1.2858 M(arcus) **Plautio(s)** T(iti) f(ilius) [*Palestrina*]
CIL 1.2869a V(ibius) **Genucilio(s)** Sen() l(ibertus) [*Lucus Feroniae*]
CIL 1.2874a **Vip[i]o(s)** Po(pli) f(ilios) [*Ortucchio*]
CIL 1.2874b L(ucius) **Vibio(s)** [[*Calvi Vecchia*]
CIL 1.2903d T(itus) **Gauio(s)** C(ai) f(ilius) [*Capena*]
CIL 1.2908 C(e)rere L(ucius) **Tolonio(s)** d(edit) [*Vei*]
CIL 1.2909 L(ucius) **Tolonio(s)** ded(it) Menerua [*Vei*]
CIL 1.2919]**neio(s)** Saluio [*Lanuvio*]
CIL 1.2923a M(arcus) **Patolcio(s)** Ar(runtis) l(ibertus) p(ondo) VIII
          [*Pizzighettone*]
CIL 1.3059 [Men]**opilu(s)** Mersei C(ai) s(eruus) [*Palestrina*]
CIL 1.3151 L(ucius) **Manio(s)** f(ilius) [*Paestum*]
CIL 1.3151 **Fadio(s)** M(arci) f(ilius) [*Paestum*]
CIL 1.3151 **Megonio(s)** C(ai) f(ilius) [*Paestum*]
CIL 1.3151 **Vibio(s)** C(ai) f(ilius) [*Paestum*]
CIL 1.3151 O(lus) **Bracio(s)** V(ibi) [*Paestum*]
CIL 1.3152 **Sextio(s)** Sex(ti) [f(ilius)] [*Paestum*]
CIL 1.3152 **Tatio(s)** L(uci) f(ilius) [*Paestum*]
CIL 1.3152 **Claudio(s)** Tr(ebi) f(ilius) [*Paestum*]

CIL 1.3152 **Statio(s)** C(ai) f(ilius) [*Paestum*]
CIL 1.3449 l M(anius) **Vibio(s)** Men(e)rua [*Tarragona*]

Other (twenty-seven)

After long vowel (fourteen)

CIL 1.454 **Canumede(s)** [Die]s pater Cupido Menerua [*Civita Castellana*]
CIL 1.500 N(e) **at(t)iga(s)** me Gemuci sum [*Velitrae*]
CIL 1.583 esse **ea(s)** res omnis [*Roma*]
CIL 1.585 is **stipendiariei(s)** det adsignetue [*Roma*]
CIL 1.593 census populi perscriptus erit **condenda(s)** curato [*Pisticci*]
CIL 1.594 II uiri quicumque erunt iis II **uiri(s)** in eos singulos [*Osuna*]
CIL 1.594 ea **re(s)** consuletur uti m(aior) p(ars) [*Osuna*]
CIL 1.1160 Seruilia a(nte) d(iem) IIX/**Eidu(s)** Mar(tias) [*Roma*]
CIL 1.1185 A(nte) d(iem) VIII ATOIBOD/**Eidu(s)** April(es) [*Roma*]
CIL 1.1187 A(nte) d(iem) IV **Eidu(s)** Oct(obres) [*Roma*]
CIL 1.2088 Caspo uix(it) **anno(s)** XX [*Volterra*]
CIL 1.2442 **aidile(s)** moltatico [*Lanuvio*]
CIL 1.2541 **ul(l)a(s)** res pos(s)it pete[re] [*Pompei*]
CIL 1.3146 sibi et **suei(s)que** uiuos fecit [*Castellamare di Stabia*]

Greek name in *-a(s)* *(five)*

CIL 1.2682 **Apella(s)** Roci L(uci) s(eruus) [*Minturnae*]
CIL 1.2682 **Aceiba(s)** Careisi L(uci) s(eruus) [*Minturnae*]
CIL 1.2683 **Sabda(s)** Aefici M(arci) s(eruus) [*Minturnae*]
CIL 1.2691 **Apella(s)** Careisi P(ubli) s(eruus) [*Minturnae*]
CIL 1.2703 **Sabda(s)** Epidi M(arci) s(eruus) [*Minturnae*]

Other *(eight)*

CIL 1.60 **nationu(s)** gratia [*Palestrina*]
CIL 1.197 **Mino(s)** Matlia [*Palestrina*]
CIL 1.442 **Coera(s)** pocolo(m) [*Orte*]
CIL 1.1614 **recta(s)** sint pus flatu [*Cumae*]
CIL 1.1861 **suauei(s)** heicei situst [*Preturo*]
CIL 1.2659 [do]no **plebe(s)** iousi(t) [*Albano Laziale*]
CIL 1.2677 **quoiu(s)** sibei e h(ac) l(ege) [*Falerone*]
CIL 1.3439 Marai(os) [G]erillano(s)/N(umerius) Varaios et s{e}i **qui(s)**
          alius eri(t) [*Delos*]

3. Lines Potentially Involving Sigmatic Ecthlipsis in Terence

This section of the Appendix is complementary to the analysis carried out in chapter V (*Sigmatic Ecthlipsis in Terence*) on the prosodic omission of final -*s* in Terence. It presents the corpus of all the instances of a sequence *short vowel* + -*s* + C- in Terence, together with a scansion of each line. The data are classified according to the metrical patterns presented in chapter V, which are reproduced in Table 7.5. For practical purposes, macron (e.g. *fēci*) and breve (e.g. *făcio*) are normally used to indicate the weight of a syllable (when it is not self-evident), not the length of its vowel (cf. e.g. *hōc = hocc*).

Table 7.5 (=Table 5.2). Metrical position and prosody of the sequence -Vs + C- in Terence

Category	1	2	3	4	5	6
ELEMENT	?	*anceps monosyllabic element*	*indifferent element*	*heavy monosyllabic element*	*one of the two syllables of a resolved element (heavy or anceps)*	*light element*
WEIGHT		HEAVY OR LIGHT		HEAVY	LIGHT	
TOTAL (1422)	30	849	34	281	205	23
%		64%		20%	16%	

3.1 Category 1: Uncertain Scansions

In this group of cases (thirty instances) it has been impossible to determine with precision the metrical value of the syllables ending in -*s*, since there are two acceptable scansions of the line, in each of which the syllable occupies a different metrical position.

An. 7   (ia⁶)   **uĕtĕris|** poē|tae mălĕ|dictis| respon|deat |

An. 21   (ia⁶)   **pŏtius|** qu(am) istō|r(um) obscū|ram dī|līgen|tiam|

An. 137   (ia⁶)   quĭd **ais|** rĕde(o) in|d(e) īrā|tŭs at|qu(e) aegrē |fĕrens|

An. 576   (ia⁷)   **ipsus|** mĭhĭ Dā|uos qu(i) in|tŭmust| eōrum| consĭli|is di|xit|

An. 665   (ia⁶)   fact(um) hō|c est Dā|uĕ fac|tŭm—hem| quĭd **ais|** scĕlus|

An. 933   (ia⁸)   certē |meas|t quĭd **ais|** quid tū—|aĭs ar|rĭg(e) au|ris pam| phĭle|

Eun. 174   (ia⁶)   **pŏtius|** quam t(e) ĭnĭ|mīc(um) hăbe|am făci|(am) ut ius| sĕris|

Eun. 176   (ia⁶)   **pŏtius|** quam t(e) ĭnĭ|mīc(um) hăbe|am s(i) is|tuc crē|dĕrem|

Eun. 223   (ia^8)   tandem| nōn ĕg(o) ĭl|lam căre|am sī |sĭt **ŏpus**| uel tō|tum trī| du(om) hūĭ|

Eun. 378   (ia^8)   quĭd **ăgis**| iŏcā|bar ĕquĭ|dem gar|ris pĕri|ī quĭd ĕ|g(o) ēgī | mĭser|

Eun. 474   (ia^6)   ĭtă mē |d(i) ămen|t hŏnes|tust quid| tŭ—**ais**| Gnătho|

Eun. 522   (ia^6)   **ecquis**| cŭm—e(a) ū|nā quĭd hă|buis|set quom| pĕrit|

Eun. 797   (tr^7)   tĭb(i) ĭllam| redda|t aut t(u) êam| tangā|s omni|(um) āh quĭd ă|gis tă|ce

Eun. 804   (tr^7)   sīcĭn ă|gis quis| tŭ—hŏm(o) es| quid tĭbĭ |uīs quid| c(um) illā |rêĭ tĭ|bist

Eun. 825   (ia^6)   quĭd **ais**| uĕnē|fĭc(a) at|quī cer|te com|pĕri|

Haut. 80   (ia^6)   mĭhĭ sī|c est ū|sus tĭbī—|ŭt **ŏpus**| factost| făce|

Haut. 118   (ia^6)   quĭd **ais**| clam mē |prŏfec|tus men|sīs trī|s ăbest|

Haut. 558   (ia^6)   uĭdē|bĭmus| quĭd **ŏpus**| sit nun|c istū|c ăge|

Haut. 628   (tr^7)   sustŭ|listī |sīc est| factum| dŏmĭn(a) ĕg(o) ĕ|rus dam|n(o) auctŭ|s est

Hec. 138   (ia^6)   quĭd **ais**| cum uir|gĭn(e) ū|n(a) ădŭles|cens cŭbu|ĕrit|

Hec. 425   (ia^6)   **pŏtius**| quam rĕde|am s(i) êō |mĭhĭ rĕde|undum| sciam|

Hec. 440   (ia^6)   **magnus**| rŭbĭcun|dus cris|pus cras|sus cae|sius|

Hec. 495   (ia^6)   mātris| seruĭ|bō com|mŏdis| quŏ—**ăbis**| măne|

Ph. 386   (ia^6)   pĕri(i) her|clĕ nō|men per|dĭdĭ |quĭd **ais**| Gēta|

Ph. 408   (ia^6)   **pŏtius**| quam lī|tis sec|ter aut| quam t(e) au|diam|

Ph. 833   (ia^8)   sed Phor|mios|t quĭd **ais**| quid quid|nam nunc| factū|rust Phae|dria|

Ad. 109   (ia^6)   **pŏtius**| qu(am) ŭbĭ t(e) ex|spectā|t(um) ēiē|cisset| fŏras|

Ad. 240   (ia^6)   **pŏtius**| quam uĕni|ās in| pĕrī|clum San|nio|

Ad. 309   (ia^8)   **sătius**| quae lŏquĭ|tur prŏpi|ŭs ob|sĕcr(o) ac|cēdā|mus Sos| trăt(a) ah|

Ad. 367   (ia^6)   **hŏmĭnis**| stultĭti|am con|laudā|uit fĭ|lium|

3.2 Category 2: Anceps Elements

In this group of cases (849 instances) the syllable ending in -*s* occupies a monosyllabic anceps element, which may be formed either by a light or by a heavy syllable. It is generally impossible to determine the weight of syllables found in such a metrical position.

An. 44   (ia^6)   quăs(i) ex|prŏbrā|tios|t **inmĕmŏ|ris** bĕnĕ|fĭci|

An. 51   (ia^6)   n(am) is pos|tqu(am) exces|sit e|x ĕphē|bis Sō|si(a) et|

An. 64   (ia^6)   ēor(um) ob|sĕqui s|tŭdii|s **aduer|sus** nē|mĭni|

An. 104   (ia^6)   ferm(e) in| **diē|bus** pau|cis quĭbŭ|s haec ac|tă sunt|

An. 108   (ia^6)   cūrā|bat ū|na **fū|nus** tris|tĭs in|tĕrim|

An. 111	(ia⁶)	caus(a) **hui**|us mor|tem tam| fert fămĭ|liā|rĭter|
An. 115	(ia⁶)	ĕgŏmet| quŏqu(e) **ei**|us cau|s(a) in fū|nus prō|deo|
An. 115	(ia⁶)	ĕgŏmet| quŏqu(e) ei|us cau|s(a) in **fū**|**nus** prō|deo|
An. 131	(ia⁶)	sătĭs cum| pĕrī|cl(o) ĭbĭ t(um) **e**|**xănĭmā**|**tus** Pam|phĭlus|
An. 134	(ia⁶)	meă Glў̆cĕ|ri(um) in|quit quĭd **ă̆**|**gis** quor| t(e) is per| dĭtum|
An. 145	(ia⁶)	indig|num **făcĭ**|**nus** com|pĕris|sĕ Pam|phĭlum|
An. 151	(ia⁶)	tūt(e) ip|s(e) his **rē**|**bus** fī|nem praes|cripstī |păter|
An. 159	(ia⁶)	sĭmul| **scĕlĕrā**|**tus** Dā|uos sī|quid con|sĭlī|
An. 159	(ia⁶)	sĭmul| scĕlĕrā|tus **Dā**|**uos** sī|quid con|sĭlī|
An. 161	(ia⁶)	qu(em) ĕgŏ crē|dō **mănĭ**|**bus** pĕdĭ|busqu(e) ob|nix(e) om|niă̆|
An. 161	(ia⁶)	qu(em) ĕgŏ crē|dō mănĭ|bus pĕdĭ|**busqu(e)** ob|nix(e) om|niă |
An. 164	(ia⁶)	mălă men|s mălŭs **ănĭ**|**mus** quem| quĭd(em) ĕgŏ |sī sen| sĕro|
An. 171	(ia⁶)	cūrā|b(o) **eā**|**mus** nun|ci(am) in|tr(o) ī prae |sĕquar|
An. 184	(ia⁸)	Dāu(e) hem| quĭd es|t ĕhŏ d(um) ad| mē quĭd hĭc| uolt quĭd **a**|**is** quā |dē rē |rŏgas|
An. 185	(ia⁸)	meùm gnā|tum rū|mor es|t ămā|r(e) id **pŏpŭ**|**lus** cū|rat scī|lĭcet|
An. 194	(ia⁸)	nōn her|cl(e) intel|lĕgō |nōn hem| non **Dā**|**uos** sum| nōn Oe|dĭpus|
An. 199	(ia⁸)	**uerbĕrĭ**|**bus** cae|sum t(e) in| pistrī|num Dā| uĕ dē|d(am) usqu(e) ad| nĕcem|
An. 203	(ia⁸)	ŭbĭuīs| **făcĭli**|**us** pas|sus sim| qu(am) ĭn hāc| rē mē |dēlū| dier|
An. 204	(ia⁸)	bŏnă uer|bă quae|s(o) inrī|des nil| mē **fal**|**lis** sed| dīcō | tĭbi|
An. 212	(ia⁸)	m(e) **infen**|**sus** ser|uat nē|quam făci|(am) in nup|tiis| fallā|ciam|
An. 222	(ia⁶)	mercā|tor nā|u(im) **is** frē|git ăpŭ|d andr(um) in|sŭlam|
An. 233	(tr⁷)	hūīc părĭ|und(i) at|qu(e) ill(i) ĭ|n ăliis| **pŏtius**| peccan|dī lŏ|cum
An. 247	(tr⁸)	nullō|n ĕgŏ Chrĕ|mētis| pact(o) ad|fīnĭ|tāt(em) ef|fŭgĕrĕ |pŏtĕro|
An. 248	(tr⁷)	quot mŏ|dis **con**|**temptus**| sprētus| facta |transac|t(a) omni|(a) hem
An. 248	(tr⁷)	quot mŏ|dis con|temptus| **sprētus**| facta |transac|t(a) omni|(a) hem
An. 249	(tr⁷)	**rĕpŭdi**|**ātus**| rĕpĕtor| qu(am) ob rem| nĭsī s(i) ĭ|d est quod| suspĭ|cor
An. 261	(ia⁸)	ămŏr mĭsĕ|rĭcor|di(a) **hui**|**us** nup|tiā|rum sol|lĭcĭtā|tio|

An. 266	(ia⁸)	d(um) in dŭbi|ost ănĭ|mus paul|lō mō|ment(o) huc| uĕl ĭllū|c impel|lĭtur|
An. 267	(ia⁸)	quĭs hĭc lŏquĭ|tur **Mȳ|sis** sal|u(e) ō sal|uē Pam|phĭlē |quĭd ăgĭt| rŏgas|
An. 282	(ia⁶)	mĕmŏr es|s(em) ō **Mȳ|sis** Mȳ|sĭs ĕti|am nunc| mĭhi|
An. 286	(ia⁶)	mī Pam|phĭl(e) **hui|us** for|m(am) atqu(e) ae|tātem| uĭdes|
An. 290	(ia⁶)	per tuăm| fĭdem| perqu(e) **hui|us** sō|lĭtū|dĭnem|
An. 292	(ia⁶)	sī t(e) in| germă|nī **frā|tris** dī|lexī |lŏco|
An. 301	(tr⁸)	quĭd **ais**| Byrri|ā dătŭr|n(e) illă |Pamphĭ|l(o) hŏdiē |nup-tum| sīc est|
An. 304	(ia⁸)	ĭtă pos|tqu(am) ădem|ptă spē|s est **las|sus** cū|rā con| fectus| stŭpet|
An. 309	(ia⁸)	făcĭl(e) om|nes quom| **uălē|mus** rec|tă con|sĭli(a) ae|grō-tīs| dămus|
An. 336	(tr⁷)	uĭdeō |quoi(u)s con|sĭliō |**frētus**| s(um) at t(u) her|cl(e) haud quic|quam mĭ|hi
An. 348	(tr⁷)	nupti|ae m(i) et|si sci|(o) hŏdi(e) **ob|tundis**| t(am) ets(i) in|tellĕ|go
An. 357	(tr⁷)	circum|spĭciō |nusquam| fort(e) ĭ|b(i) **hūius**| uĭdeō | Byrri|am
An. 360	(tr⁷)	paullŭ|l(um) opsō|n(i) **ipsus**| tristis| d(e) inprō|uīsō | nupti|ae
An. 360	(tr⁷)	paullŭ|l(um) opsō|n(i) ipsus| **tristis**| d(e) inprō|uīsō | nupti|ae
An. 361	(tr⁷)	non cŏ|haeren|t **quorsus**| n(am) istū|c ĕgŏ mē |contĭnu| (o) ad Chrĕ|mem
An. 363	(tr⁷)	rectē |**dīcis**| pergĕ |măne(o) in|tĕre(a) in|tr(o) īrĕ |nēmĭ| nem
An. 370	(tr⁷)	**lībĕ|rātus**| s(um) hŏdiē |Dāuĕ |tu(a) ŏpĕ|r(a) ac nul|lus quĭ|dem
An. 379	(tr⁷)	sed sī |tū **nĕ|gāris**| dūcĕ|r(e) ĭbĭ cul|p(am) in tē |transfĕ| ret
An. 393	(ia⁶)	haec quae |făcis| n(e) is mū|tet sŭam| senten|tiam|
An. 396	(ia⁸)	dăbĭt nē|m(o) inuĕni|et ĭnŏ|pem **pŏti|us** quam| tē cor| rumpī |sĭnat|
An. 398	(ia⁸)	ăli(am) ō|tiō|sus quae|ret in|tĕre(a) ălĭ|quĭd ac|cĭdĕrit| bŏni|
An. 412	(ia⁶)	ĕrŭs mē |rĕlic|tis rē|bus ius|sit Pam|phĭlum|
An. 434	(ia⁶)	quid Dā|uos nar|rat ae|quē quic|quam nunc| quĭdem|
An. 442	(ia⁶)	ĕtĕn(im) **ip|sus** sē|c(um) eam| rem rĕpŭ|tāuit| uia|
An. 447	(ia⁶)	**subtris|tis** uĭ|sŭs es|t ess(e) ălĭ|quantum| mĭhi|
An. 470	(ia⁶)	uix tan|dem sen|sī **stŏlĭ|dus** quĭd hĭc| sensis|s(e) ait|
An. 476	(ia⁶)	dīuĭ|să sun|t **tempŏrĭ|bus** tĭbĭ |Dāu(e) haec| mĭhin|

An. 486   (ia⁶)   pĕr ĕcas|tor scī|tus puĕ|r est nā|tus Pam|phĭlo|

An. 486   (ia⁶)   pĕr ĕcas|tor scī|tus puĕ|r est nā|tus Pam|phĭlo|

An. 487   (ia⁸)   dēos quae|s(o) ut sit| **super|stes** quan|dŏquĭd(em) ip|sest in|gĕniō |bŏno|

An. 489   (ia⁸)   uĕl hoc| **quis** crē|dat quī |tē nō|rit ab|s t(e) ess(e) or|tum quid|n(am) ĭd est|

An. 490   (ia⁸)   nōn im|pĕrā|bat cō|ram quĭd ŏ|**pus** fac|t(o) esset| puer| pĕrae|

An. 491   (ia⁸)   sed pos|tqu(am) ēgres|sast il|lis quae |sunt **in|tus** clā|mat dē |uia|

An. 495   (ia⁸)   cert(e) her|clĕ nun|c hic s(e) ip|sus fal|lĭt hau|d ĕg(o) ē| dixin| tĭbi|

An. 496   (ia⁸)   **inter|mĭnā|tus** sum| nē făcĕ|res num| uĕrĭtus| quĭd rē | tŭlit|

An. 503   (ia⁸)   cert(e) ĕnĭm| sciō |non sătĭs| mē per|nost(i) ĕti|am **quā| lis** sim| Sĭmo|

An. 509   (ia⁸)   nē t(u) hoc| **postĕri|us** dī|cas Dā|uī fac|tum con|sĭli(o) aut| dŏlis|

An. 520   (tr⁷)   **scīmus|** quam mĭsĕ|r(e) hanc ă|mārit| nunc sĭ|b(i) uxō|r (em) expĕ|tit

An. 527   (ia⁶)   quod mĭhĭ |pollĭcĭ|tust ip|**sus** gnā|tus nunc| Chrĕmem|

An. 527   (ia⁶)   quod mĭhĭ |pollĭcĭ|tust ip|sus **gnā|tus** nunc| Chrĕmem|

An. 530   (ia⁶)   nam **gnā|tus** quod| pollĭcĭ|tust haud| dŭbium|st mĭh(i) id|

An. 556   (ia⁶)   (em) id t(e) ō|r(o) ŭt an|t(e) **eā|mus** dum| tempus| dătur|

An. 560   (ia⁶)   uxō|rem **dē|mus** spē|rō con|suētū|dĭn(e) et|

An. 575   (ia⁷)   sed quĭd a|**is** quid| qui scī|s eos| nunc dis|cordā|r(e) inter| se|

An. 576   (ia⁷)   ipsus| mĭhĭ **Dā|uos** qu(i) in|tŭmust| ēorum| consĭli|is di| xit|

An. 583   (ia⁸)   quod uol|**gus** ser|uōrum| sŏlet| dŏlī|s ut mē |dēlū|dĕres|

An. 588   (ia⁸)   sĭmŭlā|uī uō|s ut per|temptā|rem quĭd a|**is** sīc| rēs es|t uĭde|

An. 591   (ia⁸)   numnam| **pĕrī|mus** nar|r(o) hūĉc quae |tū dū|dum nar| rastī |mĭhi|

An. 595   (ia⁸)   nunc t(e) ō|rō Dā|uĕ quŏni|am **sō|lus** m(i) ef|fēcis|t(i) has nup|tias|

An. 596   (ia⁸)   ĕgŏ uĕ|rō **sō|lus** cor|rĭgĕrē |mĭhĭ gnā|tum por|r(o) ēnĭ| tĕre|

An. 598   (ia⁸)   quies|cās ăg(e) ĭ|gĭtŭr ŭ|bĭ nun|c est ip|**sus** mī|rum nī | dŏmist|

An. 613   (ia⁸)   quī sum| **pollĭcĭ|tus** dū|cĕrē |qu(a) audā|ci(a) id| făcĕr(e) au|deam|

An. 616   (ia⁸)   ōh **uī|sus** s(um) ĕhŏ |dum bŏnĕ |uir quĭd a|is uĭdĕn| mē con|sĭliīs| tuis|

An. 616   (ia⁸)   ōh **uī|sus** s(um) ĕhŏ |dum bŏnĕ |uir quĭd **a|is** uĭdĕn| mē con|sĭliīs| tuis|

An. 618   (ia⁸)   nemp(e) ut| mŏd(o) im|mō **mĕli|us** spē|r(o) ōh tĭb(i) ĕ|g (o) ut crē|dam fur|cĭfer|

An. 624   (tr⁷)   namqu(e) hoc| **tempus**| praecă|uĕrĕ |mĭhĭ m(e) haud| t (e) ulcis|cī sĭ|nit

An. 640   (tr⁷)   ingĕ|ram mălă |mult(a) at|qu(e) **ălĭquis**| dīcat| nil prō| mōuĕ|ris

An. 641   (ia⁸)   multum| **mŏles|tus** cer|t(e) ei fuĕ|r(o) atqu(e) ănĭ|mō mō|rem ges|sĕro|

An. 652   (ia⁸)   haud is|tuc dī|cas sī |**cognō|ris** uel| mē uĕl ă|mōrem| meum|

An. 658   (ia⁶)   sciŏ tū |**coac|tus** tuă |uŏlun|tāt(e) es| măne|

An. 663   (ia⁸)   quĭs hŏm(o) is|tuc **Dā|uos** Dā|uŏs in|tertur|bat qu(am) ob| rem nes|cio|

An. 669   (ia⁶)   **dēcep|tus** s(um) at| non dē|fētĭ|gātus| scio|

An. 676   (ia⁶)   cōnā|rī **mănĭ|bus** pĕdĭ|bus noc|tesqu(e) et| dies|

An. 676   (ia⁶)   cōnā|rī **mănĭ|bus** pĕdĭ|bus noc|tesqu(e) et| dies|

An. 680   (ia⁶)   uel **mĕli|us** tū|te rĕpĕ|rī mē |missum| făce|

An. 702   (ia⁷)   **quis** uĭde|or mĭsĕ|r aequ(e) at|qu(e) ĕgō |consĭli|um quae|rō for|ti's|

An. 714   (ia⁷)   dŏm(i) ĕrō |tū **Mȳ|sis** d(um) e|xeō |părum|per m(e) op| pĕrĭ|r(e) hic|

An. 722   (ia⁶)   quō por|tas puĕ|rum **mȳ|sis** nun|c ŏpŭs es|t tua|

An. 748   (ia⁶)   ĕhŏ **Mȳ|sis** puĕ|r hĭc un|dest quis|u(e) hūc at|tŭlit|

An. 758   (ia⁶)   in quĭbŭs| sīc **in|lūdā|tis** uē|n(i) in tem|pŏre|

An. 772   (ia⁶)   n(e) ill(a) il|l(um) haud nō|uit **quoi|us** cau|s(a) haec in| cĭpit|

An. 776   (ia⁶)   nĭsĭ puĕ|rum **tol|lis** iăm—ĕ|g(o) hunc in| mĕdiam| uiam|

An. 780   (ia⁶)   cīu(em) At|tĭc(am) es|s(e) hanc hem| **coac|tus** lē|gĭbus|

An. 801   (ia⁶)   quem uĭde|l(o) estn(e) hic| Crītō |**sōbrī|nus** Chrĭ|sĭdis|

An. 802   (ia⁶)   ĭs es|t ō **mī|sis** sal|ue sal|uos sis| Crĭto|

An. 802   (ia⁶)   ĭs es|t ō **mī|sis** sal|ue **sal|uos** sis| Crĭto|

An. 805   (ia⁶)   ut quī|mŭs ā|iunt quan|d(o) ut **uŏlŭ|mus** non| lĭcet|

An. 809   (ia⁶)   sempĕr **ĕi|us** dic|tast es|s(e) haec at|qu(e) hăbĭtast| sŏror|

An. 817   (ia⁶)   ŏ—op|tum(e) **hos|pes** pol| Crĭt(o) an|tīqu(om) ob|tĭnes|

An. 825   (tr⁷)   uĭdĕ qu(am) ĭ|**nīquos** sis prae s|tŭdiō |dŭm—ĭd ef|fĭcias| quod lŭ|bet

An. 826   (tr⁷)   nĕquĕ mŏ|dum **bĕ|nignĭ|tātis**| nĕquĕ quid| m(e) ōrēs| cōgĭ|tas

An. 833   (tr^7)   ill(am) hinc| cīu(em) es|s(e) āiunt| puĕr est| **nātus**| nōs mis|sōs fă|ce

An. 840   (tr^7)   crēd(o) ĕ|t id fac|tūrās| **Dāuos**| dūdum| praedi|xit mĭ|h (i) et

An. 844   (tr^7)   ĕgŏ com|mŏdiō|r(em) hŏmĭn(em) ad|uentum| **tempus**| non uī|di scĕ|lus

An. 845   (tr^7)   quemn(am) hic| lauda|t **omnis**| rēs est| i(am) in uă|dō ces|s(o) ādlŏ|qui

An. 847   (tr^7)   omni|(a) adpă|rātă |iam sun|t **intus**| cūras|tī prŏ|be

An. 851   (tr^7)   cum tūŏ g|nāt(o) ū|n(a) ann(e) es|t **intus**| Pamphĭ|lus crŭci|or mĭ|ser

An. 854   (tr^7)   ĭmmŏ uē|r(o) indig|num Chrĕ|mē iam| **făcĭnus**| fax(o) ex| m(e) audi|es

An. 872   (ia^6)   **quis** mē |uolt pĕri|ī pătĕ|r est quĭd a|ĭs om|ni(um) ah|

An. 874   (ia^6)   quăsĭ quic|qu(am) ĭn hunc| iam **grăui|us** dī|cī pos|siet|

An. 875   (ia^6)   aĭn tan|dem cī|uis Glȳcĕ|rium|st ĭtă prae|dĭcant|

An. 878   (ia^6)   uĭdĕ n(um) ei(u)s| cŏlor| **pŭdō|ris** sig|n(um) usqu(am) in|dĭcat|

An. 906   (tr^7)   Andri|(um) ĕgŏ Crĭ|tōnem| uĭdeō |cert(e) ĭs ĕst| **saluos**| sīs Chrĕ|me

An. 914   (tr^7)   pĕriī |mĕtu(o) ut| subste|t **hospes**| sī Sĭ|m(o) hunc nō|ris să|tis

An. 932   (ia^8)   quĭd eam| tum suăm|n(e) ess(e) aĭ|bat non| quōi(am) ĭgĭ| tur frā|tris fĭ|liam|

An. 934   (ia^8)   quī crē|dis Phā|ni(a) il|lic frā|ter meŭs| fuit| nōr(am) et| scio|

An. 935   (ia^8)   is bel|l(um) hinc fŭgi|ens mē|qu(e) ĭn Ăsi|am per|sĕ-quen|s prŏfĭcis|cĭtur|

An. 937   (ia^8)   quĭd ĭllō |sit fac|tum uix| s(um) ăpud| m(e) ĭt(a) ănĭ|mus com|mōtust| mĕtū|

An. 941   (ia^8)   cum tūă |rēlĭgi|ōn(e) ŏdi|um nō|d(um) in scir|pō **quae**| **ris** quĭd ĭs|tŭc est|

An. 943   (ia^8)   numquid| mĕmĭnis|t(i) id quae|r(o) ĕgŏn **hui|us** mĕmŏ| riam| pătiar| meae|

An. 954   (ia^8)   quī qui(a) hă|bet ăli|ud măgĭ|s ex sē|s(e) et **mā|ius** quid| nam uin|ctŭs est|

An. 970   (tr^7)   pătĕr ă|**mīcus**| summus| nōbīs| quis Chrĕ|mes nar|rās prŏ|be

An. 970   (tr^7)   pătĕr ă|**mīcus**| **summus**| nōbīs| quis Chrĕ|mes nar|ras prŏ|be

An. 973   (tr^7)   sōlŭ|s est quem| dīlĭ|gant dī |**saluos**| sum s(i) haec| uĕră | sunt

An. 980   (tr⁷)   n(e) **exspec|tētis|** d(um) exe|ant hū|c intus| despon|dēbĭ| tur

An. 980   (tr⁷)   n(e) **exspec|tētis|** d(um) exe|ant hū|c **intus|** despon|dēbĭ| tur

An. 981   (tr⁷)   **intus|** transĭ|gētur| sīquĭ|d est quŏd| restet| plaudĭ|te

Eun. 15   (ia⁶)   **defun|ctus** iam| sum nĭ|l est quod| dīcat| mĭhi|

Eun. 16   (ia⁶)   **is** n(e) er|ret mŏne|(o) et dē|sĭnāt| lăces|sĕre|

Eun. 22   (ia⁶)   **măgĭstrā|tus** quŏm—ĭ|b(i) ădes|set oc|ceptas|t ăgi|

Eun. 31   (ia⁶)   et **mī|les** glŏ|riŏ|sŭs ẽas| sē non| nĕgat|

Eun. 45   (ia⁶)   ut **per|noscā|tis** quid| sĭb(i) eu|nŭchus| uĕlit|

Eun. 52   (ia⁶)   atqu(e) ŭbĭ |pătī |non **pŏtĕ|ris** quom| nēm(o) ex|pĕtet|

Eun. 64   (ia⁶)   et quod| nunc tū|tĕ tē|c(um) **īrā|tus** cŏ|gĭtas|

Eun. 70   (ia⁶)   ultrŏ |supplĭci|(um) ŏ—ĭndig|num **făcĭ|nus** nun|c ĕgo|

Eun. 81   (ia⁶)   mĭsĕram| mē uĕre|or n(e) il|lud **grăui|us** Phae|dria|

Eun. 83   (ia⁶)   quŏd hĕr(i) in|trŏ **mis|sus** nŏ|n est tŏ|tus Par|mĕno|

Eun. 83   (ia⁶)   quŏd hĕr(i) in|trŏ mis|sus nŏ|n est **tŏ|tus** Par|mĕno|

Eun. 90   (ia⁶)   aut quiă |s(um) ăpud| tē **prī|mus** mis|s(a) istaec| făce|

Eun. 91   (ia⁶)   quid mis|s(a) ŏ **Thā|is** Thā|ĭs ŭtĭ|n(am) esset| mĭhi|

Eun. 92   (ia⁶)   pars ae|qu(a) **ămō|ris** tē|c(um) ac părĭ|ter fĭ|ĕret|

Eun. 99   (ia⁶)   sīcĭn **ă|gis** Par|mĕn(o) ăgĕ |sĕd huc| quā grā|tia|

Eun. 111   (ia⁶)   certum| non **scī|mus** mā|tris nŏ|mĕn et| pătris|

Eun. 111   (ia⁶)   certum| non scī|mus **mā|tris** nŏ|mĕn et| pătris|

Eun. 125   (ia⁶)   intĕre|ā **mī|les** quī |m(e) ămā|r(e) occē|pĕrat|

Eun. 126   (ia⁶)   in Cā|riam|st **prŏfec|tus** t(e) in|tĕreā |lŏci|

Eun. 131   (ia⁶)   nūpĕr ĕi|us frā|ter ălĭ|quant(um) ad| remst ăuĭ|dior|

Eun. 133   (ia⁶)   et **fĭdĭ|bus** scī|re prĕti|um spē|rans ī|lĭco|

Eun. 136   (ia⁶)   inprū|dens hā|rum rē|r(um) ignā|**rusqu(e)** om|nium|

Eun. 137   (ia⁶)   **is** uē|nit pos|tquam sen|sit mē |tēcum| quŏque|

Eun. 196   (ia⁶)   meŭs fac| sis pos|trēm(o) **ănĭ|mus** quan|d(o) ĕgŏ sum| tuos|

Eun. 202   (ia⁶)   et quid|quĭd **hui|us** fē|cī cau|sā uir|gĭnis|

Eun. 203   (ia⁶)   fēcī |nam m(e) **ei|us** frā|trem spē|rŏ prŏpĕ|mŏdum|

Eun. 214   (tr⁷)   **mūnus|** nostr(um) or|nātŏ |uerbis| quod pŏtĕ|rīs ĕt ĭs|t (um) aemŭ|lum

Eun. 216   (tr⁸)   mĕmĭnī |t(am) etsī |**nullus|** mŏneā|s ĕgŏ rū|s ĭb(o) at|qu (e) ĭbĭ mă|nēbo|

Eun. 221   (ia⁸)   **uĭgĭlā|bis** las|sŭs hoc| plus făci|ēs ăbĭ |nil dī|cis Par| mĕno|

Eun. 221   (ia⁸)   uĭgĭlā|bis las|sŭs hoc| plus făci|ēs ăbĭ |nil **dī|cis** Par| mĕno|

Eun. 227   (tr⁷)   mĭnŭs ĭ|**neptus|** măgĕ sĕ|uĕrus| quisquam| nec măgĕ | contĭ|nens

Eun. 227   (tr⁷)   mĭnŭs ĭ|neptus| măgĕ **sĕ|uĕrus** quisquam| nec măgĕ | contĭ|nens

Eun. 238 (tr⁷) quō rĕ|dactus| s(um) omnes| nōtī |m(e) atqu(e) ă|mīcī |
dēsĕ|runt

Eun. 242 (tr⁷) quī cŏ|lor nī|tor ues|tītus| quae—hăbĭ|tūdos|t corpŏ|ris

Eun. 245 (tr⁷) possum| quid t(u) his| rēbus| crēdis| fiĕrī |tōt(a) er|ras
ui|a

Eun. 245 (tr⁷) possum| quid t(u) his| rēbus| crēdis| fiĕrī |tōt(a) er|ras
ui|a

Eun. 252 (tr⁷) nĕgăt quis| nĕg(o) ai|t āiō |postrē|m(o) impĕ|rāu(i) ĕgŏ|
met mĭ|hi

Eun. 253 (tr⁷) omni|(a) adsen|tār(i) is| quaestus| nunc es|t mult(o) ū|
berrĭ|mus

Eun. 253 (tr⁷) omni|(a) adsen|tār(i) is| quaestus| nunc es|t mult(o) ū|
berrĭ|mus

Eun. 265 (ia⁷) uĭdĕn ō|ti(um) et| cĭbŭs quid| făcīt| ăliē|nus sĕd ĕ|gŏ ces|
so|

Eun. 268 (ia⁷) rīuā|lis ser|uom sal|uă rē|s est nī|mīr(um) hŏmĭ|nes frī|
gent|

Eun. 275 (ia⁷) qu(am) hoc mū|nus grā|tum Thā|ĭd(i) ar|bĭtrā|r(e) ess
(e) hoc| nunc dī|cis|

Eun. 285 (ia⁷) nē t(u) is|tas fa|xō cal|cĭbus| saep(e) in|sultā|bis frus|tra|

Eun. 295 (ia⁸) incer|tus s(um) ū|n(a) haec spē|s est ŭb(i) ŭ|b(i) est diŭ |
cēlā|rī non| pŏtest|

Eun. 304 (tr⁸) sĕd ĕccum| Parmĕ|nōnem| saluē |quid tū's| tristis| qui-
due'|s ălăcris|

Eun. 313 (ia⁸) haud sĭmĭ|lis uir|gost uir|gĭnum| nostrā|rum quas| mā-
tres| stŭdent|

Eun. 318 (ia⁸) cŏlŏr uē|rus cor|pus sŏlĭ|d(um) et sū|cī plē|n(um) ann(i)
an|nī sē|dĕcim|

Eun. 318 (ia⁸) cŏlŏr uē|rus cor|pus sŏlĭ|d(um) et sū|cī plē|n(um) ann(i)
an|nī sē|dĕcim|

Eun. 326 (ia⁶) quĭd hō|c est scĕlĕ|ris pĕri|ī quid| factum|st rŏgas|

Eun. 328 (ia⁶) nostin| quidnī—|is d(um) hanc| sĕquor| fit m(i) ob|
uiam|

Eun. 334 (ia⁶) ĕhŏ non|n(e) hoc mon|strī sĭmĭ|lest quĭd a|is ma|xŭme|

Eun. 336 (ia⁶) incur|uos trĕmŭ|lus lăbi|īs dē|missīs| gĕmens|

Eun. 336 (ia⁶) incur|uos trĕmŭ|lus lăbi|īs dē|missīs| gĕmens|

Eun. 340 (ia⁶) pătr(i) ad|uŏcā|tus mā|nĕ m(i) es|s(e) ut mĕmĭ|nĕrit|

Eun. 347 (ia⁶) uērum| părăsī|tus c(um) an|cill(a) ip|sast ī|lĭcet|

Eun. 354 (tr⁷) Phaedri|ae rī|uālis| dūras| frātris| partis| praedĭ|cas

Eun. 354 (tr⁷) Phaedri|ae rī|uālis| dūras| frātris| partis| praedĭ|cas

Eun. 369 (ia⁸) quid sī |nunc tū|tĕ for|tūnā|tus fī|ās quā |rē Par|mĕno|

Eun. 376 (tr⁷) dixtī |pulchrē |numquam| uīdī |mĕlius| consĭli|um dă|ri

Eun. 379 (ia⁸) quō trū|dis per|cŭlĕris| iam tū |mē tĭb(i) ĕ|quĭdem| dīcō |
mănĕ|

Eun. 380   (ia⁸)   eā|mus per|gin cer|tumst uĭdĕ |nē nĭmi|um călĭ|d(um) hoc sit| mŏdo|

Eun. 383   (ia⁸)   dēdū|căr ĕt ĭl|lis **crŭcĭ|bus** quae |nōs nos|tramqu(e) ădŭ| lescen|tiam|

Eun. 414   (ia⁶)   1012. ĭs ŭbĭ |**mŏles|tus** măgĭ|s est quae|s(o) inquam| Strāto|

Eun. 442   (ia⁶)   intrō |**mittā|mus** cō|missā|tum Pam|phĭlam|

Eun. 443   (ia⁶)   cantā|tum **prō|uŏcē|mus** sī |laudā|bĭt haec|

Eun. 444   (ia⁶)   illī|us for|mam tŭ—hŭi|us con|trā dē|nĭque|

Eun. 444   (ia⁶)   illī|us for|mam tŭ—**hŭi|us** con|trā dē|nĭque|

Eun. 450   (ia⁶)   fructum| nēquan|d(o) **īrā|tus** t(u) ăli|ō con|fĕras|

Eun. 453   (ia⁶)   ĭd(em) hŏc tū|tĕ **mĕli|us** quan|t(o) inuē|nisses| Thrăso|

Eun. 462   (ia⁶)   ītū|ran **Thā|is** quō|pi(am) ē|s ĕhĕm Par|mĕno|

Eun. 465   (ia⁶)   ā Phae|driā |quid **stā|mus** quor| nōn ī|mŭs hinc|

Eun. 467   (ia⁶)   dăr(e) hūĭc| quae **uŏlŭ|mus** con|uĕnī|r(e) et con|lŏqui|

Eun. 485   (ia⁶)   ūbĭ **tem|pus** tĭb(i) ĕ|rit săt hă|bet sī |tum rĕcĭ|pĭtur|

Eun. 506   (ia⁶)   dŏm(i) **ădsī|tis** făcĭ|t(e) eā|mus uos| mē sĕquĭ|mĭni|

Eun. 506   (ia⁶)   dŏm(i) **ădsī|tis** făcĭ|t(e) **eā|mus** uos| mē sĕquĭ|mĭni|

Eun. 508   (ia⁶)   nīmī|rum dăbĭ|t haec **Thā|is** mĭhĭ |magnum| mălum|

Eun. 511   (ia⁶)   rŏget| **quis** quid| tĭbĭ c(um) il|lā nē |nōram| quĭdem|

Eun. 527   (ia⁶)   non mā|ior **Thā|is** quăm—ĕ|gŏ sum| maius|cŭlast|

Eun. 532   (ia⁶)   dīc(o) ĕgŏ |m(i) insĭdi|as fiĕ|rī **Thā|is** ma|xŭmo|

Eun. 536   (ia⁶)   mălam| r(em) hinc **ī|bis** s(i) is|tūc ĭtă |certum|st tĭbi|

Eun. 540   (ia⁷)   ĭn hunc| di(em) ut| dē sym|bŏlīs| **essē|mus** Chae|re(am) eī |reī|

Eun. 541   (ia⁷)   praefē|cĭmus| dăt(i) ā|nŭlī |lŏcŭs **tem|pus** con|stĭtū| tumst|

Eun. 542   (ia⁷)   praetĕri|it **tem|pus** qu(o) in| lŏcō |dictum|st parā|tī nī|l est|

Eun. 556   (ia⁸)   uestī|t(um) hunc **nan|ctus** quid| mī quae|ram sā|nus s (im) an|n(e) insā|niam|

Eun. 556   (ia⁸)   uestī|t(um) hunc nan|ctus quid| mī quae|ram **sā|nus** s (im) an|n(e) insā|niam|

Eun. 558   (tr⁸)   Chaere|ā quĭd ĕst| quod sic| gestis| quid sĭ|b(i) hic **ues| tĭtus|** quaerit|

Eun. 565   (ia⁸)   uirgō |quĭd ĕg(o) ĕi|us tĭbĭ |nunc făci|em prae|dĭc(em) aut| laud(em) An|tĭpho|

Eun. 566   (ia⁸)   qu(om) ipsum| mē nō|ris qu(am) ē|lēgans| formā|rum spec|tator| siem|

Eun. 567   (ia⁸)   ĭn hac| **commō|tus** s(um) aīn| tū prī|mam dī|ces sciō |sī uī|dĕris|

Eun. 569   (ia⁸)   ĕrăt quī|d(am) **eŭnū|chus** quem| mercā|tus fuĕ|rat frā| ter Thā|ĭdi|

Eun. 569   (ia⁸)   ĕrăt quī|d(am) eŭnū|chus quem| **mercā|tus** fuĕ|rat frā|
                    ter Thā|ĭdi|

Eun. 571   (ia⁸)   ĭbĭ **ser|uos** quŏd ĕ|g(o) arrĭpu|ī quĭd ĭ|d est tăcĭ|tus cĭti|ŭs
                    au|dies|

Eun. 571   (ia⁸)   ĭbĭ ser|uos quŏd ĕ|g(o) arrĭpu|ī quĭd ĭ|d est **tăcĭ|tus** cĭti|ŭs
                    au|dies|

Eun. 579   (ia⁸)   ĭn in|tĕriō|rĕ par|t(i) ut măne|am **sō|lus** cum| sōl(a) ad|
                    nuo|

Eun. 587   (ia⁸)   i(am) ōl(im) il|lĕ lū|d(um) inpen|diō |măgĭs ănĭ|mus
                    gau|dēbat| mĭhi|

Eun. 596   (ia⁷)   ŭbĭ nos| **lāuĕrĭ|mus** sī |uŏles| lăuā|t(o) accĭpi|ō tris|tis|

Eun. 601   (ia⁷)   intĕre|ā **som|nus** uir|gĭn(em) op|prĭmī|t ĕgŏ lī|mis spec|
                    to|

Eun. 607   (ia⁷)   sān(e) her|cl(e) ut **dī|cis** sĕd ĭn|tĕrim| dē sym|bŏlis| quĭd
                    ac|tumst|

Eun. 609   (ia⁷)   perlon|gest sed| tant(o) ō|cius| **prŏpĕrē|mus** mū|tā ues|
                    tem|

Eun. 616   (tr⁷)   nēqu(am) il|l(e) hŏdi(e) **in|sānus|** turbam| făcia|t aut
                    uim| Thāĭ|di

Eun. 619   (tr⁸)   nĕquĕ nĕ|gār(e) au|dērĕ |**Thāis|** porr(o) in|stār(e) ŭ|t
                    hŏmĭn(em) in|uītet|

Eun. 621   (tr⁷)   dē sŏ|rōr(e) ei(u)s| indĭ|cār(e) ăd e|am rem| **tempus|** nōn
                    ĕ|rat

Eun. 622   (ia⁸)   inuī|tat **tris|tis** man|sĭt ĭb(i) ĭl|lă c(um) il|lō ser|mōn(em)
                    ĭ|lĭco|

Eun. 623   (tr⁷)   **mīles|** uērō |sĭbĭ pŭ|tār(e) ad|duct(um) an|t(e) ŏcŭlō|s
                    aemŭ|lum

Eun. 626   (tr⁷)   in con|uīui|(um) illam| **miles|** tendĕ|r(e) ind(e) ad| iurgi|
                    um

Eun. 644   (tr⁸)   hoccin| t(am) audax| **făcĭnus|** făcĕr(e) es|s(e) ausum|
                    pĕri(i) hoc| quid sit| uĕreor|

Eun. 650   (ia⁸)   ădī|bō quĭd ĭs|tuc quid| festī|nās aut| quem **quae|ris** Pȳ|
                    thias|

Eun. 657   (ia⁸)   insā|nis qu(i) is|tuc făcĕ|r(e) eūnū|chus pŏtu|ĭt ĕg(o) ĭl|
                    lum nes|cio|

Eun. 662   (ia⁸)   quŏ—il|l(e) ăbĭ|r(e) **ignā|uos** pos|sĭt lon|gius| nĭsĭ sī |
                    dŏmum|

Eun. 664   (ia⁸)   pĕri(i) ob|sĕcrō |t(am) infan|dum **făcĭ|nus** meă |tū n(e)
                    au|dīuī |quĭdem|

Eun. 684   (ia⁶)   nunc tĭbĭ |uĭdē|tur **foe|dus** qui(a) ĭl|lam nō|n hăbet|

Eun. 688   (ia⁶)   hic es|t **uiē|tus** uĕtŭs| uĕter|nōsus| sĕnex|

Eun. 693   (ia⁶)   ăt ĭll(e) al|ter uē|nĭt an|nōs **nā|tus** sē|dĕcim|

Eun. 696   (ia⁶)   monstr(um) **hŏmĭ|nis** non| dictū|ru's uē|nit Chae|rea|

Eun. 703 (tr⁷) iam sătĭs| **crēdis**| sōbri|(am) essĕ |m(e) et nil| mentī|tam
tĭ|bi

Eun. 708 (tr⁷) fact(um) ĕt e|ast **in|dūtus**| fact(um) et| prō t(e) huc|
dēduc|tust ĭ|ta

Eun. 718 (tr⁷) **Parmĕ|nōnis**| tam sci|(o) ess(e) hanc| tĕchĭnam| quam
mē |uĭuĕ|re

Eun. 725 (tr⁷) **Thāis**| i(am) ădĕrit| quĭd ĭtă |quiă qu(om) in|d(e) ăbeō |
iam t(um) oc|cēpĕ|rat

Eun. 733 (ia⁸) sed **Thā|is** mul|tōn an|tĕ uē|nĭt an|n(e) ăbiit| i(am) ā mī|
lĭte|

Eun. 737 (ia⁸) corre|xit **mī|les** quŏd ĭn|telle|xī mĭnŭs| nam m(e) ex|
trūsit| fŏras|

Eun. 757 (tr⁷) ĕgŏn **for|mĭdŭ|lōsus**| nēmos|t hŏmĭnum| quī uī|uat mĭ|nus

Eun. 760 (tr⁷) mĭnŭs pŏ|tens quam| tū mĭnŭs| **nōtus**| mĭnŭs ă|mīcō|r
(um) hīc hă|bens

Eun. 763 (tr⁷) tŭ—ăb(i) at|qu(e) obsĕ|r(a) osti|(um) **intus**| dŭm—
ĕg(o) hinc| transcur|r(o) ad fŏ|rum

Eun. 780 (ia⁸) ŭb(i) ăli|ī quī |măl(um) ăli|ī sō|lus San|niō |seruat| dŏmi|

Eun. 783 (ia⁸) ĭd(em) hoc| iam **Pyr|rus** fac|tĭtā|uit uĭdĕn| tū Thā|is qu
(am) hīc| r(em) ăgit|

Eun. 783 (ia⁸) ĭd(em) hoc| iam **Pyr|rus** fac|tĭtā|uit uĭdĕn| tū **Thā|is** qu
(am) hīc| r(em) ăgit|

Eun. 792 (tr⁷) **Thāis**| prīm(um) hoc| mĭhĭ res|pondē |quom tĭbĭ |d(o)
istam| uirgĭ|nem

Eun. 804 (tr⁷) sīcĭn ă|gis **quis**| tŭ—hŏm(o) es| quid tĭbĭ |uis quid| c(um)
illā |reî tĭ|bist

Eun. 805 (tr⁷) **scībis**| princĭpi|(o) e(am) ĕsse |dīcō |lībĕ|r(am) hem cī|u
(em) Attĭ|c(am) huî

Eun. 806 (tr⁷) mēam sŏ|rōr(em) os| dūrum| **mīles**| nunc ădе|(o) ēdī|cō
tĭ|bi

Eun. 810 (tr⁷) săt hŏc tĭ|bist ĭ|d(em) hoc tū |**Thāis**| quaerĕ |quī res|
ponde|at

Eun. 811 (tr⁷) quid nun|c **ăgĭmus**| quin rĕde|āmus| i(am) haec tĭ|b(i)
ădĕrit| supplĭ|cans

Eun. 811 (tr⁷) quid nun|c **ăgĭmus**| quin **rĕde|āmus** i(am) haec tĭ|b(i)
ădĕrit| supplĭ|cans

Eun. 824 (ia⁶) quī Chae|re(a) is|t(e) **ĕphē|bus** frā|ter Phae|driae|

Eun. 829 (ia⁶) n(um) id lăcrŭ|mat uir|g(o) ĭd ŏpī|nor quĭd **a|is** săcrĭ|
lĕga|

Eun. 837 (ia⁶) quĭd ĭllō |**făciē|mus** stul|tă quid| făciās| rŏgas|

Eun. 843 (ia⁶) d(um) ant(e) os|tium| stō **nō|tus** mĭhĭ |quĭd(am) ob|
uiam|

Eun. 847 (ia⁶) fuī |fŭgĭtan|dō **nē|quis** mē |cognos|cĕret|

Eun. 848	(ia⁶)	sĕd es|tn(e) haec **Thā|is** quam| uĭde(o) ip|sast hae|reo|
Eun. 850	(ia⁶)	ădeā|mus bŏnĕ |uir Dō|rĕ sal|ue dic| mĭhi|
Eun. 864	(ia⁶)	miss(a) haec| **făciā|mus** non| tē dig|num Chae|rea|
Eun. 866	(ia⁶)	sum ma|xŭm(e) at| t(u) **indig|nus** quī |făcĕrēs| tămen|
Eun. 873	(ia⁶)	fŏrĕ **Thā|is** sae|p(e) ex hui(u)s|mŏdī |rē quā|pi(am) et|
Eun. 887	(ia⁶)	tē mĭhĭ |pătrō|nam căpi|ō **Thā|is** t(e) ob|sĕcro|
Eun. 893	(ia⁶)	in cog|noscen|dō tū|t(e) ips(e) **ădĕ|ris** Chae|rea|
Eun. 895	(ia⁶)	dŏm(i) op|pĕriā|mur **pŏti|us** qu(am) hī|c ant(e) os|tium|
Eun. 906	(ia⁶)	ăbeā|mŭs in|trō **Thā|is** nō|lō m(e) in| uia|
Eun. 943	(tr⁷)	prō de|um fĭdĕm| **făcĭnus|** foed(um) ŏ—ĭn|fēlī|c(em) ădŭles|centŭ|lum
Eun. 957	(tr⁷)	quĭd **ais|** nunc mĭ|nātur| porrō |sēs(e) id| quod moe|chis sŏ|let
Eun. 963	(tr⁷)	obsĕ|cr(o) ăn ĭs es|t nēqu(am) ĭ|n illum| **Thāis|** uim fĭĕ|rī sĭ|nat
Eun. 980	(ia⁶)	quidquĭd **hŭi|us** fac|tumst cul|pā non| factum|st mea|
Eun. 991	(ia⁶)	is pr(o) il|l(o) eunū|ch(o) ad Thā|ĭd(em) hanc| dēduc|tŭs est|
Eun. 998	(ia⁶)	nĭsĭ quiă |nĕces|sus fuĭ|t hoc făcĕ|r(e) id gau|deo|
Eun. 1021	(ia⁷)	tū iam| **pendē|bis** qui s|tult(um) ădŭ|lescen|tŭlum| nō-bĭlĭ|tas|
Eun. 1025	(tr⁷)	quid nunc| qua sp(e) aut| quō con|sĭli(o) hŭ|c **īmus|** quid coep|tas Thră|so
Eun. 1031	(tr⁷)	ō pŏpŭ|lārē|s **ecquis|** m(e) hŏdiē |uīuit| fortū|nāti|or
Eun. 1040	(ia⁸)	nōbīs| dĕdit| sē frā|trĭs ĭgĭ|tur **Thā|is** tō|tast scī|lĭcet|
Eun. 1041	(ia⁸)	i(am) hōc ăli|ŭd es|t quod **gau|deā|mus** mī|les pel|lētur| fŏras|
Eun. 1041	(ia⁸)	i(am) hōc ăli|ŭd es|t quod gau|deā|mus **mī|les** pel|lētur| fŏras|
Eun. 1055	(tr⁷)	**prĕcĭbus|** prĕti(o) ŭ|t haere|(am) in par|t(e) ălĭquā |tand(em) ăpŭd| Thāĭ|dem
Eun. 1063	(tr⁷)	uōbīs| **frētus|** scin quam| frētus| mīlĕ|s ēdī|cō tĭ|bi
Eun. 1063	(tr⁷)	uōbīs| frētus| scin quam| **frētus|** mīlĕ|s ēdī|cō tĭ|bi
Eun. 1068	(tr⁷)	făcĭtō|t(e) **audi|āmus|** tū con|cēdĕ |paull(um) is|tuc Thră|so
Eun. 1070	(tr⁷)	m(e) **hūius|** quidquid| făci(o) id| făcĕrĕ |maxŭ|mē cau|sā me|a
Eun. 1077	(tr⁷)	omni|(a) haec măgĭ|s **oppor|tūnus|** nec măgĭ|s ex ū|sū tu|o
Eun. 1079	(tr⁷)	fătuŏ|s est **in|sulsus|** tardus| stertit| noctē|s et di|es
Eun. 1079	(tr⁷)	fătuŏ|s est in|sulsus| **tardus|** stertit| noctē|s et di|es
Eun. 1082	(tr⁷)	accĭ|pĭt hŏmō |nēmō |**mĕlius|** prorsus| nĕquĕ prō|lixi|us
Eun. 1082	(tr⁷)	accĭ|pĭt hŏmō |nēmō |mĕlius| **prorsus|** nĕquĕ prō|lixi|us

Eun. 1085   (tr⁷)   rĕcĭpi|ātis| sătĭs di|(u) hoc iam| saxum| uorsō |rĕcĭpĭ|
                    mus

Haut. 22   (ia⁶)   tum quod| mălĕuŏ|lus uĕtŭs| poē|ta dic|tĭtat|

Haut. 28   (ia⁶)   făcĭt(e) ae|quī sī|tis dătĕ |crescen|dī cō|piam|

Haut. 37   (ia⁶)   nē sem|per ser|uos cur|rens ī|rātus| sĕnex|

Haut. 38   (ia⁶)   ĕdax| părăsī|tus sȳ|cŏphan|t(a) aut(em) in|pŭdens|

Haut. 39   (ia⁶)   ăuā|rus lē|n(o) adsĭdu|(e) ăgen|dī sin|t sĕni|

Haut. 42   (ia⁶)   ŭt ălĭ|quă par|s lăbō|ris mĭnu|ātur| mĭhi|

Haut. 52   (ia⁶)   uōbīs| plăcē|re stŭde|ant pŏti|us quam| sĭbi|

Haut. 64   (ia⁶)   mĕliō|rem nĕquĕ |prĕtī |māiō|ris nē|m(o) hăbet|

Haut. 70   (ia⁶)   nullum| rĕmit|tis tem|pus nĕquĕ |tē res|pĭcis|

Haut. 70   (ia⁶)   nullum| rĕmit|tis **tem|pus** nĕquĕ |tē res|pĭcis|

Haut. 72   (ia⁶)   ĕnĭm dī|ces quan|t(um) hīc ŏpĕ|ris fĭ|at pae|nĭtet|

Haut. 80   (ia⁶)   mĭhĭ sī|c est ū|sus tĭbĭ—|ŭt ŏpus| factost| făce|

Haut. 90   (ia⁶)   sĭnĕ mē |uŏcī|uom **tem|pus** nē|quod dem| mĭhi|

Haut. 91   (ia⁶)   lăbō|ris non| sĭn(am) in|qu(am) āh nō|n aequom| făcis|

Haut. 110   (ia⁶)   ĕg(o) ĭstŭ|c **aetā|tis** nō|n ămō|r(i) ŏpĕram| dăbam|

Haut. 118   (ia⁶)   quĭd ais| clam mē |prōfec|tus men|sis trī|s ăbest|

Haut. 120   (ia⁶)   ănĭmist| **puden|tis** sig|n(um) et nō|n instrē|nui|

Haut. 131   (ia⁶)   tantō|s ĕgŏ sō|lus făci|am sed| gnāt(um) ū|nĭcum|

Haut. 140   (ia⁶)   ĭtă făci|ō pror|sus nil| rĕlin|qu(o) ĭn ae|dĭbus|

Haut. 146   (ia⁶)   coē|g(i) agr(um) hunc| **mercā|tus** s(um) hic| m(e) exer|
                    ceo|

Haut. 150   (ia⁶)   nĭs(i) ŭb(i) il|l(e) huc **sal|uos** rĕdi|ĕrit| meŭs par|tĭceps|

Haut. 152   (ia⁶)   ĕt ĭll(um) ob|sĕquen|tem sī|quis rec|t(e) aut com|mŏde|

Haut. 156   (ia⁶)   nec tĭb(i) ĭl|lest crē|dĕr(e) **au|sus** qu(ae) es|t aequom|
                    pătri|

Haut. 195   (ia⁸)   atqu(e) haec| pĕrin|dĕ sun|t ŭt il|li(u)s **ănĭ|mus** quĭ—e|ă
                    pos|sĭdet|

Haut. 197   (ia⁸)   imm(o) il|l(e) fuit| sĕnĕx **in|portū|nus** sem|pĕr et| nunc
                    nil| măgis|

Haut. 198   (ia⁸)   uĕreor| quam nē|quĭd ĭn ĭl|l(um) īrā|tus plus| sătis| faxit|
                    pătĕr|

Haut. 203   (ia⁸)   huncĭn ĕ|rat ae|qu(om) ex il|li(u)s mō|r(e) ăn il|l(um) ex
                    hui|us uī|uĕre|

Haut. 222   (ia⁸)   **astū|tus** n(e) il|l(e) haud scit| quam mĭhĭ |nunc sur|dō
                    nar|ret fă|bŭlam|

Haut. 225   (ia⁸)   n(am) hic Clī|ni(a) et|s(i) is quŏquĕ |suā|rum rē|rum
                    sătă|gĭt at|tămen|

Haut. 236   (ia⁸)   făciam| sed nes|ciŏquid| prōfec|tō m(i) **ănĭ|mus** prae|
                    sāgit| măli|

Haut. 265   (ia⁶)   n(am) et uī|tast eă|d(em) ĕt **ănĭ|mus** t(e) er|g(a) ĭd(em)
                    ac| fuit|

Haut. 287 (ia⁶) ei(u)s ănu|is cau|s(a) ŏpī|nor quaĕ—ĕ|rat mor|tua|

Haut. 290 (ia⁶) căpil|lus pe|xus prō|lixus| circum| căput|

Haut. 290 (ia⁶) căpil|lus pe|xus prō|lixus| circum| căput|

Haut. 291 (ia⁶) rēiec|tus nē|glēgen|ter pax| Sȳrĕ m(i) ob|sĕcro|

Haut. 312 (tr⁷) ĕhŏ scĕ|lestĕ |quŏ—īllam| dūcis| quŏ—ĕg(o) īl|l(am) ad nos| scīlĭ|cet

Haut. 314 (tr⁷) non fit| sīnĕ pĕ|rīclō |făcĭnus| magnum| nec mĕmŏ| rābĭ|le

Haut. 334 (tr⁷) ăn eă |quŏquĕ dī|cētŭ|r hūius| s(i) ūn(a) haec| dēdĕcŏ|rist pă|rum

Haut. 338 (tr⁷) măn(e) hăbe|(o) ăliud| s(i) istuc| mĕtuis| quŏd ămbo | confīte|āmĭ|ni

Haut. 350 (ia⁶) i(am) hoc quŏquĕ |nĕgā|bis tĭbĭ |plăcē|r(e) immō |Sȳre|

Haut. 352 (ia⁶) t(u) es iū|dex nē|quĭd ac|cūsan|dus sis| uĭde|

Haut. 360 (ia⁶) ut sit| nĕces|sus mĕrĭ|tō tĕ—ă|mō Clī|nia|

Haut. 374 (ia⁶) laudā|bis uĭdĕ |sis tū|tĕmet| mīrā|bĕre|

Haut. 386 (tr⁷) omni|umqu(e) ăde|ō uos|trārum| uolgus| qu(ae) ab sē | sēgrĕ|gant

Haut. 393 (tr⁷) quoi(u)s mos| maxŭ|mest con|sĭmĭlis| uostr(um) hī |s(e) ad uō|s adplĭ|cant

Haut. 397 (tr⁷) ŭt ĕx—il|līus| commŏ|dō meŭm| compă|rārem| commŏ| d(um) ah

Haut. 431 (ia⁶) meŭs gnā|tus sī|c est uē|nit cer|te Clī|nia|

Haut. 432 (ia⁶) meŭs uē|nit di|x(i) eā|mus duc| m(e) ăd e(um) ob|sĕcro|

Haut. 443 (ia⁶) prīm(um) ō|lim pŏti|us quam| pătĕrē|rĕ fī|lium|

Haut. 454 (ia⁶) nēdum| tū pos|sīs es|tn(e) e(a) in|tus sĭt| rŏgas|

Haut. 455 (ia⁶) sensī |n(am) ūn(am) ē|ī cē|n(am) atqu(e) ei|us cŏmĭ|tĭbus|

Haut. 469 (ia⁶) quid făci|am quid|uis pŏti|us quam| quod cō|gĭtas|

Haut. 494 (ia⁶) părā|tus sum| scin quid| nunc făcĕ|re tĕ |uŏlo|

Haut. 504 (ia⁶) ăliē|n(a) ut mĕli|us uĭde|ant et| diiū|dĭcent|

Haut. 515 (ia⁶) ill(e) Clī|niă|ī ser|uos tar|dius|cŭlust|

Haut. 531 (ia⁶) dīc(o) ădŭ|lescen|tis Sȳrĕ |tĭbī |tĭmuī |măle|

Haut. 551 (ia⁶) sīquĭd hŭius sĭmĭl|lĕ for|t(e) ăliquan|d(o) ĕuē|nĕrit|

Haut. 553 (ia⁶) nōn ū|sus uĕni|et spē|rō spē|r(o) hercl(e) ĕgŏ |quŏque|

Haut. 556 (ia⁶) et n(e) ĕgŏ |tĕ s(i) ū|sus uĕni|at mag|nĭfĭcē |Chrĕme|

Haut. 557 (ia⁶) tractā|rĕ pos|sim d(e) is|toc qu(om) ū|sus uē|nĕrit|

Haut. 568 (tr⁸) uĕl hĕr(e) in| uīnō |qu(am) inmŏ|destus| fuĭstī |factum| quam mŏ|lestus|

Haut. 571 (ia⁸) at mĭhĭ |fĭdē|s ăpŭd hun|c est nil| m(e) istī|us fac|tūrum| păter|

Haut. 577 (ia⁸) n(e) ĭnep|tus nē |prŏter|uos uĭde|ar quŏd īl|lum făcĕ|rĕ crē|dĭto|

Haut. 577 (ia⁸)   n(e) ĭnep|tus nē |prŏter|uos uĭde|ar quŏd ĭl|lum făcĕ|rĕ
                    crē|dĭto|

Haut. 580 (tr⁸)   hŏmĭnis| frūg(i) et| tempĕ|rantis| functu'|s offĭci|um tăcĕ
                    |sōdes|

Haut. 580 (tr⁸)   hŏmĭnis| frūg(i) et| tempĕ|rantis| functu'|s offĭci|um
                    tăcĕ |sōdes|

Haut. 592 (tr⁷)   nĭs(i) eum| quantum| tĭb(i) ŏpis| dī dant| seruās| castī|
                    gās mŏ|nes

Haut. 614 (ia⁸)   nĭsĭ m(e) ănĭ|mus fal|lĭt hic| prōfec|tost ā|nŭlus| qu(em)
                    ĕgŏ sus|pĭcor|

Haut. 615 (ia⁸)   is quī|c(um) expŏsĭ|tast gnā|tă quid| uolt sĭbĭ |Sÿr(e) hae|
                    c ōrā|tio|

Haut. 634 (tr⁷)   tot pec|căt(a) ĭ|n hāc r(e) os|tendis| nam iam| prīmum|
                    sī me|um

Haut. 637 (tr⁷)   ăt ĭd ŏ|mittō |mĭsĕrĭ|cordi|(a) ănĭmus| māter|nus sĭ|no

Haut. 643 (tr⁷)   mĕlius| pēius| prōsĭ|t obsit| nil uĭ|dent nĭsĭ |quŏd lŭ|bet

Haut. 643 (tr⁷)   mĕlius| pēius| prōsĭ|t obsit| nil uĭ|dent nĭsĭ |quŏd lŭ|bet

Haut. 645 (tr⁷)   quantŏ |tuŏs es|t ănĭmus| nātū |grăuio|r ignos|centi|or

Haut. 654 (tr⁷)   und(e) hă|bes quam| Bacchis| sēc(um) ad|duxĭ|t ădŭles|
                    centŭ|l(am) hem

Haut. 668 (ia⁸)   nĭsĭ m(e) ănĭ|mus fal|lit mul|t(um) haud mul|t(um) ā m
                    (e) ăbĕ|rĭt in|fortŭ|nium|

Haut. 682 (ia⁷)   nil mē |fĕfel|lit cog|nĭtast| quant(um) au|di(o) hui|us
                    uer|ba|

Haut. 687 (ia⁷)   laetor| qu(am) illī|us qu(am) ĕgŏ s|ci(o) es|s(e) hŏnō|rĕ
                    quō|uis dig|nam|

Haut. 702 (ia⁷)   ăper|t(e) ĭt(a) ut| res sē|s(e) hăbet| narrā|tō quĭd a|is
                    iŭbe|o|

Haut. 715 (tr⁷)   tū for|s quid mē |fiat| paruī |pendis| d(um) illī |consŭ|las

Haut. 720 (tr⁷)   mĕtuō |quĭd ăgam| mĕtuis| quăsĭ nō|n eă pŏ|testas| sit
                    tu|a

Haut. 726 (ia⁷)   aut quom| uentū|ram di|xĕr(o) et| constĭtu|ĕrō |qu(om)
                    is cer|te|

Haut. 736 (ia⁷)   pĕri(i) her|clĕ Bac|chis mănĕ |mănē |quō mit|tĭs is|tanc
                    quae|so|

Haut. 743 (ia⁷)   eā|tur sĕquĕ|r(e) hāc heūs| Drŏmō |quis mē |uolt Sÿrŭs|
                    quĭd est| reī|

Haut. 784 (ia⁶)   ĕgŏn quŏī |dătū|rus non| s(um) ŭt eī |despon|deam|

Haut. 800 (ia⁶)   iŭbĕ pŏti|us qu(am) ob| rem qui(a) ĕ|n(im) ĭn eum|
                    suspī|ciost|

Haut. 801 (ia⁶)   translā|t(a) ămō|ris quid| tum quiă |uĭdē|bĭtur|

Haut. 805 (ia⁶)   nullast| tam făcĭ|lis rēs| quin dif|fĭcĭlis| siet|

Haut. 806 (ia⁶)   qu(am) inuī|tus făci|as uel| m(e) haec deăm|bŭlā|tio|

Haut. 813 (ia⁶)   ŭbĭ |m(e) excar|nŭfĭcē|s is t(u) hinc| quō dig|nŭs es|

Appendix 281

Haut. 815 (ia⁶) uell(em) her|clĕ fac|t(um) ĭtă mĕrĭ|tu's **mĕrĭ|tus** quō |
mŏdo|

Haut. 817 (ia⁶) qu(am) argen|t(um) hăbē|rēs quod| **dătū|rus** iam| fui|

Haut. 820 (ia⁶) iam non| s(um) īrā|tus sed| scīn ŭbĭ |sit nunc| tĭbi|

Haut. 825 (ia⁶) n(e) ĕgŏ s(um) hŏ|mō for|tūnā|tus deă|mō tē |Sȳre|

Haut. 877 (tr⁷) quae sunt| dict(a) in| stultō |caudex| stīpĕ|s **ăsĭnus**|
plumbe|us

Haut. 882 (tr⁷) sĕd ĭnte|rim quĭd ĭl|lic iam|dūdum| **gnātus**| cessat| cum
Sȳ|ro

Haut. 887 (tr⁷) callĭdĭ|tātē|s ĭtănĕ |**uoltus**| quŏqu(e) hŏmĭ|num fin|git
scĕ|lus

Haut. 888 (tr⁷) **gnātus**| quod s(e) ad|sĭmŭlāt| laet(um) id| dīcĭ|s ĭd ĭd
(em) is|tuc mĭ|hi

Haut. 894 (tr⁷) non quid| non nō|n inquam| nĕqu(e) ĭpse g|**nātus**| nil
pror|sum Chrĕ|mes

Haut. 903 (tr⁷) hūc es|t intrō |**lātus**| lectus| uestī|mentīs| strātŭ|s est

Haut. 903 (tr⁷) hūc es|t intrō |**lātus**| **lectus**| uestī|mentis| strātŭ|s est

Haut. 905 (tr⁷) **sōlus**| sōlus| tĭmeō |Bacchis| consĕ|cūtas|t ĭlĭ|co

Haut. 905 (tr⁷) sōlus| **sōlus**| tĭmeō |Bacchis| consĕ|cūtas|t ĭlĭ|co

Haut. 905 (tr⁷) sōlus| sōlus| tĭmeō |**Bacchis**| consĕ|cūtas|t ĭlĭ|co

Haut. 908 (ia⁶) fĭl(i) es|t ămĭ|ca **Bac|chis** Mĕnĕ|dēm(e) oc|cĭdi|

Haut. 937 (ia⁶) quid dō|**tis** dī|cam tē |dixis|sĕ fĭ|lio|

Haut. 947 (tr⁷) quĭd **ăgis**| mittĕ |sĭnĕ m(e) ĭ|n hāc rē |gĕrĕrĕ |mĭhĭ mō|
rem sĭ|no

Haut. 956 (tr⁷) quodn(am) ob| **făcĭnus**| quĭd ĕgŏ |tantum| scĕlĕri|s
admī|sī mĭ|ser

Haut. 957 (tr⁷) uolgō |făciun|t sciō tĭ|b(i) ess(e) hoc| **grăuius**| mult(o)
ac| dūri|us

Haut. 961 (tr⁷) quidquĭd ĕ|g(o) **hūius**| fēcī |tĭbĭ pros|pex(i) et| stultĭti|ae
tu|ae

Haut. 968 (tr⁷) **uictus**| uestī|tus qu(o) in| tectum| tē rĕ|ceptĕ|s eī mĭ|hi

Haut. 970 (tr⁷) dispĕri|i **scĕ|lestus**| quantās| turbās| concī|u(i) insci|ens

Haut. 976 (tr⁷) nec prĕ|cātō|rem **pă|rāris**| quĭd ăgis| nil sus|cense|o

Haut. 976 (tr⁷) nec prĕ|cātō|rem pă|rāris| quĭd **ăgis**| nil sus|cense|o

Haut. 987 (ia⁸) dŭm—is|tis fŭĭs|tī **sō|lus** dum| null(a) ălĭ|ă dē|lectā|tio|

Haut. 993 (ia⁸) sōlĕnt es|s(e) id non| fit uĕ|rum dī|cis quĭd ĕr|go nunc|
făciam| Sȳre|

Haut. 996 (ia⁸) aut **scī|bis** quoi|us rec|tē suā|des făci|am sāt| rect(e) hoc| mĭhi|

Haut. 996 (ia⁸) aut scī|bis **quoi|us** rec|tē suā|des făci|am sāt| rect(e) hoc|
mĭhi|

Haut. 1017 (ia⁸) quid **mĕtu|is** nē |non quom| uĕlis| conuin|cās es|s(e)
illum| tuom|

Haut. 1023 (tr⁷) sĕd ĭps(e) ē|grĕdĭtur| quam **sĕ|uĕrus**| rem quom| uĭdeas|
cense|as

Haut. 1024 (tr⁷)   s(i) umqu(am) ul|lum fŭĭt| **tempus**| māter| qu(om) ĕgŏ
uŏ|luptā|tī tĭ|bi

Haut. 1025 (tr⁷)   fuĕrim| **dictus**| fĭli|us tuŏs| uostrā |uŏlŭntā|t(e) obsĕ|cro

Haut. 1026 (tr⁷)   ei(u)s ut| mĕmĭnĕ|rīs at|qu(e) **ĭnŏpis**| nunc tē |mĭsĕres|
cat me|i

Haut. 1032 (tr⁷)   ăt ĕgo |sī mē |**mĕtuis**| mōres| cău(e) ĭn t(e) es|s(e) istos|
senti|am

Haut. 1034 (tr⁷)   gāne|o's **dam**|**nōsus**| crēd(e) et| nostrum| t(e) essĕ
|crēdĭ|to

Haut. 1035 (tr⁷)   non sun|t haec **pă**|**rentis**| dictă |non s(i) ex| căpĭtĕ
|sis me|o

Haut. 1043 (tr⁷)   făcĕrĕ |pŭduĭ|t ēhĕu |quam nunc| **tōtus**| displĭce|ō mĭ|hi

Haut. 1048 (tr⁷)   fĭli|(am) et quod| **dōtis**| dixī |firmas| mī uir| t(e) obsĕ|cro

Haut. 1051 (tr⁷)   non făci|(am) ăt id nos| non **sĭ**|**nēmus**| sī mē |uĭuom| uīs
pă|ter

Haut. 1065 (tr⁷)   quam uŏ|lō nunc| laudo g|nāt(e) Ar|chōnĭ|d(i) **hūius**|
fĭli|am

Hec. 4   (ia⁶)   ĭtă **pŏpŭ**|**lus** stŭdi|o stŭpĭ|dŭs in| fūnam|bŭlo|

Hec. 8   (ia⁶)   ălias| cognos|tĭs **ei**|**ius** quae|s(o) hanc nos|cīte|

Hec. 15   (ia⁶)   partim| s(um) eā|r(um) **exac**|**tus** par|tim uix| stĕti|

Hec. 26   (ia⁶)   ŭt ĭn ō|ti(o) es|set **pŏti**|**us** qu(am) in| nĕgō|tio|

Hec. 35   (ia⁶)   cŏmĭtum| **conuen**|**tus** strĕpĭ|tus clā|mor mŭli|ĕrum|

Hec. 35   (ia⁶)   cŏmĭtum| conuen|tus **strĕpĭ**|**tus** clā|mor mŭli|ĕrum|

Hec. 40   (ia⁶)   dăt(um) ĭ|rī glădi|ātō|res **pŏpŭ**|**lus** con|uŏlat|

Hec. 44   (ia⁶)   ăgen|dī **tem**|**pus** mĭhĭ |dătum|st uōbīs| dătur|

Hec. 79   (ia⁶)   tum dī|cas sī |non quae|ret **nul**|**lus** di|xĕris|

Hec. 82   (ia⁶)   **Phĭlō**|**tis** sal|uē mul|t(um) ō sal|uē Par|mĕno|

Hec. 84   (ia⁶)   dic m(i) ŭbĭ |**Phĭlō**|**tis** t(e) ōb|lectas|tī tam| diu|

Hec. 98   (ia⁶)   hīc **in**|**tus** Bac|chis quŏd ĕ|go num|quam crē|dĭdi|

Hec. 98   (ia⁶)   hīc in|tus **Bac**|**chis** quŏd ĕ|go num|quam crē|dĭdi|

Hec. 129 (ia⁶)   s(i) ădes|set crē|d(o) ĭb(i) **ei**|**ius** com|mĭsĕres|cĕret|

Hec. 139 (ia⁶)   plus **pō**|**tus** sē|s(e) ill(a) ab|stĭnē|r(e) ut pŏtu|ĕrit|

Hec. 140 (ia⁶)   non uē|rī sĭmĭ|lĕ **dī**|**cis** nĕquĕ |uēr(um) ar|bĭtror|

Hec. 143 (ia⁶)   quid dein|dĕ fit| **diē**|**bus** sā|nē pau|cŭlis|

Hec. 167 (ia⁶)   hīc **ănĭ**|**mus** par|t(im) uxō|ris mĭsĕ|rĭcor|dia|

Hec. 167 (ia⁶)   hīc ănĭ|mus par|t(im) **uxō**|**ris** mĭsĕ|rĭcor|dia|

Hec. 168 (ia⁶)   **dēuin**|**ctus** par|tim uic|tŭs hui(u)s| iniū|riis|

Hec. 176 (ia⁶)   quĭd ădhū|c hăben|t **infĭr**|**mĭtā**|**tis** nup|tiae|

Hec. 202 (ia⁸)   uĭrĭs es|s(e) aduor|sās ae|que stŭdi|umst **sĭmĭ**|**lis** per|
tĭnā|ciast|

Hec. 218 (tr⁷)   ĭdeŏ |qui(a) ŭt uos| mĭhĭ dŏ|m(i) **ĕrĭtis**| prōĭnd(e) ĕ|g(o)
ĕrŏ fă|mā fŏ|ris

Hec. 222 (tr⁷)   quod si s|ciss(em) il|l(a) hic mă|nēret| **pŏtius**| t(u) hinc
is|ses fŏ|ras

Hec. 227   (tr⁷)   non tē |pr(o) his cū|rassĕ |**rēbus**| nēquĭ|d aegr(e) es|set mĭ|hi

Hec. 236   (tr⁷)   ut cum| mātrĕ |plūs ū|n(a) esset| quĭd **ais**| non sig|n(i) hoc sǎ|t est

Hec. 244   (ia⁷)   qu(ae) ĕg(o) im|pĕrem| fǎcĕr(e) ĕgŏ |tǎmen| pǎtri(o) ǎnĭ| mō **uic|tus** fǎci|am|

Hec. 257   (ia⁷)   sī **mĕtu|is** sǎtĭ|s ut meâe |dŏmī |cūrē|tur dī|lĭgen|ter|

Hec. 283   (tr⁷)   hācin| caus(a) ĕg(o) ĕ|ram tan|t(o) ŏpĕrĕ |**cǔpĭdus**| rĕdeun|dī dŏ|m(um) hûī

Hec. 287   (tr⁷)   omnĕ |quŏd ĕst in|tĕreā |**tempus**| priŭs qu(am) ĭd| rescī| tumst lŭ|crost

Hec. 288   (tr⁷)   ac sic| **cĭtius**| quī t(e) ex|pĕdiā|s hīs ae|rumnis| rĕpĕri|as

Hec. 295   (ia⁸)   tǎmen| numqu(am) **au|sus** sum| rĕcū|sār(e) êam| quam m(i) ob|trūdit| pǎter|

Hec. 301   (ia⁸)   nam **mā|tris** fer|r(e) iniū|rias| mē Par|mĕnō |piĕtas| iŭbet|

Hec. 308   (ia⁸)   fǎciunt| nam sae|p(e) est quĭbŭ|s in rē|bŭs **ǎli|us** n(e) ī| rātus| quĭd(em) est|

Hec. 309   (ia⁸)   quom d(e) êā|dem cau|sast ī|**rācun|dus** fac|tŭs ĭnĭ|mīcis| sĭmus|

Hec. 310   (ia⁸)   puĕr(i) in|ter sē|sē quam| prō **lĕuĭ|bus** no|xiī|s īrās| gĕrunt|

Hec. 317   (ia⁸)   prō Iup|pĭter| clāmō|r(em) audī|uī tū|tĕ **lŏquĕ|ris** mē | uĕtas|

Hec. 318   (ia⁸)   tǎc(e) ob|sĕcrō |meǎ gnā|tǎ **mā|tris** uox| uīsast| Phĭlū| mĕnae|

Hec. 327   (ia⁶)   nōn **ū|sus** fac|tost mĭhĭ |nunc hun|c intrō |sĕqui|

Hec. 334   (ia⁶)   cǎpĭt(i) at|qu(e) aetā|t(i) illō|rum **mor|bus** qu(i) auc|tŭs sit|

Hec. 343   (ia⁷)   nam quī—ǎ|mat quôî—ŏ|di(o) ip|sŭs est| **bis** fǎcĕ|re stul| tē dū|co|

Hec. 347   (ia⁷)   hĕm—ĭstoc| uerb(o) ǎnĭ|**mus** mĭhĭ |rĕdīt| et cū|r(a) ex cor|d(e) exces|sit|

Hec. 355   (ia⁷)   quid t(u) ĭgĭ|tur lǎcrŭ|māas aut| quĭd es| tam **tris|tis** rec|tē mā|ter|

Hec. 372   (tr⁷)   mē uĕ|niss(e) ĕ|g(o) ei(u)s uĭ|dendī |**cǔpĭdus**| recta | consĕ|quor

Hec. 373   (tr⁷)   postqu(am) in|tr(o) aduĕ|n(i) extem|pl(o) **eius**| mor-bum| cognō|uī mĭ|ser

Hec. 374   (tr⁷)   nam nĕ|qu(e) ut cĕ|lārī |posset| **tempus**| spǎti(um) ul| lum dǎ|bat

Hec. 388   (tr⁷)   aduor|s(a) **eius**| per tē |tectǎ |tǎcĭtǎ|qu(e) ǎpŭd om|nis si|ent

Hec. 392   (tr⁷)   partŭ|rīr(e) e|am nec| grǎuĭd(am) es|s(e) ex tē |**sōlus**| consci|u's

Hec. 393   (tr⁷)   n(am) āiunt| tēcum| post du|ōbus| concŭbu|issĕ |mensĭ| bus

Hec. 414   (ia⁶)   hinc ā|blēgan|dus dum| părit| Phĭlū|mĕna|

Hec. 439   (ia⁶)   at non| nōu(i) hŏmĭ|nis făci|(em) at făci|(am) ut nō|uĕris|

Hec. 440   (ia⁶)   magnus| rŭbĭcun|dus cris|pus cras|sus cae|sius|

Hec. 440   (ia⁶)   magnus| rŭbĭcun|dus **cris|pus** cras|sus cae|sius|

Hec. 440   (ia⁶)   magnus| rŭbĭcun|dus cris|pus **cras|sus** cae|sius|

Hec. 444   (ia⁶)   ill(e) ăbi|it quĭd ă|g(am) infē|lix pror|sus nes|cio|

Hec. 448   (ia⁶)   nam mē |păren|tī pŏti|us quăm—ă|mōr(i) ob|sĕqui|

Hec. 459   (tr⁷)   **consō|brīnus**| noster| sān(e) her|cl(e) hŏmŏ uŏ|luptā|t(i) obsĕ|quens

Hec. 481   (tr⁷)   nunc mē |piĕtas| **mātris**| pŏtius| commŏ|dum suā|det sĕ| qui

Hec. 481   (tr⁷)   nunc mē |piĕtas| mātris| **pŏtius**| commŏ|dum suā|det sĕ| qui

Hec. 485   (ia⁶)   quĭbŭs ĭ|ris **pul|sus** nun|c ĭn il|l(am) ĭnī|quŏs sim|

Hec. 496   (ia⁶)   măn(e) in|quam quŏ—ă|bis qu(ae) hae|c est per|tĭnā|cia|

Hec. 500   (ia⁶)   ĭtă nun|c is sĭbĭ |mē sup|plĭcā|tūrum| pŭtat|

Hec. 512   (ia⁶)   quandō |nec **gnā|tus** nĕqu(e) hĭc| mī quic|qu(am) obtem|pĕrant|

Hec. 518   (tr⁷)   ĭtă cor|rĭpuit| dērĕ|pentĕ |**tăcĭtus**| sēs(e) ad| fili|am

Hec. 523   (ia⁸)   atqu(e) ec|cam uĭde|ō quĭd **a|is** Myr|rĭn(a) heūs| tĭbĭ dī| cō mĭhĭ|nĕ uir|

Hec. 534   (tr⁸)   **pŏtius**| qu(am) aduor|s(um) ănĭmī |tuī lŭ|bĭdĭ|n(em) esset| c(um) illō |nupta|

Hec. 554   (tr⁷)   nam s(i) is| posse|t ăb eā |sēsē |dērĕ|pent(e) ā|uellĕ|re

Hec. 557   (tr⁷)   et quae |mē pec|cass(e) a|īs ăbĭ |**sōlus**| sōlum| conuĕ|ni

Hec. 569   (ia⁸)   nec quā |uiā |senten|ti(a) **ei|us** pos|sit mū|tāri s|cio|

Hec. 582   (ia⁸)   nam m(i) **in|tus** tuŏs| păter| narrā|uit mŏdŏ |quō pac|tō m(e) hăbu|ĕris|

Hec. 594   (ia⁸)   d(um) **aetā|tis** tem|pus tŭlĭt| perfun|ctă sătĭs| sum săti|as iam| tĕnet|

Hec. 594   (ia⁸)   d(um) aetā|tis **tem|pus** tŭlĭt| perfun|ctă sătĭs| sum săti|as iam| tĕnet|

Hec. 600   (ia⁸)   sĭnĕ m(e) ob|sĕcr(o) hō|c effŭgĕ|rĕ **uol|gus** quod| măl(e) au|dit mŭli|ĕrum|

Hec. 601   (ia⁸)   quam **for|tūnā|tus** cē|tĕris| sum rē|bŭs ab|squ(e) ūn(a) hac| fŏret|

Hec. 614   (tr⁷)   quiă d(e) u|xōr(e) **in|certus**| s(um) ĕtiam| quid sim| factū|rus quĭ|d est

Hec. 631   (ia⁶)   nullam| d(e) his **rē|bus** cul|pam com|mĕruit| tua|

Hec. 652   (ia⁶)   qu(om) ex t(e) es|set **ălĭ|quis** quī |t(e) appel|lāret| pătrem|

Hec. 668 (ia⁶) sed quid| făciē|mus pŭē|rō rī|dĭcŭlē |rŏgas|

Hec. 670 (ia⁶) ŭt ălā|mus nos|trum qu(em) ip|sĕ nē|glexit| păter|

Hec. 671 (ia⁶) ĕg(o) ălam| quid dix|t(i) ĕh(o) ăn nō|n ălē|mus Pam|
phĭle|

Hec. 672 (ia⁶) prōdē|mus quae|sō pŏti|us qu(ae) hae|c āmen|tiast|

Hec. 672 (ia⁶) prōdē|mus quae|sō pŏti|us qu(ae) hae|c āmen|tiast|

Hec. 673 (ia⁶) ĕnĭmuē|rō pror|sus iam| tăcē|rĕ non| queo|

Hec. 681 (ia⁶) puer| quiă clam| test nā|tus nac|tŭs al|tĕr(am) es|

Hec. 688 (ia⁶) quae t(um) ob|sĕcū|tus mĭhĭ |fēcis|t(i) ut dĕcu|ĕrat|

Hec. 690 (ia⁶) quoî t(u) ob|sĕcū|tus făcĭ|s huî͡c ăde|(o) iniū|riam|

Hec. 693 (ia⁶) confin|gis fal|sās cau|sās ad| discor|diam|

Hec. 699 (ia⁶) nōn es|t nunc tem|pus pŭē|r(um) accĭpi|as n(am) is|
quĭdem|

Hec. 702 (ia⁶) tot nunc| mē rē|bus mĭsĕ|rum con|clūdit| păter|

Hec. 717 (ia⁶) ōrē|mŭs ac|cūsē|mus grăui|us dē|nĭque|

Hec. 717 (ia⁶) ōrē|mŭs ac|cūsē|mus grăui|us dē|nĭque|

Hec. 736 (ia⁷) sī uē|ră dī|cis nil| tĭbist| ā mē |pĕrī|clī mŭli|er|

Hec. 746 (tr⁸) quaer(e) ăli|um tĭbĭ |firmi|ōrem| dum tĭbĭ |tempus|
consŭ|lend(i) est|

Hec. 749 (tr⁷) pŭĕrum|qu(e) ŏb eam| rem clam| uŏluit| nātus| qu(i) est
ex|stinguĕ|re

Hec. 760 (tr⁷) inmĕrĭ|tō nam| mĕrĭtus| dē m(e) est| quod que|(am) ill
(i) ut| commŏ|dem

Hec. 767 (tr⁷) pŏtius| qu(am) ĭnĭmī|cus pĕ|rīclum| făcias| nīl ăpŭd| mē
tĭ|bi

Hec. 768 (tr⁸) dēfiĕ|rī păti|ar quin| quŏd ŏpus| sit bĕ|nignē
|praebe|ātur|

Hec. 771 (ia⁷) Phĭdip|pĕ Bac|chis dē|iĕrat| persan|ct(e) haecĭn e|ast hae|c
est|

Hec. 780 (ia⁷) miss(am) ī|ram făci|et sī|n aut(em) est| ŏb eam| r(em)
īrā|tus gnā|tus|

Hec. 785 (ia⁷) d(e) hāc r(e) ănĭ|mus meŭ|s ut sĭt| Lăchē|s illis| mŏd(o)
ex|plēt(e) ănĭ|mum|

Hec. 786 (ia⁷) quaes(o) ĕdĕ|pol Bac|chis quod| mĭh(i) es| pollĭcĭ|tă tū|t(e)
ut ser|ues|

Hec. 820 (ia⁷) quā rē |suspec|tus sûo͡ |pătr(i) et| Phĭdip|pō fuĭ|t
exsol|ui|

Hec. 842 (tr⁷) nē m(e) in| brĕuĕ cō|nĭcias| tempus| gaudi|(o) hoc fal|sō
fru|i

Hec. 848 (tr⁷) quis m(e) est| fortū|nāti|or uĕnŭs|tātis|qu(e) ădeō |
plēni|or

Hec. 856 (ia⁶) ō Bac|chĭs ō |meă Bac|chis ser|uātrix| mea|

Hec. 859   (ia⁸)   ut uŏlŭp|tāt(i) ŏbĭ|tus ser|m(o) aduen|tus tuŏs| quō-
                     quom|qu(e) aduē|nĕris|

Hec. 859   (ia⁸)   ut uŏlŭp|tāt(i) ŏbĭ|tus ser|m(o) **aduen|tus** tuŏs| quō-
                     quom|qu(e) aduē|nĕris|

Hec. 864   (ia⁸)   **perlī|bĕrā|lis** uī|sast dic| uĕr(um) ĭtă |mē dĭ—ă|ment
                     Pam|phĭle|

Hec. 874   (tr⁷)   aut quĭd ĭs|tūc est| quod uō|s **ăgĭtis**| non lĭ|cet tămĕn|
                     suspĭ|cor

Ph. 16   (ia⁶)   **is** sĭbĭ |respon|s(um) hōc hăbe|at in| mĕdi(o) om|nĭbus|

Ph. 28   (ia⁶)   **părăsī|tus** per| quem res| gĕrē|tur ma|xŭme|

Ph. 33   (ia⁶)   qu(em) **actō|ris** uir|tus nō|bīs res|tĭtuĭt| lŏcum|

Ph. 35   (ia⁶)   **ămī|cus** sum|mus meŭ|s et pŏpŭ|lāris| Gĕta|

Ph. 35   (ia⁶)   **ămī|cus sum|mus** meŭ|s et pŏpŭ|lāris| Gĕta|

Ph. 39   (ia⁶)   n(am) ĕrĭ|lem fĭ|li(um) **ei|us** du|xiss(e) au|dio|

Ph. 51   (ia⁶)   sīquis| mē quae|rēt **rū|fus** praes|tost dē|sĭn(e) oh|

Ph. 53   (ia⁶)   lectum|st conuĕni|et **nŭmĕ|rus** quan|tum dē|bui|

Ph. 58   (ia⁶)   quant(o) in| pĕrī|clō **sī|mus** quĭd ĭs|tūc es|t scies|

Ph. 64   (ia⁶)   nostin| quidnī |quĭd **ei|us** gnā|tum Phae|driam|

Ph. 76   (ia⁶)   sĕnī |**fĭdē|lis** dum| sum scăpŭ|lās per|dĭdi|

Ph. 78   (ia⁶)   **aduor|sus** stĭmŭ|lum cal|cēs coe|p(i) īs om|nia|

Ph. 87   (ia⁶)   nōs ō|tiō|s(i) ŏpĕram| **dăbā|mus** Phae|driae|

Ph. 93   (ia⁶)   **rŏgā|mus** quid| sit num|qu(am) aequ(e) in|quĭt ac|
                     mŏdo|

Ph. 94   (ia⁶)   pauper|tas mĭh(i) ŏ|nus uī|sumst et| mĭsĕr(um) et|
                     grăue|

Ph. 98   (ia⁶)   nĕquĕ **nō|tus** nĕquĕ |uīcī|nŭs ex|tr(a) ūn(am) ănĭ|cŭlam|

Ph. 99   (ia⁶)   quisqu(am) ădĕ|rat qu(i) ad|iūtā|ret **fū|nus** mĭsĕ|rĭtumst|

Ph. 102   (ia⁶)   uoltis|n(e) **eā|mus** uī|sĕr(e) ăli|us cen|seo|

Ph. 102   (ia⁶)   uoltis|n(e) eā|mus uī|sĕr(e) **ăli|us** cen|seo|

Ph. 103   (ia⁶)   **eā|mus** duc| nōs sō|dēs ī|mus uē|nĭmus|

Ph. 103   (ia⁶)   eā|mus duc| nōs sō|dēs **ī|mus** uē|nĭmus|

Ph. 104   (ia⁶)   **uĭdē|mus** uir|gō pul|chr(a) et quŏ |măgĕ dī|cĕres|

Ph. 106   (ia⁶)   **căpil|lus** pas|sus nū|dus pē|s ips(a) hor|rĭda|

Ph. 106   (ia⁶)   căpil|lus **pas|sus** nū|dus pē|s ips(a) hor|rĭda|

Ph. 106   (ia⁶)   căpil|lus pas|sus **nū|dus** pē|s ips(a) hor|rĭda|

Ph. 107   (ia⁶)   lăcrŭmae |**uestī|tus** tur|pĭs ut| nī uīs| bŏni|

Ph. 113   (ia⁶)   ut sĭb(i) **ei|us** făci|at cō|pi(am) il|l(a) ĕnĭm sē |nĕgat|

Ph. 122   (ia⁶)   quid fī|at est| **părăsī|tus** quī|dam Phor|mio|

Ph. 126   (ia⁶)   is nū|bant ĕt ĭl|los dū|cĕr(e) eă|d(em) haec lex| iŭbet|

Ph. 129   (ia⁶)   ad iŭ|dĭces| **uĕniē|mus** quī |fuĕrit| păter|

Ph. 139   (ia⁶)   (em) istuc| uĭris|t offĭci|(um) in m(e) **om|nis** spes|
                     mĭhist|

Ph. 147   (ia⁶)   pătĕr **ei|us** rĕdi|ĭt an| non non|dum quid| sĕnem|

Ph. 148   (ia⁶)   quoăd ex|spectā|tis uos|trum non| certum| scio|

Ph. 156   (tr⁸)   quĭd ĭstuc| rŏgĭtas| quī t(am) au|dācis| făcĭnŏ|ris mĭhĭ |
            consci|us sis|

Ph. 170   (ia⁸)   beā|tus n(i) ū|num dē|sĭt ănĭ|mus quī |mŏdes|t(e) istaec|
            fĕrat|

Ph. 170   (ia⁸)   beā|tus n(i) ū|num dē|sĭt ănĭ|mus quī |mŏdes|t(e) istaec|
            fĕrat|

Ph. 173   (ia⁸)   at tū |mĭhĭ con|trā nunc| uidē|rĕ for|tūnā|tus Phae|dria|

Ph. 185   (tr⁷)   quod qu(om) au|diĕrit| quŏd ĕius| rĕmĕdi|(um) inuĕni|
            (am) īrā|cundi|ae

Ph. 188   (tr⁸)   ei(u)s mē |mĭsĕre|t ei nunc| tĭme(o) is| nunc mē |rĕtĭnet|
            n(am) absqu(e) e|(o) esset|

Ph. 207   (tr⁷)   quid făcĕ|rēs s(i) ăli|ud quid| grăuius| tĭbĭ nunc| făciun|
            dum fŏ|ret

Ph. 213   (tr⁷)   nē t(e) ī|rātus| sūīs sae|uĭdĭcīs| dictīs| prōtē|let sci|o

Ph. 216   (ia⁶)   non pos|s(um) ădes|s(e) āh quĭd ă|gis quŏ—ă|bĭs An|
            tĭpho|

Ph. 230   (ia⁶)   succen|tŭriā|tus sī|quid dē|fĭciā|s ăge|

Ph. 236   (ia⁸)   inuī|tus fē|cī lex| coē|gĭt au|diō |fāteor| plăces|

Ph. 244   (ia⁸)   aut fĭ|lī pec|cāt(um) au|t uxŏ|ris mor|t(em) aut mor|bum
            fĭ|liae|

Ph. 253   (tr⁷)   Phaedri|am mēî |frātris| uĭdeō |fili|um m(i) ī|r(e)
            obui|am

Ph. 258   (ia⁶)   bŏnās| m(e) absen|t(e) hic con|fēcis|tis nup|tias|

Ph. 272   (ia⁶)   non cau|sam dī|cō quin| quod mĕrĭ|tus sit| fĕrat|

Ph. 273   (ia⁶)   sed sī|quis for|tĕ mălĭ|tiā |frētus| sua|

Ph. 282   (ia⁶)   offici|um lī|bĕrā|lis pos|tqu(am) ad iū|dĭces|

Ph. 297   (ia⁶)   dōtem| dărē|tis quae|rĕrē|t ălium| uĭrum|

Ph. 298   (ia⁶)   quā rătĭ|ōn(e) ĭnŏ|pem pŏti|us dū|cēbat| dŏmum|

Ph. 314   (ia⁶)   ut n(e) in|părā|tus sim| sī uĕni|at Phor|mio|

Ph. 324   (tr⁷)   ō uir| forti's| atqu(e) ă|mīcus| uĕr(um) hoc| saepĕ |
            Phormi|o

Ph. 349   (ia⁶)   aūdis|tis fac|t(am) iniū|riam| qu(am) haec est| mĭhi|

Ph. 359   (ia⁶)   s(i) ĕr(um) in|sĭmŭlā|bis mălĭ|tiae |măl(e) au|dies|

Ph. 380   (ia⁶)   qu(em) ămī|cum tu(om) a|is fūîs|s(e) ist(um) ex|plānā |
            mĭhi|

Ph. 383   (ia⁶)   ĕgŏ mē |nĕgō |tū quī—a|is rĕdĭ|g(e) in mĕmŏ|riam|

Ph. 400   (ia⁶)   iūdĭcĭ|bus t(um) id| sī fal|sum fuĕ|rat fĭ|lius|

Ph. 405   (ia⁶)   quandŏquĭ|dem sō|lus reg|nās et| solī |lĭcet|

Ph. 411   (ia⁶)   hăhăhae –| hŏmŏ suā|uis quĭd ĕst| n(um) ĭnī|quom pos|
            tŭlo|

Ph. 422   (ia⁶)   tuŏs est| damnā|tus gnā|tus non| tū nam| tua|

Ph. 422   (ia⁶)   tuŏs est| damnā|tus gnā|tus non| tū nam| tua|

Ph. 426	(ia⁶)	īrā|tŭs est| tū tĕ—ĭ|dem **mĕli|us** fē|cĕris|
Ph. 427	(ia⁶)	ĭtăn es| **părā|tus** făcĕ|re m(e) ad|uors(um) om|nia|
Ph. 433	(ia⁶)	sī con|cordā|bis c(um) il|l(a) hăbĕ|bis quae |tuam|
Ph. 433	(ia⁶)	sī con|cordā|bis c(um) il|l(a) **hăbĕ|bis** quae |tuam|
Ph. 438	(ia⁶)	sī t(u) il|l(am) **attĭgĕ|ris** sĕcŭs| quam dig|numst lī|bĕram|
Ph. 440	(ia⁶)	sīquĭd ŏ|**pus** fuĕ|rĭt heūs| dŏmō |m(e) intel|lĕgo|
Ph. 446	(ia⁶)	eō |**uĭdē|tis** qu(o) in| lŏcō |rēs haec| siet|
Ph. 452	(ia⁶)	ĕt ĭd **im|pĕtrā|bis** di|xī dic| nunc Hē|gio|
Ph. 461	(ia⁶)	**is** quod| mĭhĭ dĕdĕ|rit d(e) hāc| rē con|sĭli(um) id| sĕquar|
Ph. 471	(ia⁸)	et quĭd(em) ĕ|rĕ nos| iamdū|d(um) hic t(e) ab|sent(em) **in|cūsā|mus** qu(i) ăbi|ĕris|
Ph. 494	(tr⁷)	crĕdĕ |mī **gau|dēbis**| factō |uēr(um) her|cl(e) hōc est| somni|um
Ph. 496	(ia⁸)	tū mĭhĭ |**cognā|tus** tū |părens| t(u) ămī|cus tū |garrī | mŏdo|
Ph. 496	(ia⁸)	tū mĭhĭ |cognā|tus tū |părens| t(u) **ămī|cus** tū |garrī | mŏdo|
Ph. 498	(tr⁷)	ut nĕquĕ |mĭsĕrĭ|cordi|ā nĕquĕ |**prĕcĭbus**| mollī|rī que|as
Ph. 516	(ia⁸)	ĭd(em) hoc| tĭbĭ quod| bŏnī |**prōmĕrĭ|tus** fuĕ|ris con| dŭplĭcā|uĕrit|
Ph. 516	(ia⁸)	ĭd(em) hoc| tĭbĭ quod| bŏnī |prōmĕrĭ|tus **fuĕ|ris** con| dŭplĭcā|uĕrit|
Ph. 526	(tr⁷)	**uānĭ|tātis**| mĭnĭmē |d(um) ob rem| stercŭ|līnum| Dōri|o
Ph. 532	(tr⁷)	**mīles**| dărĕ sē |dixit| sī mī |priŏr t(u) at|tŭlĕris| Phaedri|a
Ph. 532	(tr⁷)	mīles| dărĕ sē |dixit| sī mī |priŏr t(u) **at|tŭlĕris**| Phaedri|a
Ph. 539	(tr⁷)	sci(o) ĕquĭ|d(em) hōc es|s(e) aequ(om) ă|g(e) ergō | **sōlus**| seruā|r(e) hunc pŏ|tes
Ph. 545	(tr⁷)	uēr(um) hic| dīcit| quĭd ĕgo |uōbīs| Gĕt(a) **ăli|ēnus**| s (um) haud pŭ|to
Ph. 547	(tr⁷)	n(i) instī|gēmŭ|s ĕti(am) ut| **nullus**| lŏcŭs rĕ|linquā|tur prĕ|ci
Ph. 553	(tr⁷)	uĭdĕ sī|quĭd **ŏpis**| pŏtĕs ad|ferr(e) huīc| sīquid| quid quae|r(e) obsĕ|cro
Ph. 561	(tr⁷)	praestos|t audā|cissĭ|m(e) **ŏnĕris**| quiduĭ|s inpō|n(e) ecfĕ|ret
Ph. 564	(tr⁷)	ĕt illam| mĭsĕram| qu(am) ĕgŏ nun|c **intus**| sci(o) ĕss(e) e|xănĭmā|tam mĕ|tu
Ph. 567	(ia⁶)	quid quā |**prōfec|tus** cau|s(a) hinc es| Lemnum| Chrĕme|
Ph. 575	(ia⁶)	sĕnec|tūs ip|sast **mor|bus** sed| uēnis|s(e) eas|
Ph. 587	(ia⁶)	ĭd res|tat n(am) ĕgŏ |meō|rum **sō|lus** sum| meus|
Ph. 596	(ia⁶)	dīs grā|tĭā|s ăgē|bat **tem|pus** sĭbĭ |dări|
Ph. 608	(ia⁶)	quam tĭme|(o) aduen|tŭs **hui|us** qu(o) in|pellat| pătrem|

Ph. 619	(ia⁶)	uīsum|st mĭh(i) ŭt **ĕi|us** tem|ptārem| senten|tiam|
Ph. 621	(ia⁶)	uĭdē|s inter| nōs sī|c haec **pŏti|us** cum| bŏna|
Ph. 622	(ia⁶)	ut **com|pōnā|mus** grā|tiā |quam cum| măla|
Ph. 635	(ia⁶)	haec hinc| făces|sat tū |**mŏles|tus** nē |sies|
Ph. 640	(ia⁶)	immō |non pŏtu|it **mĕli|us** per|uĕnī|rier|
Ph. 649	(ia⁶)	haec dē|nĭqu(e) **ei|us** fŭīt| postrē|m(a) ōrā|tio|
Ph. 667	(ia⁶)	his **rē|bus** pō|nĕ sā|n(e) inquit| dĕcem| mĭnas|
Ph. 669	(ia⁶)	nil d(o) **in|pūrā|tus** m(e) il|l(e) ŭt ĕti|(am) inrī|deat|
Ph. 680	(ia⁶)	fructum| quem Lem|n(i) **uxō|ris** red|dunt prae|dia|
Ph. 690	(ia⁶)	quid mĭnŭ|s ūtĭbĭ|lĕ fŭīt| qu(am) hōc **ul|cus** tan|gĕre|
Ph. 698	(ia⁶)	t(u) id quod| bŏnis|t **excer|pis** dī|cis quod| mălist|
Ph. 698	(ia⁶)	t(u) id quod| bŏnis|t excer|pis **dī|cis** quod| mălist|
Ph. 700	(ia⁶)	dūcen|dast u|xor ŭt **a|is** con|cēdō |tĭbi|
Ph. 716	(ia⁸)	atqu(e) ĭt(a) **ŏ|pus** fac|tost et| mātū|rā dum| lŭbī|d(o) eăd(em) haec| mănet|
Ph. 722	(ia⁸)	nōs nos|tr(o) offici|ō nil| dīgres|sōs es|sĕ quan|t(um) is uŏlu|ĕrit|
Ph. 723	(ia⁸)	dăt(um) es|sĕ **dō|tis** quid| tuā |măl(um) ĭd rē|fert mag|nī Dē|mĭpho|
Ph. 725	(ia⁸)	uŏl(o) **ĭpsi|us** quŏquĕ |uŏlŭntā|t(e) haec fiĕ|rī nē |s(e) ēiec|tam prae|dĭcet|
Ph. 731	(tr⁸)	ĭtă pă|tr(em) **ădŭles|centis|** fact(a) haec| tŏlĕrā|r(e) audi|ō uiŏ|lenter|
Ph. 735	(tr⁸)	cert(e) ĕdĕ|pol nĭsĭ |m(e) **ănĭmus|** fallĭ|t aut pă|rum pros| pĭciun|t ŏcŭli|
Ph. 741	(tr⁷)	concē|d(e) hinc ā |**fŏrĭbus|** paull(um) is|torsum| sōdēs| Sōphrō|na
Ph. 761	(ia⁷)	sĭnĕ nos|trā cū|rā ma|xumā |suă cū|ra **sō|lus** fē|cit|
Ph. 762	(ia⁷)	nunc quĭd **ŏ|pus** fac|tō sit| uĭdē |pătĕr **ădŭ|lescen|tis** uē|nit|
Ph. 762	(ia⁷)	nunc quĭd ŏ|pus fac|tō sit| uĭdē |pătĕr **ădŭ|lescen|tis** uē|nit|
Ph. 765	(ia⁶)	nĕm(o) ē |me scī|bit sĕquĕ|re m(e) **in|tus** cē|tĕra|
Ph. 791	(ia⁷)	āc **rē|bus** uī|liō|rĭbus| multō |tămĕn duŏ |tălen|t(a) hŭī|
Ph. 806	(ia⁸)	nĕqu(e) ĭntel|lĕges| sī tū |nil nar|ras **per|dis** mī|ror quĭd hŏc| siet|
Ph. 815	(ia⁸)	mănē|r(e) hanc nam| **perlĭ|bĕrā|lis** uī|sast quom| uĭdī |mĭhi|
Ph. 828	(ia⁷)	rŏgem| quod **tem|pus** con|uĕniun|dī pătrĭs| mē căpĕ|rĕ iŭbe|at|
Ph. 837	(ia⁸)	nam pō|tātū|rŭs es|t ăpud| m(e) ĕgŏ m(e) ī|rĕ **sĕnĭ|bus** Sū|nium|
Ph. 850	(tr⁷)	uāpŭ|l(a) id quĭdĕm| tĭbĭ iam| fīet| nĭsĭ **rĕ|sistis|** uerbĕ|ro

Ph. 854   (tr⁷)   nam sĭně |contrō|uorsi|(a) ab dis| **sōlus**| dīlĭgě|r(e) Antĭ| pho

Ph. 866   (tr⁷)   eûmquĕ |nunc es|s(e) **intus**| c(um) illī|s hōc ŭb(i) ĕ|g(o) audī|u(i) ad fŏ|res

Ph. 872   (tr⁷)   **pătruos**| tuŏs est| pătĕr in|uentus| Phāni|(o) uxō|rī tu| (ae) hem

Ph. 872   (tr⁷)   pătruos| tuŏs est| pătĕr **in|uentus**| Phāni|(o) uxō|rī tu| (ae) hem

Ph. 873   (tr⁷)   quĭd **ais**| c(um) ei(u)s con|sueûĭ|t ōlim| mātr(e) in| Lemnō |clancŭ|lum

Ph. 876   (tr⁷)   intel|lĕgĕr(e) ex|tr(a) osti|(um) **intus**| qu(ae) inter| sēs(e) ip|s(i) ēgĕ|rint

Ph. 881   (tr⁷)   dēnī|qu(e) ĕgŏ sum| **missus**| t(e) ŭt rĕ|quīrĕ|r(em) atqu (e) ad|dūcĕ|r(em) em

Ph. 890   (ia⁶)   nunc ges|**tus** mĭhĭ |uoltus|qu(e) est căpi|undus| nŏuos|

Ph. 898   (ia⁶)   ŭt **au|fĕrā|mus** Dē|mĭphō|nem sī |dŏmist|

Ph. 899   (ia⁶)   uīs(am) ut| quŏd at| nōs ad| t(e) ībā|**mus** Phor|mio|

Ph. 901   (ia⁶)   quĭd ad| m(e) **ībā|tis** rī|dĭcŭlum| uĕrĕbā|mĭni|

Ph. 928   (ia⁶)   qu(om) ĕgŏ uos|tr(i) **hŏnō|ris** cau|sā rĕpŭ|di(um) al| tĕrae|

Ph. 929   (ia⁶)   rĕmī|sĕrim| quae **dō|tis** tan|tundem| dăbat|

Ph. 931   (ia⁶)   fŭgĭtī|u(e) ĕtiam|nunc **crē|dis** t(e) ig|nōrā|rier|

Ph. 942   (ia⁶)   Lemn(i) hăbu|it ăli|am **nul|lus** s(um) ex| quā fi|liam|

Ph. 946   (ia⁶)   missum| tē **făcĭ|mus** fă|bŭlae |quid uīs| tĭbi|

Ph. 947   (ia⁶)   argen|tum quŏd hă|bes **con|dōnā|mus** t(e) au|dio|

Ph. 968   (ia⁶)   ĭtăn **ăgĭ|tis** mē|cum sătĭ|s astū|t(e) adgrĕdī|mĭni|

Ph. 971   (ia⁶)   nĕqu(e) hui(u)s| sīs **uĕrĭ|tus** fē|mĭnae |prīmā|riae|

Ph. 973   (ia⁶)   uĕniās| nunc **prĕcĭ|bus** lau|tum pec|cātum| tuom|

Ph. 978   (ia⁶)   nōn hoc| **pūblĭcĭ|tus** scĕlŭ|s hinc as|portā|rier|

Ph. 979   (ia⁶)   in sō|lās ter|rās ĭn ĭd| **rĕdac|tus** sum| lŏci|

Ph. 994   (ia⁶)   ăbĭ tan|gĕ sī |non **tō|tus** frī|get m(e) ē|nĭca|

Ph. 1004   (ia⁶)   in Lem|n(o) hem quĭd a|is non| tăces| clam t(e) eî | mĭhi|

Ph. 1008   (ia⁶)   prō d(i) in|mortā|les **făcĭ|nus** mĭsĕ|rand(um) et| mălum|

Ph. 1017   (tr⁷)   **uīnŏ|lentus**| fĕr(e) ăbhin|c annōs| quindĕ|cim mŭli|ercŭ| lam

Ph. 1037   (tr⁷)   heûs Nau|sistrā|tă **prius**| qu(am) huîc res|pondes| tĕmĕr (e) au|dī quî|d est

Ph. 1039   (tr⁷)   eas dĕ|dī tûo g|nāt(o) is| prō su(a) ă|mīcā |lēnō|nī dĕ|dit

Ph. 1042   (tr⁷)   nil pŭ|dērĕ |qu(o) ōr(e) il|l(um) **obiur|gābis**| respon|dē mĭ|hi

Ph. 1049   (tr⁷)   uostrae |fămĭli|(ae) hercl(e) ă|mīcŭ|s et tuŏ |**summus**| Phaedri|ae

Ph. 1051 (tr⁷) făciam|qu(e) et dī|cam bĕ|nignē |dīcis| pol mĕrĭ|tumst tu|om

Ad. 4 (ia⁶) indĭci|ō dē |s(e) ips(e) ĕrĭt| uōs ĕrĭ|tis iū|dĭces|

Ad. 7 (ia⁶) ēam com|mŏrien|tīs Plau|tus fē|cit fā|bŭlam|

Ad. 14 (ia⁶) rĕprēhen|sum quī |praetĕrĭ|tus nē|glĕgen|tiast|

Ad. 36 (ia⁶) quĭbŭs nunc| sollĭcĭ|tor rē|bus n(e) au|t ill(e) al|sĕrit|

Ad. 40 (ia⁶) atqu(e) ex| m(e) hic nā|tus nō|n est sĕd ĕx| frātr(e) ĭs ă| deo|

Ad. 43 (ia⁶) sĕcū|tus s(um) et| quod for|tūnā|t(um) istī |pŭtant|

Ad. 60 (ia⁶) uĕnĭt ad| mē sae|pĕ clā|mĭtăns quĭd ă|gis Mī|cio|

Ad. 62 (ia⁶) quor pō|tat quor| t(u) his rē|bus sum|ptum sug|gĕris|

Ad. 69 (ia⁶) mălō |coac|tus quī |su(om) of|fĭcium| făcit|

Ad. 74 (ia⁶) hoc pătri|umst pŏti|us con|suēfăcĕ|rĕ fĭ|lium|

Ad. 78 (ia⁶) sĕd es|tn(e) hic ip|sus dē |qu(o) ăgē|b(am) et cer|t(e) ĭs est|

Ad. 96 (ia⁶) null(um) hui|us sĭmĭ|lĕ fac|t(um) haec qu(om) il|lī Mī| cio|

Ad. 105 (ia⁶) ĭd lau|dī dū|cis quod| tum fē|cist(i) ĭnŏ|pia|

Ad. 111 (ia⁶) prō iup|pĭter| tŭ—hŏm(o) ădĭ|gis mĕ—ă|d insā|niam|

Ad. 115 (ia⁶) is meŭ|s est fac|tus sī|quid pec|cat Dē|mea|

Ad. 115 (ia⁶) is meŭ|s est fac|tus sī|quid pec|cat Dē|mea|

Ad. 136 (ia⁶) īras|cĕr(e) an| non crē|dis rĕpĕ|tō quem| dĕdi|

Ad. 137 (ia⁶) aēgres|t ăliē|nus non| sum s(i) ob|st(o) em dē|sĭno|

Ad. 140 (ia⁶) postĕri|us nō|l(o) ĭn il|lum grăui|us dī|cĕre|

Ad. 140 (ia⁶) postĕri|us nō|l(o) ĭn il|lum grăui|us dī|cĕre|

Ad. 159 (ia⁸) quamquamst| scĕles|tus non| commit|tet hŏdi|(e) umqu (am) ĭtĕ|r(um) ut uā|pŭlet|

Ad. 162 (tr⁸) tū quod| tē pos|tĕrius| purgē|s hanc in|iūri|am mī |nolle|

Ad. 171 (ia⁸) nē mŏră |sit s(i) in|nuĕrim| quin pug|nus con|tĭnu(o) in| māl(a) hae|reat|

Ad. 174 (ia⁸) nōn in|nuĕram| uēr(um) ĭn ĭs|tam par|tem pŏti|us pec| cātō |tămen|

Ad. 181 (ia⁸) nam sī |mōles|tus per|gĭs es|sĕ i(am) in|tr(o) abrĭpi|ēr(e) at|qu(e) ĭbi|

Ad. 185 (ia⁸) ĕgŏn dē|bacchā|tus s(um) au|t(em) an t(u) in| mē mit|t (e) ist(a) at|qu(e) ăd rem| rĕdi|

Ad. 189 (ia⁸) periŭ|rus pes|tis tămĕn| tīb(i) ā |mē null|l(a) est or|t(a) iniŭ|ria|

Ad. 189 (ia⁸) periŭ|rus pes|tis tămĕn| tīb(i) ā |mē null|l(a) est or|t(a) iniŭ|ria|

Ad. 215 (ia⁸) quī pŏtu|ī mĕli|us quī—hŏ|di(e) us|qu(e) os prae|bu(i) ăgĕ s|cis quĭd| lŏquar|

Ad. 234 (ia⁶) quor pas|sus ŭb(i) ĕ|rās ut| sit sắti|us per|dĕre|

Ad. 248 (ia⁶) ŭtŭt haec| sunt ac|tă pŏti|us quam| lītis| sĕquar|

Ad. 255 (ia⁸) uēr(um) ĕnĭm|uēr(o) id| dēmum| iŭuat| sī qu(em) ae|
quomst fắcĕ|r(e) is bĕnĕ |fācit|

Ad. 267 (ia⁸) in tū|tost om|nis rē|s ŏmit|tĕ uē|rō tris|tĭtiem| tuam|

Ad. 271 (ia⁸) ăg(e) ĭnep|tĕ quăsĭ |nunc non| nōrī|mus nō|s inter| nōs
Ctē|sĭpho|

Ad. 278 (ia⁸) Sўr(e) in|st(a) eā|mus nam|qu(e) hic prŏpĕ|rat in|
Cўprum| nē tam| quĭdem|

Ad. 284 (ia⁸) non fi|et bŏn(o) ă|nĭm(o) es|tō tū |c(um) ill(a) in|tus t(e)
ō|blect(a) in|tĕrim|

Ad. 294 (ia⁸) quin sem|per uĕni|at sō|lus mĕā|rum mĭsĕ|riā|rumst
rĕmĕ|dium|

Ad. 295 (tr⁷) ē rē |nātā |mĕlius| fiĕr(i) haud| pŏtuit| quam fac|tumst
ĕ|ra

Ad. 298 (tr⁷) ĭtă pŏ|l est ut| dīcis| saluos| nōbīs| dēos quae|s(o) ut si|et

Ad. 298 (tr⁷) ĭtă pŏ|l est ut| dīcis| saluos| nōbīs| dēos quae|s(o) ut si|et

Ad. 309 (ia⁸) sătius| quae lŏquĭ|tur prŏpi|ŭs ob|sĕcr(o) ac|cēdā|mus Sos|
trăt(a) ah|

Ad. 324 (tr⁷) ănĭmam| rĕcĭpĕ |prorsus| quĭd ĭstuc| prorsŭ|s ergost|
pĕriĭ|mus

Ad. 335 (ia⁸) ĕră lăcrŭ|mas mit|t(e) ac pŏti|us quŏd ă|d hanc r(em)
ŏpŭ|s est por|rō pros|pĭce|

Ad. 347 (ia⁸) s(i) infĭti|ās ī|bit tes|tis mē|c(um) est ā|nŭlus| quem mī|
sĕrat|

Ad. 350 (ia⁸) expĕri|ar quĭd ĭs|tic cē|d(o) ut mĕli|us dī|cas tū |quan-
tum| pŏtest|

Ad. 351 (ia⁸) ăb(i) ătq(ūe) Hē|giō|nī cog|nāt(o) hui|us r(em) ē|narrā|t(o)
omn(em) or|dĭne|

Ad. 352 (ia⁸) n(am) is nos|trō Sī|mŭlō |fŭĭt sum|mŭs et| nōs cŏlu|it
ma|xŭme|

Ad. 353 (ia⁸) n(am) hercl(e) ăli|us nē|mō res|pĭciet| nōs prŏpĕ|rā tū |
meă Can|thăra|

Ad. 360 (ia⁶) ălĭquō |persuā|sit il|l(e) inpū|rus sat| scio|

Ad. 389 (ia⁶) ell(am) in|tŭs ĕh(o) ăn| dŏmis|t hăbĭtū|rus crē|d(o) ŭt
est|

Ad. 391 (ia⁶) pătrĭs et| făcĭlĭ|tās prā|uă frā|tris mē |quĭdem|

Ad. 394 (ia⁶) tū quan|tus quan|tu's nil| nĭsĭ să|pien|ti(a) es|

Ad. 410 (ia⁶) non t(u) hō|c argen|tum per|dis sed| uītam| tuam|

Ad. 411 (ia⁶) saluos| sit spē|r(o) est sĭmĭ|lis mā|iōrum| su(om) hŭĭ|

Ad. 430 (ia⁶) ĭnep|t(a) haec es|sĕ nos| quae făcĭ|mus sen|tio|

Ad. 433 (ia⁶) tū rŭ|s hinc ī|bis rec|tā nam| quid t(u) hī|c ăgas|

Ad. 435   (ia⁶)   ĕgŏ uē|r(o) hinc ăbe|ō quan|d(o) is qu(am) ob| r(em) huc uē|nĕram|

Ad. 439   (ia⁶)   trĭbū|lis nos|ter sī |sătĭs cer|n(o) ĭs hĕrclest| uăha|

Ad. 440   (ia⁶)   hŏm(o) ămī|cus nō|bīs i(am) in|d(e) ā puĕ|r(o) ō dī | bŏni|

Ad. 441   (ia⁶)   n(e) illī|us mŏdĭ |iam mag|nă nō|bīs cī|uium|

Ad. 444   (ia⁶)   quam gau|de(o) ŭb(i) ĕ|ti(am) **hui|us** gĕnĕ|ris rĕlĭ|quias|

Ad. 444   (ia⁶)   quam gau|de(o) ŭb(i) ĕ|ti(am) hui|us **gĕnĕ|ris** rĕlĭ|quias|

Ad. 452   (ia⁶)   ăliē|nō pătĕ|r is nĭhĭ|lī pen|dĭt ei |mĭhi|

Ad. 456   (ia⁶)   tē sō|l(um) **hăbē|mus** t(u) es| patrō|nus tū |păter|

Ad. 456   (ia⁶)   tē sō|l(um) hăbē|mus t(u) es| **patrō|nus** tū |păter|

Ad. 464   (ia⁶)   nĕquĕ **lī|bĕrā|lis** fun|ctŭs of|fĭciumst| uĭri|

Ad. 466   (ia⁶)   aēquā|lem quid|nī fĭ|li(am) **ei|us** uir|gĭnem|

Ad. 478   (ia⁶)   prō cer|tō t(u) is|taec dī|cis mā|ter uir|gĭnis|

Ad. 492   (ia⁶)   sīn ălĭ|tĕr ănī|**mus** uos|tĕr es|t ĕgŏ Dē|mea|

Ad. 494   (ia⁶)   **cognā|tus** mĭh(i) ĕ|rat ū|n(a) ā puĕ|ris par|uŏlis|

Ad. 498   (ia⁶)   ănĭmam| rĕlin|quam **pŏtĭ|us** qu(am) il|las dē|sĕram|

Ad. 499   (ia⁶)   is quod| mī d(e) hāc| rē dĕdĕ|rit con|sĭli(um) id| sĕquar|

Ad. 501   (ia⁶)   quam uōs| facil|lĭm(e) **ăgĭ|tis** qu(am) es|tis ma|xŭme|

Ad. 501   (ia⁶)   quam uōs| facil|lĭm(e) ăgĭ|tis qu(am) **es|tis** ma|xŭme|

Ad. 504   (ia⁶)   ŏpor|tet sī |uōs **uol|tis** pĕrhĭ|bērī |prŏbos|

Ad. 529   (ia⁸)   clien|s ămĭ|cŭs **hos|pes** nē|most uō|bīs sun|t quid pos| tea|

Ad. 538   (tr⁷)   pătĕr es|t ipsust| Sȳrĕ quĭ|d **ăgĭmus**| fŭgĕ mŏ|d(o) intr(o) ĕgŏ |uīdĕ|ro

Ad. 542   (tr⁷)   uīd(i) is| fīli|um nĕgă|t essĕ |rūrĕ |nec quĭd ă|gam sci|o

Ad. 544   (tr⁷)   quĭd hŏc mă|l(um) **infē|līcĭ|tātis**| nĕqueō |sătĭs dē| cernĕ|re

Ad. 546   (tr⁷)   **prīmus**| senti|ō mălă |nostră |prīmus| rescis|c(o) omni|a

Ad. 546   (tr⁷)   prīmus| senti|ō mălă |nostră |**prīmus**| rescis|c(o) omni|a

Ad. 547   (tr⁷)   **prīmus**| porr(o) ob|nunti|(o) aegrē |sōlus| sīquid| fit fĕ|ro

Ad. 547   (tr⁷)   prīmus| porr(o) ob|nunti|(o) aegrē |**sōlus**| sīquid| fit fĕ|ro

Ad. 548   (tr⁷)   rīde|(o) hunc prī|m(um) aît se s|cīr(e) is| sōlus| nescĭ|t omni|a

Ad. 548   (tr⁷)   rīde|(o) hunc prī|m(um) aît se s|cīr(e) is| **sōlus**| nescĭ|t omni|a

Ad. 550   (tr⁷)   obsĕ|crō uĭdĕ |n(e) ill(e) huc| **prorsus**| s(e) inru|āt ĕti|am tă|ces

Ad. 556   (tr⁷)   quĭd ĭlle |gannit| quid uol|t quĭd **ais**| bŏnĕ uĭ|r est frā|ter dŏ|mi

Ad. 563   (tr⁷)   qu(em) ĕgŏ mŏ|dŏ puĕ|rum tan|till(um) in| **mănĭbus**| gestā| uī me|is

Ad. 569   (tr⁷)   sĕd ĕstne |frāte|r **intus**| nōn es|t ŭb(i) ĭll(um) in|uĕniam| cōgĭ|to

Ad. 572   (tr⁷)   illīŭ|s **hŏmĭnis**| sed lŏ|cum nō|u(i) ŭbĭ sit| dīc er|gō lŏ| cum

Ad. 575   (tr⁷)   **clīuos**| deōrsum| uors(um) es|t hac tē |praecĭpĭ|tātō | poste|a

Ad. 577   (tr⁷)   quodn(am) il|l(i) ŭb(i) ĕti|am **căprĭ|fĭcus**| magn(a) es|t nōu(i) hac| pergĭ|to

Ad. 585   (tr⁷)   lectŭ|lōs in| sōl(e) ī|lignis| **pĕdĭbus**| făciun|dos dĕ|dit

Ad. 586   (tr⁷)   ŭbĭ **pō|tētis**| uōs bĕnĕ |sānē |sed ces|s(o) ăd eum| pergĕ|re

Ad. 601   (ia⁸)   s(i) ĭt(a) ae|quom cen|sēs aut| s(i) ĭt(a) ŏpŭ|s est fac|t(o) eā|mus bĕnĕ |făcis|

Ad. 602   (ia⁸)   n(am) ĕt il|līc ănĭ|mum iam| **rĕlĕuā|bis** quae |dŏlō|r(e) ac mĭsĕ|ria|

Ad. 603   (ia⁸)   tābes|cĭt et| t(ūo) offici|ō **fuĕ|ris** fun|ctus sed| s(i) ălĭter| pŭtas|

Ad. 603   (ia⁸)   tābes|cĭt et| t(ūo) offici|ō fuĕ|ris **fun|ctus** sed| s(i) ălĭter| pŭtas|

Ad. 609   (ia⁸)   ĕt rec|t(e) et uĕ|rum **dī|cis** sĕquĕ|re m(e) er|g(o) hāc in| trō ma|xŭme|

Ad. 645   (ia⁶)   **ămī|cus** quī|dam m(e) ā |fŏr(o) ab|duxit| mŏdo|

Ad. 653   (ia⁶)   nil rec|tē per|g(e) **is** uĕ|nĭt ut| sēc(um) ā|uĕhat|

Ad. 677   (ia⁶)   quoī uĕ|nĕr(am) **ad|uŏcā|tus** sed| quĭd ĭst(a) Aes|chĭne|

Ad. 680   (tr⁷)   et sci|ō nam| tĕ—ămō |quō măgĕ |quaĕ—**ăgis**| cūrae |sunt mĭ|hi

Ad. 697   (tr⁷)   obsĕ|crō nunc| **lūdis**| tū mē—|ĕgŏ tē |qu(am) ŏb rem| nesci|o

Ad. 713   (ia⁶)   **dēfes|sus** s(um) am|bŭlan|d(o) ut Sӯrĕ |tē cum| tua|

Ad. 714   (ia⁶)   monstrā|tiŏ|nĕ **mag|nus** per|dat Iup|pĭter|

Ad. 734   (ia⁶)   sĭmŭlā|rĕ cer|t(e) est **hŏmĭ|nis** quin| iam uir|gĭnem|

Ad. 736   (ia⁶)   dempsī |mĕt(um) om|n(em) haec măgĕ |sunt **hŏmĭ|nis** cĕ|tĕrum|

Ad. 759   (ia⁶)   uxor| sĭnĕ dō|tĕ uĕni|et **in|tus** psal|triast|

Ad. 762   (ia⁶)   seruā|re **pror|sus** non| pŏtes|t hanc fămĭ|liam|

Ad. 765   (ia⁶)   ăbĭ sed| postqu(am) **in|tus** s(um) om|nium| rērum| sătur|

Ad. 778   (ia⁶)   est Ctĕ|sĭph(o) **in|tus** nō|n est quō|r hic nō|mĭnat|

Ad. 779   (ia⁶)   est **ăli|us** quī|dam pără|sītas|ter paul|lŭlus|

Ad. 780   (ia⁶)   nostin| iam scī|bō quĭd **ă|gis** quŏ—ă|bis mit|tĕ me|

Ad. 780   (ia⁶)   nostin| iam scī|bō quĭd ă|gis quŏ—**ă|bis** mit|tĕ me|

Ad. 793   (ia⁶)   **commū|nis** cor|ruptē|lă nos|trum lī|bĕrum|

Ad. 796   (ia⁶)   r(em) ipsam| **pŭtē|mus** dic|t(um) hoc in|ter nos| fuit|

Ad. 803   (ia⁶)   nōn ae|quom **dī|cis** non| nam uĕtŭs| uerb(um) hoc| quĭdemst|

Ad. 825   (ia⁶)   non quō **|dissĭmĭ|lis** rēs| sit sed| qu(o) is quī |făcit|

Ad. 825   (ia⁶)   non quō |dissĭmĭ|lis rēs| sit sed| qu(o) **is** quī |făcit|

Ad. 827   (ia⁶)   ĭt(a) ŭt **uŏlŭ|mus** uĭde|ō săpĕ|r(e) intel|lĕgĕr(e) in| lŏco|

Ad. 832   (ia⁶)   ăd om|ni(a) ăli|(a) aetā|tĕ **săpĭ|mus** rec|tius|

Ad. 837   (ia⁶)   et tuŏ|s ist(e) ănĭ|mŭs **ae|quos** sub|uortat| tăce|

Ad. 844   (ia⁶)   eŏ pac|tō pror|s(um) ill(i) **ad| līgā|ris** fĭ|lium|

Ad. 856   (tr⁷)   quin rē|s aetā|s **ūsus|** sempĕ|r ălĭquĭ|d adpor|tet nŏ|ui

Ad. 861   (tr⁷)   făcĭlĭ|tātĕ |nīl es|s(e) hŏmĭnī **|mĕlius|** nĕquĕ clē|menti|a

Ad. 864   (tr⁷)   clēmen|s **plăcĭdus|** nullī |laedĕ|r(e) ōs ad|rīdē|r(e) omnĭ| bus

Ad. 866   (tr⁷)   ĕg(o) ĭll(e) **ă|grestis|** saeuos| tristis| parcus| trŭcŭlen|tus tĕ|nax

Ad. 866   (tr⁷)   ĕg(o) ĭll(e) ă|grestis| **saeuos|** tristis| parcus| trŭcŭlen|tus tĕ|nax

Ad. 866   (tr⁷)   ĕg(o) ĭll(e) ă|grestis| saeuos| **tristis|** parcus| trŭcŭlen|tus tĕ|nax

Ad. 866   (tr⁷)   ĕg(o) ĭll(e) ă|grestis| saeuos| tristis| **parcus|** trŭcŭlen|tus tĕ|nax

Ad. 893   (ia⁶)   n(am) is mĭhĭ |prōfec|tost ser|uos spec|tātus| sătis|

Ad. 893   (ia⁶)   n(am) is mĭhĭ |prōfec|tost **ser|uos** spec|tātus| sătis|

Ad. 894   (ia⁶)   quoî **dŏmĭ|nus** cū|raest ĭt(a) ŭ|tī tĭbĭ |sensī |Gĕta|

Ad. 895   (ia⁶)   et tĭb(i) ŏ|b eam| rem sī|quĭd **ū|sus** uē|nĕrit|

Ad. 904   (ia⁶)   uxō|r(em) **accer|sis** cŭpi|ō uē|r(um) hoc mĭhĭ |mŏraest|

Ad. 922   (ia⁶)   aēgrō|tam nĭ|l ĕnĭm **mĕli|us** uĭ|dī mī |păter|

Ad. 945   (ia⁸)   uĭdē|tur sī |uōs tan|t(o) ŏpĕr(e) is|tuc **uol|tis** fĭ|at bĕnĕ | făcis|

Ad. 947   (ia⁸)   quid nunc| quŏd res|tat Hē|giō—|est his| **cognā|tus** pro| xŭmus|

Ad. 948   (ia⁸)   **adfi|nis** nō|bīs pau|per bĕnĕ |nōs ălĭ|quid făcĕ|r(e) illī | dĕcet|

Ad. 950   (ia⁸)   huĭc **dē|mus** quī |fruā|tur paul|l(um) ĭd au|temst sī | multum|st tămen|

Ad. 970   (tr⁷)   **uoltis|** Sўr(e) ĕh(o) ăc|cēd(e) hŭ|c ad mē |lībĕ|r estō | bĕnĕ fă|cis

Ad. 992   (tr⁷)   sed s(i) id| **uoltis|** pŏtius| quae uōs| proptĕ|r ădŭles| centi|am

Ad. 992   (tr⁷)   sed s(i) id| uoltis| **pŏtius|** quae uōs| proptĕ|r ădŭles|centi| am

Ad. 993	(tr⁷)	mĭnŭs **uĭ|dētis|** măgĭs in|pensē |cŭpĭtis| consŭlĭ|tis pă|rum
Ad. 993	(tr⁷)	mĭnŭs uĭ|dētis| măgĭs in|pensē **|cŭpĭtis|** consŭlĭ|tis pă|rum
Ad. 996	(tr⁷)	plūs scīs| quĭd **ŏpus|** factost| sed dē |frātrĕ |quid fĭ|et sĭ|no

3.3 Category 3: Indifferent Elements

This group (thirty-four examples) consists of instances in which the syllable potentially affected by sigmatic ecthlipsis occupies an indifferent element. Since for obvious reasons sigmatic ecthlipsis cannot occur at the end of a line, this group includes only instances that occupy the last element before a median caesura in ia⁷ and ia⁸.

An. 207	(ia⁸)	quant(um) in|telle|xī mŏdŏ **|sĕnis|** senten|tiam| dē nup|tiis|
An. 692	(ia⁷)	ăgĕ s(i) hic| nōn in|sānit| **sătis|** suă spon|t(e) instī|g(a) atqu (e) ĕdĕ|pol|
An. 698	(ia⁷)	rĕsĭpis|cō nō|n **Ăpol|lĭnis|** măgĕ uē|r(um) atqu(e) hoc| respon|sumst|
An. 708	(ia⁷)	ĕg(o) hănc uī|sam quid| tū qu(o) hinc| t(e) **ăgis|** uērum| uīs dī|c(am) imm(o) ĕti|am|
An. 715	(ia⁷)	quâprop|tĕr ĭtă |factos|t **ŏpus|** mātū|rā i(am) in|qu(am) hīc ădĕ|ro|
Eun. 260	(ia⁷)	ill(e) ŭbĭ |mĭser| **fămē|lĭcus|** uĭdĕt m(i) es|sĕ tan|t(um) hŏnŏ|r(em) et|
Eun. 285	(ia⁷)	nē t(u) is|tās fa|xō **cal|cĭbus|** saep(e) in|sultā|bis frus|tra|
Eun. 287	(ia⁷)	nēquis| fort(e) **in|ternun|tius|** cl(am) ā mī|lĭt(e) ăd ĭs|tam cur|set|
Eun. 547	(ia⁷)	quĭd ĭllud| mălis|t nĕqueō **|sătis|** mīrā|rī nĕquĕ |cōnĭcĕ| re|
Eun. 561	(ia⁷)	nēmos|t qu(em) ĕgŏ nun|ciam| **măgis|** cŭpĕrem| uĭdē|rĕ quam| te|
Eun. 609	(ia⁷)	perlon|gest sed| tant(o) ō|cius| prŏpĕrē|mus mū|tā ues| tem|
Eun. 656	(ia⁸)	au—ob|sēcrō |meă **Pȳ|thias|** quŏd is|tuc nam| monstrum| fuit|
Eun. 730	(ia⁸)	Chrĕmē |quĭs es|t ĕhĕm **Pȳ|thias|** uāh quan|tō nunc| formon|sior|
Eun. 753	(ia⁷)	ăbĭ tū |cistel|lam **Pȳ|thias|** dŏm(o) ec|fer cum| mŏnŭmen| tis|

Eun. 1018 (ia⁷) ĭtăn lĕpĭ|dum tĭbĭ |uĭsum|st **scĕlus**| nōs in|rīdē|rĕ nĭmi| um|

Eun. 1019 (ia⁷) sĭquĭd(em) is|tuc in|pūn(e) **hăbu|ĕris**| uērum| redd(am) her|clĕ crē|do|

Haut. 693 (ia⁷) deō|rum uī|t(am) aptī |**sŭmus**| frustr(a) ŏpĕ|r(am) ŏpī|n(o) hanc sū|mo|

Haut. 707 (ia⁷) sătĭs sā|nŭs ē|s et sō|**brius**| tŭquĭd(em) il|lum plā|nē per| dis|

Haut. 728 (ia⁷) dēcĭpi|(am) ac non| uĕniam| **Sўrus**| mĭhĭ ter|gō poe|nas pen|det|

Haut. 740 (ia⁷) ēō trans|dūcen|dast quam| r(em) **ăgis**| scĕlŭs ĕgŏ|n argen| tum cŭ|do|

Haut. 744 (ia⁷) ancil|lās om|nīs **Bac|chĭdis**| transdū|c(e) hūc ad| uōs prŏpĕ|re|

Hec. 247 (ia⁷) Phīdip|p(e) ets(i) ĕgŏ |meīs m(e) om|**nĭbus**| sci(o) ĕss(e) ad|prīm(e) ob|sĕquen|tem|

Hec. 260 (ia⁷) qu(em) ĕg(o) in|telle|x(i) ill(am) haud| **mĭnus**| quam s(e) ip|sum mag|nī făcĕ|re|

Hec. 346 (ia⁷) quĭd aĭ|s an uē|nit **Pam|phĭlus**| uēnit| dīs grā|ti(am) hăbe|o|

Hec. 357 (ia⁷) ĭtă fac|tumst quid| morb(i) es|t **fēbris**| cōtī|diā|n(a) ĭt(a) ā| iunt|

Hec. 738 (ia⁷) quō măgĭ|s omnis| res **cau|tius**| nē tĕmĕ|rĕ făci|(am) adcū|ro|

Hec. 753 (ia⁸) lĕpĭd(a) es| sed scin| quid uŏlŏ |**pŏtius**| sōdēs| făciās| quid uīs| cĕdo|

Hec. 778 (ia⁷) nōbī|s in r(e) ip|s(a) **inuē|nīmus**| porr(o) hanc| nunc ex| pĕriā|mur|

Hec. 819 (ia⁷) uxō|rem quam| numqu(am) est| **rătus**| posthac| s(e) hă-bĭtū|rum red|do|

Hec. 821 (ia⁷) hic ăde|(o) his rē|bŭs ā|**nŭlus**| fuĭt ĭnĭ|ti(um) in|uĕniun| dis|

Ph. 751 (ia⁷) mălĕ fac|t(um) ĕg(o) au|tem qu(ae) es|s(em) **ănus**| dēser|t (a) ĕgen|s ignō|ta|

Ph. 788 (ia⁷) quĭd au|tem quiă |pol meī |**pătris**| bĕnĕ par|t(a) indī|lĭgen| ter|

Ph. 791 (ia⁷) āc rē|bus **uī|liō|rĭbus**| multō |tămĕn duŏ |tălen|t(a) huī|

Ad. 254 (ia⁸) abs quī|uīs hŏmĭ|nĕ qu(om) es|t **ŏpus**| bĕnĕfĭci|(um) accĭpĕ|rĕ gau|deas|

298   *Appendix*

3.4 Category 4: Heavy Monosyllabic Elements

This group (281 instances) includes cases in which the syllable ending in -*s* occupies a monosyllabic heavy element. Syllables occupying this type of element are necessarily scanned heavy.

An. 37	(ia⁶)	scīs fē|c(i) ex ser|u(o) ŭt es|ses **lī|bertus|** mĭhi|
An. 54	(ia⁶)	d(um) aetas| **mĕtus|** măgis|ter prŏhĭ|bēban|t ītast|
An. 88	(ia⁶)	ămā|bant ĕhŏ |quid **Pam|phĭlus|** quid sym|bŏlam|
An. 99	(ia⁶)	quid uer|bīs ŏpŭ|s est hac| fām(a) **in|pulsus|** Chrĕmes|
An. 105	(ia⁶)	**Chrīsis|** uīcī|n(a) haec mŏrĭ|tur ō |factum| bĕne|
An. 192	(ia⁸)	ĭt(a) ā|iunt tum| **sīquis|** măgis|trum cē|pĭt ăd e|am r(em) in|prŏbum|
An. 228	(tr⁷)	audī|u(i) **Archy|lis** iam|dūdum| Lesbi|(am) addū|cī iŭ|bes
An. 258	(tr⁷)	quod s(i) ĕgŏ |rescis|s(em) id priŭs| quid făcĕ|rem **sī|quis** nunc| mē rŏ|get
An. 303	(ia⁸)	ŭt ănĭ|mŭs in| sp(e) atqu(e) in| tĭmō|r(e) usqu(e) an|t(e) hac **at|tentus|** fuit|
An. 304	(ia⁸)	ĭtă pos|tqu(am) ădem|ptă spē|s est las|sus cū|ra **con|fec-tus|** stŭpet|
An. 325	(tr⁷)	num quid| n(am) **ampli|us** tĭbĭ |c(um) illā |fŭĭt Chă|rīn(e) ăhă |Pamphĭ|le
An. 330	(tr⁷)	ĕgŏ Chă|rīnĕ |n(e) ŭtĭqu(am) of|fĭcium| lĭbĕ|r(i) ess(e) **hŏmĭ|nis** pŭ|to
An. 331	(tr⁷)	qu(om) is nil| mĕreat| postŭ|lār(e) id| grāti|(ae) adpō|nī sĭ|bi
An. 370	(tr⁷)	lĭbĕ|rātus| s(um) hŏdiē |Dāuĕ |tu(a) ŏpĕ|r(a) ac **nul|lus** quĭ|dem
An. 377	(tr⁷)	ipsŭs sĭ|b(i) ess(e) **in|iūri|us** uĭde|ātur| nĕqu(e) ĭd in|iūri|a
An. 393	(ia⁶)	haec quae |**făcis|** n(e) is mū|tet sŭām| senten|tiam|
An. 401	(ia⁸)	nam **pol|lĭcĭtus|** sum sus|ceptū|r(um) ō făcĭ|nŭs au|dax hanc| fĭdem|
An. 462	(ia⁶)	sĕd hĭc **Pam|phĭlus|** quid dī|cit fir|māuit| fĭd(em) hem|
An. 496	(ia⁸)	inter|mĭnā|tus sum| nē făcĕ|res num| **uĕrĭtus|** quĭd rē | tŭlit|
An. 507	(ia⁸)	sed nī|lō **sē|tius|** rĕfĕrē|tur mo|x huc puĕ|r ant(e) os|tium|
An. 536	(ia⁸)	auscul|tā pau|c(a) et quĭd ĕ|go tē |uĕl(im) et| tū quod| **quaeris|** scies|
An. 556	(ia⁶)	(em) id t(e) ō|r(o) ŭt an|t(e) eā|mus dum| **tempus|** dătur|
An. 567	(ia⁶)	nemp(e) in|commŏdĭ|tās dē|nĭqu(e) hŭ|c **omnis|** rĕdit|
An. 653	(ia⁸)	sciŏ cum| pătr(e) al|tercas|tī dū|d(um) ĕt is| nunc prop| tĕreā |tĭbi|

An. 669	(ia⁶)	dēcep|tus s(um) at| non dē|fĕtī|gātus| scio|
An. 677	(ia⁶)	căpĭtis| pĕrī|cl(um) ădī|rĕ dum| prōsim| tĭbi|
An. 686	(ia⁷)	Mȳsis| quĭs es|t ĕhĕm Pam|phĭl(e) op|tumē |mĭhĭ t(e) of| fers quĭd ĭ|d est|
An. 705	(ia⁷)	sat hăbe|ō quid| făcies| cĕdŏ di|es m(i) ut| **satis**| sit uĕre|or|
An. 731	(ia⁶)	mŏu(e) ō|cius| t(e) ut quĭd ă|gam por|r(o) intel|lĕgas|
An. 748	(ia⁶)	ĕhŏ Mȳ|sis puĕ|r hic un|dest **quis|u(e)** hūc at|tŭlit|
An. 753	(ia⁶)	ūnum| praeter| quam quod| tē rŏgŏ |**faxis**| căue|
An. 778	(ia⁶)	tū pŏl hŏ|mō nō|n es sō|brius| fallā|cia|
An. 793	(ia⁶)	ut scī|ret haec| quae **uŏlu|ĭmus**| praedī|cĕres|
An. 798	(ia⁶)	**pŏtius**| qu(am) hŏnes|t(e) in pătri|ā pau|per uī|uĕret|
An. 843	(tr⁷)	und(e) ē|grĕdĭtur| meŏ prae|sĭdi(o) at|qu(e) **hospĭ|tis** quĭd ĭl|lud mă|list
An. 851	(tr⁷)	cum tū͡o g|nāt(o) ū|n(a) ann(e) es|t intus| **Pamphĭ|lus** crŭci|or mĭ|ser
An. 855	(tr⁷)	**nesciŏ|quis** sĕ|nex mŏdŏ |uēnĭ|t ellum| confi|dens că|tus
An. 860	(tr⁷)	Drŏmŏ Drŏ|mō quĭ|d est Drŏ|m(o) audī |uerbum| s(i) **addĭdĕ|ris** Drŏ|mo
An. 887	(ia⁶)	quor meăm| sĕnĕctū|t(em) **huius**| sollĭcĭ|t(o) āmen|tia|
An. 923	(tr⁷)	**Attĭ|cus** quī|d(am) ōlim| nāuī |fract(a) ă|d Andr(um) ē|iectŭ|s est
An. 925	(tr⁷)	prīm(um) ad| **Chrȳsĭ|dis** pă|trem sē |fābŭ|l(am) incep|tat sĭ|ne
An. 926	(tr⁷)	ĭtănĕ |uĕr(o) ob|turbat| pergĕ |t(um) is mĭhĭ |cognā|tus fu|it
An. 926	(tr⁷)	ĭtănĕ |uĕr(o) ob|turbat| pergĕ |t(um) is mĭhĭ |**cognā|tus** fu|it
An. 957	(ia⁸)	prōuī|sō quĭd ă|gat Pam|philūs| atqu(e) ec|c(um) **ălĭquis**| fors mē |pŭtet|
An. 967	(tr⁷)	et quī|d(em) ĕgŏ mŏ|r(e) hŏmĭn(um) ē|uēni|t ut quod| sim **nan|ctus** mă|li
An. 970	(tr⁷)	pătĕr ă|mīcus| summus| nōbīs| **quis** Chrĕ|mes nar|rās prŏ|be
Eun. 12	(ia⁶)	qu(am) illic| quī pĕtĭ|t und(e) is| sit then|saurus| sĭbi|
Eun. 12	(ia⁶)	qu(am) illic| quī pĕtĭ|t und(e) is| sit **then|saurus**| sĭbi|
Eun. 30	(ia⁶)	Cŏlax| Mĕnan|drist ĭn e|ast **pără|sītus** cŏlax|
Eun. 45	(ia⁶)	ut per|noscā|tis quid| sĭb(i) **Eu|nūchus**| uĕlit|
Eun. 50	(ia⁶)	sĭquĭd(em) her|clĕ pos|sis nil| **prius**| nĕquĕ for|tius|
Eun. 73	(ia⁶)	**uīuos**| uĭden|squĕ pĕre|ō nec| quĭd ăgam| scio|
Eun. 105	(ia⁶)	**plēnus**| rīmā|rum s(um) hā|c atqu(e) il|lac per|fluo|
Eun. 122	(ia⁶)	nĕquĕ t(u) ū|n(o) ĕras| conten|tă nĕquĕ |**sŏlus**| dĕdit|
Eun. 169	(ia⁶)	hĕrī |mĭnās| uĭgin|tī pr(o) **am|bōbus**| dĕdi|
Eun. 190	(ia⁶)	ĭn hŏc bī|duom| **Thāis**| uălē |mī Phae|dria|

Eun. 228   (tr⁷)   sed quĭs hĭ|c est qu(i) huc| pergĭ|t attă|t hĭcquĭd(em) est|
                     părăsī|tus Gnă|tho

Eun. 229   (tr⁷)   **mīlĭ|tis** dū|cit sē|c(um) ūnā |uirgĭ|nem dō|n(o) hūĭc pă|
                     pae

Eun. 272   (ia⁷)   num quid| n(am) hic quod| **nōlis|** uĭdēs| tē crē|d(o) at
                     num|quĭd ăli|ud|

Eun. 287   (ia⁷)   **nēquis|** fort(e) in|ternun|tius| cl(am) ā mī|lĭt(e) ăd ĭs|tam
                     cur|set|

Eun. 317   (ia⁸)   ĭtăqu(e) er|g(o) ăman|tur quid| tu(a) is|taec nŏuă |fĭgū|r
                     (a) ōris| păpae|

Eun. 327   (ia⁶)   **pătris|** cognā|t(um) atqu(e) ae|quāl(em) Ar|chĭdē|mĭdes|

Eun. 353   (tr⁷)   quĭs ĭs es|t tam pŏ|tens cum| tantō |mūnĕ|r(e) hoc **mī|les**
                     Thră|so

Eun. 379   (ia⁸)   quō trū|dis **per|cŭlĕris|** iam tū |mē tĭb(i) ĕ|quĭdem| dīcō |
                     măne|

Eun. 384   (ia⁸)   hăbĕnt des|pĭcā|t(am) et quae |nōs sem|pĕr **om|nĭbus|**
                     crŭcian|t mŏdis|

Eun. 391   (ia⁶)   magnas| uēr(o) ăgĕ|rĕ grā|tias| **Thāis|** mĭhi|

Eun. 394   (ia⁶)   trium|phat hoc| prŏuī|s(o) ŭt ŭbĭ |**tempus|** siet|

Eun. 412   (ia⁶)   ill(i) in|uĭdē|rĕ mĭsĕ|rē uē|r(um) **ūnus|** tămen|

Eun. 455   (ia⁶)   atqu(e) ec|cum sal|ue mī |Thrăs(o) ō |**Thāis|** mea|

Eun. 470   (ia⁶)   exī|rĕ quos| iuss(i) ō|cius| prōcē|dĕ t(u) huc|

Eun. 507   (ia⁶)   prŏfec|tō quan|tō măgĕ |**măgis|quĕ** cō|gĭto |

Eun. 535   (ia⁶)   dum rĕde|at ip|să nil| **mĭnus|** quor mī |Chrĕmes|

Eun. 541   (ia⁷)   **praefē|cĭmus|** dăt(i) ā|nŭlī |lŏcŭs tem|pus con|stĭtū|
                     tumst|

Eun. 570   (ia⁸)   nĕqu(e) **is|** dēduc|tŭs ĕti|amd(um) ăd e|am sub|mŏnuit|
                     mē Par|mĕno|

Eun. 575   (ia⁸)   num par|uă cau|s(a) aut prā|uă răti|ost **trā|dĭtus|** sum
                     mŭli|ĕri|

Eun. 577   (ia⁸)   commen|dat uir|gĭnem| quōī tĭbĭ|nĕ mĭhĭ |**sătis|** tūtō |
                     tămen|

Eun. 598   (ia⁷)   qu(i) esset| **stătus|** flābel|lŭlum| tĕnē|rĕ t(e) ăsĭ|num tan|
                     tum|

Eun. 611   (ia⁷)   n(e) **intus|** sit por|r(o) autem| păter| nē rū|rĕ rĕdi|ĕrit|
                     iam|

Eun. 648   (ia⁸)   ŭt ĕg(o) **un|guĭbus|** făcĭl(e) il|l(i) ĭn ŏcŭ|lōs in|uŏlem|
                     uĕnē|fĭco|

Eun. 654   (tr⁸)   uirgĭ|nem qu(am) ĕ|rae dō|nō dĕdĕ|rat **mī|les** uĭti|āuit|
                     quĭd ais|

Eun. 662   (ia⁸)   quŏ—il|l(e) ăbĭ|r(e) ignā|uos pos|sĭt **lon|gius|** nĭsĭ sī |
                     dŏmum|

Eun. 671   (ia⁶)   quĭd hŭc tĭbĭ |rĕdĭti|ost quid| **uestis|** mūtā|tio|

Eun. 683	(ia⁶)	dūdum| quiă uări|ā ues|t(e) **exor|nātus**| fuit|
Eun. 688	(ia⁶)	hic es|t uiē|tus uĕtŭs| **uĕter|nōsus**| sĕnex|
Eun. 701	(ia⁶)	dīcē|bat (eūm) es|sĕ—is| dĕdit| m(i) hanc oc|cĭdi|
Eun. 776	(ia⁸)	cĕd(o) ăli|ōs ŭbĭ |centŭri|ost San|g(a) et **mănĭ|pŭlus**| fūr (um) ec|c(um) ădest|
Eun. 778	(ia⁸)	ĕgŏn **im|pĕrā|tōris**| uirtū|tem nō|uĕr(am) et| uim mī| lītum|
Eun. 781	(ia⁸)	t(u) hosc(e) in|stru(e) ĕg(o) hĭ|c ĕrŏ pos|t princĭpi|(a) ind(e) **om|nĭbus**| signum| dăbo|
Eun. 788	(tr⁷)	sĕd ĕccam| Thāĭ|d(em) ipsam| uĭdeŏ |quam mo|x **inruĭ**| **mus** mă|ne
Eun. 823	(ia⁶)	fuis|sĕ **quis**| fuĭt ĭgĭ|tŭr is|tĕ Chae|rea|
Eun. 878	(ia⁶)	mē non| fēcis|sĕ cau|sā sĕd ă|**mōris**| scio|
Eun. 890	(ia⁶)	**cīuis**| mŏd(o) haec| sit paul|lŭl(um) op|**pĕrī|rier**|
Eun. 901	(ia⁶)	non făci|am **Pȳ|thias**| non crē|dō Chae|rea|
Eun. 1023	(ia⁷)	**nullus**| s(um) hic pr(o) il|lō mū|nĕrē |tĭb(i) hŏnō|s est hăbĭ|tus ăbe|o|
Eun. 1039	(ia⁸)	**Thāis**| pătrī |sē com|mendā|uĭt in| clien|tel(am) et| fĭdem|
Eun. 1048	(ia⁸)	an mēĩ |**pătris**| festī|uĭtā|t(em) et făcĭ|lĭtā|t(em) ō Iup| pĭter|
Eun. 1052	(tr⁷)	**digni|us** quŏd ă|mētŭ|r ĭtă nos|tr(ae) omnist| fautrix| fămĭli|(ae) hūĩ
Eun. 1081	(tr⁷)	quĭd **ăgĭ|mus** prae|tĕre(a) hō|c ĕtiam| quŏd ĕgo |uel prī| mum pŭ|to
Haut. 37	(ia⁶)	nē sem|per ser|uos cur|rens ī|**rātus**| sĕnex|
Haut. 55	(ia⁶)	nēc rēĩ| fĕrē |sān(e) **am|plius**| quicquam| fuit|
Haut. 73	(ia⁶)	quŏd ĭn ŏpĕ|rĕ făci|und(o) ŏpĕ|rae **con|sūmis**| tuae|
Haut. 104	(ia⁶)	ămī|c(am) ŭt hăbe|as prŏpĕ |i(am) ĭn u|xōris| lŏco|
Haut. 198	(ia⁸)	uĕreor| quam nē|quĭd ĭn ĭl|l(um) īrā|tus plus| **sătis**| faxit| păter|
Haut. 208	(ia⁸)	uĕr(um) ŭb(i) ă|**nĭmus**| sĕmel| sē cŭpĭ|dĭtā|tĕ dē|uinxit| măla|
Haut. 219	(ia⁸)	nōn ut| **meus**| quī mĭhĭ |pĕr ăli|(um) osten|dit sŭām| senten|tiam|
Haut. 220	(ia⁸)	pĕri(i) **is**| m(i) ŭb(i) ad|bĭbit| plus paul|lō suă |quae nar| rat făcĭ|nŏra|
Haut. 226	(ia⁸)	hăbet| bĕn(e) et| pŭdī|c(e) ēduc|t(am) ignā|r(am) **artis**| mĕrĕtrī|ciae|
Haut. 290	(ia⁶)	căpil|lus pe|xus **prō|lixus**| circum| căput|
Haut. 296	(ia⁶)	uĕr(a) ĭt(a) ŭ|tī crē|dō **quis**| t(e) est for|tūnā|tior|
Haut. 299	(ia⁶)	qu(om) **eius**| tam nē|glĕgun|tŭr in|ternun|tii|
Haut. 304	(ia⁶)	ŭbĭ **dī|cĭmus**| rĕdis|sĕ t(e) ĕt| rŏgā|r(e) ŭti|
Haut. 311	(ia⁶)	**addū|cĭmus** tŭām Bac|chĭd(em) hem| quid Bac|chĭdem|

Haut. 421 (ia⁶) **nātus**| s(um) aut il|lud fal|sumst quod| uolg(o) au|dio|

Haut. 439 (ia⁶) non pos|sum sătĭs| iam sătĭs| păter| **dūrus**| fu(i) ah|

Haut. 449 (ia⁶) hăbē|rī quid|uis dărĕ |**cŭpis**| n(am) ut tu s|cias|

Haut. 459 (ia⁶) pătĕr hō|c est ăli|ŭd lē|**nius**| sōdes| uĭde|

Haut. 486 (ia⁶) tū rem| pĕrĭ|r(e) ĕt ip|sum non| **pŏtĕris**| păti|

Haut. 509 (ia⁶) Sўrŭs est| prenden|dŭs at|qu(e) **ădhor|tandus**| mĭhi|

Haut. 527 (ia⁶) uīcī|n(um) hunc nos|tīn at| quăs(i) **is**| non dī|tiis|

Haut. 540 (ia⁶) iam—huîc| mansis|set **ū|nĭcus**| gnātus| dŏmi|

Haut. 540 (ia⁶) iam—huîc| mansis|set ū|nĭcus| **gnātus**| dŏmi|

Haut. 558 (ia⁶) **uĭdē|bĭmus**| quĭd ŏpus| sit nun|c istū|c ăge|

Haut. 594 (tr⁷) fiet| sī săpi|as nam| mĭhĭ iam| mĭnŭs mĭ|**nusqu(e)** ob| tempĕ|rat

Haut. 600 (tr⁷) uāh uĭdĕ |quŏd ĭncep|tet **făcĭ|nus** fuît| quaed(am) ă|nus Cŏ|rinthi|a

Haut. 600 (tr⁷) uāh uĭdĕ |quŏd ĭncep|tet făcĭ|nus fuît| quaed(am) **ă|nus** Cŏ|rinthi|a

Haut. 614 (ia⁸) nĭsĭ m(e) ănĭ|mus fal|lĭt hic| prōfec|tost **ā|nŭlus**| qu(em) ĕgŏ sus|pĭcor|

Haut. 616 (ia⁸) quĭd ĕst **is|ne** tĭbĭ |uĭdē|tur di|x(i) ĕquĭd(em) ŭbĭ |m(i) osten|dist(i) ī|lĭco |

Haut. 637 (tr⁷) ăt ĭd ŏ|mittō |mĭsĕrĭ|cordi|(a) ănĭmus| **māter|nus** sĭ|no

Haut. 662 (tr⁷) nōmen| **mŭliĕ|ris** cĕdŏ |quid sī|t ut quae|rātur| Philtĕ|rae

Haut. 698 (ia⁷) s(i) **abdu|xĕris**| cēlā|bĭtūr| ĭtĭd(em) ut| cēlā|t(a) ădhū|c est|

Haut. 733 (ia⁷) currĭcŭ|lō per|curr(e) ăpŭ|d eum| **mīles**| Diŏnў|si(a) ăgĭ|tat|

Haut. 805 (ia⁶) nullast| tam făcĭ|lis rēs| quin **dif|fĭcĭlis**| siet|

Haut. 824 (ia⁶) **lūdis**| fortas|sĕ m(e) ip|sā r(e) ex|pĕrī|bĕre|

Haut. 832 (ia⁶) quīn **ac|cĭpis**| cĕdŏ sā|nē sĕquĕ|r(e) hac m(e) ō|cius|

Haut. 841 (ia⁶) **ălĭquis**| lăbō|r(e) inuen|tă meă |quoî dem| bŏna|

Haut. 857 (ia⁶) dătū|r(um) āh frus|trā s(um) ĭgĭ|tur **gā|uīsus**| mĭser|

Haut. 867 (ia⁶) tant(o) ō|cius| t(e) ut pos|cat et| t(u) id quod| **cŭpis**|

Haut. 896 (tr⁷) mĭră |narrās| quid Sў|rus meûs| n(e) is quĭ|dem quic| quam nĭ|hil

Haut. 896 (tr⁷) mĭră |narrās| quid Sў|rus meûs| n(e) **is** quĭ|dem quic| quam nĭ|hil

Haut. 901 (tr⁷) quĭd ĕst quŏ|d **ampli|us** sĭmŭ|lētur| uāh quĭ|d est au|dī mŏ|do

Haut. 902 (tr⁷) est mĭ|h(i) ultĭ|mīs con|clāu(e) ĭ|n **aedĭ|bus** quod|dam rĕ|tro

Haut. 914 (ia⁶) quidnĭ |quō uer|bă **făcĭ|lius**| dentur| mĭhi|

Haut. 917 (ia⁶) n(i) essem| **lăpis**| quae uĭ|dī uae |mĭsĕrō |mĭhi|

Haut. 968 (tr⁷) uictus| **uestī|tus** qu(o) in| tectum| tē rĕ|ceptĕ|s eî mĭ|hi

Haut. 1010 (ia⁸) ĭmmŏ scis| **pŏtius**| quam quĭdĕm| rĕdeā|t ăd in|tegr(um) eă|d(em) ōrā|ti(o) oh|

Haut. 1025 (tr⁷) fuĕrim| dictus| **fili|us** tuŏs| uostrā |uŏlŭntā|t(e) obsĕ|cro

Haut. 1039 (tr⁷) quaerĭ|s id quŏd hă|bes pă|rentēs| quŏd ăbes|t non **quae**| ris pă|tri

Hec. 6 (ia⁶) ĕt is| qui scrip|sĭt han|c ŏb eam| rem nō|luit|

Hec. 60 (ia⁶) uĕl hĭc **Pam|phĭlus**| iūrā|bat quŏti|ens Bac|chĭdi|

Hec. 104 (ia⁶) nōn es|t **ŏpus**| prōlā|t(o) hoc per|contā|rier|

Hec. 121 (ia⁶) pătĕr in|stat fē|cit ănĭ|m(i) ŭt in|**certus**| fŏret|

Hec. 144 (ia⁶) post **Pam|phĭlus**| mē sō|lum sē|dūcit| fŏras|

Hec. 171 (ia⁶) intĕre|(a) ĭn Im|brō mŏrĭ|tur **cog|nātus**| sĕnex|

Hec. 286 (tr⁷) nam nō|s omnēs| quĭbŭs es|t ălĭcun|d(e) ălĭquĭ|s **obiec|tus** lă|bos

Hec. 302 (ia⁸) t(um) uxō|r(i) **obno|xius**| s(um) ĭt(a) ō|lim sū͡o |m(e) ingēni|ō per|tŭlit|

Hec. 308 (ia⁸) făciun|t nam sae|p(e) est quĭbŭ|s in rē|bŭs ăli|us n(e) ī| **rātus**| quĭd(em) est|

Hec. 319 (ia⁸) **nullus**| sum quĭ|dum pĕri|ī qu(am) ŏb| rem nes|ciŏquod| magnum| mălum|

Hec. 330 (ia⁶) sī for|te mor|bŭs am|plior| **factus**| siet|

Hec. 344 (ia⁷) lābō|r(em) ĭnā|n(em) **ipsus**| căpīt| ĕt ĭllī |mŏles|ti(am) ad| fert|

Hec. 345 (ia⁷) tum **fĭ|lius**| tuŏs in|tr(o) iit| uidē|r(e) ut uē|nit quĭd ă|gat|

Hec. 385 (tr⁷) sed qu(om) ō|rāt(a) **hui|us** rĕmĭ|niscor| nĕqueō |quin lăcrŭ|mem mĭ|ser

Hec. 402 (tr⁷) **pollĭcĭ|tus** s(um) et| seruā|r(e) ĭn eō |certumst| quod di|xī fĭ|dem

Hec. 419 (ia⁶) praetĕri|ĕris| quī num|qu(am) ēs **in|gressus**| măre|

Hec. 434 (ia⁶) pĕriī |uŏuis|s(e) hunc dī|cam sī |**saluos**| dŏmum|

Hec. 493 (ia⁶) tĭb(i) ĭd in| mănust| nē fī|at sī |**sānus**| sies|

Hec. 495 (ia⁶) **mātris**| seruī|bō com|mŏdis| quŏ—ābis| măne|

Hec. 525 (tr⁷) nam s(i) ŭ|trumuī|s hōrum| mŭlie|r umquam| tĭbĭ **uī|sus** fŏ|rem

Hec. 571 (ia⁸) sī puĕ|r(um) ut tol|lam cō|git quoi(u)s| nōs quī |sit **nes**| cīmus| păter|

Hec. 593 (ia⁸) meă cau|sā nō|lō nil| pol i(am) is|taec mĭhĭ |res **uŏlŭp**| **tātis**| fĕrunt|

Hec. 614 (tr⁷) quiă d(e) u|xōr(e) in|**certus**| s(um) ĕtiam| quid sim| **factū**| **rus** quĭ|d est

Hec. 623 (ia⁶) tĭbī |quŏqu(e) ĕdĕ|pol s(um) ī|**rātus**| Phĭlū|mĕna|

Hec. 627 (ia⁶) Phĭdip|p(e) ĭn ip|sō tem|pŏr(e) **os|tendis**| quĭd est|

Hec. 649 (ia⁶) nunc nō|n est quŏm—e|am sĕquĭ|tŭr **ăli|ēnus**| puer|

Hec. 651 (ia⁶) pĕri(i) hunc| uĭdē|rĕ sae|p(e) **optā|bāmus**| diem|

Hec. 687　(ia⁶)　**tempus**| dix(i) es|s(e) inpul|sū du|xistī |meo|

Hec. 699　(ia⁶)　nōn es|t nunc tem|pus puë|r(um) accĭpi|as n(am) **is**| quĭdem|

Hec. 739　(ia⁷)　nam s(i) id| **făcis**| factū|rău(e) es| bŏnās| quod pā|r est făcĕ|re|

Hec. 748　(tr⁷)　quïs ĭd a|it sŏ|**crus** men| t(e) ips(am) et| fīli|(am) abdu|xit su|am

Hec. 751　(tr⁷)　**sancti**|us quam| iusiū|rand(um) id| pollĭ|cērer| tĭbĭ Lă|che

Hec. 766　(tr⁷)　uĕr(um) hoc| mŏne(o) ū|num **quā**|**lis** s(im) ă|mīcŭ|s aut quid| possi|em

Hec. 767　(tr⁷)　pŏtius| qu(am) ĭnĭmī|cus pĕ|rīclum| făciās| nīl ăpŭd| mē tĭ|bi

Hec. 848　(tr⁷)　**quis** m(e) es|t fortū|nāti|or uĕnŭs|tātis|qu(e) ădeō | plēni|or

Hec. 869　(tr⁷)　imm(o) ĕti|am qu(i) ho|c occul|tārī |**făcĭli**|**us** crē|dās dă|bo

Ph. 32　(ia⁶)　quom per| tŭmul|tum nos|ter grex| **mōtus**| lŏcost|

Ph. 35　(ia⁶)　ămī|cus sum|mus meŭ|s et **pŏpŭ**|**lāris**| Gĕta|

Ph. 48　(ia⁶)　porr(o) au|t(em) ăli(o) ŭb(i) ĕ|rit puĕ|rō **nā**|**tālis**| dies|

Ph. 51　(ia⁶)　**sīquis**| mē quae|rēt rū|fus praes|tost dē|sĭn(e) oh|

Ph. 56　(ia⁶)　**sīquis**| quĭd red|dit mag|n(a) hăben|dast grā|tia|

Ph. 65　(ia⁶)　tam quam| t(e) ēuē|nit sĕnĭ|bŭs am|**bōbus**| sĭmul|

Ph. 67　(ia⁶)　ăd hos|pĭt(em) an|tīqu(om) is| sĕnem| pĕr ĕpis|tŭlas|

Ph. 89　(ia⁶)　tonstrī|n(a) ĕrat| quaed(am) hic| **sŏlē**|**bāmus**| fĕre|

Ph. 102　(ia⁶)　uoltis|**n(e)** eā|mus uī|sĕr(e) ăli|us cen|seo|

Ph. 156　(tr⁸)　quĭd ĭstuc| rŏgĭtas| quī t(am) au|dācis| **făcĭnŏ**|**ris** mĭhĭ | consci|us sis|

Ph. 156　(tr⁸)　quĭd ĭstuc| rŏgĭtas| quī t(am) au|dācis| făcĭnŏ|ris mĭhĭ | **consci**|**us** sis|

Ph. 182　(ia⁸)　nam non| pŏtest| cēlā|rī nos|tră diŭ|**tius**| i(am) audā|cia|

Ph. 184　(ia⁸)　tum **tem**|**pŏris**| mĭhĭ pun|ct(um) ăd hanc| r(em) est ĕrŭ|s ădes|t quĭd ĭlluc| mălist|

Ph. 273　(ia⁶)　sed sī|quis for|tĕ mălĭ|tiā |**frētus**| sua|

Ph. 347　(tr⁷)　s(i) eͣam sus|**tĭnuĕ**|**ris** pos|tillā |i(am) ŭt lŭ|bēt lū|dās lĭ|cet

Ph. 391　(ia⁶)　nĕqu(e) ĕg(o) il|lum nō|ram nec| mĭhĭ **cog**|**nātus**| fuit|

Ph. 406　(ia⁶)　hic d(e) eͣa|dem cau|sā **bis**| iūdĭci|(um) ădĭpis|cier|

Ph. 410　(ia⁶)　**dōtis**| dăr(e) ab|dūc(e) hanc| mĭnās| quinqu(e) ac|cĭpe|

Ph. 442　(ia⁶)　**gnātus**| quī m(e) et| s(e) hisc(e) in|pĕdī|uit nup|tiis|

Ph. 457　(ia⁶)　ĕg(o) am|**plius**| dēlī|bĕran|dum cen|seo|

Ph. 458　(ia⁶)　rēs mag|nast num|quid nōs| uïs fē|**cistis**| prŏbe|

Ph. 460　(ia⁶)　rĕdis|sĕ frā|ter es|t **exspec**|**tandus**| mĭhi|

Ph. 480	(tr⁸)	mansū|rusquĕ |pătruom| pătĕr est| d(um) hūc ad|uĕniat| quĭd (eūm) ŭt ā|ībat|
Ph. 501	(tr⁷)	mĭsĕrĭ|tumst eī |uērīs| uincor| quăm—ŭter|quest sĭmĭ|lis su|i
Ph. 506	(tr⁷)	mĭhĭn dŏ|mist im|m(o) id quŏ|d āiun|t aurĭ|bus tĕne|ō lŭ| pum
Ph. 514	(tr⁷)	sī non| tum dĕdĕ|r(o) ūnam| praetĕre|(a) hōram| n(e) opper|tus si|es
Ph. 519	(tr⁷)	nĕqu(e) ĕgo |nĕquĕ tū |dī tĭ|b(i) omnē|s id quŏ|d es dig| nus du|int
Ph. 546	(tr⁷)	sed părŭm|n(e) est quŏ|d omnĭ|bus nunc| nōbīs| suscen| set sĕ|nex
Ph. 554	(tr⁷)	nēquid| plūs mĭ|nusuĕ |faxit| quod nōs| post pĭge|at Gĕ|ta
Ph. 590	(ia⁶)	dōnec| tĭb(i) id| quod pol|lĭcĭtus| s(um) effĕ|cĕro|
Ph. 604	(ia⁶)	pĕt(am) hin|c und(e) ā |prīm(o) in|stĭt(i) is| sī dat| săt est|
Ph. 618	(ia⁶)	mĭhĭ Phor|miō |quī Phor|mi(o) is| qu(i) istanc| scio|
Ph. 628	(ia⁶)	i(am) ĭd ex|plōrā|tumst hei|ă sū|dābis| sătis|
Ph. 633	(ia⁶)	sōlī |sŭmus| nunc hī|c inqu(am) ĕhŏ |quid uīs| dări|
Ph. 639	(ia⁶)	uerb(a) hŏdi|(e) inter| uōs quis| t(e) istaec| iussīt| lŏqui|
Ph. 643	(ia⁶)	quid nĭmi|um quan|tum lĭbu|it dic| sī quis| dăret|
Ph. 675	(ia⁶)	s(i) illam| dant han|c ut mit|tam n(e) in|certus| siem|
Ph. 706	(ia⁶)	intr(o) iĭ|t ĭn ae|dīs ā|tĕr ălĭ|ēnus| cănis|
Ph. 707	(ia⁶)	anguis| pĕr ĭnplŭui|um dē|cĭdit| dē tē|gŭlis|
Ph. 743	(ia⁸)	quem sem|per t(e) es|sĕ dic|tĭtas|tī st |quĭd has| mĕtuis| forēs|
Ph. 782	(ia⁷)	nĭsĭ pros|pĭcis| nunc hinc| dŏm(um) ī|b(o) ac Phā|ni(um) ē|dŏcē|bo |
Ph. 820	(ia⁷)	laetus| s(um) ŭtŭt meae|res sē|s(e) hăben|t frātr(i) op| tĭgis|sĕ quod| uolt|
Ph. 842	(tr⁷)	quam sŭbĭ|tō me(o) ĕ|r(o) Antĭ|phōn(i) ŏpĕ |uostr(a) hun| c ŏnĕras|tis di|em
Ph. 843	(tr⁷)	quidn(am) hic| sĭbĭ uol|t nosqu(e) ă|mīcō|s ei(u)s e|xŏnĕras|tis mĕ|tu
Ph. 846	(tr⁷)	num t(u) in|tellĕ|gis quĭd hĭc| narret| num tū |nil tan| tund(em) ĕ|go
Ph. 890	(ia⁶)	nunc ges|tus mĭhĭ |uoltus|qu(e) est căpi|undus| nŏuos|
Ph. 890	(ia⁶)	nunc ges|tus mĭhĭ |uoltus|qu(e) est căpi|undus| nŏuos|
Ph. 915	(ia⁶)	sătis| sŭper|b(e) inlū|dĭtis| mē quī |rŏgas|
Ph. 915	(ia⁶)	sătis| sŭper|b(e) inlū|dĭtis| mē quī |rŏgas|
Ph. 962	(ia⁶)	t(um) hunc in|pūrā|tum pŏtĕ|rĭmus| nostrō |mŏdo|
Ph. 966	(ia⁶)	ĕgŏ rĕdĭ|gam uō|s in grā|ti(am) hoc| frētus| Chrĕme|

Ph. 1005　(ia⁶)　uxō|rem du|xit mĭ—hŏ|mō dī |mĕlius| duint|

Ad. 9　　(ia⁶)　mĕrĕtrī|c(em) in prī|mā fā|bŭl(a) eūm| **Plautus**| lŏcum|

Ad. 35　　(ia⁶)　ĕgŏ quiă |non rĕdi|it **fi|lius**| quae cō|gĭt(o) et|

Ad. 39　　(ia⁶)　părā|rĕ quod| sit cā|rius| qu(am) ipses|t sĭbi|

Ad. 127　(ia⁶)　tun **con|sŭlis**| quicqu(am) ā|h sī per|gĭs ăbi|ĕro|

Ad. 166　(ia⁸)　indig|n(um) iniū|ri(a) hā|c indig|nis qu(om) ĕgŏ|met s
　　　　　　　　　　(im) **ac|ceptus**| mŏdis|

Ad. 179　(ia⁸)　quī tĭbĭ |**măgis**| lĭcet| me(am) hăbē|rĕ prō |qu(a) ĕg(o) ar|
　　　　　　　　　　gentum| dĕdi|

Ad. 221　(ia⁸)　crēd(o) is|tuc mĕli|ŭs es|sĕ uē|r(um) ĕgŏ num|qu(am) ăde
　　　　　　　　　　(o) **as|tūtus**| fui|

Ad. 226　(ia⁸)　**ănĭmus**| tĭbĭ pen|dēt ŭb(i) ĭl|linc spē|rō rĕdi|ĕris| tămĕn
　　　　　　　　　　hō|c ăges|

Ad. 226　(ia⁸)　**ănĭmus**| tĭbĭ pen|dēt ŭb(i) ĭl|linc spē|rō **rĕdi|ĕris**| tămĕn
　　　　　　　　　　hō|c ăges|

Ad. 265　(ia⁸)　ŭb(i) ĕst il|lĕ **săcrĭ|lĕgus**| mē quae|rit num| quid n(am) ec|
　　　　　　　　　　fert oc|cĭdi|

Ad. 282　(ia⁸)　quam prī|m(um) absol|uĭtō|tĕ nē |sī măgĭ|s **irrī|tātus**| siet|

Ad. 287　(ia⁸)　ĭtă quae|sō quan|d(o) hoc bĕnĕ |succes|sĭt hĭlă|r(e) hunc
　　　　　　　　　　sū|māmus| diem|

Ad. 293　(ia⁸)　pŏl is| quĭdem| iăm—hĭc ădĕ|rit nam| numqu(am) ū|n
　　　　　　　　　　(um) inter|mittit| diem|

Ad. 313　(ia⁸)　**sătis**| mĭh(i) ĭd hă|beam| supplĭ|cī d(um) il|lōs ul|ciscar|
　　　　　　　　　　mŏdo|

Ad. 320　(ia⁸)　sed ces|s(o) ĕr(am) hoc| măl(o) in|pertĭ|rī prŏpĕ|rĕ **rĕuŏ**|
　　　　　　　　　　cēmus| Gĕt(a) hem|

Ad. 326　(tr⁷)　**Aeschĭ|nus** quĭd ĭ|s erg(o) ăli|ēnŭ|s est ab| nostrā |fămĭli|
　　　　　　　　　　(a) hem

Ad. 347　(ia⁸)　s(i) infĭti|ās ī|bit tes|tis mē|c(um) est ā|**nŭlus**| quem mī|
　　　　　　　　　　sĕrat|

Ad. 366　(ia⁶)　nil quic|quam uī|dī **lae|tius**| prō Iup|pĭter|

Ad. 411　(ia⁶)　**saluos**| sit spē|r(o) est sĭmĭ|lis mā|iōrum| su(om) hūī|

Ad. 421　(ia⁶)　**nactus**| s(um) ī mĭhĭ |nē cor|rumpan|tur cau|tiost|

Ad. 458　(ia⁶)　sī **dē|sĕris**| tū pĕri|ĭmus| căuĕ di|xĕris|

Ad. 458　(ia⁶)　sī dē|sĕris| tū **pĕri|ĭmus**| căuĕ di|xĕris|

Ad. 462　(ia⁶)　quĭd au|tem mā|ior **fi|lius**| tuŏs Aes|chĭnus|

Ad. 469　(ia⁶)　uēr(o) **am|plius**| n(am) hoc quĭdĕm| fĕrun|d(um) ălĭquō |
　　　　　　　　　　mŏdost|

Ad. 496　(ia⁶)　**fuĭmus**| pauper|tāt(em) ū|nā per|tŭlĭmus| grăuem|

Ad. 496　(ia⁶)　**fuĭmus**| pauper|tāt(em) ū|nā **per|tŭlĭmus**| grăuem|

Ad. 531　(ia⁸)　**inter|dius**| sed s(i) hic| pernoc|tō cau|sae quid| dīcam|
　　　　　　　　　　Sўre|

Ad. 635	(tr⁷)	prōdit| **nesciŏ|quis** con|cēd(am) hū|c ĭt(a) ŭtī |dixī |Sos-trǎ|ta
Ad. 670	(ia⁶)	quā rǎti|ōn(e) is|tuc **quis**| despon|dit quis| dēdit|
Ad. 670	(ia⁶)	quā rǎti|ōn(e) is|tuc quis| despon|dit **quis**| dēdit|
Ad. 671	(ia⁶)	quoî quan|dō nup|sĭt auc|tŏr his| **rēbus**| quĭs est|
Ad. 678	(ia⁶)	nostr(a) aut| quid nō|bīs c(um) il|līs **ǎbe|āmus**| quĭd est|
Ad. 704	(tr⁷)	tū **pŏti|us** deôs| conprě|cārě |nam tĭb(i) e|ōs cer|to sci|o
Ad. 752	(ia⁶)	t(u) intěr e|ās res|tim duc|tans **sal|tābis**| prŏbe|
Ad. 774	(ia⁶)	quod uix| sēdā|tum sǎtĭ|s est **pō|tātis**| scělus|
Ad. 799	(ia⁶)	quor nun|c ǎpud| tē pō|tat quor| **rěcĭpis**| meum|
Ad. 810	(ia⁶)	quod sǎtĭs| pŭtā|bas tuǎ |bŏn(a) **am|bōbus**| fŏre|
Ad. 819	(ia⁶)	et mĭh(i) ět| tĭb(i) ět il|lis **dem|psěris**| mŏles|tiam|
Ad. 853	(ia⁶)	ěgŏ sen|ti(o) ā|h pergis|**ně** iam| iam dē|sĭno|
Ad. 854	(ia⁶)	ĭ—ěrg(o) in|tr(o) et quoî |reîst eî |r(eî) hunc **sū|māmus**| diem|
Ad. 866	(tr⁷)	ěg(o) ĭll(e) ǎ|grestis| saeuos| tristis| parcus| **trŭcŭlen|tus** tě|nax
Ad. 890	(ia⁶)	accer|sant sěd ěc|cum Dē|meam| **saluos**| sies|
Ad. 893	(ia⁶)	n(am) is mĭhĭ |prōfec|tost ser|uos **spec|tātus**| sǎtis|
Ad. 907	(ia⁶)	hўměnae|um tur|bas **lam|pǎdas**| tībī|cĭnas|
Ad. 911	(ia⁶)	pǎter| lěpĭdis|sĭm(e) eū|gě iam| **lěpĭdus**| uŏcor|
Ad. 993	(tr⁷)	mĭnŭs uĭ|dētis| mǎgĭs in|pensē |cŭpĭtis| **consŭlĭ|tis** pǎ|rum

3.5 Category 5: Disyllabic Resolved Elements

This group include instances (205) in which the syllable ending in -*s* must be scanned light, since it occupies one of the two places in a disyllabic resolved element. In most cases (200) the syllable ending in -*s* occupies the second place in a resolved element. There are only five instances in which the syllable ending in -*s* occupies the first place in a disyllabic element, reported at the beginning of the list.

Syllables occupying the first place of a disyllabic resolved element (5)

An. 377	(tr⁷)	**ipsŭs** sĭ|b(i) ess(e) in|iūri|us uĭde|ātŭr| něqu(e) ĭd in|iūri|a
An. 857	(tr⁷)	**tristĭs** sě|uěrĭ|tās ĭ|nest in| uolt(u) at|qu(e) in uer|bīs fĭ|des
Haut. 339	(tr⁷)	sĭně pě|rīcl(o) es|s(e) **hūiŭs** mŏ|d(i) obsě|cr(o) ǎlĭquid| rěpěrī |maxŭ|me
Haut. 812	(ia⁶)	**huiŭs** mŏ|dī mĭhĭ |res sem|per com|mĭnis|cěre|
Ph. 529	(tr⁷)	n(am) hic m(e) **hui|ŭs** mŏdi s|cība|t ess(e) ěgŏ –| hunc es| s(e) ǎlĭter| crēdĭ|di

308   *Appendix*

Syllables occupying the second place of a disyllabic resolved element (200)

An. 131	(ia⁶)	sătĭs cum| pĕrī|cl(o) ĭbĭ t(um) e|xănĭmā|tus Pam|phĭlus|
An. 150	(ia⁶)	sătĭs uĕhĕ|mens cau|s(a) ăd ob|iurgan|dum quī |cĕdo|
An. 230	(tr⁷)	nec sătĭs| dignă |quoî com|mittās| prīmō |partū |mŭlĭĕ| rem
An. 239	(ia⁸)	praescis|sĕ m(e) an|tĕ non|nĕ priŭs| commū|nĭcā|t(um) ŏpor|tuit|
An. 258	(tr⁷)	quod s(i) ĕgŏ |rescis|s(em) id priŭs| quid făcĕ|rem sī|quis nunc| mē rŏ|get
An. 262	(ia⁸)	tum pătrĭs| pŭdor| quī mē |tam lē|nī pas|sŭs es|t ănĭm(o) us|qu(e) ădhuc|
An. 311	(ia⁸)	uĭde(o) om|nĭ(a) ex|pĕrī|rī cer|tumst priŭs| quam pĕre|ō quĭd hĭ|c ăgit|
An. 337	(tr⁷)	nĭs(i) ea |quae nī|l ŏpŭs sun|t scīrĕ |fŭgĭn hin|c ĕgŏ uē|r(o) ac lŭ|bens
An. 353	(tr⁷)	tuŏs pă|ter mŏdŏ |mē prĕ|hendĭ|t aît tĭ|b(i) uxō|rem dă|re
An. 378	(tr⁷)	priŭs quam| t(u͡om) ut sē|s(e) hăbea|t ănĭm(um) ad| nup|ti|ās per|spexĕ|rit
An. 412	(ia⁶)	ĕrŭs mē |rĕlic|tīs rē|bus ius|sit Pam|phĭlum|
An. 423	(ia⁶)	sum uē|rŭs ĕrŭs| quant(um) au|di(o) u|xōr(e) ex|cĭdit|
An. 424	(ia⁶)	ī nun|ci(am) in|trō n(e) in| mŏrā |qu(om) ŏpŭs sit| sies|
An. 503	(ia⁸)	cert(e) ĕnĭm| sciō |non sătĭs| mē per|nost(i) ĕti|am quā|lis sim| Sīmo|
An. 558	(ia⁶)	priŭs qu(am) hā|rum scĕlĕ|r(a) ĕt lăcrŭ|mae con|fictae | dŏlis|
An. 577	(ia⁷)	ĕt ĭs mĭhĭ |persuā|det nup|tiās| quantum| que(am) ut| mātŭ|rem|
An. 651	(ia⁸)	meŭs car|nufex| quĭd ĭstuc| tam mī|rumst dē |tē s(i) e| xemplum| căpit|
An. 655	(ia⁶)	imm(o) ĕti|am quō |tū mĭnŭs| scīs ae|rumnās| meas|
An. 664	(ia⁸)	nĭsĭ mĭhĭ |deos sătĭs| sciō |fuis|s(e) īrā|tos qu(i) aus|cultā| uĕrim|
An. 673	(ia⁶)	imm(o) ĕti|am nam| sătĭs crē|dō s(i) ad|uĭgĭlā|uĕris|
An. 691	(ia⁷)	quĭbŭs quĭdĕm| quam făcĭ|lĕ pŏtu|ĕrat| quies|cī s(i) hic| quies|set|
An. 728	(ia⁶)	quiă sī |fort(e) ŏpŭs| sĭt ăd ĕ|rum iŭ|randum| mĭhi|
An. 736	(ia⁶)	ōrā|tiō|n(i) ut quom|qu(e) ŏpŭs sit| uerbis| uĭde|
An. 738	(ia⁶)	quod me(a) ŏ|pĕr(a) ŏpŭs| sit uŏ|bīs ut| tū plŭs| uĭdes|
An. 740	(ia⁶)	reuor|tor pos|tquam qu(ae) ŏpŭs| fuĕ|r(e) ad nup|tias|
An. 758	(ia⁶)	in quĭbŭs| sīc in|lūdā|tis uē|n(i) in tem|pŏre|
An. 820	(tr⁷)	sătĭs iam| sătĭs Sī|mō spec|tāt(a) er|gā t(e) ă|mīcĭti|ast me|a

An. 820	(tr⁷)	sătĭs iam| **sătĭs** Sĭ|mō spec|tāt(a) er|gā t(e) ă|mīcĭti|ast me|a
An. 821	(tr⁷)	sătĭs pĕ|rīcl(i) in|cēp(i) ă|dīr(e) ō|randī |iam fi|nem fă|ce
An. 934	(ia⁸)	quī crē|dis Phā|ni(a) il|lic frā|ter **meŭs**| fuit| nōr(am) et| scio|
An. 968	(tr⁷)	priŭs res|ciscĕ|res tū |qu(am) ĕg(o) ĭllud| quod tĭ|b(i) ēuē| nit bŏ|ni
Eun. 196	(ia⁶)	**meŭs** fac| sīs pos|trēm(o) ănĭ|mus quan|d(o) ĕgŏ sum| tuos|
Eun. 220	(ia⁸)	**ŏpŭs** făci|(am) ut dē|fētī|gĕr us|qu(e) ingrā|tiī|s ut dor| miam|
Eun. 222	(ia⁸)	eĭci|und(a) her|cl(e) haec est| mollĭti|ēs ănĭ|mī **nĭmĭs**| m(e) indul|geo|
Eun. 265	(ia⁷)	uĭdĕn ō|ti(um) et| **cĭbŭs** quid| făcīt| ăliē|nus sĕd ĕ|gŏ ces|so|
Eun. 310	(ia⁸)	qu(om) in cel|lŭl(am) ad| tē **pătrĭs**| pĕn(um) om|nem con| gĕrē|bam clan|cŭlum|
Eun. 333	(ia⁶)	nĭsĭ nunc| quom mĭnĭ|mē uel|lem mĭnĭ|mēqu(e) **ŏpŭs**| fuit|
Eun. 372	(ia⁸)	t(u) illis| fruā|rĕ com|mŏdis| **quĭbŭs** t(u) il|lum dī|cēbas| mŏdo|
Eun. 426	(ia⁶)	**lĕpŭs** tū|te's pul|pāmen|tum quae|rĭs ha|hăhae|
Eun. 428	(ia⁶)	tuŏmn(e) ob|sĕcrō |t(e) hoc dic|t(um) ĕrat| **uĕtŭs** crē|dĭdi|
Eun. 476	(ia⁶)	tăcent| **sătĭs** lau|dant fac| pĕrī|cl(um) in lit|tĕris|
Eun. 479	(ia⁶)	ĕg(o) il|l(um) eūnū|chum s(i) **ŏpŭs**| siet| uel sō|brius|
Eun. 541	(ia⁷)	praefē|cĭmus| dăt(i) ā|nŭlī |**lŏcŭs** tem|pus con|stĭtū|tumst|
Eun. 548	(ia⁷)	nĭsĭ quid|quĭd est| prŏcŭl hinc| lŭbet| **priŭs** quid| sit scīs| cĭtā|ri|
Eun. 645	(tr⁷)	quīn ĕti|(am) insŭ|per **scĕlŭs**| postquam| lūdĭfĭ|cātust| uirgĭ|nem
Eun. 660	(ia⁸)	ill(e) au|tem **bŏnŭs**| uir nus|qu(am) appā|ret ĕti|(am) hoc mĭsĕ|rā sus|pĭcor|
Eun. 688	(ia⁶)	hic est| uiē|tus **uĕtŭs**| uĕter|nōsus| sĕnex|
Eun. 703	(tr⁷)	iam **sătĭs**| crēdis| sōbri|(am) essĕ |m(e) et nil| mentī|tam tĭ|bi
Eun. 704	(tr⁷)	iam **sătĭs**| certumst| uirgĭ|nem uĭti|āt(am) es|s(e) ăgĕ nunc| bēlu|a
Eun. 729	(ia⁸)	postquam| surre|xī nĕquĕ |pēs nĕquĕ |mens **sătĭs** su(om) of|fĭcium| făcit|
Eun. 737	(ia⁸)	corre|xit mī|les quŏd ĭn|telle|xī **mĭnŭs**| nam m(e) ex|trūsit| fŏras|
Eun. 751	(tr⁷)	ăt ĕnĭm| căuĕ nē |**priŭs** qu(am) han|c ā m(e) ac|cĭpiā|s āmit|tas Chrĕ|me

Eun. 760   (tr⁷)   **mĭnŭs** pŏ|tens quam| tū mĭnŭs| nōtus| mĭnŭs ă|mīcō|r
(um) hīc hă|bens

Eun. 760   (tr⁷)   mĭnŭs pŏ|tens quam| tū **mĭnŭs|** nōtus| mĭnŭs ă|mīcō|r
(um) hīc hă|bens

Eun. 770   (tr⁷)   pĕri(i) hūī|c ipsis|t **ŏpŭs** pă|trōnō |quem dē|fensō|rem
pă|ro

Eun. 786   (ia⁸)   nē mĕtu|ās quid| uĭdē|tur fun|dam tĭbĭ |nunc **nĭmĭs|** uel-
lem| dări|

Eun. 1010 (ia⁷)   non pos|sum **sătĭs|** narrā|rĕ quos| lūdos| praebuĕ|ris
in|tus|

Eun. 1027 (tr⁷)   quī **mĭnŭs|** qu(am) Hercŭ|les ser|uīui|t Omphă|l(ae)
exem|plum plă|cet

Eun. 1035 (ia⁸)   inuen|tŏr in|ceptor| perfec|tor scīs| m(e) in **quĭbŭs|** sim
gau|diis|

Eun. 1051 (tr⁷)   gaude|ō **sătĭs|** crēdō |nīl est| Thāĭ|d(e) hac frā|ter tu|a

Eun. 1053 (tr⁷)   mĭh(i) ĭllam| laudās| pĕriī |quantō |**mĭnŭs** spēīst| tantō |
măgĭs ă|mo

Eun. 1085 (tr⁷)   rĕcĭpi|ātis| **sătĭs** di|(u) hoc iam| saxum| uorsō |rĕcĭpĭ|mus

Haut. 22   (ia⁶)   tum quod| mălĕuŏ|lus **uĕtŭs|** poē|tă dic|tĭtat|

Haut. 71   (ia⁶)   haec non| uŏlŭptā|tī tĭbi) ĕs|sĕ **sătĭs|** certo s|ci(o) at|

Haut. 96   (ia⁶)   est ē |Cŏrin|th(o) hīc ad|uĕn(a) **ănŭs|** pauper|cŭla|

Haut. 150 (ia⁶)   nĭs(i) ŭb(i) il|l(e) huc sal|uos rĕdi|ĕrit| **meŭs** par|tĭceps|

Haut. 153 (ia⁶)   tractā|ret uĕ|rum nec| t(u) illum| **sătĭs** nō|uĕras|

Haut. 171 (ia⁶)   nīl **ŏpŭs|** fuit| mŏnĭtō|rĕ iam|dūdum| dŏmi|

Haut. 192 (ia⁸)   quid nar|rat quĭd ĭl|lĕ mĭsĕ|rum s(e) es|sĕ mĭsĕ|rum quem|
mĭnŭs crē|dĕrest|

Haut. 194 (ia⁸)   păren|tis pătri|(am) incŏlŭ|m(em) ămī|cōs **gĕnŭs|** cognā|
tōs dī|tias|

Haut. 205 (ia⁸)   ūniŭs| mŏdī |sunt fer|mē paul|lō qu(i) es|t hŏmō |tŏlĕrā|
bĭlis|

Haut. 237 (ia⁸)   pergĭn ĭs|tuc **priŭs|** dīiū|dĭcā|rĕ quam| scīs quid| uĕrī |siet|

Haut. 264 (ia⁸)   qu(ae) hic **sŭmŭs|** lŏcū|tī Clī|ni(a) ălĭ|ter tu(om) ă|mōr
(em) at|qu(e) est ac|cĭpis|

Haut. 276 (ia⁶)   **ănŭs** quae|dam prō|dĭt hae|c ŭb(i) ăpĕru|ĭt os|tium|

Haut. 278 (ia⁶)   **ănŭs** fŏrĭ|bŭs ob|dit pes|sŭl(um) ăd| lānam| rĕdit|

Haut. 337 (tr⁷)   nil **sătĭs|** firmī |uĭdeō |qu(am) ob r(em) ac|cĭpĕr(e) hunc|
m(i) expĕdi|at mĕ|tum

Haut. 431 (ia⁶)   **meŭs** gnā|tus sī|c est uĕ|nit cer|te Clī|nia|

Haut. 432 (ia⁶)   **meŭs** uĕ|nit di|x(i) eā|mus duc| m(e) ăd e(um) ob|sĕcro|

Haut. 439 (ia⁶)   non pos|sum **sătĭs|** iam sătĭs| păter| dūrus| fu(i) ah|

Haut. 439 (ia⁶)   non pos|sum sătĭs| iam **sătĭs|** păter| dūrus| fu(i) ah|

Haut. 473 (ia⁶)   **Sÿrŭs** c(um) il|lō uos|trō con|sŭsur|rant con|fĕrunt|

Appendix 311

Haut. 479	(ia⁶)	priŭs prō|dĭtū|rum tē |tuam| uīt(am) et| prius|

Appendix   311

Haut. 479 (ia⁶)   priŭs prō|dĭtū|rum tē |tuam| uīt(am) et| prius|
Haut. 483 (ia⁶)   nam dē|tĕriō|rēs om|nes sŭmŭs| lĭcen|tia|
Haut. 506 (ia⁶)   sŭmŭs prae|pĕdī|tī nĭmi|(o) aut ae|grĭtū|dĭne|
Haut. 578 (ia⁸)   sed nos|tr(um) est in|tellĕgĕ|r(e) utquom|qu(e) atqu(e)
                   ŭbĭ|quomqu(e) ŏpŭs| sĭt ob|sĕqui|
Haut. 584 (tr⁷)   actum|st hic priŭs| s(e) indĭ|cārit| quăm—ĕg(o) ar|gent
                   (um) ef|fēcĕ|ro
Haut. 594 (tr⁷)   fiet| sī săpi|as nam| mĭhĭ iam| mĭnŭs mĭ|nusqu(e) ob|
                   tempĕ|rat
Haut. 617 (ia⁸)   e(um) es|s(e) at ut| sătĭs con|templā|tă mŏdŏ |sis meă |
                   nūtrix| sătis|
Haut. 707 (ia⁷)   sătĭs sā|nŭs ē|s et sō|brius| tŭquĭd(em) il|lum plā|nē per|
                   dis|
Haut. 723 (ia⁷)   sătĭs pol| prŏter|uē mē |Sȳrī |prōmis|s(a) hūc in|duxē|runt|
Haut. 729 (ia⁷)   sătĭs scī|tē prō|mittit| tĭb(i) at|quī t(u) hanc| iocā|rī crē|dis|
Haut. 743 (ia⁷)   eā|tur sĕquĕ|r(e) hāc hēus| Drŏmō |quis mē |uolt Sȳrŭs|
                   quĭd est| rēĭ|
Haut. 855 (ia⁶)   des qu(i) au|r(um) ac ues|t(em) atqu(e) ăli|ă qu(ae) ŏpŭs|
                   sunt com|păret|
Haut. 890 (tr⁷)   ĭtă r(em) es|s(e) aīn tū |quin t(u) aus|cultā |mān(e) hoc|
                   priŭs scī|r(e) expĕ|to
Haut. 920 (ia⁶)   non tĭb(i) ĕ|g(o) exem|plī sătĭs| sum pr(ae) ī|rācun|dia|
Haut. 939 (ia⁶)   nēquid| uĕreā|rĕ sī |mĭnŭs nil| nōs dōs| mŏuet|
Haut. 971 (tr⁷)   ēmŏ|rī cŭpi|ō priŭs| quaesō |discĕ |quid sit| uĭuĕ|re
Haut. 998 (ia⁸)   ĕrĭt tam| făcil|lŭmē |pătrĭs pā|c(em) in lē|ges con|fĭciet|
                   suas|
Haut. 1025 (tr⁷)   fuĕrim| dictus| fili|us tuŏs| uostrā |uŏlŭntā|t(e) obsĕ|cro
Haut. 1045 (tr⁷)   ĕnĭmuē|rō Chrĕ|mes nĭmĭs| grăuĭter| crŭcia|t ădŭles|
                   centŭ|lum
Haut. 1046 (tr⁷)   nĭmĭsqu(e) ĭ|nhŭmā|n(e) exe|(o) erg(o) ut| pācem| concĭli|
                   (em) optŭ|me
Hec. 204   (ia⁸)   eī lū|dō s(i) ul|lŭs est| măgis|tr(am) hanc es|sĕ sătĭs| certo
                   s|cio|
Hec. 234   (tr⁷)   sătĭs sci|ō pec|candō |dētrī|mentī |nil fiĕ|rī pŏ|test
Hec. 262   (ia⁷)   hoc sī |rescĭĕ|rĭt eō |dŏmum| stŭde(o) haec| priŭs qu(am)
                   il|lĕ rĕde|at|
Hec. 287   (tr⁷)   omnĕ |quŏd ĕst in|tĕreā |tempus| priŭs qu(am) ĭd| rescī|
                   tumst lŭ|crost
Hec. 294   (ia⁸)   priŭs qu(am) han|c uxō|rem du|x(i) hăbē|b(am) ălĭb(i)
                   ănĭ|m(um) ămō|rī dē|dĭtum|
Hec. 380   (tr⁷)   omnĭbŭs| nōbĭ|s ut res| dant sē|s(e) ĭtă mag|n(i) atqu(e)
                   hŭmĭ|les sŭ|mus

Hec. 524   (tr⁸)   uĭr ĕgŏ |tuŏs sim| tū uĭ|rum m(e) au|t hŏmĭnem| dēpŭ|tās
                     ăde|(o) esse|

Hec. 541   (tr⁷)   multō |priŭs scī|uī quam| t(u) ill(um) hă|bēr(e) ă|mīcam|
                     Myrrĭ|na

Hec. 556   (tr⁷)   nec uĭ|rum **sătĭs**| firmum| gnātae |mitt(e) ădŭ|lescen|t(em)
                     obsĕ|cro

Hec. 582   (ia⁸)   nam m(i) in|tus **tuŏs**| păter| narrā|uit mŏdŏ |quō pac|tō m
                     (e) hăbu|ĕris|

Hec. 594   (ia⁸)   d(um) aetā|tis tem|pus tŭlĭt| perfun|ctă **sătĭs**| sum sătĭ|as
                     iam| tĕnet|

Hec. 606   (ia⁸)   et mĭhĭ |quĭdem| n(am) haec res| non **mĭnŭs**| mē măl(e)
                     hă|bet quam| te gnā|tĕ mi|

Hec. 608   (ia⁸)   istū|c est săpĕ|rĕ qu(i) ŭbĭ|quomqu(e) **ŏpŭs**| sĭt ănĭ|mum
                     pos|sis flec|tĕre|

Hec. 630   (ia⁶)   nē rĕuĕ|reā|tur **mĭnŭs**| iam quō |rĕdeat| dŏm(um) ah|

Hec. 644   (ia⁶)   uxō|r(em) hăbē|s aut **quĭbŭs**| mŏrā|tam mō|rĭbus|

Hec. 647   (ia⁶)   non tĭb(i) ĭl|lud fac|tum **mĭnŭs**| plăcet| quam mĭhĭ |Lăche|

Hec. 656   (ia⁶)   aut sē|sē mē|cum nup|tam **sătĭs**| certo s|cio|

Hec. 665   (ia⁶)   remis|sān **ŏpŭs**| sit uŏ|bīs red|ductan| dŏmum|

Hec. 698   (ia⁶)   reddū|c uxō|r(em) aut qu(am) ob| rem nō|n **ŏpŭs** sit| cĕdo|

Hec. 701   (ia⁶)   **omnĭbŭs**| mŏdis| mĭser| sum nec| quĭd ăgam| scio|

Hec. 729   (ia⁸)   uĭden|dumst nē |**mĭnŭs** prop|tĕr ī|r(am) hanc im|pĕtrem|
                     quam pos|siem|

Hec. 730   (ia⁸)   aut nē|quid făci|am plus| quod post| mē **mĭnŭs**| fēcis|sĕ
                     sătĭ|ŭs sit|

Hec. 744   (ia⁸)   sĭnĕ dī|c(am) uxō|r(em) hanc **priŭs**| quam du|xit uos|tr
                     (um) ămō|rem per|tŭli|

Hec. 769   (ia⁷)   sed quom| tū sătŭ|r(a) atqu(e) ē|bri(a) **ĕrĭs**| puĕr ut| sătur|
                     sit făcĭ|to|

Hec. 783   (ia⁷)   uĕlim| quĭd(em) her|cl(e) exquī|r(e) ădest| quod **sătĭs**| sit
                     făci|et ip|sa|

Hec. 843   (tr⁷)   uīsumst| certen| certē |**deŭs** sum| s(i) hŏc ĭtas|t uĕrum|
                     rĕpĕri|es

Hec. 859   (ia⁸)   ut uŏlŭp|tāt(i) ŏbĭ|tus ser|m(o) aduen|tus **tuŏs**| quōquom|
                     qu(e) aduē|nĕris|

Hec. 877   (tr⁷)   ĭmmŏ uē|rō scī|ō nĕ|qu(e) inprū|dens fē|c(i) ĕg(o) ĭstuc|
                     sătĭs sci|(o) an

Ph. 1   (ia⁶)   postquam| poē|tă **uĕtŭs**| poē|tam non| pŏtest|

Ph. 11   (ia⁶)   **mĭnŭs** mul|t(o) audac|ter quam| nunc lae|dĭt lae|dĕret|

Ph. 13   (ia⁶)   **uĕtŭs** sī |poē|tă non| lăces|sisset| prior|

Ph. 63   (ia⁶)   **sĕnĭs** nos|trī Dā|uĕ frā|trem mā|iōrem| Chrĕmem|

Ph. 124   (ia⁶)   quĭd ĭs fē|cit hoc| consĭli|um quod| dīcam| dĕdit|

Ph. 196   (tr⁷)   **sătĭs** pr(o) im|pĕriō |quisquī|s es Ge|t(a) ipses|t quem
                     uŏlu|(i) obui|am

Ph. 208   (tr⁷)   qu(om) hoc non| poss(um) il|lud **mĭnŭs**| poss(em) hoc| nĭl
                   es|t Phaedri|(a) ĭlĭ|cet

Ph. 248   (ia⁸)   mĕdĭtā|tă mĭhĭ |sunt om|niā |me(a) ĭncom|mŏd(a) **ĕrŭs**| sī
                   rĕdi|ĕrit|

Ph. 250   (ia⁸)   **ŏpŭs** rū|rī făci|und(um) hō|rum nil| quicqu(am) ac|cĭdē|t
                   ănĭmō |nŏuom|

Ph. 271   (ia⁶)   ex quā |rē **mĭnŭs**| reî fŏrĕ|t aut fā|mae tem|pĕrans|

Ph. 337   (tr⁷)   non pŏ|test **sătĭs**| prō mĕrĭ|t(o) ăb ĭllō |tĭbĭ rĕ|ferrī |grāti|a

Ph. 338   (tr⁷)   imm(o) ĕnĭm| nēmō |**sătĭs** prō |mĕrĭtō |grāti|am rē|gī rĕ|
                   fert

Ph. 362   (ia⁶)   s(i) illum| **mĭnŭs** nō|rat quip|p(e) hŏmō |iam gran|dior|

Ph. 399   (ia⁶)   dīlū|cĭd(e) ex|pĕdī|uī **quĭbŭs**| m(e) ŏpor|tuit|

Ph. 436   (ia⁶)   **sătĭs** iam| uerbō|rumst nĭsĭ |tū prŏpĕ|ras mŭli|ĕrem|

Ph. 438   (ia⁶)   sī t(u) il|l(am) attĭgĕ|ris **sĕcŭs**| quam dig|numst lĭ|bĕram|

Ph. 454   (ia⁶)   quŏt hŏmĭ|nes tot| senten|tiae |**sŭŏs** quoî|quĕ mos|

Ph. 477   (ia⁸)   quĭd ĭs fē|cit con|fūtā|uit uer|bīs ad|mŏd(um) ī|rātum|
                   sĕnem|

Ph. 523   (tr⁷)   cert(e) her|cl(e) ĕgŏ sī |**sătĭs** com|mĕmĭnī |tĭbĭ quĭ|d(em)
                   est ō|lim di|es

Ph. 535   (tr⁷)   quoî **mĭnŭs**| nĭhĭlost| quŏd hĭc sī |pŏtĕ fu|isse|t exō|rāri|er

Ph. 547   (tr⁷)   n(i) instĭ|gēmŭ|s ĕti(am) ut| nullus| **lŏcŭs** rĕ|linquā|tur
                   prĕ|ci

Ph. 563   (tr⁷)   numquĭd ĕst| quŏd ŏpĕ|rā meâ |uōbī|s **ŏpŭs** sit| nil uē|r
                   (um) ăbĭ dŏ|mum

Ph. 623   (ia⁶)   **ĕrŭs** lī|bĕrā|lĭs es|t et fŭgĭ|tans lī|tium|

Ph. 638   (ia⁶)   ŭt ĕst il|lĕ **bŏnŭs**| uir triă |non com|mūtā|bĭtis|

Ph. 719   (ia⁸)   transī|t(o) ăd u|xōrem| me(am) ut| conuĕni|at hanc| **prĭŭs**
                   qu(am) hin|c ăbit|

Ph. 787   (ia⁷)   factum| uŏl(o) ac| pol **mĭnŭs**| queō |uĭrĭ cul|pā quam| mē
                   dig|numst|

Ph. 804   (ia⁸)   **pătrĭs** nō|mĕn ăli|ud dic|t(um) est hoc| t(u) erras|tī non|
                   nōrat| pătrem|

Ph. 811   (ia⁸)   uin **sătĭs**| quaesī|tum m(i) is|tuc es|s(e) ăgĕ fi|at quĭd ĭl|la fi|
                   lia|

Ph. 818   (ia⁸)   quō pac|tō pŏtu|it non| **sătĭs** tū|tŭs es|t ad nar|rand(um)
                   hīc| lŏcus|

Ph. 828   (ia⁷)   rŏgem| quod tem|pus con|uĕniun|dī **pătrĭs**| mē căpĕ|rĕ
                   iŭbe|at|

Ph. 852   (tr⁷)   sĕd **ĭsn(e)** est| quem quae|r(o) an nō|n ipsus|t congrĕdĕ|r
                   (e) actū|tum quĭ|d est

Ph. 860   (tr⁷)   sŭmŭs prŏ|fect(i) in|tĕreā |mittĭ|t **ĕrŭs** m(e) ă|d uxō|rem
                   tu|am

Ph. 860   (tr⁷)   **sŭmŭs** prŏ|fect(i) in|tĕreā |mittĭ|t ĕrŭs m(e) ă|d uxō|rem
                   tu|am

Ph. 897   (ia⁶)   **prius** quam| dīlăpĭ|dat nos|trās trī|gintā |mĭnas|

Ph. 923   (ia⁶)   quodn(e) ĕgŏ |discrip|sī por|r(o) illis| **quĭbŭs** dē|bui|

Ph. 1022   (tr⁷)   sed quid| spēr(em) ae|tātĕ |porrō |**mĭnŭs** pec|cātū|rum pŭ|
                 tem

Ph. 1036   (tr⁷)   ĕnĭmuē|rō **prius**| qu(am) haec dat| uĕniam| mĭhĭ pros|pĭci
                 (am) et| Phaedri|ae

Ph. 1045   (tr⁷)   **prius** quam| gnātum| uĭdĕ|r(o) ei(u)s iŭ|dĭciō |permit|t(o)
                 omni|a

Ph. 1046   (tr⁷)   quŏd ĭs iŭ|bēbit| făciam| mŭlier| săpien|s es Nau|sistră|ta

Ph. 1047   (tr⁷)   **sătĭs** tĭ|bīn es|t immō |uērō |pulchrē |discē|d(o) et prŏ|be

Ad. 12   (ia⁶)   ēam nō|s actū|rī **sŭmŭs**| nŏuam| pernos|cĭte|

Ad. 36   (ia⁶)   **quĭbŭs** nunc| sollĭcĭ|tor rē|bus n(e) au|t ill(e) al|sĕrit|

Ad. 184   (ia⁸)   sī **sătĭs**| iam dē|bacchā|tŭs es| lēn(o) au|dī sī |uīs nun|ciam|

Ad. 239   (ia⁶)   lăbas|cit ū|n(um) hoc hăbe|ō uĭdĕ |sī **sătĭs**| plăcet|

Ad. 256   (ia⁸)   ō frā|ter frā|ter quĭd ĕ|go nunc| tē lau|dem **sătĭs**| certo
                 s|cio|

Ad. 264   (ia⁸)   nil pŏtĕ |sŭprā |quidnam| **fŏrĭs** crĕpu|it mănĕ |măn(e) ip|s
                 (e) exit| fŏras|

Ad. 291   (ia⁸)   mĭsĕram| mē nē|mĭn(em) hăbe|ō sō|lae **sŭmŭs**| Get(a) au|t
                 (em) hic nō|n ădest|

Ad. 354   (ia⁸)   curr(e) ob|stētrī|c(em) accer|s(e) ut qu(om) **ŏpŭs**| sit n(e)
                 in| mŏrā |nōbīs| siet|

Ad. 379   (ia⁶)   **prius** nō|l(o) haecin| flāgĭti|ă mĭquĭ|dem non| plăcent|

Ad. 439   (ia⁶)   trĭbū|lis nos|ter sī |**sătĭs** cer|n(o) ĭs hĕrcles|t uăha|

Ad. 459   (ia⁶)   nĕquĕ făci|am nĕquĕ |mē **sătĭs**| piē |poss(e) ar|bĭtror|

Ad. 476   (ia⁶)   ill(e) **bŏnŭs** uir nō|bīs psal|triam| sī dis| plăcet|

Ad. 522   (ia⁸)   mĭsĕrē |**nĭmĭs** cŭpi|(o) ut coe|pī per|pĕtu(om) in| laetĭti|ā
                 dē|gĕre|

Ad. 525   (tr⁸)   **prius** no|x oppres|sisse|t illī |qu(am) hūc rĕ|uortī |posse|t
                 ĭtĕrum|

Ad. 544   (tr⁷)   quĭd hŏc mă|l(um) infē|lĭcĭ|tātis| nĕqueō |**sătĭs** dē|cernĕ|re

Ad. 583   (tr⁷)   īt(o) ad| dextram| **prius** qu(am) ad| portam| uĕniā|s ăpŭd
                 ip|sum lă|cum

Ad. 596   (ia⁸)   ĕt ul|tr(o) accū|sant id| quiă nō|n est ā |mē fac|t(um) **ăgĭs**
                 grā|tias|

Ad. 605   (ia⁸)   omnēs| **quĭbŭs** res| sunt mĭnŭs| sĕcun|dae măgĕ |sunt nes|
                 ciŏquŏ |mŏdo|

Ad. 605   (ia⁸)   omnēs| quĭbŭs res| sunt **mĭnŭs**| sĕcun|dae măgĕ |sunt nes|
                 ciŏquŏ |mŏdo|

Ad. 621   (ia⁸)   **sătĭs** diŭ |dĕdis|tī uer|bă săt ă|dhuc tuă |nōs frus|trātast|
                 fĭdes|

Ad. 706   (tr⁷)   ĕg(o) e(o) in|tr(o) ut qu(ae) **ŏpŭs**| sunt pă|rentur| tū făc ŭt|
                 dixī |sī să|pis

Ad. 753   (ia⁶)   prŏb(e) et| tū nō|bisc(um) ū|nā s(i) ŏpŭs| sĭt ei |mĭhi|
Ad. 760   (ia⁶)   dŏmŭs sum|ptuō|s(a) ădŭles|cens lu|xū per|dĭtus|
Ad. 803   (ia⁶)   nōn ae|quom dī|cis non| nam uĕtŭs| uerb(um) hoc|
                    quĭdemst|
Ad. 810   (ia⁶)   quod sătĭs| pŭtā|bas tuă |bŏn(a) am|bōbus| fŏre|
Ad. 822   (ia⁶)   sign(a) in|sunt ex| quĭbŭs con|iectū|rā făcĭ|lĕ fit|
Ad. 899   (ia⁶)   occī|dunt mĕquĭ|dem dum| nĭmĭs san|ctas nup|tias|
Ad. 920   (ia⁶)   quid tū—|aĭs sī|c ŏpī|nor mul|tō rec|tiust|
Ad. 938   (ia⁸)   ĕgŏ nŏuŏs| mărī|tŭs an|nō dē|mum quin|t(o) et se|xāgen|
                    sŭmo|
Ad. 971   (tr⁷)   omnĭbŭs| grāti|(am) hăbe(o) et| seōrsum| tĭbĭ prae|tĕreā |
                    Dēme|a
Ad. 993   (tr⁷)   mĭnŭs uĭ|dētis| măgĭs in|pensē |cŭpĭtis| consŭlĭ|tis pă|rum

3.6 Category 6: Light Elements

This group consists of cases in which the syllable ending in -*s* occupies a light element (twenty-two) and must be scanned light. In twenty of these cases, the element involved is the penultimate element of an ia⁶, tr⁷, or ia⁸. In two cases (listed at the beginning) the syllable ending in -*s* occupies the penultimate element before a median *caesura* in an ia⁸.

Syllables occupying the penultimate element before the median caesura (3)

An. 203   (ia⁸)   ŭbĭuĭs| făcĭli|us pas|sŭs sim| qu(am) ĭn hāc| rē mē |dēlū|dier|
An. 582   (ia⁸)   ĕgŏ dū|dum non| nil uĕrĭ|tŭs sum| Dāu(e) ab|s tē nē |făcĕrē|
                    s ĭdem|
Eun. 555   (ia⁸)   quid ges|ti(am) aut| quĭd lae|tŭs sim| quō per|g(am) und(e)
                    ē|merg(am) ŭbĭ |siem|

Syllables occupying the penultimate element of the line (20)

An. 599   (ia⁸)   īb(o) ăd e|(um) atqu(e) ēa|d(em) haec quae |tĭbĭ di|xī dī|c
                    (am) ĭd(em) il|lī nul|lŭs sum|
An. 619   (ia⁸)   tū r(em) in|pĕdī|t(am) et per|dĭtam| restĭtu|ās em| quō frē|
                    tŭs sim|
Eun. 1045 (ia⁸)   illum|nĕ quī |mĭhĭ dĕdĭt| consĭli|(um) ut făcĕ|r(em) an mē
                    |qu(i) ĭd au|sŭs sim|
Haut. 15   (ia⁶)   qu(i) ōrā|tiō|n(em) hanc scrip|sit quam| dictū|rŭs sum|
Haut. 826 (ia⁶)   sed pătĕ|r ēgrĕdĭ|tur căuĕ |quicqu(am) ad|mirā|tŭs sis|

Hec. 334 (ia⁶) căpĭt(i) at|qu(e) aetā|t(i) illō|rum mor|bus qu(i) auc|tŭs sit|

Hec. 443 (ia⁶) mănē|tō cur|rĕ non| que(o) ĭtă |dēfes|sŭs sum|

Hec. 450 (ia⁶) uĭde(o) hor|sum per|gunt quid| dīc(am) his|c(e) incer|tŭs sum|

Hec. 485 (ia⁶) quĭbŭs ī|ris pul|sus nun|c ĭn il|l(am) ĭnī|quŏs sim|

Hec. 489 (ia⁶) nam fŭĭs|s(e) ergā |mē mī|r(o) ingĕni|(o) exper|tŭs sum|

Hec. 653 (ia⁶) ēuē|nit hăbe|ō grā|tiam| dīs nul|lŭs sum|

Hec. 730 (ia⁸) aut nē|quid făci|am plūs| quod post| mē mĭnŭs| fēcis|sĕ săti|ŭs sit|

Hec. 878 (tr⁷) tĕmĕrĕ |quicquam| Parmĕ|nō prae|tĕreat| quod fac|t(o) ūsŭs| sit

Ph. 413 (ia⁶) ĭtăn tan|dem quae|s(o) ĭtĭd(em) ut| mĕrĕtrī|c(em) ŭb(i) ăbū|sŭs sis|

Ph. 660 (ia⁶) dīcam| scien|t(em) ăn in|prūden|t(em) incer|tŭs sum|

Ph. 683 (ia⁶) sătĭn es|t id nes|ci(o) her|clĕ tan|tum ius|sŭs sum|

Ph. 943 (ia⁶) suscē|pĭt ĕt e|am cl(am) ē|ducat| sĕpul|tŭs sum|

Ad. 429 (ia⁶) inspĭcĕ|rĕ iŭbe|(o) et mŏne|ō quid| fact(o) ū|sŭs sit|

Ad. 839 (ia⁶) expor|gĕ fron|tem scī|lĭcĕt ĭ|tă tem|pŭs fert|

Ad. 873 (tr⁷) illum| dīlī|gunt ăpŭ|d illum| sunt am|b(o) ĕgŏ dē|sertŭs| sum

Reference List

Abbreviations

AE — *L'Année Épigraphique* (Paris, 1888–)

CEpLat — P. Cugusi (ed.), *Corpus Epistolarum Latinarum, papyris tabulis ostracis servatarum*, 3 vols. (Florence, 1992, 2002)

ChLA — A. Bruckner, R. Marichal et al. (eds.), *Chartae Latinae Antiquiores* (Olten, etc., 1954–)

CIL — *Corpus Inscriptionum Latinarum* (Berlin, 1862–)

CILA — *Corpus de Inscripciones Latinas de Andalucia* (Seville, 1991–)

CLE — F. Bücheler and E. Lommatzsch (eds.), *Carmina Latina Epigraphica* (Leipzig, 1930)

ERPLeon — M. A. Rabanal Alonso and S. M. García Martínez (eds.), *Epigrafía romana de la provincia de León: revisión y actualización* (León, 2001)

GL — H. Keil (ed.), *Grammatici Latini*, 7 vols. (Leipzig, 1855–1880)

Hep — *Hispania Epigraphica* (Madrid, 1989–)

ICUR — *Inscriptiones christianae urbis Romae. Nova series* (Rome, 1922–)

ILAlg — *Inscriptions latines d'Algérie*, (Paris, 1922–)

ILCV — E. Diehl (ed.), *Inscriptiones Latinae Christianae Veteres* (Berlin, 1925–1967)

ILLRP — A. Degrassi (ed.), *Inscriptiones Latinae Liberae Rei Publicae*, 2nd ed. (Florence, 1965)

ILS — H. Dessau (ed.), *Inscriptiones Latinae Selectae* (Berlin, 1892–1916)

InscrAqu — J. B. Brusin (ed.), *Inscriptiones Aquileiae*, 3rd ed. (Udine, 1991–1993)

IRC — *Inscriptions romaines de Catalogne* (Paris, 1984–)

KL — Kauer and Lindsay (1958) (*see reference list*)

ML — Courtney (1995) (*see reference list*)

OBuNjem — R. Marichal (ed.), *Les Ostraca de Bu Njem* (Libya Antiqua Supplementum VII) (Tripoli, 1992)

OED — *Oxford English Dictionary*, 2nd ed. (Oxford, 1989)

OLD — *Oxford Latin Dictionary* (Oxford, 1968–1982)

P.Amh. — B. P. Grenfell and A. S. Hunt (eds.), *The Amherst Papyri, Being an Account of the Greek Papyri in the Collection of the Right Hon. Lord Amherst of Hackney, F.S.A. at Didlington Hall, Norfolk*, 2 vols. (London, 1900–1901)

P.Mich.	*Michigan Papyri* (Ann Arbor, 1931–)
PapHercul	*Herculaneum papyri* (see M. Gigante, *Catalogo dei papiri ercolanesi* (Napoli, 1979))
PItal	J. O. Tjäder (ed.). *Die nichtliterarischen lateinischen Papyri Italiens aus der Zeit 445–700*, 3 vols. (Lund, 1954–1982)
RHP	B. Lörincz (ed.), *Die römischen Hilfstruppen in Pannonien während der Prinzipatszeit. I: Die Inschriften* (Wien, 2001)
RIU	*Die römischen Inschriften Ungarns* (Budapest, 1972–)
TAlb	C. Courtois, L. Leschi et al. (eds.), *Tablettes Albertini, Actes privés de l'époque Vandale*, (Paris, 1952)
TLL	*Thesaurus Linguae Latinae* (Leipzig, 1900–)
TVindol	A. K. Bowman and J. D. Thomas (eds.), *Vindolanda: the Latin Writing Tablets* (with contributions by J. N. Adams and J. Pearce), 3 vols. (London, 1994, 2003)

Reference List

Abbott, F. F. (1909), 'Vulgar Latin in the *Ars Consentii de barbarismis*', *Classical Philology* 4, 233–47.

Adams, J. N. (1976), *The Text and Language of a Vulgar Latin Chronicle (Anonymus Valesianus II)* (Institute of Classical Studies Bulletin Supplement 36) (London).

Adams, J. N. (1977), *The Vulgar Latin of the Letters of Claudius Terentianus (P.Mich.VIII, 467–72)* (Manchester).

Adams, J. N. (1984), 'Female Speech in Latin Comedy', *Antichthon* 19, 43–77.

Adams, J. N. (1994a), *Wackernagel's Law and the Placement of the Copula esse in Classical Latin* (Cambridge).

Adams, J. N. (1994b), 'Wackernagel's Law and the Position of Unstressed Personal Pronouns in Classical Latin', *Transactions of the Philological Society* 92, 103–78.

Adams, J. N. (1994c), 'Latin and Punic in Contact? The Case of the bu Njem Ostraca', *Journal of Roman Studies* 84, 87–112.

Adams, J. N. (1999), 'The Poets of Bu Njem: Language, Culture and the Centurionate', *Journal of Roman Studies* 89, 109–34.

Adams, J. N. (2003), *Bilingualism and the Latin Language* (Cambridge).

Adams, J. N. (2007), *The Regional Diversification of Latin, 200 BC–AD 600* (Cambridge).

Adams, J. N. (2011), 'Late Latin', in Clackson (2011), 257–83.

Adams, J. N. (2013), *Social Variation and the Latin Language* (Cambridge).

Adams, J. N. and Mayer, R. (eds.) (1999), *Aspects of the Language of Latin Poetry* (Proceedings of the British Academy 93) (Oxford).

Allen, W. S. (1973), *Accent and Rhythm: Prosodic Features of Latin and Greek* (Cambridge).

Allen, W. S. (1978), *Vox Latina: a Guide to the Pronunciation of Classical Latin*, 2nd ed. (Cambridge).

Allen, W. S. (1987), *Vox Graeca: a Guide to the Pronunciation of Classical Greek* (Cambridge).

Andersen, H. (1986), *Sandhi Phenomena in the Languages of Europe* (Berlin).

Anderson, S. (1993), 'Wackernagel's Revenge: Clitics, Morphology, and the Syntax of second position', *Language* 69, 68–98.

Anderson, S. (2005), *Aspects of the Theory of Clitics* (Oxford).

Anderson, S. and Zwicky, A. (2003), 'Clitics', in Frawley, W. (ed.), *International Encyclopedia of Linguistics*, 2nd ed. (Oxford).

Arnott, W. (1970), '*Phormio Parasitus*: A Study in Dramatic Methods of Characterization', *Greece and Rome* 17, 32–57.

Austin, R. G. (1955), *P. Vergili Maronis Aeneidos liber quartus* (Oxford).

Austin, R. G. (1964), *P. Vergili Maronis Aeneidos liber secundus* (Oxford).

Austin, R. G. (1971), *P. Vergili Maronis Aeneidos liber primus* (Oxford).

Austin, R. G. (1977), *P. Vergili Maronis Aeneidos liber sextus* (Oxford).

Bader, F. (1976), 'Le présent du verb "être" en indoeuropéen', *Bulletin de la Société de Linguistique de Paris* 71, 27–111.

Baehrens, A. (1879–1886), *Poetae Latini minores*, 6 vols. (Leipzig).

Bagordo, A. (2001), *Beobachtungen zur Sprache des Terenz* (Göttingen).

Bagordo, A. (2007), 'Langversstil und Senarstil bei Terenz', in Kruschwitz, Ehlers and Felgentreu (2007), 127–42.

Bailey, C. (1947), *Titi Lucreti Cari De rerum natura libri sex* (Oxford).

Baker, M. (1988), *Incorporation: a Theory of Grammatical Function Changing* (Chicago).

Bakkum, G. C. L. M. (2009), *The Latin Dialect of the Ager Faliscus* (Amsterdam).

Baldi, P. (1999), 'Observations on Two Recently Discovered Latin Inscriptions', in Embleton, S., Joseph, J. E., and Niederehe, H.-J. (eds.), *The Emergence of the Modern Language Sciences, Volume 2: Methodological Perspectives and Applications* (Philadelphia, PA), 165–74.

Bammesberger, A. (2004), 'Lithuanian *esmí* and *esù* "I Am": on the Spread of the Thematic Present in Indo-European Languages', in Baldi, P. and Dini, P. U. (eds.), *Studies in Baltic and Indo-European Linguistics* (Amsterdam), 19–26.

Bardon, H. (1973), *Catulli Veronensis carmina* (Stuttgart).

Barsby, J. (1999), *Terence, Eunuchus* (Cambridge).

Barsby, J. (2001), *Terence*, 2 vols. (Cambridge, MA, and London).

Bauer, B. (2009), 'Word Order', in Baldi, P. and Cuzzolin, P. (eds.), *New Perspectives on Historical Latin Syntax 1: Syntax of the Sentence* (Berlin and New York), 241–316.

Beare, W. (1964), *The Roman Stage*, 3rd ed. (London).

Beeson, C. H. (1930), *Lupus of Ferrières as Scribe and Text Critic; a Study of his Autograph Copy of Cicero's De oratore* (Cambridge, MA).

Bernardi Perini, G. (1974), *Due problemi di fonetica latina* (Rome).

Bernardi Perini, G. (1983), 'Le riforme ortografiche latine di età repubblicana', *AIΩN* 5, 141–69.

Bethe, E. (1903), *Terentius: Codex Ambrosianus H. 75 inf. phototypice editus* (Leiden).

Bettini, M. (1978), 'Riflessione a proposito dell'aferesi', *Studi classici e orientali* 28, 171–4.

Bettini, M. (1990), 'La "correptio iambica"', in Danese, R. M., Gori, F., and Questa, C. (eds.), *Metrica classica e linguistica: Atti del colloquio, Urbino 3–6 ottobre 1988* (Urbino), 263–409.

Bloch, O. and Von Wartburg, W. (1968), *Dictionnaire étymologique de la langue française*, 5th ed. (Paris).

Bonfante, G. (1932), 'Lat. *sum, es, est*, etc.', *Bulletin de la Société de Linguistique de Paris* 33, 111–29.

Bonfante, G. (2000), '*esum, sum*', *Indogermanische Forschungen* 105, 21.

Bonnet, M. (1890), *Le Latin de Grégoire de Tours* (Paris).

Bottiglioni, G. (1954), *Manuale dei dialetti italici* (Bologna).

Brenot, A. (1961), *Phèdre, Fables*, 2nd ed. (Paris).

Brinkmann, O. (1906), *De copulae 'est' aphaeresi* (Marburg).

Brown, L. (1994), 'The Verb "To Be" in Greek Philosophy: Some Remarks', in Everson, S. (ed.), *Companions to Ancient Thought 3: Language* (Cambridge), 212–37.

Brown, L. (1999), 'Being in the Sophist', in Fine, G. (ed.), *Plato 1: Metaphysics and Epistemology* (Oxford), 455–78.

Brown, P. G. M. (2006), *Terence, The comedies* (Oxford).

Buck, C. D. (1904), *A Grammar of Oscan and Umbrian* (Boston, MS).

Buecheler, F. and Riese, A. (1894–1906), *Anthologia Latina*, 2nd ed., 2 vols. (Leipzig).

Burrow, C. (2002), *The Complete Sonnets and Poems* (Oxford).

Butterfield, D. J. (2006–2007), 'Emendations on the Sixth Book of Lucretius', *Eranos* 104, 386–413.

Butterfield, D. J. (2008a), '*Lucretiana quaedam*', *Philologus* 152, 111–27.

Butterfield, D. J. (2008b), 'Sigmatic Ecthlipsis in Lucretius', *Hermes* 136, 188–205.

Butterfield, D. J. (2009), 'Five Lucretian emendations', *Rivista di Filologia e Istruzione Classica* 137, 110–17.

Bybee, J. (2001), *Phonology and Language Use* (Cambridge).

Carbone, G. (2002), *Il centone De alea* (Naples).

Carnoy, A. J. (1906), *Le latin d'Espagne d'après les inscriptions: étude linguistique*, 2nd ed. (Brussels).

Carr, P. (1999), *English Phonetics and Phonology: an Introduction* (Oxford).

Castorina, E. (1950), *Appunti di metrica Classica I: la prosa di Commodiano nella storia della metrica Latina* (Catania).

Cavenaile, R. (1958), *Corpus papyrorum Latinarum* (Wiesbaden).

Chahoud, A. (2010), 'Idiom(s) and Literariness in Classical Literary Criticism', in Dickey and Chahoud (2010), 42–64.

Christenson, D. (2000), *Plautus, Amphitruo* (Cambridge).

Cipriano, P. and Mancini, M. (1984), 'Enclisi e morfologia del verbo *essere* nel latino e nell'osco', in Belardi, W. et al. (eds.), *Studi latini e romanzi in memoria di Antonino Pagliaro* (Rome), 11–62.

Clackson, J. (2007), *Indo-European Linguistics* (Cambridge).

Clackson, J. (2010), 'Colloquial Language in Linguistic Studies', in Dickey and Chahoud (2010), 7–11.

Clackson, J. (2011a), 'Classical Latin', in Clackson (2011), 236–56.

Clackson, J. (2011b), 'Latin Inscriptions and Documents', in Clackson (2011), 29–39.

Clackson, J. (2011c), 'The Social Dialects of Latin', in Clackson (2011), 505–26.

Clackson, J. (ed.) (2011), *A Companion to the Latin Language* (Oxford).

Clackson, J. and Horrocks, G. (2007), *The Blackwell History of the Latin Language* (Malden, MA, and Oxford).

Clausen, W. (1994), *A commentary on Virgil, Eclogues* (Oxford).

Coleman, R. (1999), 'Poetic Diction, Poetic Discourse and the Poetic Register', in Adams and Mayer (1999), 21–93.

Collinge, N. E. (1985), *The Laws of Indo-European* (Amsterdam and Philadelphia, PA).

Colonna, G. (1994), 'Ager Signinus', *Studi etruschi* 60, 298–301.

Conte, G. B. (2009), *P. Vergilius Maro, Aeneis* (Leipzig).

Corrsen, W. (1870), *Über Aussprache, Vokalismus und Betonung der lateinischen Sprache* (Leipzig).

Courtney, E. (1993), *The Fragmentary Latin Poets* (Oxford).

Courtney, E. (1995), *Musa Lapidaria: a Selection of Latin Verse Inscriptions* (Atlanta, GA).

Coury, E. M. (1982), *Terence, Bembine Phormio: a Palaeographic Examination* (Chicago, IL).

Crawford, M. H. (1996), *Roman Statutes*, 2 vols. (Institute of Classical Studies Bulletin Supplement 64) (London).

Crystal, D. (2008), *Think on my Words: Exploring Shakespeare's Language* (Cambridge).

Cugusi, P. (2002), 'Tradizione elegiaca latina e *Carmina Latina Epigraphica*: Letteratura e testi epigrafici', *Aufidus* 16, 17–29.

Cugusi, P. (2007), 'Ricezione del codice epigrafico e interazione tra carmi epigrafici e letteratura latina nelle età repubblicana e augustea', in Kruschwitz (2007), 1–62.

D'Angelo, R. (2001), *Carmen de figuris vel schematibus* (Hildeseim).

Dangel, J. (1995), *Accius, Oeuvres* (Paris).

de Melo, W. D. C. (2007a), *The Early Latin Verb System: Archaic Forms in Plautus, Terence, and beyond* (Oxford).

de Melo, W. D. C. (2007b), 'Latin prohibitions and the Origins of the u/w-Perfect and the Type amāstī', *Glotta* 83, 43–68.

de Melo, W. D. C. (2010–2012), *Plautus*, 5 vols. (Cambridge, MA, and London).

de Meo, C. (1986), *Lingue tecniche del latino*, 2nd ed. (Bologna).

Devine, A. M. and Stephens, L. D. (1980), 'Latin Prosody and Meter: *Brevis brevians*', *Classical Philology* 75, 142–57.

Devine, A. M. and Stephens, L. D. (2006), *Latin Word Order: Structured Meaning and Information* (Oxford).

Dickey, E. and Chahoud, A. (eds.) (2010), *Colloquial and Literary Latin* (Cambridge).

Diehl, E. (1899), *De M finali epigraphica* (Jahrbücher für classische Philologie, Supplementband 25) (Leipzig).

Dressler, W. (1973), 'Pour une stylistique phonologique du latin: à propos des styles négligents d'une langue morte', *Bulletin de la Société de Linguistique de Paris* 68, 129–45.

Drexler, H. (1969), *Die Iambenkürzung: Kürzung der zweiten Silbe eines iambischen Wortes eines iambischen Wortanfangs* (Hildesheim).

Duckworth, G. (1994), *The Nature of Roman Comedy: a Study in Popular Entertainment*, 2nd ed. (Bristol).

Dunkel, G. (1998), 'On the "Thematisation" of Latin *sum, volo, eo,* and *edo* and the System of Endings in the IE Subjunctive Active', in Jasanoff, J., Melchert, H., and Oliver, L. (eds.), *Mír Curad: Studies in Honor of Calvert Watkins* (Innsbruck), 83–100.

Dyck, A. (2004), *A Commentary on Cicero, De legibus* (Ann Arbor, MI).

Ehrhardt, C. (1985), 'A Letter of L. Lucceius', *Mnemosyne* 38, 152–3.

Ehwald, R. (1888), *P. Ovidius Naso* (Leipzig).

Eisenhut, W. (1983), *Catulli Veronensi Liber* (Leipzig).

Ernout, A. (1952–1962), *Plaute*, 3rd ed., 7 vols. (Paris).

Évrard, É. and Mellet, S. (1998), 'Les Méthodes quantitatives en langues anciennes', *Lalies* 18, 111–55.

Fantham, E. (1972), *Comparative Studies in Republican Imagery* (Toronto).

Fedeli, P. (1980), *Properzio, Il primo libro delle elegie* (Florence).

Fedeli, P. (2005), *Properzio, Elegie Libro II* (Cambridge).

Ferguson, J. (1970), 'A Note on Catullus' Hendecasyllabics', *Classical Philology* 65, 173–5.

Ferri, R. (2003), *Octavia, a Play Attributed to Seneca* (Cambridge).

Fontaine, M. (2006), 'Sicilicissitat (Plautus, *Menaechmi* 12) and Early Geminate Writing in Latin (with an Appendix on *Men.* 13)', *Mnemosyne* 59, 95–110.

Fordyce, C. J. (1977), *P. Vergili Maronis Aeneidos libri VII–VIII* (Oxford).

Formicola, C. (1988), *Il Cynegeticon di Grattio* (Bologna).

Fortson, B. W. IV (2008), *Language and Rhythm in Plautus* (Berlin and New York).

Fortson, B. W. IV (2011), 'Latin Prosody and Metrics', in Clackson (2011), 92–104.

Fögen, T. (2011), 'Latin as a Technical and Scientific Language', in Clackson (2011), 445–63.

Fraenkel, E. (1925), 'Zum Texte Römischer Juristen', *Hermes* 60, 415–43 = Fraenkel (1964) II, 417–46.

Fraenkel, E. (1964), *Kleine Beiträge zur klassischen Philologie*, 2 vols. (Rome).

Fraenkel, E. (1965), *Noch einmal Kolon und Satz* (Munich).

Gaisser, J. (2009), *Catullus* (Oxford).

Geymonat, M. (1973), *P. Vergili Maronis opera* (Turin).

Giannini, S. (1986), 'Un problema di fonosintassi in latino: la consonante -s finale', *Studi e saggi linguistici* 26, 111–36.

Goold, G. P. (1989), *Catullus*, 2nd ed. (London).

Goold, G. P. (1999), *Propertius, Elegies* (Cambridge, MA, and London).

Goold, G. P. (2002), 'Hypermeter and Elision in Virgil', in Damon, C. et al. (eds.), *Vertis in usum* (Munich), 76–89.

Grant, J. (1986), *Studies in the Textual Tradition of Terence* (Toronto).

Gratwick, A. S. (1981), 'Curculio's Last Bow: Plautus, *Trinummus* IV.3', *Mnemosyne* 34, 331–50.

Gratwick, A. S. (1993), *Plautus, Menaechmi* (Cambridge).

Gratwick, A. S. (1999), *Terence, The Brothers*, 2nd ed. (Warmister).

Haffter, H. (1934), *Untersuchungen zur altlateinischen Dichtersprache* (Berlin).

Halpern, A. (1995), *On the Placement and Morphology of Clitics* (Stanford, CA).

Hamp, E. (1959), 'Final -s in Latin', *Classical Philology* 54, 165–72.

Hamp, E. (1974), 'On the Conditioned Loss and Restitution of Latin -S', in Campbell, R. J., Goldin, M. G., and Wang, M. C. (eds.), *Linguistic studies in Romance languages* (Washington, DC), 1–7.

Happ, H. (1967), 'Die lateinische Umgangssprache und die Kunstsprache des Plautus', *Glotta* 45, 60–104.

Harris, A. C. and Campbell, L. (1995), *Historical Syntax in Cross-Linguistic Perspective* (Cambridge).

Harrison, S. J. (1991), *A commentary on Vergil, Aeneid 10* (Oxford).

Harsh, P. (1952), 'Final -s after a Short Vowel in Early Latin', *Transactions and Proceedings of the American Philological Association* 83, 267–78.

Harsting, P. (2000), 'From Melanchthonism to Mannerism: the Development of the Neo-Latin Wedding Poem in 16th century Denmark', in Haye, T. (ed.), *Humanismus im Norden* (Amsterdam), 289–318.

Haverling, G. (2000), *On -sco Verbs, Prefixes and Semantic Functions: a Study in the Development of Prefixed and Unprefixed Verbs from Early to Late Latin* (Göteborg).

Havet, L. (1884), '*Sum, s, st*', *Mémoires de la Societé de Linguistique de Paris* 5, 158–60.

Havet, L. (1891), *L's Latin caduc* (Études romanes dédiées à Gaston Paris) (Geneva).

Havet, L. (1911), *Manuel de critique verbale* (Paris).

Herman, J. (2000), *Vulgar Latin*, translated by R. Wright (University Park, PA).

Heselwood, B. (2009), 'R Vocalisation, Linking R and Intrusive R: Accounting for Final Schwa in RP English', *Transactions of the Philological Society* 107, 66–97.

Heyworth, S. J. (2007a), *Sexti Properti Elegos* (Oxford).

Heyworth, S. J. (2007b), *Cynthia: A Companion to the Text of Propertius* (Oxford).

Hofmann, J. B. and Szantyr, A. (1965), *Lateinische Syntax und Stilistik* (Munich).

Holford-Strevens, L. (2003), *Aulus Gellius: an Antonine Scholar and his Achievement*, 2nd ed. (Oxford).

Horsfall, N. (2000), *Virgil, Aeneid 7: a Commentary* (Mnemosyne Supplement 198) (Leiden).

Holmes, N. (2002), 'Metrical Notes on Vegetius' *Epitoma rei militaris*', *Classical Quarterly* 52, 358–73.

Horsfall, N. (2003), *Virgil, Aeneid 11: a Commentary* (Mnemosyne Supplement 244) (Leiden).

Horsfall, N. (2006), *Virgil, Aeneid 3: a Commentary* (Mnemosyne Supplement 273) (Leiden).

Horsfall, N. (2008), *Virgil, Aeneid 2: a Commentary* (Mnemosyne Supplement 299) (Leiden).

Hunink, V. (1996), 'Notes on Apuleius' "Apology"', *Mnemosyne* 49, 159–67.

Hunt, J. (1971a), 'An Emendation in the *Aegritudo Perdicae*', *Classical Philology* 66, 114.

Hunt, J. (1971b), 'Notes de lecture, *Aegritudo Perdicae*', *Latomus* 30, 1161–3.

Hunt, J. (1982), 'Notes on the *Aegritudo Perdicae*', *Harvard Studies in Classical Philology* 86, 117–20.

Hunt, J. (2004), 'Conjectures in the *Aegritudo Perdicae*', *Athenaeum* 92, 359–66.

Hunter, R. L. (1985), *The New Comedy of Greece and Rome* (Cambridge).

Jachmann, G. (1929), *Terentius: Codex Vaticanus Latinus 3868* (Leipzig).

Janse, M. (1994), 'Clitics and Word Order since Wackernagel: One Hundred Years of Research into Clitics and Related Phenomena', *Orbis* 37, 389–410.

Janse, M. (2000), 'Convergence and Divergence in the Development of the Greek and Latin Clitic Pronouns', in Sornicola, R., Poppe, E., and Shisha-Halevy, A. (eds.), *Stability, Variation and Change of Word-order Patterns over Time* (Amsterdam), 231–58.

Joseph, B. and Wallace, R. (1987), 'Latin *sum*/Oscan *sum, sim, esum*', *American* 108, 675–93.

Joseph, B. and Wallace, R. (1989), '*Sum*: Further Thoughts', *Classical Philology* 84, 319–21.

Kahn, C. (2003), *The Verb 'Be' in Ancient Greek* (Indianapolis, IN).

Kahn, C. (2009), *Essays on Being* (Oxford).

Kaisse, E. (1985), *Connected Speech: the Interaction of Syntax and Phonology* (Orlando).

Karakasis, E. (2005), *Terence and the Language of Roman Comedy* (Cambridge).

Katsouris, A. G. (1975), *Linguistic and Stylistic Characterization: Tragedy and Menander* (Ioannina).

Kauer, R. and Lindsay, W. M. (1958), *P. Terenti Afri Comoediae*, 2nd ed. (repr. with additions by O. Skutsch) (Oxford).

Keller, M. (1985), 'Latin *escit, escunt* at-il des correspondants?', *Revue de Philologie* 59, 27–44.

Keller, M. (1992), *Les verbes latins à infectum en -sc-, étude morphologique (à partir des formations attestées dès l'époque préclassique)* (Brussels).

Keller, O. and Holder, A. (1925), *Q. Horati Flacci Opera* (Leipzig).

Kenney, E. (1965), '*Magnum opus et tangi nisi cura vincitur inpar*', *Classical Review* 15, 55–8.

Kenney, E. (1986), 'Prodelided *est*: a Note on Orthography', *Classical Quarterly* 36, 542.

Kershaw, A. (1987), 'Prodelided *est* in Ovid', *Classical Quarterly* 37, 527.

Kruschwitz, P. (2002), *Carmina saturnia epigraphica* (Stuttgart).

Kruschwitz, P. (2004), *Römische Inschriften und Wackernagels Gesetz: Untersuchungen zur Syntax epigraphischer Texte aus republikanischer Zeit* (Heidelberg).

Kruschwitz, P. (2007), *Die metrischen Inschriften der römischen Republik* (Berlin).

Kruschwitz, P., Ehlers, W.-W., and Felgentreu, F. (eds.) (2007), *Terentius Poeta* (Munich).

Kühner, R. and Gerth, B. (1890), *Ausführliche Grammatik der griechischen Sprache* (Hannover and Leipzig).

Kühner, R. and Stegmann, C. (1955), *Ausführliche Grammatik der lateinischen Sprache*, 3rd ed. (revised by A. Thierfelder), 2 vols. (Leverkusen).

La Penna, A. (1997), 'Su una croce dell'*Aegritudo Perdicae* e pochissime altre note al poemetto', *Maia* 49, 421–4.

La Regina, A. (2010), 'Iscrizione Osca rinvenuta a Castel di Sangro', in Mattiocco, E. (ed.), *Frammenti del passato, archeologia e archivistica tra Castel di Sangro e Sulmona* (Lanciano), 45–58.

Labov, W. (2008), *The Social Stratification of English in New York City: Origins, Evolution and Variation* (Cambridge).

Lachmann, K. (1871), *In De rerum natura commentarii* (Berlin).

Langslow, D. R. (ed.) (2009), *Jacob Wackernagel, Lectures on Syntax: With Special Reference to Greek, Latin, and Germanic* (Oxford).

326   *Reference List*

Leach, J. H. C. (2009), 'Classical Scholarship in Housman's Correspondence', in Butterfield, D. J. and Stray, C. (eds.), *A. E. Housman: Classical Scholar* (London), 229–43.

Lejeune, M. (1993), 'Notes osques', in Meiser, G. (ed.), *Indogermanica et Italica: Festschrift für Helmut Rix zum 65. Geburtstag* (Innsbruck), 264–9.

Leo, F. (1895–1896), *Plauti Comoediae*, 2nd ed., 2 vols. (Berlin).

Leo, F. (1905), *Der Saturnische Vers* (Leipzig).

Leo, F. (1912), *Plautinische Forschungen zur Kritik und Geschichte der Komödie*, 2nd ed. (Berlin).

Leonhardt, J. (1988), 'Die Aphäerese bei *est* in der Geschichte der lateinischen Metrik', *Glotta* 66, 244–52.

Leumann, M. (1977), *Lateinische Laut- und Formenlehre*, 6th ed. (Munich).

Lewis, G. (2000), *Turkish Grammar*, 2nd ed. (Oxford).

Liechtenhan, E. (1963), *Anthimi De observatione ciborum ad Theodoricum regem Francorum epistula* (Berlin).

Liénard, E. (1980), *Répertoires prosodiques et métriques*, 2 vols. (Brussels).

Lightfoot, J. L. (1999), *Parthenius of Nicaea* (Oxford).

Lindsay, W. M. (1893), 'The Saturnian Metre', *American Journal of Philology* 14, 139–70.

Lindsay, W. M. (1904a), *T. Macci Plauti Comoediae*, 2 vols. (Oxford).

Lindsay, W. M. (1904b), *The Ancient Editions of Plautus* (Oxford).

Lindsay, W. M. (1922), *Early Latin Verse* (Oxford).

Lindsay, W. M. (1961), *Plautus, Captivi* (Cambridge).

Lodge, G. (1924–1933), *Lexicon Plautinum*, 2 vols. (Stuttgart).

Loewe, G., Goetz, G., and Schoell, F. (1878–1894), *T. Macci Plauti comoediae, rec. instrum. critico et prolegom. auxit Fr. Ritschl* (Leipzig).

Löfstedt, E. (1956), *Syntactica: Studien und Beiträge zur historischen Syntax des Lateins* I, 2nd ed., II (Lund).

Löfstedt, E. (1961), *Studien über die Sprache der langobardischen Gesetze: Beiträge zur frühmittelalterlichen Latinität* (Stockholm).

Lyne, R. O. A. M. (2004), *Ciris: a Poem Attributed to Vergil* (Cambridge).

Madvig, J. N. (1834), *Opuscula academica: ab ipso colleta, emendata, aucta* (Copenhagen).

Madvig, J. N. (1860), *Emendationes Livianae* (Copenhagen).

Madvig, J. N. (1871–1884), *Adversaria critica ad scriptores Graecos et Latinos*, 3 vols. (Copenhagen).

Madvig, J. N. (1876), *Ciceronis De finibus bonorum et malorum* (Copenhagen).

Maiden, M., Smith, J. C., and Ledgeway, A. (2011), *The Cambridge History of the Romance Languages* (Cambridge).

Maltby, R. (1979), 'Linguistic Characterization of Old Men in Terence', *Classical Philology* 74, 136–47.

Maltby, R. (1985), 'The Distribution of Greek Loan-Words in Terence', *Classical Quarterly* 35, 110–23.

Mancini, M. (1988), 'Sulla defixio "osco-latina" Vetter 7', *Studi e saggi linguistici* 28, 201–30.

Mancini, M. (1997), *Osservazioni sulla nuova epigrafe del Garigliano* (Rome).

Mańcsak, W. (1975), 'S final en latin archaïque', *Studii si Cercetări Linguistice* 26, 519–25.

Mariotti, S. (1952), *Livio Andronico e la traduzione aristisca* (Milan).

Mariotti, I. (1967), *Marii Victorini Ars Grammatica* (Florence).

Marouzeau, J. (1908), 'Sur l'emploi de la graphie -*st* = *est*', *Revue de Philologie* 32, 291–9.

Marouzeau, J. (1949), *L'ordre des mots dans la phrase latine* (Paris).

Marouzeau, J. (1963), *Térence, Comédies*, 3rd ed., 3 vols. (Paris).

Marshall, C. W. (2006), *The Stagecraft and Performance of Roman Comedy* (Cambridge).

Martin, J. (1959), *T. Lucreti Cari De rerum natura libri sex* (Leipzig).

Martin, R. H. (1995), 'A Not-so-Minor Character in Terence's Eunuchus', *Classical Philology* 90, 139–51.

Marx, F. (1915), *A. Cornelii Celsi quae supersunt* (Leipzig).

Massaro, M. (2007), 'Metri e ritmi nella epigrafia latina di età repubblicana', in Kruschwitz (2007), 121–68.

McCully, C. (2009), *The Sound Structure of English: an Introduction* (Cambridge).

McGlynn, P. (1963–1967), *Lexicon Terentianum*, 2 vols. (London and Glasgow).

Meiser, G. (1998), *Historische Laut- und Formenlehre der lateinischen Sprache* (Darmstadt).

Mel'čuk, I. (2009), 'Dependency in Natural Language', in Polguère, A. and Mel'čuk, I. (eds.), *Dependency in Linguistic Description* (Amsterdam, Philadelphia, PA), 1–110.

Mendelssohn, L. (1893), *M. Tullii Ciceronis epistularum libri sedecim* (Leipzig).

Mercado, A. O. (2012), *Italic Verse* (Innsbruck).

Minarini, A. (1987), *Studi Terenziani* (Bologna).

Moore, T. J. (1998), 'Music and Structure in Roman Comedy', *American Journal of Philology* 119, 245–73.

Moore, T. J. (1999), 'Facing the Music: Character and Musical Accompaniment in Roman Comedy', *Syllecta Classica* 10, 130–53.

Moore, T. J. (2008), 'When did the Tibicen Play?: Meter and Musical Accompaniment in Roman Comedy', *Transactions and Proceedings of the American Philological Association* 138, 3–46.

Moore, T. J. (2012), *Music in Roman Comedy* (Cambridge).

Moro, A. (1997), *The Raising of Predicates* (Cambridge).

Mueller, C. F. W. (1896–1898), *M. Tulli Ciceronis scripta quae manserunt omnia: Pars III, Epistulae*, 2 vols. (Leipzig).

Munari, F. (1955), *Epigrammata Bobiensia*, 2 vols. (Roma).

Müller, L. (1894), *De re metrica*, 2nd ed. (Leipzig).

Mynors, R. A. B. (1958), *Carmina C. Valerii Catulli* (Oxford).

Mynors, R. A. B. (1972), *Vergili opera*, 2nd ed. (Oxford).

Mynors, R. A. B. (1990), *Georgics* (Oxford).

Nettleship, H. (1889), *Contributions to Latin Lexicography* (Oxford).

Neue, F. and Wagener, C. (1892–1905), *Formenlehre der lateinischen Sprache*, 3rd ed., 4 vols. (Berlin and Leipzig).

Niedermann, M. (1937), *Consentii Ars de barbarismis et metaplasmis* (Neuchâtel).

Norberg, D. (1944), *Beiträge zur spätlateinischen Syntax* (Uppsala).

Norden, E. (1957), *P. Vergilius Maro Aeneis Buch VI*, 4th ed. (Darmstadt).

Nougaret, L. (1966), *Analyse verbale comparée du De signis et des Bucoliques* (Paris).

Nyman, M. (1974), *Ubi est and ubist: the Problem of Latin Aphaeresis and the Phonology of esse* (Turku).

Nyman, M. (1975), 'Ist der *rest* Typus möglich?', *Arctos* 9, 61–73.

Nyman, M. (1977), 'Where does Latin *sum* come from?', *Language* 53, 39–60.

Palmer, A. (1890), *The Amphitruo of Plautus* (London).

Panayotakis, C. (2010), *Decimus Laberius: The Fragments* (Cambridge).

Parsons, J. (1999), 'A New Approach to the Saturnian Verse and Its Relation to Latin Prosody', *Transactions of the American Philological Association* 129, 117–37.

Pasquali, G. (1981), *Preistoria della poesia romana* (Florence).

Peitsara, K. (2004), 'Variants of Contraction: The Case of It's and 'Tis', *International Computer Archive of Modern and Medieval English Journal* 28, 77–94.

Penney, J. (2011), 'Archaic and Old Latin', in Clackson (2011), 220–35.

Perret, J. (1957), 'Prosodie et métrique chez Commodien', *Pallas* 5, 27–42.

Perret, J. (1981), *Virgile, Énéide*, 2nd ed., 2 vols. (Paris).

Pesce, L. (1997), *Amedeo Peyron e i suoi corrispondenti: da un carteggio inedito* (Treviso).

Petersmann, H. (2002–2003), 'Bedeutung und Gebrauch von lateinisch *fui*: eine soziolinguistische Analyse', *Die Sprache* 43, 94–103.

Pezzini, G. (2011), 'Contraction of EST in Latin', *Transactions of the Philological Society* 109, 327–43.

Pezzini, G. (2015), 'Consonance of final -*s* and Asyndetic Accumulation in Latin poetry', *Mnemosyne* 68.

Pighi, G. B. (1964), *Lettere latine d'un soldato di Traiano: PMich 467–472* (Bologna).

Platnauer, M. (1960), 'Prodelision in Greek Drama', *Classical Quarterly* 10, 140–4.

Posani, M. R. (1990), *Terenzio, Andria* (Bologna).

Postgate, J. P. (1904), 'The Latin Future Infinitive (*Crambe repetita*)', *Classical Review* 18, 450–6.

Postgate, J. P. (1920), *Phaedri Fabulae Aesopiae* (Oxford).

Powell, J. G. F. (2011), 'Legal Latin', in Clackson (2011), 464–84.

Prete, S. (1970), *Il codice di Terenzio Vaticano Latino 3226* (Vaticano).

Probert, P. (2002), 'On the prosody of Latin enclitics', *Oxford University Working Papers in Linguistics* 7, 181–206.

Proskauer, C. (1910), *Das auslautende -s auf den lateinischen Inschriften* (Strassburg).

Questa, C. (1995), *Titi Macci Plauti cantica* (Urbino).

Questa, C. (2007), *La metrica di Plauto e di Terenzio* (Urbino).

Quirk, R. (1985), *A Comprehensive Grammar of the English Language* (London).

Raffaelli, R. (1982), *Ricerche sui versi lunghi di Plauto e Terenzio* (Pisa).

Raven, D. S. (1965), *Latin Metre* (London).

Reynolds, L. D. (ed.) (1986), *Texts and Transmission: a Survey of the Latin Classics*, 2nd ed. (Oxford).

Ribbeck, O. (1866), *Prolegomena critica ad P. Vergili Maronis opera maiora* (Leipzig).

Ribbeck, O. (1871–1873), *Scaenicae Romanorum poesis fragmenta*, 2nd ed., 2 vols. (Leipzig).

Ribbeck, O. (1894–1895), *P. Vergili Maronis Opera*, 2nd ed., 4 vols. (Leipzig).

Rietveld, T. and van Hout, R. (2005), *Statistics in Language Research* (Berlin, New York).

Riggsby, A. (1991), 'Elision and Hiatus in Latin Prose', *Classical Antiquity* 10, 328–43.

Ritschl, F. (1848–1854), *T. Macci Plauti Comoediae* (Bonn).

Rix, H. (1992), 'Zur Entstehung des lateinischen Perfektparadigmas', in Krisch, T. and Panagl, O. (eds.), *Latein und Indogermanisch: Akten des Kolloquiums der Indogermanischen Gesellschaft, 23–26 September 1986* (Innsbruck), 221–40.

Rix, H. (2001), *Lexikon der indogermanischen Verben: Die Wurzeln und ihre Primärstammbildungen*, 2nd ed. (Wiesbaden).

Rix, H. (2002), *Sabellische Texte: die Texte des Oskischen, Umbrischen und Südpikenischen* (Heidelberg).

Roach, P. (2000), *English Phonetics and Phonology: a Practical Course*, 3rd ed. (Cambridge).

Rohlfs, G. (1966–1969), *Grammatica storica della lingua italiana e dei suoi dialetti*, 3 vols. (Torino).

Roller, M. (1996), 'Ethical Contradiction and the Fractured Community in Lucan's *Bellum Civile*', *Classical Antiquity* 15, 319–47.

Rubio, G. (2009), 'Semitic Influence in the History of Latin Syntax', in Cuzzolin, P. and Baldi, P. (eds.), *New Perspectives on Historical Latin Syntax 1: Syntax of the Sentence* (Berlin and New York), 195–240.

Salanitro, G. (2007), *Alcesta: Cento Virgiliano* (Acireale).

Sampson, R. (2010), *Vowel Prosthesis in Romance* (Oxford).

Sandbach, F. H. (1977), *The Comic Theatre of Greece and Rome* (London).

Schenkeveld, D. M. (2001), *Review of D'Angelo 2001, Bryn Mawr Classical Review* 2001.10.34.

Schindel, U. (1999), 'Entstehungsbedingungen eines spätantiken Schulbuchs: zum *Carmen de figuris*', in Döpp, S. (ed.), *Antike Rhetorik und ihre Rezeption* (Stuttgart), 85–98.

Schmalstieg, W. R. (1998), 'Latin *sum* and the Slavic First Person Singular Present', *Historische Sprachforschung* 111, 286–95.

Schuchardt, H. (1866–1868), *Der Vokalismus des Vulgärlateins*, 3 vols. (Leipzig).

Shackleton Bailey, D. R. (1977), *Cicero, Epistulae ad familiares*, 2 vols. (Cambridge).

Shackleton Bailey, D. R. (1987), 'A Letter of L. Lucceius', *Mnemosyne* 40, 419–20.

Shipley, F. (1924), 'Hiatus, Elision, Caesura, in Virgil's Hexameter', *Transactions and Proceedings of the American Philological Association* 55, 137–58.

Shipp, G. P. (1960), *P. Terenti Afri Andria*, 2nd ed. (Oxford).

Siedow, G. A. (1911), *De elisionis aphaeresis hiatus usu in hexametris latinis* (Greifswald).

Siefert, G. J. (1956), 'Meter and Case in the Latin Elegiac Pentameter', *Language* 28, 9–126.

Sihler, A. (1995), *New Comparative Grammar of Greek and Latin* (New York and Oxford).

Skutsch, F. (1892), *Forschungen zur lateinischen Grammatik und Metrik, Bd. 1: Plautinisches und Romanisches, Studien zur Plautinischen Prosodie* (Leipzig).

Skutsch, F. (1914), *Kleine Schriften* (Leipzig and Berlin).

Skutsch, O. (1985), *The Annals of Q. Ennius* (Oxford).

Sommer, F. and Pfister, R. (1977), *Handbuch der lateinischen laut- und Formenlehre*, 4th ed. (Heidelberg).

Soubiran, J. (1966), *L'Élision dans la poésie latine* (Paris).

Spencer, A. and Luís, A. R. (2012), *Clitics: An Introduction* (Cambridge).

Stroh, W. (1990), 'Arsis und Thesis oder: Wie hat man lateinische Verse gesprochen?', in von Albrecht, M. and Schubert, W. (eds.), *Musik und Dichtung: Neue Forschungsbeiträge, Viktor Pöschl zum 80 Geburtstag gewidmet* (Frankfurt am Main), 87–116.

Studemund, W. (1889), *T. Macci Plauti fabularum reliquiae Ambrosianae* (Berlin).

Sullivan, J. P. (1970), *Final -s in Early Latin* (PhD Dissertation, Yale, CT).

Svennung, J. (1941), *Compositiones Lucenses: Studien zum Inhalt, zur Textkritik und Sprache* (Uppsala and Leipzig).

Svennung, J. (1932), *Wortstudien zu den spätlateinischen Oribasiusrezensionen* (Uppsala).

Timpanaro, S. (1978), *Contributi di filologia e di storia della lingua latina* (Rome).

Tordeur, P. (1994), 'Le monosyllable élidé et l'aphérèse en latin', *Revue informatique et statistique des sciense humaines* 30, 183–222.

Traina, A. (1973), *L'alfabeto e la pronunzia del latino* (Bologna).

Traina, A. and Bernardi Perini, G. (1998), *Propedeutica al latino universitario*, 6th ed. (Bologna).

Trappes-Lomax, J. (2007), *Catullus: a Textual Reappraisal* (Swansea).

Tränkle, H. (1960), *Die Sprachkunst des Properz und die Tradition der lateinischen Dichtersprache* (Wiesbaden).

Untermann, J. (2000), *Wörterbuch des Oskisch-Umbrischen* (Heidelberg).

Väänänen, V. (1966), *Le latin vulgaire des inscriptions Pompéiennes*, 3rd ed. (Berlin).

Väänänen, V. (1981), *Introduction au latin vulgaire*, 3rd ed. (Paris).

Van Kemenade, A. and Vincent, N. (1997), *Parameters of Morphosyntactic Change* (Cambridge).

Verdière, R. (1964), *Cynegeticon libri I quae supersunt* (Wetteren).

Vetter, E. (1953), *Handbuch der italischen Dialekte* (Heidelberg).

Victor, B. (1996), 'A Problem of Method in the History of Texts and its Implications for the Manuscript Tradition of Terence', *Revue d'Histoire des Textes* 26, 269–87.

Victor, B. (1999), 'The Colometric Evidence for the History of the Terence Text in the Early Middle Ages', *Revue d'Histoire des Textes* 29, 141–68.

Victor, B. (2007), 'New Manuscript Sources of the Terence Text', in Kruschwitz, Ehlers and Felgentreu (2007), 1–14.

Villa, C. (1984), *La 'Lectura Terentii'* (Padova).

Vine, B. (1993), *Studies in Archaic Latin Inscriptions* (Innsbruck).

Vine, B. (1998), 'Remarks on the Archaic Latin Garigliano Bowl Inscription', *Zeitschrift für Papyrologie und Epigraphik* 121, 257–62.

Viparelli, V. (1990), *Tra prosodia e metrica: su alcuni problemi del Carmen de figuris* (Naples).

Vitale, M. T. (1999), 'Alcuni rimedi testuali all' *Aegritudo Perdicae*', *Athenaeum* 87, 215–42.

Vogel, I. (1986), 'External Sandhi Rules Operating between Sentences', in Andersen (1986), 55–64.

Wachter, R. (1987), *Altlateinische Inschriften: Sprachliche und epigraphische Untersuchungen zu den Dokumenten bis etwa 150 v. Chr.* (Bern).

Wackernagel, J. (1892), 'Über ein Gesetz der indogermanischen Wortstellung', *Indogermanische Forschungen* 1, 333–436.

Wallace, R. (1982), 'A Note on the Phonostylistics of Latin: (*s*) in Plautus', *Glotta* 60, 120–4.

Wallace, R. (1984), 'The Deletion of -s in Plautus', *American Journal of Philology* 105, 213–25.

Wallace, R. (2011), 'The Latin Alphabet and Orthography', in Clackson (2011), 9–28.

Watt, W. S. (1992), 'Notes on the Text of the *Aegritudo Perdicae*', *Rivista di Filologia e Istruzione Classica* 120, 205–11.

Weiss, M. (2009), *Outline of the Historical and Comparative Grammar of Latin* (Ann Arbor, MA).

West, M. L. (1982), *Greek Metre* (Oxford).

Williams, R. D. (1960), *P. Vergili Maronis Aeneidos liber quintus* (Oxford).

Williams, R. D. (1962), *P. Vergili Maronis Aeneidos liber tertius* (Oxford).

Winterbottom, M. (1970), *Problems in Quintilian* (London).

Woods, A., Fletcher, P., and Huges, A. (1986), *Statistics in Language Studies* (Cambridge).

Wright, R. (2011), 'Romance Languages as a Source for Spoken Latin', in Clackson (2011), 59–79.

Wunder, E. (1830), *M. Tulli Ciceronis Oratio pro Cn. Plancio* (Leipzig).

Zurli, L. (1987), *Aegritudo Perdicae* (Leipzig).

Zwicky, A. (1970), 'Auxiliary Reduction in English', *Linguistic Inquiry* 1, 323–36.

Zwicky, A. (1977), *On Clitics* (Bloomington, IN).

Zwicky, A. and Pullum, G. K. (1983), 'Cliticization vs. Inflection: English n't', *Language* 59, 502–13.

General Index

contraction(s) (*cont.*)
    in formal and/or prose
        texts 72–3, 125
    with existential or locational
        esse 147–53, 178–80, 241–3
    at the end of the clause 160–4
contracted forms (-*stl's*), *see also*
    contraction
    as clitic forms of *esse* 106–8, 160–8,
        237, 239–41, *see also*
        contraction, clitics
    in Latin speech 30, 90, 132–9, 237–8
    in Latin spelling 30, 90, 123–32,
        138–9, 235–6
    in Terence 31–4, 36–7, 141–80,
        249–55
    as abbreviations 99–101
    in manuscripts of literary
        authors 37–50, 91–4
    misunderstood by scribes 56–65,
        93–4, 236
    in inscriptions 65–75, 97
    commented on by
        grammarians 75–84
    in non-literary corpora 132 n. 109
    required by metre 52–6, 94–7
    phonology 30–6
        after vowel or -*m* 31–2, 176–80
        -*ust* = -*umst* 50–1, 70
        's after -*m* 32–3
        -*stl's* after short vowel + -*s* 31–2,
            37, 106–7, 141–2
        after long vowel + -*s* 34
        after consonant other than -*m* and
            -*s* 34–5
        -*est* = ? -*īs* + *est* 108–23
    non-univerbated in spelling 107 n. 37
    parallels in Sabellian languages 85–6
    style and register 13, 40–1, 154–9
        as archaisms 40–1, 73–4, 236, 238
        as markers of and/or reflecting
            speech 47, 73–80, 126, 132–8,
            159, 235–8
        as poetic and/or metrical
            forms 47–9, 72–3, 125–6,
            127–8, 235–6
    alternating with uncontracted
        forms 7–11, 142–91, *see also*
        contraction, blocking of
        contraction
    syntactic features 9, 159–70, 243–6
    analogous to verbal inflection 245 n. 53

copula
    as function of *esse* 147–9, 241–2
    in Latin, see *esse*
    in Oscan 85–6
    bond with the host word 160, 229–30,
        243–5
    replaced by clitic suffix in
        Turkish 244
    omitted in Russian 244 n. 51
    syntactic marginality 244 n. 50
Carmen de figuris uel
    schematibus 49–50, 131, 199,
        201–2

ecthlipsis 81–3, *see also* elision, sigmatic
    ecthlipsis
elision
    and contraction 101–5, 237
    as a sandhi phenomenon 102–3, 138
    involving merging rather than
        omission of vowel 28 n. 10
    before *est/es* 94–5, 180 n. 108, 186
    before *et* 104 n. 25
    impossible after -*s* 52, 105 n. 28
    of long vowels 89, 95 n. 173
    between monosyllables 183
    avoidance of elision 89–90, 184–5
    word-internal 101
    frequency in imperial
        poetry 89 n. 153
    in grammatical texts 81–4, 101,
        133–4
    providing evidence for cliticization of
        est/es 149–50, 177
    elided spellings 29–30, 70 n. 95, 103,
        (before *est/es* in
        inscriptions) 69–70, 74, 97
        n. 181
Ennius
    contractions 42
    sigmatic ecthlipsis 201–5
epenthesis 77 n. 122
esse, see also copula, contracted forms
    stem of *esse* 22–4
    cliticization of *esse* 88, 106–8, 160–8,
        227–31, 239–41
    contraction of *(e)st/(e)s, see*
        contraction, contracted forms
    sum as a clitic, derived from
        esum 23–4
    semantics of *esse* 147–53, 178–9,
        241–3

Index of Words

Index Locorum Potiorum

89: 304
93: 286
94: 286
98: 286
99: 286
100: 174
102: 209, 286, 304
103: 286
104: 286
106: 286
107: 286
113: 286
122: 286
124: 217, 312
126: 286
129: 286
139: 286
147: 286
148: 287
156: 287, 304
170: 287
173: 287
179: 162, 168
182: 304
184: 304
185: 287
188: 287
196: 312
204: 172
207: 287
208: 313
213: 287
215: 162
216: 287
227: 171
230: 287
236: 211, 287
244: 287
247: 250
248: 313
250: 313
253: 287
258: 287
271: 313
272: 287
273: 287, 304
282: 287
295: 92, 160, 251, 252
297: 287
298: 287
303: 173
314: 287

324: 92, 251, 252, 287
332: 152
337: 313
338: 313
346: 251
347: 304
349: 287
350: 162
359: 287
362: 313
380: 287
383: 287
386: 266
391: 304
399: 313
400: 287
405: 287
406: 304
408: 266
410: 304
411: 287
413: 222, 316
421: 188, 250
422: 153, 162, 287
426: 162, 288
427: 288
433: 288
436: 313
438: 288, 313
440: 288
442: 304
446: 288
452: 288
454: 313
457: 304
458: 304
460: 304
461: 288
471: 288
477: 217, 313
480: 209, 305
482: 152
494: 288
496: 288
498: 288
501: 305
506: 305
514: 305
516: 288
519: 305
523: 313
526: 288

529: 215, 222, 307
532: 288
535: 313
538: 174, 252
539: 288
545: 288
546: 251, 305
547: 288, 313
550: 92, 168
553: 288
554: 209, 305
555: 162
557: 171, 172
559: 170
560: 172
561: 288
562: 162, 167
563: 313
564: 288
567: 288
575: 288
584: 172
587: 288
590: 305
596: 288
604: 305
608: 288
618: 305
619: 289
621: 289
622: 289
623: 313
628: 305
633: 305
635: 289
638: 313
639: 305
640: 289
643: 305
649: 289
660: 222, 316
661: 53, 169, 250, 252
665-6: 174
666: 172, 173
667: 289
669: 289
675: 305
680: 289
683: 222, 316
690: 289
698: 289
700: 289

Inscriptions and papyri

(for the abbreviations see List of Abbreviations)

Sabellian Languages

(Texts and abbreviations as in Rix 2002 and La Regina 2010)